GOOD HOUSEKEEPING

DECORATING

AND DO-IT-YOURSELF

GOOD HOUSEKEEPING

DECORATING

AND DO-IT-YOURSELF

PUBLISHED BY GOOD HOUSEKEEPING BOOKS NEW YORK

Contents

Whether you own or rent your home, you will want to plan and carry out new decorations or improvements. As a modern home maker you may find the options open to you bewildering. Moreover, the skills needed for improvements or repairs may appear daunting while the costs involved in employing others to do them may be even more so.

The Good Housekeeping Decorating and Do-It-Yourself *book has been specially designed to provide practical as well as economical solutions. You will find at the beginning sections dealing with overall home planning, the principles of interior design and the wide range of available decorative finishes. For specific areas turn to the last sections which not only show you how to plan for the individual needs of each area but which include many money-saving projects. Finally, the central section is your guide to all the tools and techniques necessary for improvements, maintenance and repairs.*

The editors trust that by using this book you will make your home into a better place to live.

Manufactured in the Netherlands.

ISBN 0-87851-019-2
Library of Congress Catalog Card Number: 77-71606.

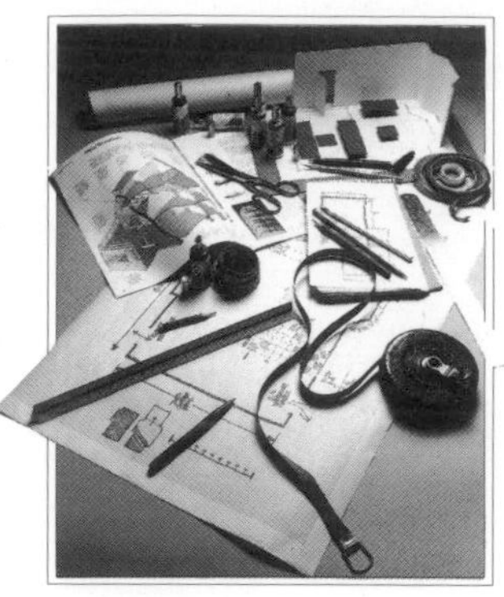

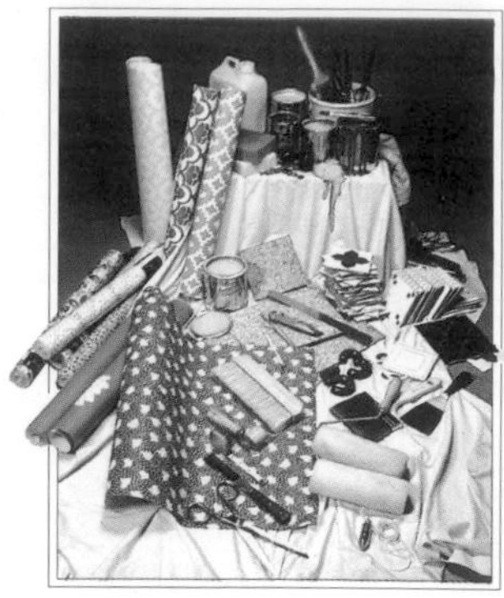

Tools and Techniques continued

Cooking and Eating Areas 161

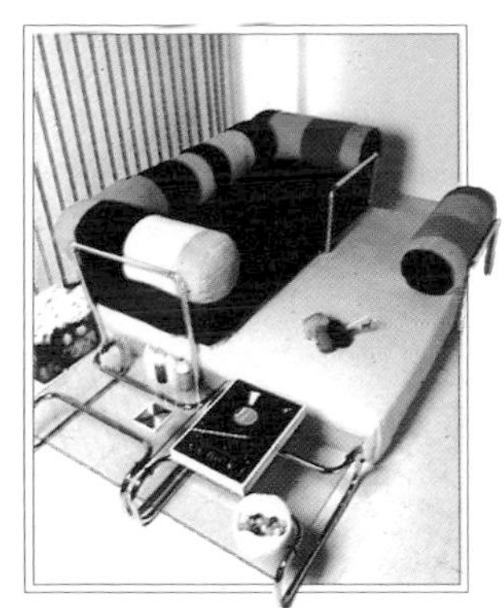

Leisure Areas 177

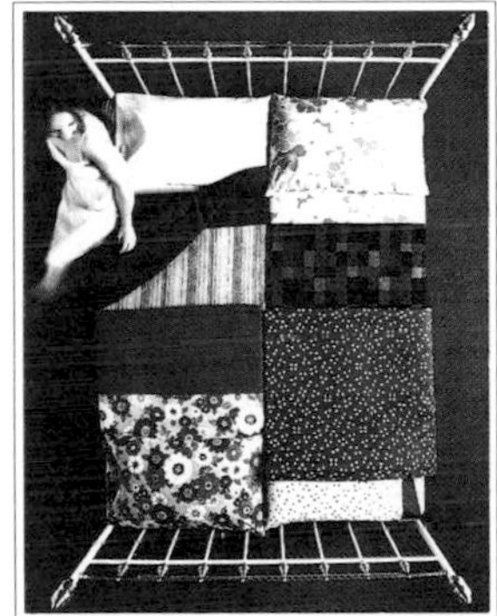

Bedrooms 191

Bathrooms 197

Children's Rooms 205

Storage 211

Storage continued

Work Areas 225

One Room Living 235

Glossary and Index 241

Defining Areas

Planning your home
While areas for specific use are essential to any home, the traditional labeling of rooms need not apply. A bedroom can have a practical daytime use while a living room may have many functions: it can contain a work area, an eating area as well as an area to relax in, each being defined by the position or type of furniture, or merely by a change in floor level or material. Consider your home as a series of areas rather than a group of rooms to enable you to make the best of your available space.

Sleeping areas
If you live in a small apartment or even a single room, your sleeping area tends to perform several functions. These areas need to be carefully planned to provide a measure of privacy and comfort. (See pp. 235-240.)
Where a family is involved you will need specifically to define the areas used for sleeping and privacy, even though they can be used for additional activities. It makes sense to think of sleeping areas having other uses, when you consider the large amount of space given over to a single activity. Convention has always allowed parents the largest bedroom, yet children of a household could put such a room to better use both as a play area during the day and as a sleeping area at night. Consider the actual location of sleeping areas and keep them as far away as possible from sources of noise. Situate them away from the sunny side of the house leaving those areas for daytime use.

Bathrooms
A bathroom is unlikely to be incorporated as part of another activity area. If you intend to add another bathroom to the home, its position is best determined by existing plumbing in order to achieve economical pipe runs. If you have only one bathroom, it is wise to site the toilet separately.

Kitchens
The number of functions required of a kitchen, whether large or small, are considerable. In addition to essential areas for preparation, washing and cooking (see pp. 162-165) you will almost certainly use part of the kitchen for eating, if only for breakfast or children's meals. If you have a separate dining room, plan to include a service hatch. This arrangement will eliminate delays from kitchen to table, keep the food hot, and reduce the risk of accident

1

2

3

1 Open plan space
The visual interest of any interior is increased if one area can be glimpsed from another. This can be achieved by dividing a large open-plan space through a change in floor levels.

2 Playroom and bedroom
A large bedroom divided into playing and sleeping areas will leave other parts of the house free from children's activities.

3 Extra work surface
A simple breakfast bar situated in the kitchen is convenient for children's meals as well as breakfast. It also doubles as an extra surface when preparing meals.

4 Providing access
A large hatch between the kitchen and the dining room allows for safe and easy service without isolating one area from another.

5 Creating privacy
In a small apartment it is sometimes an advantage to provide private areas within a larger space. A free standing screen is an ideal solution, particularly where it is not possible to make structural alterations.

6 Multi-purpose areas
One living area for daytime use can be furnished with practical hard-wearing furniture and materials. A small work space can be included without disturbing other activities.

4

5

6

when carrying food from one place to another.

Living areas

Every family differs in its requirements of a living area, although certain functions are common to all: conversation; the playing of games; watching television; listening to music and entertaining friends. In addition you may use the living area for study and possibly for eating in. (See pp. 176-179.)

In order to plan it efficiently consider what you and your family require of a living area. Do you really want just one area – or would two be more practical? With two areas, one can be casually furnished for daytime use by the whole family, with easy access to the kitchen and perhaps a yard. The other would be for evening use, comfortable and well equipped for adult relaxation and entertainment.

Work areas

There are a number of activities that are carried out in the average domestic environment such as sewing, carpentry and a variety of hobbies which may be classed as "work." Where these are generally quiet and inoffensive there is no reason why they should not be performed anywhere in the house, either in a specifically designed area or as part of another activity area. If, however, the activity either requires the use of noisy machinery or creates a certain amount of litter, or demands a ready supply of materials, then a separate work area must be allowed for away from the mainstream of family life. (See pp. 226-234.)

Remember that if bulky materials are needed for such work, a storage area should be provided adjacent to the work area, and preferably in such a way that the materials do not have to be carried through the main part of the house.

Thinking Ahead

Flexible design considerations
Ideally, a home should be based on a flexible design so as to accommodate future expansion or changes in interest. There should be enough space for additional children and occasional or even permanent guests; provision for hobbies or work done at home; ample storage for a growing family; adequate bathroom and laundry facilities and so on. When it comes to planning your own home, *you* are the expert; no one else has such detailed knowledge of your family's lifestyle and ambitions. Although there are bound to be a few influential factors imposed on any planned scheme that may limit certain requirements, the needs of you and your family must come first. It is therefore very important to have a clear idea of your collective working and leisure environment, especially if you are contemplating making alterations to your home. Observe and note down how your home is coping with the present needs of your family. Make a list of essential repairs and alterations, so that you can plan priorities and estimate costs. If you intend carrying out most of the work yourself, a well-planned scheme will ensure efficient use of time and materials, and will help you to avoid mistakes. If you want to employ professionals to carry out some stages of the work, make sure that detailed instructions are given – alterations made later can prove very expensive. Most professional builders and decorators prefer an accurate or at least explicit brief, so that they can carry out the work to your complete satisfaction. A professional will also advise you on local building codes and help you apply for any permits, if necessary. Structural changes or major alterations should only be considered if you plan to maintain your present home over a long period. If an early move is possible, it is unwise to make a permanent alteration which might jeopardize an easy re-sale. It is relatively unimportant from this aspect if your home has built-in shelves rather than an adjustable system but converting the entire basement to a sauna might limit its appeal considerably.

No area need be completely divorced from another area – encourage dispersion and flexibility by having intercommunicating areas, or rooms that are easily adaptable to a variety of functions.

Division of family activities
This block schematic diagram shows how the home may be satisfactorily divided, and in some areas combined, to cope with the daily activities of your family at various stages.

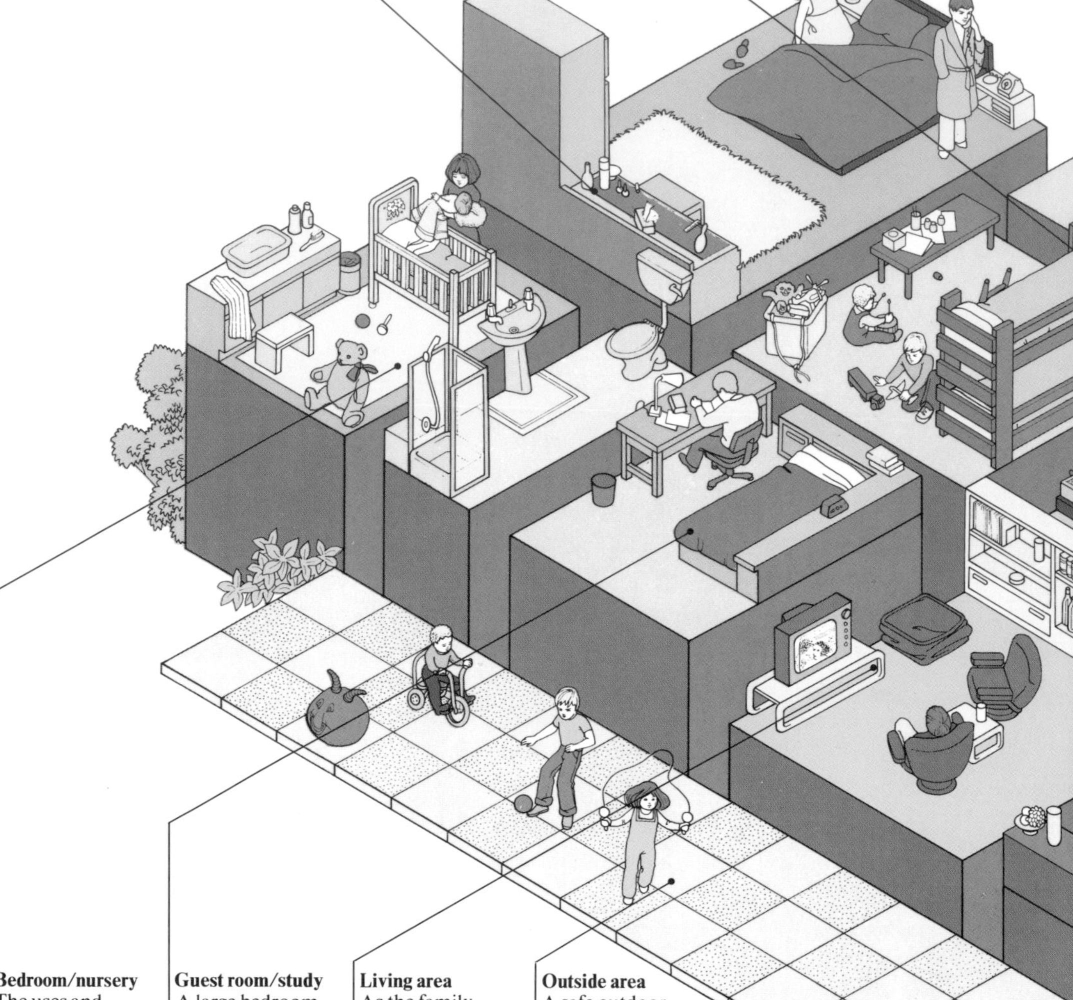

Master bedroom
The principal bedroom as occupied by the parents or the head of the family is often the largest bedroom in the house. Space is needed for adequate storage facilities. The room should be within easy reach of the children's room so that the parents can be alerted and it should have access to a bathroom.

Bedroom
Older children will need separate rooms for sleeping, study and play. And while it is ideal that children have their own rooms, it is sometimes necessary or desirable for them to share. Storage and beds should be planned to provide enough floor space.

Bedroom/nursery
The uses and functions of this room will change over the years. If used initially as a nursery, its position close to the parents' bedroom is ideal so that the child can be easily supervised and so that he or she will not disturb other members of the family. If used as a guest room, a nearby bathroom will provide more privacy.

Guest room/study
A large bedroom may be used by guests or an elderly relative, but may also serve as a study or workroom. At a later time it could be converted into private quarters for a growing child. In any case, it should have convenient washing facilities.

Living area
As the family develops and bedrooms are used for individual requirements, the living area may have to be zoned to provide for varying activities. An open plan arrangement allows children to be supervised from other areas. You will need to provide adequate seating, lighting and a certain amount of storage.

Outside area
A safe outdoor play area is one that can easily be viewed from the living areas – or from the most frequently used rooms in the house.

Dining area
This should be adjacent to the kitchen, and spacious enough for the family and guests to dine comfortably. If your house or apartment is an open plan, install independent lighting or a screen to isolate the kitchen area while dining.

Bathroom
This should be sited conveniently close to the bedrooms. You should try to separate the toilet from the washing facilities and also to have more than one bathroom to ease the demand, especially in the mornings. Plan bathrooms so that there is ample room to wash and dress. Provide safety precautions if there are elderly people in the house.

Kitchen
In many modern homes, the kitchen and dining area are combined, or interlinked by an opening in a dividing wall. This permits easy carrying of food from kitchen to dining area and also allows parents to supervise children's meals. Provide a safety gate between kitchen and dining area to keep children away from danger zones.

Hallway
Outdoor clothing and umbrellas should be stored in the hall for convenience. Fairly spacious hallways can easily be fitted with storage closets and perhaps a telephone table. Floor-to-ceiling units may be sited in the "dead" area behind the entrance door along the flanking wall.

Work areas
Tasks that need a lot of space, or create a lot of mess – laundry, for example, wood and metalworking- should be relegated to more isolated areas such as basements or garages. If the basement is large, part of it can be furnished to accommodate an extra recreational area so that other members of the family are not inconvenienced.

The changing home

The way a family can alter and adapt their four bedroom house to suit changing needs is shown below.

Stage 1 Parents occupy master bedroom. One bedroom serves as a nursery. The guest room doubles as a study, the remaining room is used for sewing or other activities.

Stage 2 Master bedroom still occupied by parents. Older child takes over guest room. Extra room doubles as guest room. Study becomes part of living area, includes storage system. Dining area doubles as play area.

Stage 3 Master bedroom still occupied by parents. Children might share a bedroom, which doubles as play room. Both the beds and clothes storage convert to adult requirements. Nursery becomes the guest room. Extra "sewing" room remains.

Stage 4 Master bedroom still occupied by parents. Children have one room each with facilities for hobbies and study. Elderly relative has own room. Living area adapted to provide different zones for different activities. Bathrooms and kitchen have been made safe for use by elderly person.

Using Spaces

Creating more space
The only real way to create more space is to extend your home, either outward or upward, but you can achieve an illusion of spaciousness by rearranging the available space or furniture to greater advantage.
The traditional sofa and two chairs, for example, could be replaced by a more economical seating arrangement altogether. (See pp. 178-179.)
Consider replacing individual storage units with a wall of modular units; the result would certainly be more space-saving. These concepts also apply to kitchens, work areas and bedrooms. You can take this a stage further by actually removing walls to allow greater freedom with furniture layout.
By removing a wall between the hall and other rooms, you can convert what has until now been simply an access space into extra living space, possibly opening up a staircase view of both levels at the same time.

Dividing an area
It is sometimes an advantage to emphasize or isolate one area from another - lightweight, folding or adjustable screens are flexible in their use, and can be moved from room to room.
If you need regular screening, you might consider installing drapes, shades, curtains or venetian blinds. Certain types of curtain tracks can be bent to provide curved screening. This type of room divider will not close off sound; you may need to consider more permanent interior walls. (See p. 91.)
If you have rooms with high ceilings, consider changing the proportions of the room by installing a false ceiling. If you have really high ceilings you can re-plan an interior by building a gallery above the existing floor level to be used as a study or sleeping area, leaving the floor level free for other activities. Before planning a structure of this kind, it is best to seek professional advice.

1

2

3

4

5

6

1 Room divider
Create a room divider by grouping storage units together in the center of a room; this will be more space-saving than individual cabinets. A glassed-in center section will give a room divider a lighter appearance.

2 Extra space
Simple seating units arranged against the wall will provide extra space, particularly important in a smaller room. A white interior together with the use of glass always creates a light, airy effect.

3 Wall-hung units
Wall-hung units allow the floor covering to run from wall to wall. This will make the room appear much larger.

4 Removing a wall
Knocking down a wall into a landing area creates additional living space.

5 Integral staircase
A staircase which is included in a living space will link the whole house visually, and provide interesting viewpoints at all levels.

6 Split-level
A sleeping area built into a gallery leaves the whole floor area beneath for other activities. This is an advantage in a one room apartment and allows a measure of privacy in the sleeping areas.

Drawing Up Plans

Making plans
Whether you intend to combine one area of your home with another, divide one space into two, or merely re-arrange your furniture layout, it will be easier if you can plan out your scheme on paper, or make a model. There is no need to think in terms of sophisticated plans involving elaborate models finished in every detail, but more of simple methods that will enable you to see the whole scheme at a glance, and to test out your ideas. If you visualize a more complex scheme that involves structural alterations, you should consult with a professional designer or architect, who will carry out the entire job, including the preparation of detailed plans. Even so, drawing your own plans or making a model beforehand will give an architect a much better idea of your own personal requirements.

Measuring up a room
Use as long a tape measure as possible, and measure the main dimensions of the room. These include the length of the walls, the height of the ceiling, plus any other structural features that the room might have, such as alcoves, fireplaces, closets, windows and doors. Make a note of the way in which the doors and windows open. For the purposes of planning your interior you can assume that corners are square, although in actual fact they rarely are. If you want to draw a more accurate plan, or if you have a room that is obviously out of square, measure the diagonals to check against other measurements.

Additional considerations
There are certain features in every room that must be taken into account in case your scheme is affected by their position: these include radiators; any visible pipework; plumbing facilities; light fittings, switches and sockets; baseboards and ceiling moldings. You may decide at this stage to make alterations to these features, or to eliminate some of them altogether.

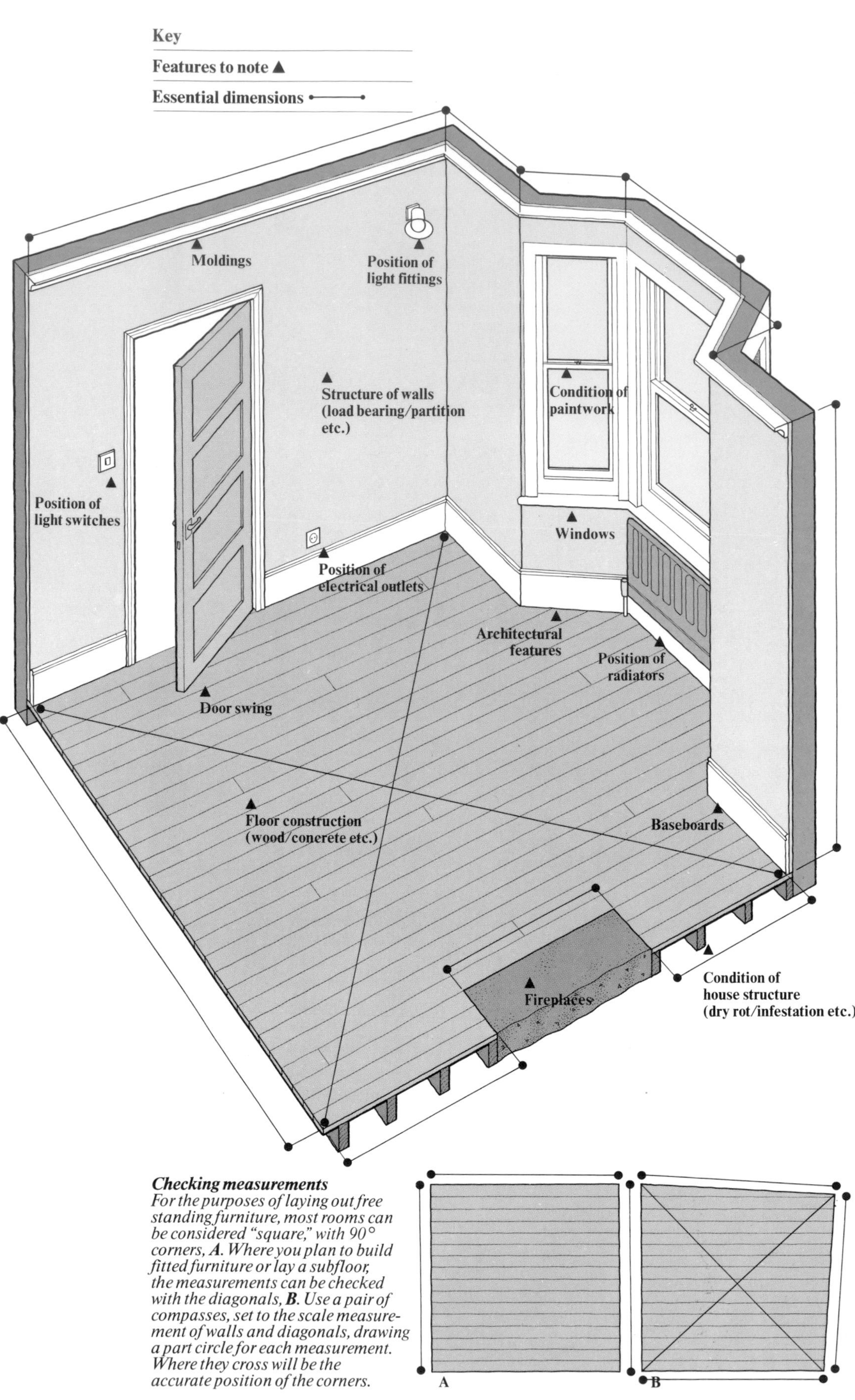

Checking measurements
*For the purposes of laying out free standing furniture, most rooms can be considered "square," with 90° corners, **A**. Where you plan to build fitted furniture or lay a subfloor, the measurements can be checked with the diagonals, **B**. Use a pair of compasses, set to the scale measurement of walls and diagonals, drawing a part circle for each measurement. Where they cross will be the accurate position of the corners.*

Drawing the plans

The easiest method of drawing plans and elevations is to use squared graph paper. Transfer your measurements on to the paper, using the squares to scale the drawing. When you have drawn the position of the walls and structural features, plot the positions of the additional features – radiators, fireplaces, light fittings, etc., as carefully as possible. Now cut out pieces of paper to represent your furniture, making them to the same scale as the drawing. These can be very easily moved around in your plan, allowing you to establish their best position. If you want to make structural alterations, measure up the area and draw it on graph paper in the same way; this will enable you to see which walls or parts of walls you will need to remove, and how it will affect other features, and how your furniture will fit into the new space. Similarly, if you plan to divide an area, you will be able to see if the new rooms are the correct size and shape, and whether access is satisfactory.

Making a model

An even better method of helping you to visualize your scheme is to make a model; the three dimensional nature of the model may help you to clarify many points. Paste down your plan on to a base of plywood, particle board or stiff cardboard. Using the same technique as described for making plans, transfer your measurements on to graph paper to construct elevations of all the walls in the room. After cutting and marking out the shapes, whether of the same material or polystyrene tiles, fasten the walls to the plan. You can put a flat piece of cardboard or another tile on top to create a ceiling and with holes punched in the walls you can get an impression of what the room will look like full-size. With block models of your furniture you can arrange them within the available space to plan your internal layout. It is not necessary to make recognizable pieces as long as they are of the correct scale and mass to make accurate planning possible.

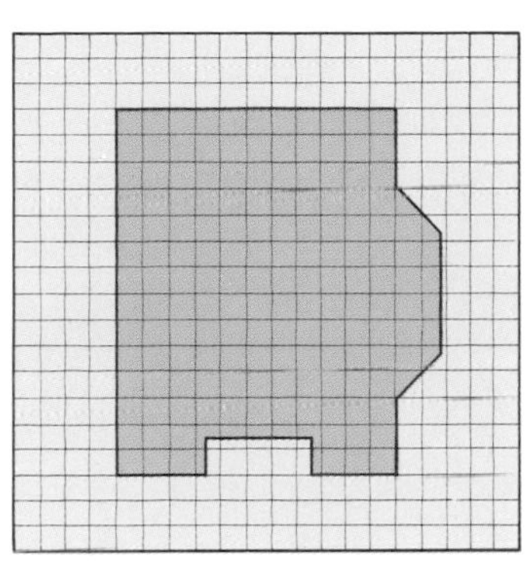

Plan view
This is a measured drawing made of the horizontal plane of an area.

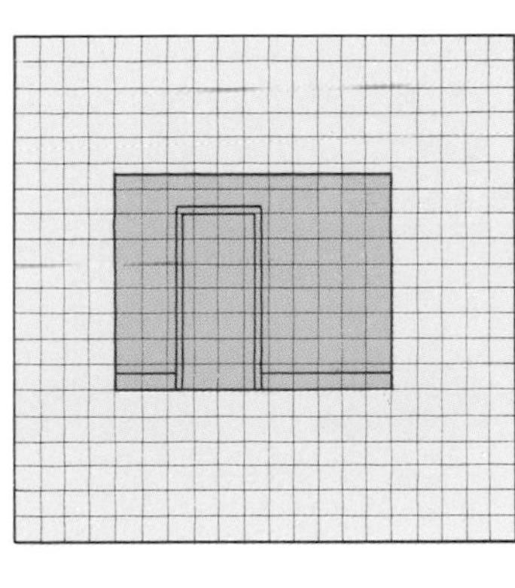

Elevation
This is a measured drawing made of the vertical plane of an area.

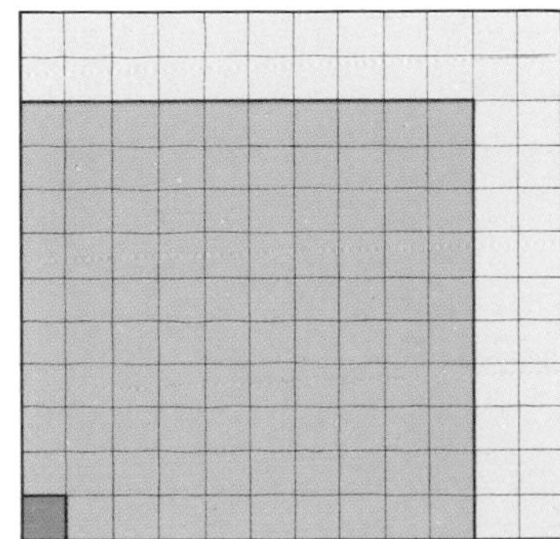

Scale
In order to transfer your measurements on to paper, you need a scale to make the drawing's dimensions proportional to those of the full-size room. A convenient scale to use is 1 unit representing 10 units.

Providing a firm base
Paste down your plan on a piece of plywood, particle board or stiff cardboard.

Transfer measurements
Draw the scaled-down measurements on graph paper, and mount the paper on thin cardboard or polystyrene tiles.

Cutting the shapes
Draw in features such as windows and doors with a felt tip pen. Then cut out main shapes with a sharp knife.

Fastening the parts together
You can use scotch tape or paper glue to attach the walls to the plan.

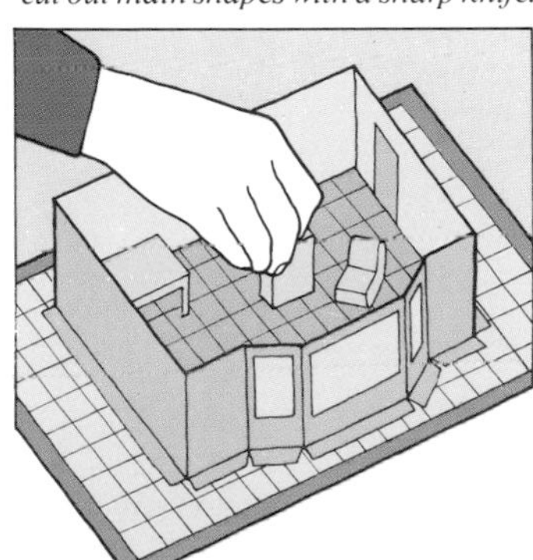

Furniture models
Make models of the furniture from pieces of polystyrene or cardboard.

Life size impression
Drill or punch small holes in the walls at scale "eye-level".

Lighting

Creating a mood
Apart from its many functional applications, well-planned lighting can contribute a great deal to the atmosphere in your home. The position and style of the lamps and fixtures determines the kind of light they give. Candle light and oil lamps have long been associated with a warm and cosy atmosphere, and you can create an almost identical mood with modern lighting, using small spotlights, or shaded lamps to make isolated pools of light around the room. The mood may be enhanced where a dark floor or ceiling absorbs the light rather than reflects it. If, on the other hand, you want to create a fresh, airy appearance, use reflected light from pale-colored ceilings and walls. Ideally, lighting should be as flexible as possible so that you can arrange it to suit the occasion; this cannot be achieved merely by fitting dimmer switches.

Well-balanced lighting
When you plan your lighting, first consider the size and position of the windows, and the amount of natural light they bring to the interior. Some areas may have poor illumination and will need subsidiary lighting during the daytime. The most efficient method of achieving the correct balance is with a light-sensitive switch: when the natural light level falls below a certain point, artificial light is automatically switched on. This is particularly useful in areas of potential hazard such as a stairway, where light should be thrown on to the stairs, so that the edge of the tread is well-defined. Ideally, the light source should be to one side so that your shadow does not obscure the stairs when you are going up or down. Always avoid sudden changes in light level.

Planning installations
Plan your lighting first before you decorate or build any furniture into a room. Position outlets carefully, to give you as much flexibility as possible. Place light switches within easy reach as you enter a room – a point to remember if you intend re-hanging a door. Three-way switches are very useful placed at the top and bottom of a staircase, or by the side of the bed. Bear in mind that light fixtures have to be cleaned and maintained, so if you need a light in a normally inaccessible area, consider installing a flush-fitting or a recessed light that will require less cleaning.

1

1 Creating atmosphere
Create small pools of atmospheric light by strategically positioning lamps at a low level around the room.

2 Reading lights
Reading lights are provided in this bedroom, by positioning strip lights behind a batten running across the headboard. Provide a separate light and switch for each side of the bed so that one person can read without disturbing the other.

3 Reflecting light and textures
Position your light fittings to make the most of textural surfaces in the room. Supplement low level lamps by using reflected light from the ceiling.

4 Reinforcing natural light
Directional spotlights reinforce natural light from a skylight, while at the same time picking out pictures hung on the wall.

2

3

4

Lighting

A good source of light
Plan carefully to create an overall, harmonious effect that will at the same time satisfy individual activities. You should arrange your light sources so as to avoid throwing shadows into activity areas while reducing glare from a direct light source.

Reading light
A centrally placed ceiling light as in **1** is unsuitable for reading, since it casts shadows on the page. A better arrangement is shown in **2** where a lamp is positioned behind and to the side so that light is thrown on to the page. Another low-level light should be used to reduce contrast between the well-lit page and the darkened background.

Television viewing
Low-level, indirect light adjacent to the set, **3**, reduces eye strain.

Lighting a dining area
Avoid light fixtures in which the naked bulb is visible to diners as in **4**. If possible, install a light with a wider shade that can be adjusted up and down thus preventing glare. Additional lighting may be necessary for long tables as in **6**.

Lamps for writing
Avoid a light that throws your own shadow on to the page as **7**. Much better is a concealed light as in **8**, which causes less shadow by partially reflecting on the wall. An adjustable lamp such as in **9** provides the best illumination and combined with another room light will reduce eye strain.

Bedroom lighting
A reading light should be positioned to one side of the bed, or behind it, as in **10**, shaded to avoid glare. Indirect light in a child's room can be provided from an adjoining area **11**, or a dimmer switch **12**.

Bathroom lighting
Position the light to shine on you – not the mirror, **13**. Place the light either side of the mirror or around the perimeter and avoid lights which will reflect in it.

Lighting closets and shelves
Interior closet lighting can be controlled by a switch operated by the opening and closing of the door. Use a concealed or shaded strip light, as **14**. Position a light above shelves as in **15**.

1 Central light casts shadows

2 Reading lamp positioned behind

3 Indirect lighting near television

4 A naked bulb can annoy diners

5 Extender lamps are more versatile

6 A long table needs two lamps

7 A high lamp casts shadows

8 Concealed lamp gives better light

9 Use an adjustable lamp for typing

10 Position reading light behind bed

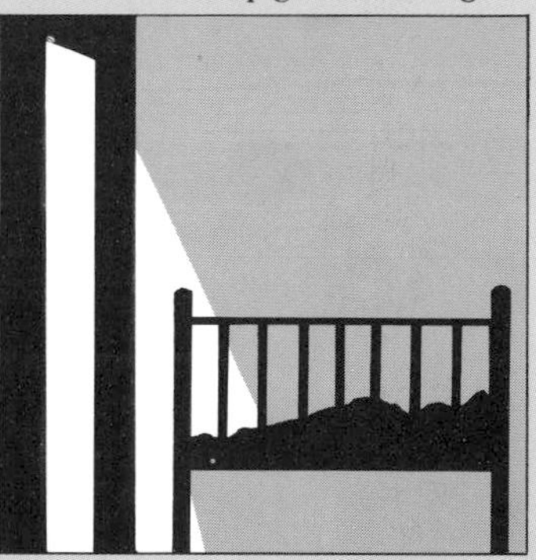
11 Indirect light from adjoining area

12 Install a dimmer switch

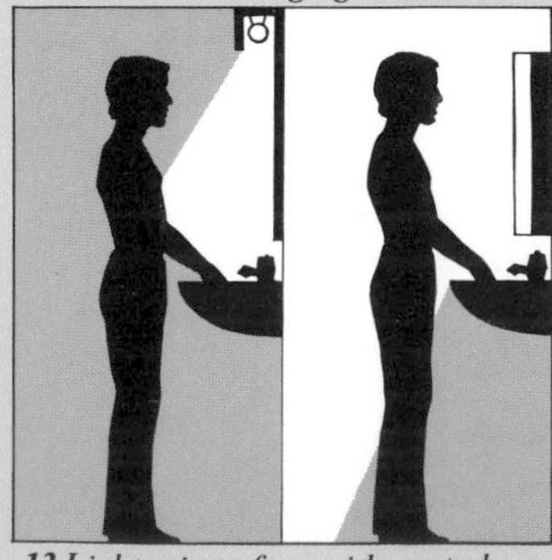
13 Light mirror from side, not above

14 Illuminate closet interiors

15 Light shelves from above

Interior Design

Creating an Atmosphere

1

2

3

1 Comfortable kitchen
Warm dark tones create a cosy atmosphere in a large kitchen. The ruffled curtains and louvered wood cabinets soften the utilitarian look of the modern appliances.

2 Unexpected décor
The use of bold, lively colors completely transforms a traditionally designed and furnished room thus producing an unexpected interior.

3 Light, airy bedroom
The crisp, geometric patterns on wall, window and bedspread go well with the natural foliage. They work together to give this bedroom a light, airy look.

4 Inviting interior
The patterned wallpaper and natural wood paneling produce a rich, warm effect, making this bathroom as inviting as any other room in the house.

5 Dramatic corner
The decorative shapes of flowers and vases are augmented by the carved screen. They all combine to turn an awkward corner into something more dramatic.

6 Fresh feeling
A yellow daffodil motif against a white background creates a fresh, invigorating atmosphere. The soft pillows are a comfortable contrast to the sturdy wicker.

4

5

6

Creating an Atmosphere

Selecting colors and textures
Working out a new color scheme, or modifying an existing one, will need considerable thought since you are faced with an almost limitless range of possibilities. A good scheme relies not only on the successful combination of colors but of textures too. But the "rules" that govern color combinations are infinitely flexible. Making a selection from possible colors and textures is very much a matter of personal taste, so it is difficult to formulate any but the simplest guidelines to help you in your choice. Nevertheless, there are a few factors that relate the nature of colors and textures to the fundamentals of decoration and design and which may make your task somewhat easier. For example, a gloss painted surface will reflect more light than one painted with latex, so although they might appear identical on the color chart, they will certainly appear different in practice.

Warm and cool colors
Colors have certain temperature associations and we can categorize them as either warm or cool. These characteristics reflect elements of a simple, natural kind with which we are most familiar. For example, warm colors such as reds, yellows and oranges we associate with the sun and fire; browns reflect earth and wood, both of which are warm to the touch. On the other hand, cool colors such as blues and greens we associate with water, ice, forests and shadows. Our emotions and responses can be affected by the use of these colors.

How color influences atmosphere
You can use dominating colors – dark blues, strong reds and yellows, mid-browns, to change or emphasize the atmosphere and character of a room. A room decorated in warm colors feels warmer and more welcoming than one painted white or pale blue, although the temperature itself remains the same. Warm colors will also make a poorly lit room seem almost sunny. Bold splashes of reds, browns or oranges will warm up even a predominantly "cool" room. Remember, too, that we respond emotionally to color. Warm colors are stimulating, while cool colors are used where a calm, relaxed atmosphere is needed. It is therefore very important to consider carefully the function of each area before you finalize your scheme.

Relaxing areas

Of all the rooms in the house, the relaxing and entertaining areas present the most problems in creating the right atmosphere. This is mainly because of the variety of practical functions and the divergence of family tastes. To create a lively, fresh atmosphere for daytime use, yet one that can become cosy and intimate for the evening, depends mainly on lighting, furnishings and fabrics more than the use of color schemes. This will enable you to compromise, and to change the interior to suit the occasion: screens are useful to provide a definite color bias when needed, or to hide a certain feature when not needed. Drapes and shades can be employed in a similar way to add warmth to the scheme; large cushions can accent areas with bright colors and patterns, or display a more somber tone when reversed. Color, if emphasized in wood, fabrics and fittings, is thus more usefully employed and adaptable, to suit the mood of a party, a relaxed conversation between friends, or any other mood dictated by the moment.

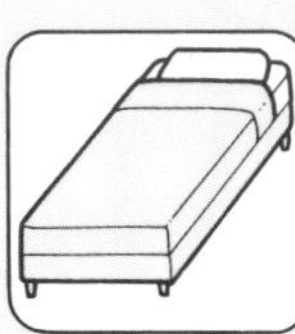

Bedrooms

The bedroom is an area which should be decorated to suit the personal taste of its occupants. A child's bedroom needs to be stimulating, particularly if it is also a playroom and this can be provided by the use of more adventurous color combinations, such as undiluted primary colors. A bedroom decorated with cool colors is conducive to a relaxed atmosphere, but you may wish to include some darker tones or patterns in order to create a comfortable and cosy feeling. Alternatively, you might prefer the use of exotic colors and textures, and a strong emphasis on drapes and plants. Any guest room should above all be welcoming, but it should also suit the taste of different age groups, and make visitors feel at home.

Cooking and eating areas

A kitchen is essentially a workroom, but it often has to combine several functions within one area – it might double as a dining room or family room. In any event, the kitchen area is a place where a lot of time will be spent, and the color scheme should make it comfortable to work in. If it is situated so that it receives strong sunlight for most of the day, this, coupled with the heat from cooking, may make the area uncomfortably warm. By choosing colors from the cool range, along with proper ventilation and insulation, you can give the kitchen a sunny but fresh atmosphere. Very modern, clinical kitchens, however, may be enhanced by a warm decor, and possibly the use of wood. A breakfast room needs fresh, stimulating colors, whereas a separate dining room may benefit from dark tones which create a more intimate mood.

Work areas

The colors used in a study should be stimulating, but not distracting. Neither should a particular pattern or texture predominate. Since the purpose of a study is mainly devoted to reading and writing in one small area of the room, you can divide the room decoratively, so that the work area has a calm, relaxed feeling – mid blues or browns, perhaps, while the remaining area is more lively. Workshops, often situated in the basement or the garage, might benefit from a bright, warm treatment. Color can emphasize danger areas – red or orange could be used to call attention to emergency power switches, fire extinguishers, and first aid equipment. Walls can remain in fair-faced, warm brick, which gives both color and texture. Concrete floors may be painted in special paint, usually available in a range of primary colors.

Bathrooms

Bathrooms as well as other less frequently used areas of the house, such as hallways, stairs and landings can be much more dramatic in their color schemes. Those strong colors which may be tiring to live with in regularly occupied areas can be used to good advantage in such areas and where there are large expanses of wall. Bathrooms should feel warm, both physically and decoratively. Here is an opportunity to try out murals of brightly-colored tiles and mosaics, and to make use of boldly patterned curtains and shades. If your bathroom is small take care not to overpower it by over-emphasis of dark and powerful tones although small touches can work well.

Visual Effects

Wall surface treatments
You can use tone and the warm and cool characteristics of color to give the illusion of changing shape and space. A wall painted with a warm color tends to advance into an area, while a cool color will recede; a dark tone will also advance more than a light tone, and a combination of both tone and color will emphasize the illusion. This basic law of color can change the proportion of a room to a certain extent, without your having to modify the structure.

Dark tones project
A wall painted in dark tones will appear to advance into a room.

Light tones recede
A wall painted in a cool color or a light tone will recede.

Combining tone and color
A combination of tone and color will increase any illusion.

Ceiling treatments
Small rooms with very high ceilings may need a lower ceiling to improve their appearance and atmosphere. Paint the ceiling a dark tone. This effect can be enhanced by painting the top section of the walls in the same color; the more wall you paint, the lower the ceiling will appear. Conversely, a low ceiling may benefit from a light tone, which will tend to recede and also increase the amount of reflected light.

Lowering a ceiling
1 If you want to lower a ceiling optically, paint it a dark tone.

2 You can further emphasize the effect of lowering a ceiling by painting top section of wall.

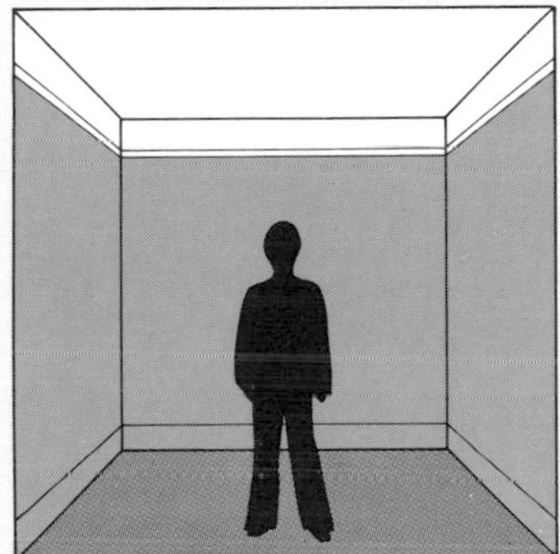

Heightening a ceiling
This effect is brought about by painting it white.

Corridors and narrow areas
Narrow areas painted in light, cool colors will seem less confined. If the wall at the end of the corridor is painted in a warm, dark tone, it will appear to shorten the length. Juxtaposition of light and dark tones will help to alter proportions, so that you can alter a wide corridor by having dark ceiling and floor, but light-colored walls, thus emphasizing the width of the floor and lowering the ceiling.

Widening corridors
Give a feeling of spaciousness by painting corridor white.

Shortening corridors
Paint the wall at the end of a light corridor a dark tone.

Changing a corridor's proportions
Paint the ceiling and floors a dark color but leave the walls white.

Total room areas
A dark tone will make a room seem cosier and restful and will draw attention to certain features, but where there are areas of artificial light there is a tendency for walls and ceilings to disappear altogether. A contrast in tone makes focal points of objects such as fireplaces, windows, pictures, etc. Painting ceiling and walls white mutes the corners and angles of the room. The monotony of a wall can be interrupted by painting certain areas in a tone or color, perhaps to blend with other features.

Light tones
An open, airy effect is achieved by destroying angles.

Dark tones
A large room becomes cosier and warmer.

Painted panels
The proportions of a wall can be altered by color panels.

Visual Effects

1

2

3

1 Unifying unusual shapes
Co-ordinate sloping walls and ceilings by painting them all one color.

2 Adding space
Make a small hall appear larger by emphasizing the verticals, which gives an illusion of height, and "doubling" the width with a mirror.

3 Enlarging perimeters
Painting a room white will destroy the lines made by walls and ceilings and give an open light effect.

4 Emphasizing decorative features
Use the warm and cool characteristics of color, or the contrast of tones, to bring out certain features such as windows, moldings and beams.

5 Scaling down space
You can make a large room appear smaller by painting the walls a dark tone. Gloss paint will reflect more light to compensate for the darker surfaces.

4

5

Relating Colors & Materials

Color schemes
How can colors be successfully matched or contrasted? The most basic colors are described as primaries; red, yellow and blue; it is their mixtures which give orange, green, and violet. Complementary or contrasting colors–violet and yellow, orange and blue, red and green–are the most powerful and stimulating when used together. Colors or hues that match or shade into each other – blue into green, yellow into orange – are described as harmonies. Those colors that lie on either side of a primary in the spectrum are discords, and are tricky to use in combination: blue-green and blue-violet, red-orange and red-violet. There remain the neutral colors, and the grays, blacks and whites, which need to be used for their own special contrast to color. An all-white or cream room, with a single color carpet and fabrics that echo or contrast with that color, can be very stimulating and also very fresh. Similarly, colors against a black background become intensified and brilliant.

You can take each room as a separate problem in terms of color selection, but where you can view one area from another, even if only through open doors, the colors in both areas will be mutually influenced. Make your selection of colors and arrange them against some unifying hue or shade to link them visually: blue in one room can merge into green in the next, while fabrics and furnishings can be of many subtle variations of both colors, co-ordinating the whole. This co-ordination is very successful in small houses, where variations of one color – browns, for example – can be used throughout. If separate areas or rooms need different carpets, try and match one main feature to make a unifying theme; let the pattern be similar, or the color harmonious. Paint windows, doors and baseboards in one color. This not only integrates areas, but also makes door frames easier to paint in that you do not have to stop one color exactly where another begins.

Monochromatic schemes

Most people find that a monochromatic or a single color scheme is the easiest to handle. The technique is to use one basic color as the dominating factor throughout the scheme, and it requires well-arranged tones, patterns and textures. To some extent, a neutral is simplest to use, since all you need consider are the tonal values – the "strength" or "weight" of a tone, while still being able to employ the warm or cool characteristics of color by use of those grays which are biased toward one or the other. Strictly speaking, few schemes are entirely monochromatic. Although any color can be used as a basis, most interiors benefit from the addition of a neutral to emphasize color details, and small touches of contrasting color to add relief. The general effect is to soften the interior and to modulate strong accessory colors.

Colors with similar characteristics

Another approach is to use two related colors, those which occur side by side in the spectrum and which reinforce each other. For inspiration, you only have to look at naturally occurring combinations of color to see which appear pleasing when viewed together. Blue and green, both from the cool range, are demonstrated in combination whenever you see a green field or a row of trees against a blue sky. You can also see how a neutral in the form of clouds adds contrast to the combination. The two colors do not have to be used equally throughout the scheme. One can be dominant, while the other can be supplementary and emphasize details, or be featured as part of a specific area, such as the carpet or curtains. Perhaps one color is used in a strong form while the other only in its dark or light tones. It is important to consider the tonal balance between colors as this gives depth to the scheme.

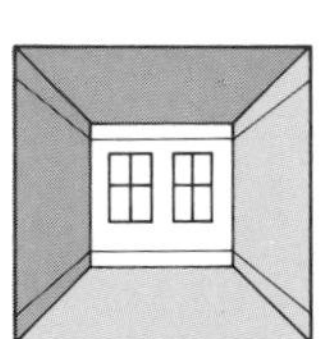

Contrasting colors

A more dramatic combination is achieved with two colors having opposite characteristics. If you place pure complementary colors side by side, one will appear to advance, while the other attempts to recede, thus producing a vibrating effect. This happens most vividly where one primary color is used against a mixture of the other two: red against green, blue against orange, yellow against purple; the technique is sometimes used in store signs, and on posters. Only use these color combinations in pure form when you want the contrast to be vibrant. You can counteract the effect by toning down one or both colors, or by separating them in the scheme with a related color or a neutral. Remember that artificial light will influence colors considerably, and those that appear discordant by day may be quite harmonious at night.

Multi-colored schemes

It is not easy to arrange a variety of different colors in one space to gain a pleasing effect, but if successfully done it can be very stimulating. One method is to use a limited number of pure colors, relying instead on subtle combinations of those colors in a toned-down form – hues or shades, in fact, but with areas of brighter colors in the detail. Another successful approach uses either a monochromatic scheme, or a color-related one (all blues, all greens together) as a basis, gradually building up areas with lots of patterns in the form of cushions and curtains. Some manufacturers produce basic sets of designs in a range of colors, and the common pattern adds the necessary sense of unity to the total scheme. You can obtain quite a pleasing effect if you run through a range of colors in the spectrum, in the order in which they naturally occur, gradually changing in tone from one to another.

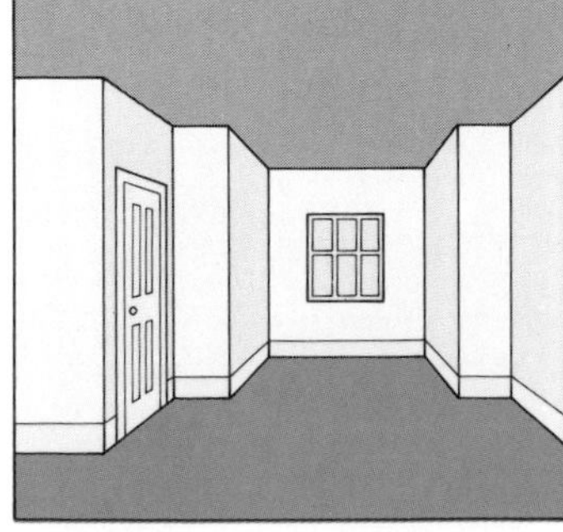

Unifying areas
Link intercommunicating areas with the same color, or with similar tones and hues.

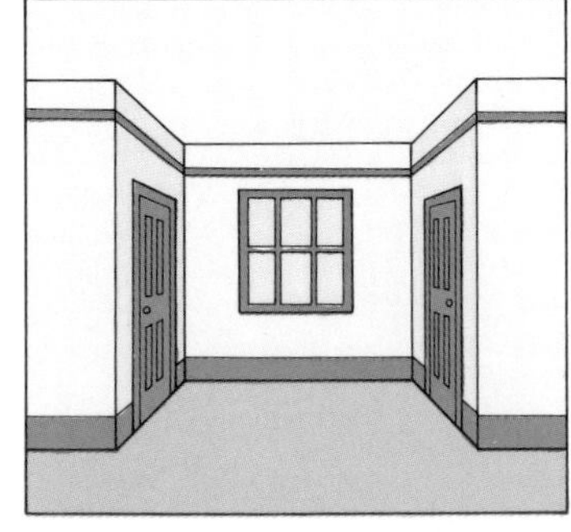

Painting woodwork
Similarly, areas can be integrated by having the doors and windows painted the same color.

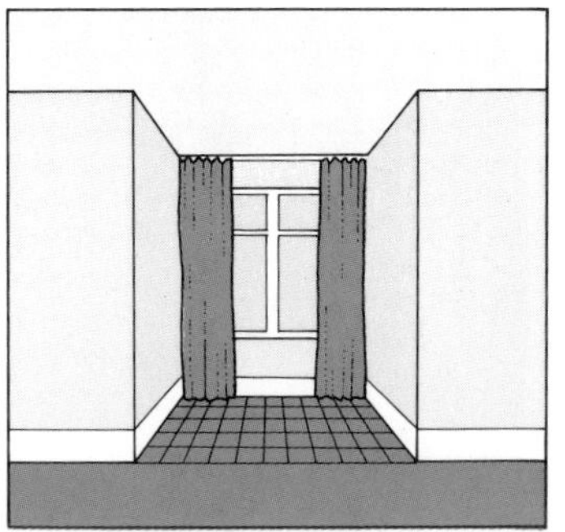

Co-ordinated materials
Texture, pattern or color of carpets and curtains can also unify.

Collecting samples

Having decided on the color scheme of your room, gather as many relevant samples of furnishing fabrics and materials as you require to make your final selection, and compare them with the scheme. Professional designers do this by mounting the samples on to a piece of cardboard, each sample in the proportion in which it is to be used. If the walls are to be painted or papered in one dominant color, this will certainly be the main factor in your selection. The contrasting molding, if you have any, will be less important, so the samples should reflect the same sense of proportion. Remember that most patterned materials look quite different when handled as large samples, so try and obtain generous lengths when possible.

Making a sample board
Mount samples close together, as the color of cardboard in between will alter their relationship.

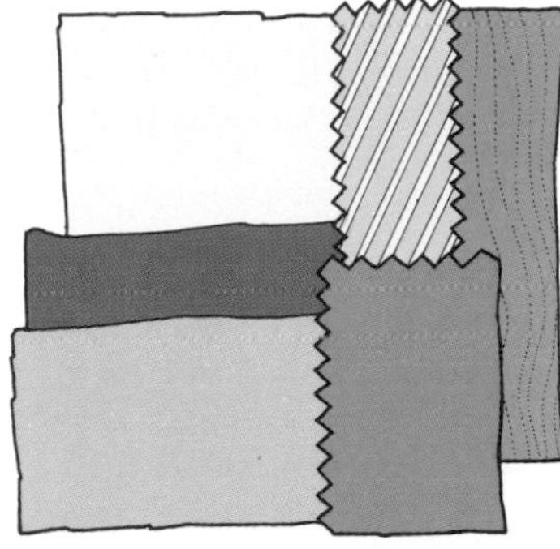

Proportion of materials
Make board large enough to take materials displayed in proportion to their final use.

Matching to fitted materials
Leave space in cardboard for hole to view samples next to existing materials.

Floor covering: cork tiles

Wall covering: paper

Paintwork

Furniture

Furnishing fabrics and accessories

Drapes

Floor covering: carpet

Effect of light conditions
*Quality and direction of light will affect the appearance of materials and fabrics. The color and texture will change, so compare your sample board in full daylight **1**, artificial light **2**, and shadow **3** before making your final choice.*

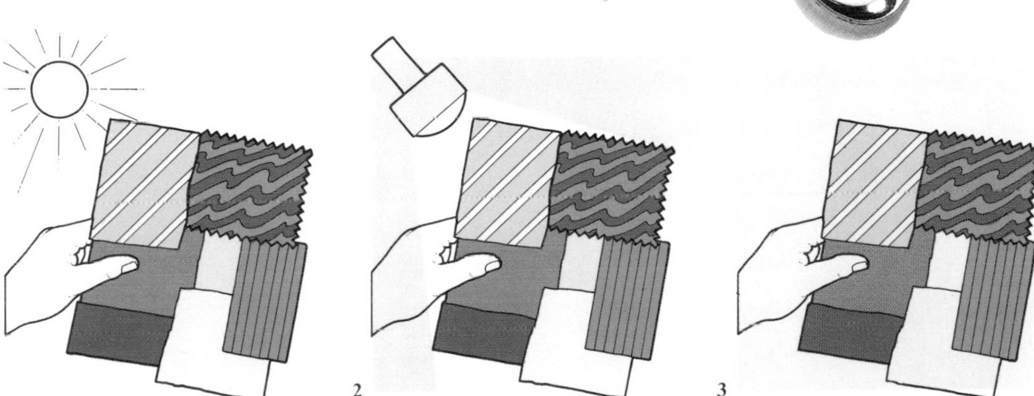

Relating Colors & Materials

1

1 Neutral colors
The careful choice of tone or strong pattern is essential to create sufficient contrast, especially where a scheme relies heavily on neutral colors.

2 Contrasting colors
Primary colors used together are always very striking. The addition of white adds a feeling of freshness and prevents the primary colors producing unwanted vibrant effects.

3 Unifying areas
To avoid unwanted combinations use the same carpet and ceiling color to unify areas while creating an illusion of greater space.

4 Related colors
Closely related reds and browns produce a feeling of harmony and warmth, which is strengthened by the deep brown carpet and ceiling.

2

3

4

Texture & Pattern

Cool textures
Shiny, smooth surfaces such as marble, glass, mirrors, ceramic tiles, stainless steel, gloss paint and plastic are regarded as cool textures. Such surfaces are cold to the touch and similarly make a room feel colder than usual.

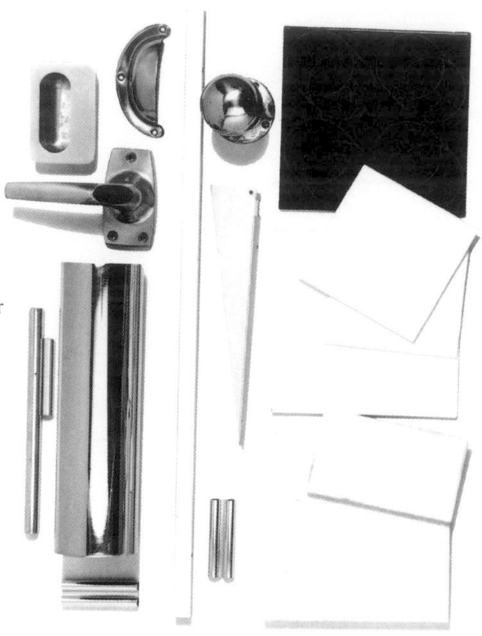

Warm textures
Rough, non-reflective surfaces such as wood, cork, brick, wool and other natural fibers are regarded as warm materials. They contribute to a soft, cosy atmosphere.

Contrasting textures
By contrasting one texture against another, we can create visual interest without the need of color: brick against plaster, gloss paint against stone, a wool rug against wood. Cool materials must be relieved by some contrasting warm ones, while warm materials can be used with little or no cool contrast.

Combining effects

Texture and pattern combined with color and tone give us all the elements needed to produce decorative effects. Both the color and the special tactile characteristics of a texture are affected by light and its direction. Shadows darken color and make texture more obvious. Textured wallpaper will show up better adjacent to a window than opposite it. Such effects can be both an advantage and a problem – rough surfaces such as bare brick or cork will benefit from side lighting whereas any imperfections in a gloss surface will be exaggerated. Small and subtle textures may be lost altogether unless they are appropriately illuminated.

Unexpected textural interest can be provided by a wall of bookcases, groups of small objects, a selection of plants or perhaps a collection of small photographs placed on a wall. Like colors, textures possess similar characteristics in terms of warmth and coolness, as shown on the opposite page.

Pattern, on the other hand, depends for its effect on a deliberate arrangement or repetition of shape. This may be a printed surface motif or a combination of modular shapes – parquet flooring for instance. Used correctly, pattern imposes a sense of order and purpose. Scale must be carefully considered, as a large pattern over a small or uneven surface can become mere patches of broken color.

Some of the effects of pattern are shown on the right. If used unwisely, pattern effects can become safety hazards as when they camouflage raised or covered steps.

Manufactured patterns
A rich variety of patterns results from embossing or surface printing on to fabrics, paper and tiles.

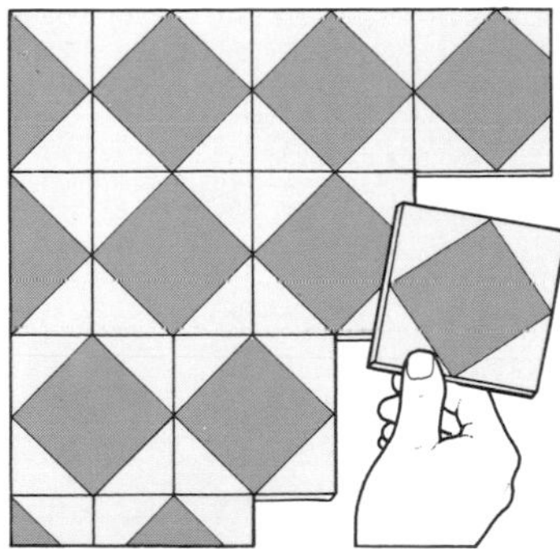

Using modules for pattern making
Even a simple repetitive module can be the starting point for a large number of different patterns.

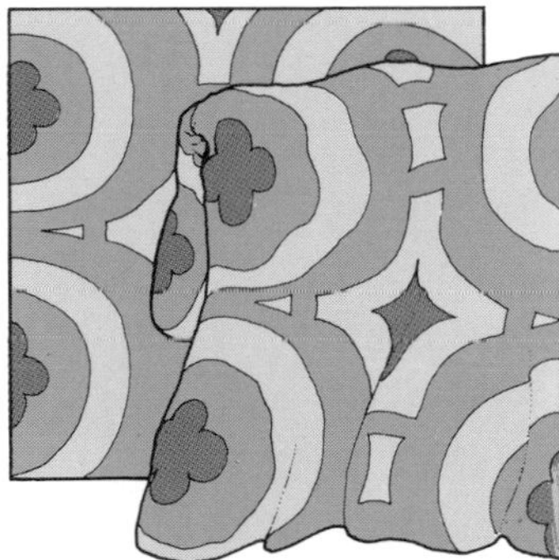

Matched fabric and wallpaper
A unified effect is produced by having wall and window coverings of the same design.

Small patterns
Small repeat patterns create the illusion of space by making surfaces recede.

Large patterns
Large patterns will optically reduce the appearance of large areas and wall surfaces.

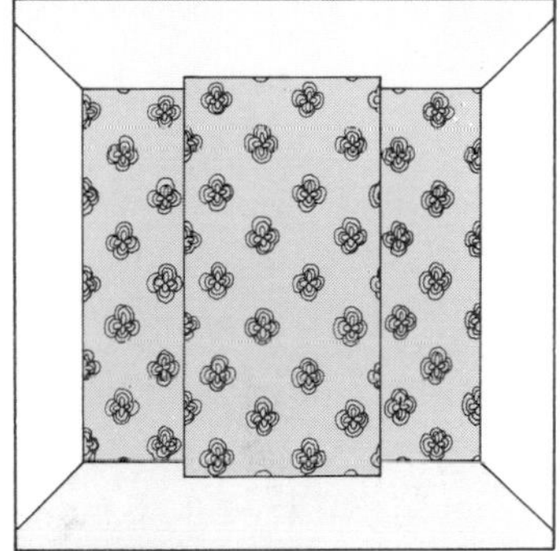

Pattern as camouflage
Carefully arranged patterns can be used to disguise or mute certain unattractive features.

Geometric patterns
Three-dimensional designs can be used to create the illusion of depth.

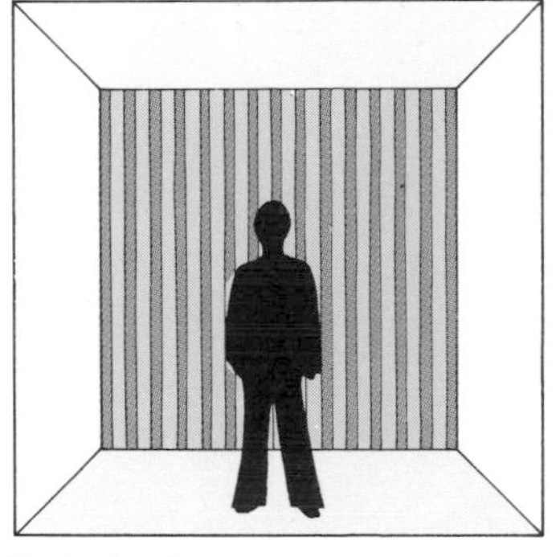

Vertical stripes
Vertical wall coverings will create or emphasize a feeling of height.

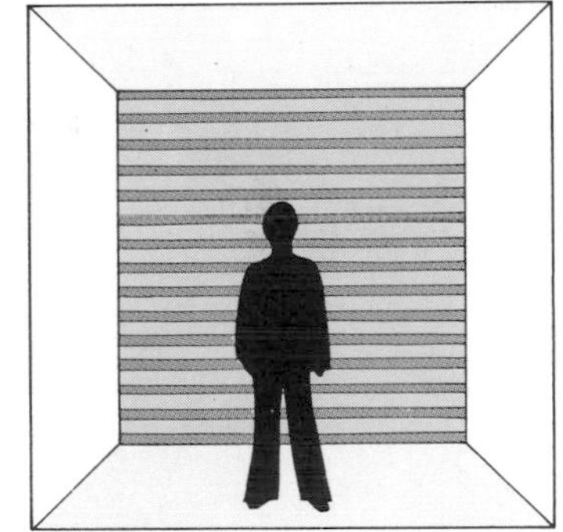

Horizontal stripes
In a similar way, horizontal stripes create a feeling of width.

Highlighting a texture

A full, general light has the effect of flattening the surface of a texture, **A.** An acute, raking light reveals the depth or tactile feeling, **B.** As the direction and intensity of the light change, the texture becomes softer, **C.**

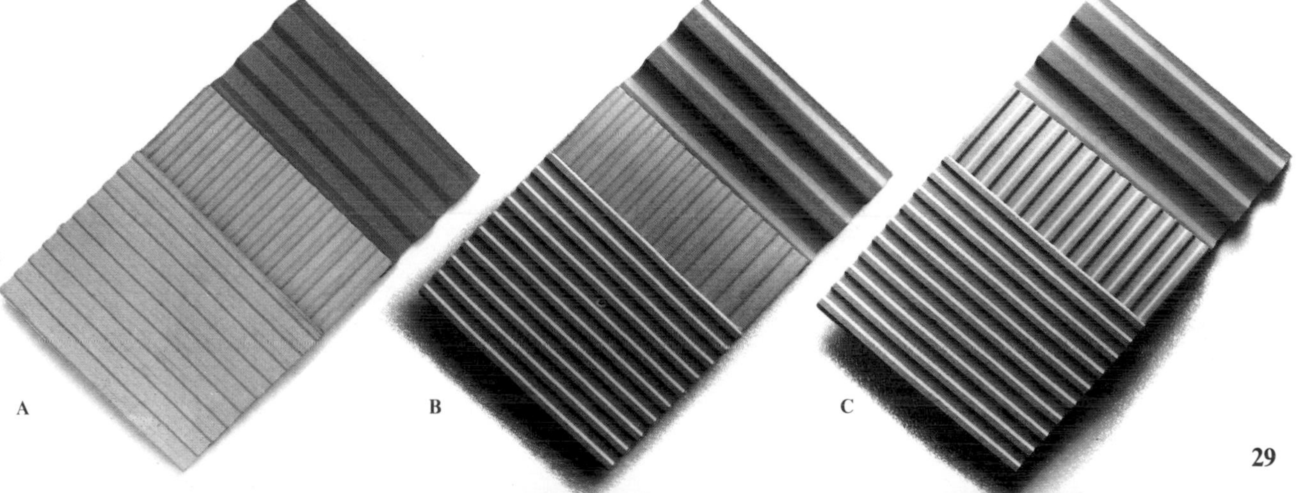

Texture & Pattern

1

2

3

4

5

1 Contrasting textures
Textures can be used in juxtaposition. Here, smooth contrasts with rough, cold with warm.

2 Complementary pattern
Patterns should suit the required atmosphere of a room. A geometric pattern, which gives a sense of order and regimentation, blends very well with a group of militaria in a collector's den.

3 Pattern and scale
This corner of a room shows a sensitive use of small scale patterns, which work equally well on the furniture, cushions, drapes and even the picture frames.

4 Unexpected textures
Spontaneous collections of objects often provide unlooked for visual interest.

5 Co-ordinated pattern
The use of an identical pattern transforms a corner into a light and airy alcove seat.

6 Using plants
The flowing shapes and textures of plants are echoed in floral fabric prints and pictures.

7 Overall effects
Rough plaster walls complement the quarry floor tiles and wooden louvered shutters. The furniture also contrasts with the clean, white bookshelves.

8 Pattern and atmosphere
A collection of decorated objects displayed against a delicate, flowered wallpaper combine to create an unmistakable atmosphere of cosiness and charm.

6

7

8

Organizing Work

Relative costs

The information given in these charts is based on an average price per unit and on an average quality material. Any assessment of true value for money must equate the cost with the durability of the material.

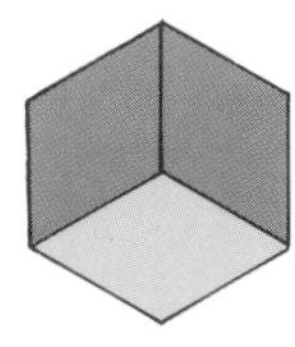

Wall coverings

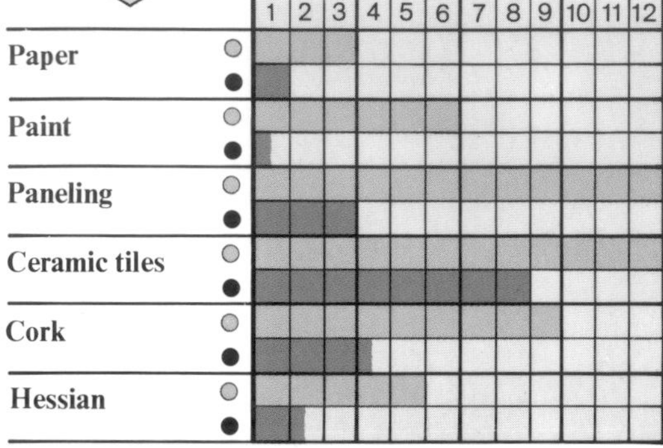

○Durability ●Relative cost

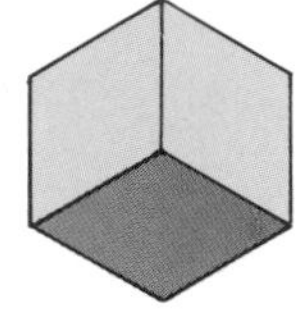

Floor coverings

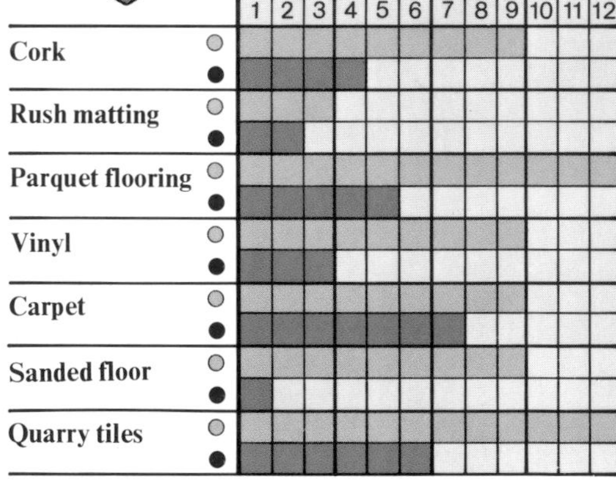

○Durability ●Relative cost

Window treatments

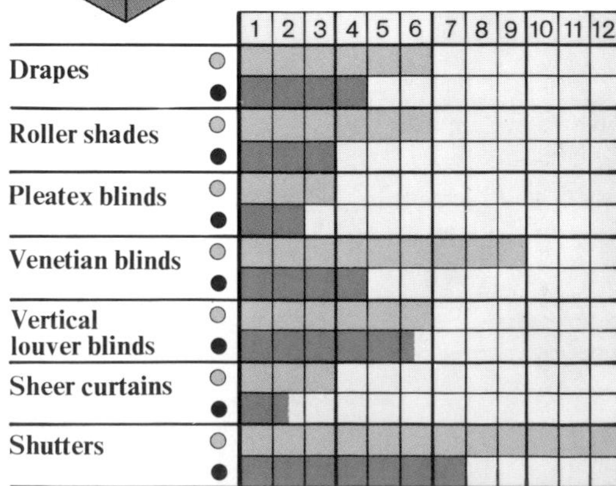

Key: ●Relative cost. ○Durability 1-3 Fair: 4-6 Good: 7-9 Very Good: 10-12 Excellent.

Starting points

When you are faced with creating a new interior decoration scheme, a lot depends on whether you aim to make major alterations, to modify existing finishes, or to start from scratch. You may want to decorate a new extension to your home, or perhaps you are moving into a new house, or you intend changing the function of an area where the decoration and furniture are no longer suitable. The information set out below describes the important planning stages, and how to organize the various elements-colors and textures, materials and furniture, fabrics, paints, fixtures and fittings. Having reached the right decision and plotted the broad outlines, you only need to fill in the details.

The budget

First of all, decide on your priorities. The charts on the left make a comparison between the durability and expense of materials for various decorative treatments. If you begin a scheme without a firm idea of how much you can afford to spend on each separate item, you may end up choosing materials which you will have to reject because they are too costly: you might spend a lot of time planning a color scheme only to discover that the main item - a rug of a particular shade - is way beyond your budget. Perhaps the best solution is to choose the carpeting first; the balance of the budget can then be apportioned to other items in order of priority.

Practical requirements

Make notes of both the decorative and structural requirements of the interior. Would you prefer that it be made warmer, cooler, more stimulating, or relaxing? Is the lighting suitable, and should it be slightly improved - or radically altered? Could the proportions of the room be changed by raising or lowering the ceiling, or by emphasizing a particular wall or feature? Are the present decorative finishes suitable? As your scheme progresses, keep these basic points in mind; it is easy to get so carried away with a multitude of detail that your main objectives become eclipsed.

Utilizing existing materials

Most items of furniture and carpeting will probably remain. Curtains or shades could be re-used by moving them to another room, unless they have been specially made to fit a particular window. You may also have to retain certain features that were originally an expensive outlay - wood-paneled walls, ceramic tiled floor, or perhaps a costly wallpaper; these cannot be discarded like a coat of paint. Any of these features could be the starting point for a new scheme, so do not regard them as restrictive. Modern furnishing fabrics and materials offer an almost limitless choice - many will blend very successfully with your existing scheme. Alternatively, consider which items could be refurbished by stripping off old finishes, re-upholstering or re-painting.

Relating colors and materials

Consider the approach you wish to pursue: monochromatic, related or contrasting colors, and gather your selected materials together to make sample boards. As we have seen, it is advisable to budget for the expensive items first, because the choice is likely to be more limited than your choice of wall fabrics, paint and furnishing fabrics. Now take the larger areas of color and texture that remain - they must be chosen as the background to everything else. When selecting patterns at this stage, check back to your practical requirements to see that they do not conflict with your original aims for the scheme. Finally, fill in the details by obtaining color samples of paintwork, materials for cushions and lampshades; small items can make a surprising difference to the final look of any decorative scheme.

Proceeding with the work

Once you have made your final selection, order the materials from the suppliers. Try to plot the progress of the work by stages, so that large bulky items like rugs and furniture do not arrive before they are needed. For this reason, if your work includes decorating a hallway, leave it until last in case deliveries of furniture damage the new paintwork in passing. The order in which you should tackle the actual decoration so as to get the best results is suggested in the chart on page 35. Above all, if work may be affected by local regulations, ensure that you are acquainted with these and that you have any necessary permits before starting construction.

Decorative Finishes

Painting & Papering Tools

Preparation
Invest in excellent equipment if you can: it will repay you in the end. You will need two scrapers, one with a three-inch blade for stripping off old wallpaper, the other one inch wide for removing old paint; for molded surfaces you will need a hook-shaped scraper. A three-inch filling knife is best for cracks and small holes. A soft-bristled brush will remove dust from both flat and molded surfaces, while a putty knife will give you a nicely beveled finish if you have to replace window frames. Paint can be removed with a gas blowtorch and surfaces can be smoothed down with a sanding block bound with abrasive paper.

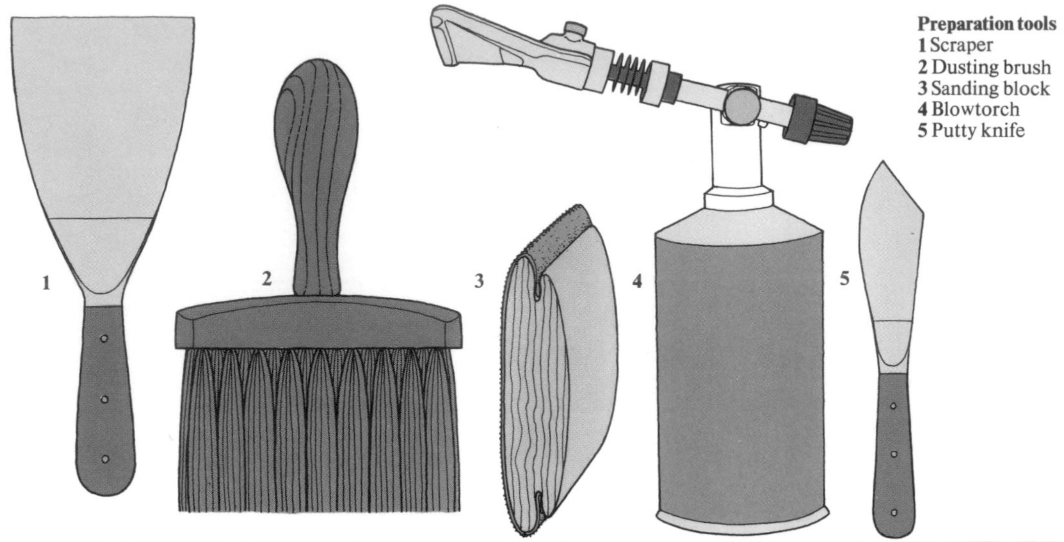

Preparation tools
1 Scraper
2 Dusting brush
3 Sanding block
4 Blowtorch
5 Putty knife

Wallpapering
Wallpapering scissors are made up to 12 inches in length: choose the longest pair you can comfortably handle. A hardwood seam roller ensures that, once pasted, seams remain firmly stuck down. A plumb bob makes for accurate vertical hanging of paper; a large and good quality paste brush will apply paste evenly, without shedding bristles. You can cut around light fixtures and other protrusions or moldings with a trimming knife. A hanging brush will smooth paper on to the wall, allowing you to release trapped air bubbles without tearing the paper. Finally, a steel tape is essential if measuring is to be accurate.

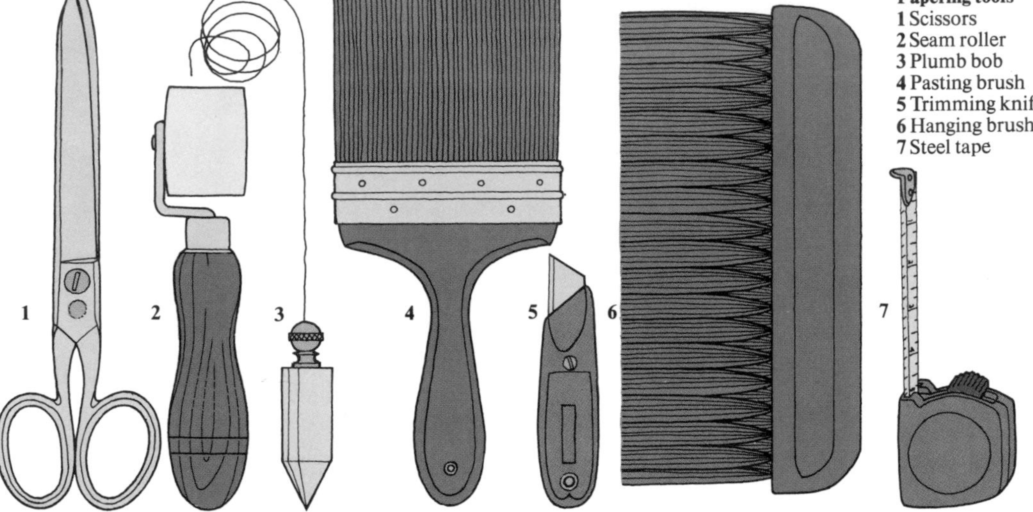

Papering tools
1 Scissors
2 Seam roller
3 Plumb bob
4 Pasting brush
5 Trimming knife
6 Hanging brush
7 Steel tape

Workstations
Before you begin work, take drapes and pictures from walls, remove furniture, and cover floor with a dust sheet. Make a platform with stepladders and a plank.

Stepladders
Choose the aluminum variety, which is light to handle and very hardwearing. Ideally, buy a model with a small platform for paint rollers and brushes. A pair of these ladders, with a stout board between them, is essential for papering and painting ceilings.

Paste tables
Paste tables usually fold out to a convenient length, and have either wood or metal key frames. The length and width of the average table makes the job of cutting and pasting as easy as possible. As an extra guide to measurements, mark the edge of your paste table at six-inch intervals.

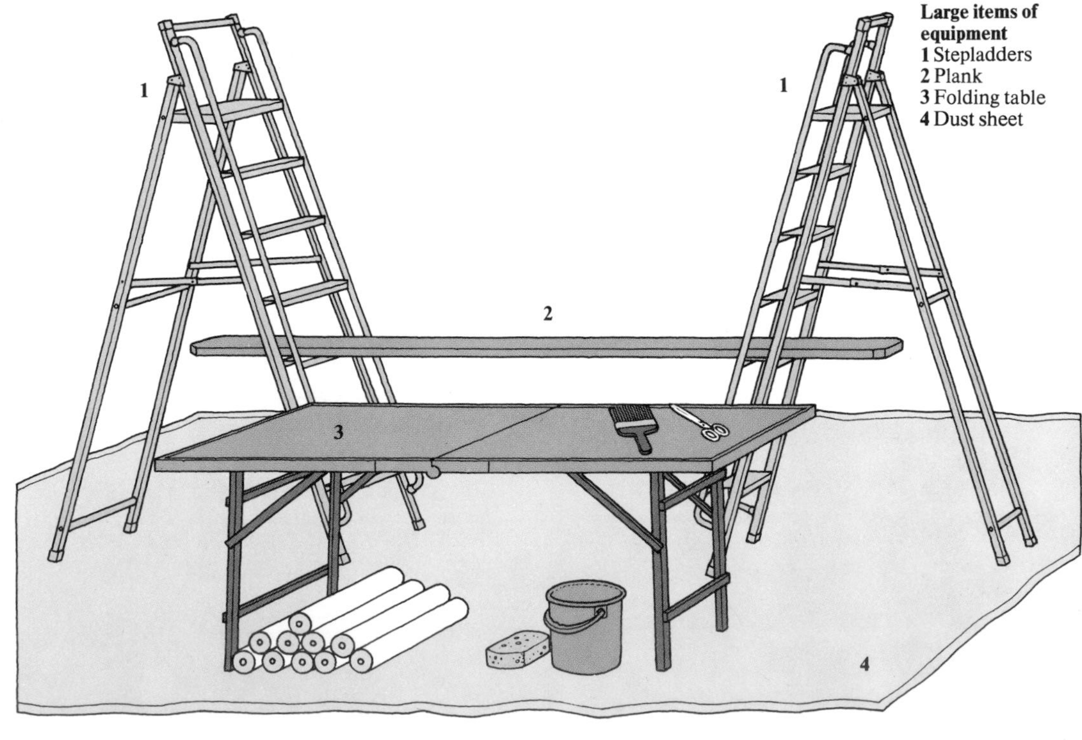

Large items of equipment
1 Stepladders
2 Plank
3 Folding table
4 Dust sheet

Painting tools

A paint shield for windows stops paint getting on to the glass, but a razor blade scraper will remove it if it does. A paint roller ideally has three 9-inch removable covers: mohair for gloss paint, short pile dacron for latex, long-haired dacron for textured surfaces. Use a roller tray for holding paint. Buy the best brushes you can, as cheap ones shed hairs and do not apply paint evenly. For latex paint choose a 4-inch brush, and a 1, 2 and 3-inch selection for finer work. An alternative to the brush is now popular: a paint pad of plastic foam with a layer of fine mohair bristles.

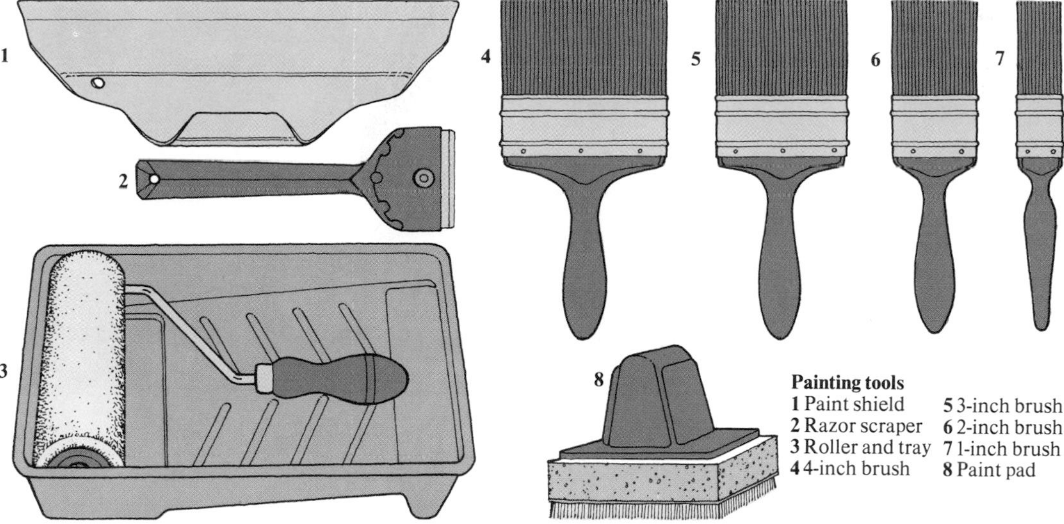

Painting tools
1 Paint shield
2 Razor scraper
3 Roller and tray
4 4-inch brush
5 3-inch brush
6 2-inch brush
7 1-inch brush
8 Paint pad

Care of brushes

Always clean a brush immediately after use with the appropriate solvent: for oil-based paints use turpentine or paint thinner, for latex paints use clean warm water. Comb out the bristles with a metal comb, and work the comb into the bristles where they meet the handle - the paint becomes deposited here, dries hard, and soon spoils the brush's efficiency. When the brush has been cleaned and is dry, store it wrapped in brown paper or foil; this helps it to retain its shape.

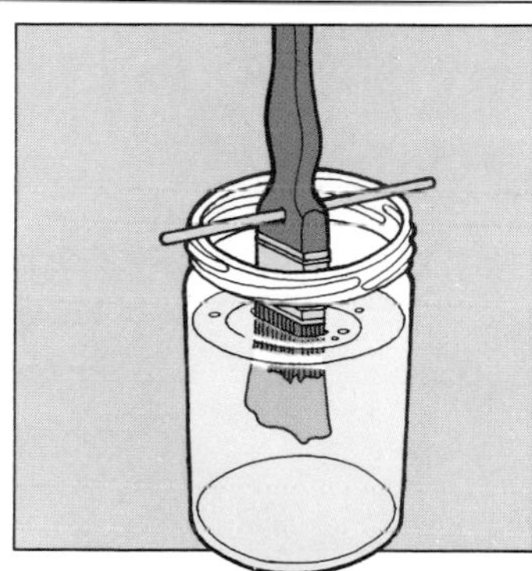

1 Suspend brushes for overnight protection in containers of solvent by means of a rod passed through a drilled hole in the handle.

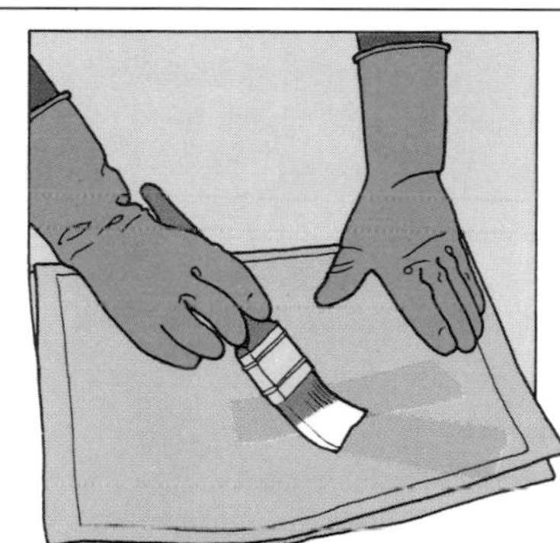

2 When you have finished a job, wipe excess paint off the brush with newspaper before soaking.

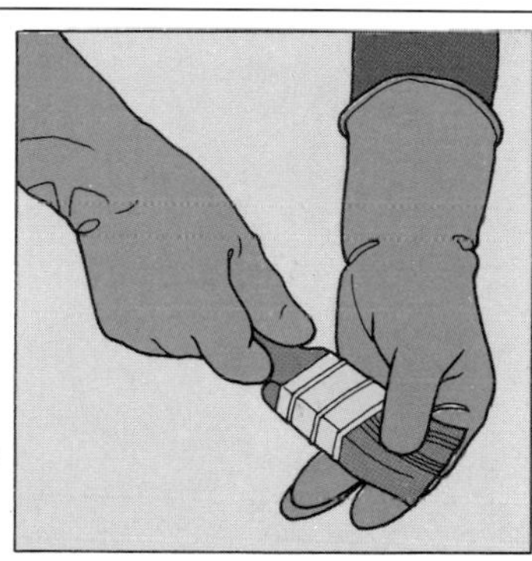

3 Work out remaining paint by squeezing the bristles with your fingers, fanning them out. Then wash brush in warm soapy water.

Care of rollers

Like brushes, rollers repay careful maintenance. Make sure you clean the roller as soon as you have finished work. The fabric holds a surprising amount of paint. With oil based paints you will have to remove this surplus with turpentine before washing the remainder away with warm soapy water. Thorough drying is important with rollers and brushes, as some have metal parts that will rust, discoloring the paint next time you use it. Because of this always dry the roller handle and ferrule carefully after washing.

1 At the end of a job, roll out excess paint on newspaper. Pour solvent (water for latex paint) into tray and soak both tray and roller.

2 Remove cover from roller, and wash it and the tray in warm, soapy water to remove partially dissolved paint.

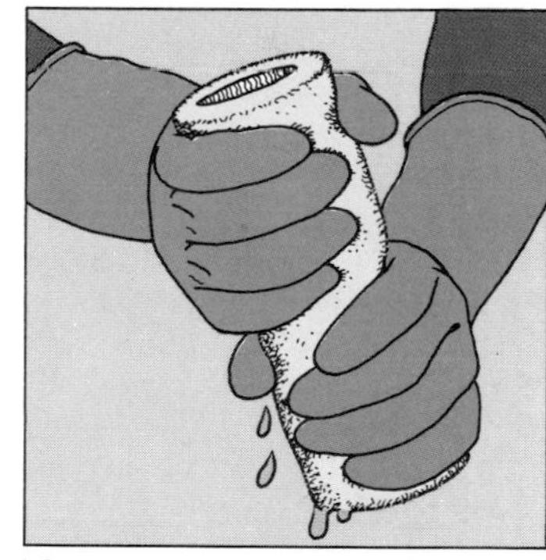

3 Squeeze out the cover and dry it with a rag. When thoroughly dry, store it in brown paper or foil.

Working sequence

For successful painting and papering, it is most important to proceed logically. The chart on the right lists the correct order of work, depending on the type of wall or ceiling covering you intend to use. It is vital to complete the preparation first so that you do not contaminate any finished work.

Preparation

Remove old ceiling and wall coverings
Rake out cracks and holes in plaster prior to filling
Wash walls to remove old paste and sizing
Make good any defective plaster
Size or seal walls as required

Painted walls and ceiling	Papered walls and ceiling	Painted ceiling and papered walls
Hang lining paper on walls and ceiling	Apply first undercoat to woodwork	Paper and paint ceiling
Paint walls and ceiling	Apply second undercoat	Apply first undercoat to woodwork
Apply first undercoat to woodwork	Apply gloss coat	Apply second undercoat
Apply second undercoat	Hang lining paper where necessary	Apply gloss coat
Then apply gloss coat	Hang ceiling and wall covering	Hang lining paper on walls
		Hang final wall covering

Walls

Practical considerations
Your choice of wall finishes should depend on the condition of the walls and the function of each particular room or area. Those parts of the house normally subject to wear – hallways, for example, where a constant flow of traffic passes through, will need very durable materials. Obviously, the more durable the material, the longer it will last and the more economical it will prove. Before deciding on a wall finish, try and familiarize yourself with the range of materials available, so that you can combine the decorative with the functional. Kitchens and bathrooms, areas in which a lot of moisture is present, should be painted with a gloss rather than a mat finish latex paint. The gloss is more likely to show up condensation but can be washed to remove grease and smoke stains. Similarly, vinyl wallpapers are both washable and waterproof and can be easily removed. However, they should not be placed in direct contact with running water as in a shower unit, for instance. Ceramic or plastic tiles should be used on walls around sinks and bathtubs to provide a fully waterproof seal.
Living areas tend to have their decor changed frequently; a fresh coat of paint is the most economical treatment, but textured or thick vinyl wallpaper is better able to camouflage imperfect walls. Wood paneling is more expensive but it is the most long-lasting finish and it can be used on walls in bad repair. Stains or dyes can add a permanent color finish. More fragile wall treatments can be used in bedrooms, which are less subject to wear and tear. Fabric stretched over panels such as silk or hessian materials can be fixed directly to the wall. Cork tiles can provide an element of soundproofing. Children's rooms require more durable wall coverings and ones that are easy to clean. A cork or softwood wall here can be used for displaying artwork while plastic laminates can be wiped free of crayon marks.
Hallways, stairs and landings, should be covered with heavy vinyl papers or a combination of textured paper and latex paint. You can clad the lower half of a wall with paneling, and paint the wall above. A workroom, especially one sited in a basement or garage, can be left with "fair-faced" brick or block walls, or simply painted with latex.

1

2

1 Plastic veneered board
This finish is good for walls in bad repair and is especially useful for bedrooms where it will provide extra sound and heat insulation.

2 Wood paneling
Consider covering the lower half of the walls which take most wear with paneling, then painting or papering the wall above. Such paneling is less expensive and provides a long-lasting covering.

3 Brick and wood
Brick and wood go well together and require very little care to maintain although dust can adhere to a textured brick surface. Brush down, and where necessary, wash the bricks with warm water using a bristle brush, not wire which will mark the surface.

4/5 Panels and tiles
The narrow strip of wall between kitchen counter and upper cabinets can be easily scratched by cooking utensils or appliances. Provide a hard-wearing surface of wood paneling, wall tiles or plastic laminate.

6 Mosaic tiles
Mosaic tiles provide an easy-to-clean surface in areas which have to be water-proofed. They can also be shaped to fit curved walls.

3

4

5

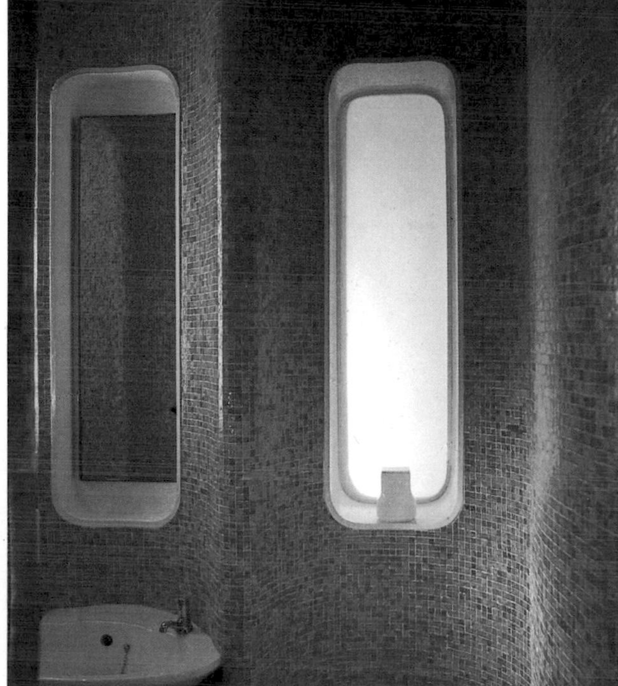

6

Papering Walls

Preparing the surfaces

Even a heavy paper will fail to disguise large cracks and bumps, so most wall surfaces need preparing before they can be papered. Newly plastered walls require a coat of sizing, which, after it has dried, provides a non-porous surface for the paste. A sealer coat should be applied to wallboard after any nailheads have been treated with rust inhibitive primer. It is best to remove old wallpaper with warm water, although vinyl and ready-pasted papers strip off in entire lengths without pre-soaking. The vinyl's backing paper which remains stuck to the wall is an ideal surface for repapering. Wash the wall after stripping off pasted papers. Latex and glossy painted surfaces need to be washed with warm, soapy water, and the surface scraped with sandpaper before pasting. After washing off old whitewash, apply a coat of stabilizing primer. Never hang paper on walls affected by damp. Treat mold growth with fungicide, but efflorescence, a white, powdery deposit, should be rubbed down with coarse burlap, then painted with an alkaline resistant priming material.

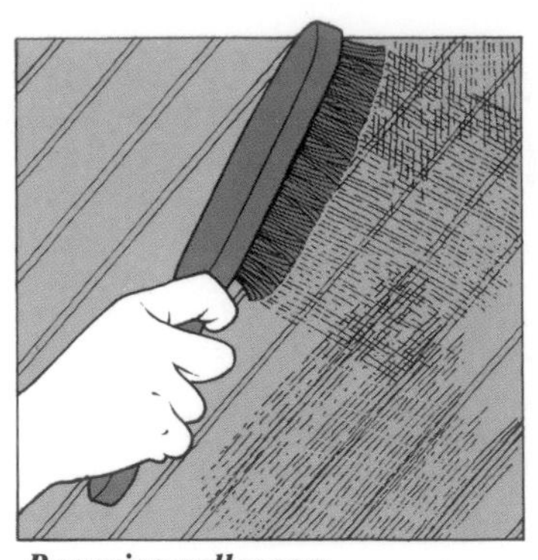

Removing wallpapers
1 Scour washable papers with a wire brush. Soak with stripping solution.

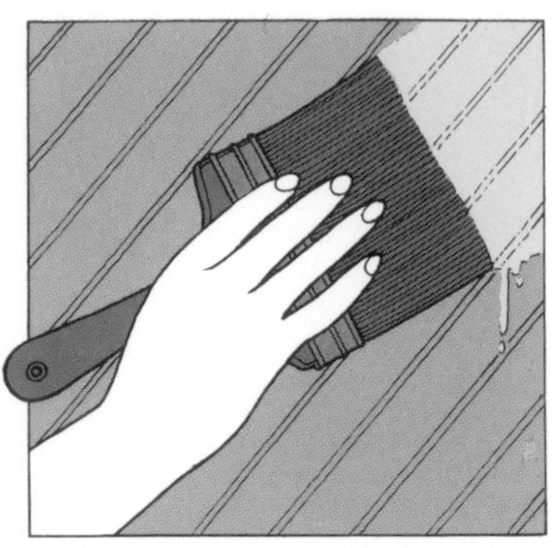

2 Using a clean paste brush, apply adequate amounts of warm water to porous papers (or use a brand-name stripping solution).

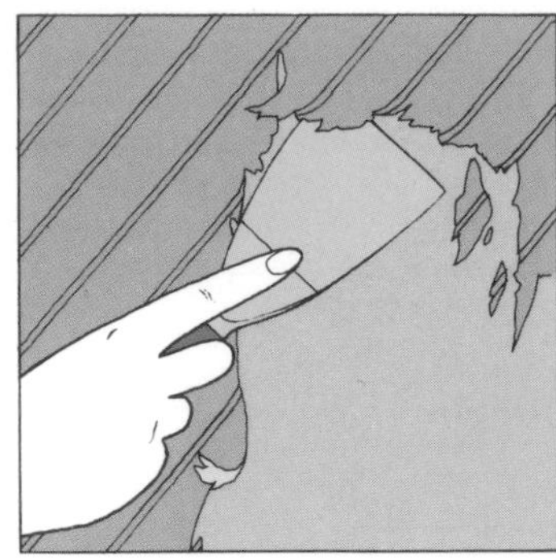

3 Use a scraper with a broad blade for stripping ordinary papers. Do not dig its corners into the plaster. Re-soak stubborn patches.

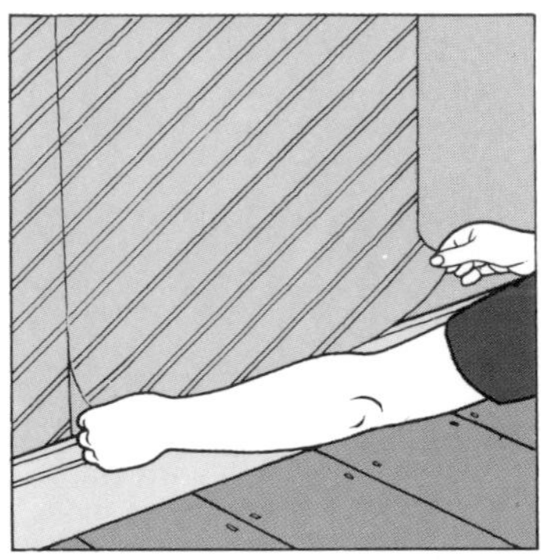

4 To remove vinyl papers, lift the bottom corners and pull the entire length away from wall. If paper tears, strip off backing paper.

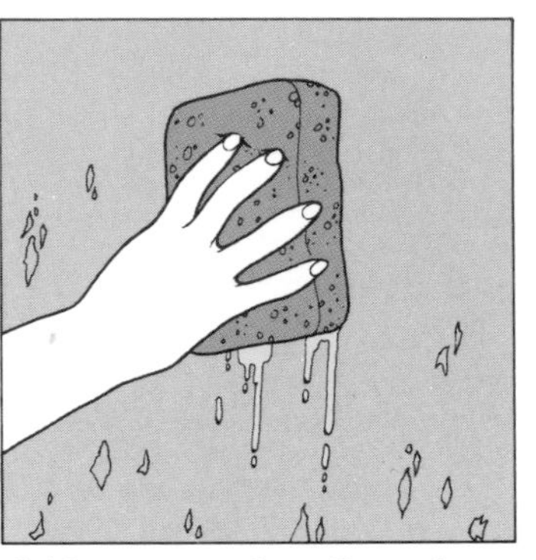

5 After stripping the walls, wash them with clean, hot water to remove any residue of paste or paper. Clear away all waste.

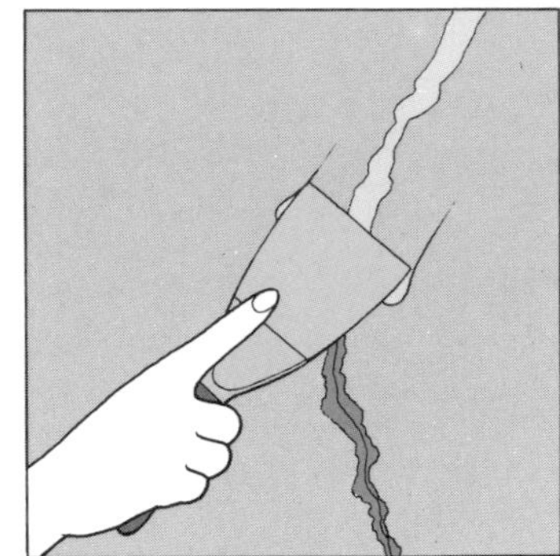

6 Rake out and fill small cracks with spackle and large holes with patching plaster. When dry, rub down with sandpaper.

Estimating and buying wallpaper

Make use of the chart below to calculate the amount of paper you will need, and buy it all at the same time. This ensures that the color is constant throughout the batch. Even so, it is sensible partly to unroll the lengths of paper at home and to check on any color variations. Return any odd rolls to your dealer or plan your work so that they can be used on a window wall, or in a corner. Ask your dealer for help in estimating large, repeating designs (see opposite page) as they often mean more wastage.

Cutting and pasting

Set up your pasting table in the center of the room, and lay a dust sheet underneath it. Have a sponge and water handy to wipe off excess paste. Choose the paste to match the paper; vinyl, for example needs a slow drying paste with a fungicide. Mix your paste to the maker's instructions; make sure there are no lumps. The pasting sequence is shown on the right: line paper up with the far edge of the table and paste in sections brushing away from you **1.** Then bring paper to front edge and brush toward you **2.** Fold the ends paste side inward **3.**

1

2

3

Estimating chart

Wall height	Wall widths including doors and windows													
in feet	30	34	38	42	46	50	54	58	62	66	70	74	78	82
7 –7½	4	5	5	6	6	7	7	8	8	9	9	10	10	11
7½–8	5	5	6	6	7	7	8	8	9	9	10	10	11	11
8 –8½	5	5	6	7	7	8	9	9	10	10	11	12	12	13
8½–9	5	5	6	7	7	8	9	9	10	10	11	12	12	13
9 –9½	6	6	7	7	8	9	9	10	10	11	12	12	13	14
9½–10	6	6	7	8	8	9	10	10	11	12	12	13	14	14
10 –10½	6	7	8	9	9	10	10	11	12	13	13	14	15	16
	Number of rolls required													

Deciding where to begin
If your paper is plain or has a small pattern, start in a corner near a window, and work in both directions toward the door (see **A** right). Center a large-patterned paper in a prominent place such as above the fireplace and work outward, **B**. Always align adjacent lengths so that the pattern registers correctly. When cutting lengths allow an extra 2 in. top and bottom for positioning and trimming.

Hanging the paper
If you are hanging a thin paper, or if the wall surface has been extensively patched, cover the wall horizontally with good quality lining paper; leave it to dry thoroughly before hanging the wallcovering. Cut the lengths according to your estimates (remembering to allow for trimming waste). Keep the short ends of rolls to put above doors and windows. Mark each piece on the reverse so that you hang it right way up; errors in small patterns especially may go unnoticed. To hang, follow the sequence illustrated on the right. Make sure paste has soaked in enough on thicker papers. Always have a cloth or sponge on hand for wiping away excess paste, but take care not to spoil the finish. If a portion of the edge will not stay down, push a little extra paste under it, and press flat. Treat external corners in the same way as internal ones (see below right), but allow 1 in. extra instead of ½ in. Waste should be trimmed with scissors as a knife will tear wet paper.

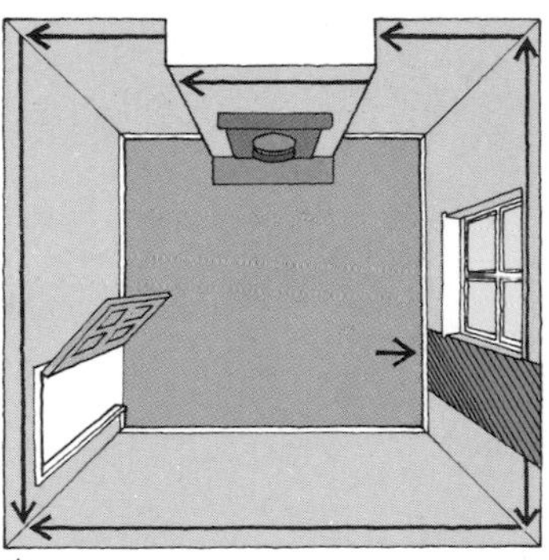
A

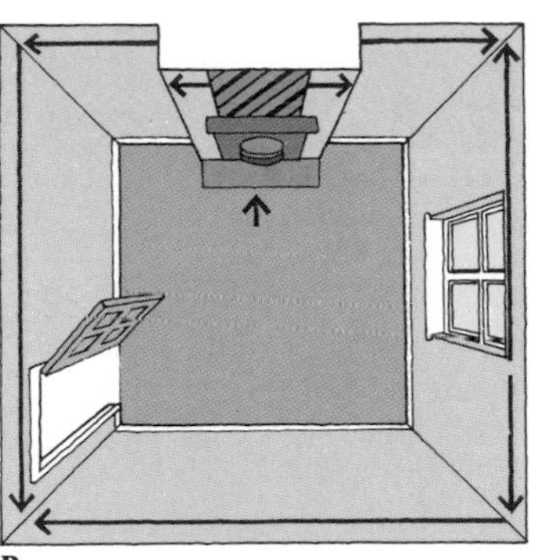
B

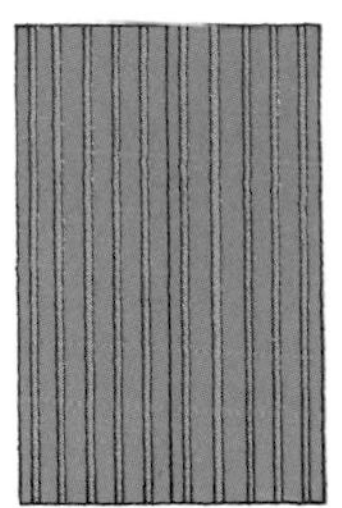
Straight patterns
4 in. waste is usually enough to match pattern repeats.

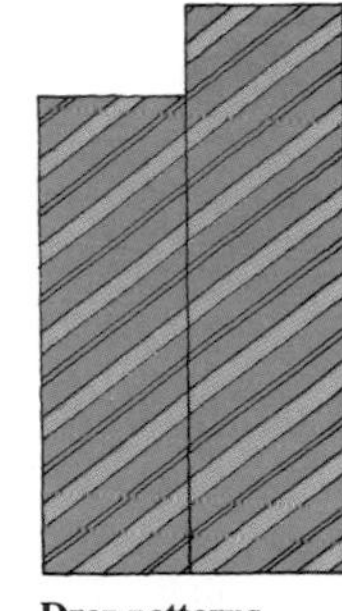
Drop patterns
Always check design matches before cutting out lengths.

Hanging wallpaper
1 To hang first strip accurately, mark the position of a plumb line on the wall.

2 Line up edge of first strip with vertical mark, lightly brushing the top. Adjust by sliding paper or peel off and re-position.

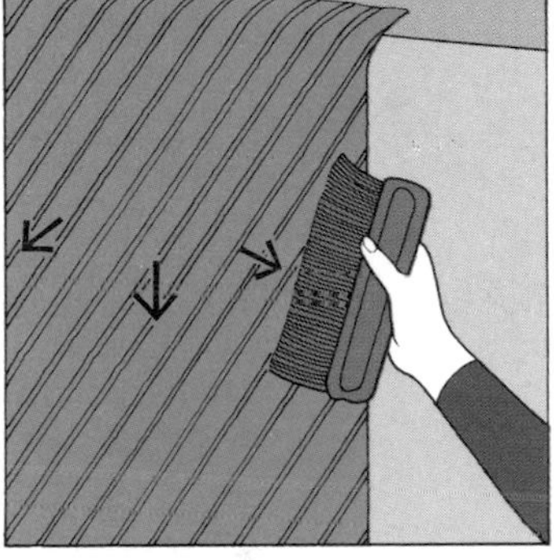
3 When the paper is in place, brush it out systematically from the center, smoothing out any creases or air bubbles.

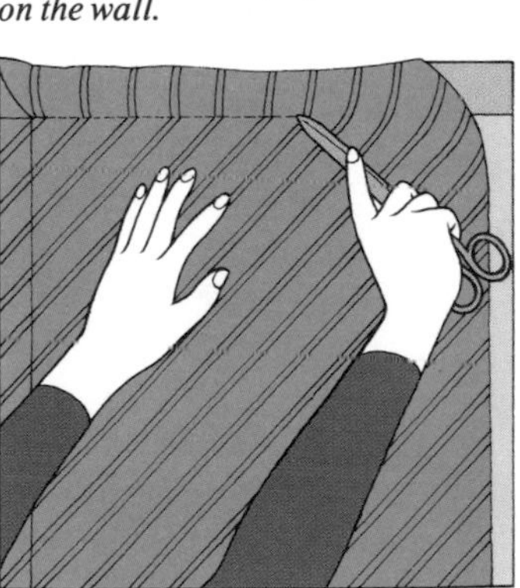
4 Brush the top of the paper into the angle between the wall and ceiling, and gently mark a trimming line with a pair of scissors.

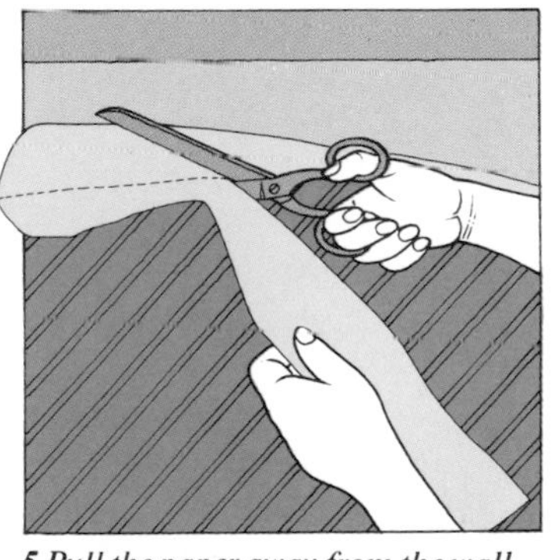
5 Pull the paper away from the wall. Cut along the crease with scissors and brush back in place. Unfold the bottom section and repeat.

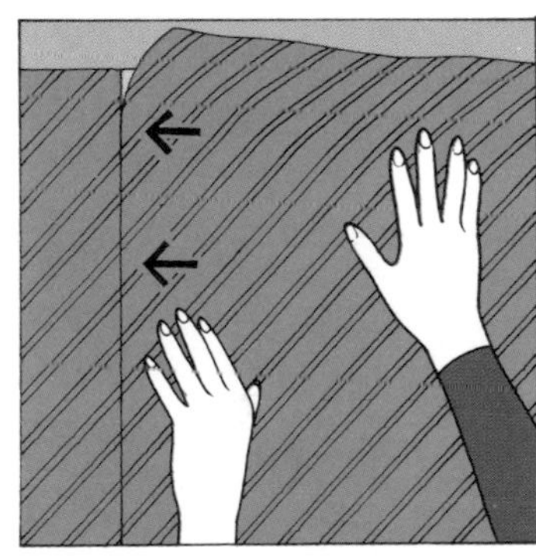
6 Hang the next length, butting it against the edge of the first one. Match the pattern by sliding the paper with the palms of your hands.

Carrying pasted paper
Hold the paper so that there is a large fold at the top and a smaller one on the bottom with the pasted surfaces together. Carry the paper to the wall. Grasp the top end by the corners and allow it to unfold.

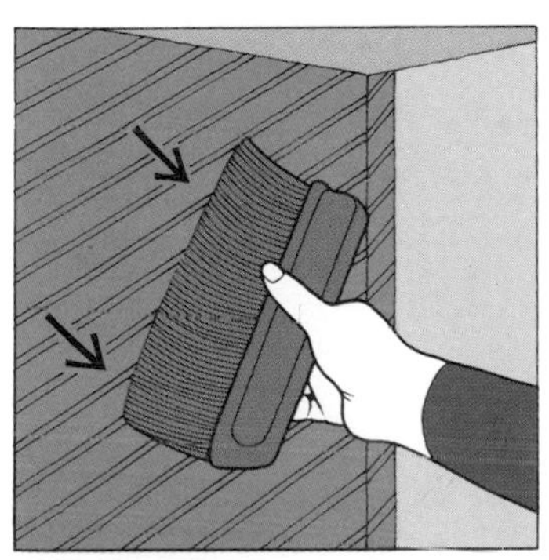
Papering into a corner
Never hang a complete length so that it goes around a corner. As you approach a corner, measure the distance and cut to this width, plus ½ in. Brush well into the corner so that the ½ in. laps the adjoining wall.

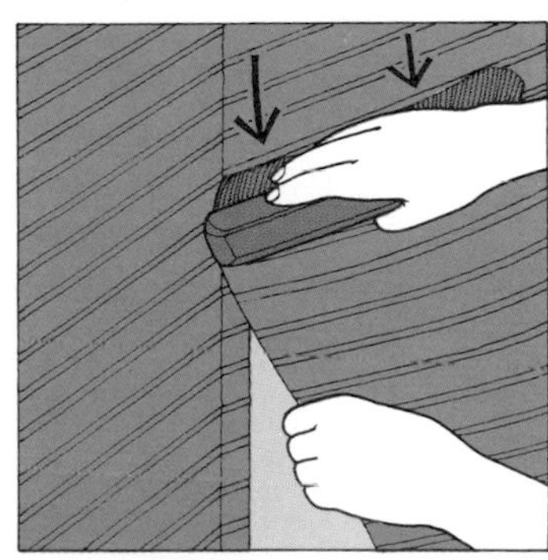
Papering out from a corner
Set the plumb line along the adjoining wall to establish another vertical; overlap the previous length, either with the remaining piece from the corner strip, or with another full width of paper.

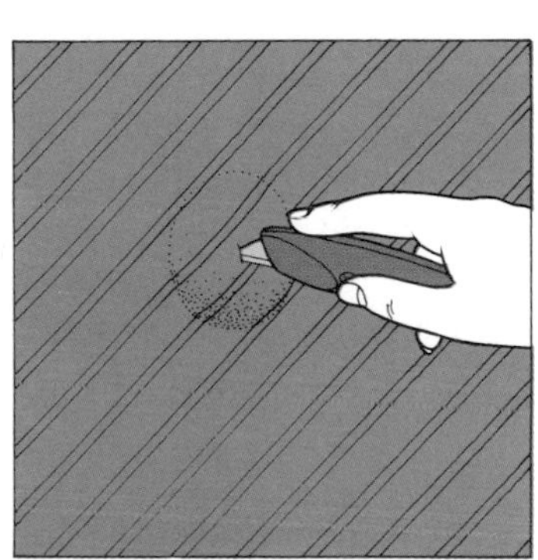
Removing air bubbles
Some air bubbles may prove difficult to eradicate. Use a knife with a sharp point to prick stubborn ones and then brush out the paper flat.

Wall Coverings

Wall coverings
There is an enormous range of wall covering materials available. You might consider a few of the more unusual alternatives before committing yourself. A very special covering, even if used only on a small area of wall, can transform an otherwise commonplace interior.

1 Co-ordinated ranges
Many manufacturers produce fabrics and paper which are matched for color and pattern.

1

2 Stretched fabric
Fabric can be used very successfully as a wall covering. Stretch it over sheets of plywood or hardboard, gluing it on the reverse. Cut away as much bulk material at the corners as possible. Nail the completed panels to the wall, losing the nail heads through the weave.

3 Foil papers
There is a wide range of foil finished papers, often with over-printed patterns, which add extra brilliance to a room. Check to see that the paper is pre-trimmed.

2

3

4 Patchwork
Old pattern books or odd lengths of paper can make a patchwork effect. Either trim them carefully and butt joint them as shown here, or overlap the edges using random sizes of paper. Rolls of brown paper, magazines and comic books, and, of course, lining paper can also be used.

5 Textured papers
Textured materials like silk, grass cloth and, in this case, hessian are also found. Unbacked hessian can be pasted to the wall, but pre-trimmed, paper backed hessians, along with many other materials, are much easier to use.

6 Complementary papers
Papers with complementary motifs can be used to highlight various features in a room. Sections can be cut out and pasted over doors, between moldings or in alcoves.

7 Bedspreads or sheets
Printed cotton, Indian bedspreads make exotic but quite inexpensive wall coverings. Either mount them or stretch and pin them directly to the wall. You can paste them if they are color-fast.

8 Cork faced paper
Thin layers of paper backed cork are available in many beautiful colors and textures. Be careful when applying cork paper to the wall, as the surface can easily be damaged.

4

5

6

7

8

Papering Problem Areas

Papering a stairwell
Before you begin papering you will need a safe working platform. An arrangement of ladders and scaffold planks can be adapted to suit most common situations. Remove the stair carpet; cut a batten and screw it into a stair to keep the bottom of the ladder from slipping (see arrangement A below). Always use a plumb line to establish a true vertical, and position the longest length of paper first. This way any irregularities will show up at an early stage. The long lengths of paper required will tear with the weight of paste; get somebody to support them from below.

Special ladders
You can buy or rent extension ladders, stepladders and stair ladders: some multi-purpose aluminum ones convert into all three. The stair ladder shown right stands on two surfaces at different levels and can be used with a plank. If special ladders are fixed at a point half-way up the stairs, they should have their legs secured in the same way as normal ladders (see below) to prevent them slipping.

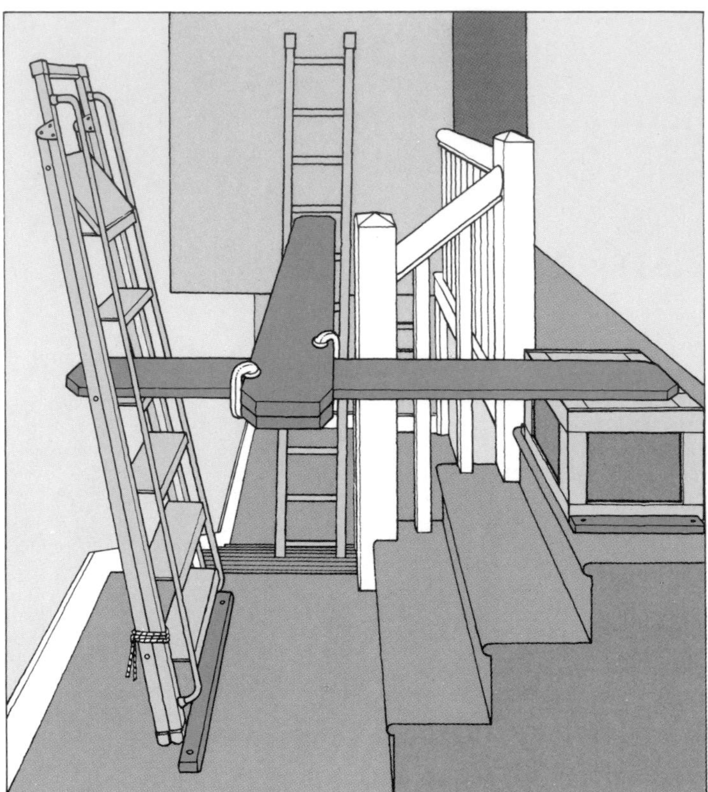

Arrangement B
You can make this platform with scaffold boards, two ladders and a strong box. Clamp the top board to the other to prevent it slipping.

Arrangement A
This is suitable for a single flight staircase with a landing at the top. Make sure the step ladder is fully open and the main ladder secure.

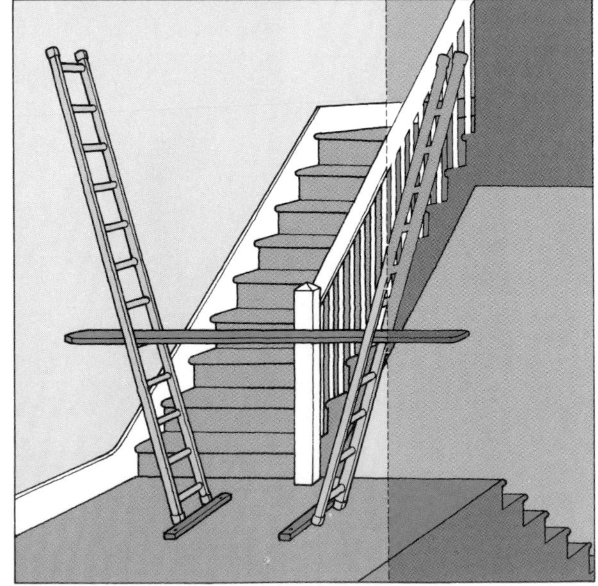

Arrangement C
For a double staircase use two tall ladders and a scaffold plank. If distance between ladders is over five feet use two planks.

Papering around a door

If wallpaper falls short of the door, cut a narrower strip to fill space. Carefully measure from last pasted strip to both the top and bottom of the door frame and cut length to fit. Paste strip in place, brushing well into frame. The waste can be used for finishing the top of the door.

A more professional method is to paste a full length strip over the door, butting against the previous length. Make a diagonal cut from the outside edge to the casing corner. Mark the position of the frame and cut off excess paper.

Papering around a door
1 The waste piece over the door is cut from the fill-in strip, so if carefully butted the join is invisible.

2 Placing an entire pasted length over the frame may be harder to do, but it eliminates the need for accurate cutting beforehand.

3 If the frame butts into a corner, use a waste piece to fit remaining space above door, overlapping the corner by ½ in. (see p. 39).

Papering around a fireplace

Papering around the mantelpiece of a fireplace is similar to papering around a door. Hang your first length centrally over the mantelpiece, as this area is often the focal point of a room. Trim to fit between ceiling and mantelpiece. Trim the side pieces, cutting diagonally from the outside edge along to the end of the mantelpiece. Cut around any molding, paste down and trim off the waste paper.

Papering around a fireplace
1 Measure and mark the position of the first length, to be hung in the center over the mantelpiece.

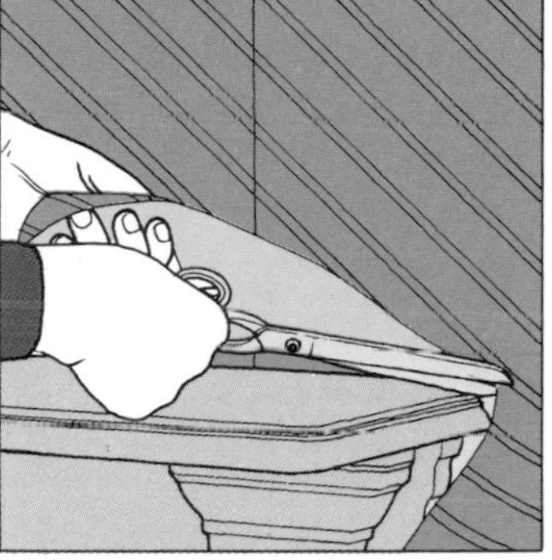

2 Hang a length to each side of the central piece; cut diagonally from the edge to the corner of the mantelpiece without tearing paper.

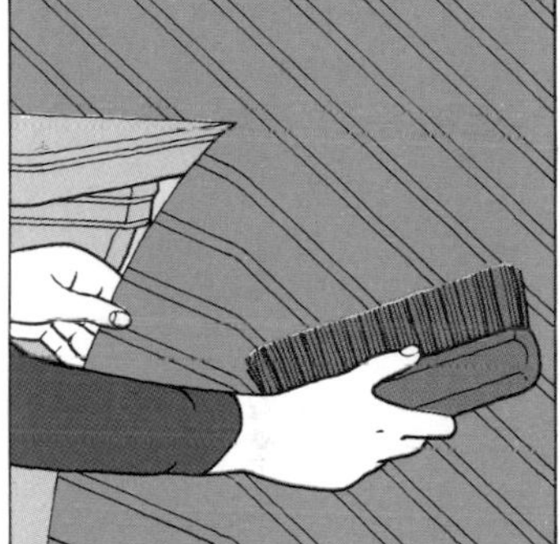

3 Trim away as much waste as possible and carefully cut the paper to fit around the molding of the mantelpiece. Paste down the edges.

Papering around wall fittings

When unscrewing any electrical outlet from the wall, first shut off the main power supply. Remove the switch or outlet plate and paper behind it, rather than cutting around it. Cut away just enough waste for the cut edges to fit under the cover plate, then replace the plate. Papering around a wall light may be easier if you leave the light attached to its wires. Cut an X large enough to pass the light through. Although the base plate may not finally cover the cuts, the joins will not show if carefully pasted down.

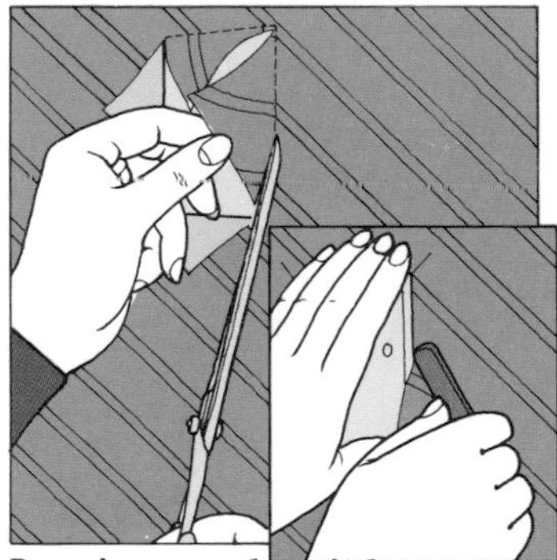

Papering around a switch
Remove switch plate. Mark and cut an X in paper over switch; trim paper enough to fit under plate.

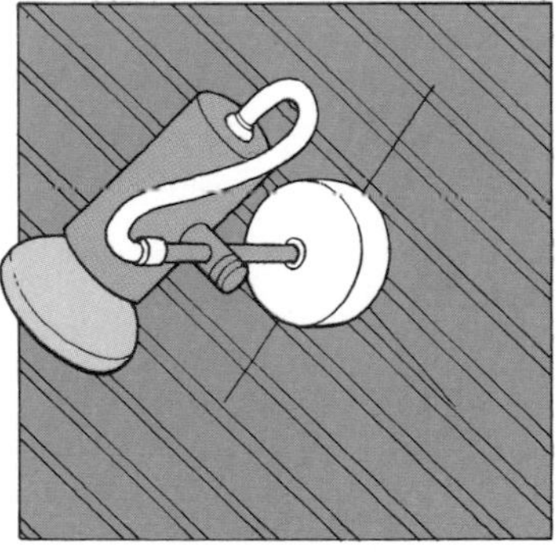

Papering around a wall light
Cut an X large enough for the fitting to pass through. Paste down and replace the base plate.

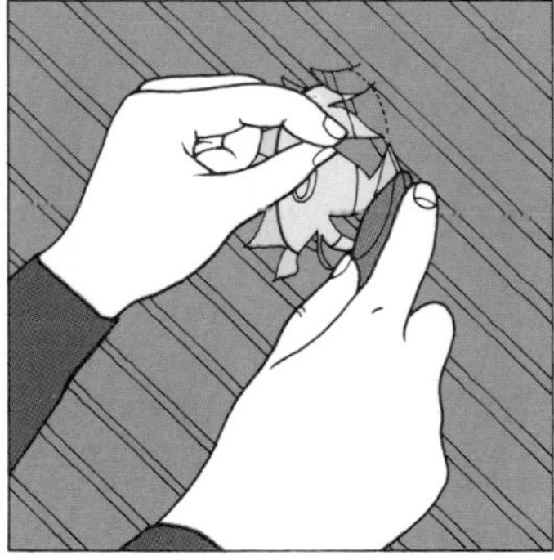

Papering around a circular fitting
Make triangular-shaped cuts around fitting. Brush tongues well into fitting and trim off excess with knife.

Papering around windows and radiators

Paper around a window in the same way as a door. Where the window is recessed, paste an excess around the edge, so that the surrounding lengths overlap neatly.

If possible remove radiators before papering, if not, make sure the heat is turned off. Try to hang paper right behind the radiator, as otherwise the heat may make ends and edges curl around the top and sides. Wet paper tears easily, so make a tool from a wire coat hanger to push the paper carefully into place.

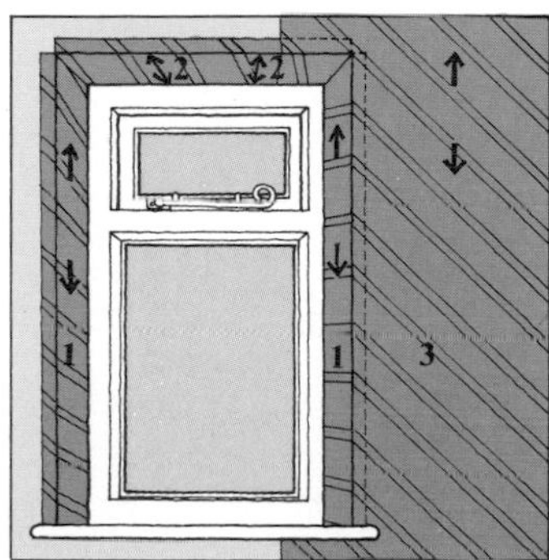

Papering a window recess
*Paper inside walls **1** and top inside **2**, allowing overlap as usual. Paste lengths **3** to match.*

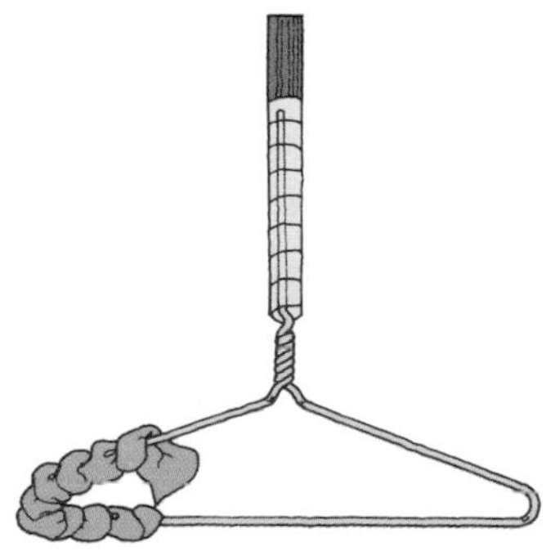

Papering behind a radiator
A cloth covered wire coat hanger taped to a wooden handle can ease paper down behind a radiator.

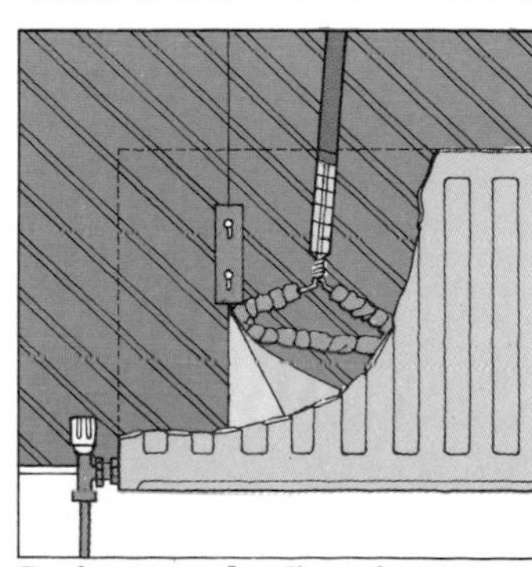

Cutting around radiator brackets
Cut a length of paper up to bracket level. Paste down either side, and rejoin beneath the bracket.

Painting Walls

Preparing the surfaces
New plaster, brick or concrete
Allow about three months for any of these to dry out. Efflorescence, a white powdery deposit, can be rubbed off, and the affected areas treated with an alkali-resistant primer. Porous or rough-textured surfaces must have a coat of thinned paint and be left for twelve hours before a full-strength coat can be applied.
Old brick or concrete
Scrub with detergent solution, then apply a coat of stabilizing primer. When painting, stipple with the brush to ensure paint penetrates the texture, then "lay off" with normal strokes. Use a long-napped roller to cover the texture.
Wallboard
Prime any nail heads with a rust inhibitive primer to stop rust seeping through paint. Wallboard is porous, so apply at least two coats of paint.
Existing paintwork
Where surface is sound, wash down with a weak detergent solution. Rinse and dry thoroughly before applying paint. Rub down old gloss paint with fine grade wet and dry paper to produce an even surface and a grip for new paint.
Flaking paintwork
Remove flaking paint with a scraper. Use a block and sandpaper to feather the edges of damaged areas. Where you find extensive flaking, apply a coat of stabilizing primer.
Wallpaper
If the wallpaper is not in good condition, strip off and re-line the wall. Apply a solution of 1 part wood alcohol to 4 parts shellac to dark-colored paper before painting. Apply two coats of latex paint.
Mildew and damp
Having located the cause and cured the problem (see p. 88), allow the area to dry thoroughly, then apply a multi-purpose primer. Treat any mold growth with 1 part bleach to 16 parts water. Leave for four hours, repeat, and then leave for three days before painting.

1

2

1 Children's rooms
You could let your children paint their own room. Divide a flat wall into pencilled squares and invite them to fill in each square as they wish. If you cover the wall with lining paper first, it can be stripped for redecorating.
2 Contrasting trim
A boldly painted scheme is the cheapest method of producing an exciting interior. Strong colors painted on to doors, fireplaces, moldings, or furniture create a striking contrast to a flat, light colored wall.

Latex paint
To give quick coverage to a wall, use a combination of brush and roller. With the roller, paint horizontal bands from the ceiling downward, filling in the edges with the brush.

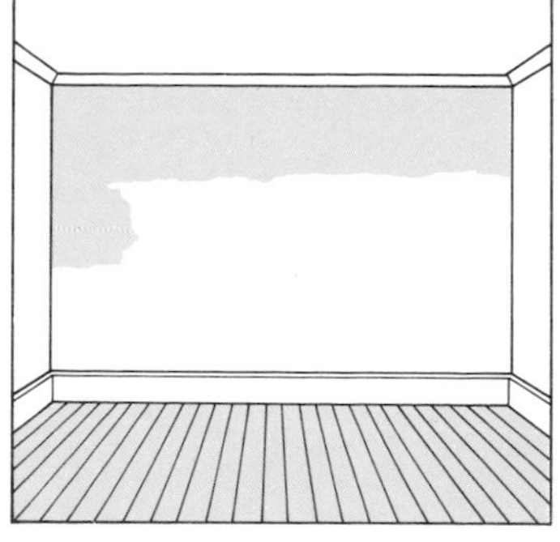

Gloss paint
Gloss paint shows brush marks if allowed to dry out at unfinished edges – unlike latex paint. Paint in vertical bands starting from the ceiling and moving quickly and evenly across the wall. Pick up and blend in wet edges as you go.

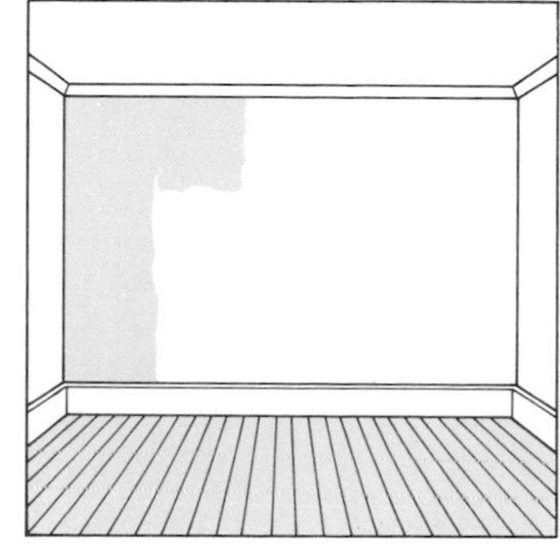

Using a brush
Holding the brush as illustrated, load it with paint and apply with vertical strokes, changing the direction of the stroke to achieve an even spread. Finish each area with light upward strokes – this is essential with gloss paint. If paintwork looks patchy when dry, apply a second or even a third coat. Gloss paint should have two under-coats and a top coat, and be rubbed down in between each one.

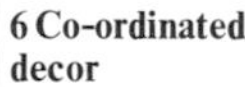

Using a roller
Dip the roller in the paint and roll it out on the textured area of the tray to obtain even saturation. Paint in vertical strokes, moving across the area and back again with an even pressure. To get thorough cover-age, change direction of strokes. Finish with vertical strokes if using gloss paint.

3 Creating a mural
Draw squares on a favorite picture and copy the image on larger scale squares pencilled on to a wall. Fill in the shapes with paint. If you prefer, paint the mural on hardboard and fasten it to the wall.

4 Zig-zag stripes
Paint a wall with gloss paint and use colored scotch tape to produce this dramatic striped effect. Take care to keep the tape straight, particularly over door or window moldings.

5 Taped effects
To reproduce this effect, mark out the design and mask the edges of the dark areas with tape. Rounded corners are cut out from the tape with a sharp knife. Rub down edges and paint the wall in between. When the paint is thoroughly dry, peel off the tape leaving a crisp painted edge.

6 Co-ordinated decor
To copy a simple fabric design on to a wall lay the fabric out flat on the floor, and trace the image; it is only necessary to trace the "repeat" of the pattern. Tape the tracing to the wall, and prick through the design with a pointed tool. Join up the marks with a pencil, and fill in the shapes with the correct paint.

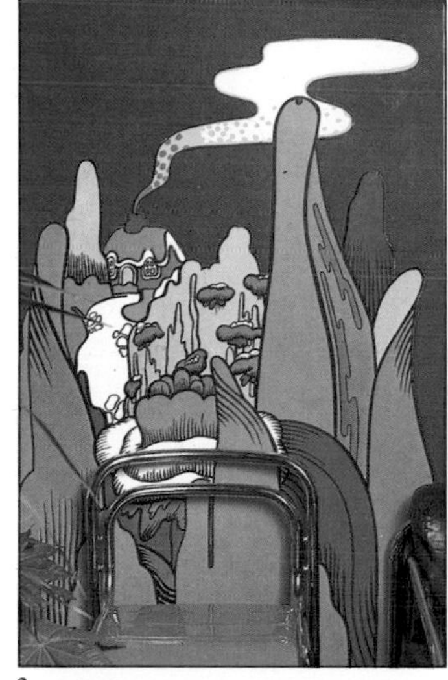

3

4

5

6

Paneling Walls

Preparation
Cure any mildew in the wall, and make good structural defects. Remove the baseboard and line the entire wall area with a waterproof membrane, such as polyethylene sheet. As an extra precaution, treat the wood with a preservative. Note that vertical lines make a wall appear higher, whereas horizontal lines make it seem wider.

Erecting a frame
Wall paneling must be fixed to a wall-mounted frame (as illustrated), made out of softwood battens 2 in. x 1 in. at 16-inch centers. Battens should be horizontally mounted for vertical paneling, and vertically mounted for horizontal paneling. Fix the frame to the wall. You can use masonry nails if you are driving directly into masonry, otherwise use wallplug and no. 8 screws, 2 to $2\frac{1}{2}$ inches long, at 16-inch centers along the batten. Use a level to check that the battens are all on one plane; pack out with strips of veneer or cardboard if necessary. Store the paneling in the room where it is to be used so the moisture content of the wood has time to stabilize. See diagram (top right) for method of nailing solid boards, such as tongue and groove or shiplap, to battens so as to avoid them warping or splitting when temperature changes cause them to shrink.

Fixing vertical boards
Begin at one end, butting the grooved edge of a board against the wall; check that it is vertical. Nail it in the center through its face, then fit the next board, nailing through the tongue as shown in the diagram top right. Proceed along the wall, cutting the boards to fit. Cut final board to fit so it clears the wall by $\frac{1}{4}$ in. and nail it through its face on the center line. Replace the baseboard. Nail a $\frac{3}{4}$ in. molding strip to cover the joints between walls and ceiling. This applies to horizontal boards as well as vertical ones.

Fixing horizontal boards
Butt the grooved edge of a board against the ceiling, and check if level. If wide gaps occur, scribe the board to the ceiling. Work down the wall, nailing as shown in diagrams and cutting boards to fit. The final board should finish just below baseboard level. Nail remnants of board to the bottom of battens to level the baseboard, which you then replace.

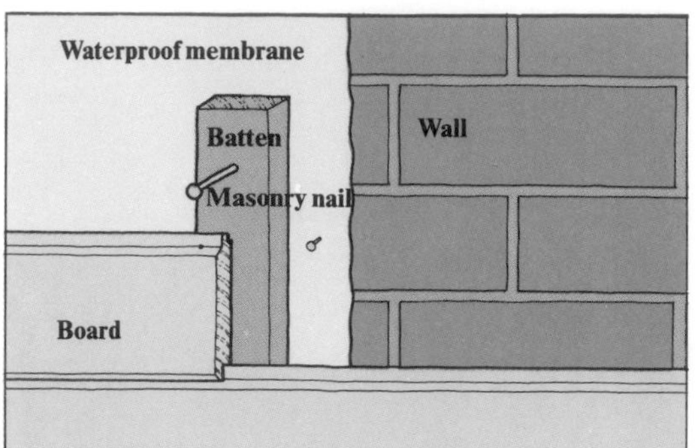

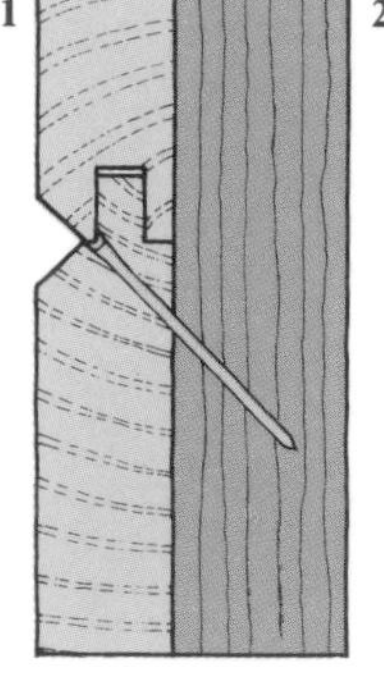

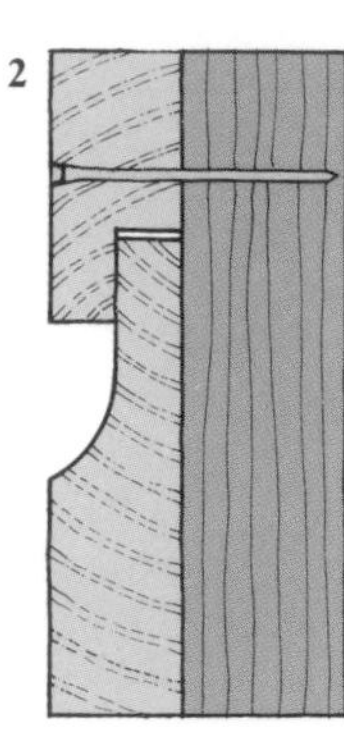

1 Nailing a tongue and groove board
Drive a brad through tongue at an angle, and below the surface with nail set. Slip groove over tongue.
2 Nailing shiplap board
Nail through face of board just behind lap. Punch below surface and fill holes.

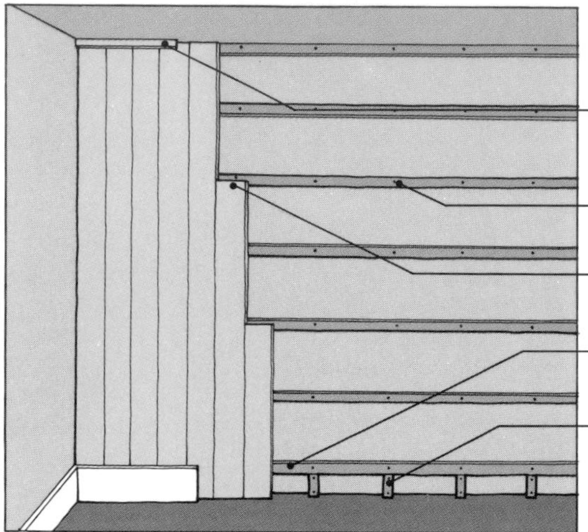

Checking for level
When fixing battens to the wall check level both horizontally and vertically, packing out where necessary.

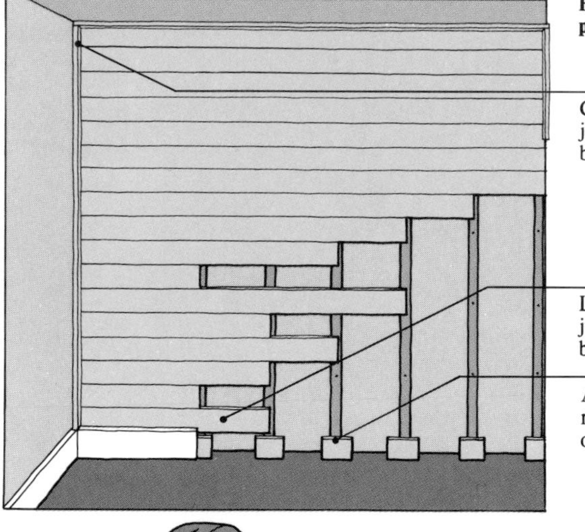

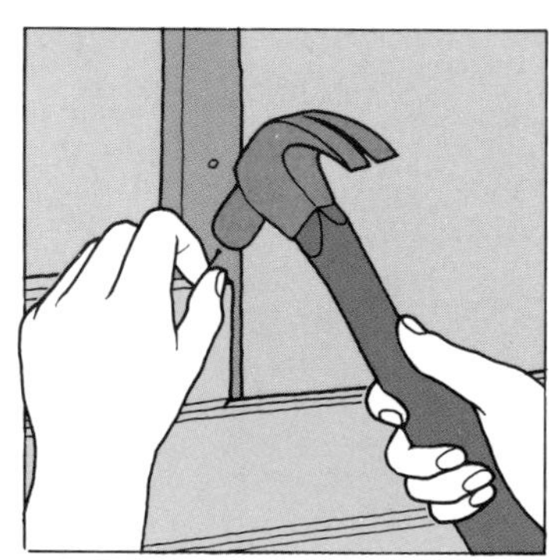

Butt jointing short lengths
It is not necessary to have every board the full length of the wall. Where possible, use up short lengths of board, and butt joint them on a batten.

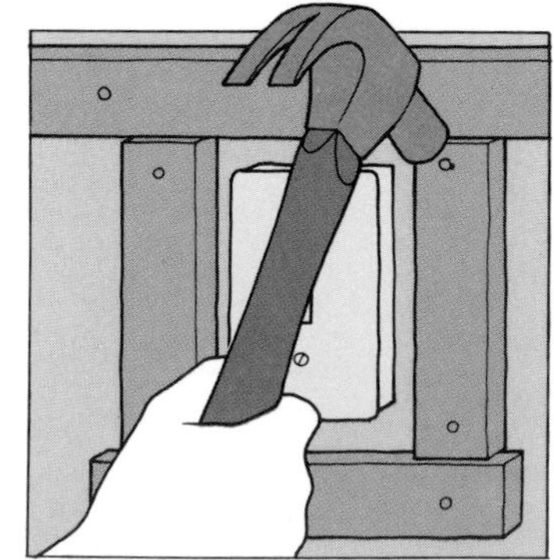

Fitting around a switch or outlet
1 Replace old fitting with metal box to fit flush with paneled surface. Nail short battens around box first.

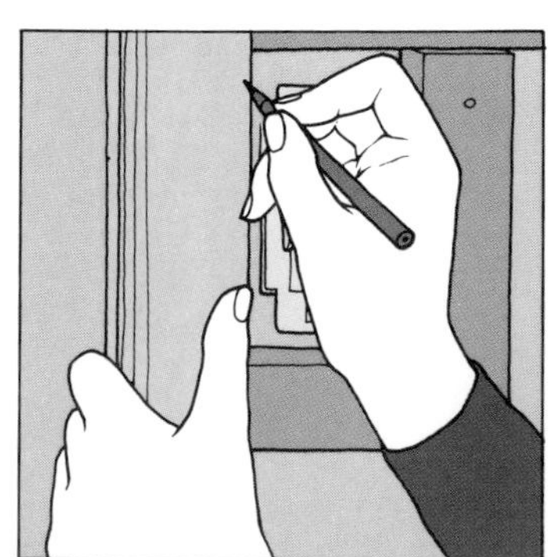

2 Mark the boards to fit snugly around the box, cut and nail them to the battens.

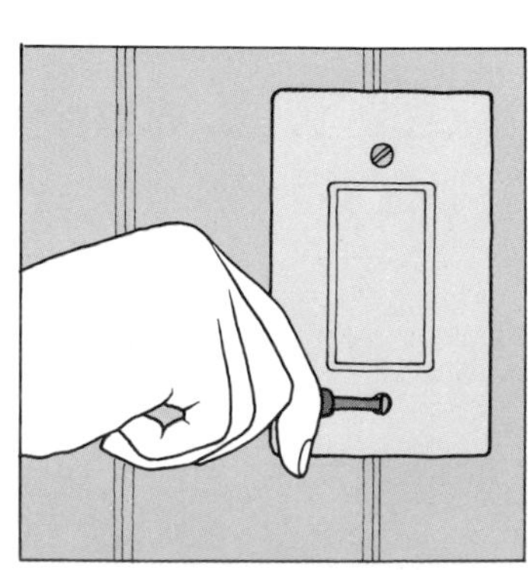

3 The boards fit around the box so that the cover plate overlaps and hides the cutout. Align with the box and screw tight.

Fixing around a door

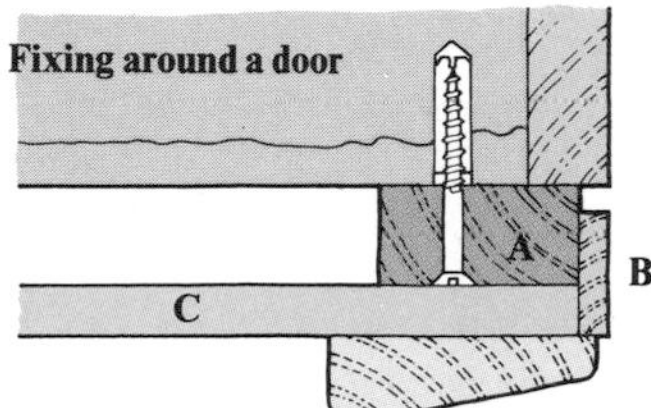

Remove casing from around the door. Fix a wall batten **A** to the wall, offset to the left to take thickness of cover strip **B.** Nail board **C** flush to the edge of batten. Nail a 1¼ in. x ¼ in. cover strip **B** to the batten. Nail door casing back in place.

Fitting boards to corners

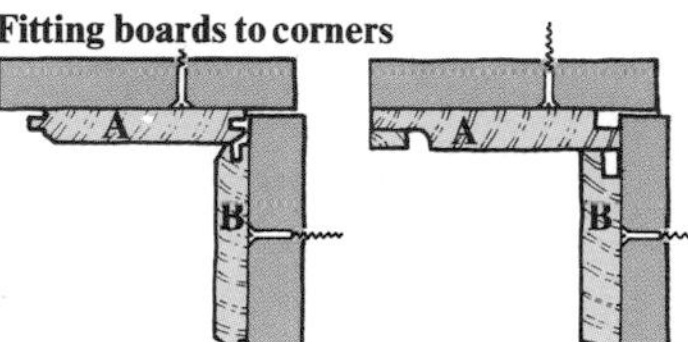

Vertical tongue and groove
Butt board **B** against board **A** and check for vertical. Nail through board on center line.

Vertical shiplap
Nail board **A** to batten just behind lap. Butt board **B** against it, check for vertical. Nail and continue as already shown.

Horizontal boards
Run board **A** into corner. Butt board **B** against it. If necessary, nail a triangular cover strip into corner.

Fixing boards to external corners

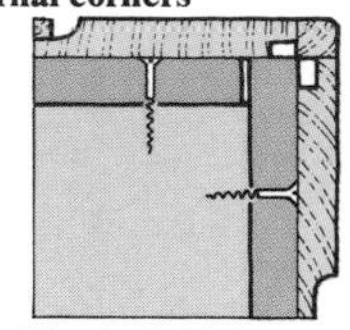

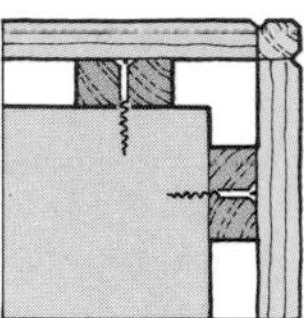

Vertical tongue and groove
Begin each wall from the corner, with groove flush fitting as above. Fix a matching batten to finish.

Vertical shiplap
Proceed as for vertical tongue and groove. The matching corner batten will fit flush with the boards.

Horizontal boards
Fix two battens flush with corner and nail boards so they meet at corner, as above. Nail a square cover strip.

Fitting sheet material
Sheets of plywood and hardboard measuring 8 ft x 4 ft are manufactured for paneling walls. Both materials are finished in a range of wood veneers, both real and simulated, and some are covered with plastic laminates.
Plywood or particle board both provide an excellent surface as a base for ceramic wall tiles.

Establishing a frame
If you are paneling a stud partition, you can nail directly into the studs. With a masonry wall, you will need to line it with horizontal battens at 16-inch centers. Estimate the position of the vertical battens between the main ones to correspond with these positions, as shown on the right.

Fitting the panels
Work out the most economical way of cutting the panels, and number the back of each one to note its position. When installing them, start from one corner, scribing the edge where necessary. Unless you paper over the panels, it is difficult to hide the joints. With V-grooved panels, the edge is chamfered to match adjacent grooves when the ends are butted together. Another method is to finish the front face of the vertical batten to match or contrast with the panels, leaving a ¼-inch gap between panel edges, showing the finished batten in between.

Fitting to the battens
If a panel is to be tiled or papered, nail it to the battens. V-grooved panels should be nailed in the grooves, one of which is provided every 16 inches for this purpose. Where you are unable to nail a panel without spoiling the surface finish, glue the panel to the battens using a name brand glue designed for this purpose. Take particular care at the joints; the technique is illustrated on the right. Where the panels meet the ceiling and floor, finish in the same way as for wood boards.

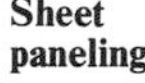

Sheet paneling

Horizontal battens every 16 inches

Short supporting battens need to correspond with vertical edges of sheets

Work with whole sheets from one end to other. Cut and scribe final board

Attach cover strip and baseboard if needed at bottom

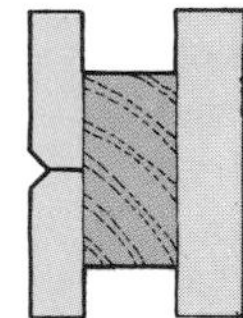

Chamfer joint
Plane a chamfer along edge of each board or panel to give defined break.

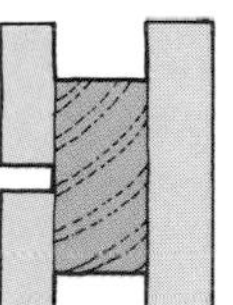

Sheet panel joints
Emphasize the joint by fixing panel edge to a matching or contrasting batten leaving a ¼ inch gap.

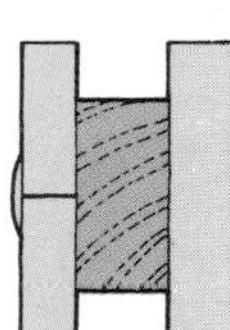

Cover strip
Hide the butt joint with a cover strip of wood or plastic.

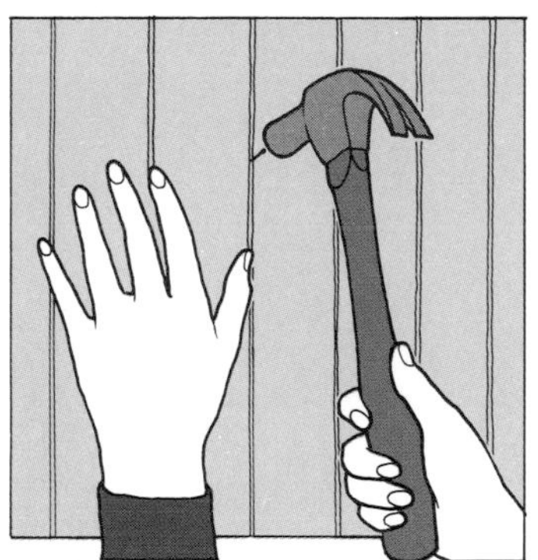

Nailing through joins
Simulated tongue and groove plywood appears almost invisible if you drive nails into grooves.

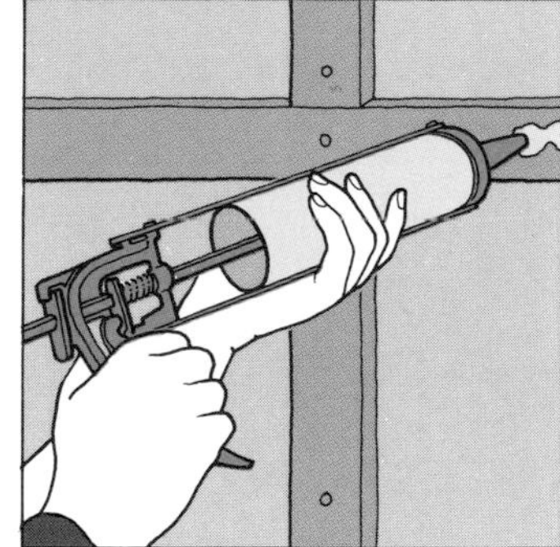

Fixing with adhesive
Apply glue to battens and press panel in position. Support panel, if short of the floor, until glue sets.

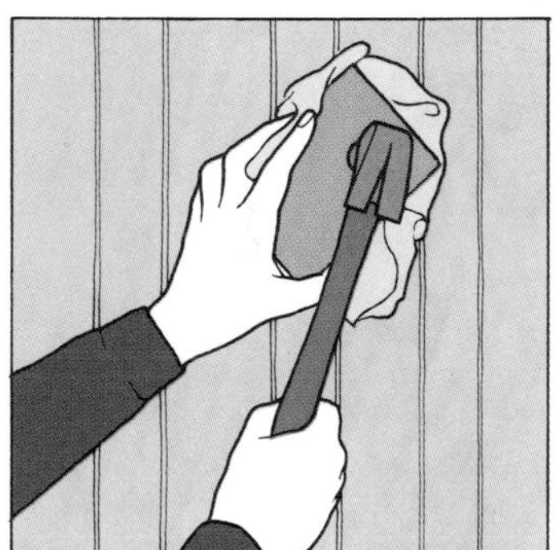

Bonding the joints
Spread the adhesive by hammering on top of the panel, using a cloth-protected block.

Fitting around switches
Mount electric boxes as described for wood paneling. Measure the position of the box and mark out.

Making an aperture
Drill a pilot hole in one corner of marked rectangle. Cut out the hole and trim the edges.

Fitting the panel
Check that the aperture fits exactly over the box. When cover plate is screwed in place it should overlap.

Panels & Tiles

1

2

3

4

5

6

1 Plastic panels
Particle board panels covered with plastic laminate can be cut to match the width of the furniture.

2 Cork tiles
Pre-sealed cork floor tiles are continued over the walls of the bathroom to provide a warm, moisture-resistant surface.

3 Mirror panels
The mirrored wall panels are large sliding doors which conceal built-in clothes storage.

4 Mirror tiles
Mirror tiles are easier to handle and to work with than large sheets, particularly if plumbing fixtures have to be accommodated.

5 Brick tiles
These rectangular quarry type tiles are laid in courses over block walls to simulate fair-faced brickwork.

6 Plywood panels
A plywood covering hides two rough finished chimney stacks in this attic conversion. One side has been extended to match the height of the other and contains a display area.

7 V-grooved panels
V-grooved panels cut and painted to match the storage create a continuous wall treatment.

8 Rough boards
The strong texture of roughly sawn boards adds a rustic quality to a country home.

9 Pine boards
The gaps between the pine boards produce strong horizontal lines making the room appear wider while masking the plumbing in a simple way.

7

8

9

Ceramic Tiling

Ceramic tiles
Ceramic wall tiles are generally 4¼ x 4¼ inches and serve either as decoration for which they are ideally suited, or as a functional domestic surface in bathrooms and kitchens. Furthermore, tiles are one of the easiest ways of achieving a professional finish, requiring no more than careful setting out and a little accurate cutting around the edges. There is an extremely wide range of designs and colors available, including special-purpose packs for finishing off tiled areas; these contain edging tiles curved on one or two edges. There are also cove tiles to seal the joint between bathtub, or sink unit, and wall. If the gap is small, run a silicone rubber sealant along the joint instead.

Tools
Scriber is used for tile cutting, with a tungsten carbide tip for scoring the line across the glaze.
Tile nippers are used to nibble the edge of a tile when reducing a very narrow or small section. A pair of ordinary pincers is adequate.
Adhesive spreader or trowel must be notched to ensure even application of adhesive over the area.
Spreader with a rubber blade fitted to a wooden handle is the best tool for applying grout to the tiled area.
Sponge cleans off excess grout.
Additional tools could be a level, scraper, whetstone, try square.

Preparation of surfaces
1 Brick and concrete
Scrub the surface to remove loose material. You may have to screed the wall if the surface is uneven.
2 New plaster or wallboard
Make sure the surface is dry. Coat the wall with a multi-purpose primer to make quite sure it will absorb no moisture from the tile adhesive.
3 Old plaster
Rake out loose plaster and fill any cracks or holes.
4 Painted surfaces
Wash off dirt and grease. Scratch the surface with sandpaper. Remove flaking paint with a scraper and apply a coat of stabilizing primer.
5 Wallpaper
Do not tile over wallpaper. Strip off old paper and prepare surface plaster as above.
6 Old tiles
This is a good surface for new tiles. Wash down with detergent, and repair any loose tiles or cracks.

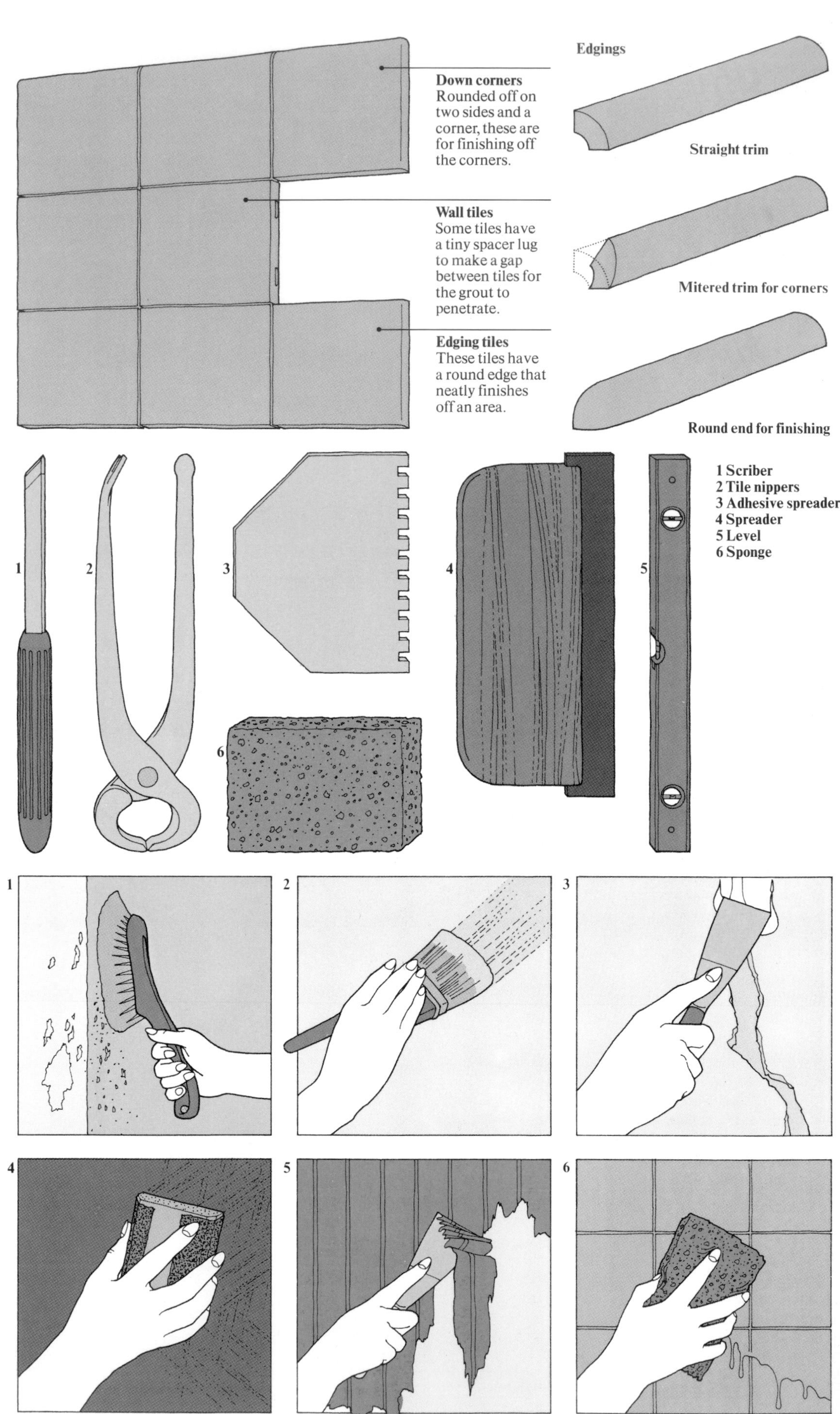

Tiling a wall

Begin tiling at the level of the floor or the baseboard, or from the edge of the bathtub.

1 Place a tile on the bottom level and mark a line along its top edge. Do this at several intervals along the wall, then hold a batten top edge along the line. **2** Check the horizontal with a level, and nail the batten to the wall in such a way that you can easily remove the nails later. Center a tile on the nailed batten, and mark tile widths from end to end. **3** Use another batten, marked off in tile widths, for centering. If the tiles do not have spacers, estimate with a thin piece of cardboard, and make allowances for the spaces in the final measurement.

Applying adhesive

4 Mark a vertical line at each end of the wall, from the edge of the end tile, and nail an upright batten along it. Dry lay a few tiles to check right angles. **5** Use a spreader to apply adhesive where battens meet, then spread with a notched trowel to cover an area of about 1 sq. foot. **6** Apply the tiles by pressing them into the adhesive, and check the level of each section as you go.

Cutting tiles

7 If gaps occur at the ends of the wall you may have to cut tiles to fit. Set the tile against the wall and, on the reverse of the tile, mark the line to be cut. **8** Use a try square and tile cutter to score the glazed surface along the line. Make several cuts, particularly on the edges. **9** Place the tile glazed side up, the line resting along a thin stick, and press either side to break the tile.

Cutting shapes

10 To cut a very small piece, score the line and nibble the edge with nippers; finish with a whetstone. **11** To cut a narrow strip, plane a shallow angle up to a marked line on a square of softwood. Rest the scored tile on the wood so marks align. Stand on the tile, using a cloth or cork tile to spread the weight and give a clean break. **12** To cut indents, score with the cutter and snip away the waste with nippers. **13** When tiling around external corners, make sure the edging cap aligns with the edge of the adjacent tile.

Grouting

14 Leave the wall to dry for 24 hours before grouting. Mix grout to maker's instructions, and spread across tiles so that gaps are filled. **15** Wipe off excess with a damp sponge before it dries.

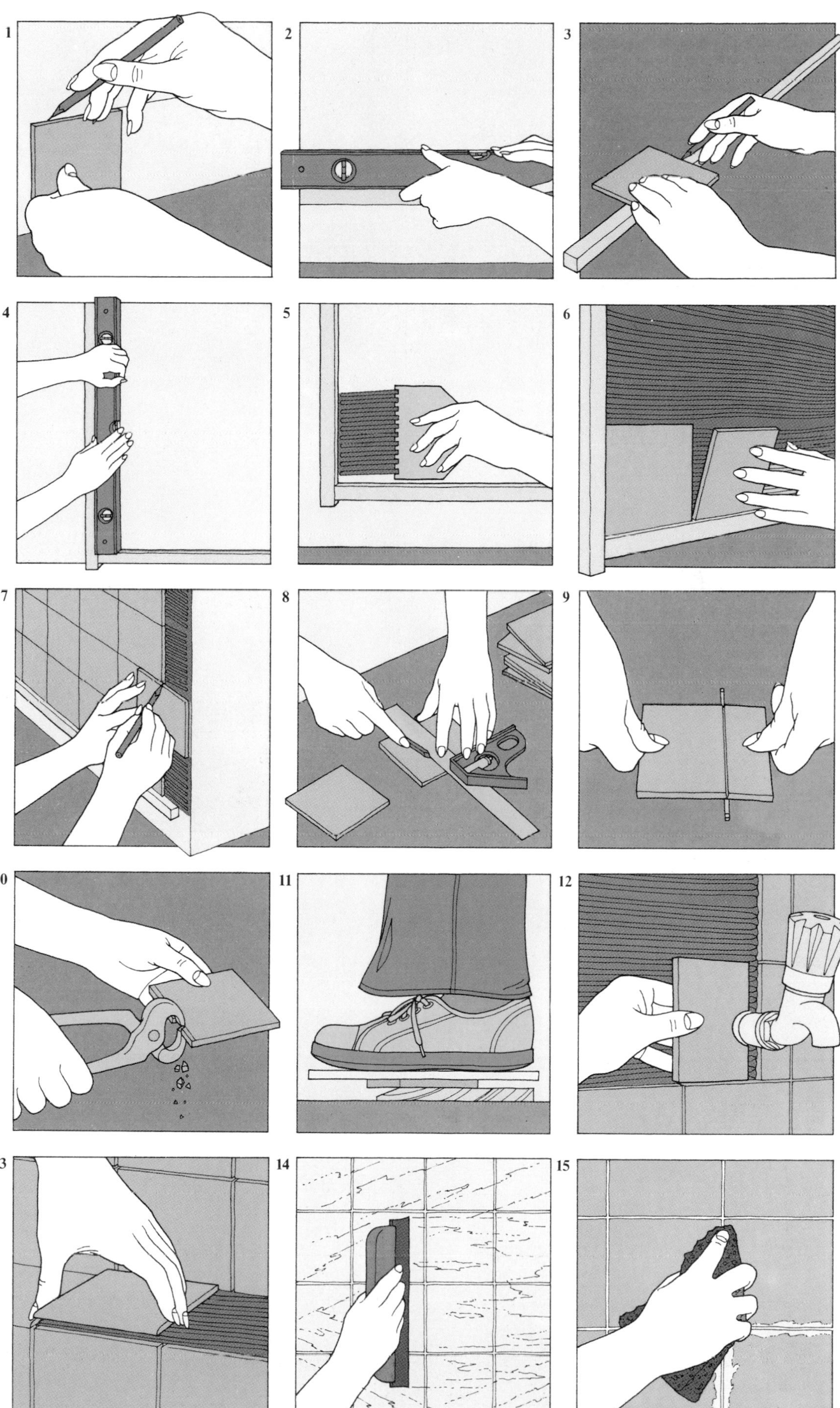

Ceilings

Practical considerations

Any work carried out on a ceiling will be more difficult than working on a wall using the same material, and this is why paint has always been the most popular finish.

Even with a newly-plastered ceiling, it is better to cover it with lining paper before painting, if you want to get a good finish. Lining a ceiling is not an easy job, and certainly needs skill to do single-handed – a non-professional should always have someone to help. On the other hand, you will have no pattern to align, and the coat of paint will hide most small faults in your technique. Textured paper, used for ceilings where the plaster may be badly cracked and uneven, is more difficult to hang than regular paper. Do not be too ambitious and try hanging an expensive paper, unless you have had some experience.

Although ceilings are traditionally painted white, they show discoloring, particularly above light fittings where airborne dust is carried up by the column of hot air. This is less likely to show with darker tones. Another method of disguising a badly cracked ceiling is with lightweight tiles, as long as the surface is basically sound. Tiles have good insulation properties, but you should avoid using polystyrene, as they will give off poisonous fumes if burned. Wood paneling will also hide a damaged ceiling; if the surface is flat, fix paneling directly to ceiling joists. Alternatively, level the surface with battens, packing out where needed, and fix the panels to the battens. Using tongue and groove boards is much easier than using plywood sheet panels. If the ceiling is beyond repair, remove old plaster to reveal the joists and the floor above. Either resurface with wallboard, or clean up the woodwork and finish with paint. Where a ceiling has a roof space above, you should insulate against loss of heat; where there is another living space above, remember that noise is more likely to penetrate an exposed ceiling.

Lowered ceilings have several advantages: they will reduce the cost of heating, particularly if you install an insulating material in the ceiling and they insulate against sound while hiding plumbing and wiring. A false ceiling can be covered in any suitable material, or the entire ceiling can be fitted with translucent panels which both conceal and diffuse lighting.

1

2

3

1 Converting a roof space
When converting a roof space, cover insulation between roof timbers with hardboard sheets. These panels have been painted gloss white to reflect as much light as possible.

2/3 Wood paneling
Wood paneling is an ideal method of covering a damaged ceiling. For painting, choose good quality knot-free lumber, or be prepared for a lot of filling and rubbing down. Alternatively, finish with a clear lacquer or wood stain.

4 Lowered ceilings
This lowered ceiling fills the space between a row of closets and a high ceiling, while concealing wiring and light fittings.

5 Economical paneling
Standard planed lumber is more economical than tongue and groove boards. Fix furring strips, painting them and the original surface mat black to conceal ceiling irregularities. Nail the panels to strips, leaving a gap in between.

6 Exposed beams
If you are building a new extension, consider leaving the beams exposed and finish with a clear lacquer.

4

5

6

Tiling & Paneling Ceilings

Preparing the ceiling
Tiling is an ideal method of covering a ceiling in poor condition, but a crumbling or damp ceiling should not be tiled before being repaired. Locate and repair the fault which is causing the damp and leave ceiling to dry thoroughly, or if the plaster is saturated remove it completely and nail a softwood framework directly to the joists. Ceiling tiles are usually manufactured from man-made fibers chosen for their acoustic, insulating and fireproof qualities. Polystyrene is quite common but is highly inflammable, and gives off poisonous fumes as it burns. Most ceiling tiles are 12 x 12 in. although larger dimensions are made. Some have a tongue and groove edge so they can be easily stapled to a ceiling frame.
You can line the ceiling with softwood battens to which you staple the tiles, or cover it with hardboard to make a surface for adhesives. To prepare the surface, scrape off flaking paint and rake loose plaster from any cracks, then fill and rub down with sandpaper. Wash the ceiling with a detergent to remove dust and grease. Gloss-painted surfaces should be scraped with coarse sandpaper.
Whitewash should be removed and the surface coated with a stabilizing primer. Turn off electricity; remove light fittings and insulate the ends of wires before turning on current again. When you tile that particular area, cut a hole in the tile to pass the wires through. Establish a center point at each end of the ceiling across the narrowest width. "Snap" a center line across the ceiling. Measure the center point, and bisect it with a right angled line.

Prefabricated systems
Acoustic tiles or translucent panels for diffusing light are lowered into a grid made up of metal cross-sections.

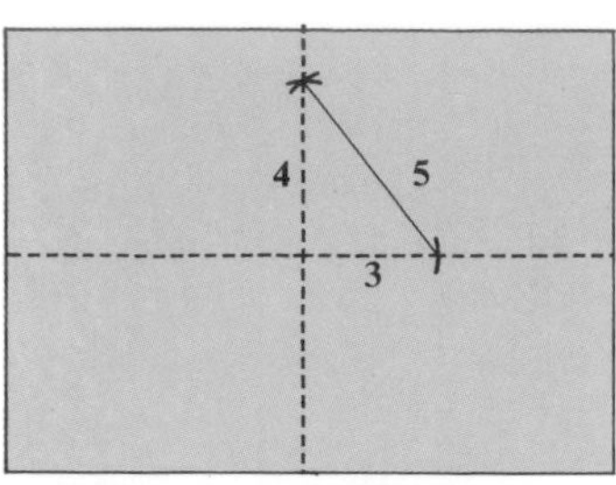

Attaching tiles with adhesive
1 Measure from the center 3 ft one way and 4 ft the other. A line joining the two forms a 90° angle.

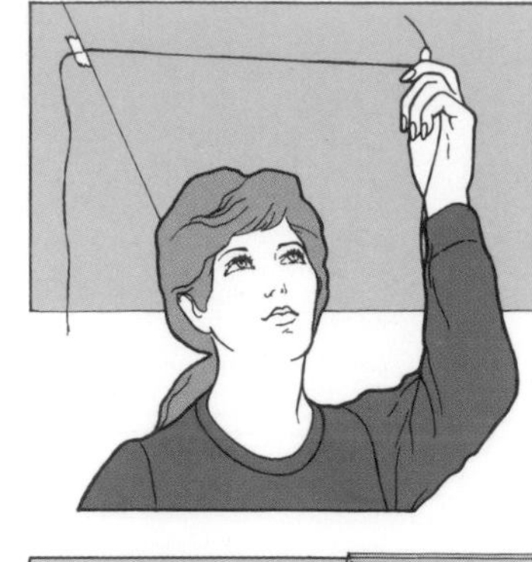

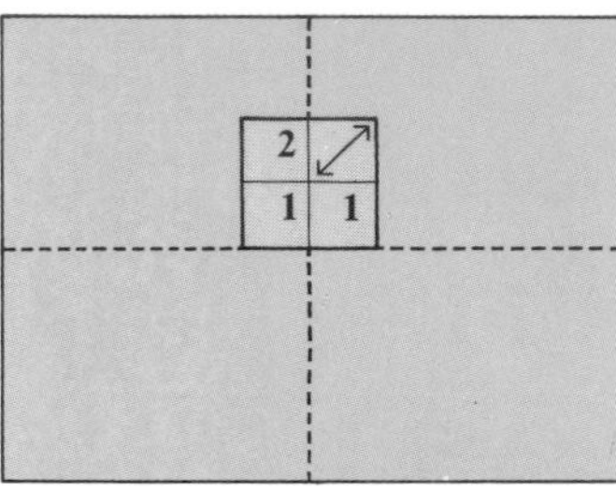

2 The first two tiles should fit into the angle formed by the bisecting lines. Then lay two more to form a square.

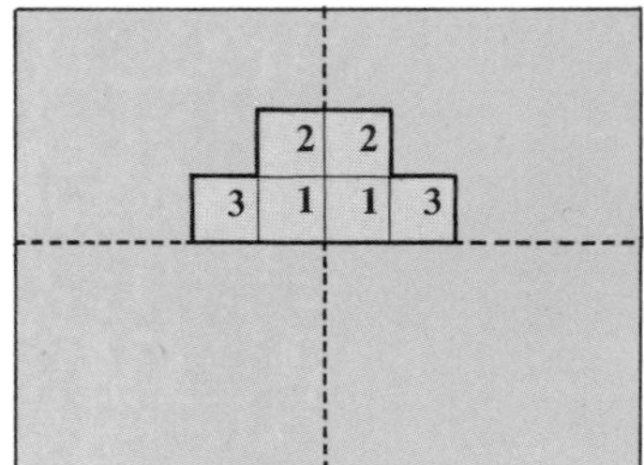

3 Form a shallow pyramid, by working outward, filling in the steps. Mark off each border tile from the last whole one.

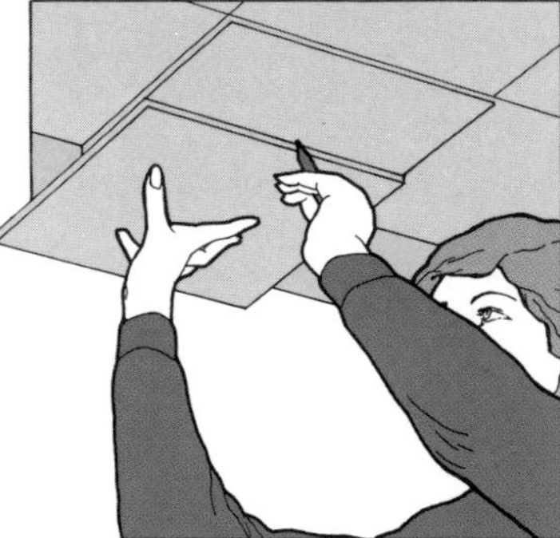

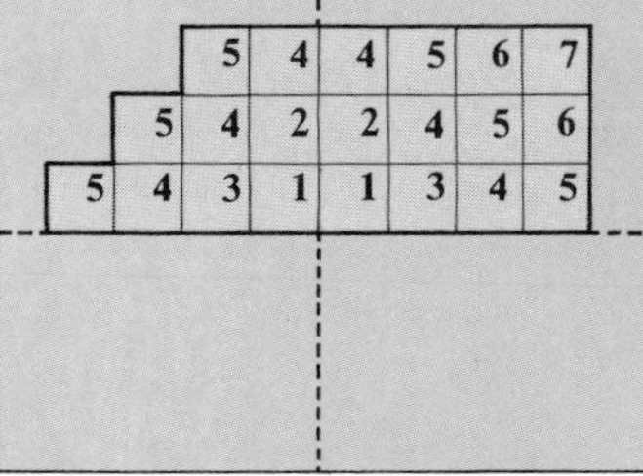

4 Complete one half of the room, then repeat process. Border tiles can be scored with a knife and broken over an edge.

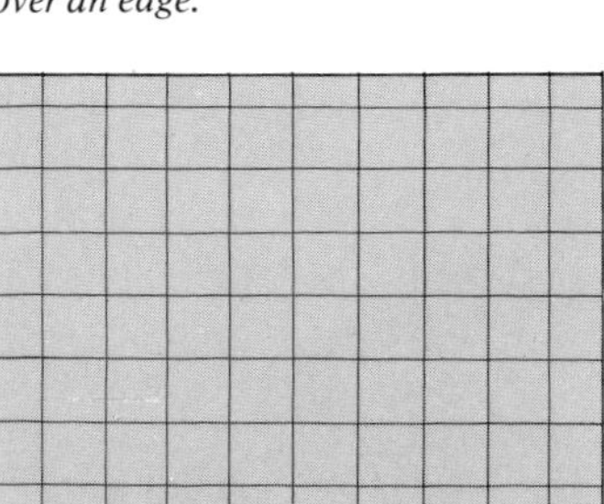

5 Having marked and cut the border tiles, fit them into position. Finish off the edges with wooden moldings.

Attaching tiles with adhesive
Estimate the number of tiles between the center point and each wall. If you are left with anything less than half a tile at the edges, move your marking line 6 in. in either direction, and set up a new line. Use a ready-mixed brand name adhesive, and apply some to each corner of the tile. Press the tile on the ceiling, moving it to spread the adhesive evenly. Place the next tile, and butt the edges together. Fit four tiles into the square centered on the bisecting lines as shown left, and fill out with the remaining tiles as illustrated. Mark and cut border tiles as shown in **3** and **4**, left.
Attaching tiles with staples
Mark out center lines on ceiling, **1** right. The tiles need to be stapled to 3 x 1 in. furring strips sited at right angles to the joists. See p. 91 for locating joists. Estimate the number of whole tiles it will take to span the ceiling and check that the border tiles will be the same width all around. Butt the first strip in the angle formed by wall and ceiling to support the border tiles. The second strip will be placed according to the width of the border tile. The stapling edge of the tile must be centered on it. Nail subsequent strips at 12 in. centers; check that they are level, and pack with wedges if needed. The last two strips should be positioned like the first ones. The next-to-last one should be the same distance from the wall as the second strip and the last one should be flush with the wall. As an edge guide for the border tiles, snap a chalked cord on the furring strips, parallel to both bisecting center lines. Cut and fit first corner tile, and proceed as illustrated right, nailing to the first strip as close to the wall as possible. The nail heads will be covered by edge molding. Place tiles so that you can staple through the tongue, bottom right, and work across the ceiling. Check the line with a ruler as you go. Fit the remaining border tiles working outward in both directions.

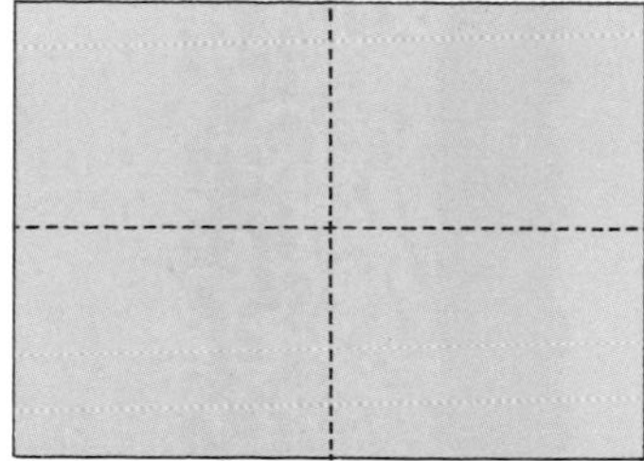

Attaching tiles with staples
1 Snap a chalked cord to establish bisecting lines as described on opposite page.

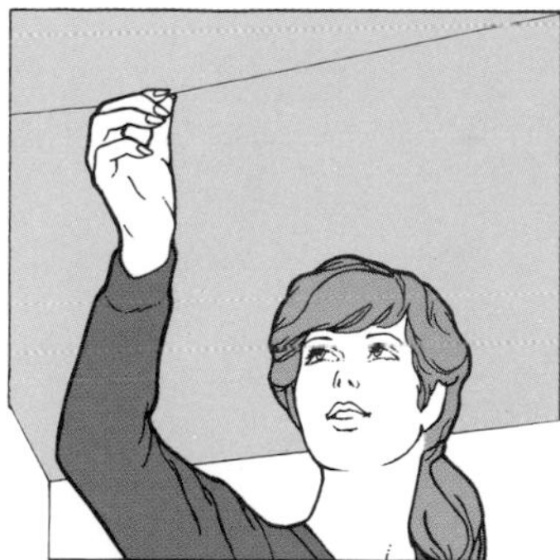

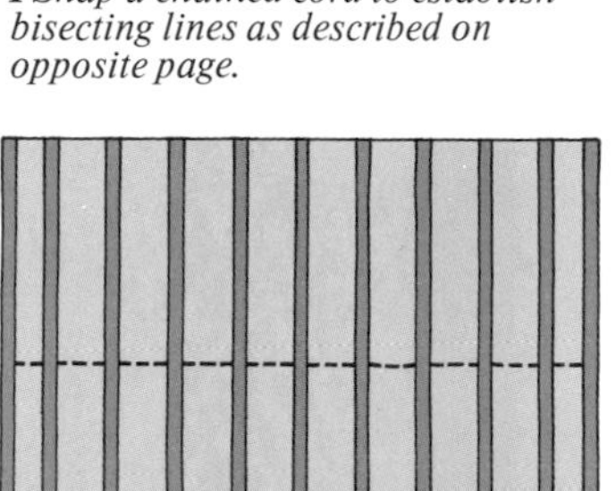

2 Fix 3 x 1 in. furring strips 12 in. apart across the ceiling, at right angles to the joists. A spacer will make the job easier.

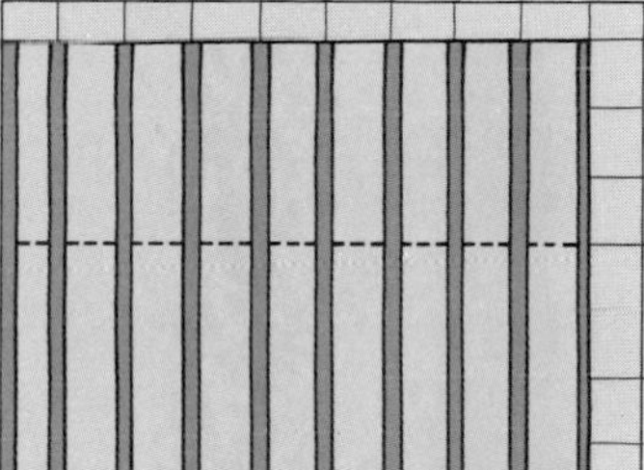

3 Cut and fit a corner tile first, and nail it to first strip. Fix remaining border tiles, working outward in both directions.

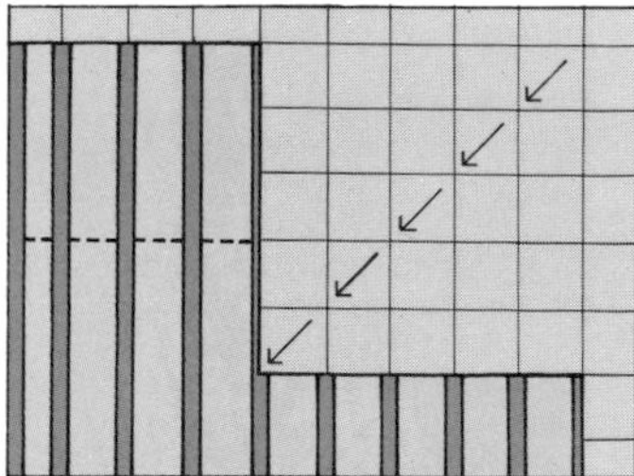

4 Fit the second row corner tile, and work outward as before. Staple through the tongue of each tile into the furring strips.

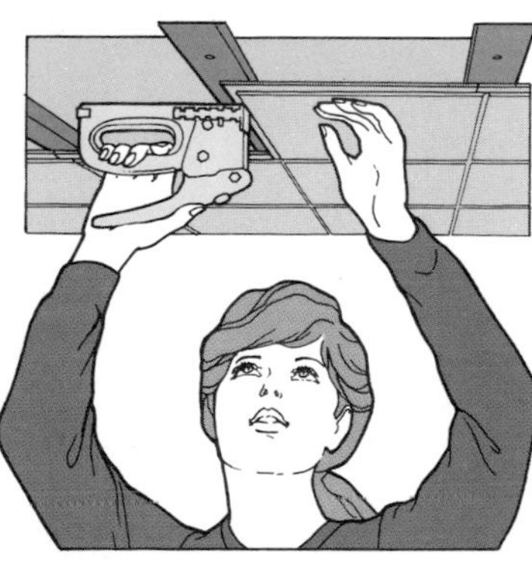

5 Work from one side of room, so stapling edge of each tile faces center. Position mating edges and staple. Fit remaining tiles.

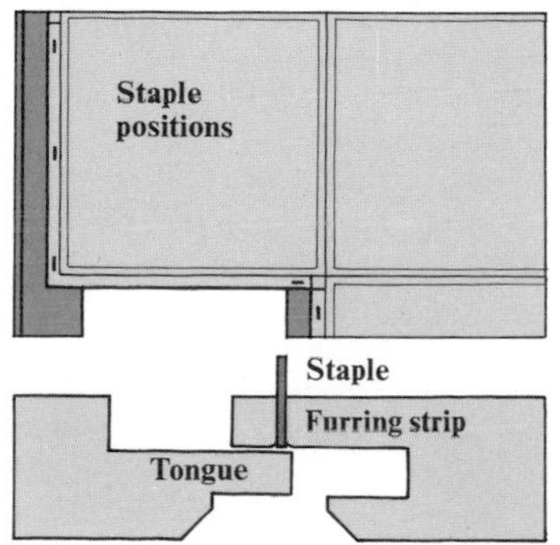

Paneling a ceiling
Establish the direction of the ceiling joists: the floorboards above will run in the opposite direction from the joists. Panels can be nailed directly to the joists. If you want panels to run in opposite directions from the joists, nail 2 x 1 in. furring strips at 16 in. centers to the joists (see below). Fix panels as described on pp. 46-47.

Lowering the ceiling
1 Mark the height of the intended ceiling on a clear wall. Deduct the thickness of the paneling, and screw a 3 x 2 in. furring strip to the wall, using a level to establish the line. Continue adding strips around the room at the correct height, checking with the level.
2 Before screwing the strips in place, cut notches for half-lap joints (see pp. 128-131) at 16 in. centers in the two parallel strips which run in the direction of the paneling (see small diagram); these notches will take the cross battens. Cut a lap in the ends of the cross battens. Check the length of each batten before cutting the joints, in case the walls are not completely parallel. Toe nail the joints together. The cross battens will need intermediate support between the joists and the battens themselves, to prevent the ceiling from sagging and to prevent the battens from springing when you nail up the panels. In **3** and **4** the method of fixing the intermediate strips for panels running perpendicular or parallel to the joists is shown. Cut 3 x 2 in. furring strips to the required length and screw them at 4 ft centers to the nearest floor joists. Nail short hanging battens to these joist strips and to the cross battens. The length of the hanging supports is determined by the distance from the frame to the ceiling above. Cover finished framework with panels (see pp. 46-47).

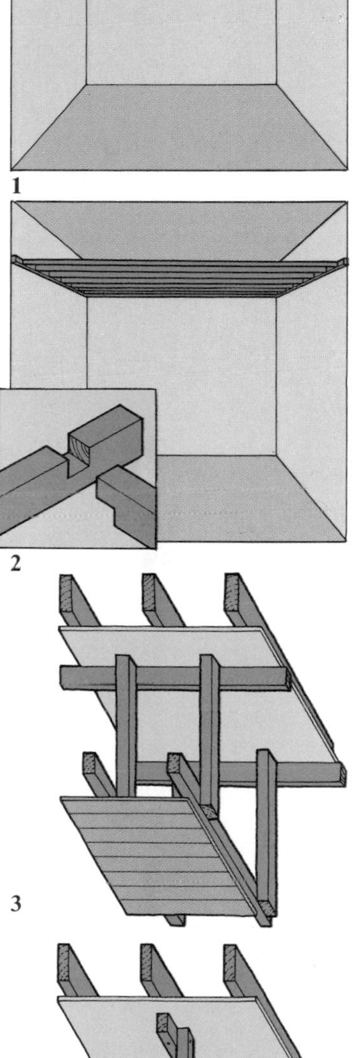

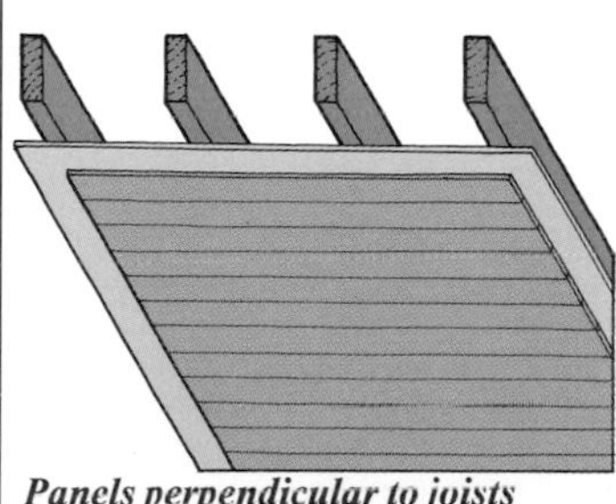

Panels perpendicular to joists
After establishing position of joists you can fix ceiling panels directly to them at right angles.

Panels parallel to joists
Battens must be fixed to the joists before panels are attached.

Papering & Painting Ceilings

Ceiling treatments
A ceiling can be turned into a decorative feature by an imaginative use of paint or paper. Such treatment can also highlight favorable attributes in a room or tone down defects. Always remember to paint the ceiling before tackling the walls.

1 Ceiling moldings
Highlight ceiling moldings by painting them a contrasting color. The use of both gloss and latex paints adds further interest.

1

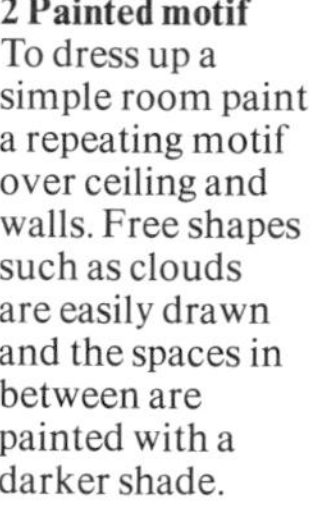

2 Painted motif
To dress up a simple room paint a repeating motif over ceiling and walls. Free shapes such as clouds are easily drawn and the spaces in between are painted with a darker shade.

2

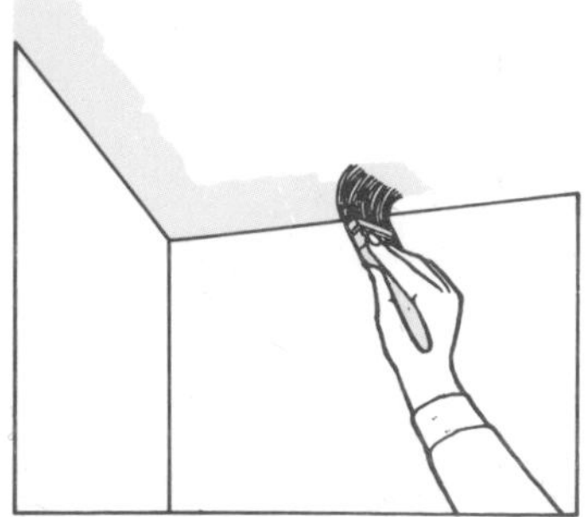

Using a brush
Start at the window, and use a 2-inch brush to paint into corners and around light fixtures. A larger brush is needed to cover the ceiling.

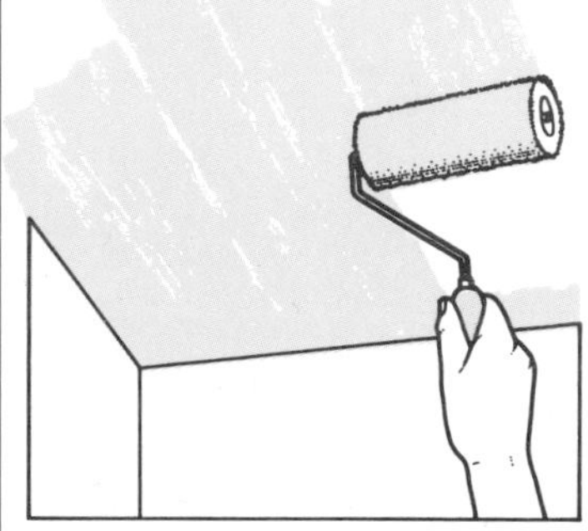

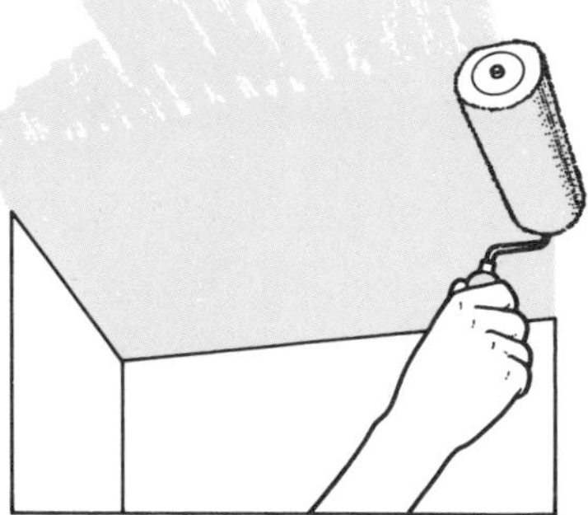

Using a roller
Paint ceiling in strips 2 ft wide in one direction, then cross at right angles for maximum cover. Apply gloss paint toward the window.

Extended roller
If you fit the roller with a long handle you can paint the ceiling from the floor.

3 High level window
Where windows run up to the ceiling special care is needed in painting as the light will show up any defects.

4 Decorative borders
You can lower the ceiling line by painting a decorative border. Make a pattern by cutting out a repeat motif in thin cardboard. Stick pattern to wall with masking tape and apply the paint with a brush or better still, an aerosol can. Keep paint off walls and ceiling by masking with newspaper.

5 Striped effect
Snap a chalked line, and mask the edges of stripes with masking tape. Paint lighter areas first and overlap with darker stripes.

6 Papered ceilings
If you plan to cover the ceiling and walls with the same paper, choose a small pattern, to avoid a matching problem where ceiling meets wall.

Papering ceilings
Prepare the surface as described on pp. 38-39. Take the longest width measurement adding two inches and cut the required lengths. Snap a chalk line at the window end of the room for the first strip. Pasting, brushing and trimming are as described on pp. 38-39, but fold concertina fashion. Hanging paper is easier if one person supports it while another positions and brushes it flat **A**. If possible, begin in such a way that the edge of a strip coincides with any light fixture. Make star shaped cuts for fitting **B**.

3

4

5

6

A

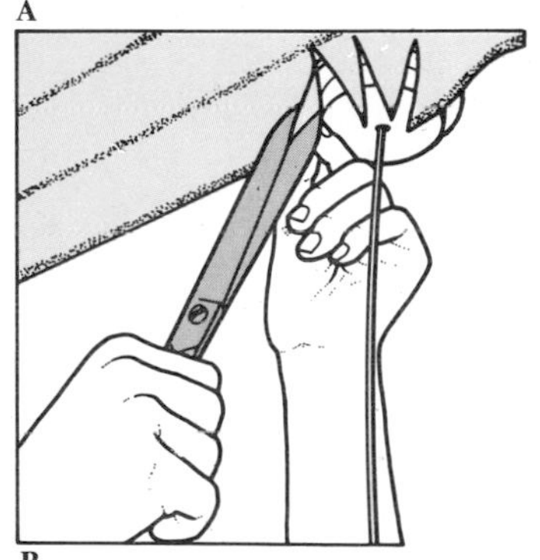
B

Painting Woodwork

Preparing the Surfaces

New woodwork
Lightly sand the surface to smooth it off. Apply shellac coating to knots in the wood to prevent any resin seeping through finished paintwork. Now paint with primer which will highlight scratches, dents and open grain. Fill these with a fine surface filler and rub down when set hard. Fill cracks with putty. Fit any new glass to windows, remembering that putty takes a week to be sufficiently hard to paint with undercoat.

New woodwork
1 Coat any knots in new wood with shellac coating before priming, to prevent resin from seeping through.

2 Primer reveals irregularities in new wood such as scratches, dents and open grain. Be sure to prime moldings and rabbets thoroughly.

3 Fill dents and scratches with a fine surface filler, applied with a filling knife. Rub down, then fill large cracks with putty.

Old paintwork
Wash down paintwork with detergent. Fill any cracks with filler, and rub down the area with wet and dry paper. If the surface is really bad, remove old paint with a blowtorch, or chemical paint-stripper if a natural, lacquered finish is needed. When using a gas torch make sure you do not aim it at any inflammable materials, or at glass which will crack. Never hold the flame in one place for too long, as this will result in charred woodwork. Slight scorching is inevitable but can be rubbed down. When stripping is completed, treat as for new wood.

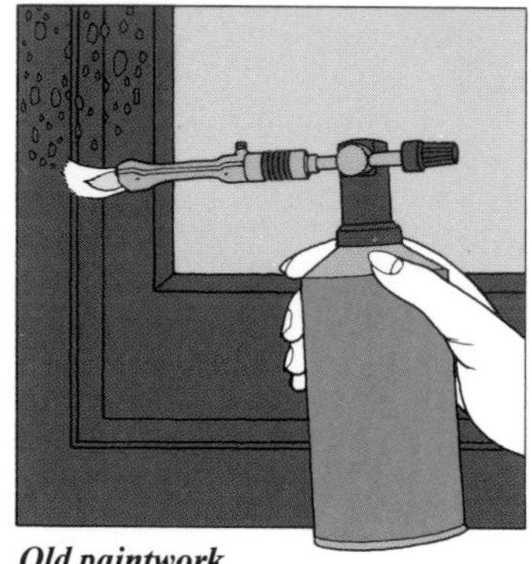

Old paintwork
1 Burn off old paint with a blowtorch. Move blowtorch across paint until it blisters.

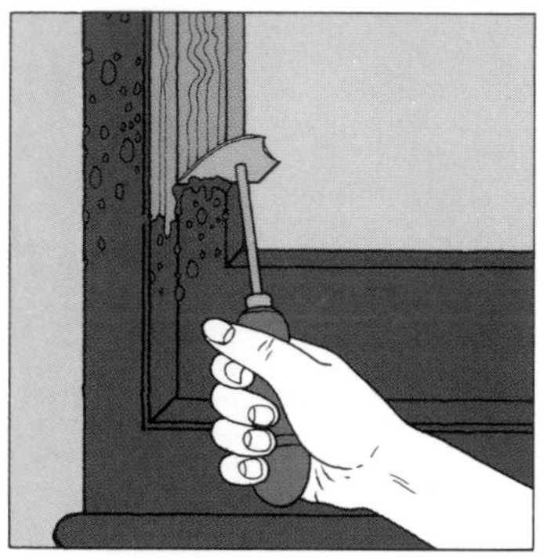

2 Before paint has had time to harden, remove it with a scraping tool, starting from top of moldings.

3 Strip off flat areas of paint. Take great care, for falling scraps of burning paint can easily cause substantial damage.

Chemical stripper
If you use a chemical stripper, wear protective clothing, and keep children and animals away from the area. Apply stripper liberally with an old paint brush and leave it for 10 to 15 minutes. Now remove softened paint with a scraping tool or stripping knife. Very old or deep layers of paint may need a further application of stripper. Wash the surface down with paint thinner to remove any traces of stripper. Finally, sand down and treat it as if it were new woodwork.

Chemical stripper
1 Wear protective clothing and rubber gloves to apply chemical stripper, which is very corrosive.

2 Leave for 10 to 15 minutes, then scrape off softened paint with a stripping knife. Difficult areas may need extra applications.

3 Rub down the surface with a paint thinner to remove all traces of stripper. Finally, sand down and treat as for new woodwork.

Preparation and application
If a skin has formed on the paint, cut it away, then stir the paint. All paints need stirring except for the thixotropic "jelly" type. When the paint has a smooth, even-colored surface, apply as described on the right. Interior woodwork normally requires one undercoat. Leave for about 16 hours before rubbing down with fine sandpaper, then apply one or two gloss coats. The order of the work is **1** window frames and sills, **2** cabinets, shelves and fireplaces, **3** doors and frames, **4** baseboards.

Application of paint
1 Dip one third of the brush into paint, then touch it against the can side, so that it does not drip.

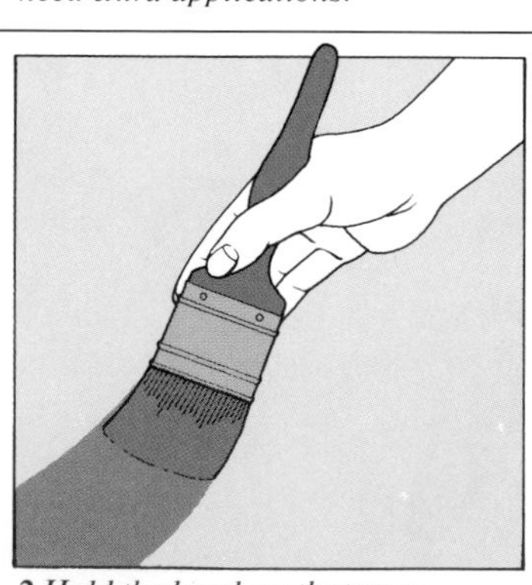

2 Hold the brush so that your wrist is free to move in both directions. Apply with even strokes, flexing the bristles against the surface.

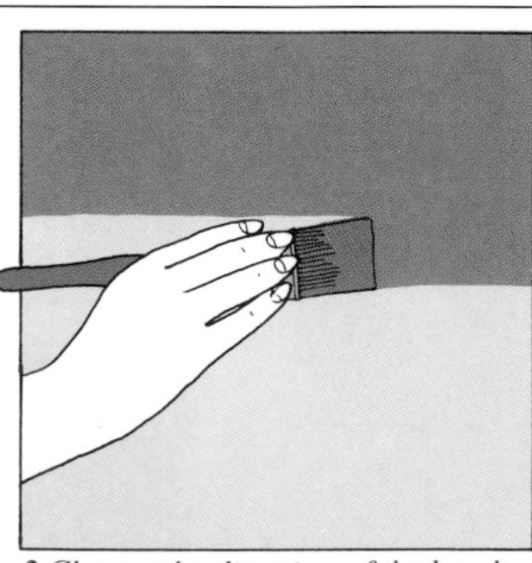

3 Change the direction of the brush strokes to achieve an even cover, finishing off with light upward strokes to avoid any running paint.

Painting Techniques

Painting around glass
When painting windows, work right up to the glass with a steady, freehand stroke and make sure you cover the gap between putty and glass. You can mask the glass around the frames with tape before starting the job, or protect it with a paint shield as you paint. You can always remove excess paint from the glass with a razor blade scraper after finishing the job.

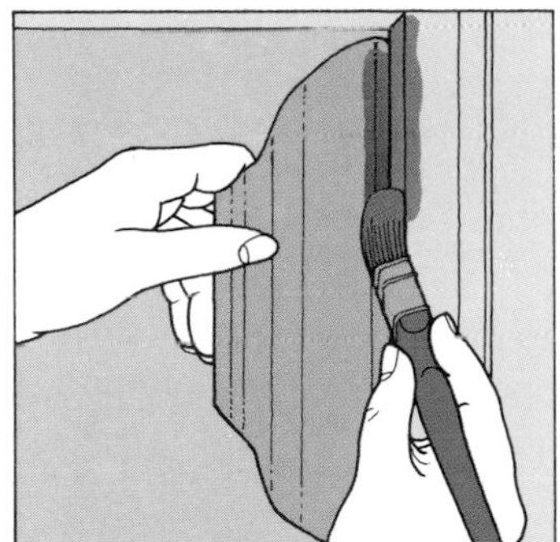

Painting window frames
1 A paint shield prevents paint from getting on to the glass.

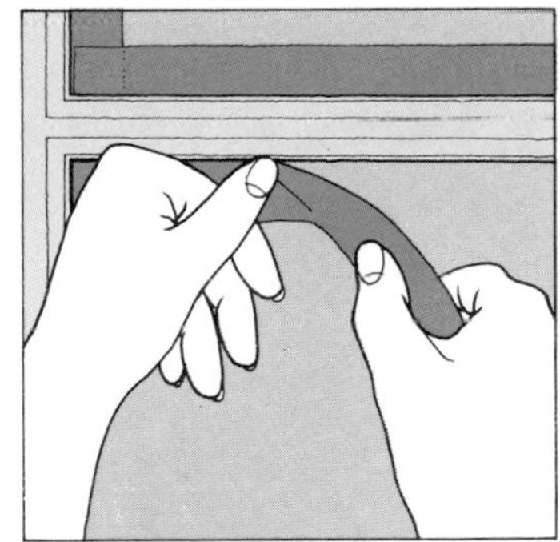

2 Alternatively mask the edges of the glass with tape before painting. Do not remove tape until paint is completely dry.

3 Painting right up to the glass seals the gap between glass and putty. Paint on the glass can be removed with a razor blade scraper.

Painting the frames
Windows should be painted in a certain order: see diagram, right, for casement and double-hung windows. If you are painting the window lock or crank, leave them until last so that you control the window as you work. With double-hung windows it is important not to get paint on the sash cords, as it will harden and weaken them. As the paint dries, move the window up and down several times, as otherwise it will become difficult to open.
Painting doors
Remove all the fittings from the door and wedge it in an open position. Work at a reasonable speed to avoid join marks between sections of paint. If one side is a different color from the other, paint it and the frame so that only one color is visible at a time when the door is open. The sequence of painting a panel door differs from a flush door (see right).
Painting baseboards
Mask off the junctions between baseboard and the floor and wall. When painting is completed, close the door and windows and try not to use the room until the paint is dry, as dust will be kicked up and settle on the wet paint.

Casement windows
*You should paint in the following sequence: **1** Muntins, where the molded wood meets the glass, **2** Crossbars, **3** Top and bottom cross-rails, which should be painted with the window open and the lock secured, **4** Window frame, **5** Casing.*

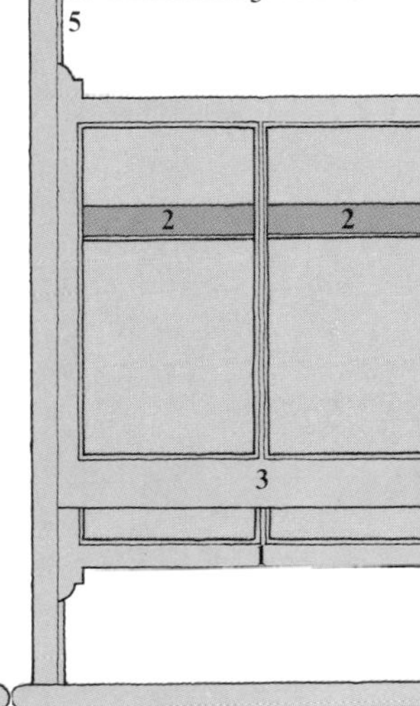

Double-hung windows
*Push bottom window up and top one down. Paint in the following sequence: **1** Bottom meeting rail, and all the vertical sections, **2** Rest of top sash, with the window almost closed, **3** Bottom sash, **4** Window frame, **5** Outside and inside runners.*

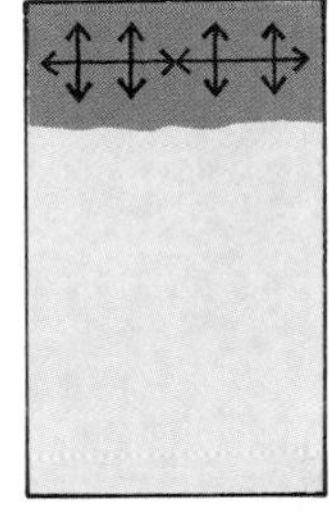

Painting flush doors
1 Divide the door into seven or eight similar sections. Apply paint along the top section with vertical strokes brushed out with horizontal strokes.

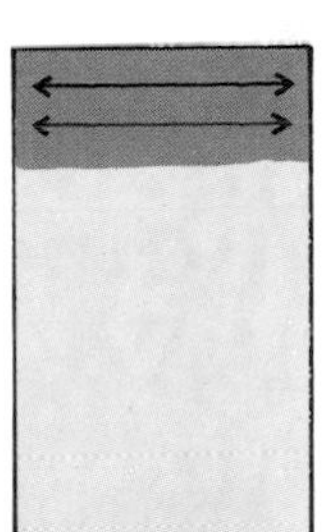

2 Without reloading the brush, smooth out the entire section with firm, horizontal strokes.

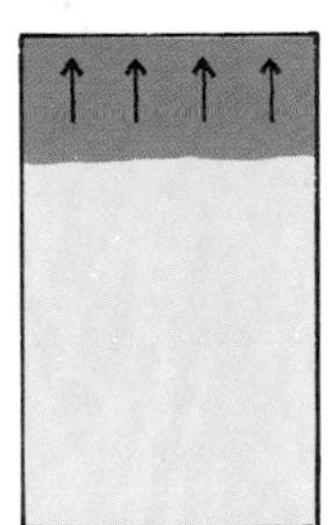

3 Finally, complete the section in hand by smoothing it out with light, vertical strokes.

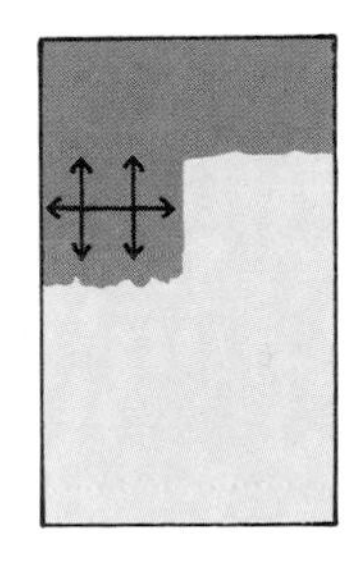

4 Continue in the same way with the remaining sections. Work quickly, as speed will eliminate join marks, which are more obvious in a flush door than a paneled one.

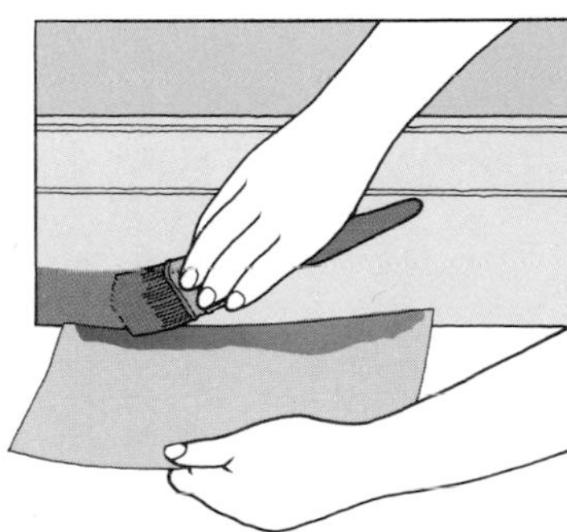

Baseboards
Always use a cardboard mask as a protective measure for floor and walls when painting a baseboard.

Panel doors
*Paint: **1** Moldings, **2** Panels, **3** Center uprights, **4** Horizontal rails, **5** Stiles, **6** Edges.*

Stairs
If you are carpeting your stairs, you only need to paint the sides of the stair treads. Check to see that the carpet overlaps the painted area, as shown left. If you are not carpeting the stairs, paint alternate treads, so that you can make use of the stairs while paint is still wet.

Floors

Practical considerations
Before laying the final floor material, it is important that the subfloor be in good condition and well prepared. A particle board, plywood, or even a hardboard floor can, in some areas, be used as a finished surface if laid well.
Where floors need to be regularly wiped clean, or need to be waterproof, tiles are an obvious choice. Ceramic and quarry tiles provide a very hardwearing and easy to clean finish. Cork tiles are softer on the feet and waterproof if well-sealed. Vinyl is also durable and less expensive, but is apt to be slippery when wet. A better choice for a bathroom would be wall-to-wall carpeting which is rubber backed, or carpet tiles, which can be cleaned in the washing machine.
More than one floor covering may be used in living areas, both to provide visual interest or perhaps to zone off certain sections. A wooden floor, sanded and sealed, with carpet squares or rugs strategically placed, can be a good compromise between the elegant and the functional. Wood block or parquet floors are very hardwearing, and need only the occasional polishing. Wall-to-wall carpeting is expensive and good-quality material is essential if you want the covering to be durable. It does, however, unify an area and make it appear more spacious. An alternative is to lay cork or vinyl tiles in those areas where liquids are in use, such as the dining room, and to carpet the seating section. Carpets are particularly suitable to bedrooms where they create a warm, comfortable atmosphere by eliminating drafts. Short-pile carpet tiles can even be used in children's rooms, or you can lay vinyl or cork tiles which are easy to keep clean and provide a flat surface for games. In hallways and passage ways, sanded floorboards are a practical choice, likewise sealed floor tiles. Stairs really need fitted carpeting, for sound absorption and safety. Unless a good quality carpet and underlay is used, wear will eventually show on stair treads. In workrooms, a smooth clear floor is the most practical. Finely-textured and painted concrete is suitable, but hard on the feet. Particle board or hardboard is better than floorboards; if you want vinyl tiles, lay down wood slats near the workbench, as vinyl can become slippery. Laundries need waterproof flooring.

1

2

3

4

1 Ceramic tiles
Ceramic tiles provide a sturdy and easy to clean floor covering. They are particularly useful in a room which opens directly on to the garden.

2 Quarry tiles
Areas which are used a great deal during the daytime, such as family rooms, will benefit from a hardwearing floor covering such as quarry tiles.

3 Cork floor tiles
Cork floor tiles are ideal in a child's playroom. They are warm to the touch, and therefore comfortable to sit on, and yet easily cleaned if properly finished.

4 Vinyl tiles
These tiles are ideal for a sewing room where small scraps of fabric and threads would be difficult to remove from a carpet.

5 Strip floor
A hardwood strip floor, if properly sealed and maintained, may prove cheaper in the long run than less expensive coverings which have to be replaced at regular intervals.

6 Parquet floor
Hallways benefit from an overall finish which makes them appear roomy and integrates them visually with those corridors leading off them. Rugs are a colorful addition.

7 Slats
The slatted lumber sections in this laundry area cover a concrete floor which can be cold and hard on the feet. Seal the wood well to protect it.

5

6

7

Wood Floors

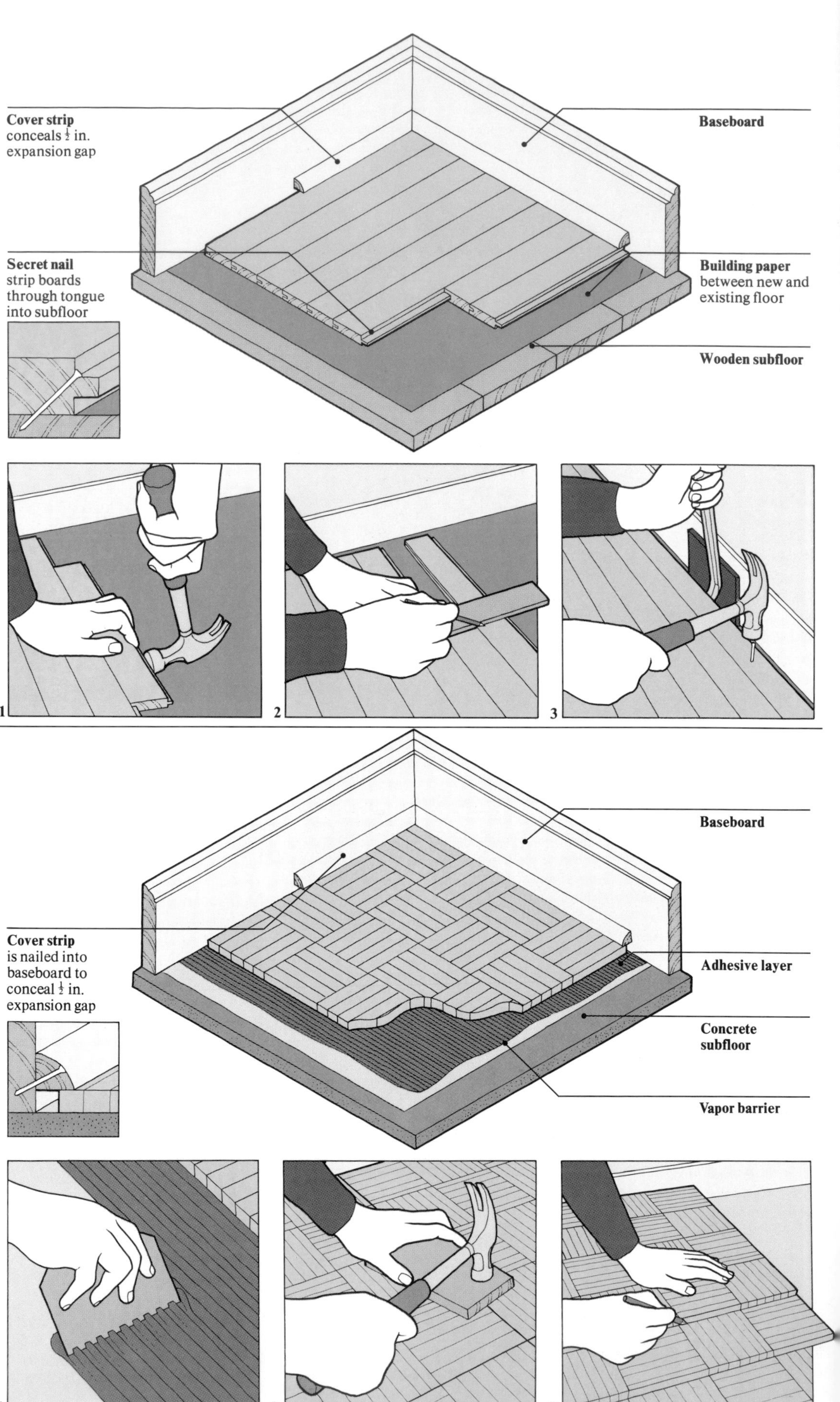

Strip floors

A strip floor is constructed from hardwood tongue and groove strips laid at right angles to the subfloor which must be flat. Nail down loose boards and punch nail heads below surface. A subfloor can be constructed by laying thick sheets of plywood (see pp. 96-97) on the joists. Cover with building paper, sheets overlapping 4 in.

Mark a line a board's width plus ½ in. from the baseboard and lay first board along it, groove edge toward wall. Nail through center, punching head below surface. When laying subsequent boards, lap the edge with a piece of stripping **1** so as to protect the edge while securing flooring. Nail the boards at an angle through the corner of the tongue as in small diagram, right. Butt joint all ends which must be cut or planed square. Stagger joints to prevent them lining up. When finishing the end of a strip, mark off additional length with new board ½ in. from wall as in **2**. Cut last strip lengthwise to fit ending ½ in. from baseboard. If necessary, lever piece on to tongue of its neighbor using scrap hardboard to protect baseboard, as in **3.** Nail last board through center. Fix cover strip to baseboard.

Block floors

The easiest way to install a block floor is to buy manufactured parquet panels which are waterproofed and pre-sanded. Lumber subfloors should be lined with hardboard, textured side up. Blocks can also be laid on concrete, provided it is level and protected against damp.

Mark out the floor as for laying ceramic tiles (see pp. 68-69). Work from center of room and spread 4 sq. yds of adhesive at a time, using a notched spreader and mastic, **1**. Press the blocks into the adhesive, butting them carefully together and checking alignment. Use a piece of scrap wood to knock neighboring panels flush when necessary, **2**. Border panels should be marked out leaving a ½ in. gap between them and the baseboard. Lay the panel to be cut over an adjacent whole tile. Lay another panel on top of it, **3**. Mark the cutting line and saw block to fit. When the floor is complete, finish with a light sanding to remove any dirt, and fix a cover strip between edge and baseboard. Nail cover strip to baseboard as in diagram above.

Sanding Floors

Drum and rotary sanders

Sanding machines finish both old and new floors quickly and with a minimum of mess. They are obtainable from hire shops. Allow a day to sand each room.

Use a *drum sander* for the main bulk of the work, and the smaller *rotary sander* for finishing the edges and small areas. Both these machines can be plugged into domestic electrical supply, both take varying grades of sandpaper and both suck waste material into attached dust bags.

Sandpaper is usually supplied with the machine; coarse grades clean and level the surface, finer grades are used for finishing. Make sure machines are unplugged before changing paper. Lay drum sander on its back and open guard. Using key supplied, loosen the bar clamp screws until the bar is $\frac{3}{8}$ in. clear of drum. Insert a new sheet under the bar wrapping it around drum and tucking end in slot. Tension paper by tightening clamps with key. Never use machine if paper is slack. Replace the guard. To change the paper on a rotary sander, unscrew the retaining clamp in the disk's center with a key or wrench. Replace the worn disk and tighten the clamp.

Sanding techniques

Close up any gaps in floorboards and make sure flooring is secure. Punch nail heads below the surface. Remove any loose material. Tilt the machine backwards so that roller is lifted off floor. Switch on machine and gradually lower it. As it comes into contact with the surface, move it across floor at an angle to the boards. At the end of a strip tilt back and turn it around to sand a parallel section, overlapping the previous strip. When the floor is finished, sand at an opposite angle to initial run to complete leveling process. Fit a medium grade of paper followed by a finer grade and finish sanding in the direction of the floorboards.

The rotary machine is now used to finish off edges and hard-to-reach spots. Grip the handles and switch the machine on, keeping it moving to avoid oversanding. To get into very small areas, use a sanding disk attached to a power drill or use a sanding block. Vacuum all loose dust from the floor and surrounding surface and complete with your chosen finish.

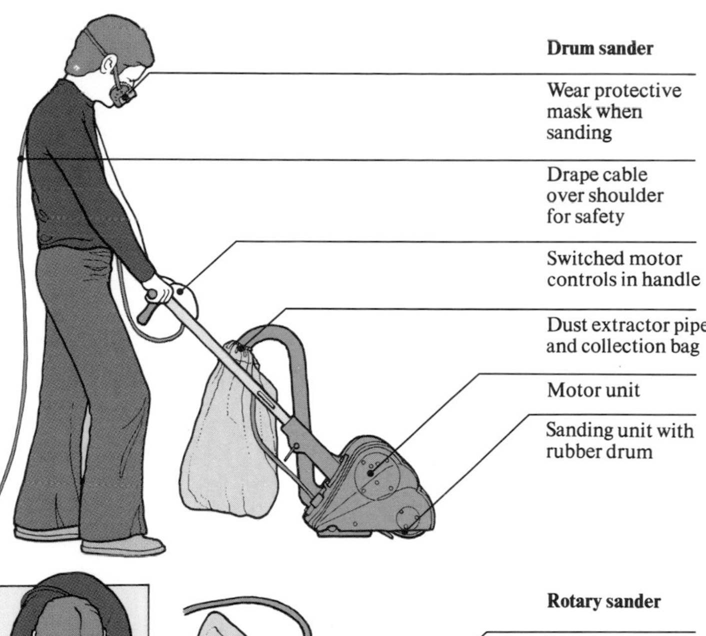

1

Changing the drum sander
1 Push back guard and locate keys in clamp screws.

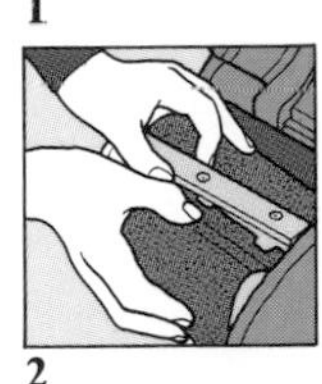
2

2 Turn keys to release drum bar clamp; take out the worn paper.

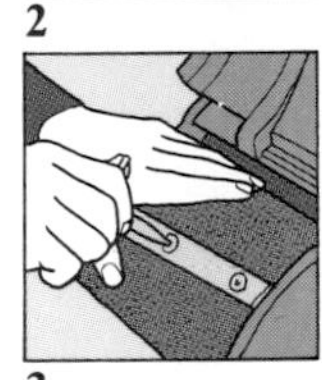
3

3 Insert a new sheet under the clamp bar, tighten the screws and replace guard.

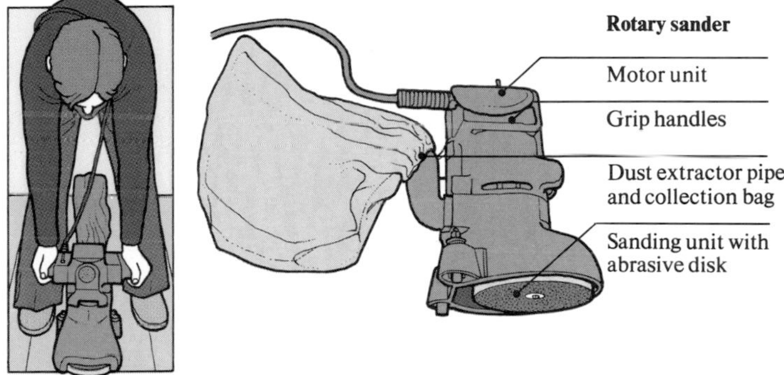

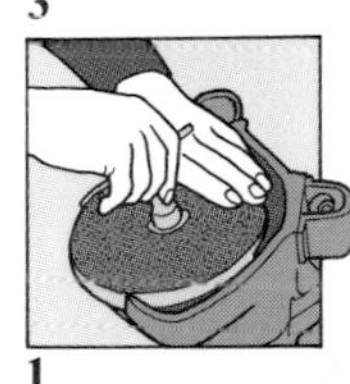
1

Changing the rotary sander
1 Unlock and remove the bolt and disk washer with a wrench.

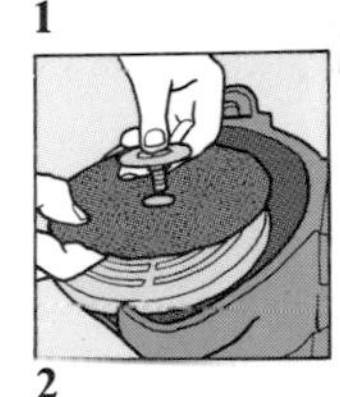
2

2 Replace worn disk. Insert bolt through hole in new disk and tighten.

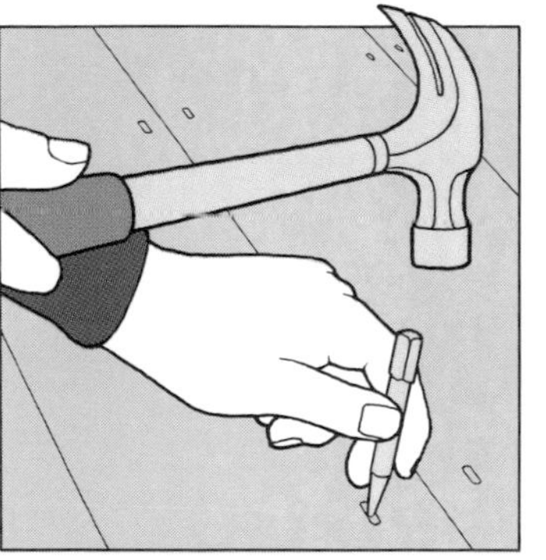

Preparing floor
Use a nail set to punch nail heads well below surface. A nail head could tear paper or damage drum.

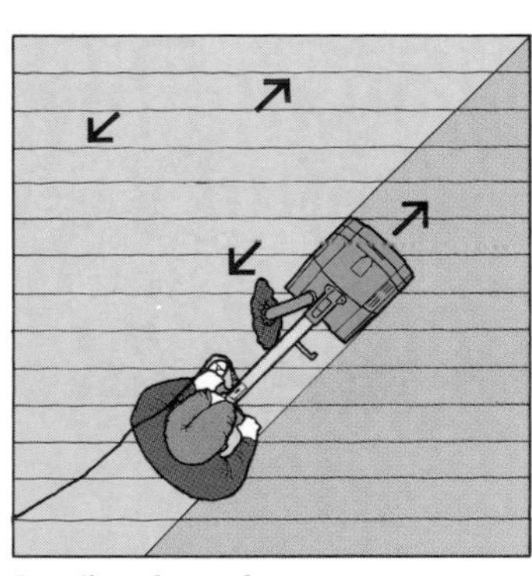

Leveling the surface
Sand at an angle to the boards. This will level any high points on the boards, instead of following them.

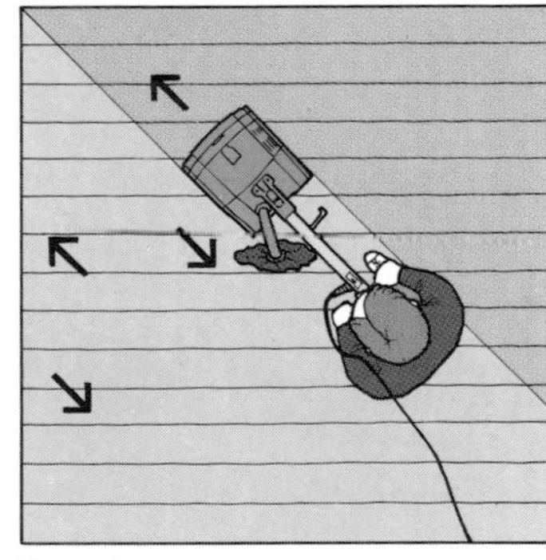

Second run
Having covered the entire floor with the drum sander, change direction and sand across the other way.

Final finish
When the surface has been sanded flat, use medium to fine papers and work along the grain of the boards.

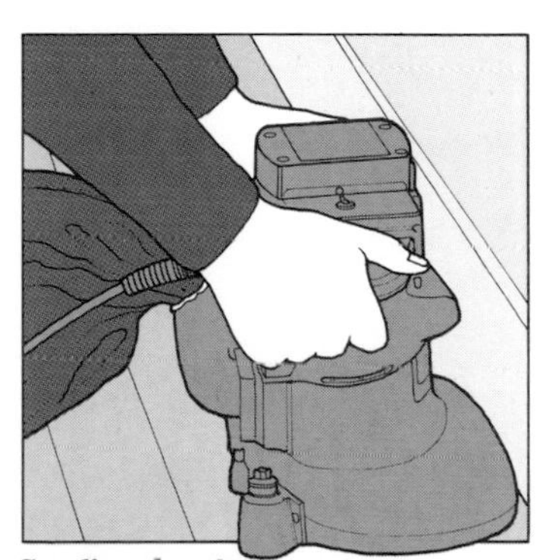

Sanding the edges
Use the rotary sander to finish off the edges by the baseboard. Change disks from coarse to fine.

Awkward corners
Use a disk sander attachment on a power drill or a sanding block for small, awkward corners.

1

2

1 Wood stains
The three top softwood sample strips on the left illustrate color changes after applying two coats of wood stains to simulate more expensive hardwoods, before the application of a sealer. They are, top down, teak, Indian rosewood, black oak. The fourth sample is finished with a clear varnish. The first coat darkens the wood to a noticeable degree, subsequent coats will not greatly change the color but should be applied to protect the wood's surface. The darker wood stains will also tone down after the application of the sealer.

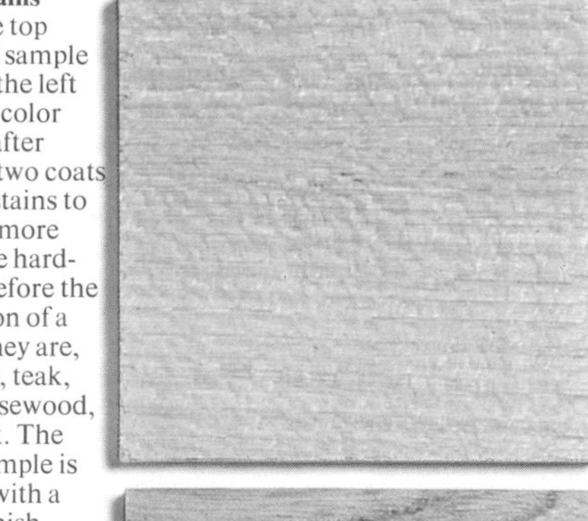

2 Color stains
Stains for wood are also available in a wide range of colors. Like the simulated hardwood stains, the depth of color will change between coats.

3 Other woods
Wooden floors, either in strip form or blocks, are laid for their durability and natural color. Some of the woods used, shown right from top to bottom, include beech, oak, pine, teak and mahogany. These are generally sealed with a clear finish. For most woods this can be a polyurethane varnish or wax. For a teak floor use teak oil; the natural oils in this wood will reject most other floor finishes.

3

Wood Finishes

Preparing the floor
Clean floor of dust before applying a sealer; avoid sweeping adjacent areas after applying it.

Applying the stain
Use a large brush to apply stain or sealers, and follow the grain of the flooring lumber.

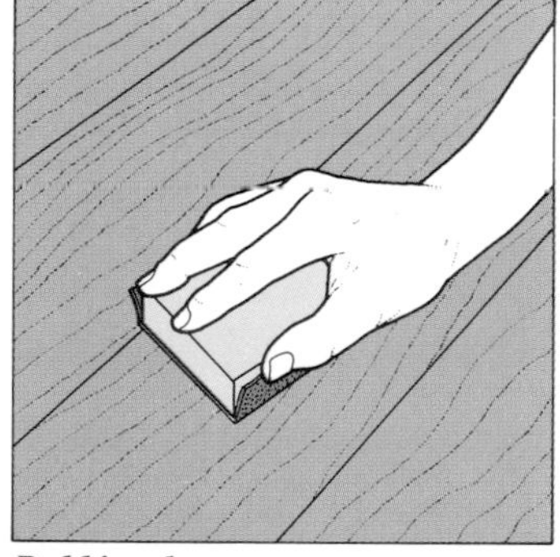

Rubbing down
Sealers and water-based stains need to be smoothed off with a fine abrasive paper between coats.

Painting in sections
Work in easily-manageable sections, and avoid overlapping by finishing on the edges of boards.

Wood stains

Stains alter the color of wood while still allowing the grain to show through. You can, however, use several coats of a very dark stain to cover the grain as well. A stain is applied either to match up a piece of lumber with the surrounding wood or to disguise the character of a certain wood type. You can buy stains the approximate color of most wood varieties, and mix them to a fairly accurate match. Colors can also be used which merely decorate the wood, without disguising their nature.

Most stains need to be built up with one or two layers to produce the desired depth of color. It is wise to prepare a test piece of similar lumber before tackling the floor; apply successive coats and slightly overlap each coat to see how the color is changing. Remember that most stains appear lighter when dry than when applied. Use a large brush and follow the grain.

Work along floorboards in easily handled sections, finishing each time on the edges of boards to avoid overlapping. An even, liberal coat is essential for a uniform effect. When the stain has dried, go over the floor with a soft cloth. Finish with a coat of clear sealer, but check first that it will not affect the stain. If you use a water-based stainer, rub down with fine abrasive paper between each coat.

Wood sealers

A sealer is a form of protection that acts in much the same way as a primer coat on paintwork. Some types should be applied initially so that they soak into the grain and prevent other finishes from doing so; others act as a protective top coat for both finish and wood. Modern sealers are very easy to apply – they are brushed on – and are made in a range of finishes from gloss through to semi-mat and mat. Several light coats are better than one heavy one and floors must be dust-free on application. All sealers will darken the wood to a certain extent, but this enhances grain characteristics and gives an added warmth to the color.

Polyurethane sealers are extremely hard wearing and are manufactured in a clear finish, as well as translucent colors. These colors do not penetrate as far as a wood dye and remain on the surface.

Wax polishes

Wax polishing produces a very pleasing "satin" finish on a wooden floor although it looks better on dark rather than light woods. Waxing must be repeated at regular intervals – depending on the amount of wear on the surface. The wax should contain silicone, as you will need a durable finish.

If the wood is untreated, apply a coat of sealer with a paint brush to prevent wax soaking into boards. Work it well into the surface. Let floor dry, then sand it down with a fine abrasive paper. Apply a liberal coat of liquid wax polish with a brush or a soft cloth. Rub well into the grain, leave it to dry and apply a second, lighter coat. Let harden before buffing with a cloth or an electric polisher. If the floor is old, or has been thoroughly sealed, you may need several applications, allowing each to harden before applying the next.

Before waxing a new floor, make a few test strips on the same type of wood, first applying a coat of stain and then the wax polish. Never over polish a floor, as it can become slippery and dangerous.

Painted floors

An increasingly popular solution to the problem of floor covering is to use paint, since traditional floor coverings are becoming more expensive, and tough and durable paints are now widely available. You can buy special hard paints for much-used floors, but a good quality oil-based paint is adequate where there is little traffic – such as the outside area of stair treads. The best floor paints have a base of polyurethane or epoxy resin. Painting a floor tends to show up the gaps between the floorboards, so you must decide first if you are going to fill these gaps with wood putty, or some other suitable type of wood filler.

Before painting, the floor surface must be clean and dry, free of dust, grease or oil. Sand down, if necessary, before applying the first coat, which should be thinned down about 20%. When this has dried, follow with one or more unthinned coats. If the wood is new flooring lumber, it may have some large knots which should first be treated with a knot sealer. Finally, apply the paint as described on pp. 58-59.

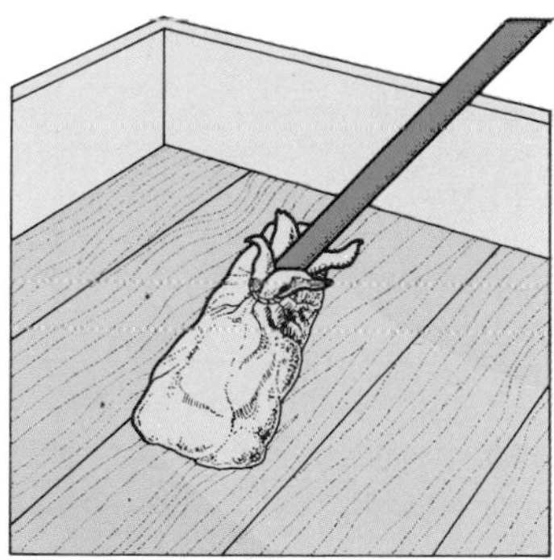

Cleaning off residue
After staining, you may notice a powdery residue. Remove it with a cloth wrapped around a broom.

Wax polishing
After sealing and rubbing down apply liberal coats of liquid wax, using a soft cloth.

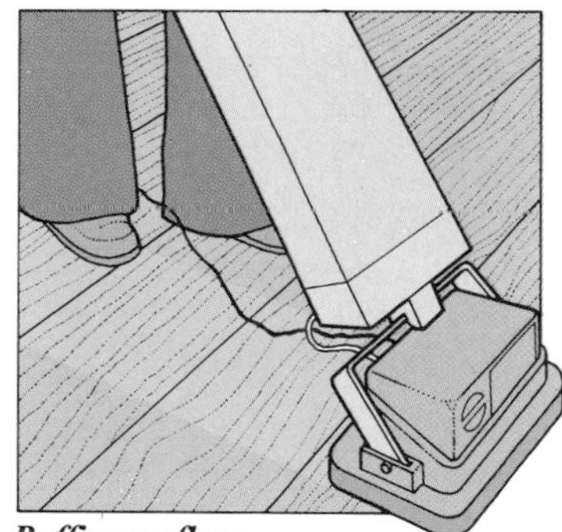

Buffing up floor
After the second, lighter coat of wax has hardened, buff the floor with an electric polisher.

Using a sealer
Wood sealers preserve finishes by forming a protective covering. They also prevent wax being absorbed.

Tiles

Making patterns
Even a simply designed tile can be used in several ways. The diagrams below show two variations.

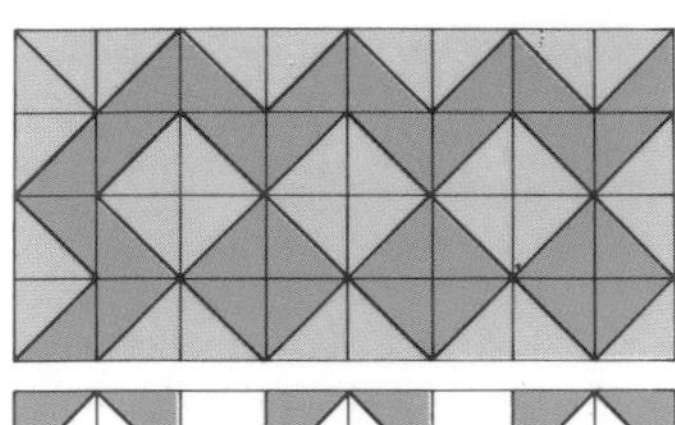

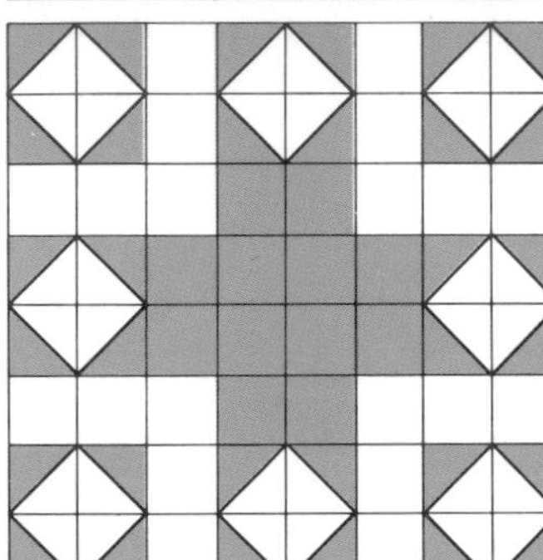

Shaped tiles
Patterned floors can also be constructed by using shaped tiles. The diagrams below show shapes used singly or in combination. The pattern is strengthened by using different color tiles.

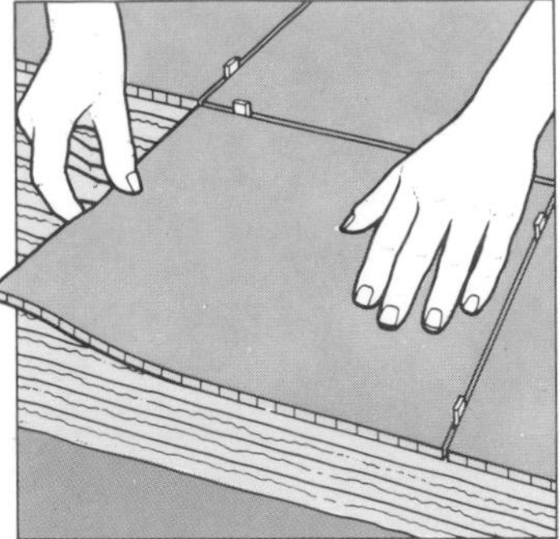

Laying mosaic tiles
1 Set out as for cork tiles, see p. 68. Lay tiles paper backing uppermost, with same spacing as between the individual tiles.

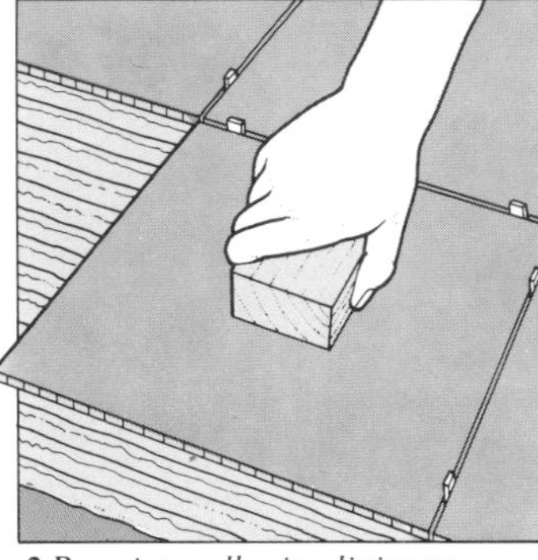

2 Press into adhesive, lining up joints. Tamp down with block to level tiles. Cut border tiles by scoring and nibbling waste with pincers.

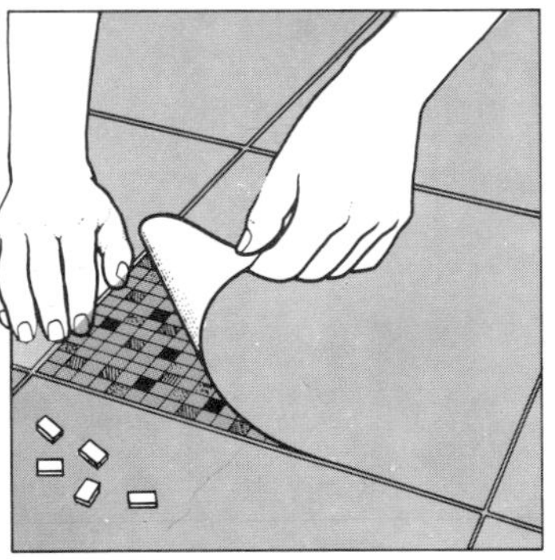

3 Allow adhesive 24 hours to set. Remove spacers and soak backing with warm water, and when ready, gently peel it off.

4 Apply grouting to the entire surface with a rubber bladed trowel, pushing it well into gaps – wipe off the excess with a damp sponge.

2

1 Vinyl tiles
Different colored vinyl tiles are often used to form checkerboard or linear patterns – here they have been laid on the floor of a playroom to form gamesboards and roadways.

2 Patterned vinyl
A combination of patterned and plain colored vinyl tiles make a strong decorative feature. The tile motif has been repeated on the dining table surface.

3 Complicated patterns
This floor admirably demonstrates the amount of pattern which can be achieved by using a tile similar to that shown top left on the opposite page, in combination with a plain square. When planning a pattern of this kind, work out your design first with colored pencils on graph paper.

4 Slate
Slate is beautiful, hardwearing but expensive. Here, its natural coloring and texture are enhanced by laying it in conjunction with rectangular quarry tiles. Both materials are laid on a cement base and should be sealed.

5 Stone
Lay stone slabs on a cement base as for quarry tiles. The slabs should be leveled by tamping down with a heavy section of wood. If the cement is stubborn, brush a little water between the stones. Finally fill between the slabs with a cement mix which can either emphasize the irregular shapes or be colored to match the stone.

3

4

5

Tiling Floors

Laying Tiles

Ceramic tiles
Tiles must be laid square with joints aligning correctly. As when tiling a wall, you will need to fix two marker battens, in case walls are out of square. First establish the desired direction of the joints and set up battens accordingly. In the plan on the right square tiles are to be laid square to the room. Measure and mark a center line down the main axis of the floor. Mark out on a batten the position of a row of tiles, allowing space for grouting between each. Use this batten to establish the position of the tiles on the floor. You can either mark it out starting from the center line running to each wall, ending with equal gaps at either end, or you can begin with whole tiles, at a prominent point in the room where they will look more attractive than cut border tiles, such as a door. Establish the position of the last whole tile on the center line, and nail a batten at right angles to it (see pp. 54-55). Set out another batten at right angles to the first at one end of it; dry lay a group of nine tiles to check accuracy of the battens, as shown in diagram top right: the final appearance of the job depends on this last check.

Vinyl and cork tiles
Mark and set out vinyl and cork tiles in exactly the same way as ceramic. You can fix a straight batten along the center line to which you can butt the tiles for the first half of the room. Apply adhesive and carefully press tiles into position. Try not to allow adhesive to seep between joints. If it does, wipe off immediately with a damp cloth, or clean with solvent. This is particularly important when laying uncoated cork tiles.

Cutting tiles
Cork and vinyl tiles can be shaped with a sharp knife. You will get a straight cut with the help of a steel ruler. A goscut (see p. 141) will cut odd shapes in vinyl, but cork is too thick. Cut border tiles as described on p. 62. Some shops will rent you a tile cutting machine, or cut tiles for you, in which case all you need to do is mark the cutting line, and number each tile and its position on the floor. If you are cutting tiles yourself, use a glass cutter or tile scriber, and always take care to wear protective gloves and goggles. Score the line as deeply as possible on the upper surface. Score the

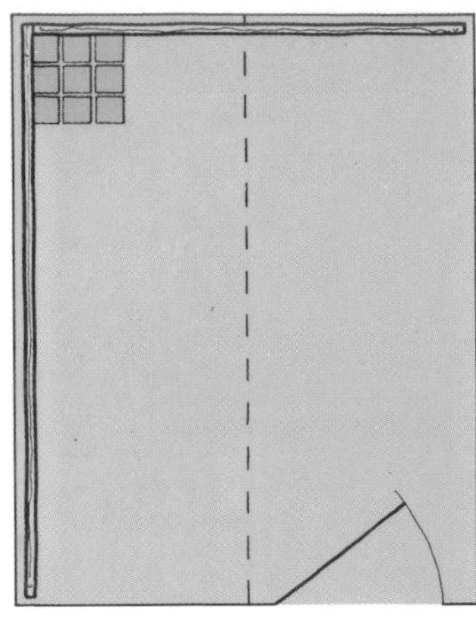

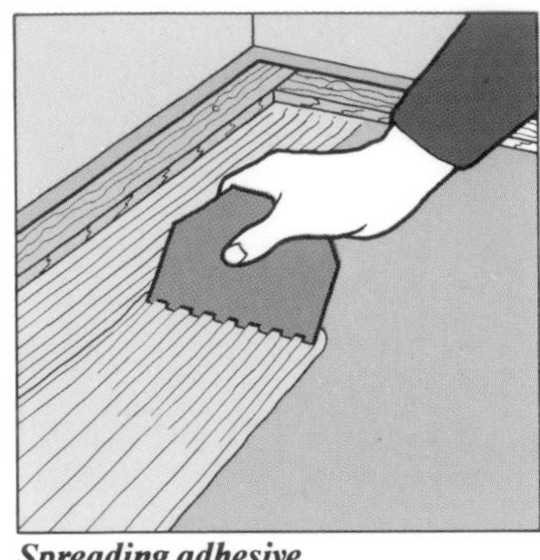

Spreading adhesive
Use a notched trowel and spread enough adhesive to lay nine tiles at a time.

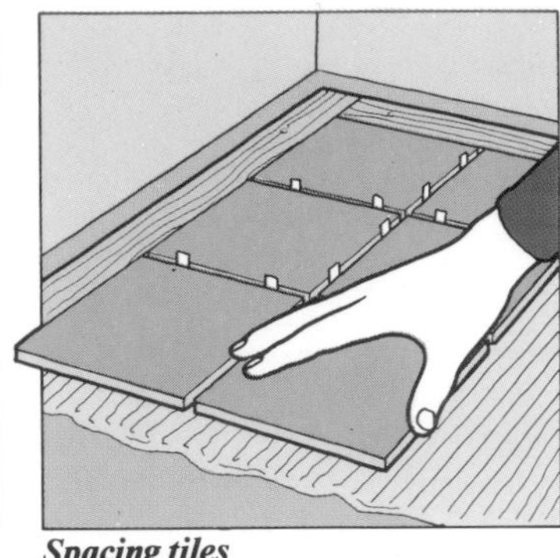

Spacing tiles
If tiles do not have integral spacers to keep them apart, use wood strips 1/16 or 1/8 in. thick.

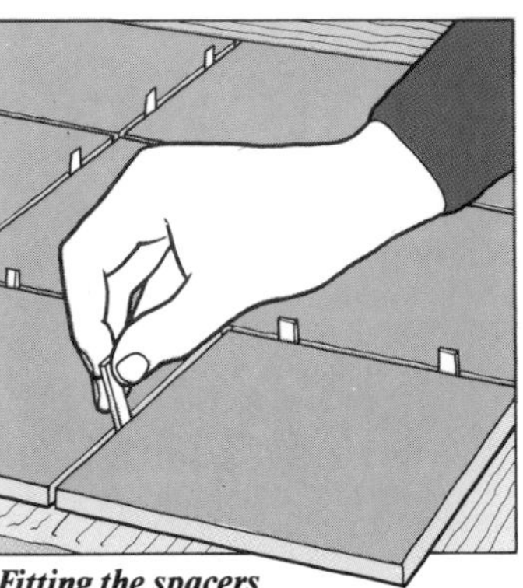

Fitting the spacers
Press the tile into adhesive. Insert the spacers in between to keep tiles square to each other.

Using a straight edge
Lay tiles in batches of nine. Check each group for square with a straight edge. Wipe off excess adhesive.

Fitting border tiles
Before laying border tiles leave main area to set, and remove spacers and battens. Grout entire area.

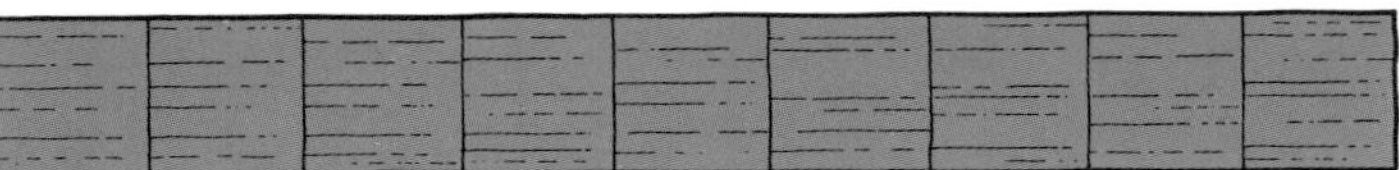

Going with the grain
Lay nine tiles on the floor to see if there is a grain or noticeable pattern on the surface. Most cork tiles have a "face" with a slight sheen to it. Lay the tiles with the grain going in the same direction.

Going against the grain
Unless the pattern on the tiles is obviously meant to align, you can create a deliberate contrast with grain or pattern going in opposite directions. Lay tiles alternately, as shown above.

Resetting a tile
To reset a tile, run a thin blade underneath it before adhesive sets and pry it up from the floor.

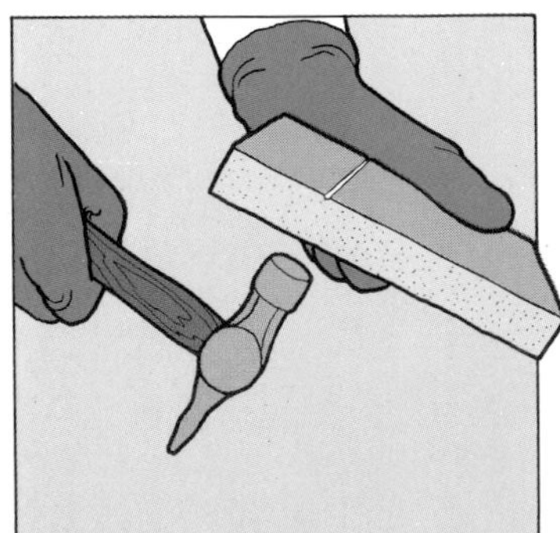

Three ways of cutting quarry tiles
1 After scoring the tile hold it with the waste facing you, and tap the underside with a hammer.

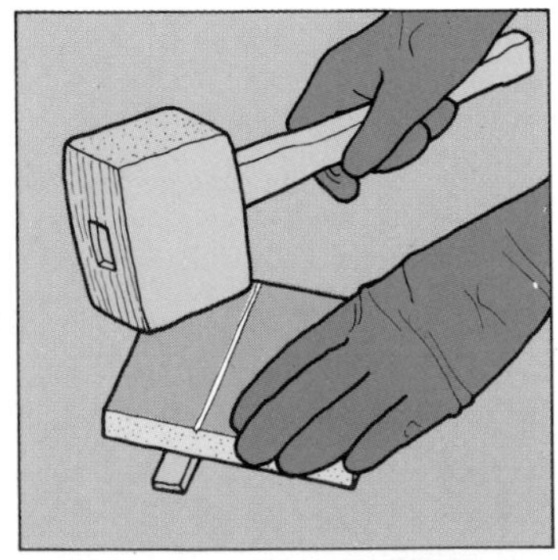

2 Alternatively place the tile face up on a firm edge in line with the intended cut. Hold it firmly and strike sharply with a mallet.

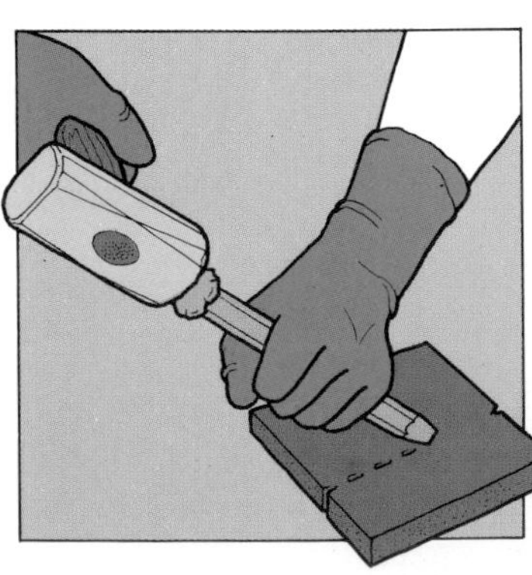

3 Lastly, the edges can be notched with a cold chisel in line with the intended cut.

edges, too, either with the scriber or with a cold chisel, cutting a small notch. To break, hold the tile face upward on each side of the scored line, and tap the underside smartly on the line with a hammer.

Laying quarry tiles

Set out two corner battens in the same way as described for laying ceramic tiles but with the battens twice the thickness of the tiles. Use a level to check the battens, packing them with cardboard where necessary, and nail them to the floor, leaving nail heads protruding so they can be removed later. Mark out a batten the length of four tiles, allowing ⅛ in. gaps between them. Use this measure to establish the position of a second batten parallel to the first (see diagram top right) also to be nailed to the floor after leveling. Cut a strikeoff board as described right. Before making up the bedding mixture, let the tiles soak for a while in water. Make up the bedding mortar with a 1:3 cement to sand mixture; the consistency should be smooth but not so wet that the tiles sink.

Leveling the mortar

Spread enough mortar between the battens for a 2 ft square of tiles. Level with strikeoff board, and sprinkle surface with dry cement to provide better adhesion. Lay the tiles as illustrated, leveling them flush with the battens by using the back of the strikeoff board. If the mortar is stubborn, soften it by brushing water between the joints of the tiles. Wash off any additional mortar on or between tiles with water. Work along the first batten laying a square of sixteen tiles at a time, until you have completed the first wall to wall section, less the border. Re-position the parallel batten, and repeat the process to lay the second section. When you have completed the entire area, leave for 24 hours before laying the border tiles, which should be measured and cut as described earlier. Remove the original battens, fill gap with bedding mortar and level down. Then position the border tiles, and tamp down with a heavy block of wood. These final tiles should be left to dry before you grout the floor.

It should be kept in mind that all tiles raise the floor level and it may be necessary to cut or plane off the equivalent amount from the bottom of any door (see p. 106).

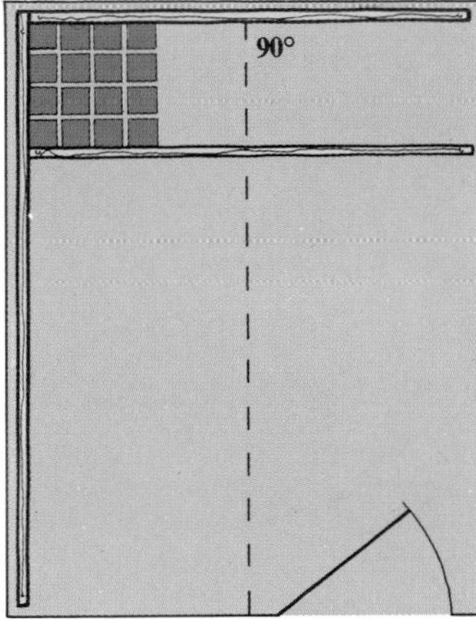
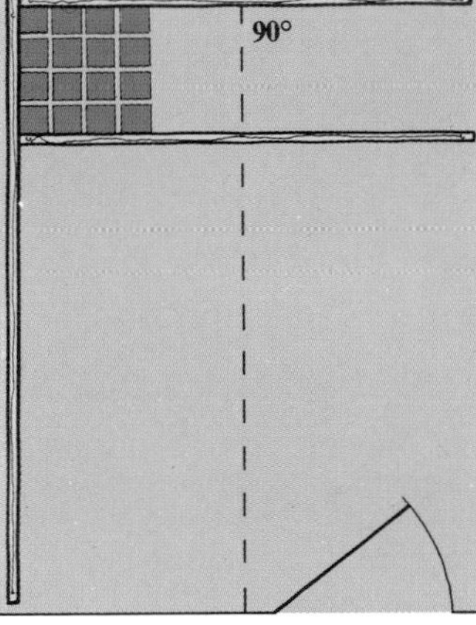

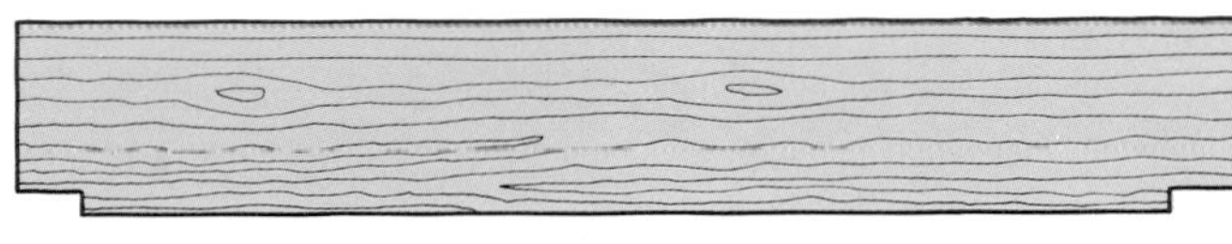

Making a strikeoff board
The purpose of this board is to level the mortar bedding, and it should therefore be long enough to bridge the floor battens. Cut the board from a stout length of straight softwood, and at each corner of the straight edge cut a notch, as deep as the thickness of a tile, less ⅛ in. For detail see picture right.

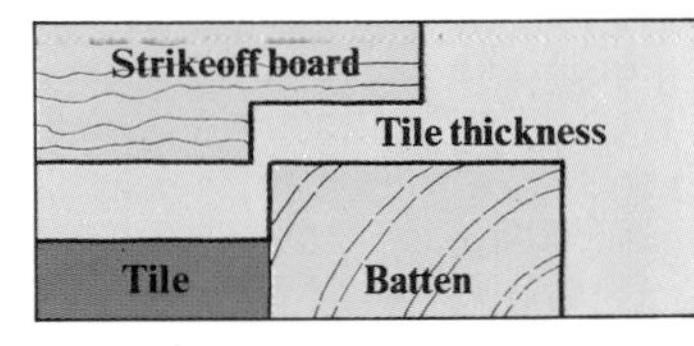

Setting out battens
Before nailing battens down, check that they are level, packing with strips of cardboard if necessary.

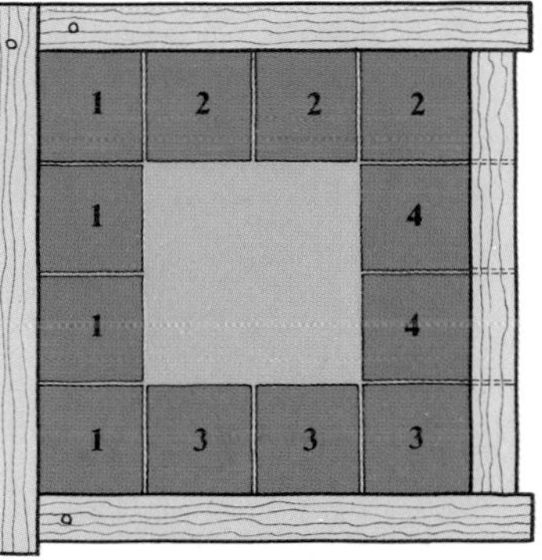

Using the measuring batten
Position four tiles along one batten evenly spaced, three tiles along the other two, and fill gap with two more.

Tamping down
Fill in the remaining four tiles, and level them flat with the strikeoff board, correcting spacing.

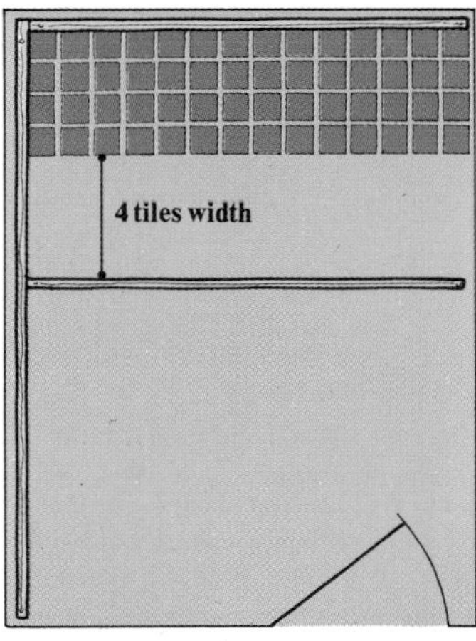

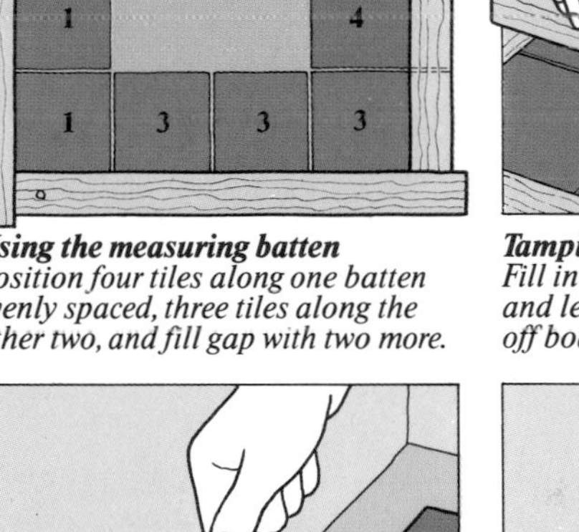

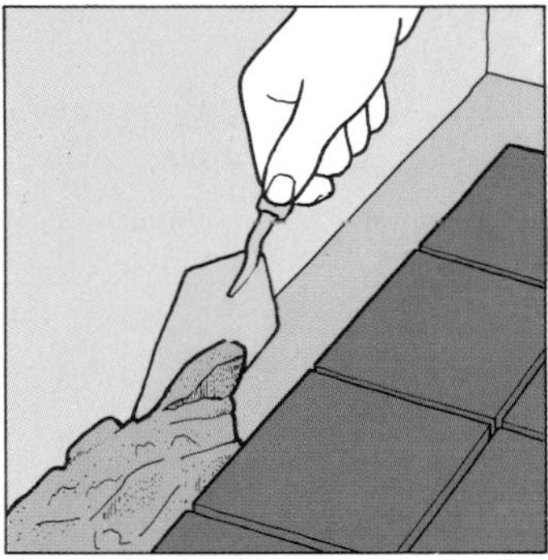

Laying border tiles
You are left with a border area when you remove the battens. Use a pointed trowel to put down the mortar bedding.

Leveling off mortar
Cut a hardboard leveler with a notch the depth of a tile, and a leveling edge the width of border.

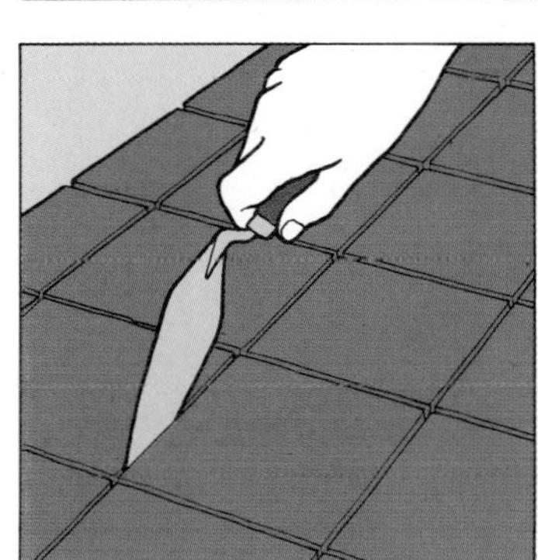

Spacing the tiles
Even up spaces between tiles by placing the point of a trowel in the gap and twisting it.

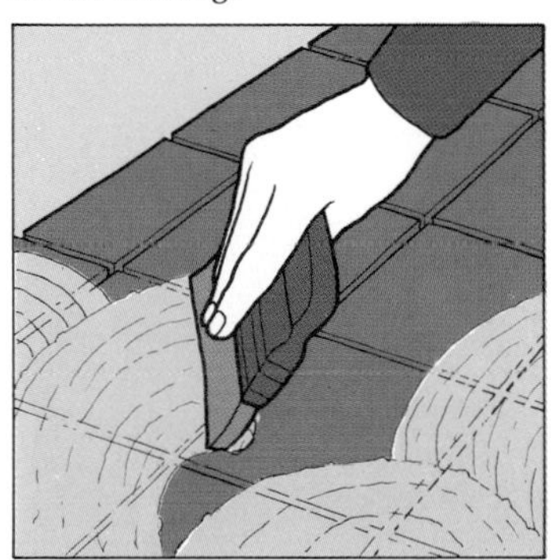

Applying grout
Mix grout to a thick, creamy consistency, using a cement base. This can be colored to match tiles.

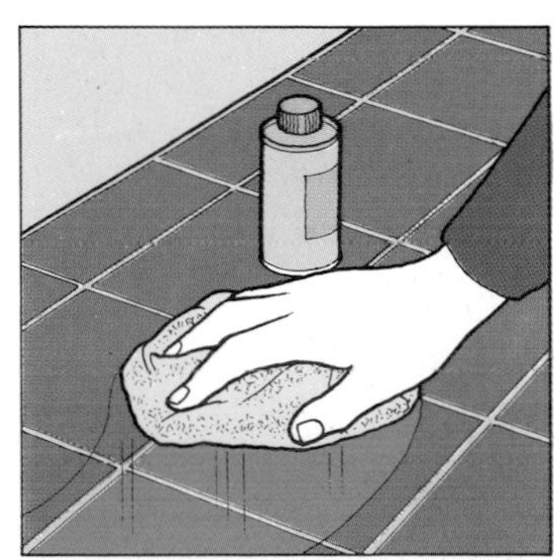

Cleaning off the surface
Wipe away excess grout with a sponge. When floor is clean and dry, seal with a brand name tile polish.

Carpeting

Soft floor coverings

Carpets are now available in a great many materials, both natural and man-made. Some alternatives to the traditional wool carpets are rush and cane mattings, nylon piles and harder wearing indoor-outdoor carpeting. Many of these materials are sold in the form of squares or individual tiles which are easily joined together and just as easily replaced if damaged.

Good quality carpet usually has the cost of fitting included in the purchase price, but even where this is not the case, it is advisable to hire a professional to cut and lay an expensive carpet. This is particularly important when laying an unbacked carpet, where lengths may need to be sewn together and the edges hemmed to prevent fraying. With this type of carpet you will also need an underlay, which is essential to increase its life and comfort. This consists of rolls of resilient materials which are laid prior to the carpet and protect it from wear from the floor and make it softer on the feet. It also provides extra insulation. Underlay is commonly made from latex, foam rubber and a combination of natural or man-made fibers.

Fitting carpet into most rooms inevitably means an element of wastage which unfortunately has to be paid for. There are, however, some companies which will measure up for you and pre-cut the carpet from one piece which will exactly fit the shape of your room.

If you decide to lay your own carpet it is advisable to choose a good quality foam backed variety. The normal underlay is an integral part of the carpet which prevents the carpet from stretching or shrinking.

1

2

3

4

1 Rush matting
Rush matting is woven in squares which are sewn together to form larger units. If you cut for fitting, the edges must be bound to prevent fraying.

2 Split cane matting
With this type of floor covering it is essential periodically to vacuum the dust which will filter through the weave.

3 Cut pile carpet
The yarn is cut on the top surface to produce a smooth tufted finish. The length of the tufts can vary from a short velvet-like pile to a long shaggy variety.

4 Looped pile
The uncut yarn gives a pronounced texture to the carpet. This might be an even ribbed form or a random heavy knotted surface.

5 Fitting patterns
This room ideally demonstrates the advantage of a fitted carpet in an open plan area. Where it has a strong linear pattern it should be carefully fitted to avoid distortion by over stretching.

6 Carpet tiles
Carpet tiles are ideal for children's rooms in that they can be replaced one tile at a time should they become damaged or stained. Choose a man-made fiber which has been treated to eliminate the build up of static electricity.

7 Striped carpet
You can make your own striped carpeting using two or more contrasting colors. Use the same quality to avoid a difference in thickness.

5

6

7

Laying Carpets

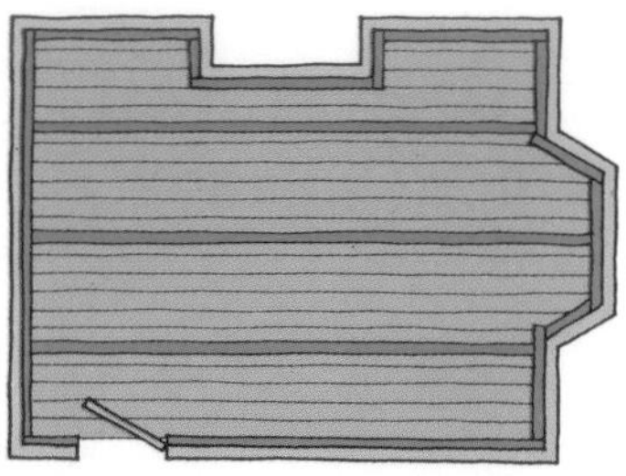

Laying a bedroom carpet
1 Stick double-faced tape around edges, down center line and 3 ft each side of it, saving backing paper.

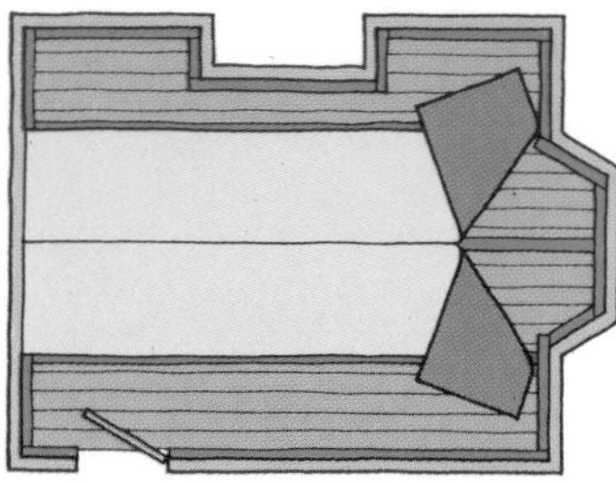

2 Cut two lengths of carpet to size plus 1 in. spare each end. Butt together and peel back sides of carpet pieces to center.

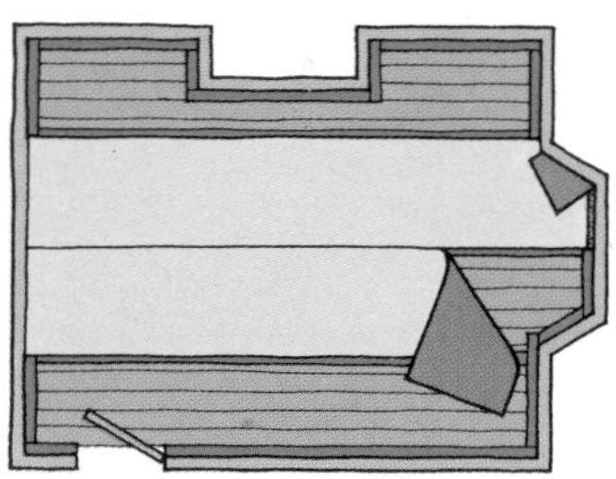

3 Strip backing paper from tape to center and replace one carpet strip carefully keeping to line. Fold excess back from window.

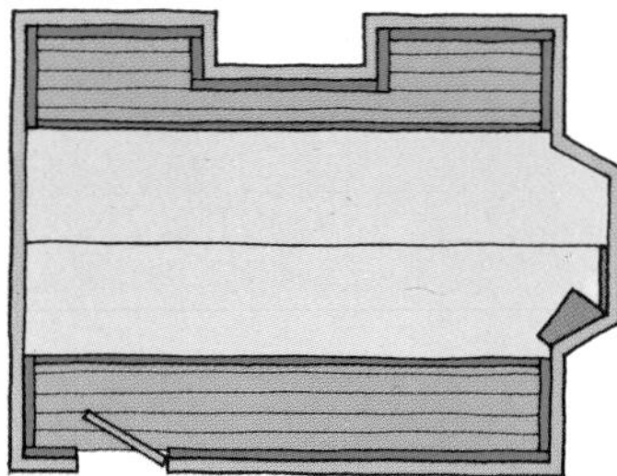

4 Trim excess at window, repeat process for second strip. 'Peel back these lengths from opposite end, strip tape, lay and trim as before.

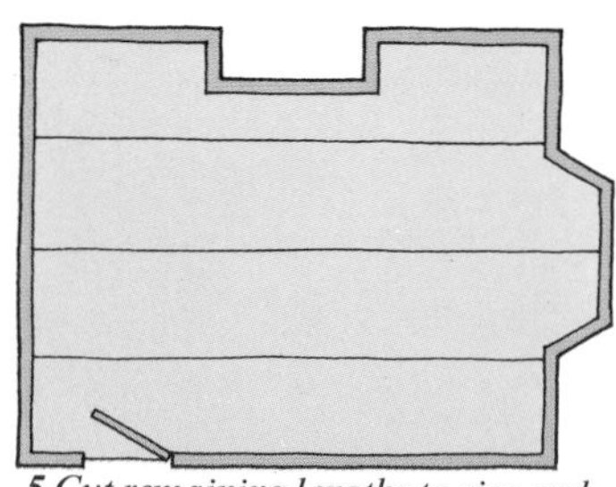

5 Cut remaining lengths to size and butt lay against first two center pieces sticking down tape at all joins. Fit into corners.

Estimating the amount
Measure the room carefully (see pp. 12-13) to calculate the amount of carpet you will need; remember to allow enough to fit into a door opening. Measure in the direction the carpet will be laid. If your choice of carpet specifies narrow widths to be joined together, calculate for laying toward the window where the light is less likely to reveal the join. When joining strips, make sure that the pile lies in the same direction on all of them, to avoid unevenness when viewed against the light. Find the direction of the pile by brushing it with the flat of your hand. If it brushes up you are going against the pile. If the strips are laid in the direction of the longest dimension of the room, the joins will be fewer.

Preparing floor surfaces
Foam-backed carpet can be successfully laid on wood or concrete floors, so long as they are level and clean. Any unevenness in the floor, such as a warped floorboard, will eventually wear a patch in the carpet. Use a nail set to drive protruding nail heads below the surface, otherwise they will tear the foam backing. If necessary, level the floor (see pp. 96-97).
Where concrete floors are uneven, they may need to be leveled with concrete, or perhaps with a latex based compound which also acts as a barrier against damp. Concrete floors can be insulated with a number of brand name treatments and by laying plastic sheeting. However, plastic sheet and vinyl tiles are both likely to accumulate moisture unless the room is well ventilated.

Laying the carpet
How to lay a carpet is demonstrated in the diagrams, left, with fitting details shown on the right. The carpet used comes in 3 ft wide strips and is of a plain, foam-backed design. The bedroom has a bay window at one end and a fireplace along the wall. An extra inch of carpet is included all around for accurate trimming and double-faced tape is placed around the room's edges and underneath each join. After marking a center line on the floor, proceed as shown in the laying sequence. Finally, work around the door frame pushing the carpet into place and trimming it to fit. Cover with an edging strip, making sure door clears carpet.

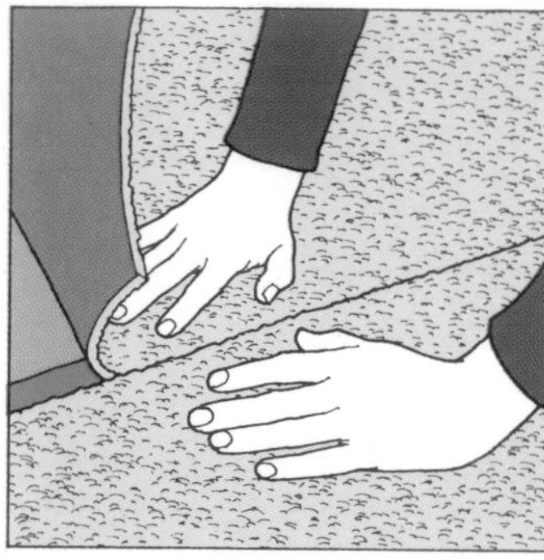

Butting strips together
Push carpet pieces firmly together pressing down hard so tape has a good grip.

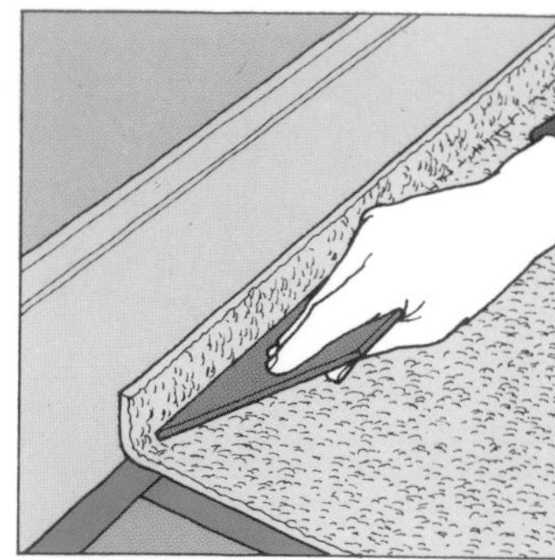

Fitting into edges
Peel back paper from edge tape and using a piece of hardboard press carpet well into joint.

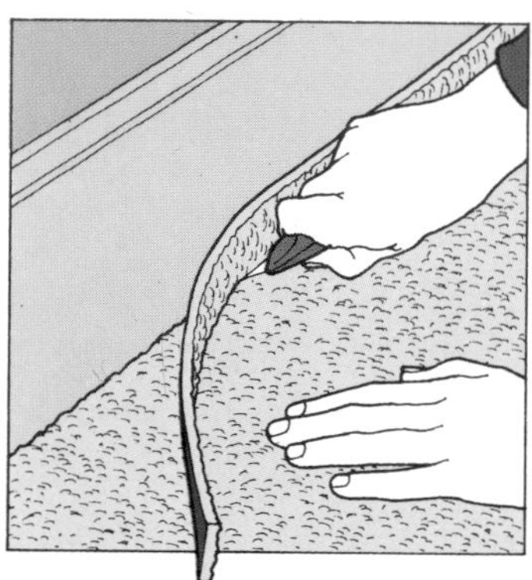

Trimming edges
Push a sharp knife tight into angle formed by floor and baseboard. Take care not to damage baseboard.

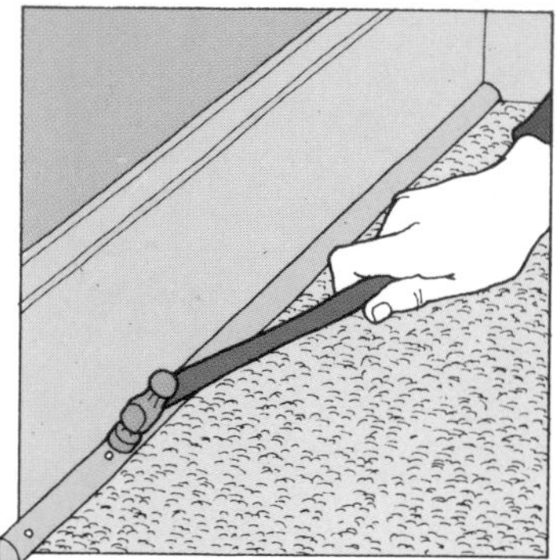

Fixing a cover strip
You can cover the joint with a molding nailed to the baseboard and painted to match.

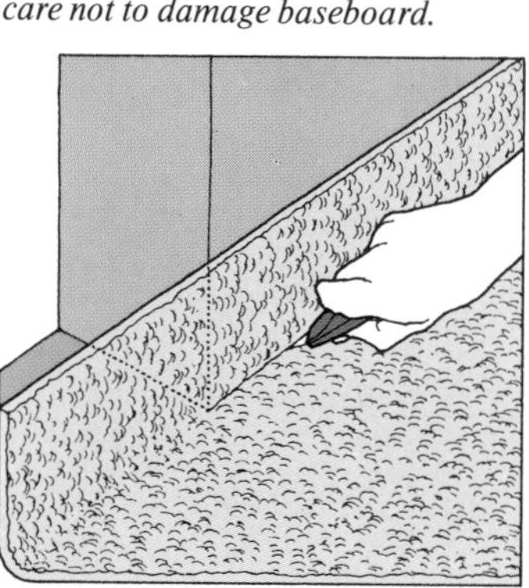

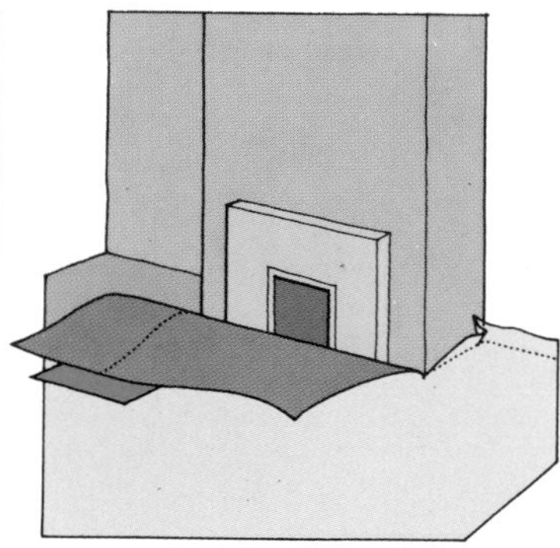

Trimming around a fireplace
Roll out carpet and press it into front edge with hardboard. Trim along front edge with knife. Fold back carpet slipping a piece of hardboard underneath to protect carpet while cutting along from corner of fireplace to alcove.

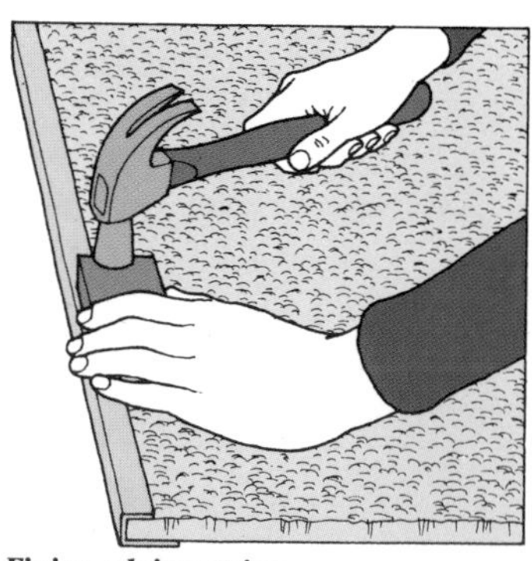

Fixing edging strips
Nail or glue edging strip to floor, insert carpet and hammer down with protective softwood block.

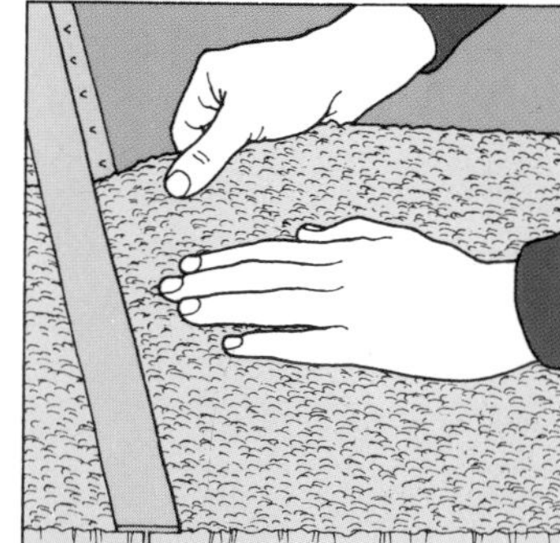

Double edging
Use a double edging strip for joining one type of carpet to another.

Laying a stair carpet

Stairs are usually carpeted from strips of standard widths, either fully fitted or centered with the painted tread showing on both sides. You can easily lay your own carpet on straight stairs; winding stairs will require practice. It is advisable to choose a foam-backed carpet as this avoids your having to bind any cut edges. Include an extra 9 in. for carpet wear.

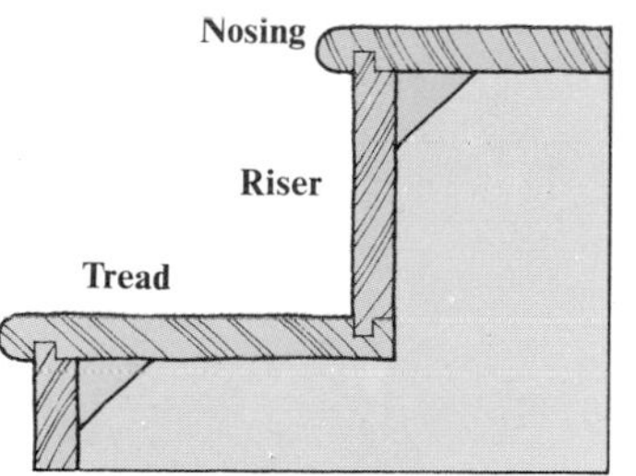

Measuring straight stairs
Measure from riser to nosing then to tread and multiply by number of steps. Add on 9 in.

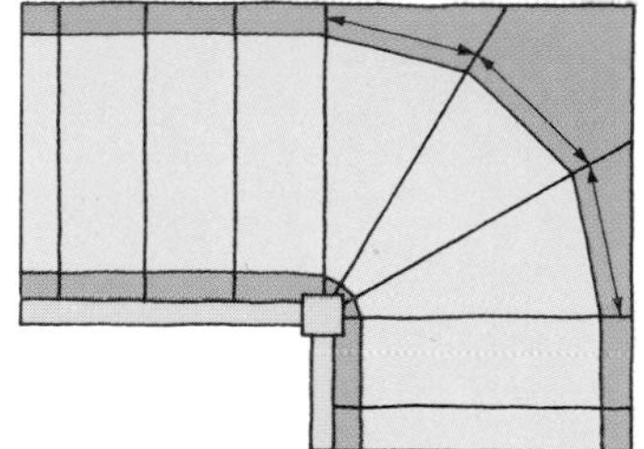

Measuring winding stairs
Measure distance across the tread at its widest point and add to total for straight stairs.

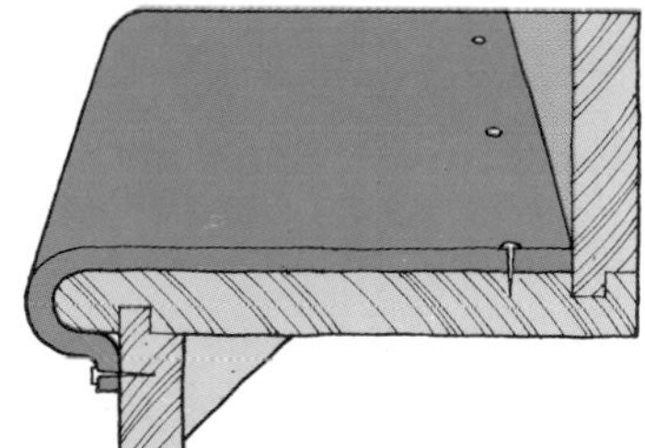

Laying underlay sections
Butt padding against riser and tack every 3 in. to tread. Wrap other end under nosing and tack.

Carpeting a straight staircase

Underlay can either be laid as a continuous strip following the carpet or in sections as shown right. It should be slightly narrower than the carpet's width. The carpet's pile should face down the stairs. The principal means of securing stair carpet are rods, which are often decorative, tacks or gripper strips, designed specially for staircases. Gripper strips are made as flat strips or in angled sections; the pointed teeth face away from the pull of the carpet to hold it in place, and are nailed through the underlay. Rods and tacks are suitable for any type of carpet, but gripper strips should not be used with the foam-backed kind of carpeting.

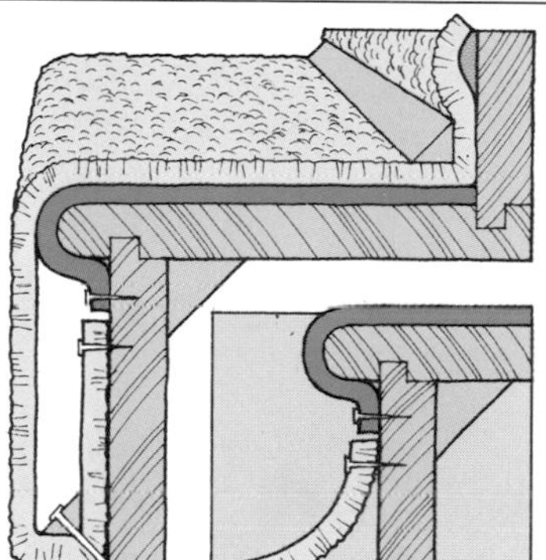

Using stair rods
Screw rod retainers $\frac{3}{4}$ in. each side of carpet. Position carpet face inwards against bottom riser, butted under nosing and tack. Drop carpet to bottom of riser, secure with a rod. Reverse carpet and pull over nosing, fixing to next riser with new rod.

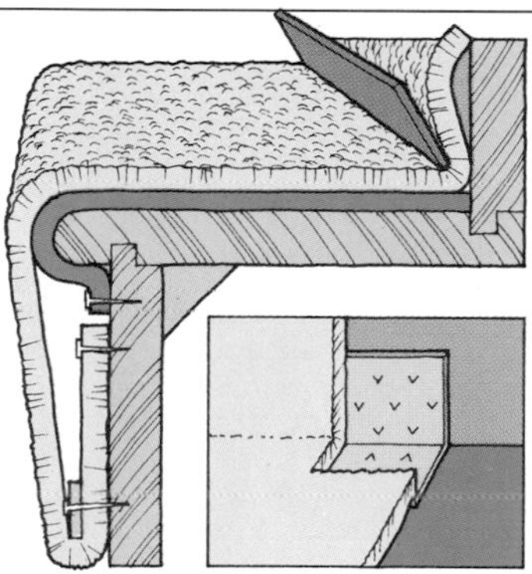

Fitting gripper strips
Nail angled strips into riser/tread joints. Tack carpet end under first nosing along length of riser. Nail flat gripper teeth downwards, through fold. Pull carpet tightly over nosing. Use hardboard to stretch carpet into angled strip.

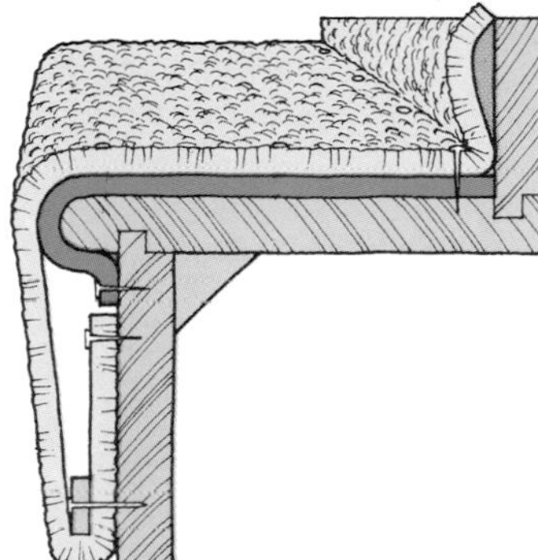

Fixing with tacks
Fit bottom edge of carpet, nailing a thin wooden batten through carpet to riser base. Pull carpet over nosing and stretch tightly into riser joint with hardboard. Hammer tacks close to riser at intervals of 3 in. across the tread.

Carpeting a landing

Where a staircase changes direction at an intermediate landing, treat each flight as separate and lay the carpet as described for a straight staircase. Run the carpet from the first flight over the landing to fit with the line of carpet on the next flight as shown right.

Carpeting a winding staircase

Fitting a winding staircase is more difficult because of the quantity of slack carpet taken up. This has to be folded with the slack tucked under the nosing on the riser. If you are using stair rods, position them so that they hold the slack against the riser, and run the remaining carpet over the rod and up the riser, as you did on the very first step. When using gripper strips, fix a flat strip on the tread to hold the carpet in place, take up the slack and nail it to the riser. Use another flat strip to hold both slack and remaining carpet, which should then be pulled up over the stair's nosing.

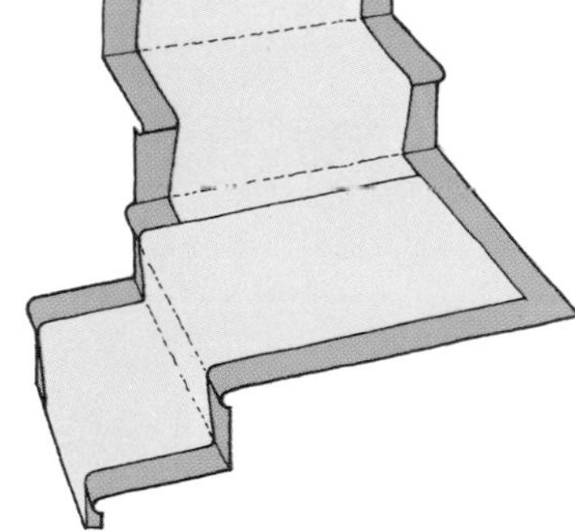

Laying landing carpeting
Where a staircase changes direction at a landing, treat each flight separately. Run the carpet over the landing from the first flight and fit with the line of carpet on the next, ascending flight. Secure with double-faced tape or tacks.

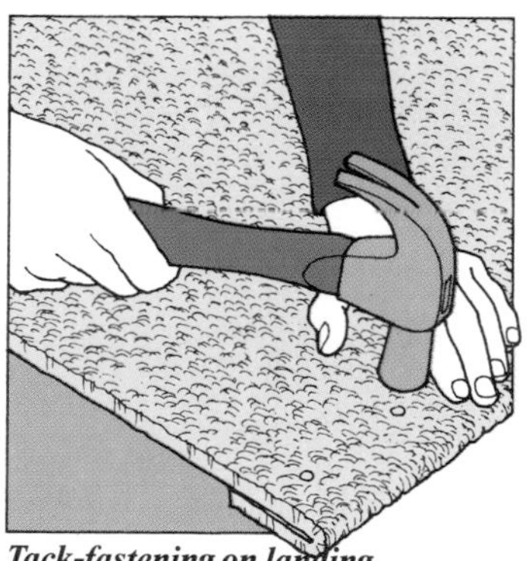

Tack-fastening on landing
If using tacks, fold carpet edge under 3 in. and fasten through double layer. Underlay should have been cut short of turned edge by 3 in. to allow for the fold and so as not to produce any bumps.

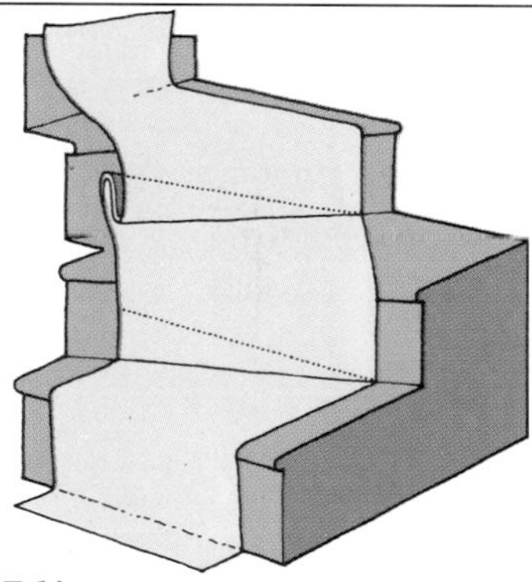

Taking up excess on winding stairs
Where stairs wind to change direction you will have to take up slack at the narrow end of the tread. Position the carpet so that it fits both treads, with the slack hidden against the riser.

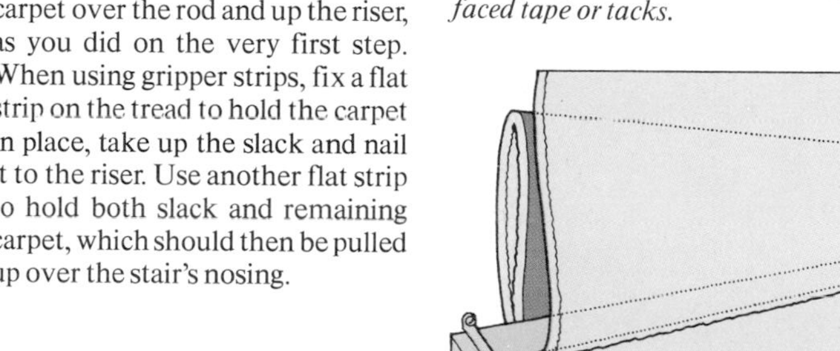

Taking up slack with stair rods
Hold slack in place on riser, positioning rod at joint and fixing retainers.

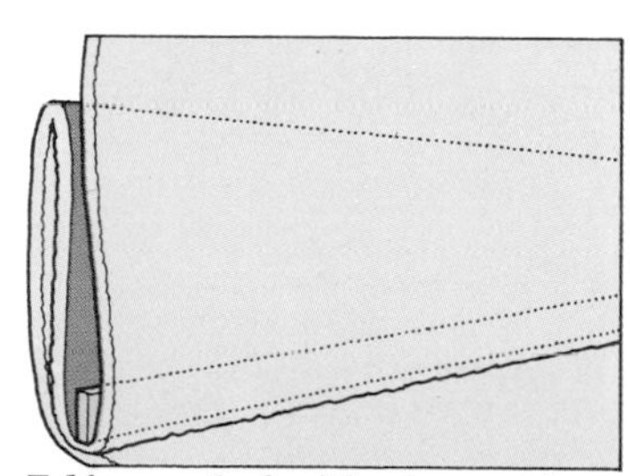

Taking up slack with gripper strips
Two lengths are needed. One holds carpet in position on tread and one takes up slack on riser.

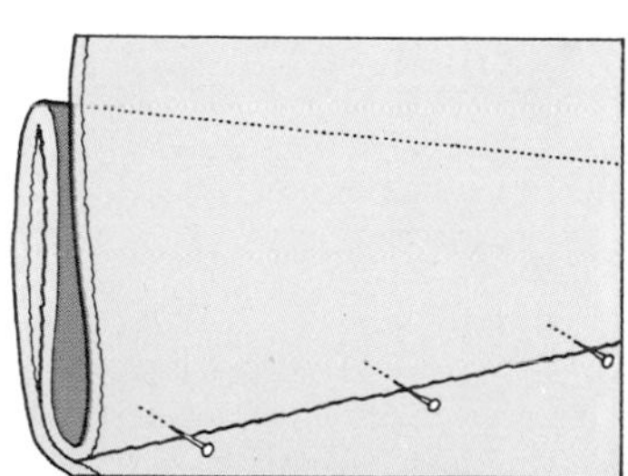

Taking up slack with tacks
Fit long tacks to pin right through folded section at base of risers.

Window Treatments

Practical considerations

Give the decorative treatment of your windows careful thought. Fabrics for curtains and drapes as well as shades and shutters can be very expensive, and should be considered as an integral part of the scheme, not as an afterthought. Light falling through any window draws attention to it and the way it is covered, so that your choice of treatment will become immediately obvious. This same light can be used to create a particular atmosphere, or accentuate a certain feature. The color and texture of a fabric used for curtains or blinds, for instance, will modify the light to a great extent. This is especially obvious at a window which receives strong sunlight where you would perhaps have curtains or blinds partially closed during the hottest part of the day. "Sheer" or net curtains diffuse the light, making it softer and toning down the shadows, without losing the view outside. Colored nets will modify the light further by giving it a bias to produce a cool or warm effect (see p. 18). Light passing through a printed fabric adds brilliance to the colors. For the strongest effect use unlined fabrics. Remember that your room lights will create the same brilliance at night, only this time viewed from the outside. For this reason, some people use matching fabrics in all windows which show from one side of a house to co-ordinate them.

Another possible treatment, which is viewable from either side of the window, is the positioning of plants in a window box, or on a shelf placed on the inside at sill level. As well as providing a screen, which can be changed as often as you wish, the plants will benefit from the direct light. Alternatively, hang plants in baskets suspended in the window, or on shelves running across the opening supported on brackets either side of the frame.

The window glass does not have to be completely clear. There is a wide range of designs etched or molded into the glass itself, which can be used to screen part or whole of the window while stained glass can be substituted for clear.

1

2

3

1 Finely printed fabric
This window, reduced to a light source, becomes an integral part of the decoration by the use of finely printed fabric which hangs completely across the wall.

2 Drapes and plants
The amount of window area in this unusually shaped room makes the treatment vitally important. The windows are partially screened by drapes which are reinforced by strategically placed plants.

3 Brightly colored fabric
The atmosphere of this room is entirely dominated by the sunlight shining through the brilliant colors of the window fabric.

4 Open-weave fabrics
Apart from finely woven net screening, you can use a wide range of heavier, open-weave fabrics.

5 Decorative screen
This narrow sash window, which needs no screening, has been completely transformed by a decorative facade.

6 Plant screen
A well-planted conservatory or secluded garden, preferably lit after dark, is all the embellishment needed for some windows.

4

5

6

Curtains & Drapes

Window treatments and tracks
Before you buy any fabric and measure up for curtain tracks, carefully consider your rooms and windows, and decide what type of curtains will be best suited to a particular room. Full length curtains in a bold print can make an attractive feature in an otherwise large and rather dark room; sill length curtains with a floral pattern can make a child's room light and airy. Match your curtains to the environment, but remember the golden rule: make them either full length or sill length, but never anything in between.
Modern tracks for curtains are so unobtrusive that they hardly show even when the curtains are drawn back. This is especially true if the track matches the color of the frame; when the curtains are closed, the track will not show at all if you choose a "stand-up" heading. Track fixings remain well hidden, even when viewed from the side, as the curtain can be made to wrap around the end bracket. Runners are sometimes located on the reverse of the track or form part of the curtain hook itself, simply clipping over the track.

Estimating for fabric
Fix your curtain track in position so you can more easily estimate the quantity of fabric you will need. The general rule is that the fabric should be twice the width of the track; this gives a luxurious, full appearance. Never economize on the amount of fabric – better to choose a less expensive quality that will give you the required fullness than a limited quantity of a more expensive kind. Very lightweight unlined and sheer curtains and casement cloths should be three times the width of the track. Allow extra for the seams: 1¼ in. for each join, 1½ in. for each side hem. Divide this measurement by the width of the fabric to give you the number of fabric widths needed. The length of the curtain should be measured from the top edge of the heading to 1 in. from floor level. Add to this an allowance for the hem and the heading, also an extra inch per yard if fabrics are neither pre-shrunk nor man-made. Also allow for matching pattern repeats, see next page. Finally, multiply this sum by the number of fabric widths, to find the fabric required – and then double-check.

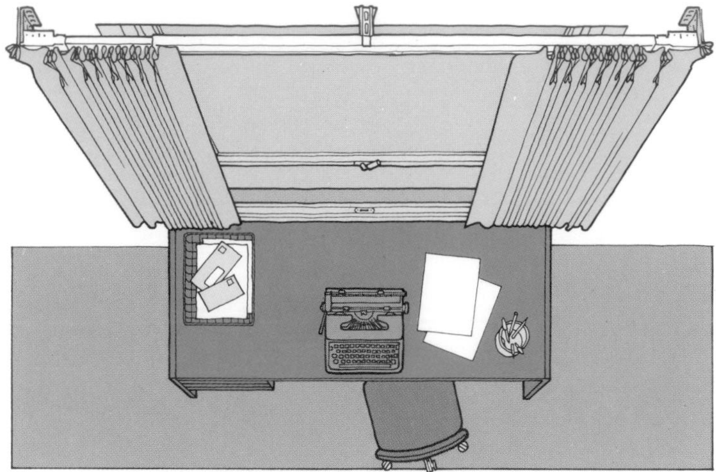

Sill length curtains
Sill length curtains (which should just clear the sill), are ideal where a piece of furniture or a radiator is sited immediately below the window. This length is also good for small rooms such as kitchens or bathrooms, where a large amount of wall space is taken up by fittings and appliances. Unlined curtains with a simple heading and a plain track are the most suitable types for such rooms.

Full length curtains
Full length curtains should hang an inch short of the floor. Fix your track and extend it beyond the window frame at each end, to make the window appear wider; this will also permit maximum daylight when curtains are pulled back. Tracks for bay windows, as shown left, follow the bends of the frame. You can soften the angular appearance of a bay window by dividing the fabric into four separate curtains, so that two sections can hang at the inner corners of the bay, the other two at the ends.

Closing off bay windows
An alternative treatment for a bay window is to use a brass or wooden pole to span the entire recess. Hang the curtains from the pole with decorative brass or wooden rings. This will screen off the bay when the curtains are closed. Hang casement curtains in the bay itself. These will give you privacy and also a pleasantly diffused light during the daylight hours.

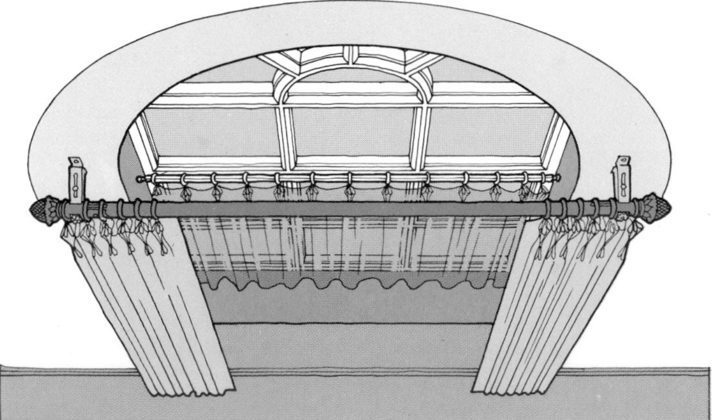

Decorative curtains
You can feature an unusual or well-proportioned window, either by the use of a brass pole, as previously described, or a modern decorative track. These offer a variety of knobs which plug into a standard track. The runners look like rings, but are located on the reverse of the track; use an appropriate heading so that the track remains visible. Hang half-lengths or cafe curtains inside the recess. Some tracks are spring-loaded so that they fit between the recess walls.

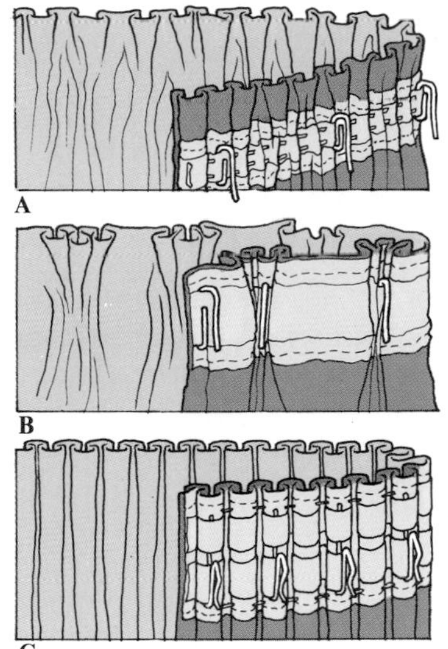

Curtain headings

Various headings require different types of heading tape and hooks. A gathered heading **A** needs tape which simply gathers the fabric along the top edge to give a full folded look. Pinch pleats **B** are formed by pronged hooks inserted into the pockets of another tape. The number of pockets per hook determines whether the pleat is single, double or treble. The height of the heading is determined by the length of the prongs, use long hooks for a wall-hung track, short ones for a decorative or ceiling track. Pencil pleats **C** are narrow, regular pleats which look particularly good with lightweight fabrics.

Cutting curtains

If your chosen fabric has a repeat pattern, it must be matched in the same way as you would match lengths of wallpaper. If your estimations are correct, you will have allowed extra material for the repeats. Cut your first curtain, including the hem and heading allowances, composing any dominant features of the design accordingly. Now lay this length on top of the remaining fabric to match the pattern exactly. Mark and cut other lengths in the same way.

Squaring up

Curtains will not hang properly unless the fabric is cut square to the weave. As an accurate guideline, pull a thread out from the cross weave of the fabric. This will provide you with your cutting line.

Finishing raw edges

1 With right sides facing stitch fabric pieces together ½ in. from the selvage.

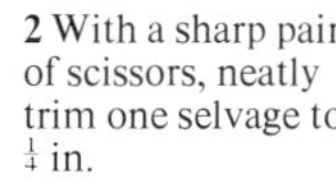

2 With a sharp pair of scissors, neatly trim one selvage to ¼ in.

3 Turn the other selvage over the trimmed one, smooth and flatten, then machine-stitch in place.

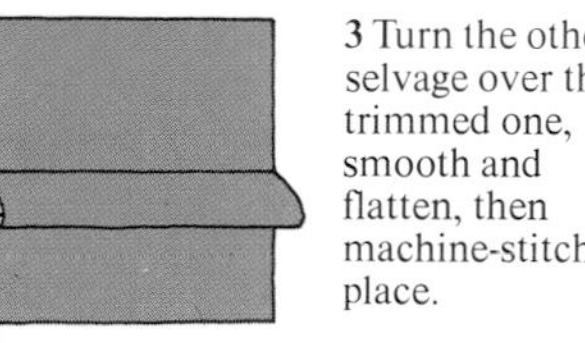

Making a double hem

1 Fold over and press down one edge of fabric ¼ in. from end.

2 Now fold, press and baste a second, ½ in. hem to envelop the first. Machine-stitch.

Unlined curtains

These are the simplest kind of curtains to make. You should choose a closely-woven fabric, otherwise the curtains will let in too much light. Where you need to join two widths of material, make a seam which will envelop raw edges (as shown left). Use a double hem as illustrated for the sides of the curtains. Fold down a 2 in. hem at the top edge of the curtain and pin a heading tape to cover the raw edge. Machine-stitch the tape in place (the exact position may differ according to maker's instructions). Pull the tape cords to the required fullness and width, then knot them, tucking or pinning the extra cord out of sight. Do not cut it off as you will need the full length when you come to wash or dryclean the curtains. Square off the bottom edge of the curtains, as previously described. Make a ½ in. hem and machine-stitch it. Hang the curtains from the track so that you can determine the hem length, then pin and baste. Leave curtains to hang for a few days for the fabric to "drop", or, in the case of fabric that is not pre-shrunk, until after the first cleaning, then adjust the hem accordingly.

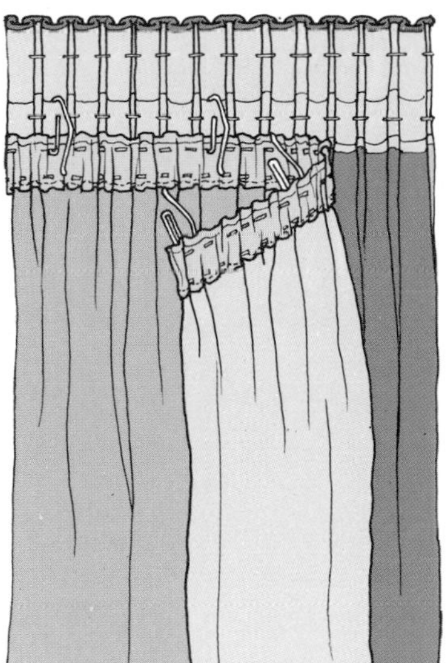

Separate curtain linings

By making the curtain thicker, a lining keeps out more light and is also more draft-proof. It protects the finished fabric from fading as a result of strong sunlight. The usual fabric for a lining is shiny on the outside so that dust is shed more easily. Because the linings of curtains face outward toward the window, they naturally become more soiled and faded than the curtains themselves. In a city environment, or one where you can expect a certain amount of pollution, it is wise to make separate curtain linings. These can be removed for more frequent cleaning than the curtains normally need. Use a special heading tape, which is sewn to the top edge of the lining. The lining is then attached to the bottom edge of the curtains' heading tape by hooks or directly to the hooks that fix the curtain to the track. The second row of hooks will only be visible from outside the window.

Mitering corners

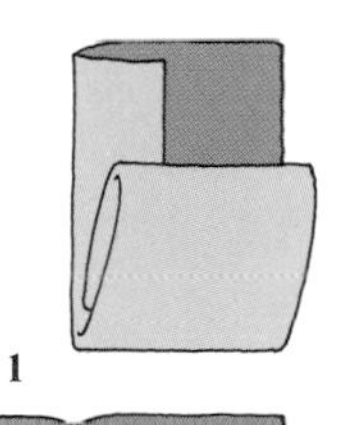

1 Fold and press a 1½ in. hem on both curtains' edges and a 3 in. double hem on bottom.

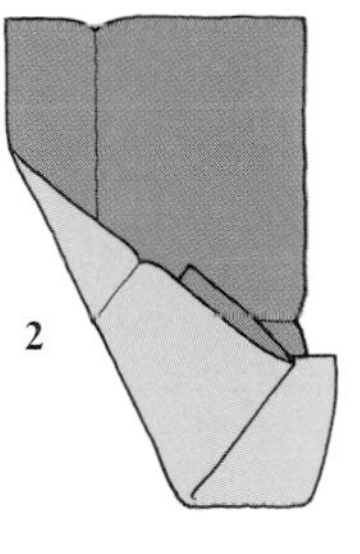

2 Unfold all but one half of the bottom hem, and fold in the corner as shown.

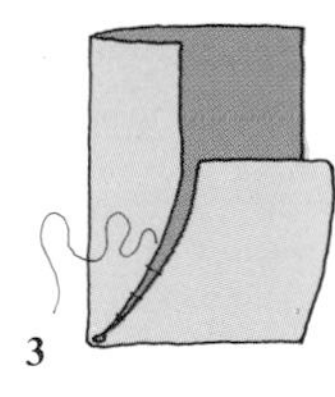

3 Now fold both side and bottom hem to meet as a miter at the corner, and slip stitch them together.

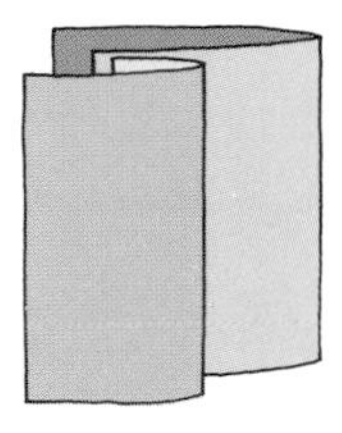

Position of lining

Place lining on fabric, right sides facing out and turn under lining edges 1 in. short of curtain borders.

Integral linings

Because of the additional material, lined curtains both hang better and look more attractive. To line curtains, cut lengths of curtain and lining fabric, making the lining 1 in. shorter in length, and 1 in. narrower on each side. To join widths, use a plain seam, as the edges will not show with lined curtains. You can achieve a really professional finish by mitering the curtains at both corners as shown left, **1-3**. Press and machine stitch a 3 in. double hem along the bottom edge of lining. Position curtain and lining as on the left and then pin and baste it in place. Slip stitch side edges of lining to the fabric but do not sew lower edge as this will remain free to avoid uneven hanging. Fold top edges of lining and fabric inward to required length of curtains. Press and baste in position. Sew on the proper heading tape as previously described. Remove all basting stitches.

Making sheers

Fabrics for sheer curtains can differ in the amount of light they let in and many contain some pattern. It is advisable that you buy fabric that is wide enough to fit your windows without having to make seams. If the fabric is too narrow, simply hang fabric widths side by side without sewing, allowing the fullness of the curtains to hide the fact that there are no seams. Use a double hem at the top as this looks better against the light, and masks the outline of the heading tape. Make sure that you buy one of the special lightweight drip-dry heading tapes, specially made for sheer fabrics. When you are estimating material yardage, allow an extra-deep bottom hem – this will help to weight the fabric, and make the curtains hang better. You can also buy decoratively hemmed sheers.

Shades, Blinds & Shutters

Simple window coverings
The simple, usually linear, forms of shades, screens or shutters are becoming increasingly popular in the modern home.

1 Shades
Shades can be an effective window treatment and require relatively little fabric as compared with drapes which appear skimpy if not fully gathered.

2 Screens
To block out an uninteresting view fit a fixed translucent screen across the window. Use plexiglass or tracing paper glued or tacked on to the back of a frame.

3 Printed shades
The designs on printed fabric, which may be lost in gathered drapes, are shown to advantage in flat roman or roller shades.

1

2

3

4 Shutters
Folding shutters can still serve a useful purpose as draft excluders, although in these days of central heating and storm windows their continuing popularity is mainly for their visual appeal. Also, they seldom, if ever, need replacing.

5 Louvers
Louvered doors and shutters protect a room from strong sunlight without making the room darker.

6 Slatted screen
Make your own screen by nailing and gluing strips of plywood to a softwood frame. This can be permanently fitted, designed to be lifted off, or hinged to the window frame.

7 Vertical louver blinds
Disguise a small window by screening the whole wall with vertical louvered blinds. They can be adjusted to admit light as required or to seal the window off completely.

8 Venetian blinds
Venetian blinds work on the same principle as vertical louvers except that they withdraw upwards instead of sideways. Venetian blinds, made from thin metal or plastic blades, are available in a wide range of colors.

4

5

6

7

8

Making Roller Shades

Choosing your materials
Kits for making window shades are readily available and include standard length rollers which can be cut to size as well as all necessary hardware. Choose closely woven fabrics for the shade as these are less likely to stretch and hang unevenly. Fabric stiffeners are necessary to condition the material and to give the shade a crisp, even appearance while sealing the weave so that the fabric won't fray when cut. Some manufacturers supply ready-conditioned fabric along with their kits.

Positioning the shade
Shades can be hung inside the window frame or outside for more effective draft and light control. The fabric should be 2 in. wider than the frame if the shade is to be hung outside. If positioned inside the frame, you should allow 1 in. either side for brackets.

Installing the roller
Position the brackets and roller first so that you can make the shade fit. The bracket with the hole should be to your right as you face the window. Using a fine-tooth saw cut the roller to length on the end cap side and replace the cap, chamfering the roller end if necessary. Check that the roller runs smoothly; if it wobbles, the end pin is probably off-center or at an angle.

Making up the shade
Choose a material wide enough to fit the roller width between caps without a join. If you must add to the fabric, it is best to have two narrower strips each side of the central piece. Use plain seams, press flat and oversew the edges. The shade must be cut square, otherwise it will run unevenly. Pull a thread out across the fabric to mark the cut line. If you are using a stiffener, spray the fabric before cutting it to width. If the fabric is not to be stiffened, make sure enough material is available for hems. Measure the depth of the window, and add an extra 8 to 12 in. for fitting to the roller and hemming the bottom. Turn up a $\frac{1}{4}$ in. hem to make sleeve for wooden batten. After sewing up the sides attach the shade pull to the batten. Some kits include a plastic edge trim. Lay the roller with the spring mechanism to the left on the right side of fabric. Match the material to printed line on roller. Glue and tack the material on to the roller. Roll up the shade and fit to the brackets.

1 Roller with spring and end caps
2 Material
3 Fabric stiffener
4 Brackets/left and right
5 Cord
6 Pull knob

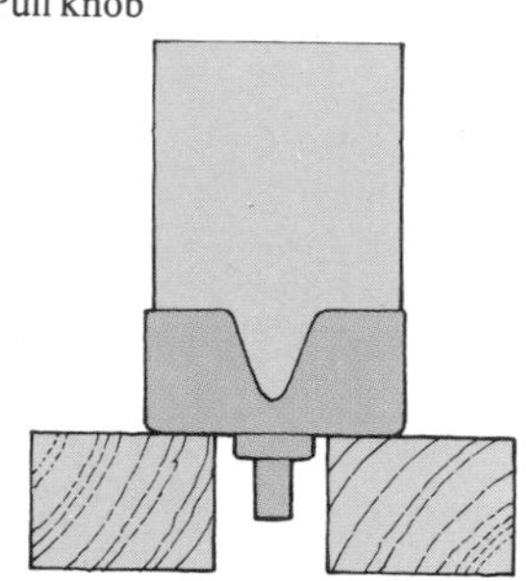

Plastic end cap
Plastic rollers have a cap which is designed to fit over the end opposite the projecting flat pin. This cap has a round pin molded into it.

Metal cap
Wooden rollers have a metal end cap with a center hole into which the round pin is driven. This round pin fits into the hole in the bracket.

Fitting the pin
Place cap on end after supporting flat pin on battens. Tap pointed end of pin squarely through hole in cap to secure this firmly to the roller.

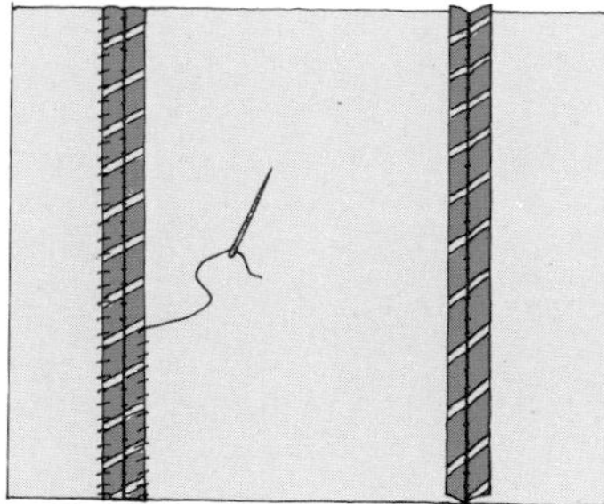

Seaming fabric
Symmetrically placed seams allow the shade to roll up evenly.

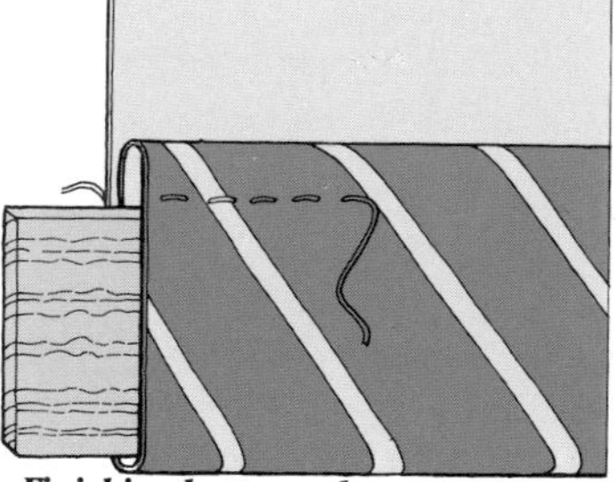

Finishing bottom edge
1 Make a $\frac{1}{4}$ in. hem on the bottom edge. Turn up edge to form a sleeve to hold batten.

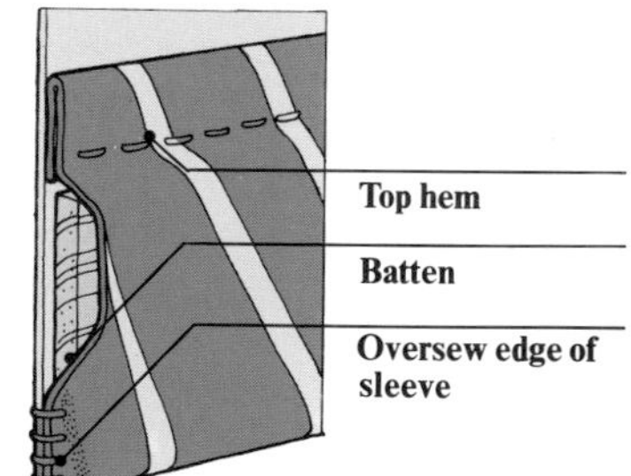

2 Sew up both ends of the sleeve after batten has been inserted. Fix shade pull to batten.

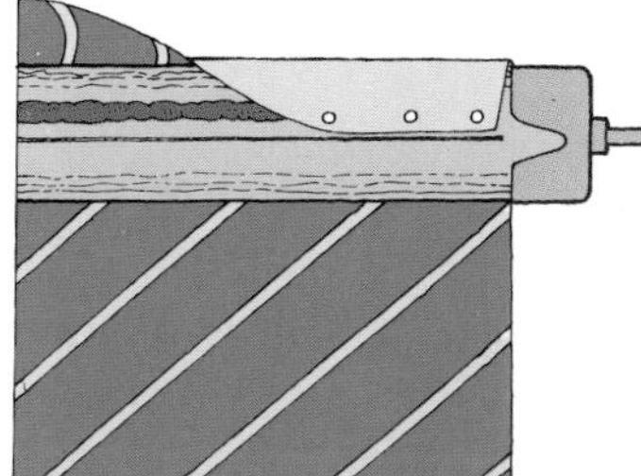

Fitting the shade to the roller
Square the roller to the top edge of shade material, right side up. The spring mechanism is to the left. Match fabric edge with roller line and glue fabric edge to roller, securing with tacks every 2 in.

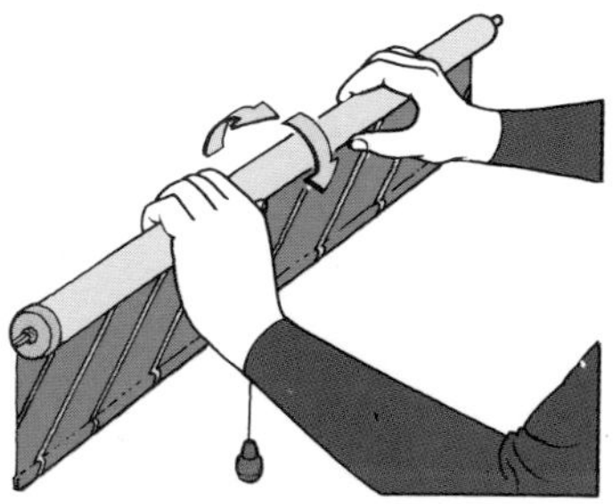

Tensioning the return spring
Roll up shade with the face on the inside. Join roller to the brackets and pull shade down until it stops. Remove and re-roll as before, and replace on brackets. The shade should now unroll with a steady pull.

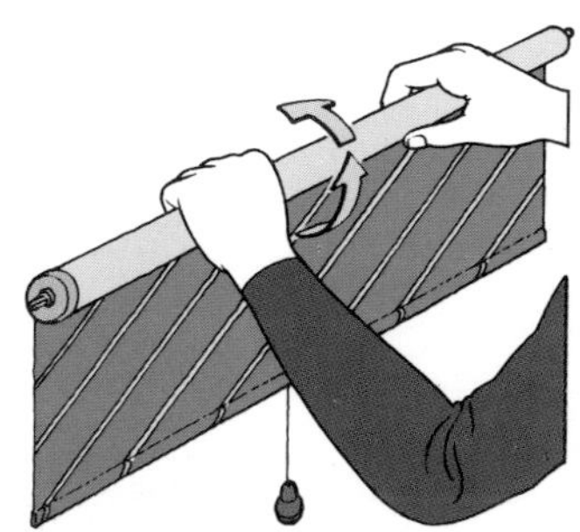

Overtension
If the roller mechanism does not work smoothly or if the spring is overtensioned and the shade returns too fast, remove shade from the brackets, unroll it a little by hand, then replace shade on the brackets.

Tools & Techniques

Structure

The various types of walls, both load and non load bearing found in new as well as old houses are shown below. Load bearing walls are usually external, and carry part of the weight of the structure above. The wall may be built of brick, stone, concrete blocks or of lumber, framed and braced for maximum strength. A wall that does not necessarily support any weight from above, but acts as a structural tie between two flank walls, is considered to have a load bearing capacity if built of brick or stone. Non load bearing walls are more frequently of the wooden frame type, and are usually for internal use only.

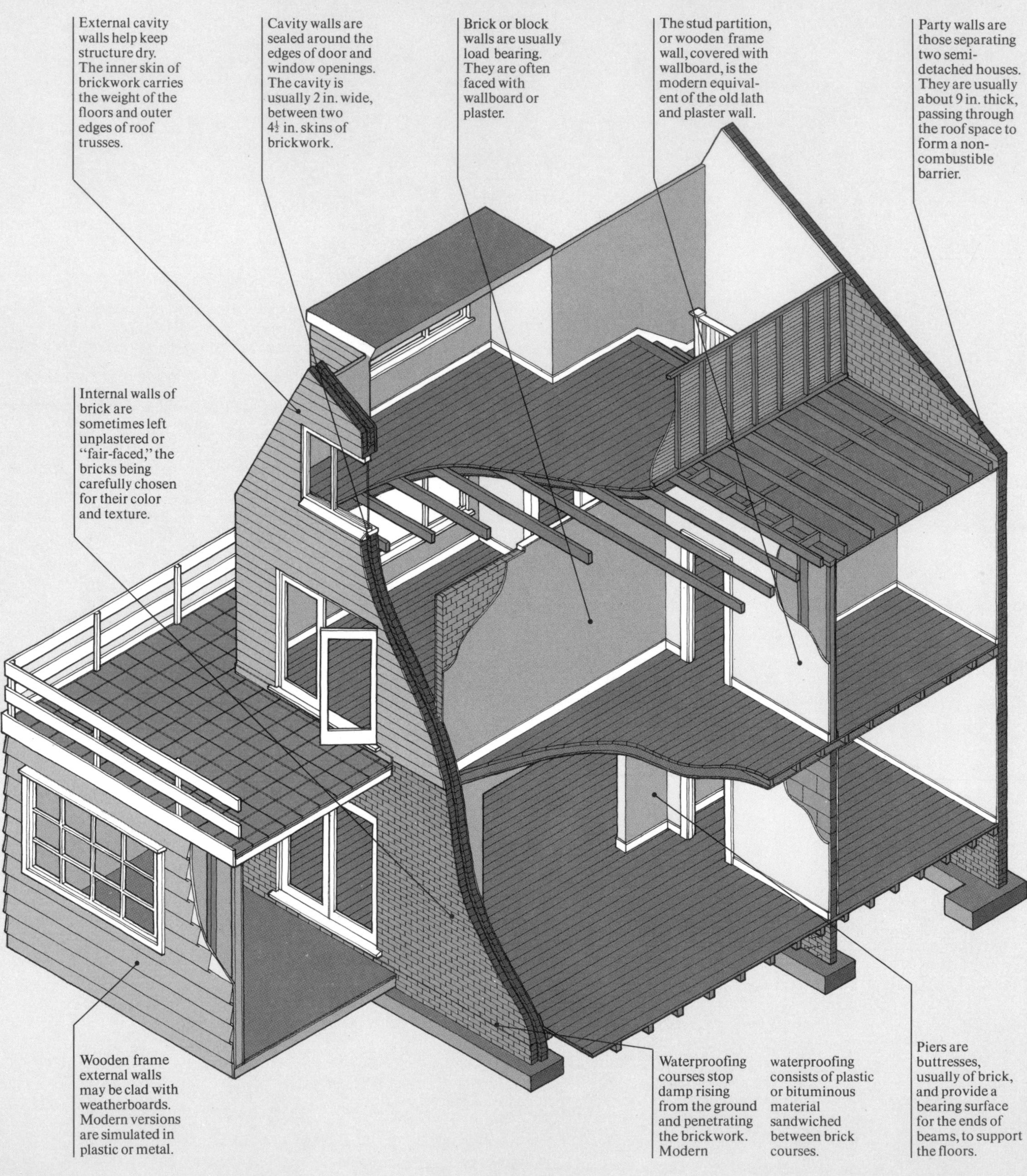

Infestation

Termites, the furniture beetle, the powder post and death watch beetle all damage most types of woodwork. Small areas of infestation can be dealt with by cleaning the infected wood and adjacent timber, and treating with a brand name insecticide. This may be in the form of an aerosol spray, powder or fluid to be brushed on the wood. If you are uncertain of the extent of the damage, and its nature, there are specialist firms who will inspect the property, and submit an estimate for treatment. Most such firms supply a generous guarantee.

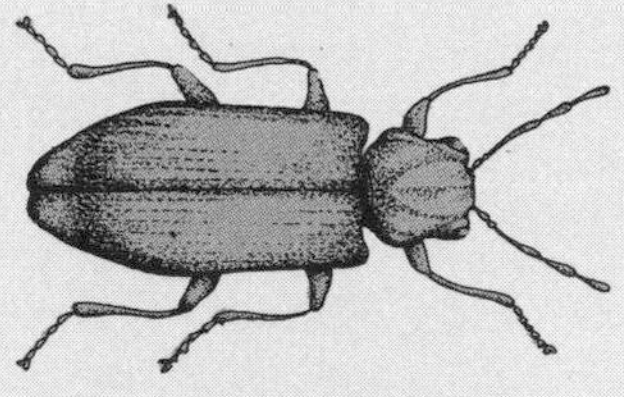

Furniture beetle

Anobium punctatum

The furniture beetle is more popularly known as woodworm. It is partial to most kinds of furniture and also attacks structural timbers. The adult beetles lay their eggs in cracks and crevices in the surface of the wood, or the edges of plywood. When the larvae hatch out they spend three years tunnelling through the timber, finally making small cavities near the surface to pupate. They emerge after two or three weeks as fully grown beetles, leaving behind them characteristic flight holes – about 1/12 in. diameter – and powderings of fine dust.

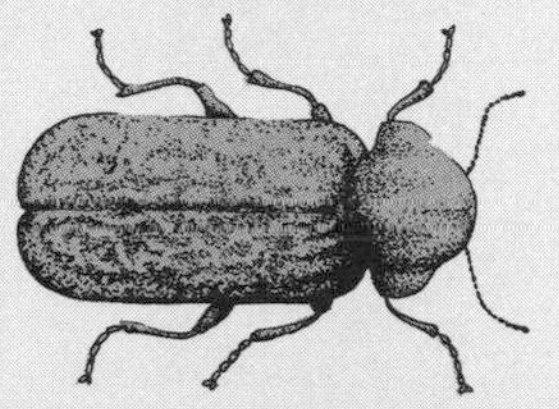

The death watch beetle

Xestobium rufovillosum

This insect does not attack sound and newly seasoned timber, preferring old and decayed hardwoods, and is therefore mainly found in the roofing timbers of old buildings. The adult beetle lays its eggs on the surface of the wood. After some two to eight weeks the larvae hatch, spread over the surface of the timber and then burrow in, tunnelling for an average of four years – stubborn ones can be active for as long as ten years. They emerge as beetles in the spring, leaving behind $\frac{1}{8}$ in. exit holes.

Powder post beetle

Lyctus brunneus/Lyctus linearis

Also called the Lyctus beetle, of which there are two species, Lyctus brunneus and Lyctus linearis. The beetles are fond of certain hardwoods, especially those used in floors and paneling, parquet floors being a favorite. Although a household pest, the powder post beetle is found most frequently in warehouses and lumber yards. The eggs are laid in the spring, and the larvae hatch out within a few weeks, remaining in the wood for about a year, where their tunnelling causes serious damage. The flight holes left by adult beetles are about $\frac{1}{16}$ in. diameter. The bore dust left behind has the texture of flour.

Termite

Prorhinotermes simplex

Unlike the above pests, termites do not always reveal any outward signs of infestation; there can be as many as several thousand termites at any one time in a cubic foot of lumber – whether softwood or hardwood. The discarded wings of *Prorhinotermes simplex*, pearl white and opaque, can be a clue to their presence, as can the small earth tunnels they make to bridge the gap between moist earth or old and new supplies of wood. The tunnels are about $\frac{1}{2}$ in. in diameter, and can be found almost anywhere, so check basement window sills, thresholds, staircases and any scrap timber that may be in basement areas.

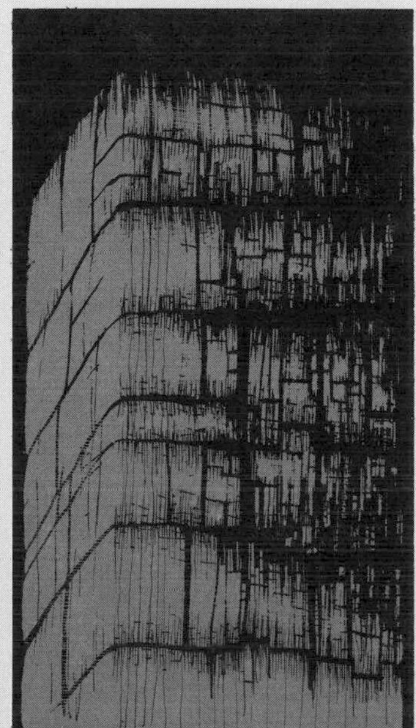

Wood rotting fungi

Various fungi will attack timber in a house, but the two main forms are those known as dry rot and wet rot. Both are usually the result of damp conditions and poor ventilation. The treatment for wet rot is to cut out all affected lumber at least 2 ft beyond limits of attack, and burn decayed wood. Hack away affected plaster, heat exposed bricks with a blowtorch, spray surrounding wood with insecticides. For dry rot, cut away affected lumber and treat with insecticides. Finally, you must eradicate the conditions that attract attacks of wet and dry rot.

Dry rot is identified by a characteristic cube-like splitting of the timbers, often hidden beneath a painted surface.

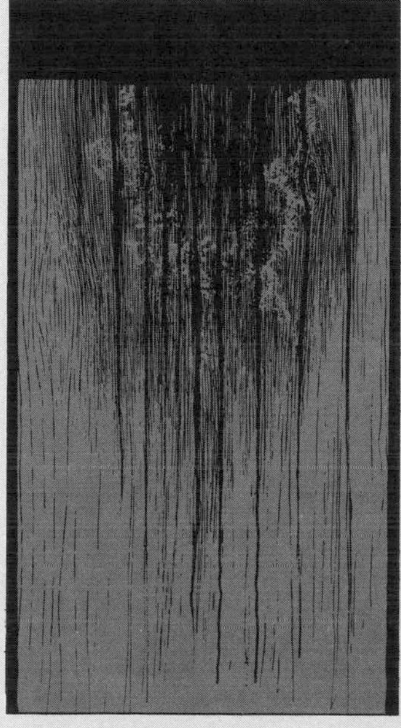

Dry rot

Merulius lacrymans

Merulius lacrymans attacks woodwork such as baseboards, window frames and door surrounds, often leaving the surface unaffected, although it may develop waves or splits. Try pressing a knife blade into the wood which gives easily if it is rotten.

Wet rot

Coniophera cerebella

Coniophera cerebella is less serious than dry rot, and will only occur with saturated or very wet timbers. Once the damp conditions have been eradicated it is likely to stop. Wet rot splits the wood in one direction only; the wood may appear charred.

Wet rot is revealed as saturated wood which has split with the grain.

Brickwork

Tools

For all types of brick construction you need a basic selection of tools, for cutting bricks, laying mortar, and checking that the wall is true.
Heavy-duty hammer is essential; choose one weighing $2\text{-}2\frac{1}{2}$ lb. Any other kind of hammer will not only be too light, but will hurt the wrist with its vibrations.
Wide chisel, also known as a bricklayer's chisel, is the companion of the hammer, used for cutting bricks, or demolishing old brickwork. Choose a 4-inch chisel.
Trowels should include one with a 10-12 inch blade for holding the mortar - you can buy them either right-handed or left-handed. The smaller pointing trowel is useful for "pointing", finishing the layers of mortar between bricks.
Level and **plumb line** are vital. Choose a lightweight metal level which has both vertical and horizontal gauges.

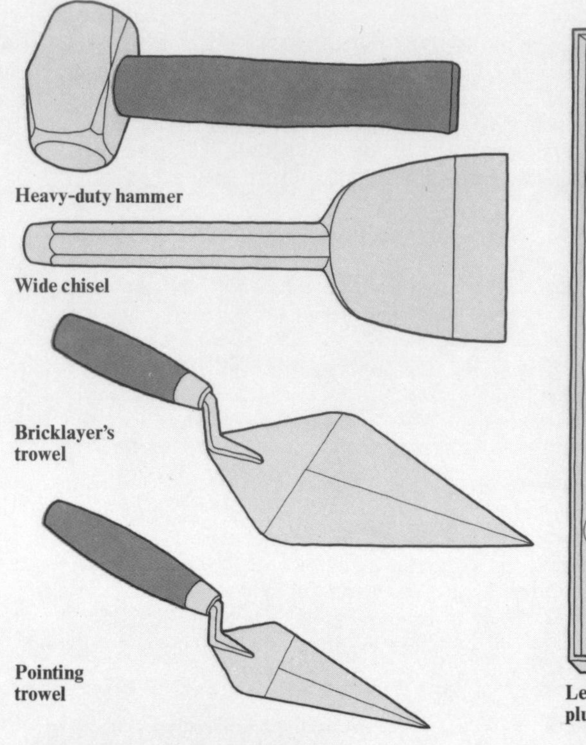

Preparation for Brickwork

Mortar mix
For small areas, use ready-mixed, purchased in bags. To mix your own mortar, use 1 part Portland cement, 1 part lime and 6 parts building sand. Measure by volume, and mix dry constituents thoroughly before adding water. Add water sparingly until mortar retains the impression of a trowel serrated on its surface.
Preparation
In warm, dry weather first wet bricks by soaking in a bucket. Keep a supply of water nearby to clean hands and tools. Only mix sufficient mortar for the job.
Cutting bricks
Score the bed face of the brick with the chisel, then use chisel and hammer to cut a small chip from edge of brick at each end of the line. Lay chisel blade along the line and strike firmly with hammer. To cut an odd shape from part of a brick, chop gently by hand with the chisel.

Techniques

Brickwork must be built on a firm foundation of concrete. In addition to the above basic tools, you will find the following useful:
A spot board for holding the main reserve of mortar, a hawk for carrying mortar to the wall, and a story pole to check the correct height of each brick course.
Make a quantity of mortar on the spot board, but never slice off more than you can handle easily. Work the mortar into a sausage shape and scoop it up on the flat of the trowel blade. Place it on the concrete base, for first bed joint. Flatten the mortar with the blade, and recess it slightly in the center. Place the first brick, straight down on to the mortar, pressing the brick until the joint is about $\frac{1}{2}$ in. thick. If you are going to have the first brick against an existing wall, place a dab of mortar on one end of the brick. Hold it in an approximate position, then with a flick of the wrist, turn and bed the brick against the wall. Lay the second brick against the first in the same way.
Make continual checks to see that the course is level, that the wall is vertical and the thickness of the joint constant. Tap bricks down if they are too high, add a little mortar if too low. Use the story pole to check height and regularity; slice off surplus mortar from brickwork as you go.

1

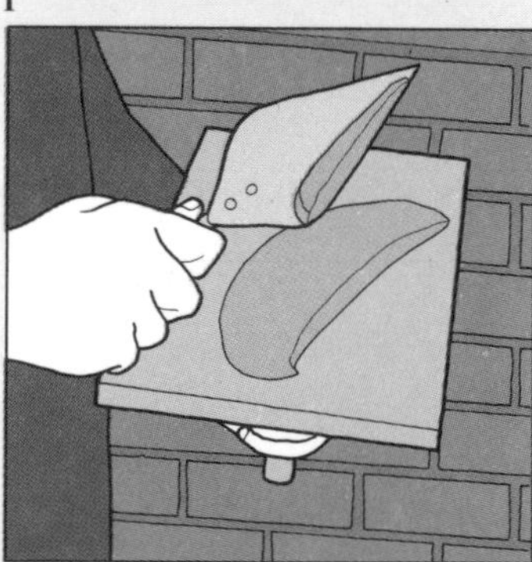
2

3

Pointing

The finish that is applied as a new wall is being built is called pointing. This is the shape given to the mortar joint for decorative purposes which also acts to compress the mortar and to waterproof the joint at the same time.
1 To repoint part of an old wall, first rake out the loose mortar with a cold chisel to a depth of $\frac{1}{2}$ inch.
2 Brush joints and dampen with water. Mix mortar and put a quantity on a hawk.
3 Make a small "sausage" of mortar and roll it into the joint, pressing it into vertical joints, then horizontals.

Types of Joints

Weathered
This is the most practical joint for draining off rainwater. Work with the edge of the trowel slightly angled inwards; uprights can be sloped in either direction. Level off bottom of joint using batten as a template.
Flush
This is good for old brickwork where bricks have spalled, or corners have crumbled. As mortar starts to dry, rub it flush to face of brickwork with sacking or a piece of flat wood.
Concave
Attractive when used with new, sharp-cornered brickwork, the joint is finished flush then rubbed while wet with curved length of $\frac{3}{4}$ in. barrel piping or metal rod.
Raked
Appearance is pleasing but unsuitable in exposed areas. Joint is finished flush then recessed when almost dry.

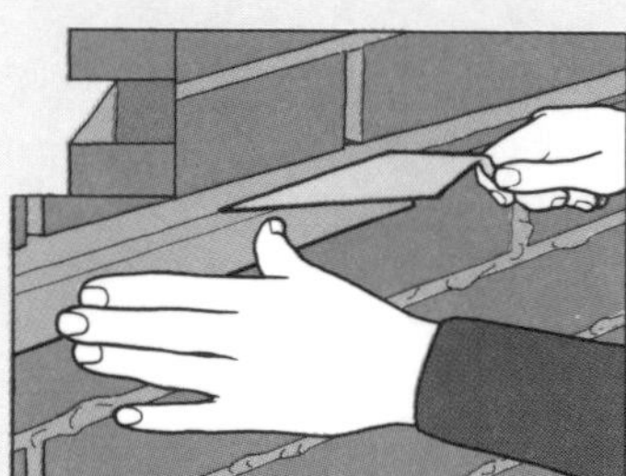
Weathered joint

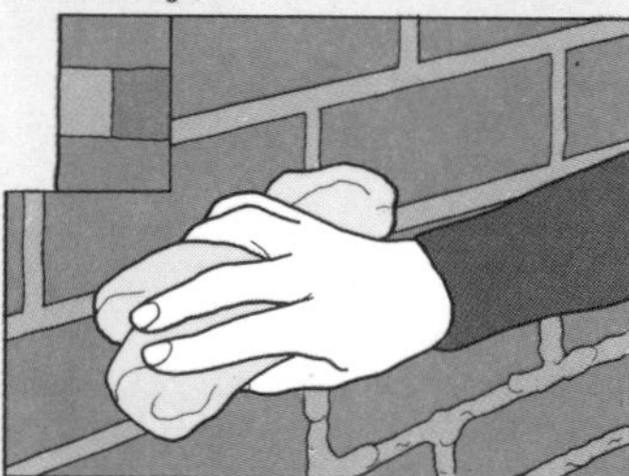
Flush joint

Concave joint

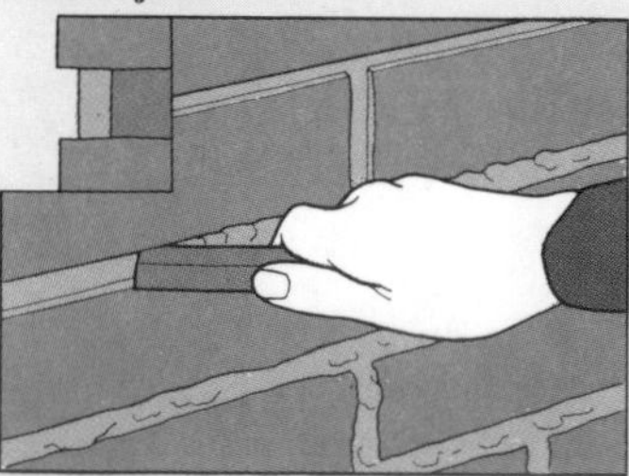
Raked joint

Types of Bricks

Common
Common, or building bricks, are the cheapest kind, but the least attractive for facing purposes. They come in three grades – SW (severe weathering), MW (medium weathering), NW (no weathering). Use SW grade for extremes of temperature, NW for internal walls.

Facing
Facing bricks have a more attractive finish, and come in a wide range of textures and colors. They have all-round weathering properties.

Reclaimed
New bricks rarely match the color of existing brickwork but reclaimed ones which have aged to the same degree are often available from local demolition contractors. Check carefully to see that they are not extensively damaged.

Cut
Bricks which are cut to regulate the bond are either known as "bats" or "closures."

Stretcher and header
Stretchers are bricks laid parallel to the line of the wall while headers are those laid at right angles.

Bonding Brickwork

Strong brickwork requires that bricks are laid in a staggered fashion. This "bonding" ensures that the vertical joints of one course do not align with those of the course immediately below. The vertical joints should match exactly, however, in alternate courses in most bonds. Different bondings are used for their decorative effect. Load bearing brickwork should only be tackled by a competent bricklayer. However, the "running bond" (shown right) is suitable for partition walls and for blocking up unwanted doors or fireplaces.

Head face
Stretcher face
Bed face/underside
Stretcher
Header

Efflorescence
This appears as a fine white powder over the surface of the brickwork, usually in large patches. It is caused by soluble salts in the brickwork and mortar, crystallizing on the surface as the moisture dries out. It can be removed from time to time by vigorous brushing with a stiff, bristle brush. Persistent cases of efflorescence can be treated with two or three coats of a brand name neutralizing fluid.

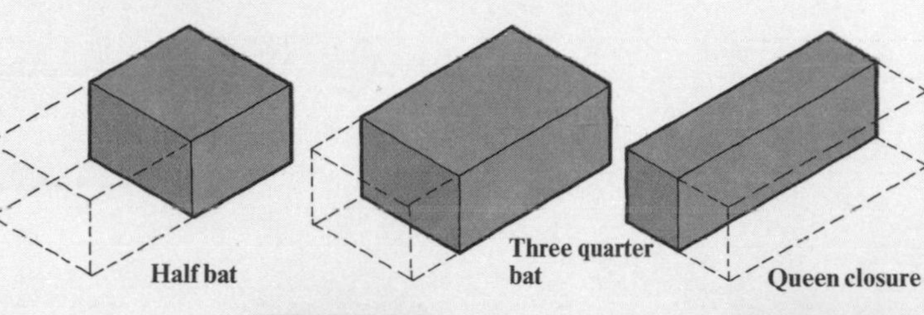

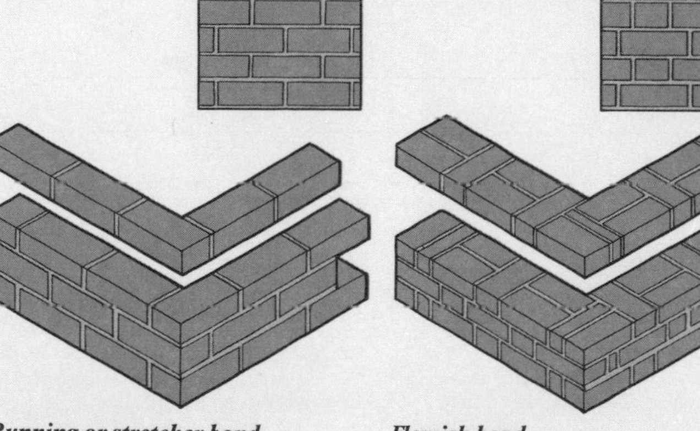

Running or stretcher bond
Used for a dividing internal wall, or a cavity wall, cut bricks are not needed, only half bats at the ends of the wall; the corners use the header face.

Flemish bond
Considered more attractive than English bond, this is slightly weaker. Closures are used to start alternate courses. It is also used for 8 inch thick wall.

English bond
Alternate rows of headers and stretchers are used with a closure at the beginning of the course showing the header faces. It is used for 8 inch thick walls.

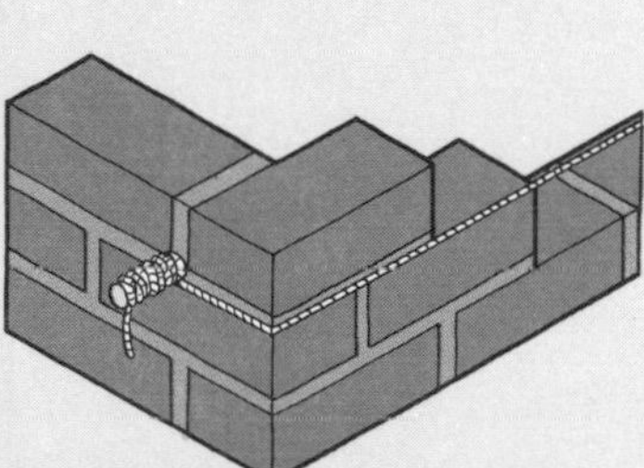

Lining up courses
Use a taut line to regulate the level of courses. Begin the course at either end of wall and drive large nails into mortar joint at either end. Stretch a line between the two nails to give a straight line.

T junction wall
Use headers to key a junction wall into a new "running bond" wall. The bond should be evened out with $\frac{3}{4}$ bats.

Piers
The running bond has limited transverse strength. It should be supported at intervals by laying in a pier with headers at alternate courses. The bond is evened off with $\frac{1}{2}$ and $\frac{3}{4}$ bats.

Bonding into an existing wall
Mark a vertical line on old wall with a plumb line. Cut out a half brick from every fourth course. These indents provide anchoring for a new full brick. Try and match up brick color and type of pointing.

Plasterwork

Tools and Techniques

Covering large areas of wall with plaster is a difficult job for the non-professional; it requires special skills and techniques to obtain a smooth, satisfactory finish. Most small areas and hairline cracks are within the scope and abilities of most householders. All plaster faults must be repaired before other wall finishes are added. The tools you will need are shown on the right. A steel hand trowel and a filler knife are both useful for applying plaster or filler, the trowel can be used to smooth off small areas. Floats are needed when applying larger areas of rendering – either cement or plaster, the plaster being "floated" on the wall with generous sweeps. The bat and hawk both serve a similar purpose to an artist's palette – they allow you to take the material to the wall. The brush is used to apply various finishes to the wall.

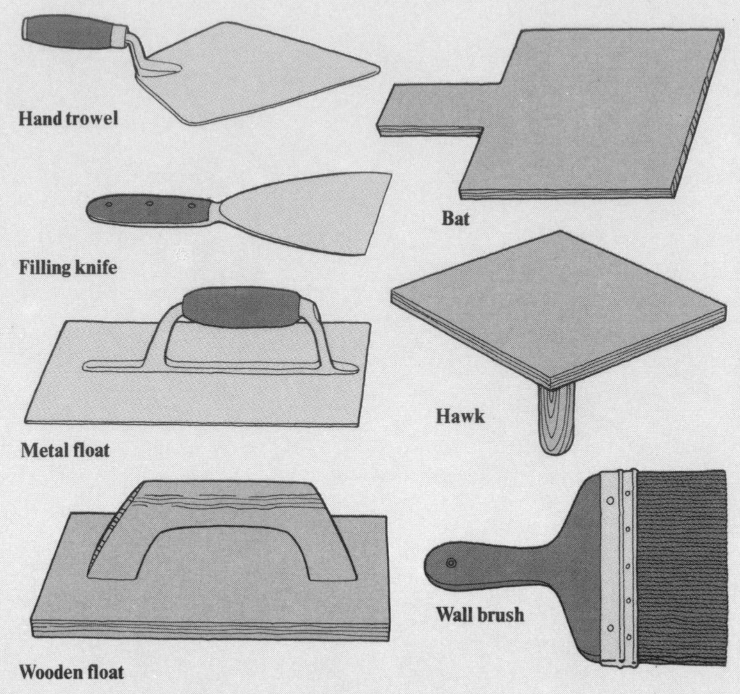

Types of Plaster and Filler

The many different types of plaster available all have varying qualities related to setting and hardening times. Plaster is generally applied in two coats. The first coat, or "rendering" makes a good bond with the wall. The second "skim" or "set" coat provides a smooth surface for decorating. The first coat is usually scored to provide a grip for the second. Repair all large holes and cracks with mixed patching plaster, it takes longer to set than the regular sort, and can be used for both coats. When buying plaster, check the setting time, and never make up more than you can use within that time. Fillers, the most popular being the cellulose-based type, are for small repairs, and they only need mixing with water to form a malleable paste that is unworkable after 30 minutes. Use a plaster filler for hairline cracks and a cellulose one where movement might be expected.

Filling hairline cracks

These generally occur as a result of new plaster drying out, or through vibration. You will need to enlarge the crack by scoring with a filler knife to provide a firm grip for the filler. If you are using a plaster-based filler, dampen the crack with water on a clean brush, just before applying the filler. Because fillers often contract as they dry out, it is a good idea to apply the paste so that it overspreads the surrounding surface. After the filler has dried, you can rub it down flush with fine sandpaper before applying primer coat and final finish.

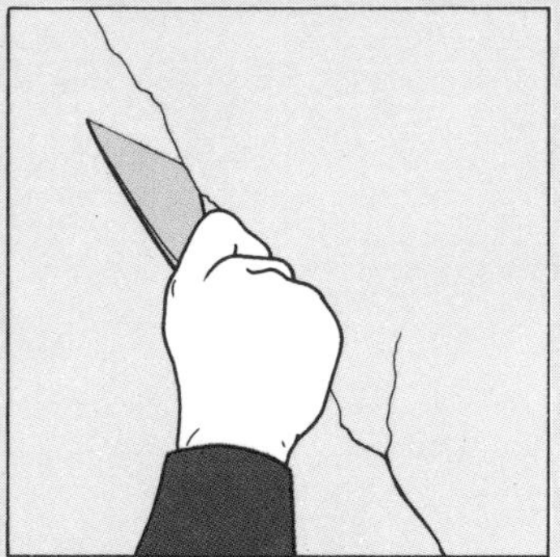

Filling hairline cracks
1 Scrape away loose material, score the crack and brush free of dust.

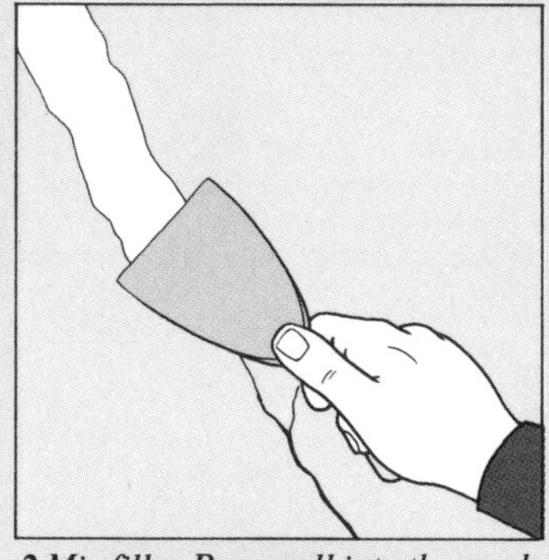

2 Mix filler. Press well into the crack so the paste spreads and makes a good bond.

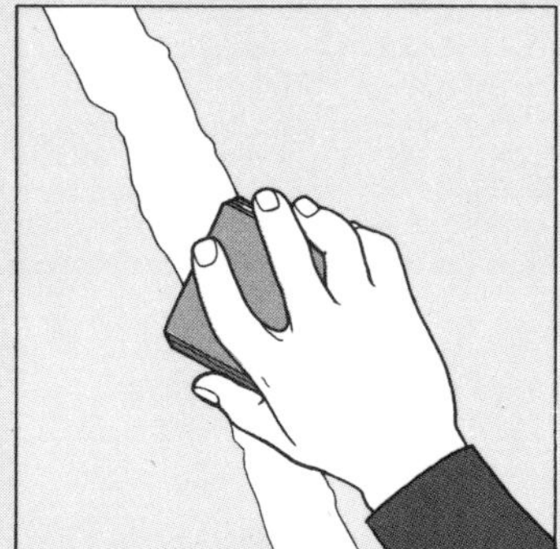

3 Leave filler to dry for about an hour. Rub down flush with fine sandpaper on a small sanding block.

Patching chipped corners

The corner of a wall can easily be damaged when moving furniture, or doing building work. For small areas, apply filler in thin layers and finish so that it is slightly raised. Rub down with sandpaper when dry; avoid using a power tool to sand down plaster as it will damage the surface. For larger areas, use a metal edging or corner bead which will protect corners against future damage. Some beads have paper wings and some have metal wings. These wings support the beading which then becomes the apex of the corner.

Patching chipped corners
1 Trim damaged plaster away from corner. Fix reinforcing bead with dabs of plaster, removing excess.

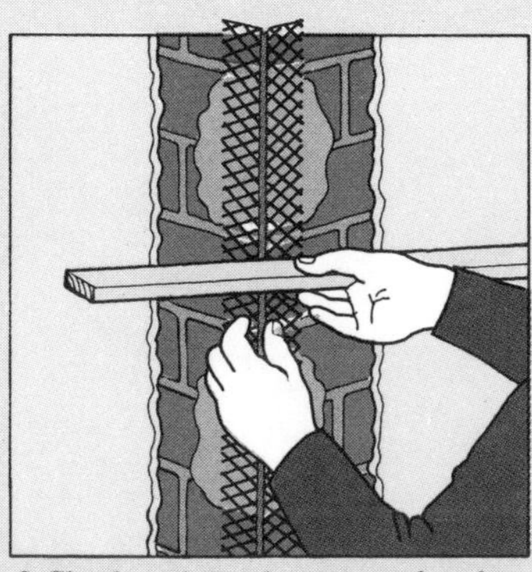

2 Check with level to ensure bead is vertical, and with the ruler to ensure the nose is flush with the surrounding undamaged wall surface.

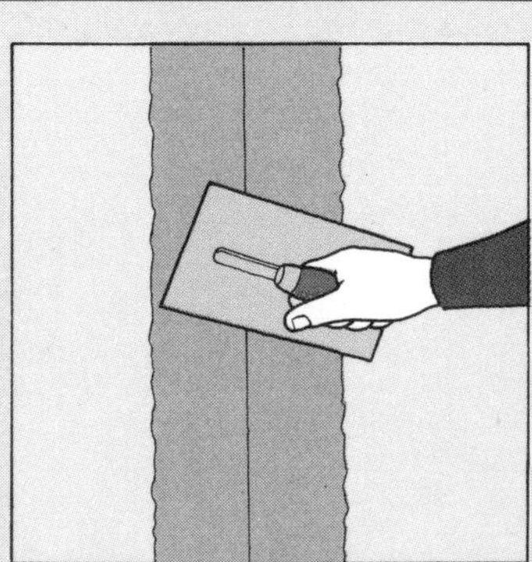

3 When bead is firmly fixed, apply plaster to wall so that it is flush with existing plaster and nose of the bead. Finish with skim coat applied by trowel dipped in water.

Patching large holes
While small holes can be filled with a cellulose filler, and sanded flush with the surrounding wall, larger holes require more careful building-up techniques. The hole can be packed with crumpled paper, first soaked in water and then dipped in a creamy mixture of plaster filler. Cover this plug with a layer of plaster, leave to dry and apply a second coat. Smooth flush with sandpaper. Holes in lath and plaster walls should be patched with expanded metal under two coats of plaster between lath and plaster.

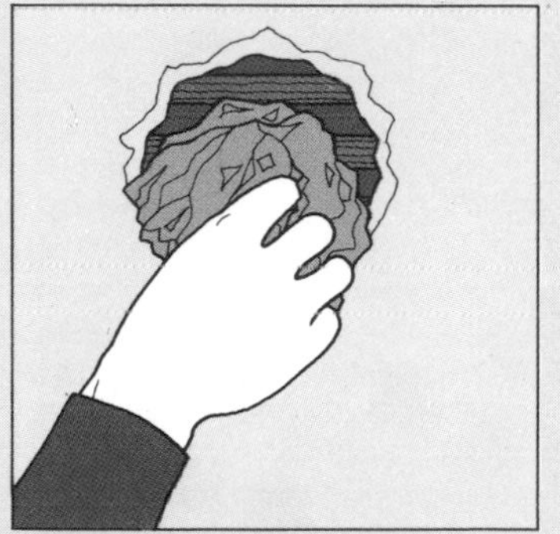

Patching a large hole
1 Use crumpled paper as a plug. Paper can be made pliable by dipping it in water.

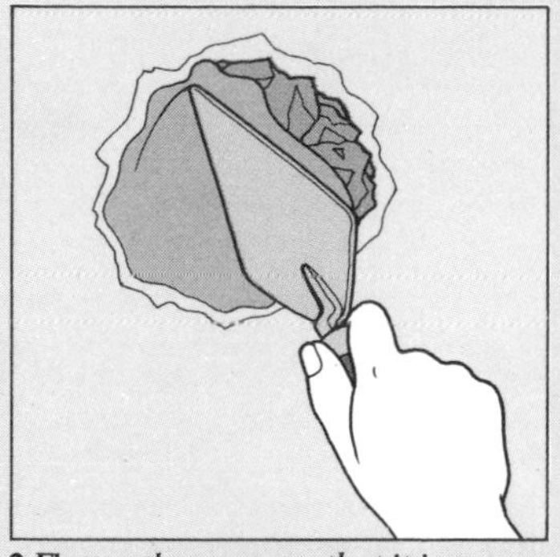

2 Flatten the paper so that it is more or less flush with the surrounding surface, apply a coat of plaster.

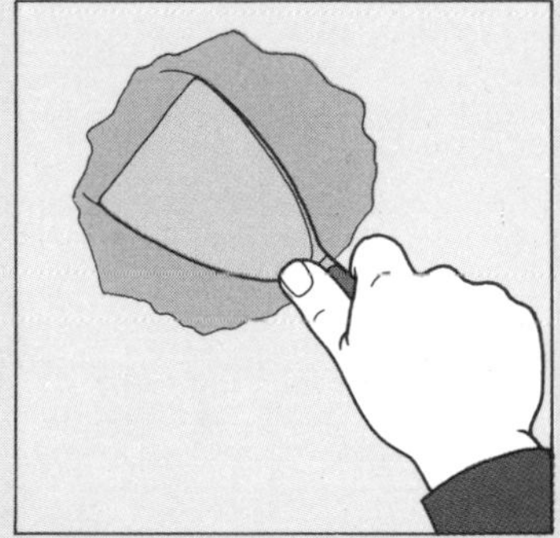

3 Apply second coat, leaving a slightly raised surface. When dry, sand flush with fine sandpaper.

Applying wallboard
An unattractive wall surface, or one that may be in poor condition yet still of sound construction, can be replastered or covered with wallboard. Plastering is a skilled technique, but applying wallboard is within the scope of the non-professional. It conceals the existing wall behind a covering of paper-covered gypsum, and also adds to the insulation of the room. The wall must be dry, and should first be prepared by removing the baseboards, and by hacking off old plaster with a wide chisel and hammer. Wire brush the surface of the wall and, if needed, repoint any bad patches of brickwork (see pp. 84-85). Some wallboards are manufactured with tapering or beveled edges, and additional assembling materials are sold with the boards. You will also require a quantity of wallboard joint compound used as an adhesive. The process consists of attaching the boards to the existing wall by means of intermediate supports–small squares of wallboard fixed to the wall with adhesive. (For batten method see p. 46.) To do this, first mark vertical lines on the wall at 16 in. intervals, and then a horizontal line 6 in. up from the ground. The gap this creates will be hidden by the replaced baseboard, always assuming that it is of average width. Using this line as your base, draw a horizontal centerline for the wallboard. Position the squares on the intersections between the lines, and put up dabs of fresh compound just before positioning each board. Although the wallboards are fixed to the wall, air can circulate between, minimizing the risk of damp and increasing insulation. Nail up individual boards, and cut to fit any remaining gaps.

Applying wallboard
1 Carefully mark intended position of boards across wall; compound does not allow for margins of error.

2 Prepare a number of 6 in. squares of wallboard, as many as there are intersections. Apply a dab of compound to back of each square.

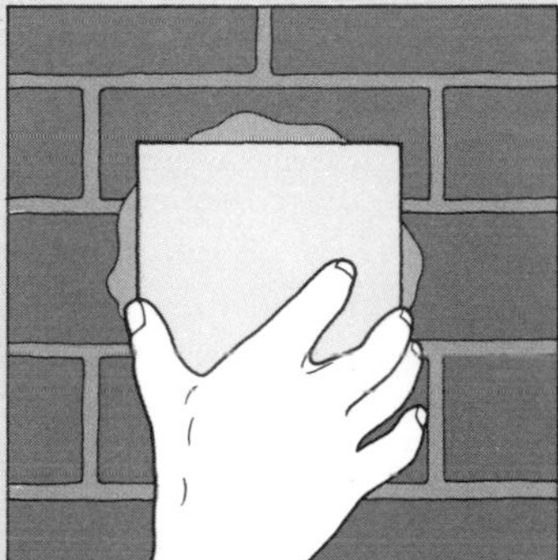

3 Press the square on the wall, centered on an intersection. Do the same with remaining squares.

4 Place dabs of fresh compound to provide points of adhesion for each wallboard.

5 Press board to wall, using a scrap-wood lever to raise it off floor.

6 Nail wallboard to squares with duplex head nails. Fix remaining boards, using full width ones in middle. Cut to fit sides.

7 After an hour, remove nails carefully, using scrap of wood as a lever support.

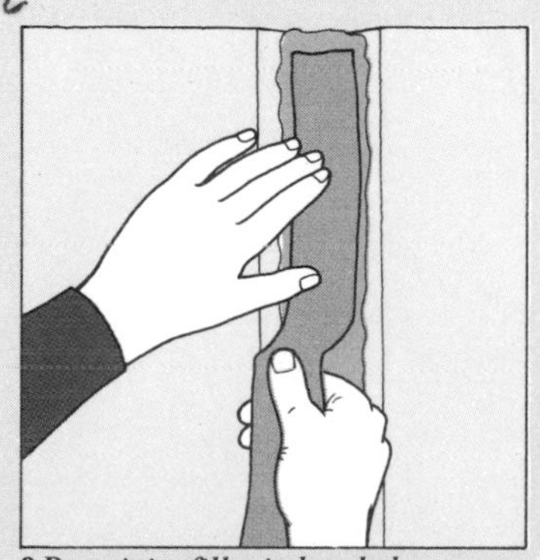

8 Press joint filler in beveled spaces, leaving surface flat and smooth. Press jointing tape into this.

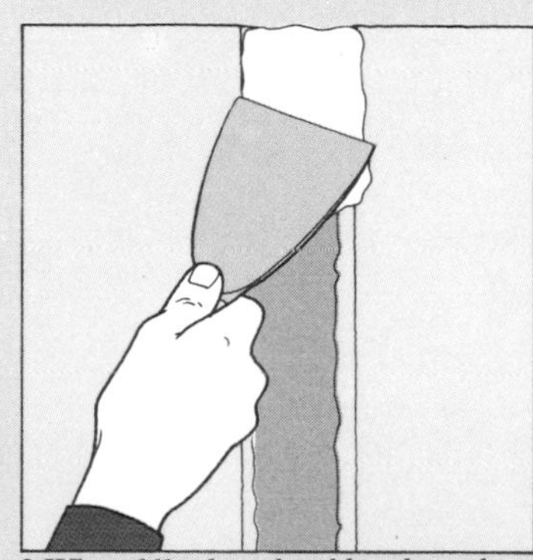

9 When filler has dried hard, apply thin coat of joint compound, about 6 in. wide, over joint.

Waterproofing Walls

Causes of Damp

Dampness is the prime cause of decay. Exposed on the outside to extremes of weather, and internally to moisture rising from the earth, the fabric of a house needs lasting protection. Many building materials are porous: lumber, concrete and bricks soak up moisture like a sponge and can become saturated to an extent that can damage the internal finishes, even causing fungal decay and weakening of the structure. Dampness is usually easy to detect, either by sight or by smell. Rising damp from the sub-soil is the most common, but damp is also caused in older houses by deterioration – broken downspouts, leaks in shingles and flashings; it is a good idea to check possible weak spots every six months.

Rising damp and condensation

You can recognize the presence of rising damp, which usually appears as a crescent of discoloration that spreads above the baseboards to a height of two or three feet, causing wallpaper to peel away from the plaster or, in bad cases, even the plaster itself to crumble. Rising damp is usually due to the absence of a proper waterproofing treatment, or one that has deteriorated. Condensation is another major cause of mildew. The best way to cure condensation is to achieve an efficient balance between heating and ventilation, and to have insulated walls, ceilings and pipes. Exhaust fans in kitchens and bathrooms will considerably reduce the level of condensation. Weep holes in an outer wall, louvered windows and window vents all contribute toward making a good cross-flow of ventilation. Pipes can be effectively lagged with insulating materials.

Treatment of walls

Junctions are usually waterproofed with flashings and caulked with sealants. Caulking is the most efficient means of sealing the shrinkage gaps that occur around door and window frames, and of weatherproofing the top of a flashing where it fits into the brickwork. For small jobs, use caulking compound in tubes. For larger jobs, cartridges of compound that fit into caulking guns will simplify application. Whichever type you use, hold the nozzle at 45° to the work surface, and apply the compound so that it adheres to both surfaces.

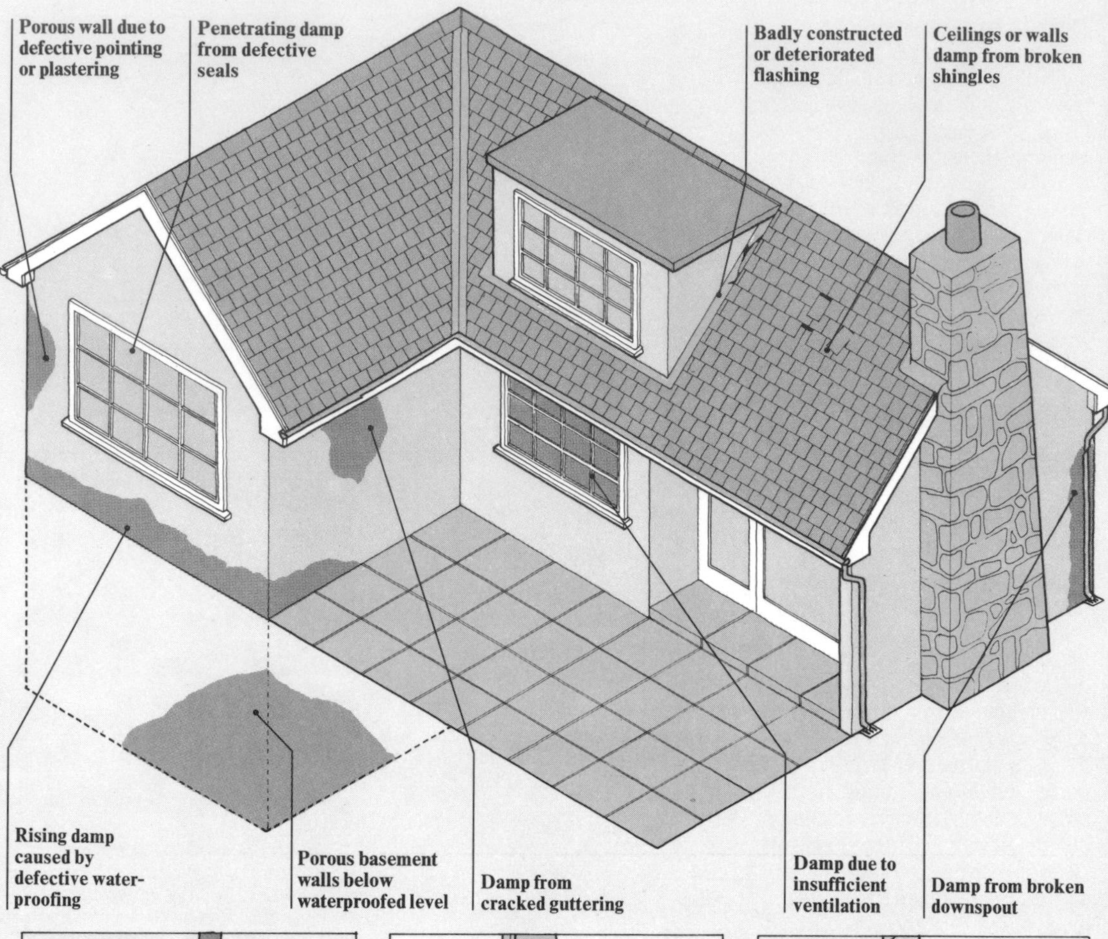

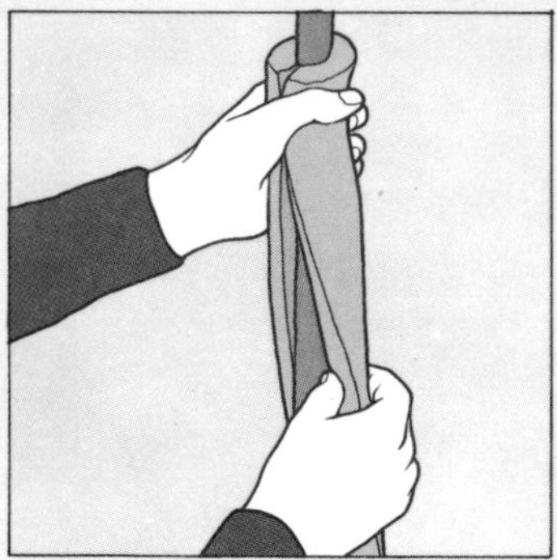

Curing condensation on pipes
Foam plastic sleeves are ideal. You may have to cut along one side of the sleeve, to slip around the pipe.

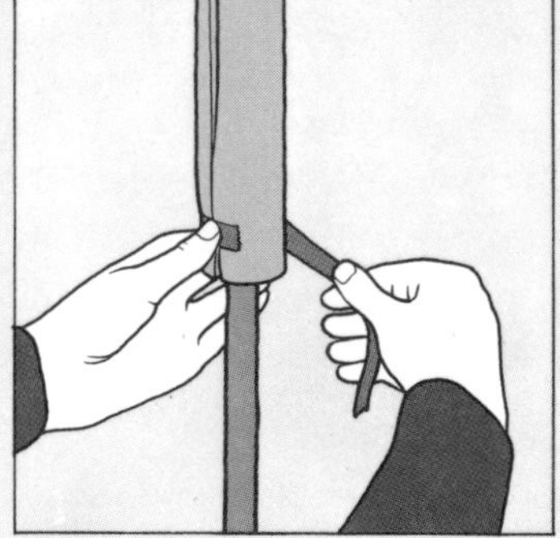

Sealing the joints
Use adhesive tape to seal up the joints, including those between adjacent lengths of foam insulation.

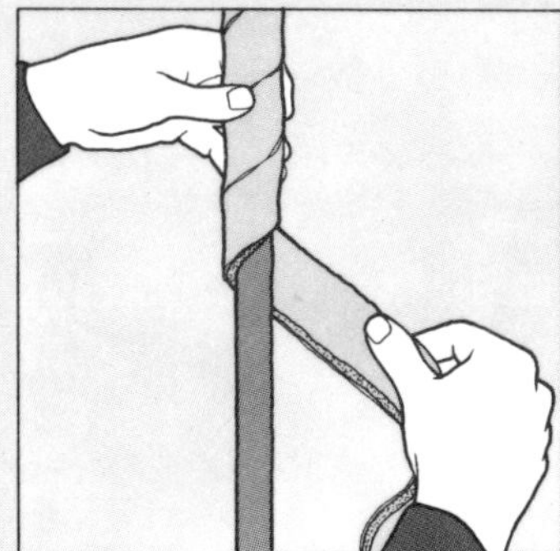

Fiberglass bandage
Another method is to wrap strips of fiber insulaton around pipes. Fix ends with tape or galvanized wire.

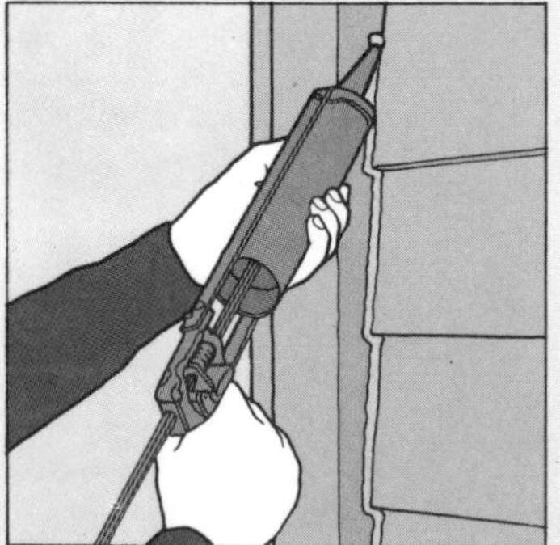

Sealing door frames
Gaps between door frame and wall can be filled with mastic caulking compound. Squeeze through nozzle.

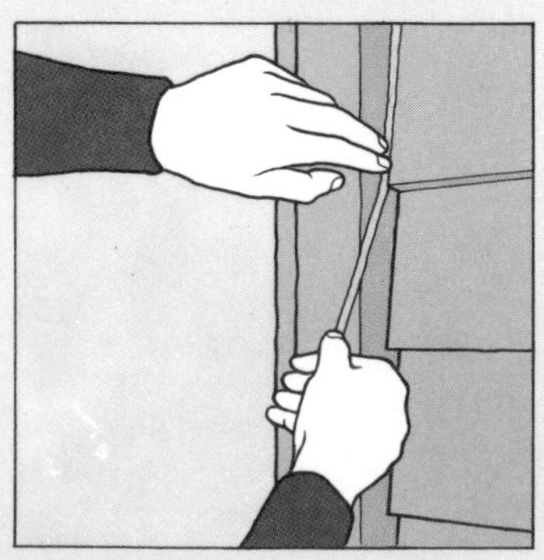

Coiled caulking compound
This can be bought in rope form, and may be used instead of caulking tube or gun. Press into gaps with fingers.

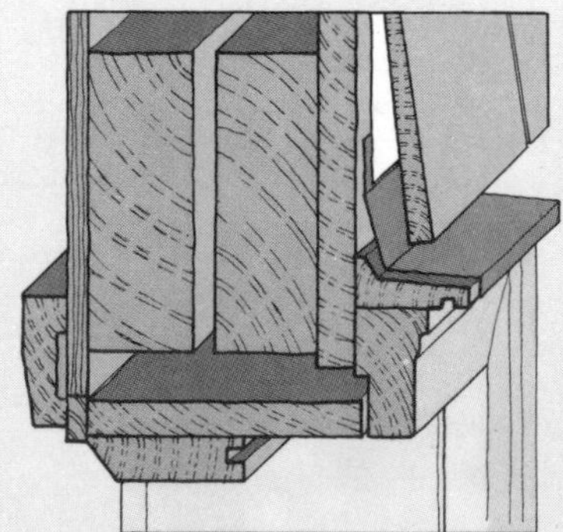

Defective flashings
Where shrinkage has occurred around door and window frames, plug gap with caulking compound.

Basement waterproofing

Basement walls are particularly prone to the penetration of damp, mainly through cracks in foundation walls, or due to faulty drainage, or water seeping through junctions between the floor and base of the wall. To repair cracks, you will have to treat them from the outside. This will mean excavating down to the level of the footing to reveal the foundation wall. Clean off loose debris from around cracks and fill with a 1:1:6 mix of cement, sand and lime. Then apply a layer of asphalt paper or roof cement, and if the sub-surface water level is high, put in a drain tile. Lay the tiles at a gradient of about 1:24, with the drain leading to a dry well or storm sewer. Cover the tiles with 6-8 in. of crushed stone or coarse gravel, and return topsoil to ground level. If the soil is periodically very wet in your area, it is worth giving the wall an extra coat of bituminous asphalt before returning the topsoil. Stains that occur near the bottom of a basement wall may be cured with a liquid sealer. Dig a shallow trench alongside the foundation in the proximity of the stain and pour the sealer in.

Treating interior walls

Waterproofing compounds can be used on the inside of basement walls to keep out the damp. There are many different brands, but application is usually the same: dampen the wall beforehand – a dry wall will affect the quality of adhesion. Apply as shown on the right, and wash the brush immediately after use. When the first coat is dry, dampen wall again and apply a second coat. Cracks can be cured with quick-setting cement even if they are continuously leaking. Form the mix into a plug, and hold it into place for the final stage of setting, and at the last moment, use a trowel to smooth the surface flush with the wall.

Building a secondary wall

Weatherproofing walls needs professional attention, although you can combat damp to a great extent by building a secondary wall surface; this is particularly suitable for cellar walls below waterproofed level.

Use pitch-impregnated fiber sheets, which can afterwards be plastered. The sheets are a branded product, and supplied with fixing instructions. Alternatively, you can use aluminum foil, pasted on the wall.

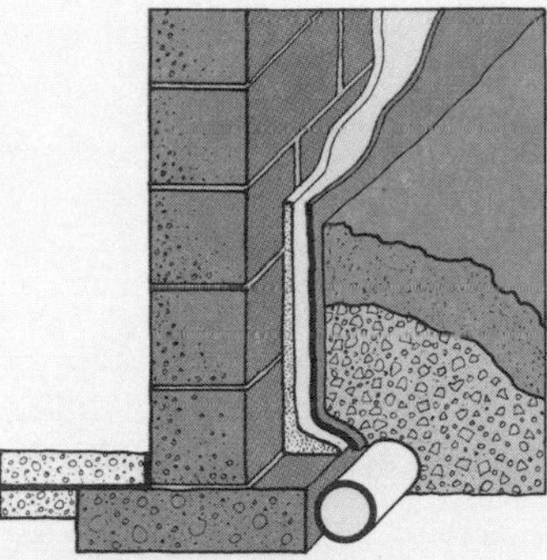

Waterproofing walls
This diagram shows the correct waterproofing construction, with asphalt paper or otherwise with cement and drain tiles.

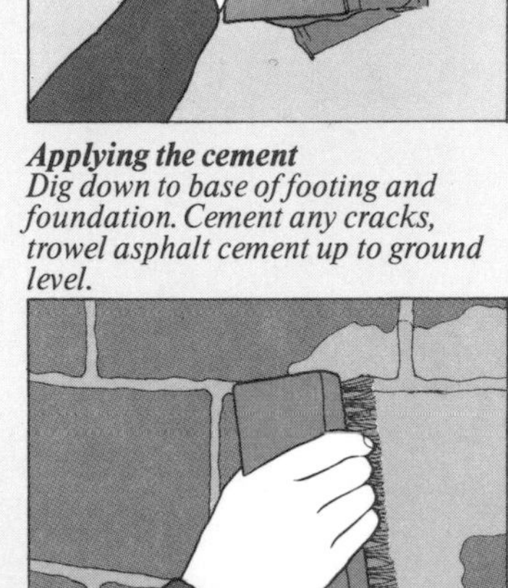

Applying the cement
Dig down to base of footing and foundation. Cement any cracks, trowel asphalt cement up to ground level.

Dispersing ground water
Lay 4 in. tiles along the footing with a ¼ in. gap between them. Cover gaps with tar-paper, the whole with gravel.

Preparing walls for compounds
First dampen the wall surface with a brush or hose. Mix the compound according to maker's instructions.

Applying compound
Use a stiff bristle brush to rub the compound well into the wall surface. After 24 hours, repeat procedure.

Waterproofing basement floor
Where damp shows between concrete slab and wall, cut wedge shape groove at junction. Fill with 2-part epoxy.

Sealing cracks in walls
Undercut the crack with chisel, so it is wider inside than out, making a wedge shape. Clear out loose material.

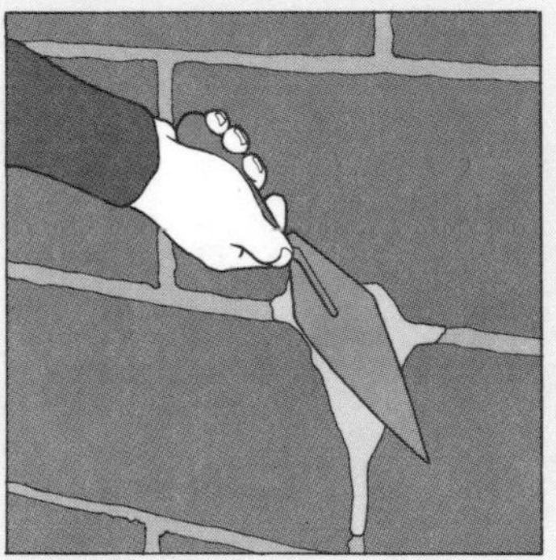

Filling with epoxy
Plug the hole with brand name epoxy, forcing well into the crack; finish flush with the trowel.

Quick-setting cement
In wet weather, use hydraulic cement. As mix starts to set, roll into plug and press into hole. Trowel flush.

Building a secondary wall
1 Hack off any existing deteriorated plaster material with a wide chisel and hammer.

2 Nail fiber sheets, cut to size, directly on to wall with wall nails.

3 Leave a 1 in. gap top and bottom for ventilation. Render with plaster as for normal wall.

Blockwork

Building a Block Wall

Basic blockwork

Building blocks are made of concrete, and can be a useful alternative to bricks for an internal partition wall, whether it is load bearing or non load bearing. While they are heavier than bricks, building blocks are quicker and easier to lay, and some types are cheaper; blocks can also have a higher insulation value.

Types of blocks

Stretcher blocks are the most commonly used and weigh about 30 lbs. Their dimensions are 8x8x16 inches with two or three internal cores and half core ends. Use them for an internal, load bearing wall.

Corner blocks match the stretcher blocks, but they have one smooth end. Dealers usually supply a proportionate number with an order of stretcher blocks.

Solid top blocks should be used for the course that provides direct support for floor slab or joist. They are made with a top which is at least 4 inches thick.

Partition blocks are ideal for an internal, non load bearing wall, having a cellular core, dimensions of 16x8x4 inches, and a weight of about 15 lbs. They are smooth on both ends.

Laying concrete blocks

Plan the position of windows or doors before laying so as to avoid cutting; half blocks are designed to facilitate openings in walls. As there are fewer joints than in brickwork there is less opportunity to absorb awkward shapes. Lay blocks as for bricks (the blocks must be dry) with $\frac{3}{8}$ in. mortar joints made with 1:3 mix of cement to sand. Use a stiffer mix than for brickwork. Lay first course "dry", using a piece of $\frac{3}{8}$ in. wood as a spacer. Complete a course, and chalk position of joints on the floor. Use stretched string as a guide 6 in. above floor for correct alignment. Begin mortaring blocks from corner or end blocks. The technique is illustrated in the pictures on the right.

Fair-facing and stucco

If the blocks are to be left fair-faced, you should avoid excess mortar smearing the surface of the blockwork. Try lifting mortar with a trowel, rather than scraping. If necessary, brush off smears once mortar has started to dry. If blockwork is to be stuccoed, apply a $\frac{1}{2}$ in. rendering of mortar to provide an adhering surface.

Stretcher

Corner

Solid top

Partition

Basic Construction

Control joints

Block walls are subject to a greater degree of movement than are bricks, and so elastic control joints are needed at intervals of 20 ft, at all door and window openings, and at the junctions between walls and columns. These joints eliminate the cracking that might otherwise occur. Rake out each control joint when the mortar is nearly dry, to a depth of about $\frac{3}{4}$ in. and fill with a caulking compound.

Wall junctions

Junctions between one load bearing wall and another must be reinforced with galvanized metal tie bars which have a right angle bend at each end. They are installed at maximum vertical intervals of 4 ft, the ends embedded in the mortar-filled cores of the blocks; the mortar is supported on a piece of metal lath. Junctions between non load bearing block walls must have every alternate course reinforced with metal lath, or with $\frac{1}{4}$ in. galvanized hardware cloth.

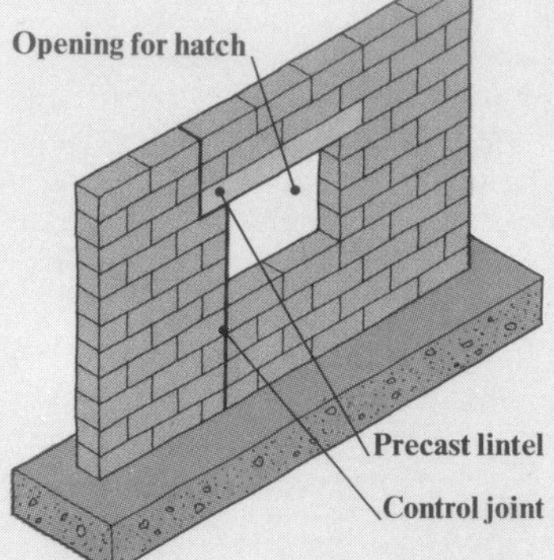

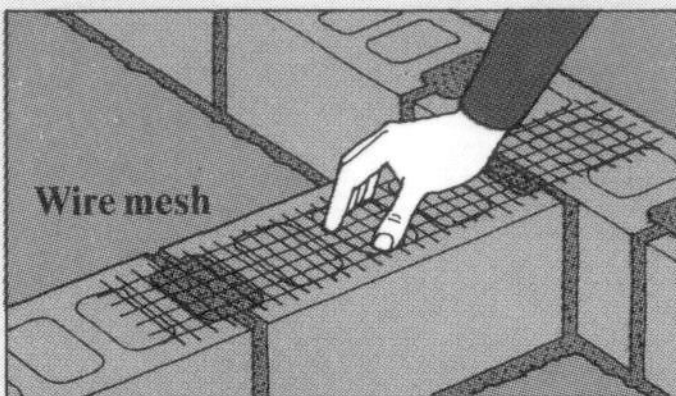

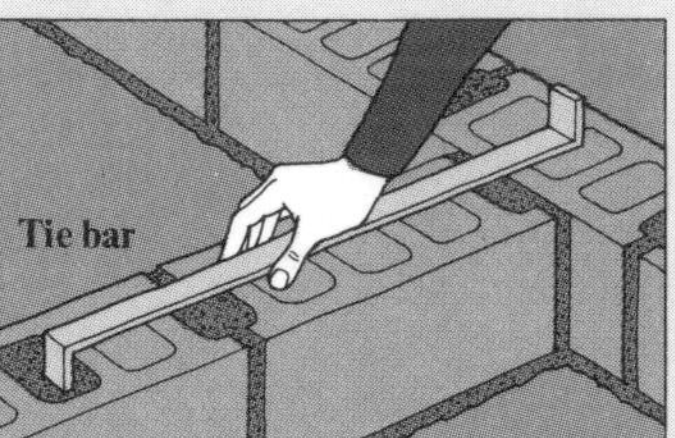

Wall junctions
Non load bearing walls are tied with metal lath; load bearing walls are strengthened with tie bars.

Laying concrete blocks
1 For best results, pre-planning is essential. Lay the first course "dry" using a $\frac{3}{8}$ in. piece of wood in place of mortar.

2 Chalk the position of joints on the floor, after completing the first course.

3 Align the blocks flush by stretching a line between ends of the course, about 6 in. above the floor.

4 Remove corner or end blocks, and mortar the flat or projecting ends. Lay $\frac{1}{2}$ in. bed of mortar and replace corner blocks.

5 Press down until mortar is about $\frac{3}{8}$ in. thick and check with level. Re-lay if too low, tamp down with handle of trowel if too high.

6 Continue through remainder of blocks in same way, removing them from the "dry" position in pairs.

Partitions

Building a Stud Partition

The stud partition

A wooden frame wall, usually called a "stud partition," can be surfaced with any one of a range of materials: wallboard, fiber board, tongue-and-grooved boards. Remember to check your local code before starting any structural work; your plans may contravene fire or ventilation requirements. The main advantages of a stud partition are its lightness and ease of construction; openings such as serving hatches or doors are fairly simple to add or remove.

Building a partition

You can locate joists either from above, by removing floorboards, or from below, by tapping ceiling with a hammer, to ascertain the approximate position. To locate exact position, drill ⅛ in. holes across marked areas. The sole plate – the bottom horizontal piece of the partition – can be fixed to the floorboards, unless the partition is load bearing, when it must have a joist below, strong enough to support it. The head plate – the horizontal top piece – is fixed to the joists in the ceiling. The entire frame is strengthened by cross beams, or spreaders, to provide lateral support, and to which the lining material can be fixed. The upright studs should be 16 in. to center, so that 4 ft wide sheets of wallboard can be fixed to the studs without having to be cut. The joints in the end studs, and the ends of the sole plate should be rabbeted (see pp. 128-131), and plain dado joints should be cut for the intermediate studs in the head plate. For lumber use 3x2 in. softwood: the widest dimension is the width of the partition.

Stud partition with door

If you intend to build a door opening in the partition, leave out the sole plate where the door is to be located, allowing the width of the door plus the thickness of the lining wood in the opening. Fit a header – the piece that squares off the top of the door opening – allowing for the height of the door, plus the top lining wood.

Load bearing stud partition

You will need a builder or surveyor to check the load bearing capacity of the floor above and below the site of your partition. Use 4x2 in. lumber throughout, with studs placed 16 in. to center. Reinforce with additional diagonal bracing to studs and cross beams.

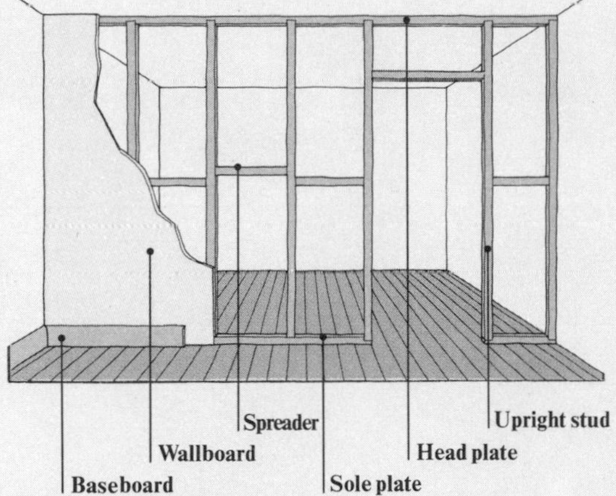

Deciding the position

Your decision will be influenced by the direction of floor joists above the ceiling. If parallel with the joists, position the partition so that the head plate can be fixed to a joist through the ceiling **1**. If the partition must be arranged between the joists you will have to nail 2x2 in. cross beams between the joists to anchor the head plate **2**. Locate the joists by removing the floorboards in the room above. If the partition runs at right angles to the joists, the head plate can be fixed to each one.

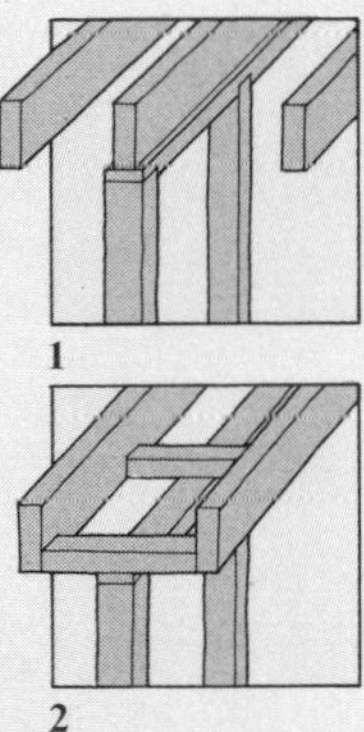

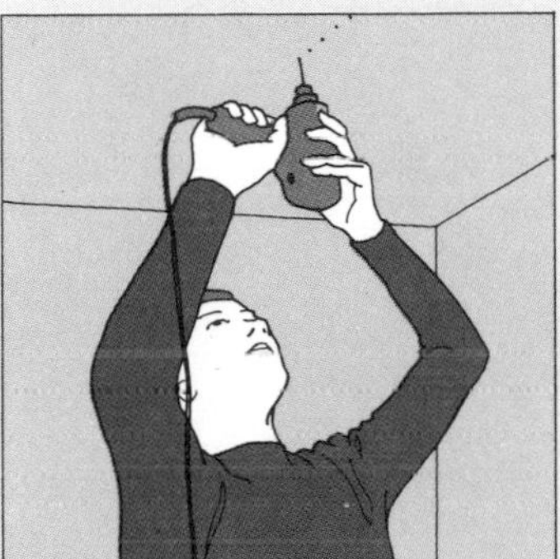

Building a partition
1 Tap ceiling with hammer for the approximate position of joists. Drill ⅛ in. holes for exact position.

2 With a pencil, mark the width of head plate on the ceiling. Also mark walls for position of end studs.

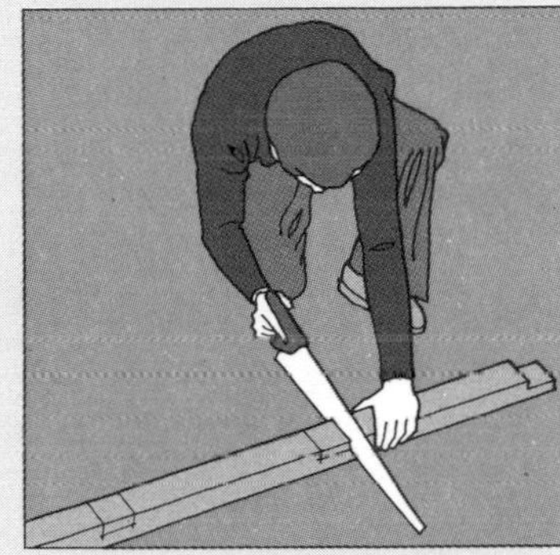

3 Cut head plate to length, mark position of intermediate studs. Cut plain dado joints to take stud ends.

4 Cut sole plate to length, cut rabbeted joints in each end. Screw to floor with 2½ in. screws, screw end studs to walls with expanding plugs.

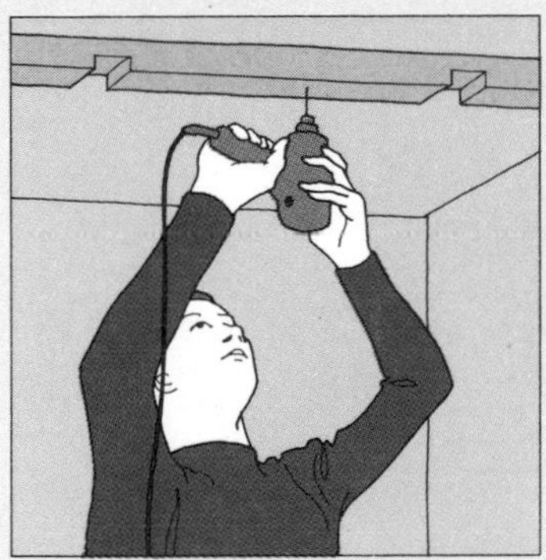

5 Mark position of head plate screws and drill clearance holes through ceiling. Place head plate in position and screw to joists.

6 Cut each intermediate stud. Locate tops in dado joints of head plate. Nail diagonally to head plate and also to sole plate.

7 Cut cross beams to make a tight and level fit between studs. Fit them about 3 ft apart, nailing diagonally.

8 Fix wallboard to studs with drywall nails. Start with first board flush against ceiling and wall.

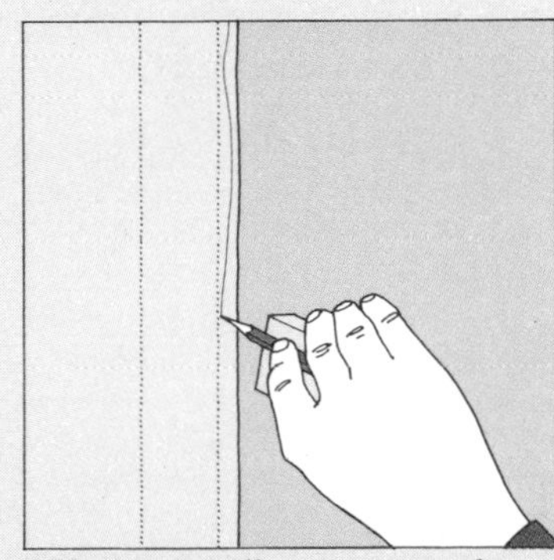

9 If existing walls are not straight, scribe wallboard to the wall.

Structural Alterations

Altering Existing Walls

When converting an interior, you may find it necessary to alter existing walls, either by removing part or the whole wall, or perhaps by filling in an opening. Anything which affects the load bearing capacity of a structural wall is potentially dangerous, even though the alteration may appear to have little or no effect on the wall's stability. Work of this nature should be done by a builder or contractor.

Making an opening in a non load bearing brick or block wall

Before you make an opening in an external wall, you must check your local building regulations. If you remove a triangular section of bricks from either an external or internal wall, of a sufficient width to allow for a service hatch, a door or window, the aperture will be self-supporting, provided that the wall is sound; this is a characteristic feature of all brickwork. Removing a triangular section enables you to insert a lintel without having to support the structure above with temporary joists, and before increasing the size of the aperture below. Let us imagine, for example, that you want to install a doorway in a solid brick wall. You need to plan the exact position, and observe the particular structure - the bond - of the brickwork. You then knock out a brick above the intended position of the lintel, determined by the height of the doorway - the brick forms the apex of a triangle made by the width of the lintel as representing the triangle's base. The technique is described in drawings right (1-6 above). Take care, when altering walls, not to disturb any adjacent structure such as ceilings, or any plumbing or electrical fittings. If in doubt, always ask a builder or contractor for advice.

Filling in an opening in a non load bearing brick or block wall

All brickwork is "bonded" - that is, laid in a pattern to avoid having joins running in a continuous vertical line. When you fill in an existing opening - a doorway or a service hatch - you must keep to the bonding pattern of the brickwork, or the strength of the wall may be impaired. If the wall is "fair-faced" where the bricks are to remain unrendered, you will have to use matching bricks where possible, to avoid a noticeable patch.

Opening up a brick wall
1 Mark out the position. Using a hammer and chisel, hack off 4 in. of plaster to expose mortar joint.

2 Measure width of opening accurately, and drill holes of ½ in. diameter through the mortar joint.

3 From these holes, measure down the height of the opening. Drill holes through the bottom two corners.

4 Hack off all the plaster as far up as four courses of brickwork above the top of the opening.

5 Remove bricks with chisel, taking the first from top center of the four courses, then from the second and third and finally four from bottom.

6 Cut out sufficient brickwork on each side of opening to take lintel, allowing a maximum bearing surface of no more than 6 in.

7 Fit lintel on a bed of cement mortar, packing out if necessary with small pieces of slate. Lintel must be level and flush with wall.

8 Use original bricks to fill in the triangular opening above lintel. Leave mortar for 24 hours to dry.

9 Working downwards, clear remaining bricks from opening. Make sides good with ½ or ¼ bricks.

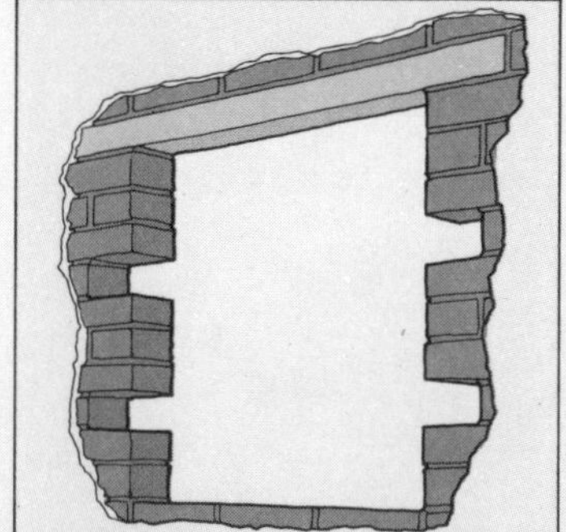

Infilling a brick wall
1 Remove quarter bricks from every 4th course at sides of opening, or alternate course if wall is blockwork.

2 Build and bond in bricks to match course heights, using same type material, and cement mortar.

3 Leave raked joints (see pp. 86-87) if wall is to be plastered to match existing finish.

Making an opening in a non load bearing wooden frame wall
Some internal walls are made of a wooden frame, covered on both sides with wallboard, and finished with a plaster rendering. These walls are called "stud" walls or "stud partitions" and the upright timbers or studs are usually 16 or 18 in. apart. To make a wider opening you will have to cut out part of one or more studs and insert horizontal cross beams, or spreaders, top and bottom of the opening; these anchor and strengthen the cut studs. Wherever possible, make the width correspond with an upright to give the finished opening greater stability, otherwise you will have to insert short uprights between the horizontals. When removing wallboard, make sure that you do not damage any electric wiring that is in the partition. As a precaution, turn off the power at the mains switch.

Filling in an opening in a non load bearing wooden frame wall
The opening, a door or perhaps a window, will have lining timber fixed to the studs at each side and above the opening – in other words, the wooden door frame or window frame. This will need to be removed in order to expose the upright studs to which the frame is fixed. A wide opening will have to be provided with extra studs and spreaders. Should the existing wallboard conceal the face side of the studs, nail 1 in. strips of wood the length of the studs to provide a fixing surface for the new wallboard. Cut the wallboard to fit the size of the opening, and nail it to the upright studs, bearing in mind that it may have to be slightly recessed to take a coat of plaster that will make it flush with the existing wood.

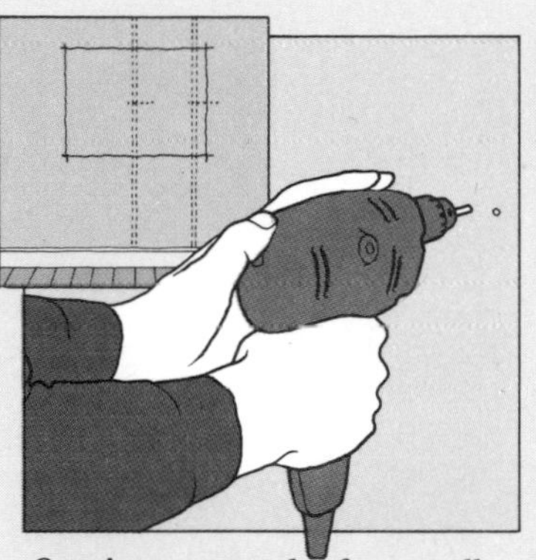

Opening up a wooden frame wall
1 Mark out opening. Drill a horizontal line of $\frac{3}{4}$ in. holes centrally across to find position of studs.

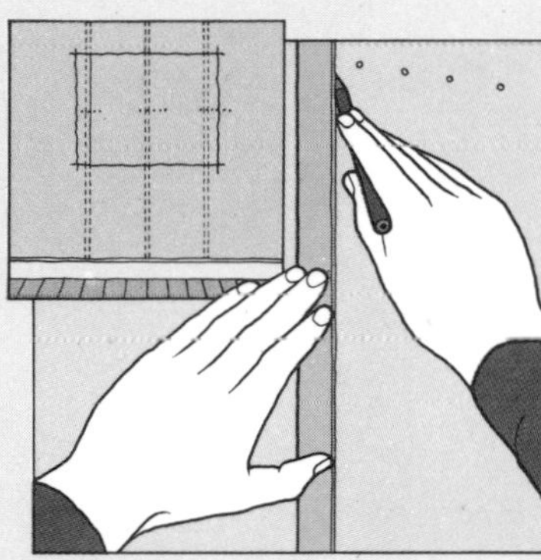

2 Mark out exact size of opening and remove area of covering material.

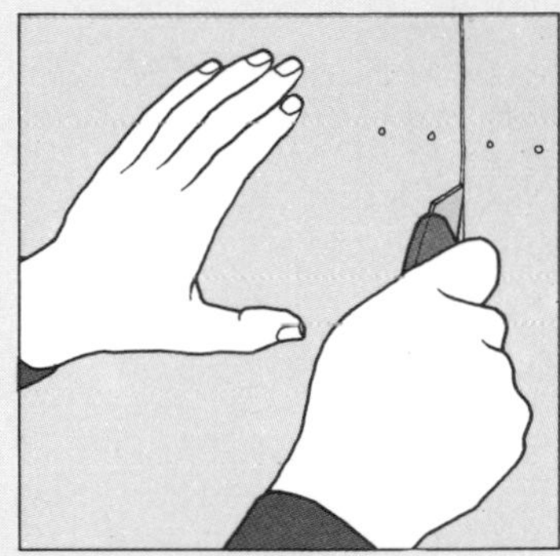

3 Remove wallboard with a sharp trimming knife, or old wood chisel and hammer.

4 With old lath and plaster walls, first remove plaster with chisel, then cut through lath with wallboard saw.

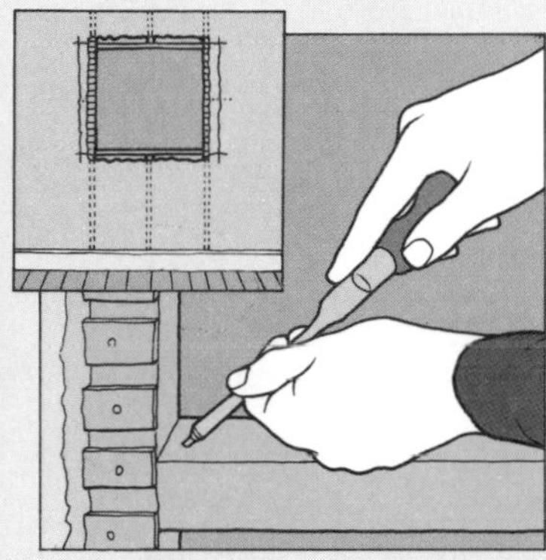

5 Cut softwood horizontals and studs from same size lumber. Screw into position, horizontals first, then the uprights.

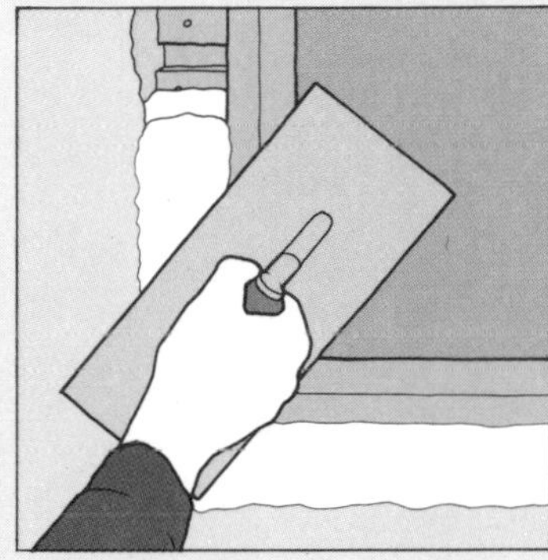

6 Make good sides of opening with wallboard: finish them off with plaster rendering.

Infilling a wooden frame wall
1 Remove lining from around opening, using same size wood for the infill.

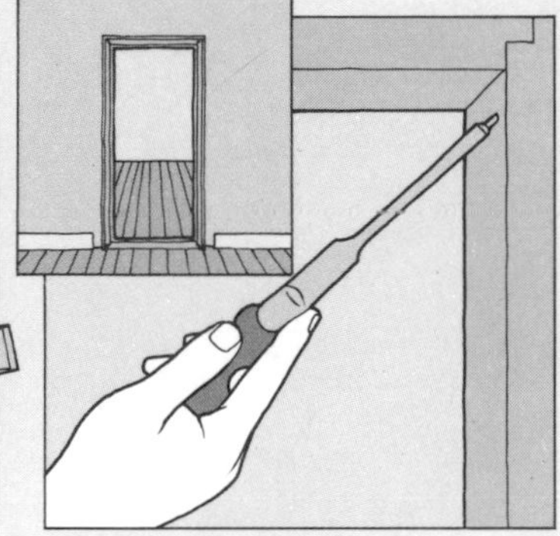

2 Cut wood for opening, with rabbeted joints at ends. Screw uprights to edges, also wood above and below opening.

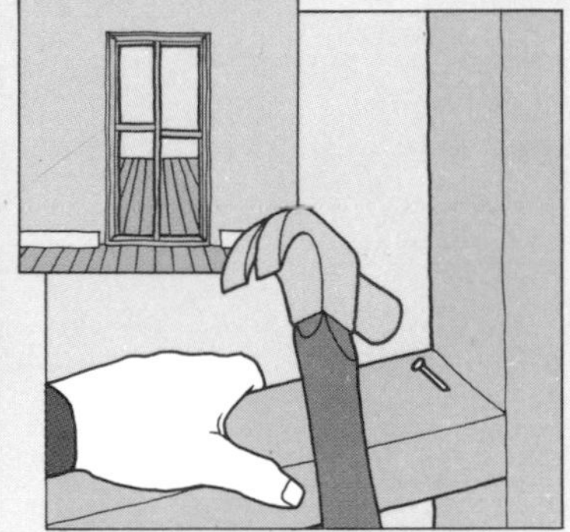

3 If several uprights are needed, strengthen by nailing horizontal spreaders. Cover frame with wallboard.

Making an opening in a load bearing brick or block wall
All alterations to load bearing walls must be done by a builder. When an opening is planned for such a wall he must first assess whether the triangle of self-supporting brickwork above the intended opening will be sufficient to carry the structure while inserting a lintel; temporary support is almost sure to be needed. With an external cavity wall he will probably need to include a water proofing course around all the edges of the opening.

Making an opening in a load bearing wooden frame wall
The only likely case where an opening may need to be made in a load-bearing stud partition is when a new door or service hatch is installed. The job must be done by a builder, who will first establish the method used, and if necessary adjust the position of the opening so that it will not affect the overall stability of the wall.

Filling in existing openings – brick or block load bearing walls
The sides of the opening must be prepared, and the lintel, if any, removed. New brickwork must be bonded into the sides of the opening, complete with wall ties (see pp. 84-85). Unless the outer skin is rendered, matching brickwork – in texture and color – should be laid to the same bond as the existing wall and finished with the same pointing.

Removing a load bearing wall
Demolishing a load bearing wall is a major undertaking, and must be left to a builder. A beam of precast concrete or an RSJ (rolled steel joist) will have to be provided to support the structure above, once the wall has been removed. If the wall is soundly constructed, parts may be retained either side of the intended opening, to act as piers to support the beam; otherwise new piers will have to be built.

Concrete Work

Ingredients

Concrete consists of Portland cement, sand and aggregate (gravel or crushed stone) mixed together with water. The addition of water creates a chemical reaction with the cement, so that when the mixture dries it forms a hard, dense material. Concrete is strong in compression but weak when under tension, so that it is occasionally reinforced with mild steel. The proportions of the ingredients therefore may vary according to the type of job and these are expressed in figures, thus 1:3:4 concrete is made with one part cement, three parts sand, and four parts aggregate.

Portland cement has a texture of fine powder and it is important to store it in a dry place. When exposed to damp it develops lumps, but if these can easily be crushed with your fingers, it is still usable. Cement dries gray, but for more ornamental work and pavings, choose white Portland cement.

Sand is really a fine aggregate and should be clean and free-flowing; beach sand is unsuitable.

Aggregates determine the strength of the mix and can be coarse or lightweight, i.e., slag, clay or shale.

Water must be free from impurities.

Mixing concrete

Either a 1:2:3 mix or a $1:2\frac{1}{2}:3\frac{1}{2}$ mix can be used for basement floors, paths, steps and terraces. In each case the aggregate should be not more than $1\frac{1}{2}$ in.; $\frac{3}{4}$ in. is ideal.

Obviously it is more practical to mix concrete in or near where you are laying it; wet concrete is heavy and awkward to carry. Work on a concrete or paved surface, and measure out the sand and aggregate first. Mix by turning with a shovel, then add the cement, mixing until the whole becomes an even color, minus any streaks. Now turn the mix over three more times; thorough mixing is very important to the finished product. Add water gradually, as too much will spoil the mix. As you near the correct consistency, add water by sprinkling rather than pouring.

Placing concrete

If the ground where concrete is to be laid is dry, dampen with water. Avoid dropping concrete into position, as aggregates will sink to the bottom. Large areas, those longer than 10 ft long, need expansion joints of $\frac{1}{2}$ in. board. These prevent the concrete cracking as it dries and shrinks.

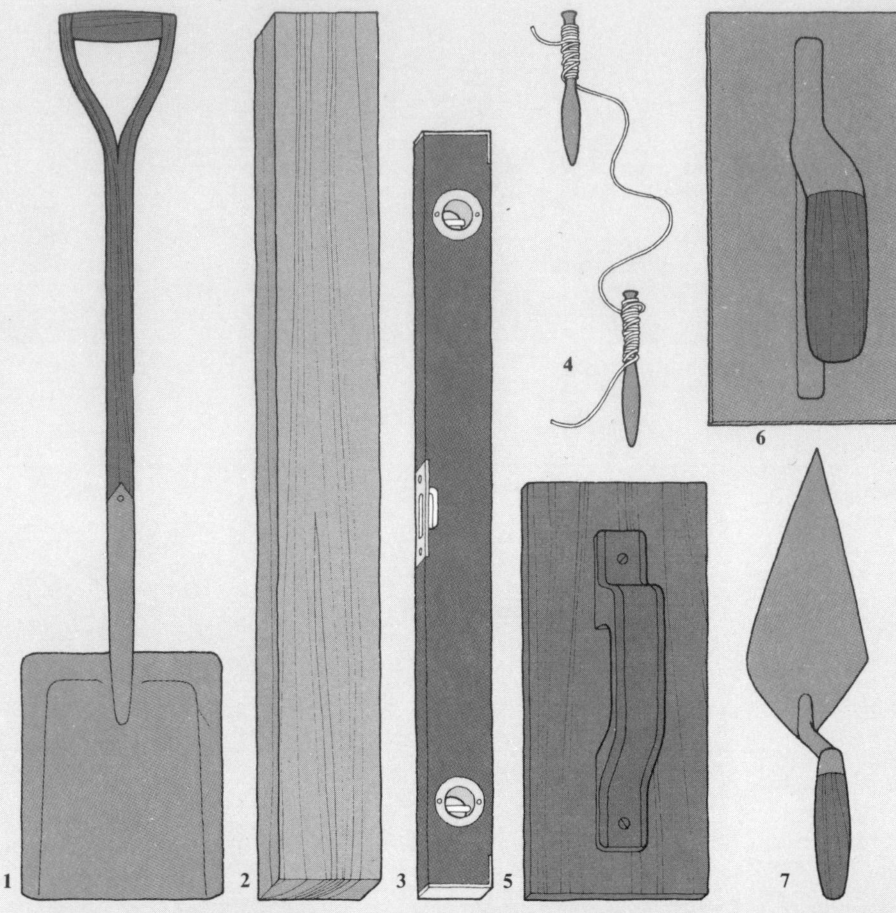

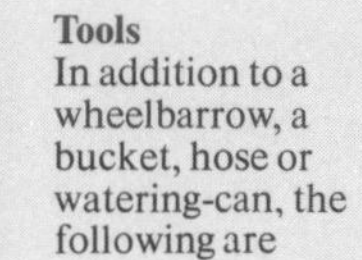

Tools
In addition to a wheelbarrow, a bucket, hose or watering-can, the following are needed:

1 Square shovel
This is ideal for mixing and placing concrete.

2 Strikeoff board
A straight length of lumber about 4 in. x 2 in. thick, this should project 6 in. beyond laying area.

3 Level
This should be about 4 ft long.

4 Lines and pins
These are used for setting out forms.

5 Wooden float
Use in same way as steel trowel, but for rough finish.

6 Steel trowel
Use for a smooth hard surface.

7 Trowel
This places small amounts of concrete.

Measuring ingredients
Use a bucket to measure out proportions, scrape off excess with a straight length of wood.

Adding water
Make a hole in pile of mix, and fill this with water. Add gradually, as too much water can spoil the mix.

Mixing ingredients
Gradually turn dry mix into the water until the whole becomes moist. Add water as needed.

Testing consistency
Draw shovel across top of mix, then make a series of ridges. When ridges remain well-defined, mix is ready.

Spreading concrete
Start in one corner and use shovel to spread as you go. Do not agitate concrete much at this stage.

Providing expansion joints
Control joints should be placed every 10 ft apart over large areas, to prevent concrete cracking.

Forms

These are the wooden frames that confine wet concrete to an appropriate shape. Make the forms from scrap lumber and cheap boards; the width of the wood should be as the depth of the concrete, and about 2 in. thick. Place dividing boards to fit width of the form, and at every 10 ft along the length of the concreting. Then have ½ in. softwood expansion boards butting against them on the side concreting is to begin. If concreting is to run along the wall, insert ½ in. thick asphalt-impregnated fiber strips between wall and concrete, as additional expansion joints. Drive stakes for the side boards and dividing boards into the ground to a depth of 12 in. and every 3 ft apart. Fix boards to the stakes. One side of the form should be slightly lower to allow for a slope on the surface of the concrete to disperse rain water - about ⅛ in. per foot of the path's width. Alternatively the form's sides should be set parallel at a similar angle to shed water over their length. Lay sections of concrete at a time, allowing the first section to harden so that you can remove dividing boards - the expansion joints remain. Finish surface with the appropriate trowel, or brush, during the two hour setting period.

Repairing concrete floors and steps
A cracked or holed floor can be patched with concrete to give it new life. If badly cracked, break up the entire surface with a sledge hammer, otherwise the new surface will swiftly crack and craze. Compact the broken material firmly, and fill depressions with a similar hardcore. Dampen the surface and lay a 1:2:2 mix.

Patch small areas with either a brand name compound, or a 1:2:3 mix. First remove loose material with a chisel, and finally a brush. Dampen surfaces, make a paste with cement powder and water, and apply to surfaces. Before this has dried, fill with the patching compound or mix, pushing well under edges. Finish small areas with a slightly raised surface to compensate for shrinkage. To patch damaged steps, cut the edge as shown (right). Brush out loose material and seal with a brand name compound, or cement paste. Fill with a 1:2:2 mix, and trowel it into the recess. Leave at least a week before removing the supporting board and using the step.

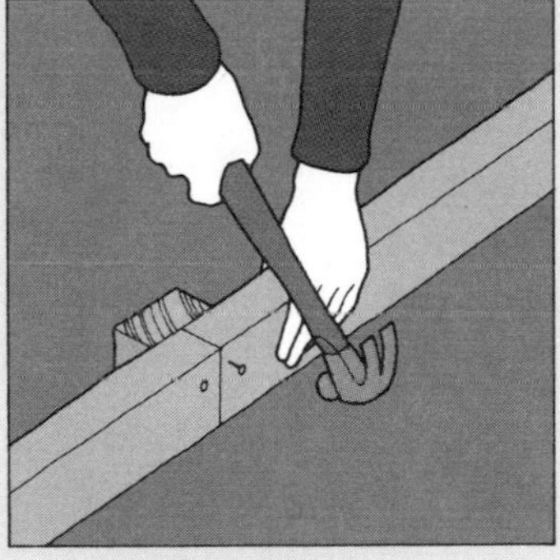

Securing form boards
Nail these to insides of stakes. Avoid leaving gaps between adjacent board lengths.

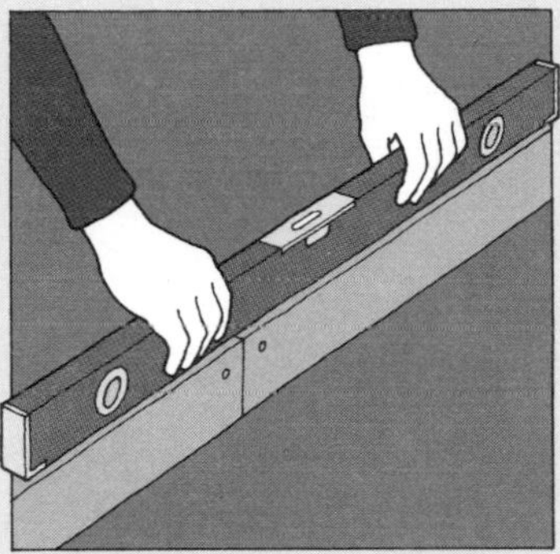

Leveling boards
Make frequent checks with the level to see that top edges of boards are at the same height.

Using the strikeoff board
Tamp down surface of the concrete flush with tops of boards. Strike off any excess concrete.

Leveling with the float
Use a wood float to smooth over the surface of the concrete, and to give it a slightly rough finish.

Surfacing concrete
Use a bristle brush for a skid-resistant surface, or a steel trowel for a smooth surface.

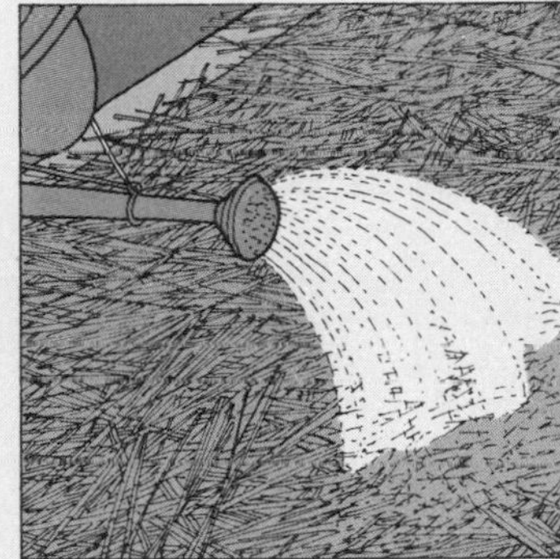

Retarding the drying
Wet concrete frequently and cover with plastic sheet. Do not remove forms for at least 6 days.

Repairing a damaged area
Remove all loose material to a depth of about 1 in. with a chisel. Undercut edges of sound concrete.

Filling in cavity
Dampen surfaces and apply cement paste. Fill with concrete, pushing well under edges. Finish with float.

Leveling off with strikeoff board
For a large area, use the strikeoff board with a sawing motion to remove excess. Finish with float.

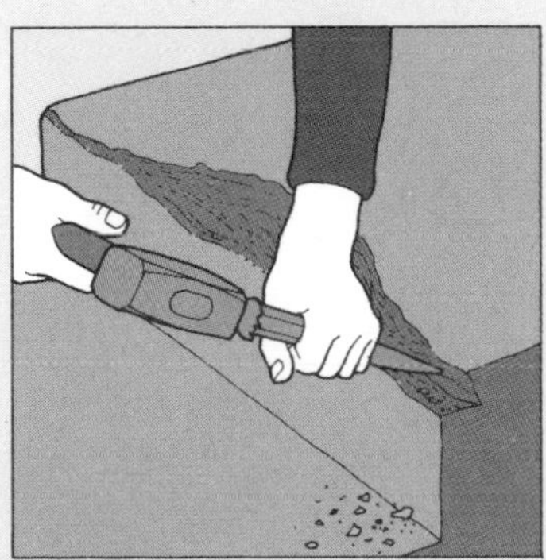

Undercutting front edge of step
Use a cold chisel to cut away about 1 in. from top of sound material. Undercut to grip new concrete.

Mounting a support board
Place a board in front of riser with top of board flush with top of step. Keep board in place with brick.

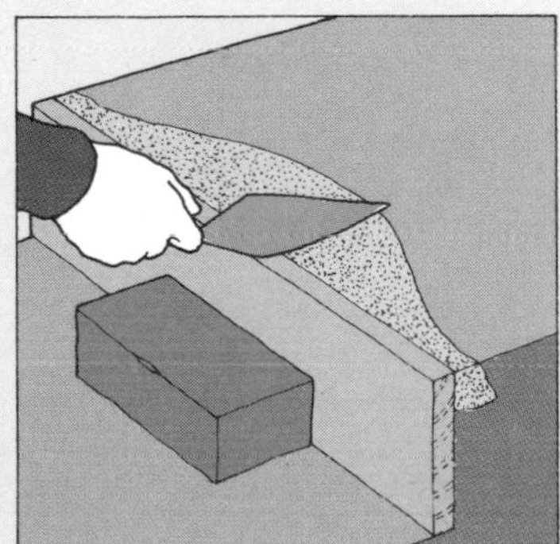

Filling new concrete
Leave surface slightly raised to allow for shrinkage when drying. Smooth with a wet trowel.

Repairing & Renovating Floors

Wood Floors

Types of floorboards
Floorboards are either square edged or tongued and grooved. The first kind butt tightly against each other, the second kind interlock and are the more efficient. The point where a floorboard covers a joist is fixed with two cut floor brads, their heads punched below the surface. Brads prevent the wood from splitting.

Filling gaps between boards
Gaps not only create drafts, but cause floor coverings to wear unevenly: vinyl or linoleum will mold itself to the profile of the floor, revealing every imperfection in the surface. There are two things you can do: either you fill the gaps between the boards, or you lift the boards and re-lay them. How you fill gaps depends on the width: large gaps can be filled with strips of softwood, gaps less than ¼ in. can be filled with papier mache, or a more expensive brand name filler paste. Scrape out the gaps, then sweep the floor. Make sure all the boards are securely fixed to the joists and all nail heads punched beneath the surface. Shred a number of newspapers into a bucket and add boiling water to make a thick pulp. When the mixture is cool, add wallpaper adhesive powder and stir until thick and stiff. Use a putty knife to press the paste between boards. After two or three days, the surface can be rubbed down with sandpaper. To fill large gaps, cut strips of wood each slightly wider than the gap, to be planed to a tight fit. These should have a slight wedge shape to assist hammering. Ends of strips must come to the centers of joists, and be fixed with a 1½ in. nail.

Re-laying boards
Start by lifting the first board next to the one beneath the baseboard. Lift near the joist (where the floor brads are located) and follow the sequence as shown on the right. Tongue and groove boards have first to be unlocked with a backsaw: saw carefully in case you cut a cable or pipe beneath. As a precaution, turn off the services. Use the wedge technique to tighten the boards together. Cut three pairs of wedges. Position one pair on the edge of the board at the center, with other pairs at each end. Hammer wedges until the boards bind evenly, then nail boards to the joists. When you have driven all nail heads beneath the surface, the floor can be sanded.

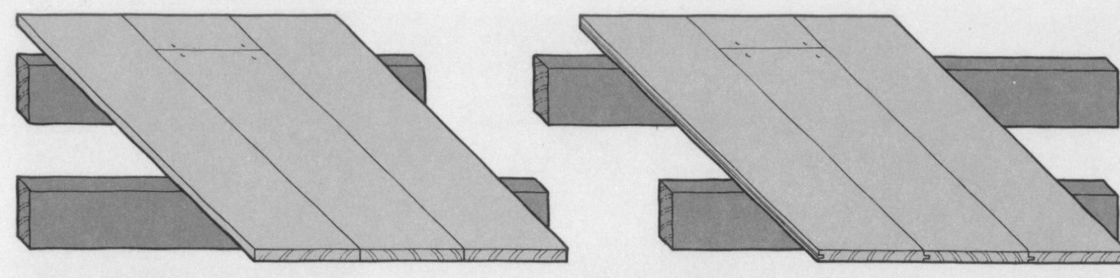

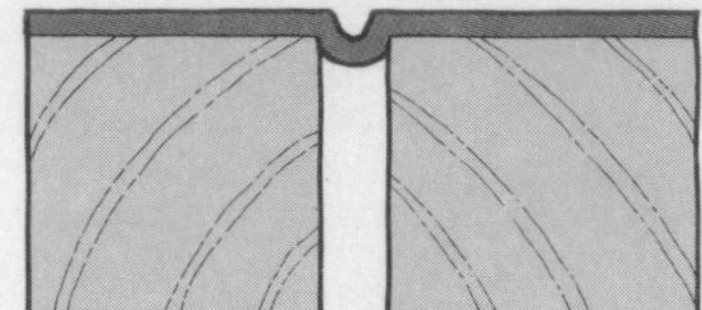

Square edge
These boards butt against each other. Where gaps occur, floor coverings like vinyl wear unevenly.

Tongue and groove
Off-center tongue creates a deep shoulder. Lay this side uppermost to gain maximum wear.

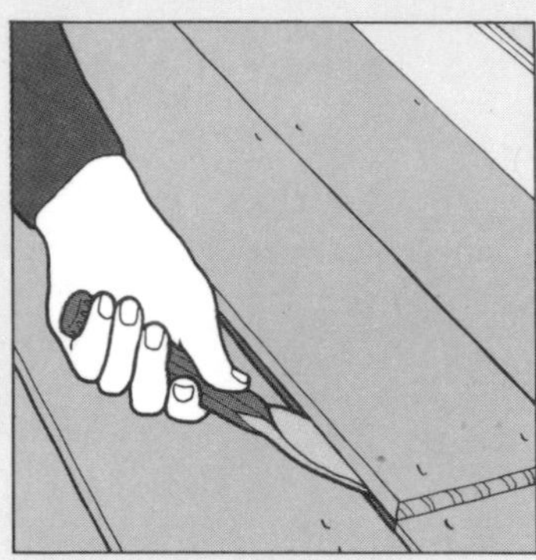

Lifting square edge boards
Insert the chisel between two boards near a joist. Lever to and fro until board begins to lift.

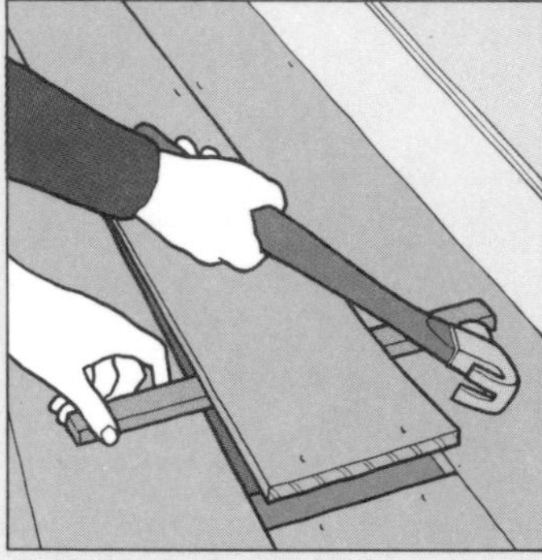

Wedging the free end
Use the claw of a hammer and the chisel together. Ease up end until you can slip a length of wood under.

Lifting tongue and groove boards
Cut through the tongue of the first board with a backsaw, then use the chisel technique as before.

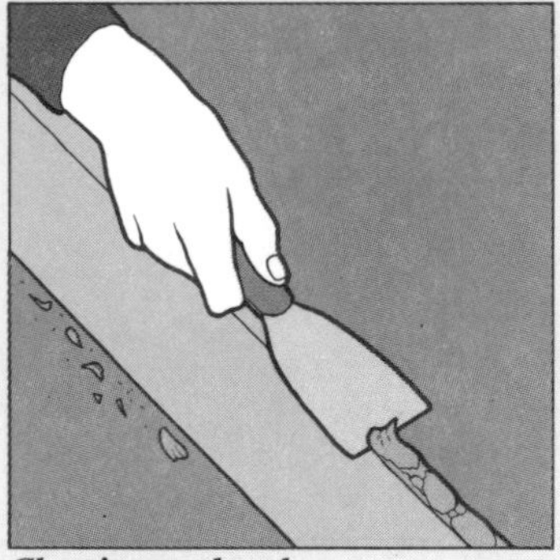

Cleaning up the edges
When all the boards have been lifted, clean them with a scraper to ensure a tight fit when re-laying.

Re-laying the boards
Begin where the last boards were lifted. Lay four boards on the joists and a pair of wedges as shown.

Securing the wedges
Use a spare piece of board and nail it to the joists so that the wedges are tightly clamped between boards.

Hammering wedges together
Use a pair of hammers to drive wedges against each other. This will tighten up loose boards.

Securing the boards
When the boards are binding evenly, nail them to the joists. Repeat wedge technique with remaining boards.

Finishing off
When you are left with a gap less than a board's width, cut and plane a board to fit. Punch down all nails.

Wood and Concrete Floors

Replacing a worn floor
Badly-worn floorboards should be replaced or covered with flooring-grade particle board, usually sold in sheets 8ft x 4ft and ¾ in. thick. Remove a few floorboards to determine the distance between joists. If they are either 16 in. or 24 in. apart, you can use full-size sheets without cutting, except for length and when fitting around projections or into recesses. Particle board must be supported on all edges, and fixed so that the edges rest along the center line of the joists; edges at right angles to joists must be supported by cross members, fitted flush with the joists and toenailed with 3 in. wire nails.

Covering floorboards
Use ½ in. particle board and secure it to the floor with 2½ in. wire nails, spaced 12 in. apart. Before laying the board, the floorboards must be well nailed to the joists, the surface smooth and sound. If necessary, plane off high points. Use a punch to drive all nail heads beneath the surface. If some floorboards are too springy, screw them to the joists with 1½ in. screws, countersunk.

Lifting the floor
Remove the baseboard and floorboards and pull out any projecting nail heads from the joists.

Cleaning up joists
Scrape tops of joists clean, and brush away any loose material.

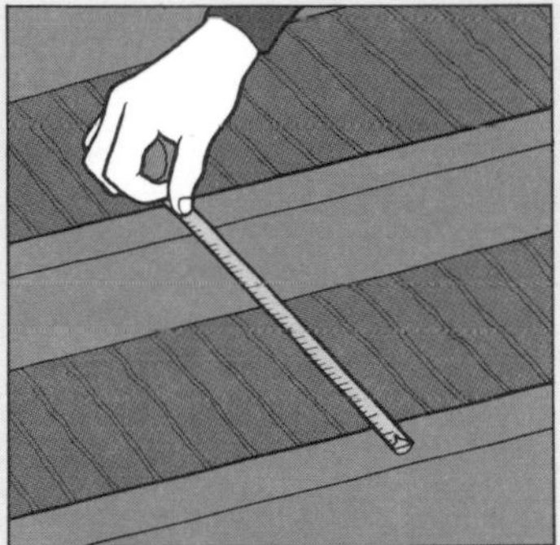

Calculating amounts of board
Measure space between joists (usually 16 or 24 in.). Boards 4 ft wide will span joists without being cut.

Fixing cross supports
Nail 3 x 2 in. softwood cross members where needed to support edges of boards.

Positioning boards
Lay boards on joists. Drill countersunk pilot holes at 12 in. intervals, except at the corners.

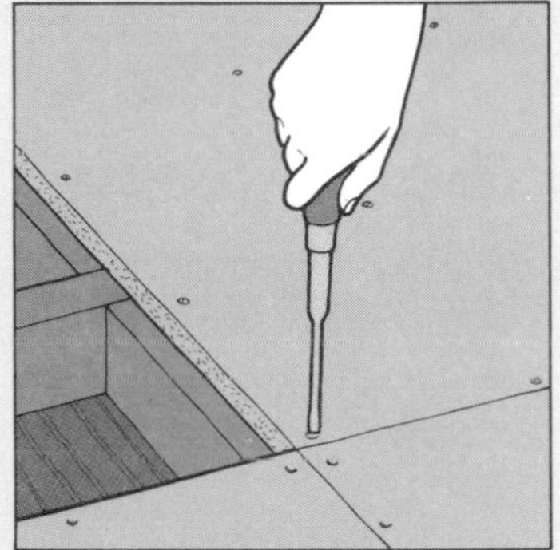

Securing firmly to joists
Use 2 in. screws, staggering the position of screws in adjacent boards except at corners.

Hardboard flooring
Hardboard should be laid rough face up, unless you intend it as a finished surface. Sheets are made in standard sizes, 8ft x 4ft x ⅛ in. thick. Cut them into 4ft squares. The floor must be prepared as for particle board. Hardboard should be allowed to stand on edge for 48 hours where it is to be laid. If there is no central heating, sponge the sheets with water beforehand. Set them out as shown on the right, nailing down with hardboard nails, 6 in. apart. If used as a finished surface, seal with polyurethane.

Preparing the surface for hardboard
Punch all nail heads below the surface. Plane level any high points.

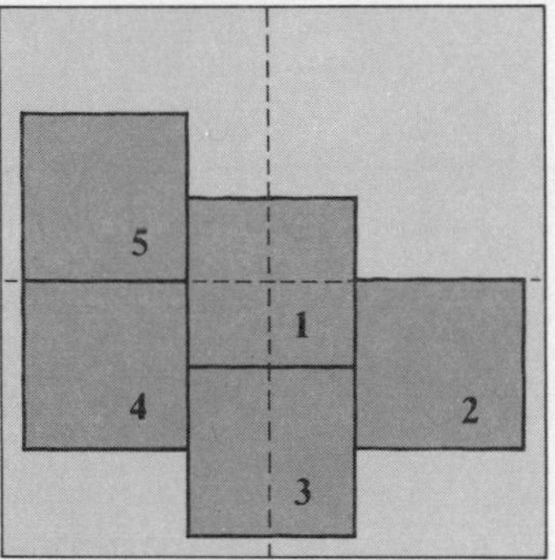

Setting out the boards
Mark center lines of room. Position first board to bisect these lines. Lay successive boards clockwise.

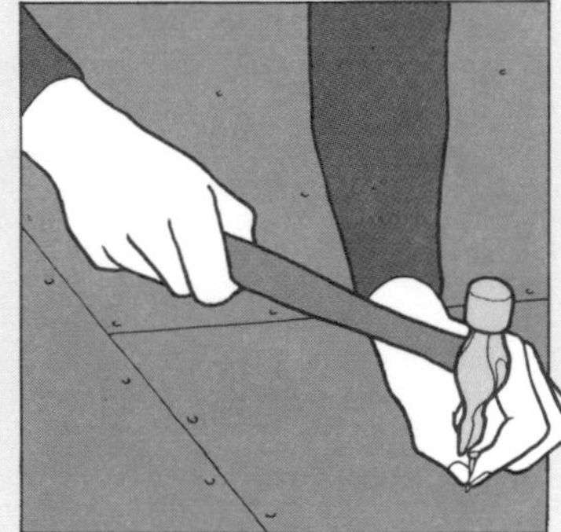

Securing the boards
Nail each board, starting at the center and work outward evenly toward the edges.

Re-surfacing a concrete floor
A concrete floor may need to be smoothed and leveled before you can lay wood block, cork or vinyl tiles. Use a self-leveling compound, sold in a powder form. This will mix with water to the consistency of thick cream. If floor is already tiled, loose ones must be re-laid. Fill any holes with sand and cement mix. Smooth rough surfaces. Coat quarry tiles with adhesive primer; damp concrete with water. Pour compound on floor a yard at a time, and spread with a float, work toward the door. Leave for 7 hours.

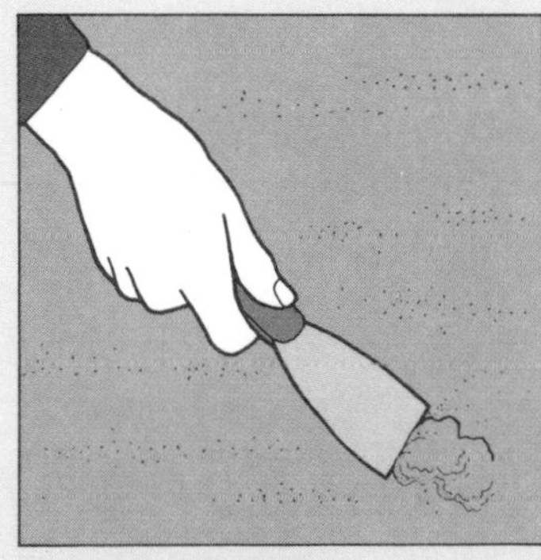

Smoothing the surface
Scrape off any projections on the existing floor with a paint scraper. Sandpaper rough patches.

Treating the surface
Give non-absorbent surfaces a coat of adhesive primer; dampen absorbent ones with fresh water.

Re-surfacing with compound
Apply self-smoothing mixture with a steel float; spread evenly a yard at a time, to about ⅛ in. thickness.

Fireplaces

Improving Fireplaces

Removing the framing
Fireplace framing can be unexpectedly heavy, so two people may be necessary to remove it. First have the chimney swept. Next, find the metal fixing bolts that secure the framing to the wall: cast iron, tiled or wood fire framings are usually invisibly fixed with screws through lugs. Locate the screws by tapping the plaster with the handle of a screwdriver, listening for a difference in sound. Unless the framing is made of marble, it will come away in one piece. Brick framings must be broken up in situ.

Filling in a fireplace
The best way of blocking up an opening is to use bricks, covered to match the existing finish. The new bricks do not need to be bonded to the surrounding ones (see pp. 84-85), but the brickwork should be slightly recessed so that when plastered the new surface is flush with the existing one. If possible, provide ventilation with a perforated terracotta brick, eventually to be covered with a plastic grille. Before plastering rake out the brick joints to a depth of about ½ in. to make a rough surface for the new plaster.

Curing faults
Chimneys in regular use should be swept once every two years, and appliance flues must also be cleaned. Both too little and too much air will cause a fire to smoke or burn poorly. If your room is insulated against drafts, there is probably insufficient ventilation for the fire. Smoke may be caused by an adjacent exhaust fan and boiler sucking air out: fit a perforated brick in the wall, near the boiler. Regularly check pointing on the chimney stack; faulty brickwork causes the flue to become saturated with rainwater, resulting in condensation.

Repairing fire chambers
Fire chambers are made of fireproof clay, but small cracks sometimes develop and need to be filled. These repairs should not be made for 48 hours after there has been a fire in the grate, in order to give the fire chambers time to cool down thoroughly. Before filling, the cracks need to be slightly undercut with the tip of a pointing trowel, and brushed to clear out all loose particles. Use fireclay cement to fill the cracks, pressing it well in. Clean off excess with the trowel. Leave the fire chamber for at least 24 hours before lighting a fire.

Exposing the screws
Pry away molding or hack off plaster around the fireplace to expose screw heads securing bolts. Remove the screws.

Removing the framing
With an assistant steadying the framing, use a crowbar to ease it away from the wall, starting at the top and sides of the mantel.

Removing a stone or brick trim
Hack out the mortar between joints with a ¼ in. cape chisel and hammer. Remove pieces individually, using a crowbar and working downward.

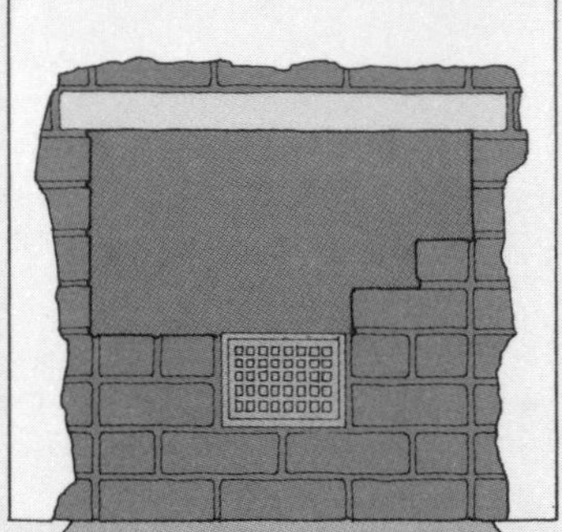

Filling with bricks
Hack off plaster to expose 3 in. of brickwork around opening. Lay 4½ in. thick brickwork in opening, slightly recessed.

Securing the brickwork
Center perforated brick in the opening, above baseboard level. Cut and nail 2 in. strips of metal across junctions of new and old brickwork.

Plastering the surface
Plaster entire surface with the exception of perforated brick, so that it lies flush with the surrounding plaster. Cover with plastic grille.

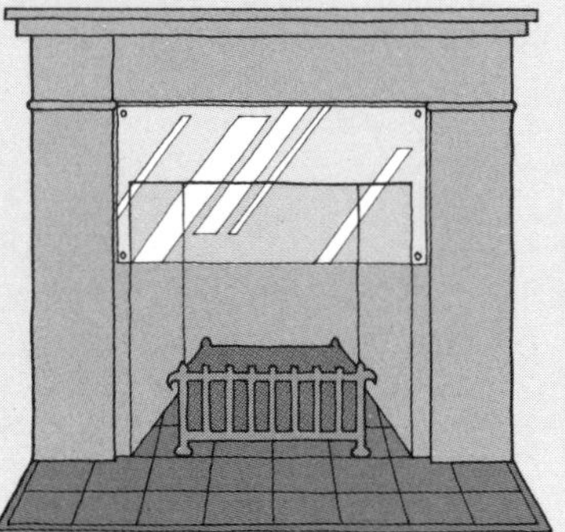

Improving the draw
If the draft is too strong, fit a metal hood or toughened glass screen across top of opening.

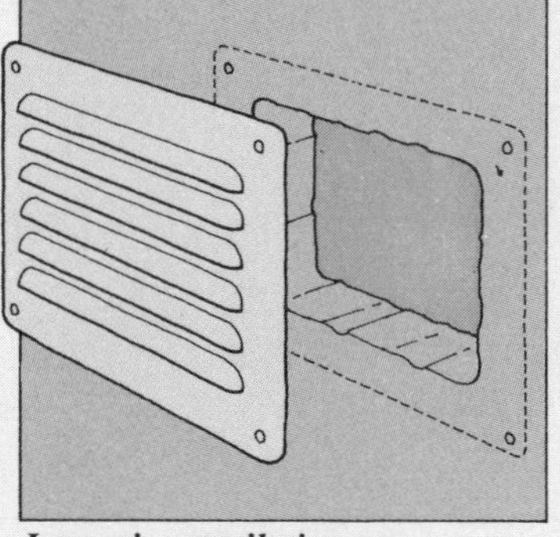

Improving ventilation
Bore a hole through the top of room's door to provide a through draft. Cover with a slotted plate.

Fitting a cap
Condensation may mean rainwater is entering the chimney flue. Fit a rain or draft deflector to it.

Cleaning off soot
Close the damper, and brush off any deposits from the fire chamber with a brush before filling cracks.

Filling cracks
Soak the surface of the fire chamber with clean water. Fill cracks while still wet, using a trowel.

Smoothing the finish
Clean off any excess filler with the edge of the trowel. Then gently rub surface of cement with a wet finger.

Replacing a lintel
An old fireplace can be revitalized if you hack off the surrounding plaster to expose the original brickwork. Bring out the natural colors of the bricks with a coat of clear polyurethane or, if the brickwork is in poor condition, paint it white or a strong color. When removing the plaster, a concrete lintel spanning the opening may be revealed. As long as the opening is no wider than about 39 in. the lintel and the bricks above it can be safely replaced with a brick arch supported on an iron bracket, as shown right. Mortar the bricks in place, and point to match the framing.

Fitting a stove
Most free standing stoves need to be linked with an airtight seal to a conventional flue. A stove with a rear outlet as opposed to a top outlet is the most suitable. Remove the existing appliance and the framing, and have the chimney swept. It is easier to cut an accurate hole for the outlet sleeve after the opening has been bricked up than to build the brickwork around it. Plaster the new brickwork flush with the surrounding plaster. When dry, position the stove on the hearth, and seal the sleeve in the outlet.

Creating a display space
Remove the appliance and the fire chamber, and have the chimney swept. Fit a terminal or cap to the chimney flue. If the opening is high and wide, you can improve the proportions by raising the hearth level. Joints between old and new brickwork will need to be reinforced with expanded metal if you want a plaster finish. With fair-faced brickwork, cut out alternate courses to bond in with new bricks (see pp. 84-85). Fill in the recess with rubble and finish the top flush with a weak mix of sand and cement.

Removing stains
Soot stains can be shifted from brick or stone with clean water and vigorous scrubbing with a fiber (not wire) scrubbing brush. Clean slate with pumice powder and mild detergent. Rinse with fresh water and buff the surface with a lint-free cloth. Marble can be cleaned with a paste made of hydrogen peroxide and powdered whiting, with a few drops of ammonia. Apply paste to the stain, leave a few minutes, then rinse off with hot water. Polish afterward. Remove fine scratches with wet or dry paper. If stains are very obstinate, rub a cut lemon on them and rinse.

Making a brick arch
1 If the fireplace lintel is concrete, remove it after taking out the triangle of brickwork above it. You can then build a new brick arch.

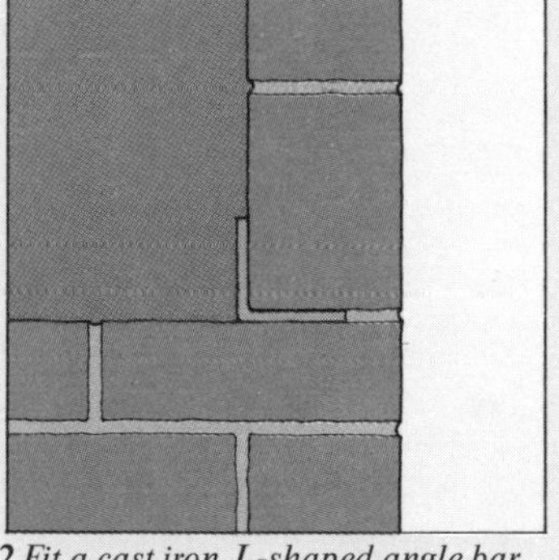
2 Fit a cast iron, L-shaped angle bar across the opening to support the bricks. It should be 2x2 in., ¼ in. thick, and wide enough to bear at least 3 in. on each side.

3 Choose matching bricks if possible. Should the width of the fireplace opening be narrower than its height cut the bricks so that they are about 6 in. long.

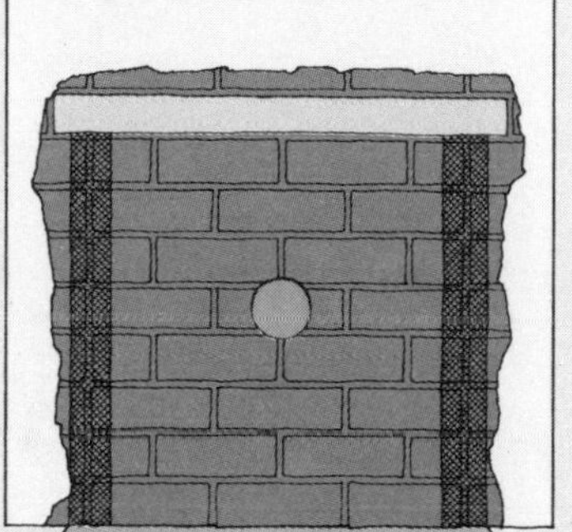
Installing a free standing stove
1 Block up the opening with bricks. Leave brickwork to dry before cutting the outlet. Use a chisel and hammer; cut the hole to match the sleeve.

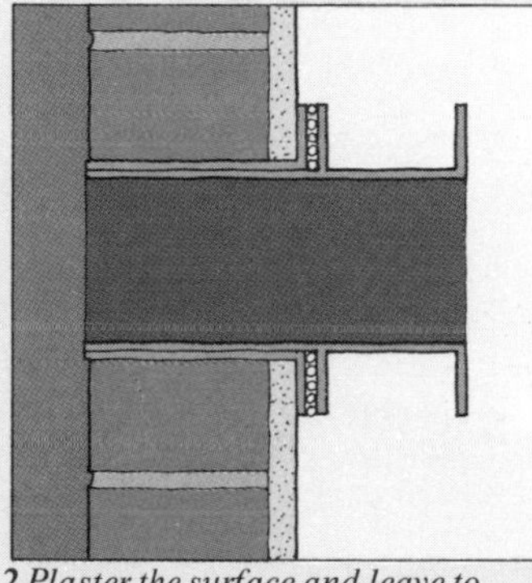
2 Plaster the surface and leave to dry. Fit sleeve outlet. This may be either cemented or glued to the plaster to make an airtight seal between sleeve and wall.

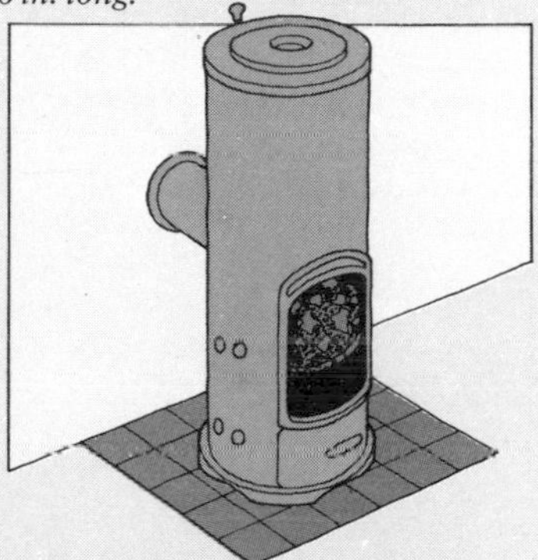
3 Fit the flue into the sleeve outlet, and seal the joint between them with soft asbestos rope. Joint with fireclay cement.

Making a display space
1 Remove the existing hearth and lay two courses of bricks across opening, flush with brickwork framing.

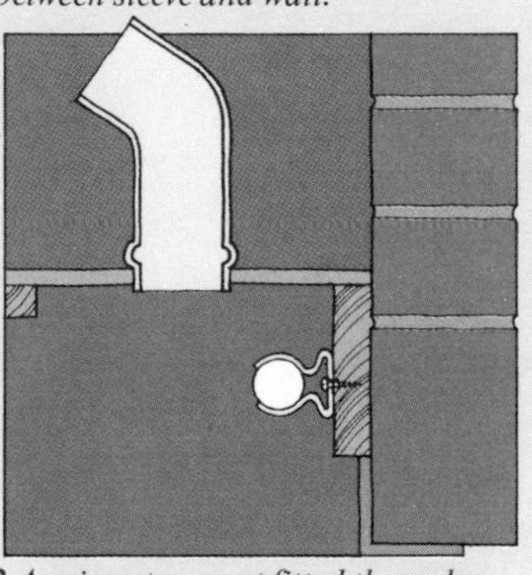
2 A rainwater spout fitted through a board will provide ventilation and prevent grit falling through; a strip light can be fixed behind the lintel.

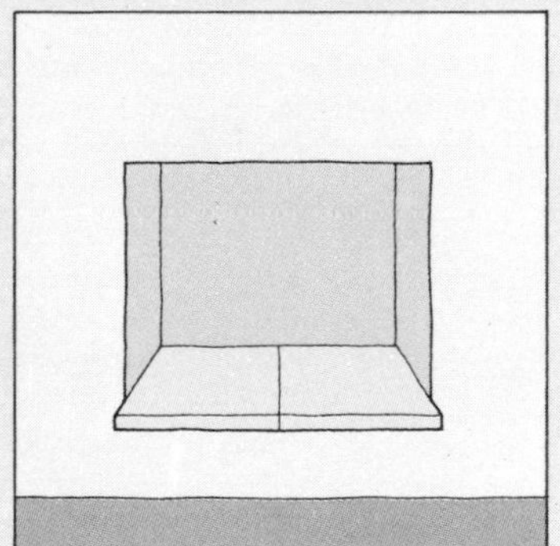
3 The bottom and sides of the opening can be lined with stone, slate or marble, which can project in front by about 4 in.

Removing stains on brickwork
1 Use a scrub brush or a medium grade sandpaper. Avoid detergents, soap or abrasive powders.

2 Remove stubborn stains with muriatic acid and water. Wear rubber gloves and goggles when using acid.

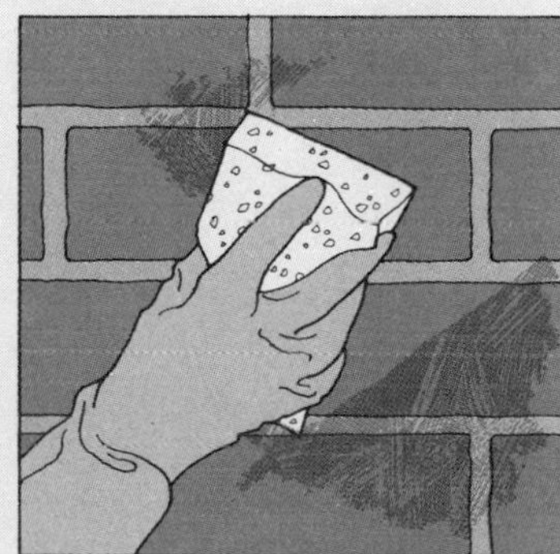
3 After applying acid with a soft brush, leave it for a few minutes; then wash it off with plenty of water to ensure it is neutralized.

Repairing Window Frames

Sash Windows

A double-hung window has two sashes which are counterbalanced by springs or weights. The type counterbalanced by weights has a recess on the top outer edge to which the cord is secured by knots or nails; some have a chain fixed by screws. A different type of balance is provided by the spring balanced and spring lift mechanisms. The former has a spring inside a revolving drum, recessed into each side of the framework. Attached to the end of the spring is a nylon tape with a metal loop on the end. The loop fits over a hook on an L-shaped metal bracket screwed to the top corners of the sash. A spring lift sash has a metal spiral rod inside a metal tube, fixed to the sides of the framework. The rod is attached to a spring within the tube, tensioned to balance the weight of the window. Both mechanisms are easier to replace than cords or chains, and it may be worth replacing a broken cord with a spring mechanism.

Fitting new sash cords

In time sash cords fray and eventually break. The fracture causes the weighted end to drop down the side channels in the framework, to the bottom of the sash weight pockets. If one cord breaks it is advisable to replace the other three at the same time, since you will have to remove the windows anyway. It is a simple matter to remove the molding nailed to the side of the framework and to lift the window out. The technique is shown on the right. If you intend fitting a replacement cord, be sure to use the special plaited kind, that is also waxed and rot-proof. Measure and cut new cords according to the lengths of the old ones. Check the pulley to see that it revolves freely, and lubricate with a drop of oil. Feed the new cord over the pulley and down the channel to the weight pocket. If this proves difficult, tie a piece of twine to the cord, and a small weight, such as a bent nail, to the twine and pass it over the pulley. Slip the cord through the counterweight, using a figure of eight knot to secure it. Prepare the cord and weight on the opposite side in the same way. Get an assistant to help you support the sash while fixing the other ends of the cords. If you are replacing the cord with a chain, attach the chain to the counterweight with wire, and screw the other end to the sash frame.

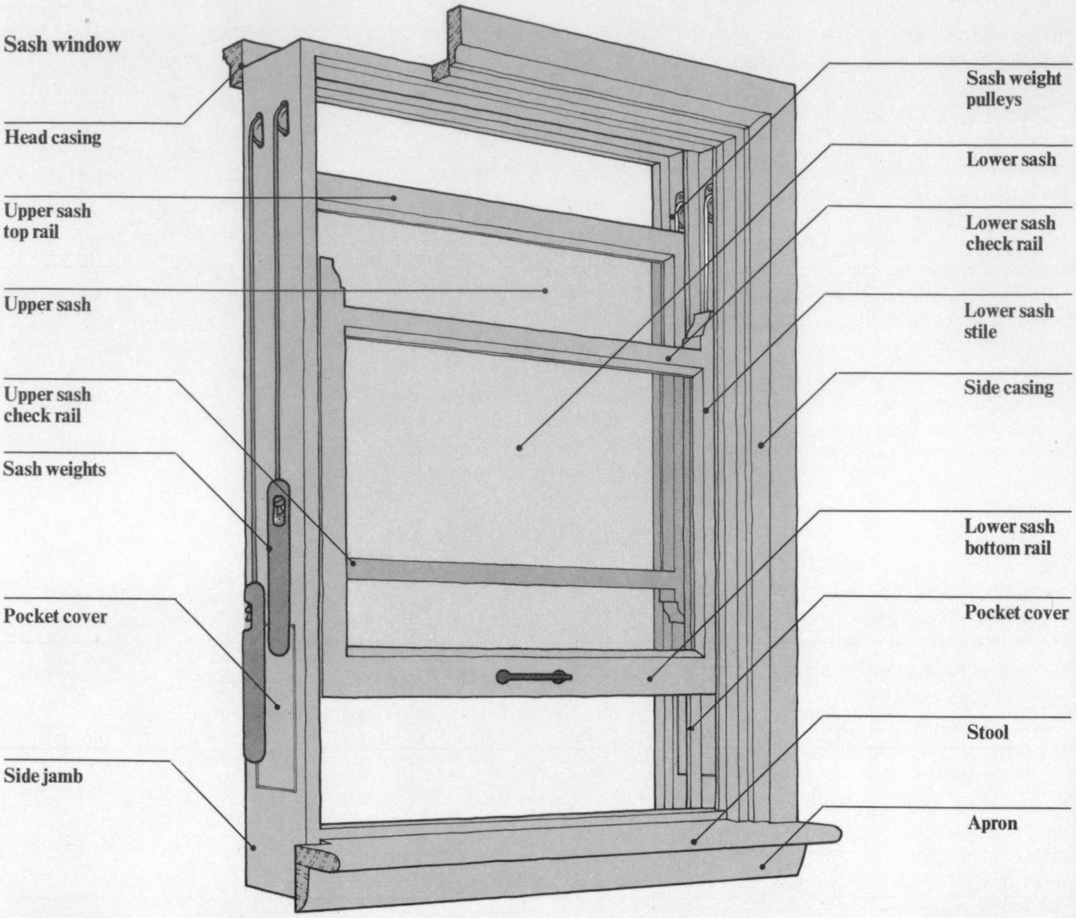

Sash window
Head casing
Upper sash top rail
Upper sash
Upper sash check rail
Sash weights
Pocket cover
Side jamb
Sash weight pulleys
Lower sash
Lower sash check rail
Lower sash stile
Side casing
Lower sash bottom rail
Pocket cover
Stool
Apron

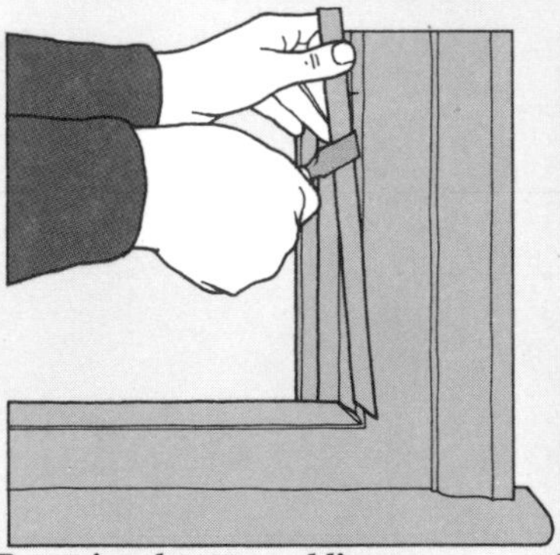

Removing the stop molding
Gently pry off the molding or the stop with an old chisel or a broad screwdriver.

Taking out the sash window
If there is an intact sash cord, cut it and lower the weight. Lift out the sash and put it aside.

Removing the top sash
Next take off the parting strip that separates the two sash windows, and remove the upper sash.

Taking out the weight
Unscrew or lift out the small covers at the bottom of the sash weight channels; lift out the weights.

Replacing a new cord
Slip the old cord from the eye in the weight. Feed new cord over pulley to channel bottom. Knot into weight.

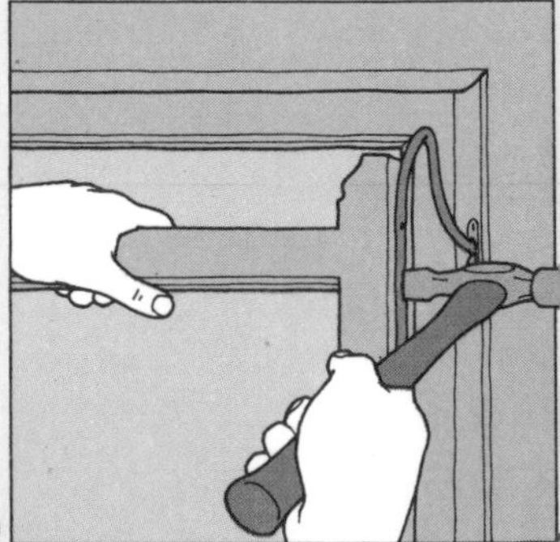

Nailing to the sash
Sash fixing is either knotted or nailed. If the latter, use three nails through centerline of cord spaced apart.

Fitting a spring lift sash

After a time, spring lift sashes lose their tension, or occasionally break. They are easily re-tensioned by unscrewing the tube holding the spring from the window frame. Keep a firm hold of the tube, otherwise it will unwind. A weak tension is evident by the sash window failing to ascend satisfactorily; turn the tube clockwise a few times to tighten the spring. If the spring is too tight, unwind by turning it anticlockwise. Should the spring break you will have to take the window out and remove the mechanism – not a difficult job. The sash windows having spring lift mechanisms slide up and down in twin-channel aluminum sections. The metal parting strip will need to be hammered flat to get the window out. With the window removed, you can unscrew the L-brackets from the bottom of the sash frame, ready to replace with a new unit: raise the sash to its half height position, with the new unit attached to the sash frame. Insert the screw through the tube, and turn it the number of times recommended by the makers, in a clockwise direction. Screw the tube back to the frame, and straighten the metal parting strip.

Tensioning the spring tube
1 Undo the screw securing the top of the tube to the side of the frame.

2 Now turn the tube until the required tension is reached, and replace the screw.

Replacing a broken spring
1 Flatten the metal strip with a wood block and a hammer.

2 Remove the tube as before, using a thin bladed knife to ease the sash past the metal parting strip.

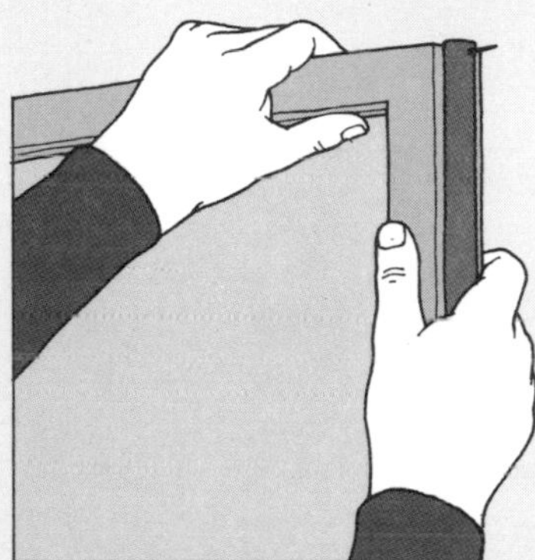

3 The tube travels in a groove along the edge of the sash. The twist rod is fixed at the bottom by an L-bracket.

4 Unscrew L-brackets to remove entire mechanism. Tension replacement unit, then screw into place.

Fitting a spring balance

To replace counterweights, first remove the sash cords and weights as previously described and the two pulleys. Locate the hook adaptor bracket over the cord channels in the top of the sash frame, and secure in position with flat head screws. The spring drum should fit into the pulley recess, but you may need to cut a shallow housing for the base plate with a chisel. Screw the drum into place, then hook the tapes over the adaptor hooks. When you buy a spring balance, make sure it suits the weight of your window.

Fitting a spring balance
1 Fit the two adaptor hooks over the cord channels each side of frame.

2 Insert the spring drum into the pulley hole, cut a housing if needed, and screw into position.

3 Pull the tape loops over the hooks on the brackets, and hang the sash, fit back the molding or parting strip.

When windows stick

This is invariably due to fresh paint hardening between the moving parts, or a new window where the wood has swollen. Tap around the sash frame with a hammer and small block of wood. Alternatively, use a broad bladed knife. Should either of these fail, remove the sash frame and rub down surfaces with coarse sandpaper, or plane them flat. Oil any crank handles and hinges at least once a year. If damp patches appear around the window, this may be caused by an external gap. Fill the gap with mastic.

Windows stuck with paint
Tap edge of a broad-bladed scraper between the sash and frame.

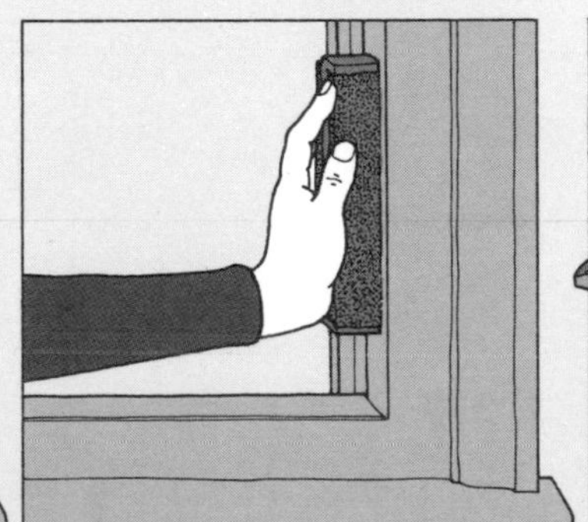

Sanding down
Take out the sash frame and rub channel with coarse sandpaper.

Planing a sash frame
Rub a pencil over the edges to reveal irregularities, then plane flat.

Replacing Glass

Broken Window Panes

Take care when you re-glaze a broken window to wear protective gloves and to handle glass properly. If you are inexperienced, it is better to leave repairs to upper floor windows to a professional. To remove broken glass, start at the top and work down, easing each part out piece by piece. The technique is described on the right, below. Open the window, or adjacent window if the frame is fixed. When all glass and old putty has been removed, clean out the frame down to the bare wood or metal with sandpaper or a wire brush.

Repairs to wood framed windows
Brush away dust; coat frame's surface with linseed oil or thinned primer. This will prevent the wood absorbing oils in the putty or glazing compound and causing it to dry out and crack. Leave four or five hours before installing new glass. Measure frame's inside edges at top and bottom both vertically and horizontally, and check that the frame is square. Have glass cut to size, less ⅛ in. overall to ensure glass is not too tight a fit. Apply a thin layer of putty or glazing compound in the rabbets of the frame. The purpose of putty is to seal the glass in the frame, but the seal must be resilient, otherwise the brittle glass might crack.
As further security, small headless nails or glazier's points hold the glass in place either secured by a

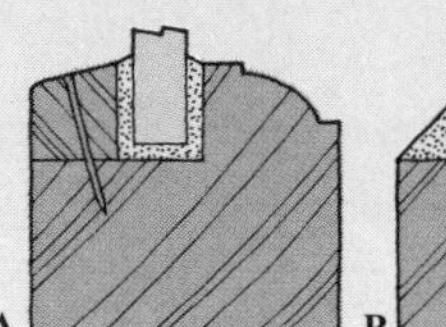

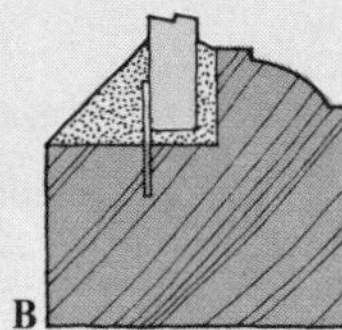

batten **A**, or by putty, **B.** Remove excess putty from the back. With additional putty or compound, make a rope of about ½ in. diameter, rolling it between your hands, and press it into the frame. Smooth the surface with a putty knife, and finish at a beveled angle so that it slopes from the glass down to the edge of the frame. Dip the knife in water as you work, and finish by mitering the corners. Clean the glass with thinner before smear marks dry hard. Leave the putty for about three to four weeks or more, in order to develop a hard skin, and paint it to match the framework. Take the paint beyond the putty and on to the glass, to seal the joint.

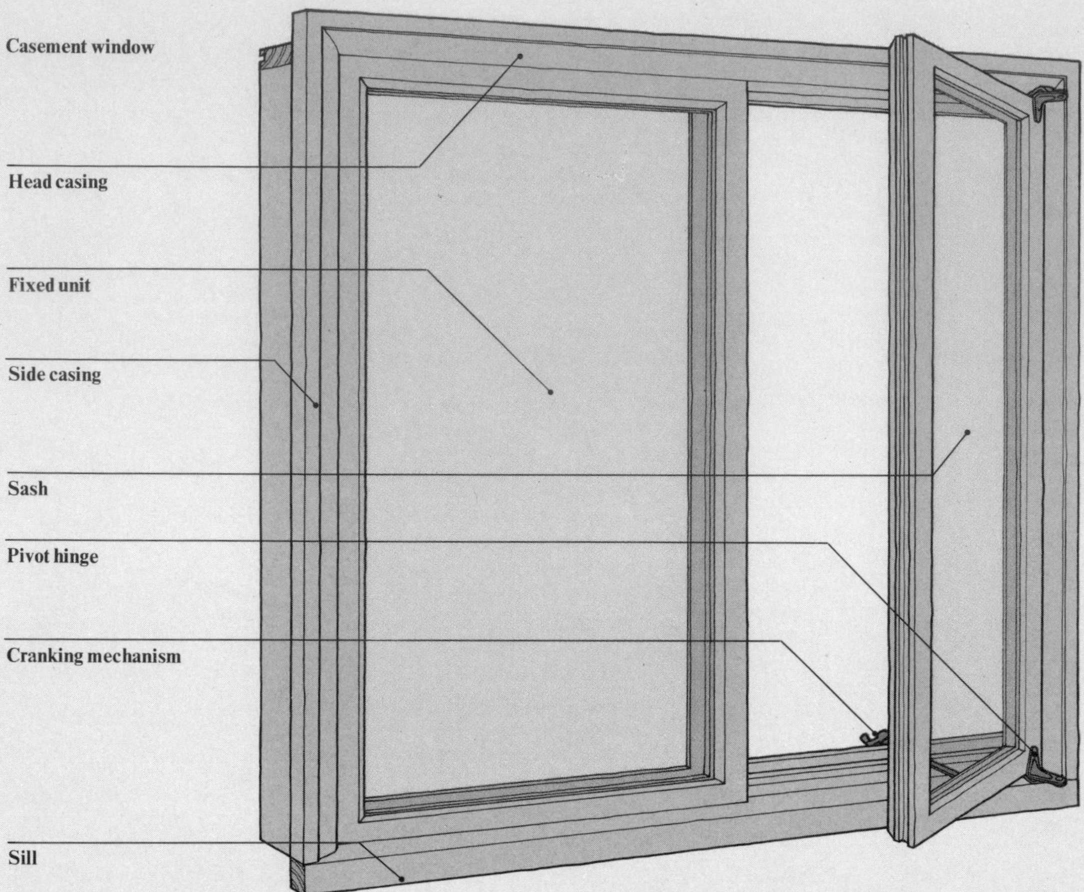

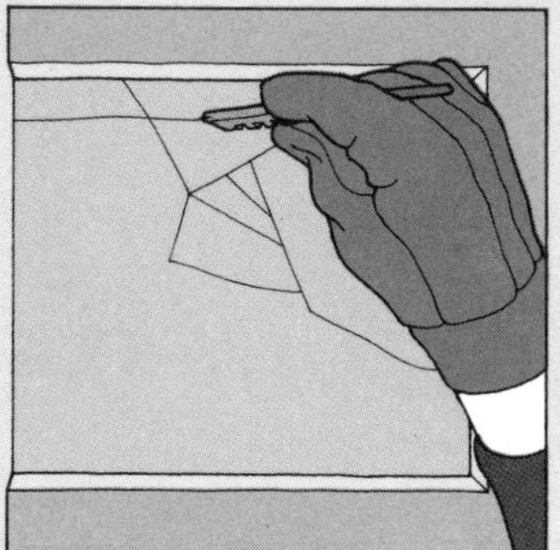

Replacing a broken pane
1 If the glass is cracked, use a glass cutter to score a line around the edge, about 1 in. from the frame.

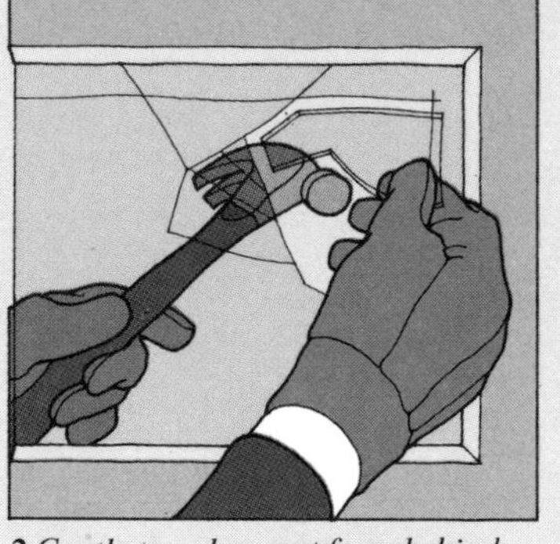

2 Gently tap glass out from behind, steadying it from the front with the other hand. Break glass out in small fragments.

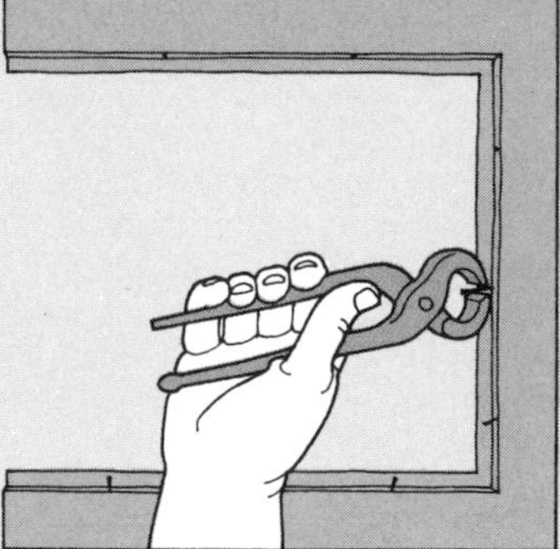

3 Remove all remaining glass and putty from frame using an old chisel or screwdriver. Use nippers to pull out glazier's points or nails.

4 Mold putty with fingers to make it pliable. Press putty into the frame using your fingers or putty knife. Make a bed ⅛ in. thick for glass.

5 Install glass, bottom edge first, pressing edges into putty until well bedded. Bevel the edge, miter corners and remove excess putty.

6 Gently tap glazier's points in front of glass. Leave for 3 weeks before painting. Seal joint by painting beyond putty.

Decorative windows

Small panes of glass are frequently held in place by double and single channeled lead rods. To replace a broken pane, cut the corner and fold back the outer edges of the rod **1** to expose the glass and tap it out from the opposite side. Clean out any debris from the grooves. Make a template from a piece of heavy paper to establish the shape of the new pane. Hold the paper against the empty space, and rub the impression through with a wax crayon. Cut out the shape and test it in place. Transfer the shape to a fresh piece of paper, lay the glass on it, and cut the glass a fraction smaller than the template pattern, using a straight edge ruler **2.** Mix a little gold size with a little putty, sufficient for the pane, to accelerate drying and reduce shrinkage. Press this mixture into the open grooves with a putty knife. Press the pane in place and fold back the lead flat against the glass. Scrape off excess putty, and finally smooth the lead rod with the round handle of a screwdriver, **3.** Rub the corner joints externally with medium-grade sandpaper. Now apply a little solder to the cut corners with flux and a moderately hot soldering iron. This is necessary to stop the window leaking. If the window panes are unbroken but leak during wet weather, mark the spot with a crayon. Cut the corners and fold back the lead, renew the putty and replace the metal.

1

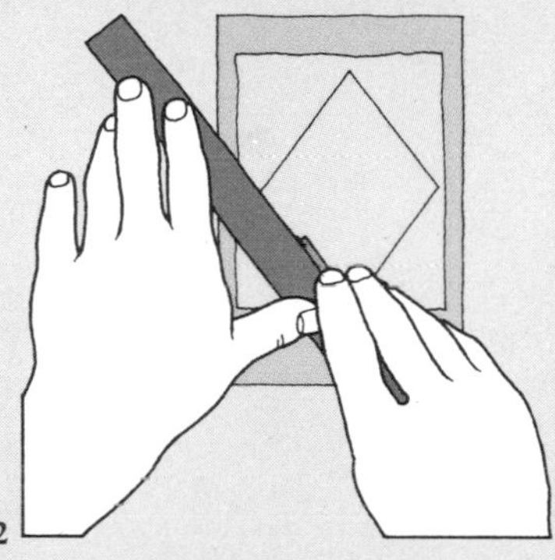
2

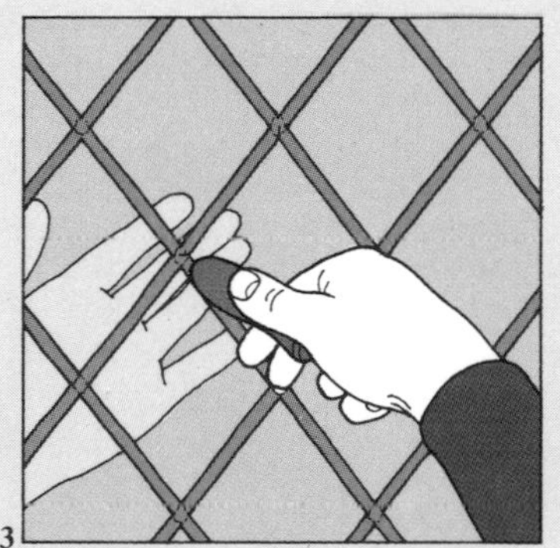
3

How to cut glass

To cut small pieces of glass you will need a glass cutter as shown below. Always make sure that it has a well-lubricated wheel. First practice on a spare piece of glass and then rest the sheet on a flat surface, such as a piece of lumber core plywood covered with a blanket, and clean the glass with paint thinner; greasy glass will not cut evenly. Measure and mark the glass with a wax pencil. Hold the glass cutter at an

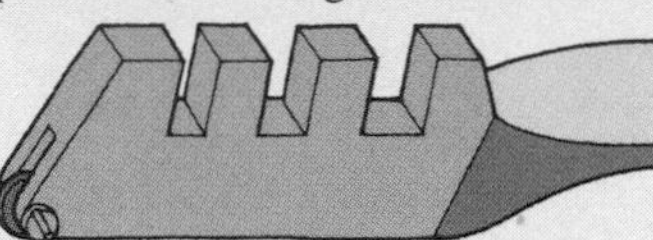

angle **1,** and make a small nick in the glass at the beginning of the line. Hold the cutter against a straight-edge and draw the cutter smoothly and firmly across the surface. The aim is to score the glass from end to end with a continuous movement. Let the cutter run off the glass, with a slight lessening of pressure, otherwise the edge may fragment. When you have scored the surface, lift the glass and gently tap the underside with the toothed side of the cutter, directly beneath the line. Now lay the glass on a thin strip of wood, in line with the score-cut, and press down firmly on each side of the line until the glass breaks cleanly, **2.** Thin strips of glass can be removed by snapping them off, holding each side of the score line with gloved hands, **3.**

1

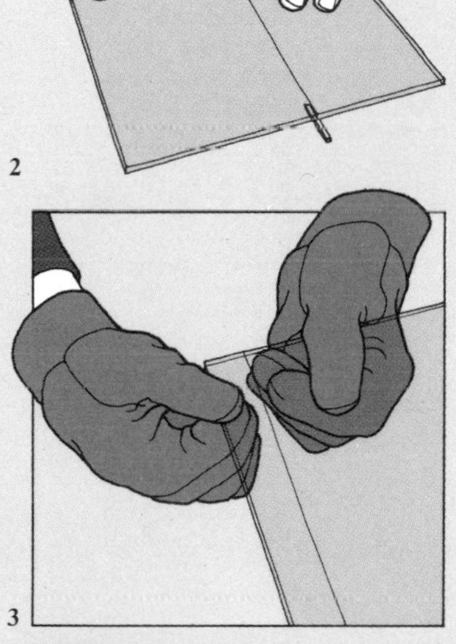
2

3

Metal framed windows

The glass in metal framed windows is also sealed with putty, but held secure with spring clips instead of glazier's points. These U-shaped clips **1** fit into holes in the edge of the frame, and hold the glass in place. When you are removing a broken window pane, first take out the glass and putty and retain the clips for future use. Clean out clip holes, and also clean the metal rabbet or groove, then give it a coat of aluminum paint to prevent rust. If the existing frame is rusty, wire-brush clean before painting. Use special self-hardening glazing compound, and provide a thin bed for the glass. Have the glass cut to size as for a wood framed window, and press it into place using the retained clips **2**, then putty the outside as on the opposite page. Replacing glass in a sliding metal framed window should be left to a professional: the strains imposed on the glass are greater, and unless correctly fitted it will crack. Whatever the type or size of window replace the broken glass with a similar type; use double strength glass for areas larger than $1\frac{1}{2}$ square feet.

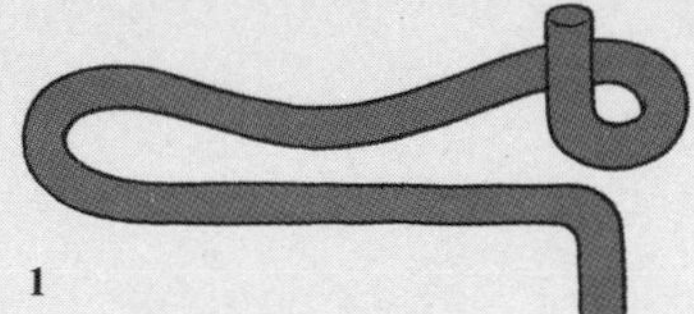
1

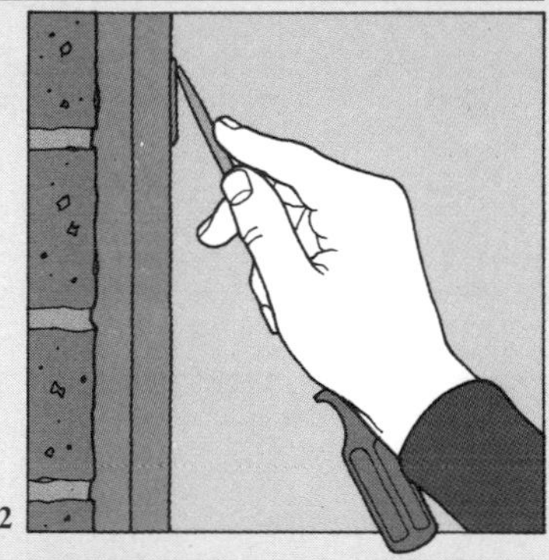
2

Temporary covering for a broken window

First purchase enough polyethylene sheet to cover the area, with an extra few inches overall. Cut four battens 1 in. x $\frac{1}{4}$ in. to frame four sides. Nail top edge of sheet above the window. Now fix the top batten, nailing through batten and edge of sheet with small nails, **1.** Secure remaining sides, **2** and the bottom **3** in the same way, keeping polyethylene taut.

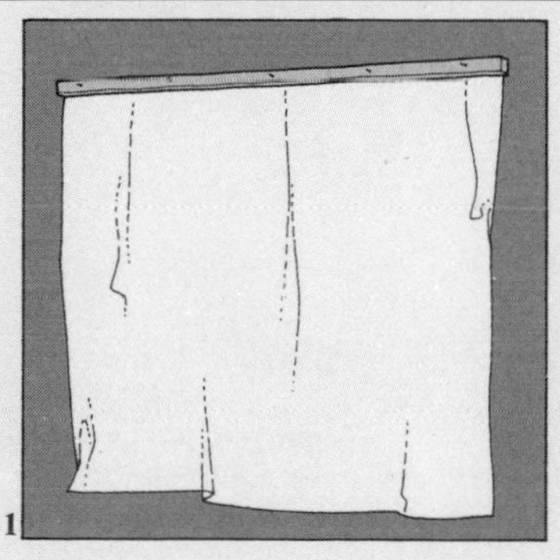
1

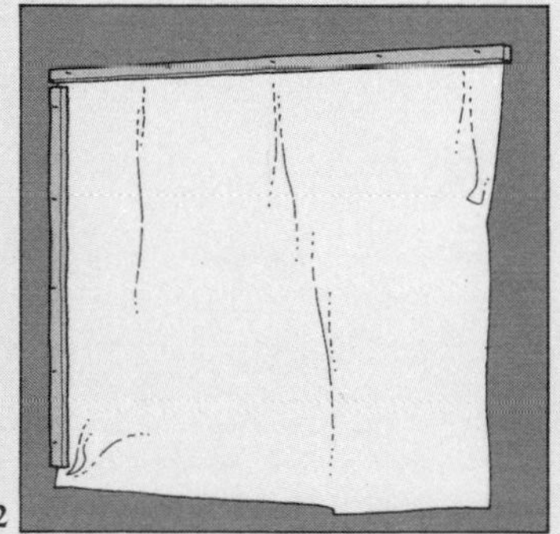
2

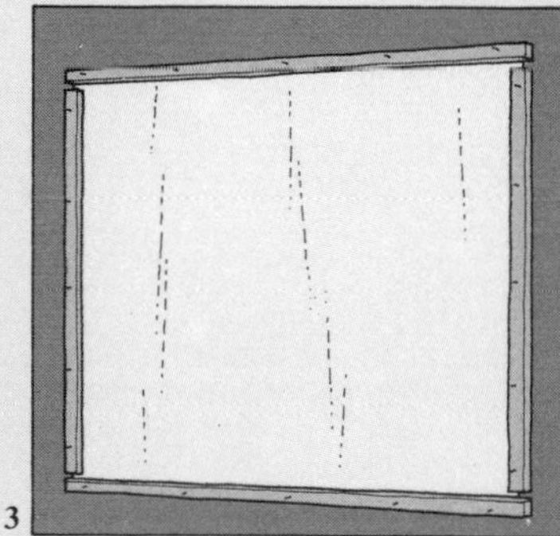
3

Refitting & Insulating Windows

Replacing an existing window
The majority of houses have standard-sized windows and replacements can be bought ready-made. You can install these yourself, or have a builder do it for you. If on measuring a window you find that it is non-standard, you will have to order a custom-built replacement from a builder or manufacturer, and submit accurate measurements. How to do this is described on the opposite page; a new window should be ¼ in. smaller than the aperture in the brickwork.

Removing the existing window
First take out the glass (see p. 102) to lighten the weight, and make the window safer to handle. Next, remove the frame following the procedure described below, right. The frame may be screwed to plugs in the wall, screwed to metal lugs cemented in the wall between brick courses, or nailed in position. To remove a screwed frame, scrape off any putty covering the screws, and remove them with a screwdriver. Long established screws may have seized, so use a drop of penetrating oil; give the driver a smart tap, try to turn the screw a fraction, then turn it sharply anticlockwise. Next, hammer the window frame out from the inside. Work down the frame from the top to bottom – this is really a job for two people. If the frame cannot be budged, take a hand saw and cut through the stiles just above sill level, and pry off top portion. Cut through the center of the sill and knock it out with a mallet.

Fitting a new frame
Wooden windows are usually supplied ready primed. Paint those surfaces to be embedded in the wall with an undercoat and a gloss finish. If the frame is hardwood, only use polyurethane unless you want a paint finish. Clean a metal frame with turpentine; take care not to damage a galvanized one, as this impairs its rust-proofing qualities. Install the window as described on the right. Secure with screws or nails to the plugs in the brickwork. Install a metal window by the side lugs. Rake out joints to the same depth as the lugs and slide the window in place. Mortar the joints, and provide a bed of mortar along the bottom edge of the frame. The gap between the wooden or metal window and the brickwork now needs to be filled. Apply mastic under pressure, removing the wedges as the work proceeds.

Sliding windows
The double hung window, left, has two sashes that slide up and down in the frame, held open by friction, springs or balances. Horizontal sliding windows, right, have two or three sashes which slide within the frame.

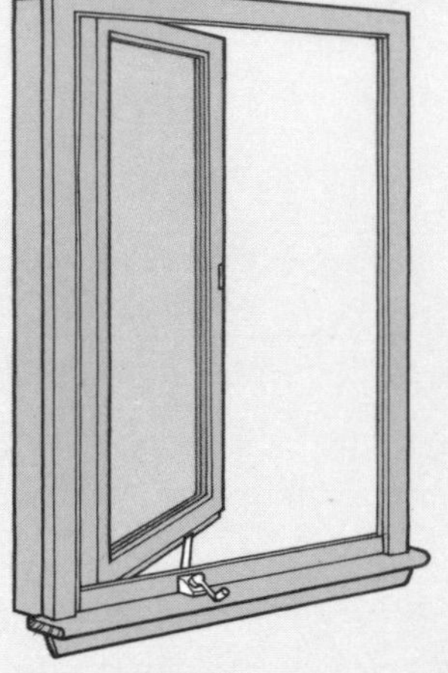

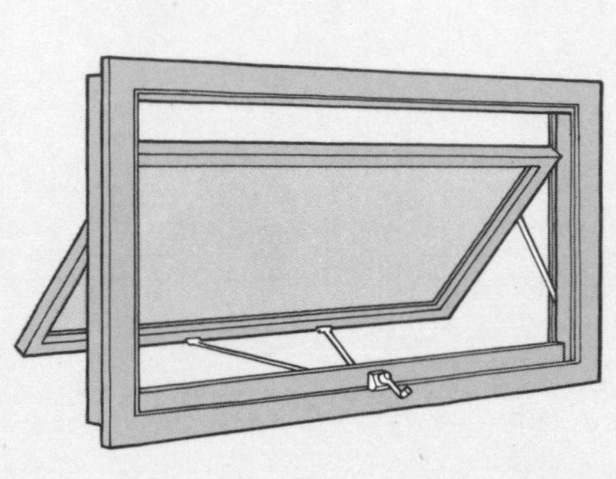

Swinging windows
Casement windows, left, are hinged vertically on the side so the sash swings outward, operated by a crank or push-bar. Awning windows, right, are hinged horizontally with sashes on a sliding track, operated by crank or push-bar.

Unscrewing the frame
Remove the screws with a strong, long-shanked screwdriver. Use easing oil if screws will not move.

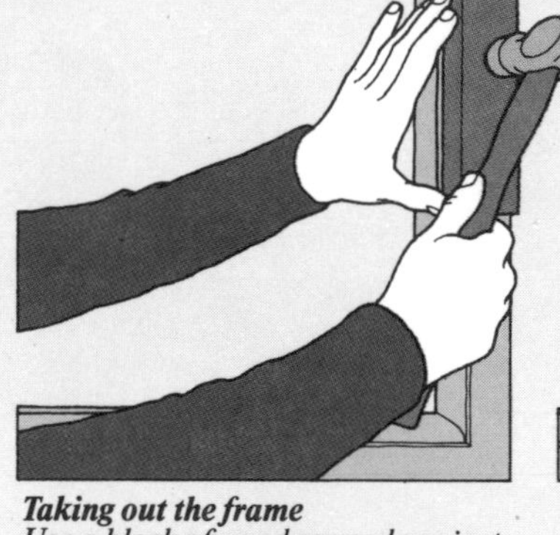

Taking out the frame
Use a block of wood pressed against the frame, and hammer frame out from the opening, from the top down.

Removing a nailed frame
Cut between wall and frame with a mini hacksaw, or use a chisel and hammer.

Cutting through stiles
If you cannot move frame by hammering, cut through stiles with hand saw, then lever off top part.

Aligning new frame
Install new window frame, use small wedges between frame and wall to get even spacing. Check with level.

Repairing surfaces
Fill any cracks or holes where plaster has been disturbed, also finishing outer walls. Repoint joints.

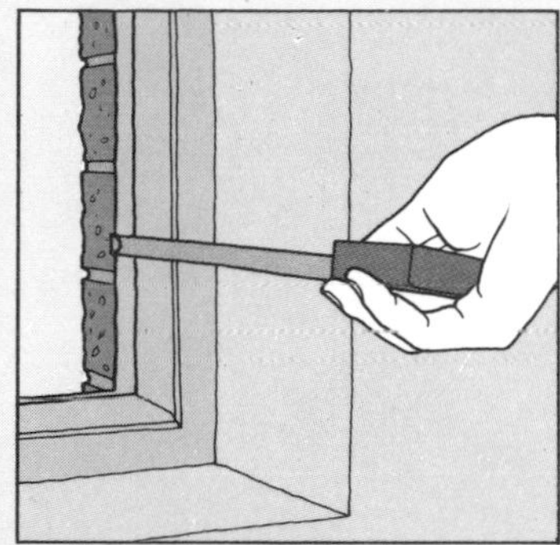

Measuring a window
Getting the measurements accurate for a replacement window is very important. First, open the window and measure the overall thickness of the frame from the recess.

Depth of outside recess
Close the window, and from the outside, measure the depth of the brickwork from the front face of the wall to the front edge of the frame.

Taking the overall width
Now take the overall dimensions, beginning with the width from wall to wall. Take these measurements at the center in case the opening is not a true rectangle.

Measuring the height
For a window larger than 3 ft square, take measurements at each end and in the middle. Finally, measure the height from the top of the frame to underside of sill.

Storm windows

Without insulation, windows are the weak spots through which 20% of the heat generated in a house can escape, and through which outside noise can penetrate. By installing storm windows, the heat loss and the noise level can be considerably reduced, and condensation eliminated. The ideal distance between panes of glass is $\frac{3}{4}$ in. and this can save up to 50% of heat loss, although the size and position of the window may affect this figure. Greater distance will greatly improve sound reduction. Here, the ideal distance is between 4 in. and 8 in.; triple glazing, using three panes, doubles the noise reduction. Give priority to sky lights and windows facing north and east.

Home-made storm windows

Cut $\frac{3}{8}$ in. rabbeted lengths of softwood to the dimensions of the existing opening and miter corners. Drill pilot holes for screw fixings to window, 10 in. apart. Cut glass to size and add self-stick, draft-proof foam strip to all edges. Drill two 3/16 in. holes through the bottom of the existing frame from the inside, and near frame stiles. Angle holes so water cannot enter, push a little steel wool in each to keep out insects. Clean glass on both windows. Fix bottom length of rabbeted framing in place, but do not tighten screws. Insert glass in rabbet, then fix side and top lengths. Gradually tighten the screws until the foam strip has insulated the gap between. Rub down the frame with fine sandpaper and paint or seal with polyurethane. If the frame is likely to be removed fairly frequently, use brass cups and screws to fix framing.

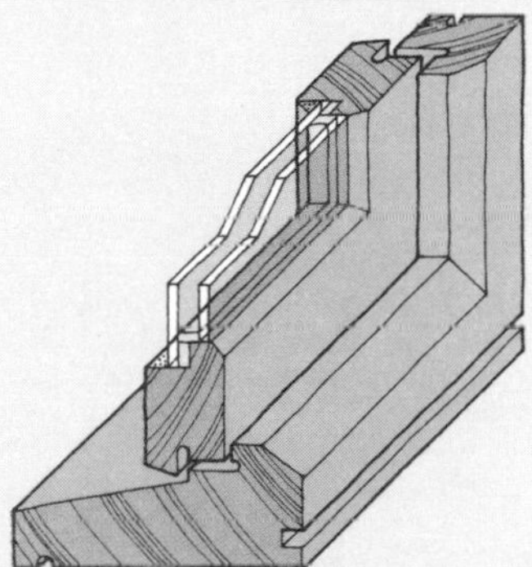

Stepped factory unit
Two panes of glass are hermetically sealed together with a plastic or metal edging strip so that condensation will not form in the space between. A stepped unit such as this where the inner pane of glass is smaller than the outer will fit most standard sash frames.

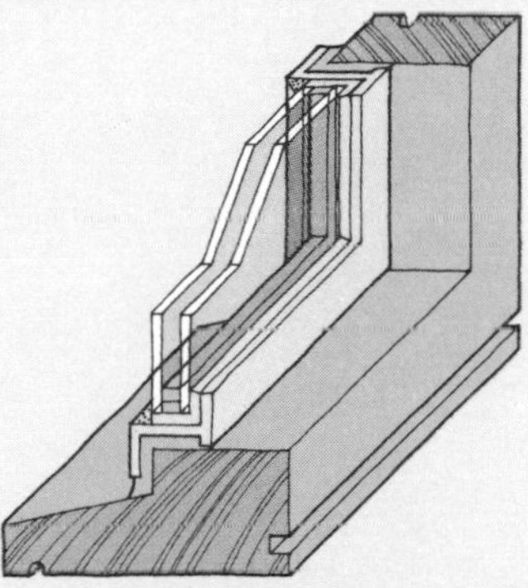

Factory sealed unit in metal window
Both this type and the stepped unit are made in a variety of window sizes. Sealed units are efficient and easy to install, except that you may need to enlarge the rabbet on the existing window sash bottoms and stiles to take extra thickness of glass or install a stepped unit.

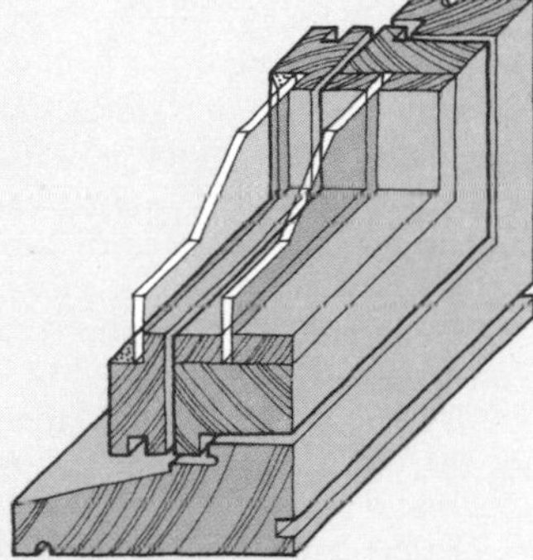

Coupled windows
A coupled window has two sash frames linked as a single unit. The auxiliary window is on the outside, and hinged so that the two can be separated for cleaning, but they can be opened together as a single window. An advantage is that Venetian blinds can be installed between the frames, with a simple system of operation from inside the room.

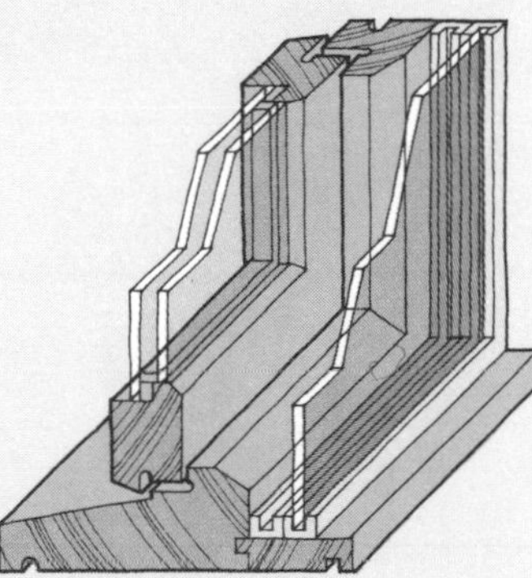

Triple glazing
A secondary window can be fitted either to the sash frame or to the measurements of the entire window frame. They can be made to measure and installed by the makers, or by you, or bought in kit form. As used above, a secondary window added to a double one results in triple glazing and improved heat and sound insulation.

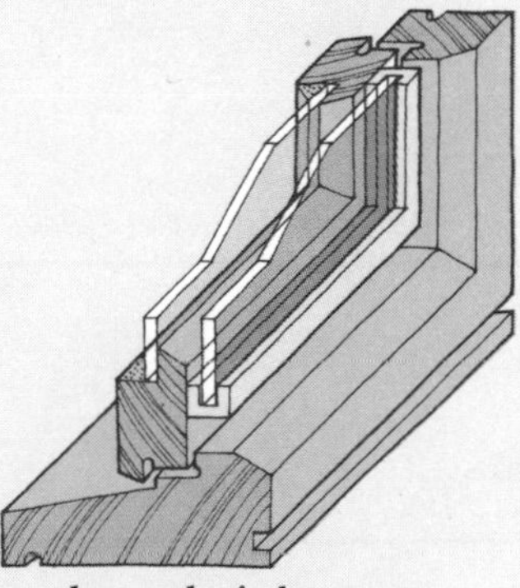

Secondary sash window
This type of secondary window is less obtrusive since it is fixed to the sash frame, usually hinged to the stile. Like the window to the left, the frame can be of aluminum, wood or plastic. There are different kinds of fixings for secondary windows, but whether they are sliding, hinged or double-hung, they need to be installed so that access is available to the existing window frame.

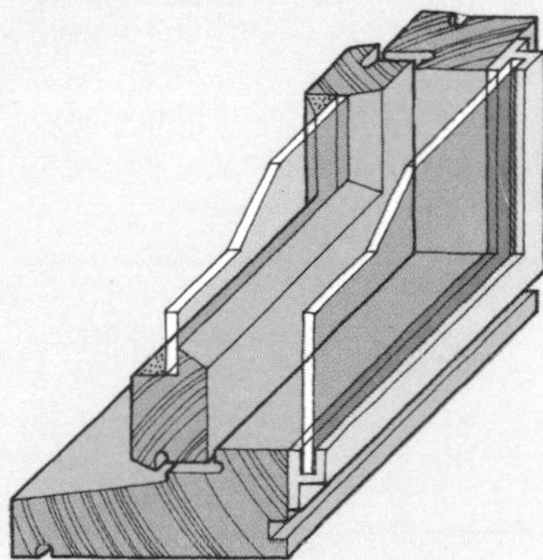

DIY units
DIY units usually comprise flexible plastic channels or lightweight aluminum frames to hold the second pane of glass. The metal or plastic parts usually have mitered corners or special covering clips. Glass has to be bought as a separate item, the entire unit is then assembled and fixed to the back of existing windows with fixings supplied with the outfit.

Hanging Doors

Types of doors
A panel door has vertical stiles, solid cross rails and filler panels which are usually solid wood, but may be plywood or glass. The surrounds are often molded. Panel doors are made for internal and external use, either in hardwood or softwood. Flush doors have a lighter wooden frame, surfaced on both sides with plywood or hardboard. Both panel and flush doors can have asbestos panels or lining as a fire precaution. External flush doors have a heavier framework and are bonded with a resin adhesive.

Frames and casings
The illustrations on the right depict internal doors and casings. An external door should be hinged to a rabbeted frame–a single piece of L-shaped softwood 3 in. x 2 in. – which is better able than a lining to resist weathering. Use galvanized steel angles, built into the brickwork, to secure the jambs, or patent lugs mortared into brick joints. Waterproof gaps between wall and frame with mastic compound.

Hanging a door
Try the door to see if it fits: there should be a clearance of ⅛ in. at the sides and top, and ¼ in. at the bottom. If you need more clearance, plane edges from the outside toward the center to avoid splitting corners. Wedge door in place, and mark position of hinges. On a panel door they should align with the edges of top and bottom rails; on a flush door the top hinge should be 6 in. down, the bottom hinge 8 in. up. When fitting the hinges, the barrel should project slightly beyond the inner face of the door. Cut the mortise with a sharp chisel, beveled face down. The recess should be the depth of the hinge leaf. Fit the hinge, and screw in one screw for each leaf through center hole. Test door for easy opening and closing before fitting remaining screws. Adjustments can be made by chiseling recess slightly deeper, or by packing it out with cardboard.

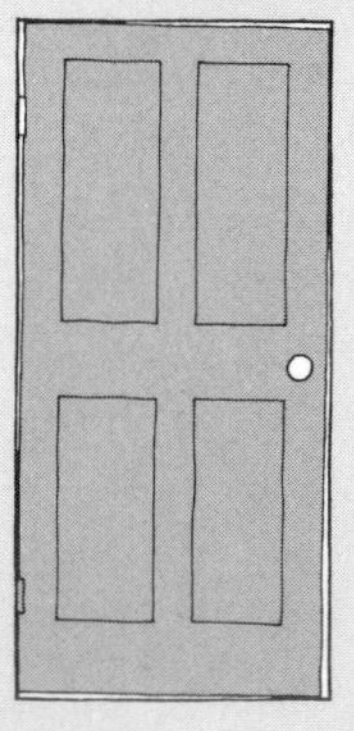

Sticking doors
Worn hinges often cause doors to stick. You can plane wood from the door or fit new hinges if they are identical to the present ones. The best solution is to switch the top and bottom hinges.

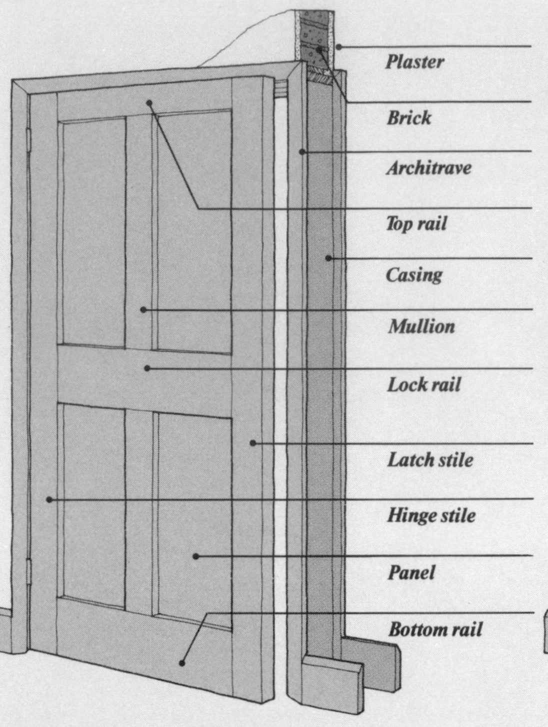

Panel door in a brick wall
Panel doors are inclined to be heavier than the flush type and may need a stronger frame. The casing should be the same width as that of the plastered wall, and nailed to the brick or block face of the wall with masonry nails. The gap between casing and wall may be concealed with a plain or decorative molding.

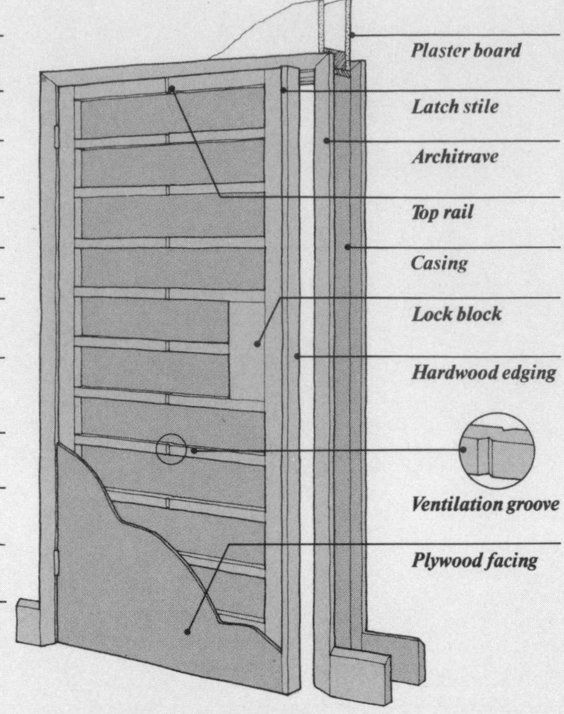

Flush door in a stud partition
In a stud partition, the door casing can be nailed to the upright stud, which also provides a fitting for the wallboard. For a thin partition wall, construct a frame with casings from floor to ceiling, and a double header fixed at door height. The area above the door can either be glassed-in, or filled with wallboard.

Hanging a door
1 *Cut off the extended stile ends from a new door, then plane ends from outside toward center.*

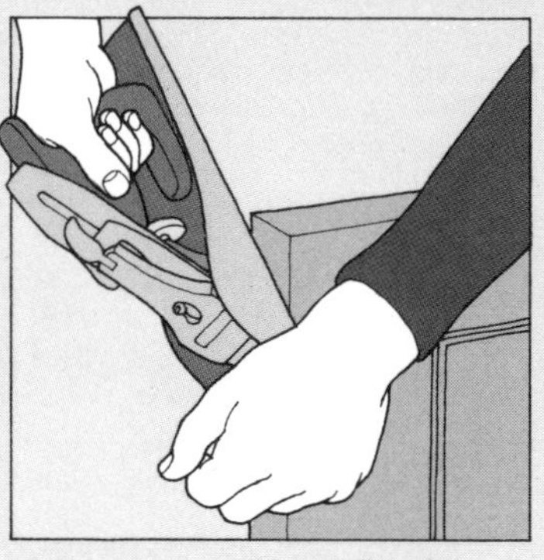

2 Plane hinge stile first. Bevel the latch stile slightly toward the door stop. Plane top and bottom edges toward center.

3 Site door in frame, tapping in the wedges until they hold the door in the correct position.

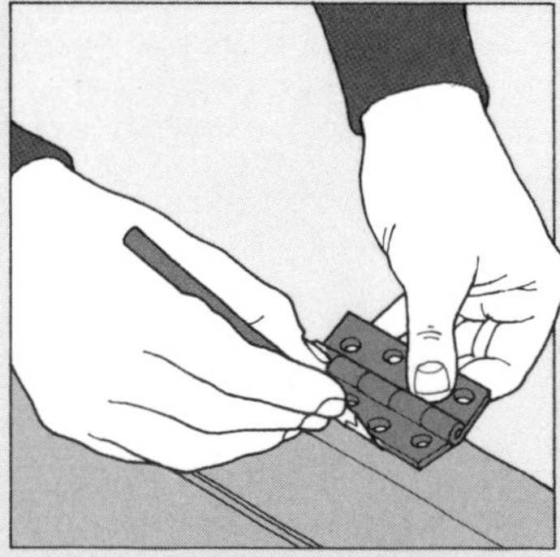

4 Use a pencil to mark hinge positions on both door and jamb. Use hinge leaf to outline recess.

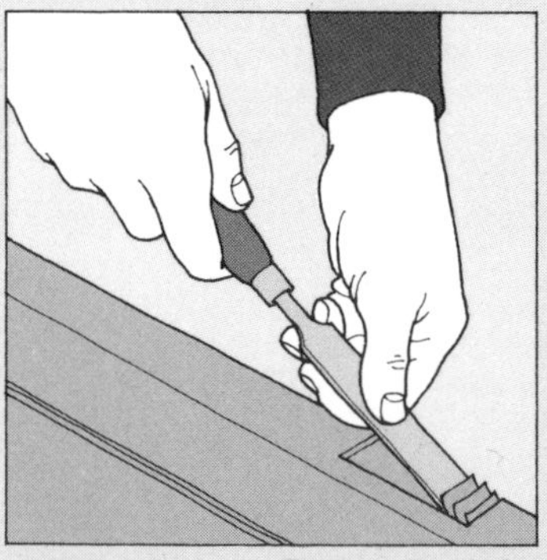

5 Score marks with sharp chisel, then make series of shallow angle cuts, and pare off down to depth of hinge.

6 Make a starter hole with a bradawl. Screw both hinges in place. Remove wedges and test fitting.

Locks

Mortise lock
First mark a line on the edge of the door along its center, on the stile and in line with the lock rail. Flush doors have a deep stile behind the facing for this purpose. When marking up, use a try square and marking gauge for accuracy. Cut the mortise and fit the lock according to the diagrams on the right, and then align the strike plate with the lock on the door jamb. Finally test that the closed door can be operated by latch and key. Mortise locks vary considerably in depth, depending on whether you want the handle to be near or away from the door edge. These locks are secure but can weaken the lock stile if the door is very thin.

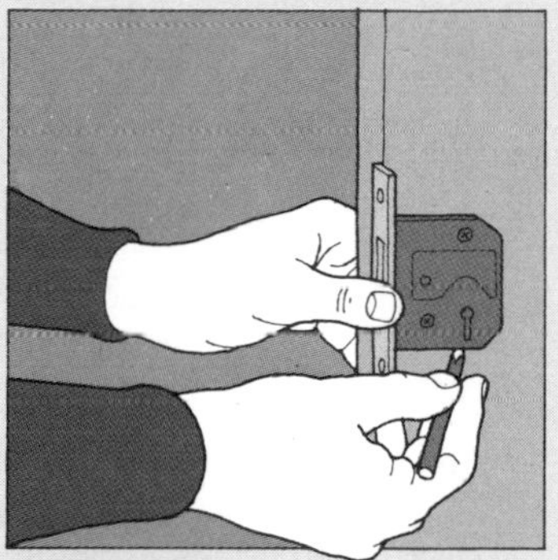

Fitting a mortise lock
1 Carefully measure and mark position of face plate. Rest the lock on edge of door, and mark its width and length.

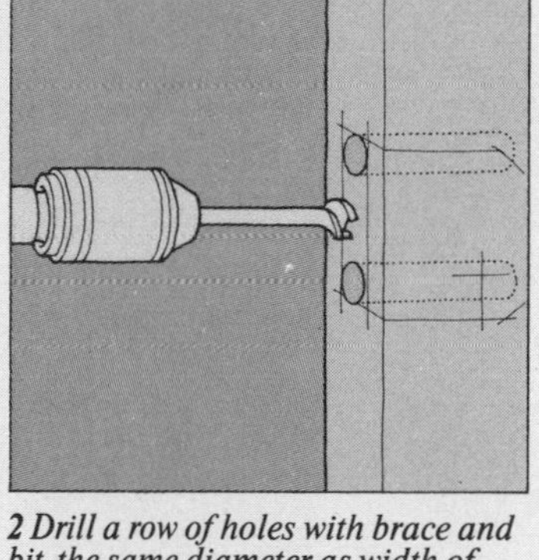

2 Drill a row of holes with brace and bit, the same diameter as width of lock. Use depth gauge to ensure that holes are as deep as lock.

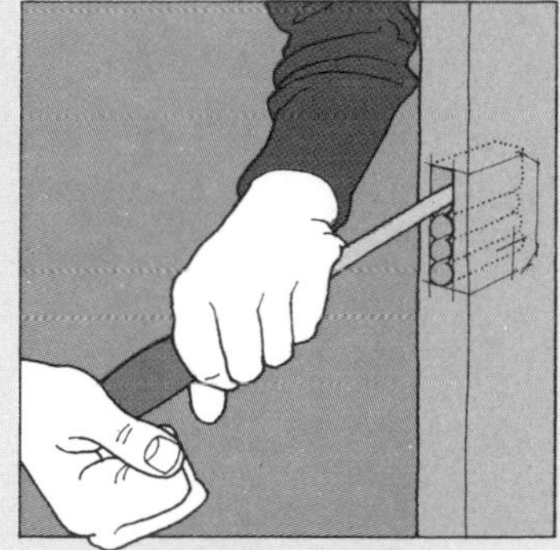

3 Clean out waste and clear edges of holes with a sharp chisel. Test fit lock. Chisel out recess for face plate to the same depth as the plate.

4 Mark out positions of screws for the face plate. Mark position of spindle hole and keyhole, measuring their depth from front of plate.

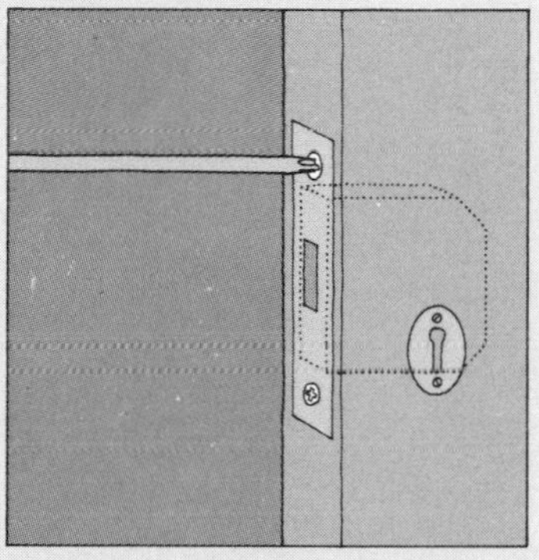

5 Drill out the hole for the spindle to the appropriate diameter. Shape keyhole with a ¼ in. chisel. Test fit lock, also test the key.

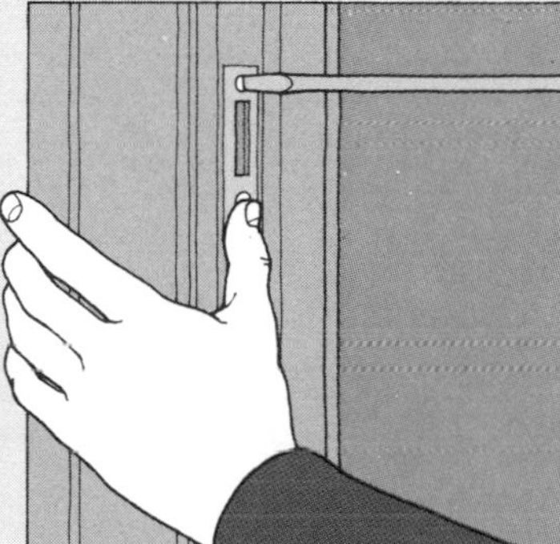

6 If everything aligns, screw front plate into place. Insert spindles, fit handles.

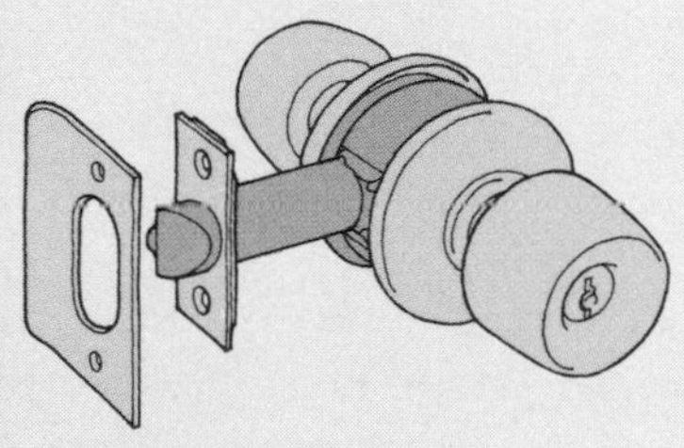

Cylinder mortise lock
Accurate measuring and marking is vital for a cylinder lock to operate correctly. In this type of lock, the mortise consists of a hole drilled to receive the latch bolt, and a larger hole for the cylinder barrel. Some locks are provided with a template to allow easy siting of the lock in the stile. Alternatively, follow the diagrams on the right. It is particularly important in this case that the holes in the door are drilled true. Get someone to check from the side that the drill is horizontal, while you check from above. Clean up any misalignment of the holes with a half-round rasp. Check that the lock button is set to allow the door to open from both sides before closing it while you are working.

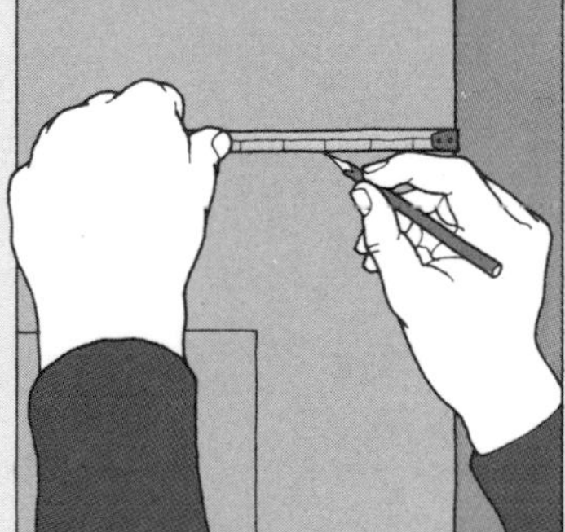

Fitting a cylinder lock
1 Measure distance from centerline of cylinder to outer edge of lock case. Mark this distance on door face.

2 Use a brace and bit, or a hole saw, and drill hole same diameter as lock cylinder through the stile of the door. Work from both sides.

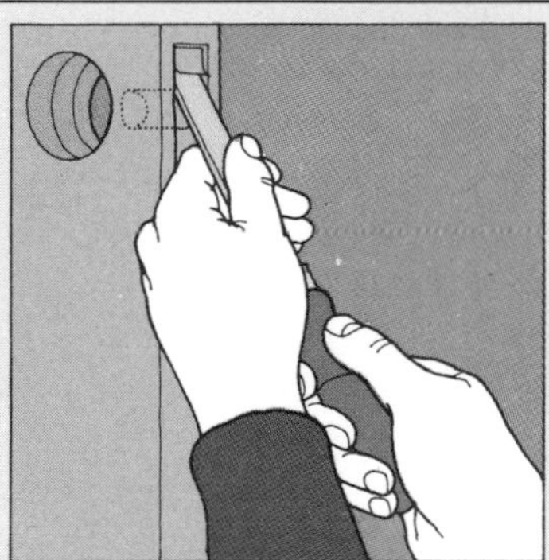

3 Drill smaller hole through edge of door on center line to take latch bolt. Chisel recess for face plate after marking its position.

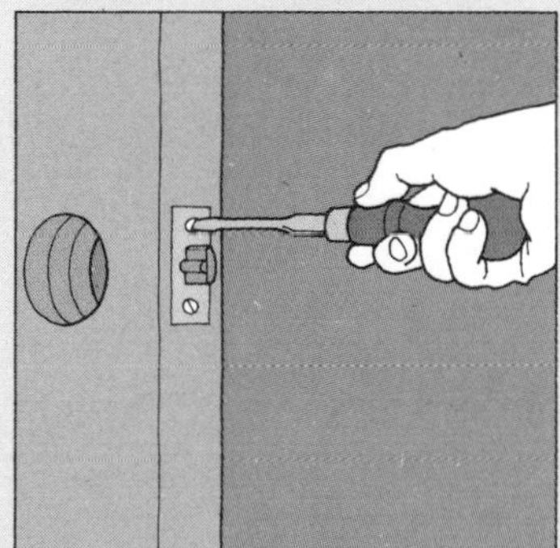

4 Insert latch bolt, making sure that the sloping edge faces outside of door, and screw into position.

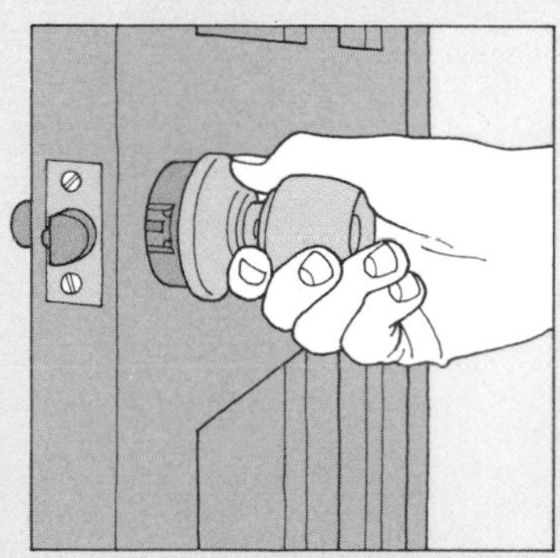

5 Insert cylinder from outside of door. Align latch retractor with latch bolt. Attach rose to door.

6 Partly close door and mark position of strike plate. Cut recess and screw plate to door jamb.

Lumber & Boards

The structure of wood

Wood is not only one of the most attractive building materials, but also the most versatile. The cellular structure of wood is responsible for its great strength and relative light weight. A tree's cells are tiny – long and narrow in shape – and contain strands of cellulose bonded together by an aromatic compound called lignin. Seasonal differences account for the characteristic grain pattern when lumber is cut into boards: the faster growing spring cells are larger and lighter than the small, dark summer growth.

Types of wood

Wood can be classified into two types, hardwood and softwood, depending upon the parent tree and cellular size (a softwood cell is larger). Both evergreen or needle-leaved trees and cone-bearing conifers produce softwoods, while hardwoods come from deciduous trees which grow broad leaves and shed them in winter. Not all hardwoods are hard (balsa being remarkably light and soft) but they are usually stronger and more decorative than softwood and generally more expensive. Softwoods, which include hard types, are more common and are widely used for structural work.

Seasoning

Seasoning is the process of reducing the moisture content of lumber. This makes the wood more stable and more easily workable by tools. But even seasoned wood reacts to atmospheric conditions and will give off or absorb moisture accordingly. This is why doors can swell and bind in wet weather and why furniture often cracks from central heating. Bare wood is especially susceptible and should be protected with paint or varnish. Before using new wood it is a good idea to allow it to adjust to the surrounding conditions. Make sure that it is properly stacked to prevent it from becoming distorted.

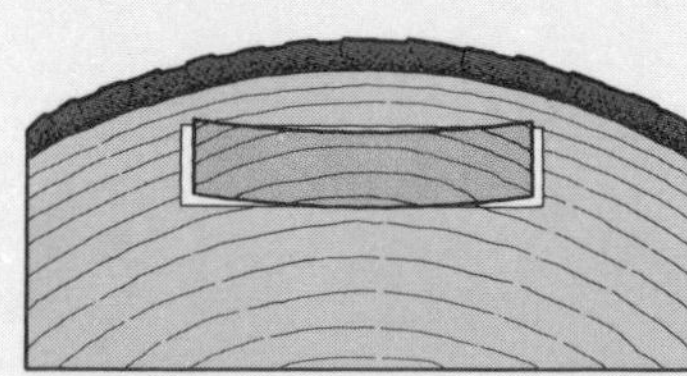

Shrinkage
Shrinkage resulting from the seasoning process may cause the wood to warp. This mostly occurs around the tree's annual rings but the degree of distortion can be lessened by a carefully controlled drying process.

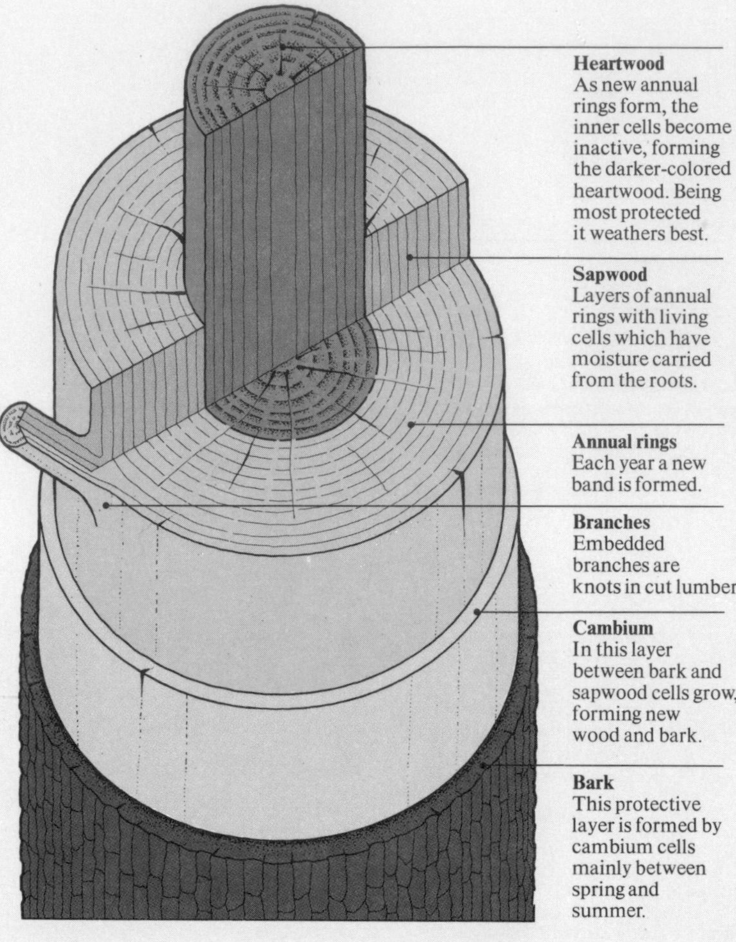

Buying lumber

Wood is sold by the foot, sawn or planed in a variety of standard sizes. The width and depth measurements are nominal, not actual, because the machined waste is included. Thus, if you order a board of 2 in. x 2 in. lumber, you get a board of 1½ in. x 1½ in. When ordering lumber, tell the merchant the dimensions you are working to as he may be able to supply you, more economically, from stocks that are already cut.

Dimension chart
The diagram below shows the quoted nominal measurements of lumber as it is sawn. The actual measurements shown in the line below are what the buyer receives.

1 inch									
Nominal 1 ×	1	2	3	4	5	6	8	10	12
Actual ¾ ×	¾	1½	2½	3½	4½	5½	7½	9½	11½
2 inch									
Nominal 2 ×		2	3	4		6	8	10	12
Actual 1½ ×		1½	2½	3½		5½	7¼	9¼	11¼
4 inch									
Nominal 4 ×			3	4		6			
Actual 3½ ×			2½	3½		5½			

Knots
Knots, found mostly in softwood, can weaken the lumber. Live knots, which are an integral part of the wood, are usually hard and contain a lot of resin. Dead knots are loose and can fall out, leaving a hole.

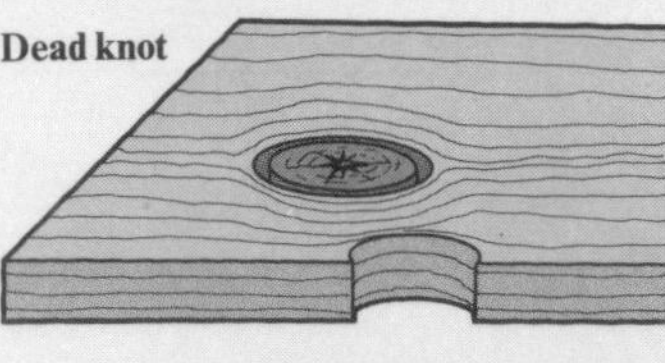

Dead knot

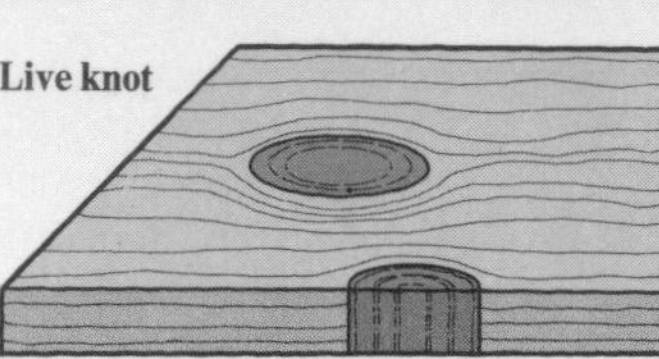

Live knot

Care must be taken to prevent damage when planing a knotty surface. The plane should be very sharp to avoid tearing the grain out. Knots should be primed to seal in the resin.

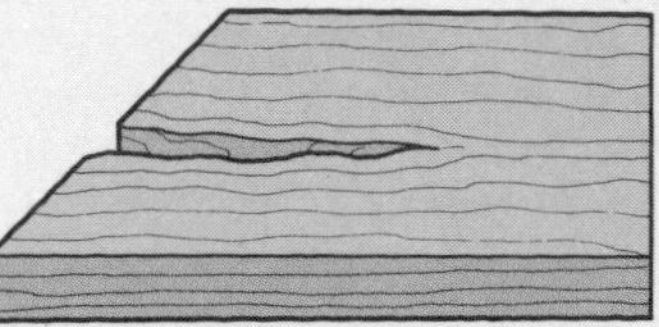

Shakes
Shakes are splits caused by uneven shrinkage, which results in a separation of fibers along the grain between the annual rings.

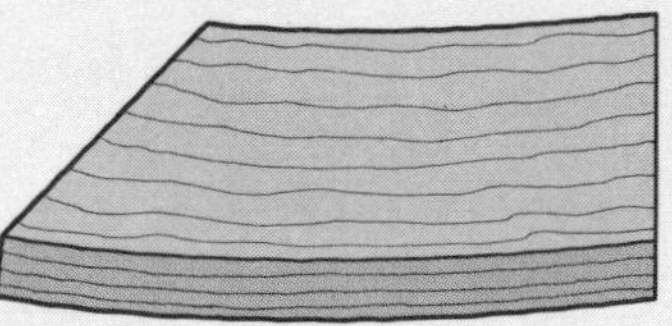

Warping
Warping is caused by irregular seasoning or poor stacking, and results in boards being twisted or bowed in width or length. When buying long square or rectangular pieces, you should sight along them to see if they are out of true.

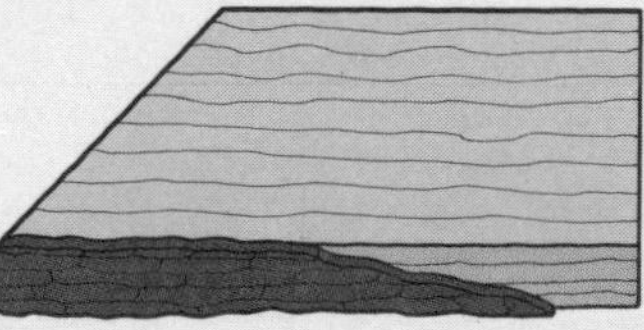

Wanes
Wanes are uneven, beveled edges or layers of rough bark which may be present on some boards. Unless these edges are planed off, the workable width of the lumber can be effectively reduced.

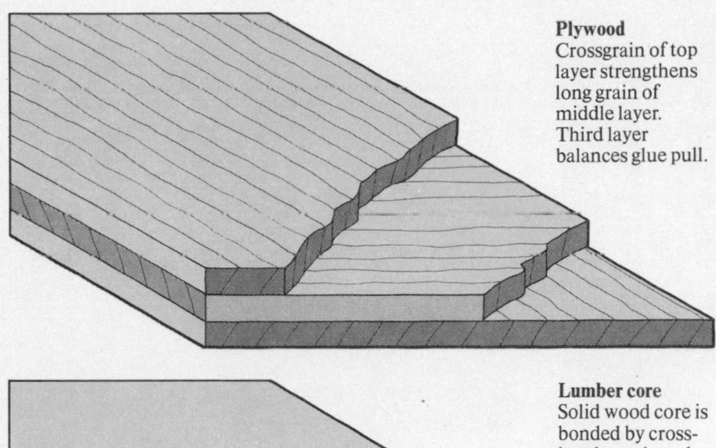

Plywood
Crossgrain of top layer strengthens long grain of middle layer. Third layer balances glue pull.

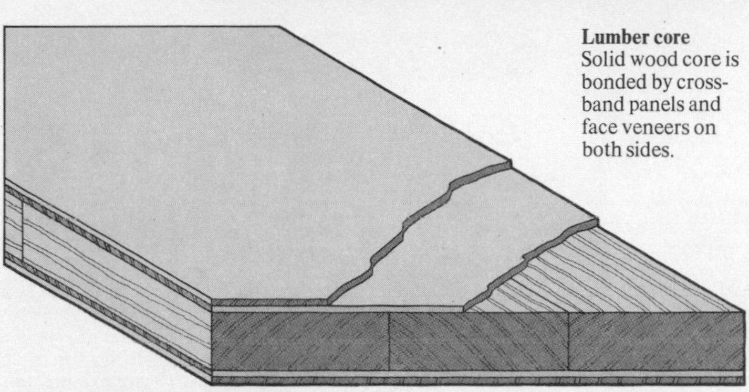

Lumber core
Solid wood core is bonded by cross-band panels and face veneers on both sides.

Sheet boards

Woodbased manufactured boards provide large sheet materials for building work and furniture making. The wood can be converted into thin layers or veneers, thin strips or battens, wood chips or wood pulp. Different processes and adhesives produce brands of different thicknesses and properties. Sheets are usually sold in standard measurements but can be cut to size; the cost is calculated by the square foot.

Plywood is made of at least three layers of wood or veneers which are bonded together with the grain direction set at right angles in each alternate layer. Such alternating grain combats warping and increases tensile strength as the long grain of one layer reinforces the cross grain of the next. A third layer provides balance to the pull of the glue and the opposite grain direction. The number of veneers varies according to the thickness of each layer and the total thickness of the board, although there will always be an odd number. Plywood is available in both soft and hard woods and is graded according to the quality of the outer veneers and type of glue. Exterior grade plywood is bonded with a waterproof adhesive, whereas the interior grade is only suitable for low humidity conditions. Sheet sizes vary, the average being 8 ft x 4 ft with thicknesses ranging from $\frac{1}{8}$ in. to 1 in. Non-standard sizes are also available.

Lumber core plywood has a thick core of solid wood and an outer skin of two bonded veneers. It is used mainly for furniture making since it not only cuts easily, but it securely holds screws driven into its edges such as for cabinet door hinges.

Lumber core board is strongest in the direction of the long grain of the core and when used for table tops the core should run lengthwise. For doors, the grain should be vertical.

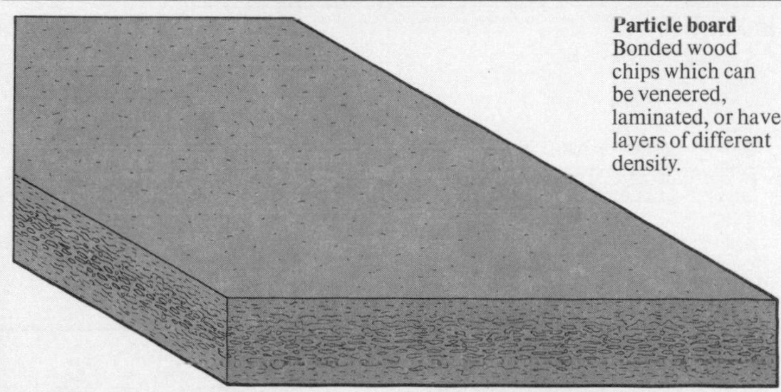

Particle board
Bonded wood chips which can be veneered, laminated, or have layers of different density.

Particle board

This inexpensive board is made of fine wood chips bonded under pressure with resin adhesive. It is thicker than hardboard, but lighter in weight and color. Particle board may also be manufactured in layers, coarse chipboard being sandwiched between veneers of fine chipboard to produce greater strength and a finer finish. Particle board is available in 4 ft x 8 ft sheets, usually $\frac{1}{2}$ in. to $\frac{3}{4}$ in. thick. It is not suitable for outside use. It is, however, very stable and can be used around heating systems and radiators as well as in cabinet-making as a core for wood and plastic veneers. Although it has good compression it has poor tensile strength and needs supporting when used in shelving. Screws can be driven into the surface in the normal way, but plastic inserts are necessary on the edge.

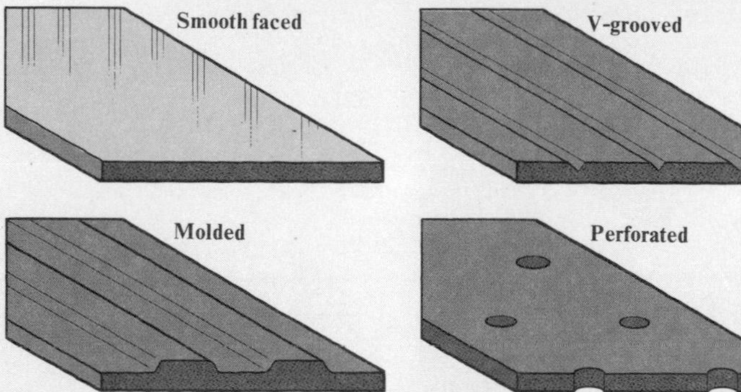

Hardboard

Hardboard is a hard, dense sheet material made of pulped wood fibers bonded together with resin glues under heat and pressure. It has many applications, including wall panels, screens and linings. Standard or oil tempered types exist, the latter being water resistant. Regular hardboard has a single, smooth face with a textured back. A board with two smooth faces is also manufactured. Many sheet sizes exist and thicknesses range from $\frac{1}{8}$ in. to $\frac{3}{8}$ in. Hardboard is a comparatively brittle material and should be handled with care to avoid any damage to corners and edges or to its smooth surface. Thin boards need supporting with a frame; if the surface is painted the board back must be sealed to prevent warping. Types of special hardboard are shown at left.

Edge lippings

All manufactured boards need edge lipping. You can buy manufactured boards that have laminate or veneer on the edges but these are in standard sizes. Cut board especially needs its edges masked. This can be achieved by solid wood battens butt jointed or tongue and grooved. A simple edging can be applied using an iron-on veneer or plastic edging. Aluminum edging is also available.

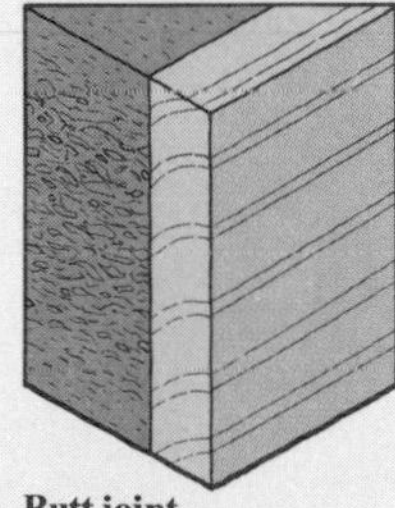

Butt joint
Wood, metal or plastic nailed or glued.

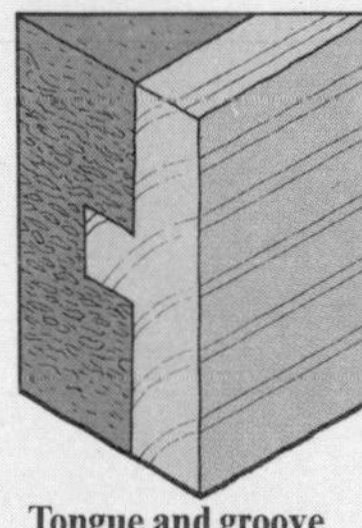

Tongue and groove
Increased gluing area for wooden lipping.

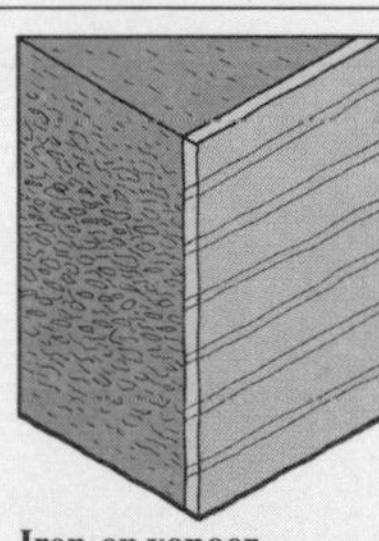

Iron-on veneer
Self-sticking when heated.

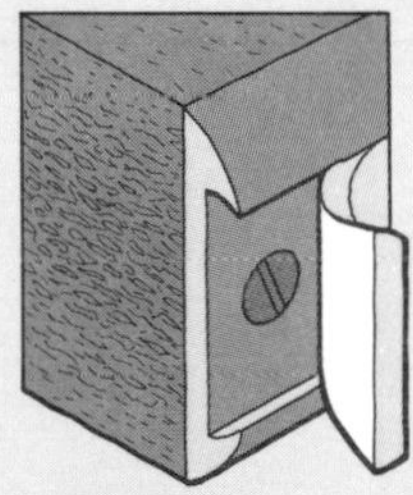

Aluminum edge
Screw fixed. Plastic insert hides screws.

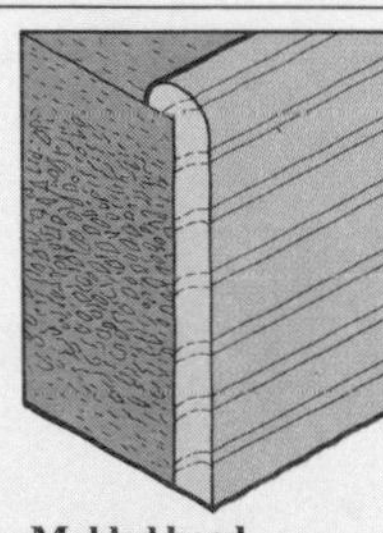

Molded bead
Wood, metal or plastic, screwed or glued.

Measuring & Marking Lumber

Tools

Working with lumber demands accurate measuring and marking, using the tools described below, and cutting true to the marks. Lumber is sold in standard sections, and many projects can be made entirely from these – all you have to do is cut lengths and angles – very little trimming or planing is needed.

Try square determines right angles, checks that a cut edge is square.
T bevel's adjustable blade can be set and locked to mark any angle.
Combination square is several gauges in one: try square, miter, ruler, depth gauge, straight edge.
Level checks vertical and horizontal surfaces.
Mortise gauge has two scribers to mark width of mortise joint.
Marking gauge scribes parallel lines.
Marking knife scribes for cutting.
Folding ruler opens out and retains rigidity while measuring.
Retractable tape measures around objects, and within restricted spaces.

Techniques

Lengths of lumber for woodworking need to be straight and true: it is worth bearing in mind that some types of lumber, especially softwood, can arrive warped. To true up a rectilinear section, first check that the wood is flat along its length with the aid of a straight edge. On wider boards, make sure that the wood is not twisted by placing a straight batten across the board at each end, and sighting along the top edges from one to another – if they are parallel the board is flat. If curved you will have to plane down the high points. Check the adjacent sides with the try square. When cutting several lengths of lumber to a standard size, measure and cut one piece, and use it to mark off the lengths of the others, remember to allow for the width of the sawcut. It is better to mark and cut each length as you go.

If you intend to cut several recesses or rebates in lumber for joints, measure and mark several of the same type of joint at the same time. Hold the lengths in a clamp or vise, and use the lumber being jointed, i.e., the piece to be fitted in the housing, as a gauge to get exact widths, rather than transferring dimensions with a ruler.

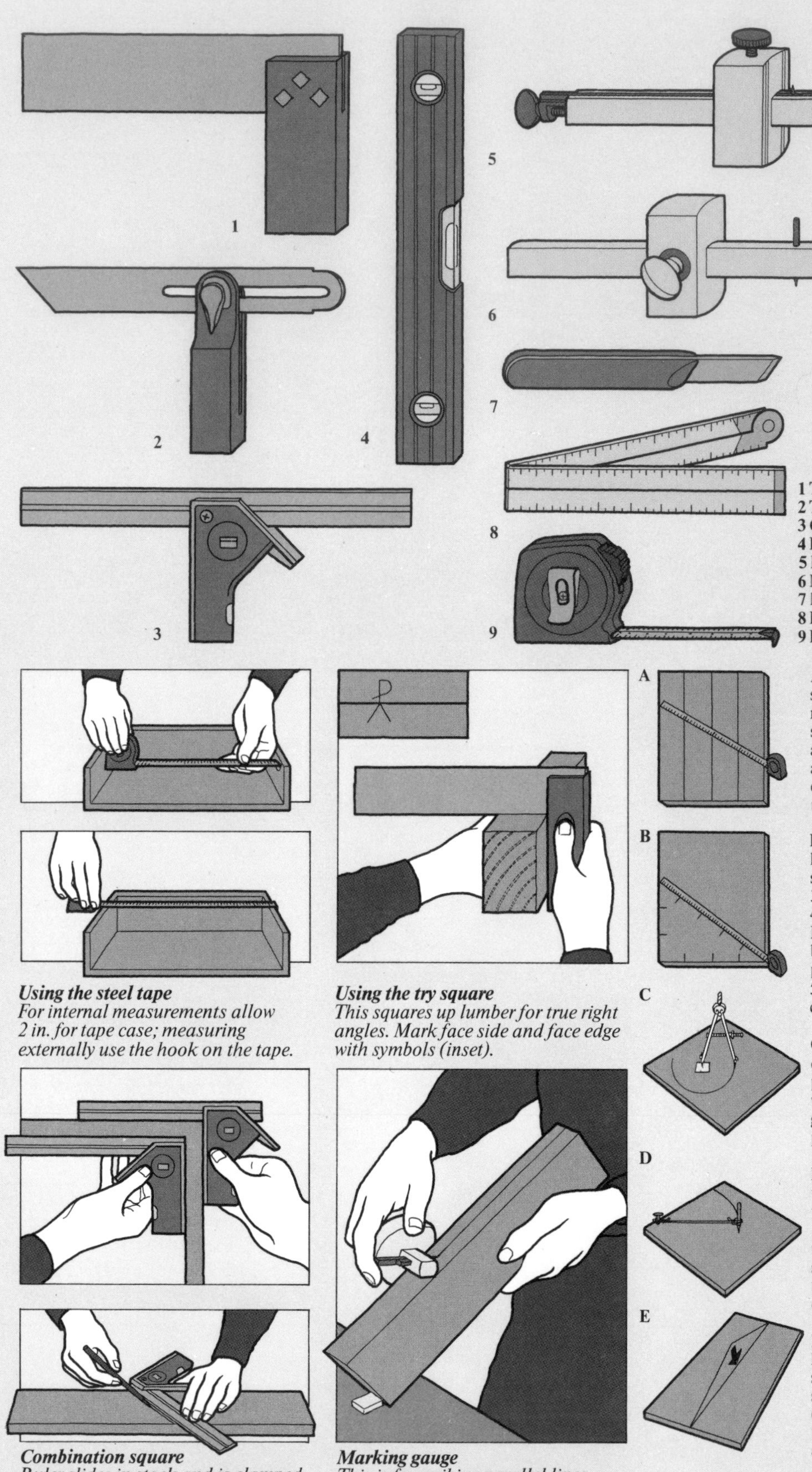

1 Try square
2 T bevel
3 Combination square
4 Level
5 Mortise gauge
6 Marking gauge
7 Marking knife
8 Folding ruler
9 Retractable tape

Using the steel tape
For internal measurements allow 2 in. for tape case; measuring externally use the hook on the tape.

Using the try square
This squares up lumber for true right angles. Mark face side and face edge with symbols (inset).

Combination square
Ruler slides in stock and is clamped by means of a knurled nut. Checks inside and outside angles, also 45°. Has vials for checking horizontal and vertical.

Marking gauge
This is for scribing parallel lines at a set distance. The stock guides scribing point along work. Use scribing gauge to mark across grain before cutting with a saw.

A To subdivide any size board into any number of equal strips, set ruler at angle across board and mark off equal units of measure.

B For checking a large corner for square, measure 3 units one side, 4 units the other. If line drawn between these points measures 5 units, then the corner is square.

C When using a compass on wood, protect surface with a piece of glued card to take point.

D Draw large circles using string tied to a pencil at one end, and nailed at the other. String should be under tension as the circle is drawn.

E Mark long, straight lines with chalked string. Fasten string taut between each end, then pluck string against surface.

Holding Lumber

Tools

The tools shown on the right will hold a wide variety of simple and complicated shapes and joints.
Woodworking vise has wide, flat jaws that spread the grip on the lumber to prevent undue bruising. Jaws are drilled for fixing with wooden facings.
Clamp-on vise is useful for light work, fits to the workbench with a screw clamp.
Workmate is a very useful, portable metal bench with built-in vise.
Sash clamp holds several large pieces of lumber.
C clamps are made in a range of sizes. A tightening screw holds the work in place.
Hold down is a bench-mounted clamp for holding work of awkward shape.
Miter clamps hold mitered joints accurately for nailing or gluing. Ideal for making picture frames.

Techniques

The vise is probably the most frequently applied method of securing lumber while woodworking. A vise set flush with the front edge of the bench, fixed with hardwood facings for the jaws, gives additional support to long pieces of lumber (see right). When using a vise, always clamp the work at the center of the vise to avoid distortion; the alternative is to place a piece of wood of a similar thickness on the opposite side of the work. Do not overtighten the screw as this could strain the jaws. This same rule applies to all vises and clamps: overtightening can damage both work and tool.
The lightweight, clamp-on vise has the advantage of being portable, so that it can also double as a clamp. The workmate's vise has long jaws – about 30 in. – and operates either in parallel or with a taper action to hold pieces of an awkward shape. Smaller jobs of this kind can be secured with the versatile C clamp: if you are gluing two wedge-shapes together, for example, and the joints tend to slip out of place, use another C clamp to sandwich the joint edges, with a piece of polythene sheet between the clamp heads and the joint to protect them from glue. Remember when using a clamp to place "softening" between the work and the clamp heads to avoid bruising.

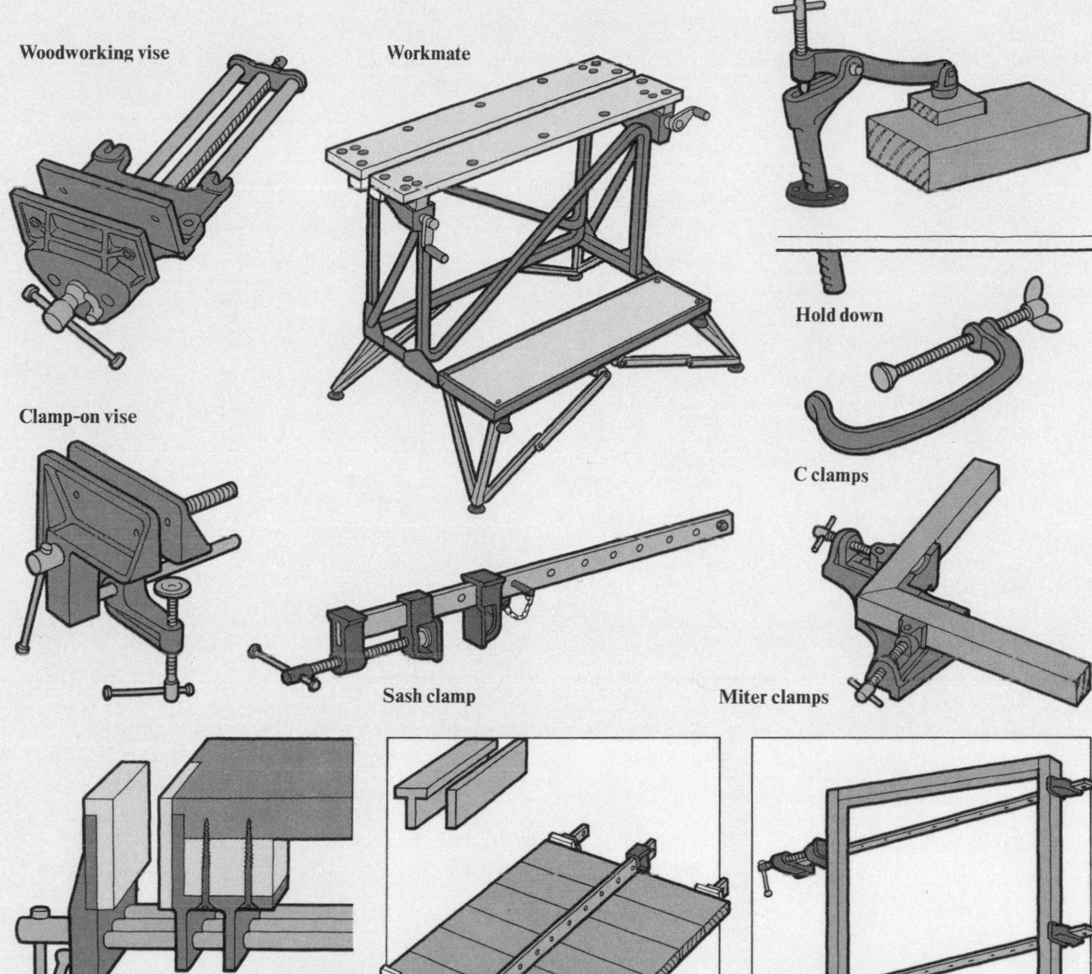

__Fitting a vise__
Cut a housing in front edge of work-bench, deep enough to accept rear jaw of vise, plus its hardwood facing, so that facing is flush with front edge and surface of work top. Screw vise to underside of bench using a spacer block.

__Correcting bowing__
Distortion sometimes occurs when gluing planks to make a wide board. Place sash clamps alternately over and under the board to counteract bowing action.

__Clamping frames__
Distortion can also occur when clamping frames. If the frame is out of square, set the clamps at a slight angle in the direction of the pull. Lightly tighten up screw until the frame is pulled square and true.

__Making your own sash clamp__
Use a pair of clamp heads, and fit the heads to a 1 in. thick hardwood rail. Drill holes to take the steel dowels – one near the end of the rail for one clamp head, the others at intervals or where needed.

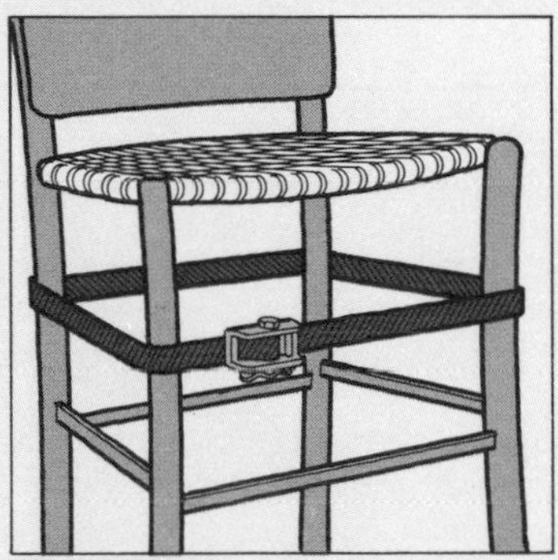

__The web clamp__
A band of webbing fitted with a ratchet clamp enables you to maintain all-round pressure on frames. The final tension is applied to the ratchet with a wrench or a screwdriver.

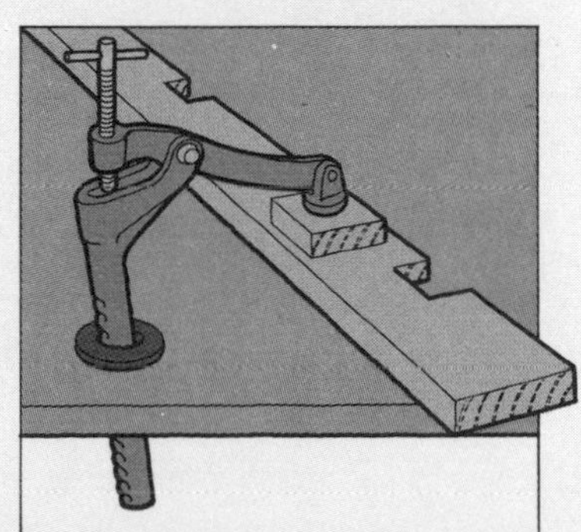

__The hold down__
Some hold downs are mounted to the bench with countersunk screws. Others have a metal collar set flush on the bench top, a notched pillar and turning screw provide the clamping power.

Saws

Tools

Rip saws and **Crosscut** saws have thin, flexible and unbacked blades for cutting lengths or panels of wood, hard or particle board. The set, pitch and number of teeth per inch determines saw's function (see right).
Panel saw is a smaller version of the crosscut and also cuts with the grain.
Tenon saw is strengthened along top edge, and used for cutting large joints, especially in softwood. It is the most versatile backsaw.
Dovetail saw is finer than the tenon, useful for cutting hardwood joints.
Compass saw blade slots in the handle. It cuts panels where coping saw is restricted by the frame.
Coping and **fret saws** both have a frame to provide tension for the thin blade. Coping saw cuts lumber and panels with equal ease.
Bench hook is essentially a cutting board. It secures wood for crosscutting.

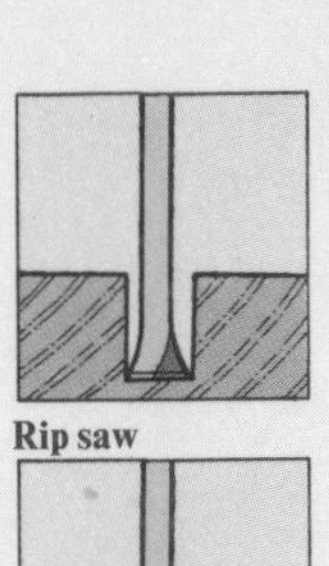

Rip saw's teeth shave like miniature plane blades so you can saw with the grain. Crosscut's teeth "scribe" two lines, cutting across the grain.

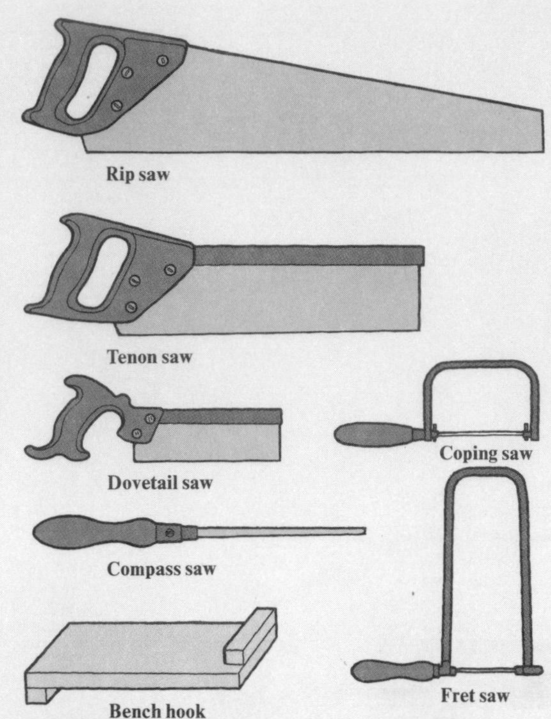

Cutting with the fret saw
The deep frame of the scroll or fret saw allows plenty of freedom for cutting shapes from plywood or other types of wood panel, while the thin blade enables you to cut fine and intricate patterns. You will probably need to lay the panel on a bench, and use the saw as shown above. The blade should be fitted to the saw with the teeth facing backward, so that the bench supports the panel during the cutting stroke.

Techniques

Not so long ago, all sawing was done by hand, planks being cut from the tree trunk in a saw pit with a two-handed saw. In spite of the widespread use of the modern power tool, a hand saw remains the most efficient means of cutting wood. Because sawing jobs sometimes promise to be lengthy, most people prefer to use a power tool. But where the wood section is deeper than the power saw blade, or when fine and accurate cutting is needed, you must use a hand saw. Remember that a sawing job requires much less effort if the saw is kept sharp, and the teeth are correctly set.
When you have marked the wood for cutting, always saw on the waste side of the line, starting the cut with the butt end of the blade (the tip of the blade if it's a rip saw). If the saw jams in the cut you may find the blade has wandered, or you are not holding the saw firmly (see right), or the wood is not secure. Lengths of wood must be supported on a bench, or on trestles, and panels should be well supported on either side of the cut.
With plywood or particle board panels, you should use a panel saw. When cutting straight across a thick section, first mark a continuous line at 90° on adjacent sides of the wood, using a try square. Then cut to the waste side of the line.

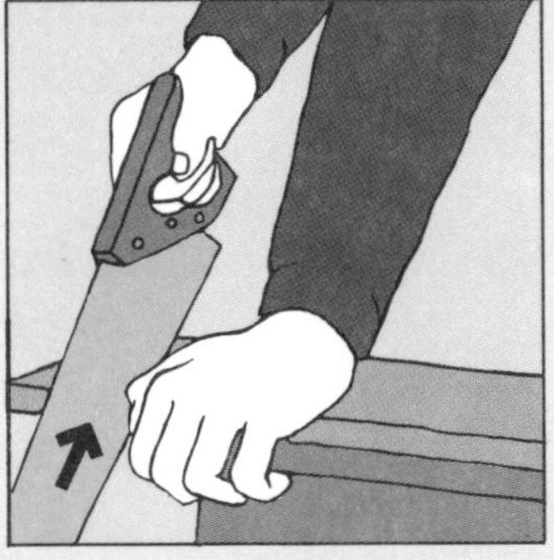

Using a hand saw
Grip the handle, steadying the blade with the forefinger, the blade in line with the forearm. Hold saw at an angle to the work, using the thumb as a guide to start the cut. Establish cut with backstrokes. Saw with regular strokes, using the full length of the blade.

How to prevent splitting
When you approach the end of the cut, support the wood on the waste side. This will prevent the weight of the waste from breaking off and splitting the edge of the work. Make your final strokes slowly and carefully to ensure success.

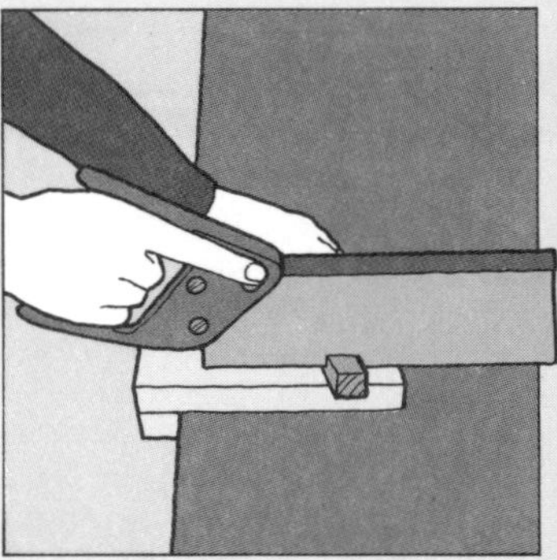

Using a backsaw
Apart from establishing the cut, a backsaw should be held square to the work, especially when you need accurate crosscutting for joints. For short lengths of wood, use a bench hook, which is held firm by the edge of the bench, and provides a shoulder to support the work.

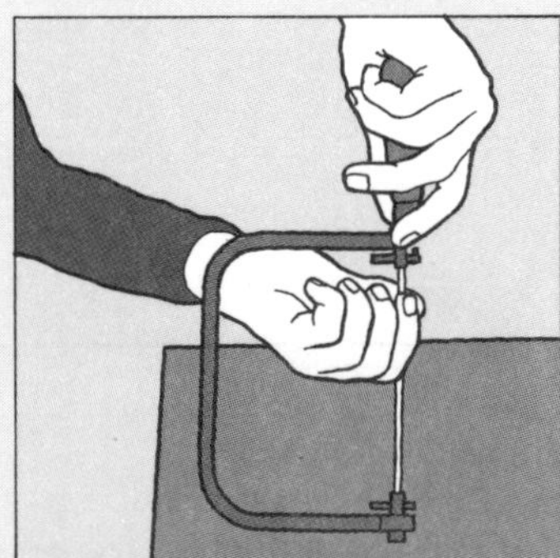

Fitting a blade in a frame saw
Locate the blade in the front end of the frame, the teeth facing forward. Press frame against a firm surface until you can attach other end of the blade. Most saws have a handle that unscrews to release blade tension.

Cutting shapes
Blades can be adjusted to any angle so that the frame does not restrict movement. To cut shapes in a panel, drill a starting hole and pass blade through hole before connecting it to the frame.

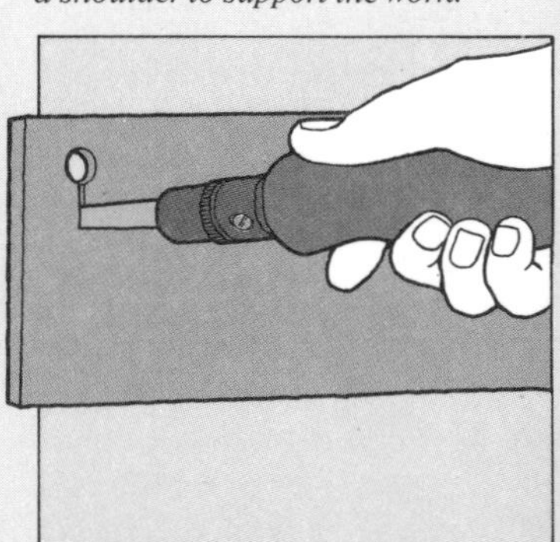

Using the compass saw
The wider and stronger blade of the compass saw allows you to cut through fairly thick panels, and is better suited than the coping saw for cutting straight lines. Start the cut by drilling a hole in which you can locate the blade.

Chisels & Gouges

Tools

Chisels and gouges are designed for those cutting jobs that cannot be tackled with a saw or plane. Chisels cut holes and recesses in wood, and are essential for most joining jobs. Gouges, which are available in great variety, have a curved section, and are very useful for carving hollow shapes.

The bevel edge chisel is particularly versatile in that it can perform most cutting operations, and undercuts shoulders for dovetail joints.

The firmer chisel is stronger due to its squarer section, and is used for heavier cutting work.

The mortise chisel can cut narrow, deep holes, and is designed to lever the waste wood out of the recess.

The firmer gouge, like its chisel relation, is for heavy work, and can be ground on either side of the curve.

The scribing or **paring gouge** is usually longer than the firmer, and ground on the inside only.

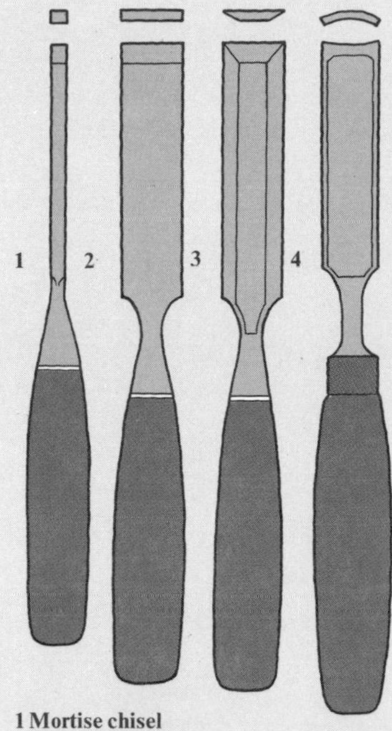

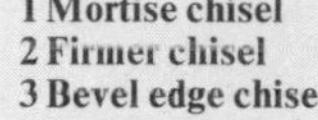
1 Mortise chisel
2 Firmer chisel
3 Bevel edge chisel
4 Paring gouge

Techniques

The bevel of a chisel or gouge should always face away from the finished edge of the work, so that the waste material is pushed clear. Because a chisel will always cut deeper when the bevel is uppermost, cut shallow recesses with the bevel face down. This also allows the blade to clear the sides. When chopping out a mortise, remove most of the waste before cutting on the line, otherwise the bevel will drive the chisel edge over the line.

Fine paring

A straight line is more easily cut with a wide chisel than with a narrow one. A golden rule when handling chisels is never to have your hand in front of the cutting edge – grip the chisel by the handle, and hold the blade between thumb and forefinger. Use a whetstone to keep chisels sharp, you can feel a burr by running your thumb along the underside of the edge.

Driving a chisel

Where particularly heavy cutting work is involved, you will need a mallet – never a hammer – to drive the chisel. Otherwise, strike the end of the handle with your hand, while maintaining your grip on the blade. Cutting across the grain usually needs extra effort: hold the chisel in one hand and put the weight of your shoulder behind the cut. Rest the other hand on the work, the blade between thumb and forefinger.

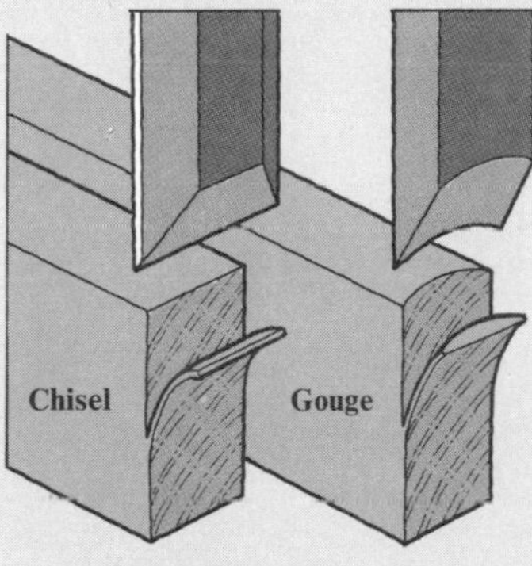

Drills

Tools

The brace is designed to drill large diameter, deep holes using an auger bit, and is particularly useful for clearing away mortise waste. The size of the brace is determined by the sweep or arc of its offset handle; an arc can be up to 14 in. The larger the sweep the easier the brace is to operate, except in confined spaces where the ratchet brace is best.

The hand drill makes smaller holes – down to 1/32 in. diameter. The cranked handle is geared to produce high speeds. Long shank twist drills are used.

Auger bits. The most common variation of bit is the *solid center bit,* designed to drill fairly shallow holes, with a cutting edge that prevents splitting of the wood. The *Jennings* or *twist bit* drills deeper, clearing the waste as it goes. *Expansive bits* have an adjustable diameter, while *countersink bits* have a recess for flathead screws.

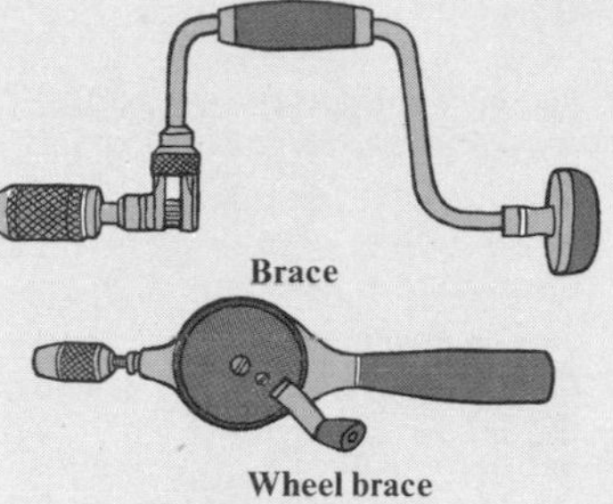

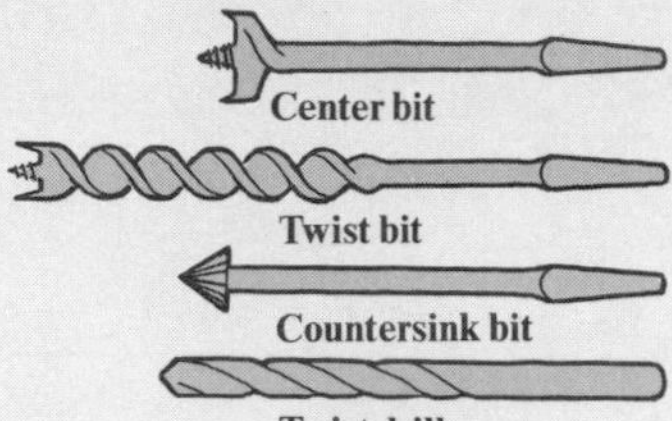

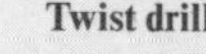

Techniques

If the brace is fitted with a ratchet you can drill with short sweeps of the handle rather than having to turn it in a complete arc. This is very useful for drilling holes in narrow spaces. By holding the head of the brace, you can control the drilling angle, and by leaning your weight on the head exert greater driving power to the drill. When drilling deep holes, back off counterclockwise periodically in order to remove impacted waste material. If you want to drill small holes in wood, metal or plastic, use a hand drill with the appropriate twist drill. You can control the speed of a hand drill, which requires no electricity. Auger bits start a hole with the threaded point, but you must use a bradawl or center punch to start a twist drill. Auger bits should be sharpened with a bit file; twist drills with a whetstone, or a power grinder.

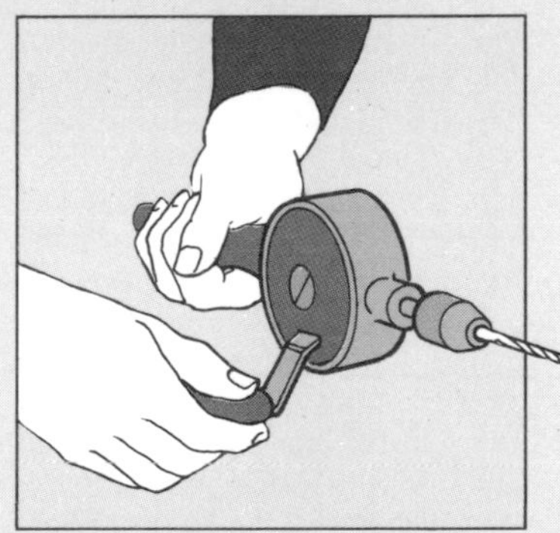

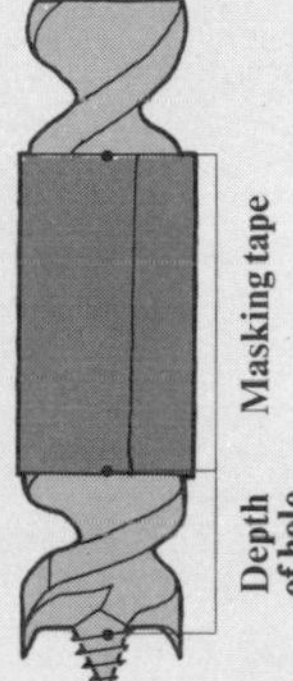

Gauging the depth of a hole
Wrap a piece of masking tape around the bit, to establish depth of hole. Remember to allow extra depth for lead screw. Don't let the tape ride up the bit when drilling.

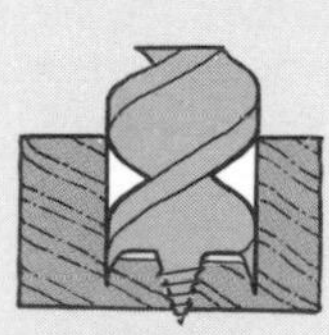

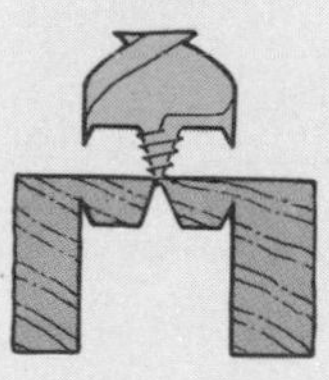

How to avoid the grain splitting
As soon as the lead screw breaks through the wood, back off the drill and meet the hole on the other side.

Shaping & Joining Lumber

General Purpose Planes

Planing lumber is the most effective means of leveling, or reducing the thickness to produce a smooth finish. Three similar planes with removable blades for sharpening are the *smooth plane,* 7 to 10 in. long, the *jack plane,* 12 to 15 in. long and the *jointer plane,* up to 24 in. The *smooth plane* is useful for finishing small jobs and cleaning up surfaces. The *jointer* will level long pieces of lumber, while the *jack plane,* which is the most versatile, fills the gap between the two and will do either job fairly well.

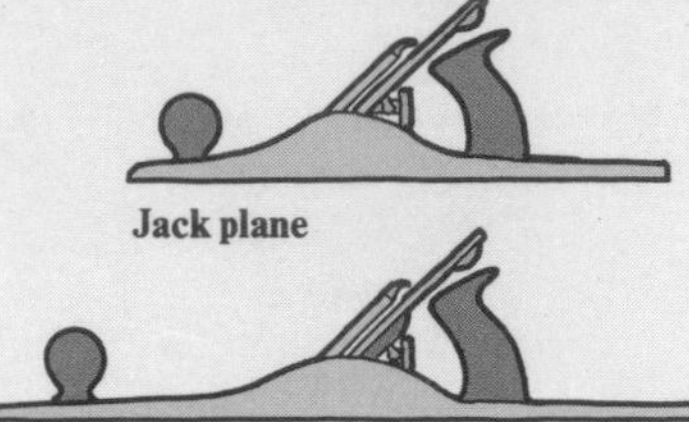

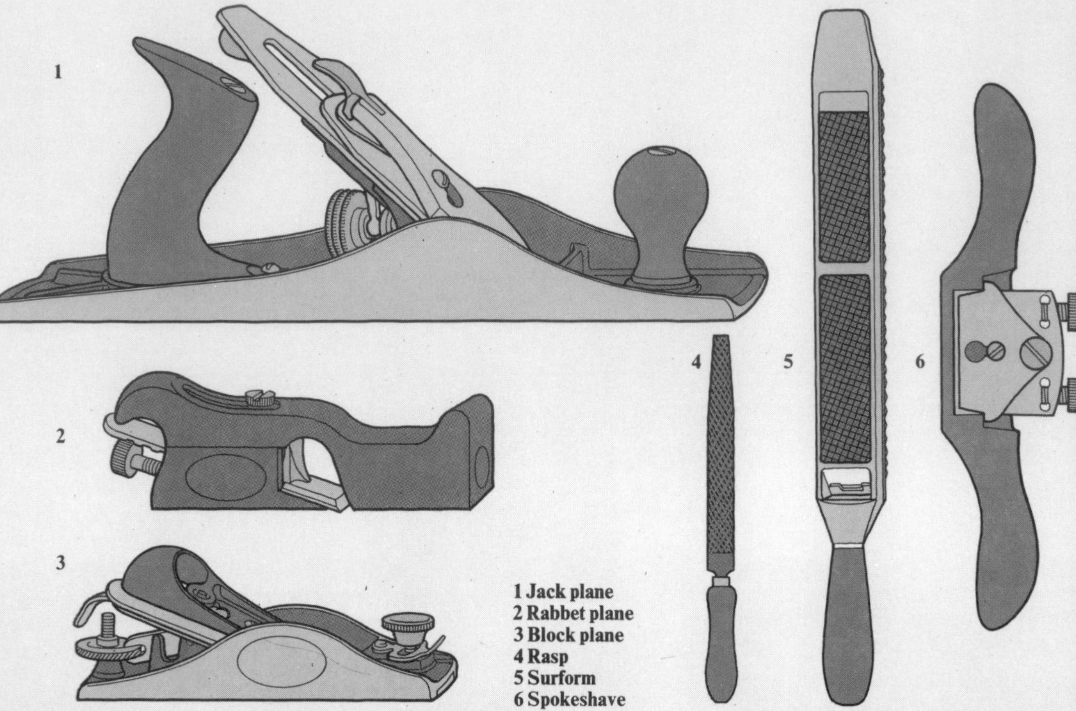

Special Purpose Planes

Special purpose planes cut grooves, curves and molded sections. A particularly useful addition to any toolkit is the lightweight, block plane used for planing end grain and finishing small areas, it can be used single-handed if needed. If you anticipate doing a lot of joining you will need a rabbet plane, which has a blade the full width of the sole, enabling you to finish a surface right up into a corner. Some types have a removable nose which is used for trimming stopped rabbets. Shaping lumber can be done with a rasp, a spokeshave or a surform. The spokeshave is used for cutting curves, either concave or convex; the surform is a modern development of the rasp, the cutting surface consists of many small blades pressed from sheet metal in the form of a mesh, and fitted with specially-designed handles. Lumber shaped with a rasp or surform usually requires further finishing to get a smooth surface. When using a plane or a spokeshave, always work in the direction of the grain. If in doubt, test a length by planing with a finely-set blade. Waxing the sole of a plane with a candle will help it to slide more easily over the surface. Before planing, check that the wood is flat. Mark any irregularities, then plane them flat. Use a shooting board to get a true, square edge.

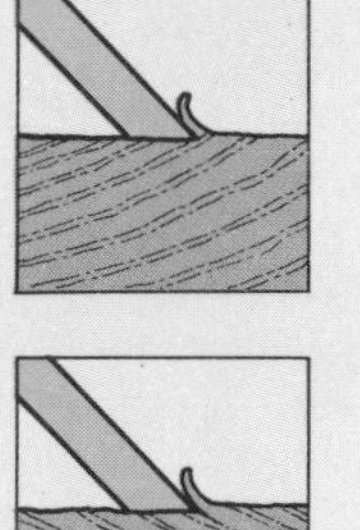
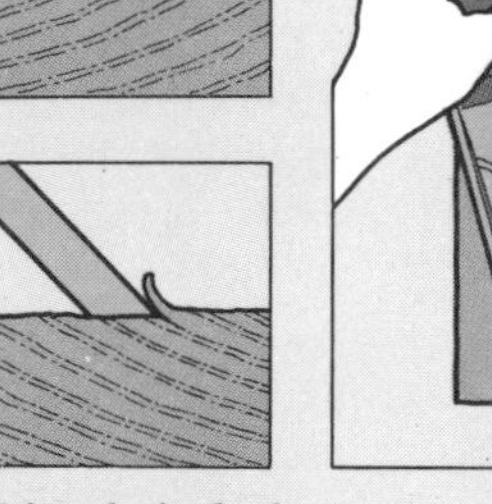
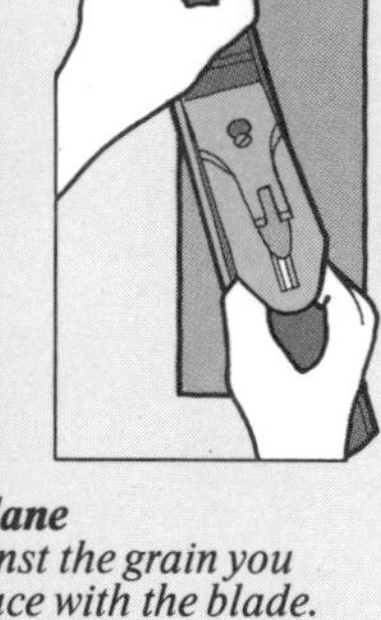

Using the jack plane
If you plane against the grain you will tear the surface with the blade. Planing with the grain and at an angle in the direction of the cut will encourage the blade to slice evenly through the lumber.

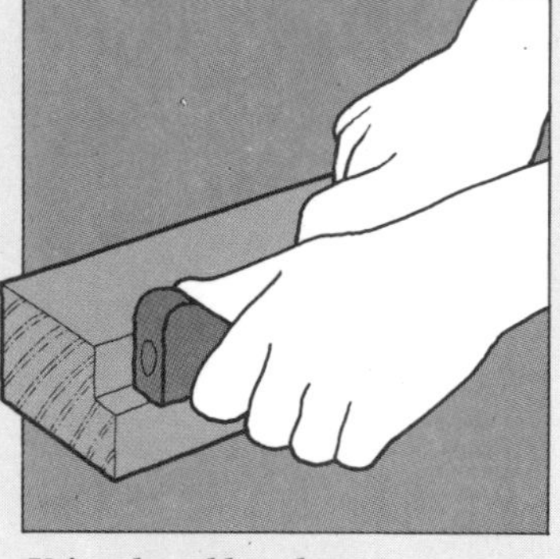

Using the rabbet plane
This will trim large tenon or rabbet joints. To cut a rabbet along the edge of a board, clamp a straight batten as a guide to the width of the cut. For deep rabbets, remove the batten after establishing the cut.

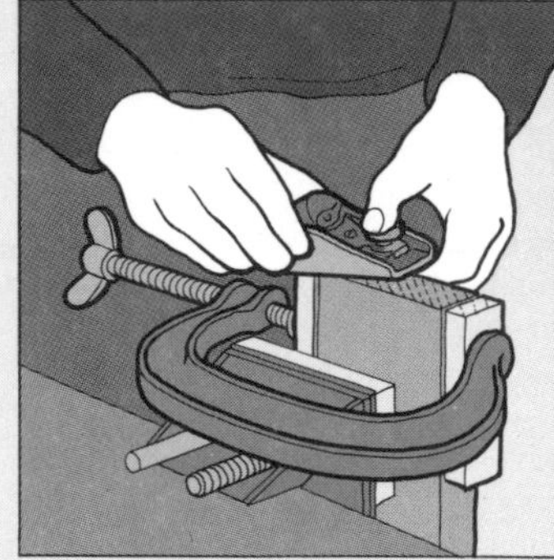

Using the block plane
When cutting across the end grain, see that the blade is as sharp as possible; unlike jack planes the blade is located bevel uppermost. Clamp two pieces of waste lumber on either side of the board to avoid splitting the wood.

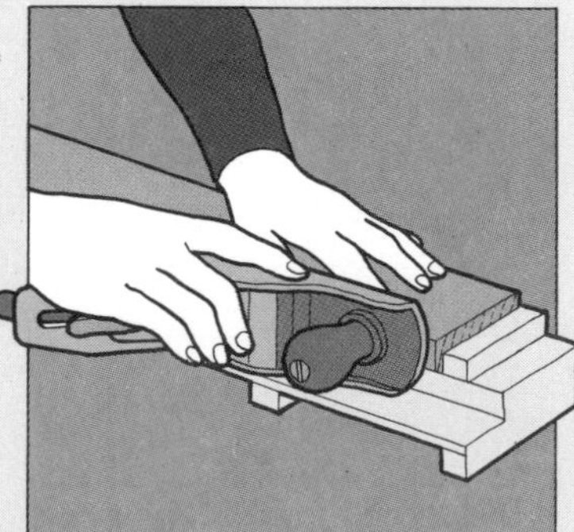

The shooting board
A shooting board is a platform mounted on a baseboard. The work rests against a stop on the platform. The plane is set on its side on the baseboard, the edge of the platform acts as a guide.

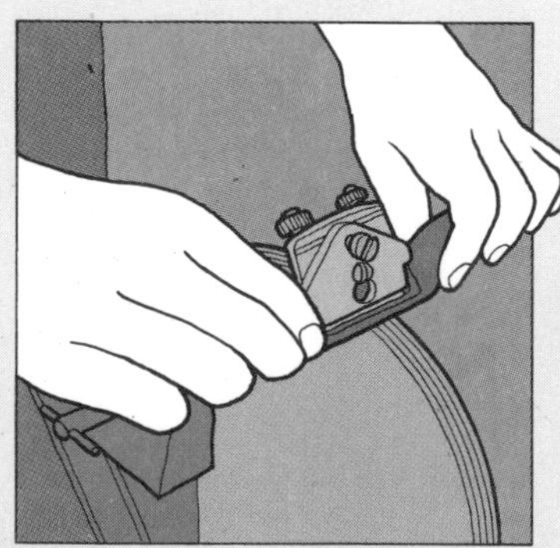

The spokeshave
As with the plane, you must use the spokeshave to cut with the grain, which usually means working from both ends of the lumber toward the center. Always keep the blade as sharp as possible.

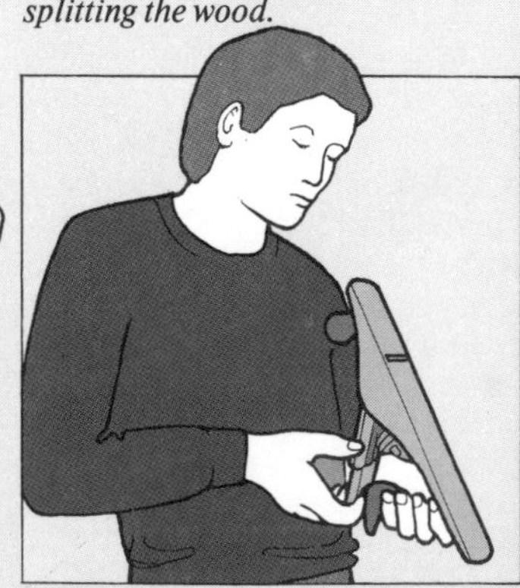

Plane adjustment
Align the blade square by sighting along the sole, and correcting with the lateral lever. Back off the knurled knob to obtain the required depth of cut.

Tools

Most jobs can be tackled with a modest selection of hammers and screwdrivers; in addition you need a nail set and bradawl. The basic tool kit may include the following:
Claw hammer is heavy enough to drive in large nails and combines a claw for nail removal.
Cross peen drives small nails and tacks. Tapered end is used to start off nails held between the fingers.
Set drives nail head below surface of lumber.
Ratchet screwdriver allows you to drive in screw without changing grip.
Spiral-ratchet drives in screw when you push against the handle.
Standard screwdriver is the most useful tool for general purpose work.
Philips screwdriver is for driving crossed-slot, matching screws.
Bradawl makes a pilot hole for screws.

1 Claw hammer
2 Cross peen hammer
3 Nail set

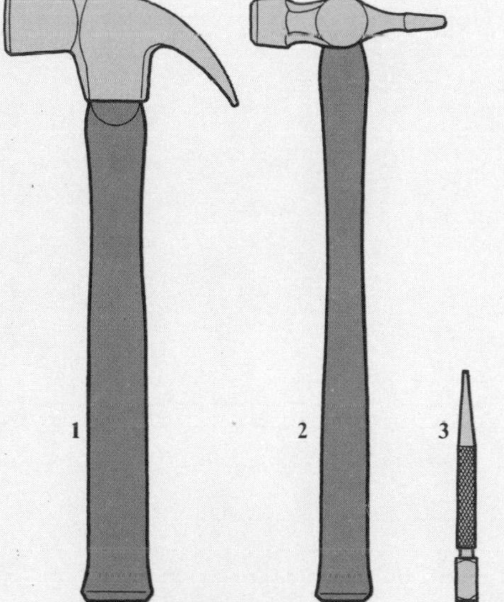

4 Ratchet screwdriver
5 Spiral-ratchet
6 Standard screwdriver
7 Philips screwdriver
8 Bradawl

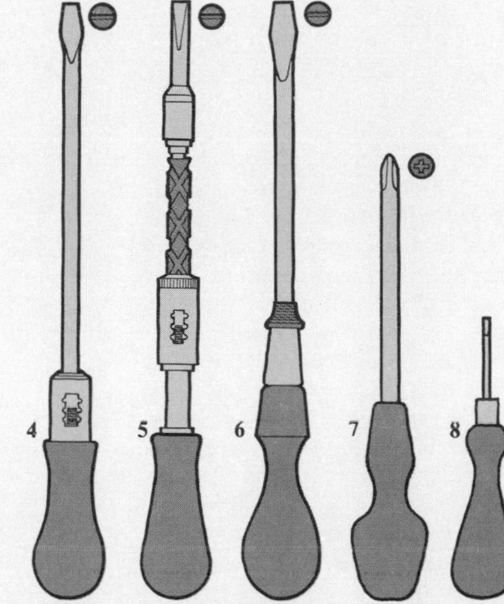

Techniques

Nails are used in greater variety than are screws, for fixing hardboard, wallboard, floorboards, cladding, roofing, joinery, and so on; there is a nail to suit nearly every kind of job.
To drive in a nail, start off with gentle taps until it is firmly seated. If you bend the nail, straighten it by tapping sideways, or remove it and start again.
If the hammer slips and bruises the lumber, soak the area with warm water so that the lumber can swell and raise the bruise; sand the raised grain when dry.
Screws are used in place of nails for those jobs requiring a tighter, more secure join. Nails can sometimes split the wood, while a screw will not cause splitting if you first drill a pilot hole.
The size of the screw should always match the size of the screwdriver – it is difficult to drive a large screw with a small screwdriver. On the other hand, if you use too wide a screwdriver for the screw head, you may damage the surrounding lumber as well as the screw head. Damage to a screw head can even occur with a Philips screwdriver if tool and screw are not correctly matched in size.
If the screw starts to bind as you work, it is in danger of stripping. The best solution is to remove it and grease the shank lightly.

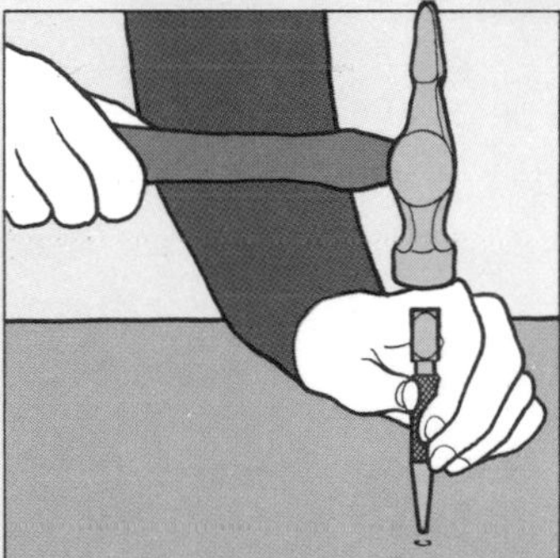

Using the set
The set is used to drive the heads of finishing nails, casing nails and brads below the surface of lumber. Set tip should be slightly smaller than nail head. Keep the set square to the nail and use a heavy hammer, even when you are only sinking small brads.

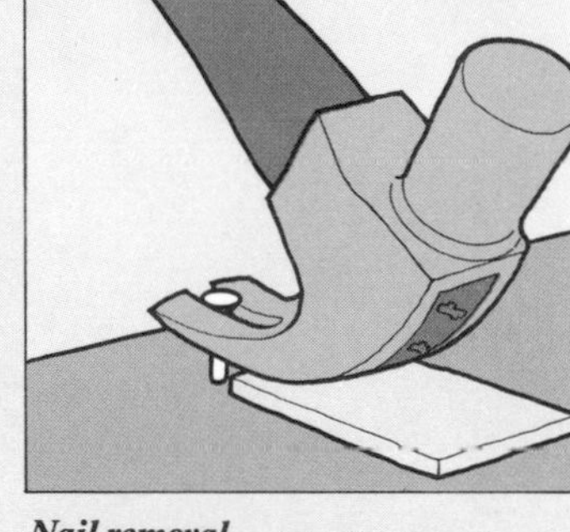

Nail removal
Nails can be removed with end-cutting pliers, or with a claw hammer. If the nail is stubborn and refuses to budge, you may have to resort to a wrecking bar. Avoid damaging the lumber by placing a block of wood under the tool while you are levering.

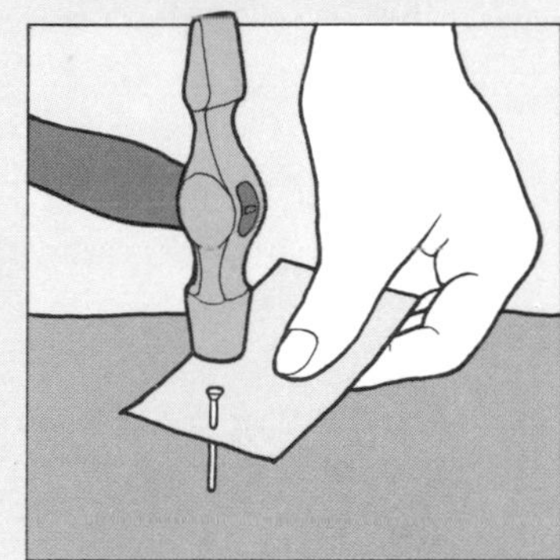

Driving brads
It is not easy to hold a small brad without hitting your fingers, unless you use a card to grip the nail. Cut a slot in a thin piece of card and slip it around the brad, or simply drive the brad through the card and then pull the card away.

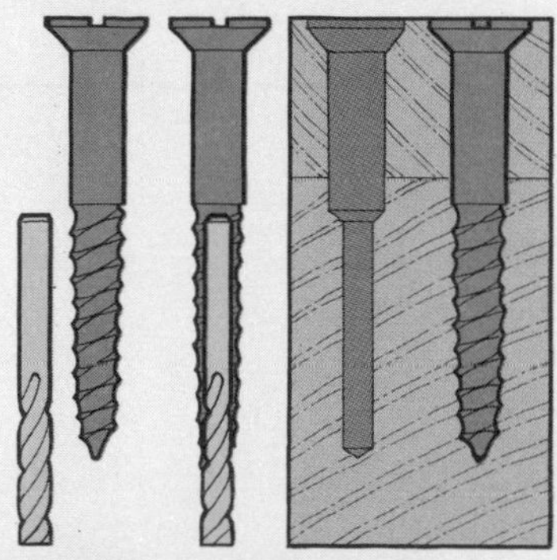

Drilling pilot holes
Driving a screw is less tiring if you make a pilot hole with a drill slightly narrower than the screw thread.
The shank of the screw will need its own wider clearance hole.

Removing damaged screws
Screw heads are sometimes solid with rust or paint, and you may have to re-cut the slot. Either use a hacksaw, or place the corner of a screwdriver in the slot and tap along it with a hammer.

Using the bradawl
Small screws can be started by making a hole with a bradawl. Press the tapered point of the bradawl into the wood, using a twisting action. Be sure not to make the hole too large.

Finishing Lumber

Using Scrapers

The majority of carpentry jobs need to be rendered smooth to perfect the finished appearance. Cabinet makers, who work mainly with hardwoods, use a steel scraper to smooth off wood surfaces after planing. This removes the fibers and gives the surface a silky finish. Scrapers are employed to give a finish to veneers, the burr on the cutting edge acts as a blade which removes the surface in fine shavings. Unlike sandpaper, it avoids creating dust which can clog the grain, and which would dull the luster of a wax or french polish. Should the scraper produce dust rather than shavings, it probably needs sharpening. The amount of pressure applied to the scraper will produce a varying curve in the cutting edge, localizing the cut. Scrapers are either rectangular and between 4 and 6 in. wide, or shaped, for giving a finish to concave and convex surfaces or molded sections.

Sanding Techniques

After you have planed wood, you can get a smoother finish with one of the many types of abrasive paper. Sanding should only take place after all the cutting has been completed – the residue of abrasives can blunt the edge of planes and chisels – to take away slight tool marks and dirt that may have built up on the surface. Sandpaper is no longer manufactured, but the term is still in general use. Flint paper is the most popular abrasive for finishing wood – this has a yellow color the appearance of sand. Red garnet paper gives a better finish, and is longer lasting. Black emery paper or cloth is used to prepare metal, while silicon carbide paper is sold as "wet-or-dry", and is used dry for rubbing down bare wood, or lubricated with water to give a smooth surface to painted wood or metal. Flat surfaces should be sanded with a sanding block, made of either cork or rubber, so that the entire surface of the paper is in contact with the work. When sanding up to the edge of a board, the block keeps the paper flat, and can overshoot without rounding off the edge. Don't let the paper become clogged with dust, so periodically tap the block on the edge of the bench. The same applies to the wet paper technique, which should be rinsed in water to clear impacted paint.

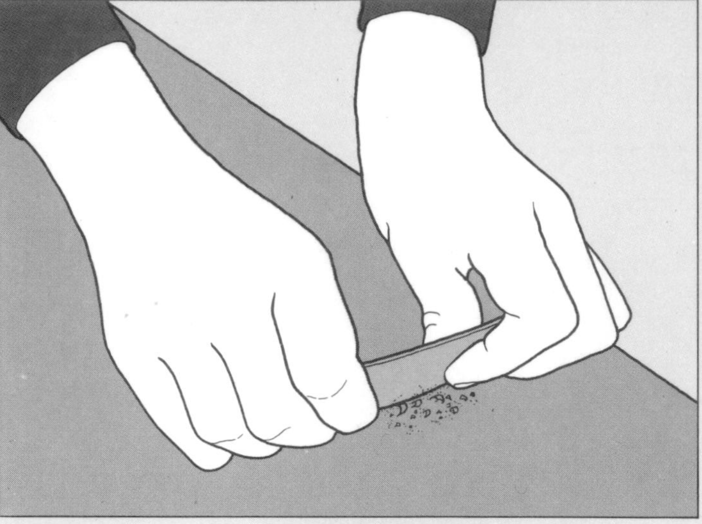

The cabinet scraper
Hold scraper with both hands, the thumbs pressed firmly against the back face, close to the bottom edge. Hold scraper at a slight angle and work with the grain.

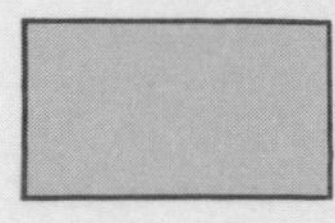

Square scrapers are about 1/16 in. thick, with two cutting edges for flat surfaces.

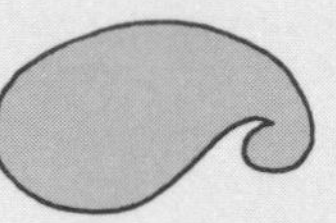

Shaped scrapers have an all-round cutting edge, for molded sections.

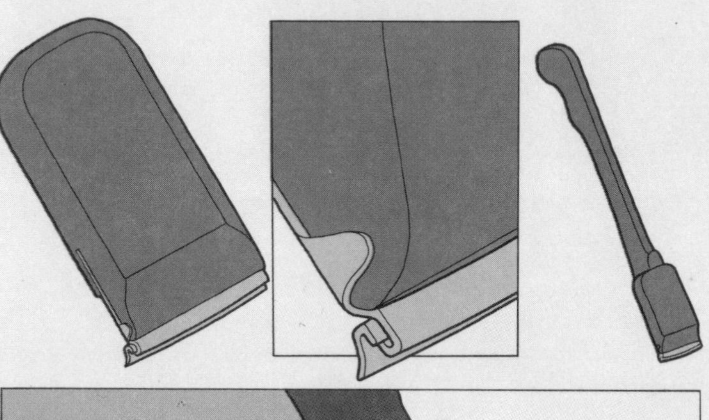

The hand scraper
The tool is designed for smoothing surfaces to varying degrees of finish. The blades are disposable and slot into a lip on the handle, some blades being finely toothed. The long-handled version of the scraper is used for heavy jobs, such as smoothing floorboards, especially in awkward corners, or stripping paint from clapboard.

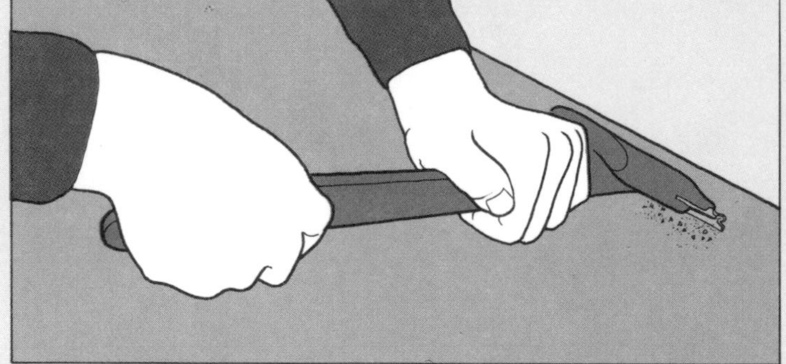

Scraper technique
Unlike the cabinet scraper, which works in one direction only, the hand scraper can be held to work with a pulling or pushing action, using one or both hands. When the blade becomes worn, slide in a new one from the side, which will automatically eject the old blade.

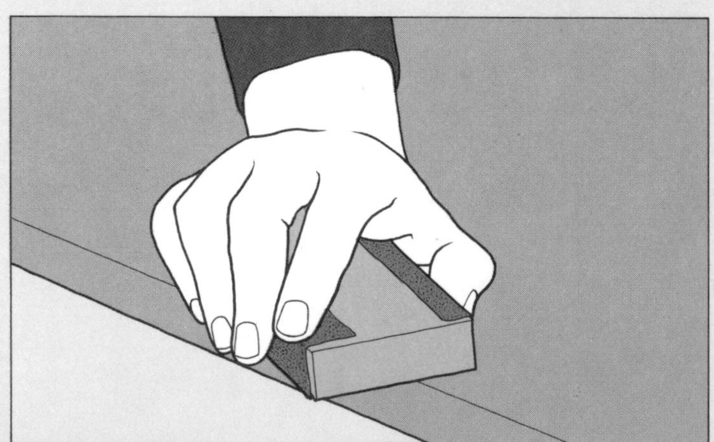

Using the sanding block
Always sand in the direction of the grain. Lines across the grain show up badly when lacquer is applied.

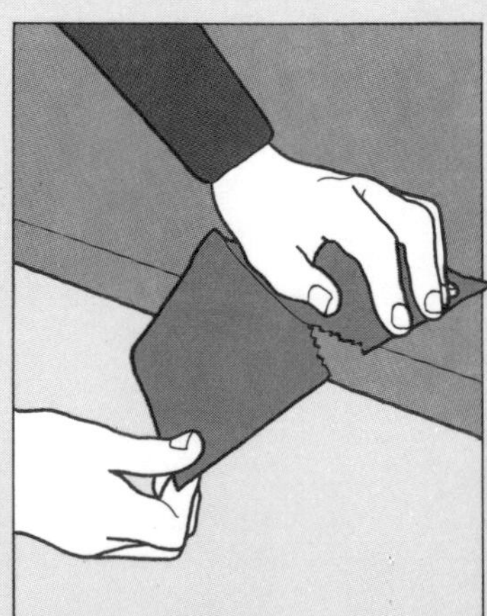

Dividing sandpaper
Never cut paper. Fold and tear to required size along edge of bench.

Sharpening Chisels & Planes

Using Sharpening Stones

Chisels and planes are sharpened on whetstones, and these come in three grades: coarse, medium and fine. Combination stones have a different grade on each side. The coarse surface is for regrinding a damaged blade; the medium and fine for getting a sharp edge. Choose a stone at least 8 in. long and 2 in. wide. Clean the stone's clogged surface with a stiff brush.

Regrinding a whetstone
Use carborundum powder, lubricated with water, rubbed against a flat, smooth surface.

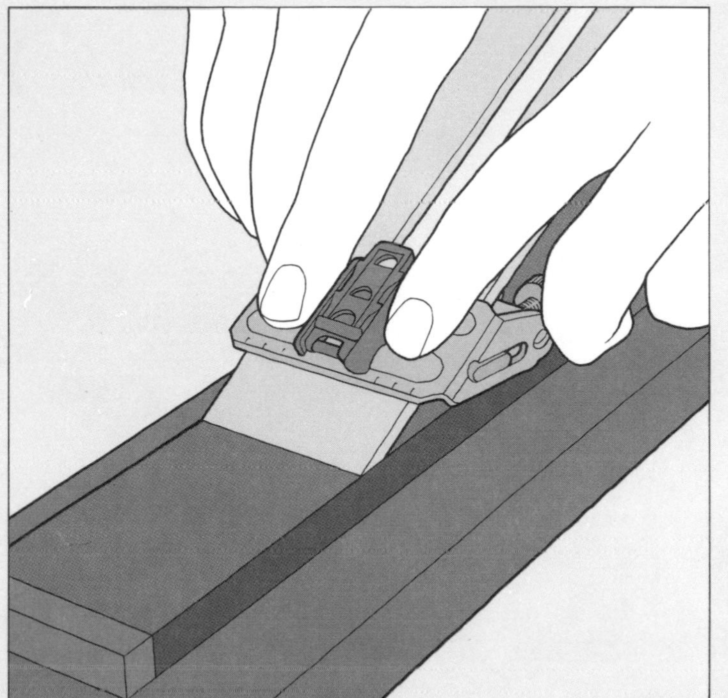

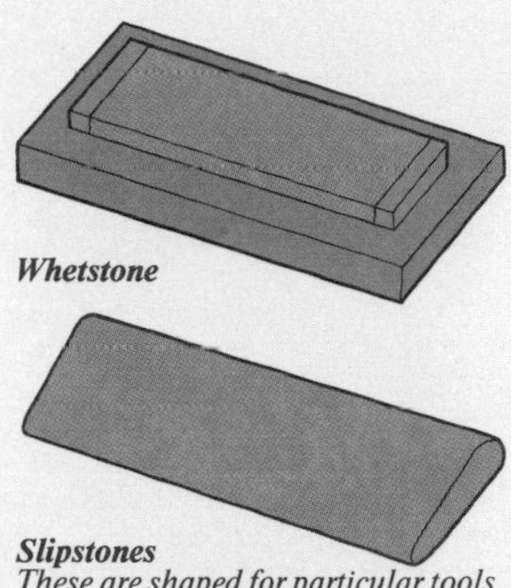

Whetstone

Slipstones
These are shaped for particular tools and are rubbed along edges.

Honing gauge
This clamps plane and chisel blades to correct angle, without rocking the blade in the process.

Sharpening Methods

Honing a new blade
A new plane blade, or chisel, has an angle of 25° ground on the cutting edge. You will need to put a finer edge on the blade by honing an angle of approximately 30°. See diagram **1.** Put a little oil on the whetstone **2.** Now hold the blade bevel face down, pressing against the back of the blade with your fingers **3.** Maintain the blade at the estimated angle, and rub it up and down the stone in an X pattern, to avoid wearing the surface in one place. When you can feel a burr on the flat side of the cutting edge **4,** hold the flat of the blade on the stone and move it from side to side a few times **5.** By alternately raising and returning the burr, it will break off, leaving a sharp edge. For a final keenness to the edge, strop on a leather strap **6.**

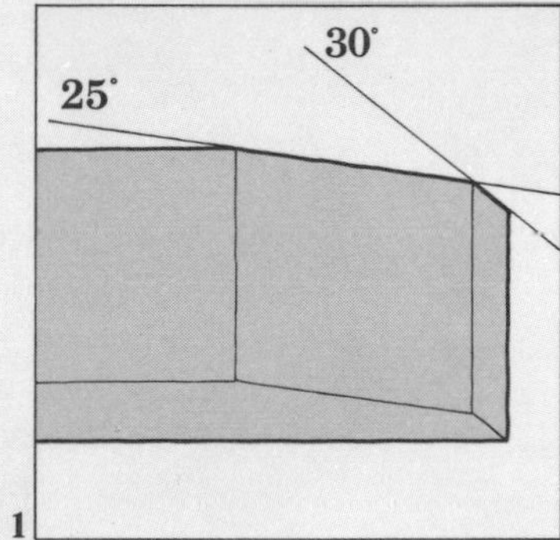

1

2

3

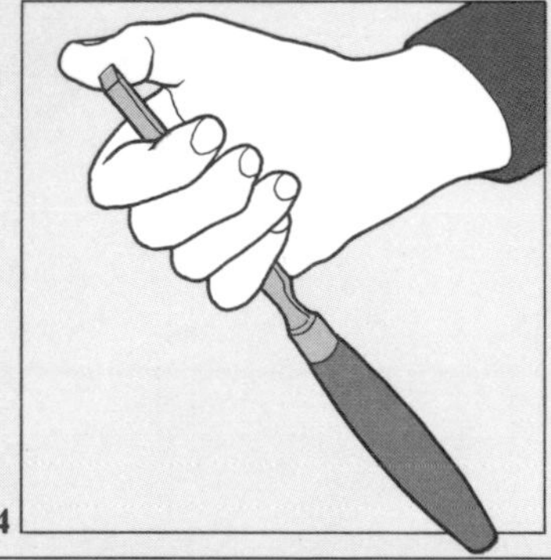

4

5

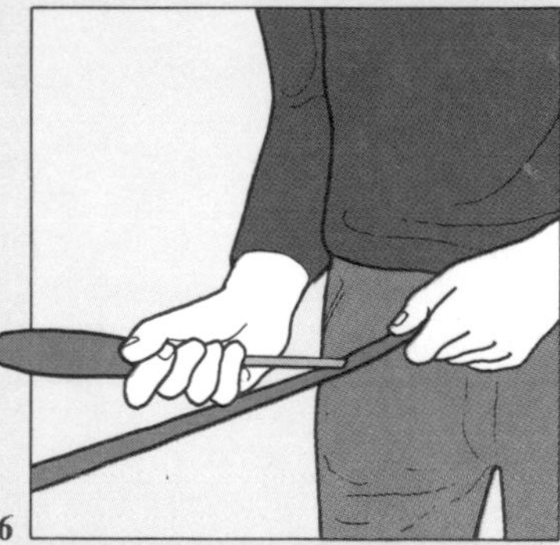

6

Regrinding an old blade
The quickest method of regrinding a worn or chipped blade is with a grindstone on a power tool **1.** Fit the tool-rest of the stone at 30° to the wheel surface **2.** Move the blade from side to side across the revolving wheel, maintaining a light but constant pressure **3.** If you press too hard you may "burn" the blade, which makes it impossible to sharpen. Keep the blade cool, lubricate with water.

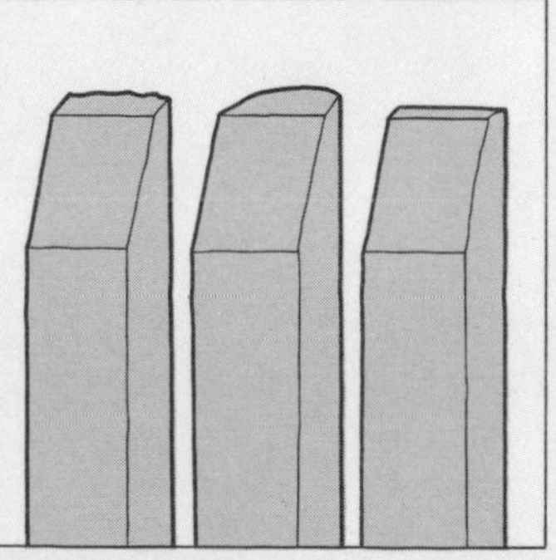

1

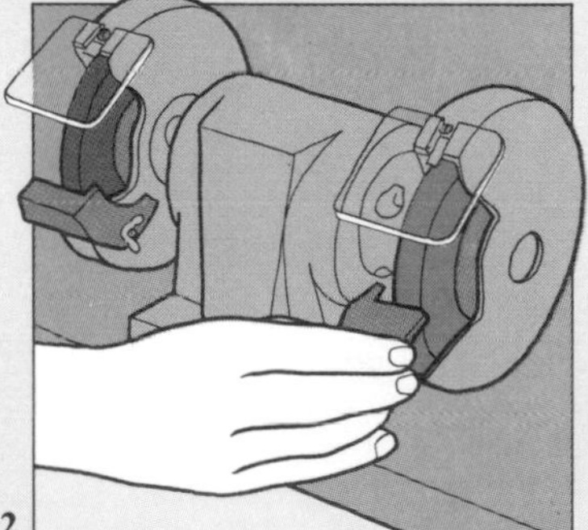

2

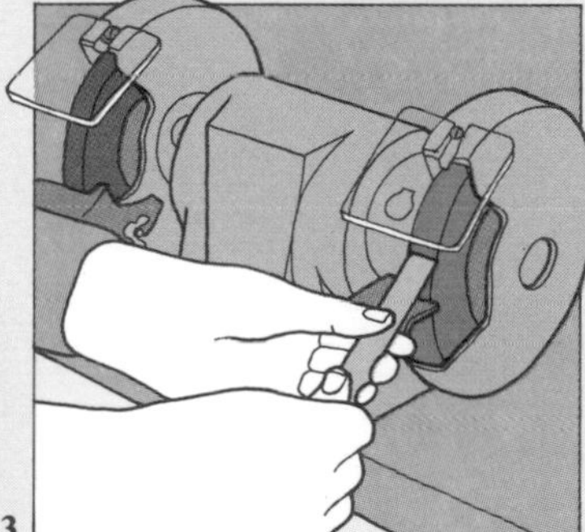

3

Sharpening Gouges, Scrapers & Bits

Sharpening a firmer gouge

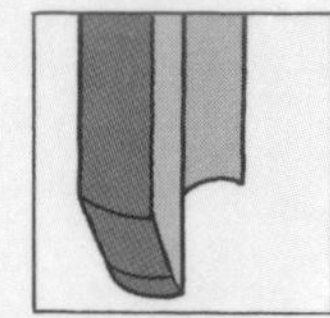

1 Place the gouge flat and at right angles on a whetstone. 2 Press firmly on the gouge and move it from side to side, rocking the tool to produce a burr. 3 Return the burr by rubbing the oiled slipstone up and down the inside face.

1
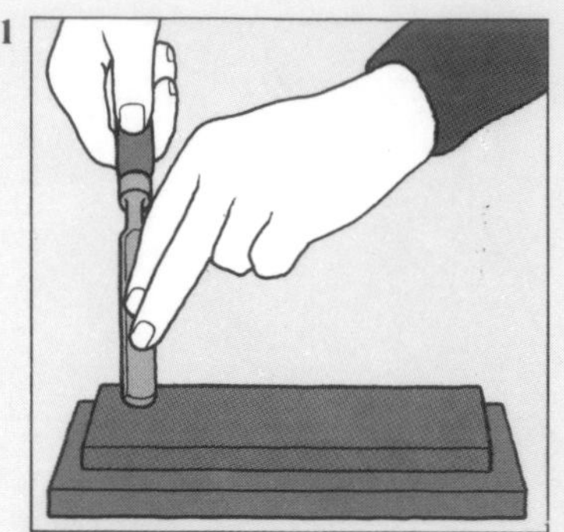

2
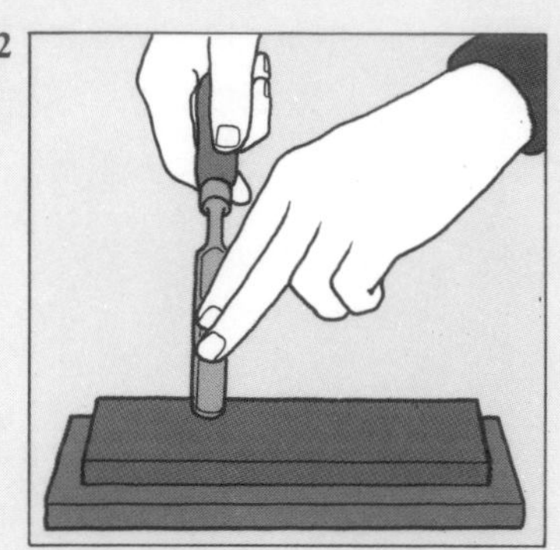

3
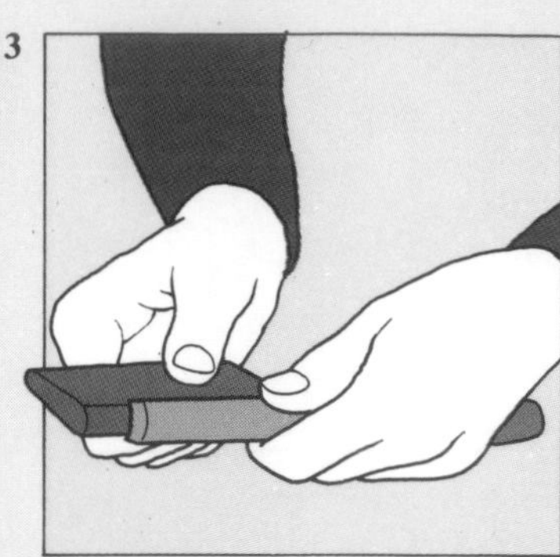

Sharpening a paring gouge

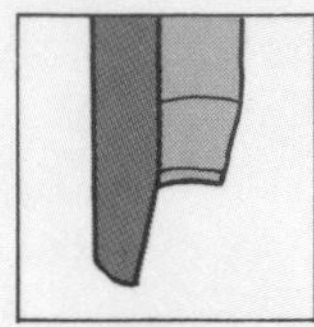

1 Put a few drops of oil on the inside of the blade. 2 Rub with a slipstone, held at about 30° to the edge, in order to raise a burr. 3 Rub the outside flat against the whetstone, rocking from side to side. Repeat both techniques until tool is sharp.

1

2

3

Sharpening scrapers

1 Clamp the scraper in a vise, and file the edges square. 2 Hold the scraper at an angle on a whetstone and raise a burr on all edges. 3 Rub the edge with the back of a gouge to turn over the burr, which must not be rounded (see above, right).

1
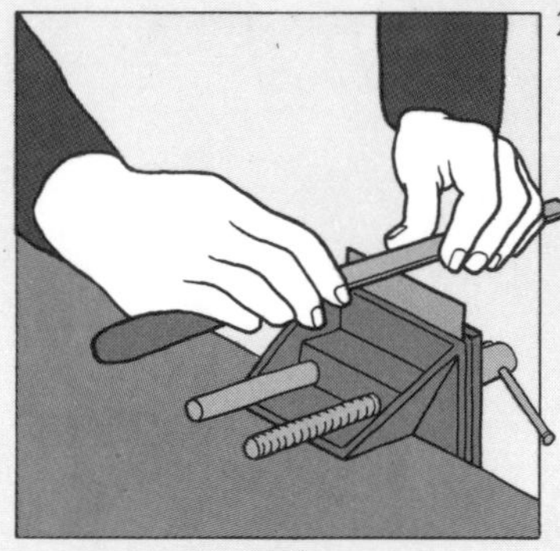

2

3
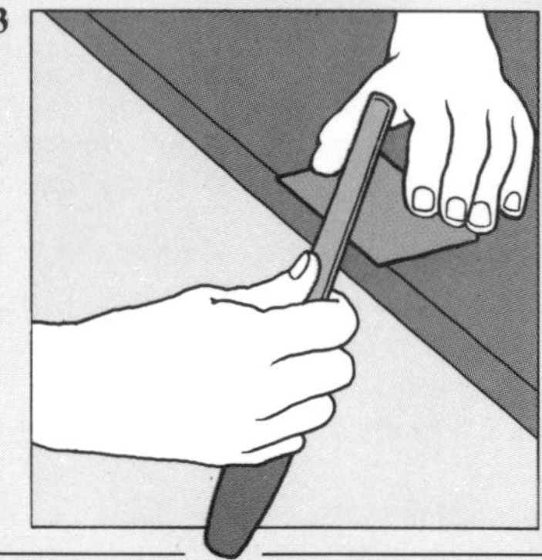

Sharpening a solid center bit

1 To function correctly the drill must retain its shape, so try to remove as little metal as possible when sharpening. 2 Sharpen cutting edges with a flat or auger bit file. 3 Carefully hone the small, projecting spur, but avoid touching the lead screw.

1
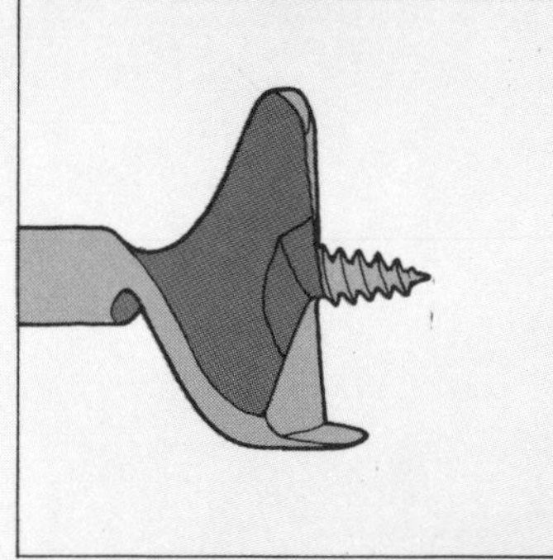

2
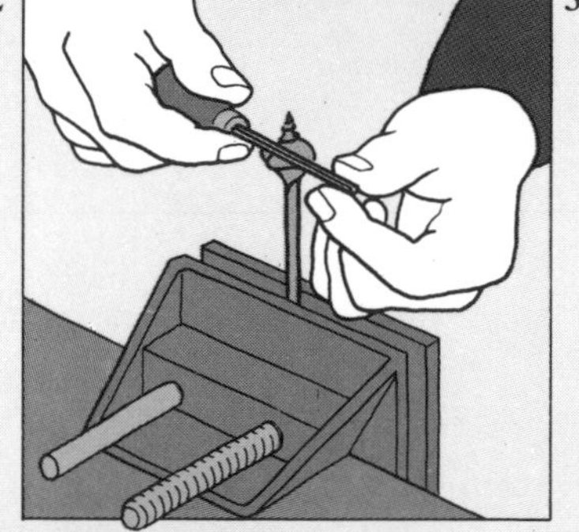

3
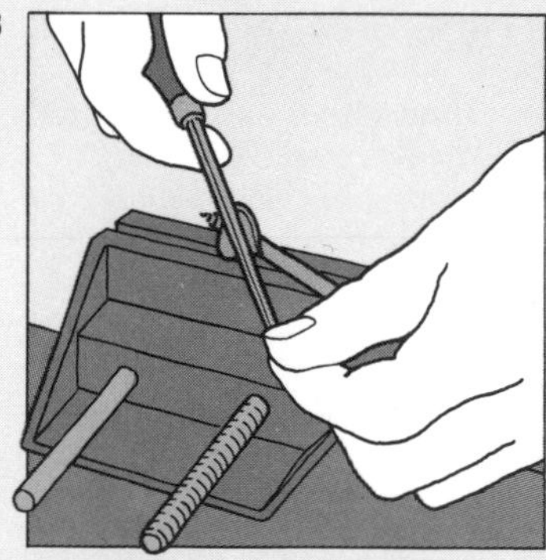

Useful sharpening hints

1 When the blade of a plane is wider than the whetstone, sharpen by holding it at an angle to the stone. 2 Before sharpening saw teeth, clamp saw in a vise and render teeth level with a whetstone. 3 A distorted screwdriver blade will jump out of a screw slot, or perhaps damage it. Keep drivers in good condition by grinding them square.

1

2

3
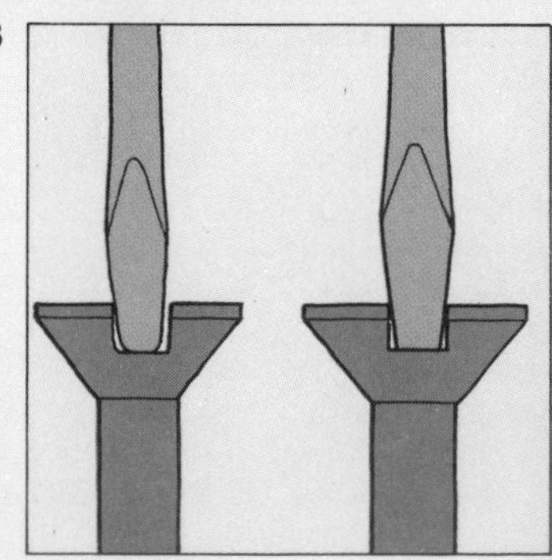

Sharpening Saws

Tools

Saw teeth must be sharpened by a file with a triangular section. The larger size of saw file is used for hand saws while the small size is for backsaws; compass, fret and keyhole saws are usually replaced rather than sharpened. A saw set is used to correct the angle of each tooth along the blade.

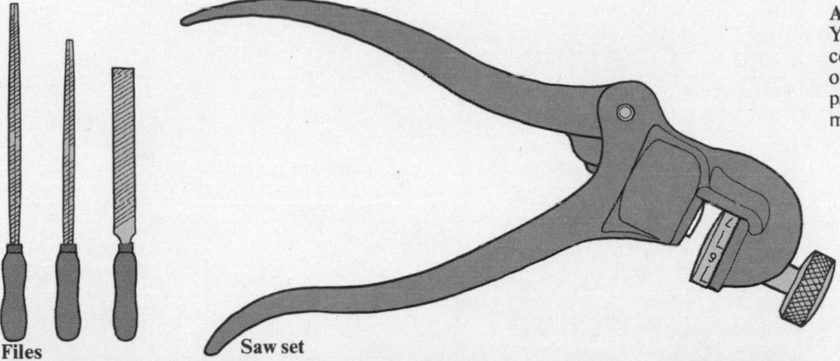

Adjusting the saw set
You adjust the set to correspond with the number of teeth per inch of the particular saw, usually by means of a graded dial.

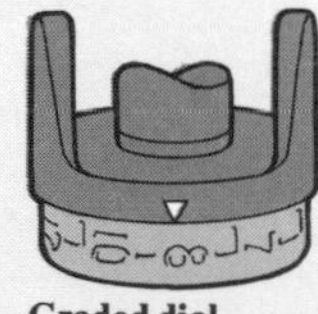

Graded dial

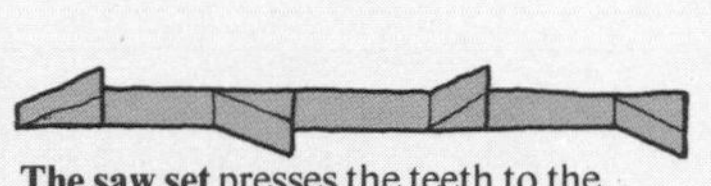

The triangular file is used to bring the teeth to a point.

The saw set presses the teeth to the correct angle or set.

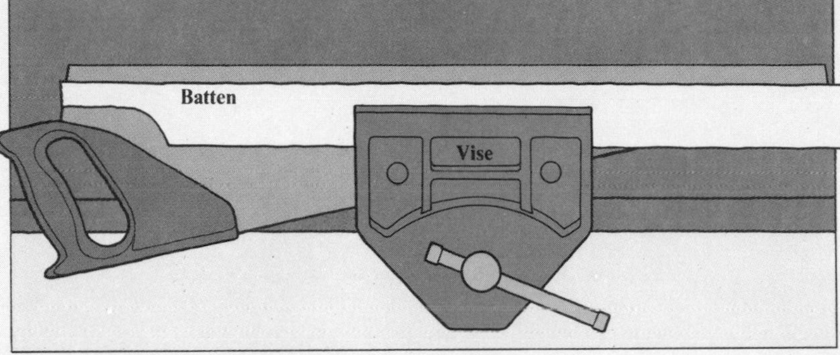

Securing the saw for sharpening
The saw must not vibrate while being filed, so the blade is best secured between two appropriate lengths of wood, clamped in a vise as shown on the left. The wood battens should support the blade as close to the teeth as possible.

Technique

A saw needs sharpening when it becomes an effort to cut with it, or you find that the cut is constantly wandering off course, or out of square. Do not allow the saw to become too worn before sharpening as it is then very difficult to obtain an even row of teeth. Some hardware or tool stores will sharpen saws, but with a little practice you can do it yourself. Saws with coarser teeth are easiest for the beginner as the angle at which you must file is more obvious.

Getting a cutting edge
First, clamp the blade in a vise, and between two battens of wood. Start filing from the left hand end of the saw, on the first tooth that is bent away from you. Position the file carefully, according to the angle of the tooth – at right angles to the blade if it is a rip saw, and at approximately 60° for crosscut or other types of saw.

Setting the cutting angle
File the teeth as described on the right, reversing the saw to repeat the sequence. The teeth are now sharp, but need to be set correctly so that the blade has sufficient clearance when cutting. The saw set is a hand tool, rather like a plier-wrench, and bends the teeth of the saw to the required setting by means of a plunger set opposite an anvil. Pressure is applied by squeezing the handles.

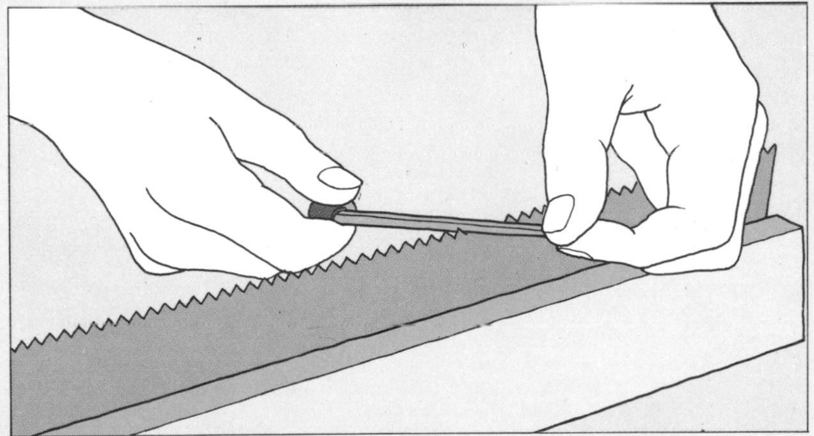

How to file the saw teeth
Hone each tooth with firm strokes, until bright metal appears along the whole face of the tooth. Move from left to right, filing alternate teeth. When you reach the end reverse the saw and repeat.

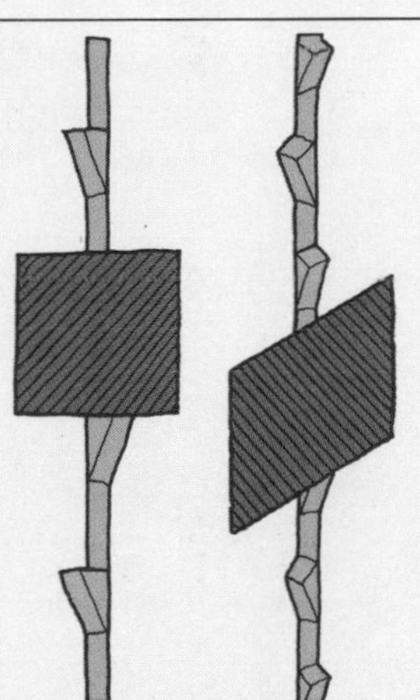

Correct filing angles
These two diagrams show how to position the file at the correct angle matching the pitch of the tooth.

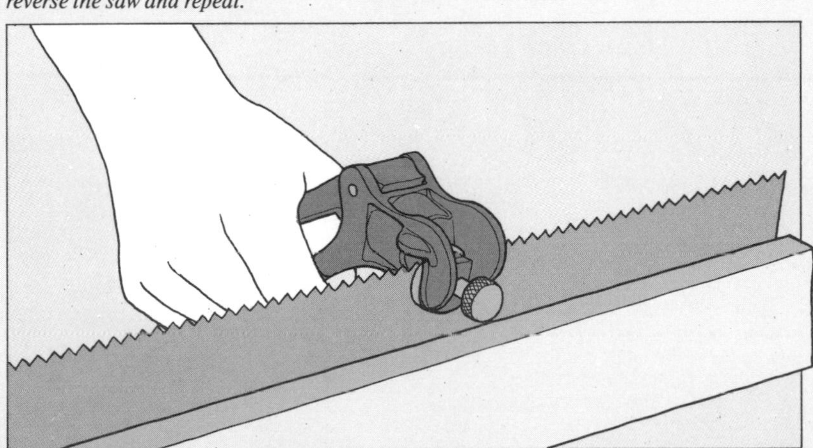

Using the saw set
Position the tool over each alternate tooth on the blade, and set to the required angle by squeezing the handles.

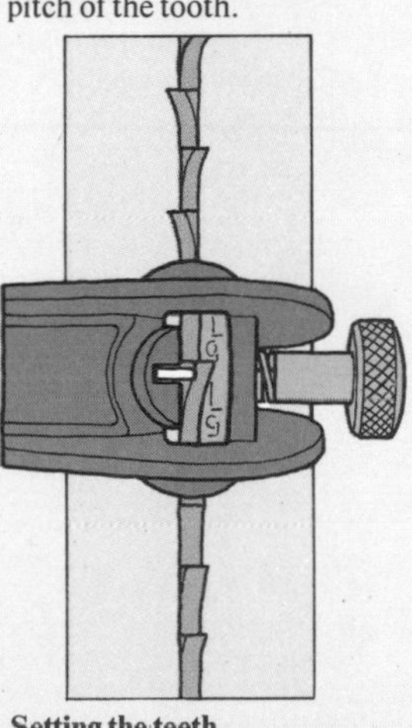

Setting the teeth
The saw set corrects the angle of each alternate tooth on one side of the blade.

Power Drills

The hand drill

The most versatile and certainly the most popular modern tool, the power drill can be applied to a wide range of activities from drilling masonry to stirring paint. Your choice of drill depends on the type of work you expect it to do. For the average household, a drill with one or perhaps two speeds is adequate; at maximum speed the motor runs at about 2500-3000 rpm. Drills with additional speeds are very useful because of the different resistance of materials: in general you need a high speed for drilling wood, a medium speed for metal, and a slow speed for drilling masonry and glass. The motor drive shaft is fitted with a chuck to receive drill bits or attachment shanks. These chucks are made in three sizes to take a range of drill bits. When combined with its various attachments and drill bits, the applications of the hand drill are virtually without limit.

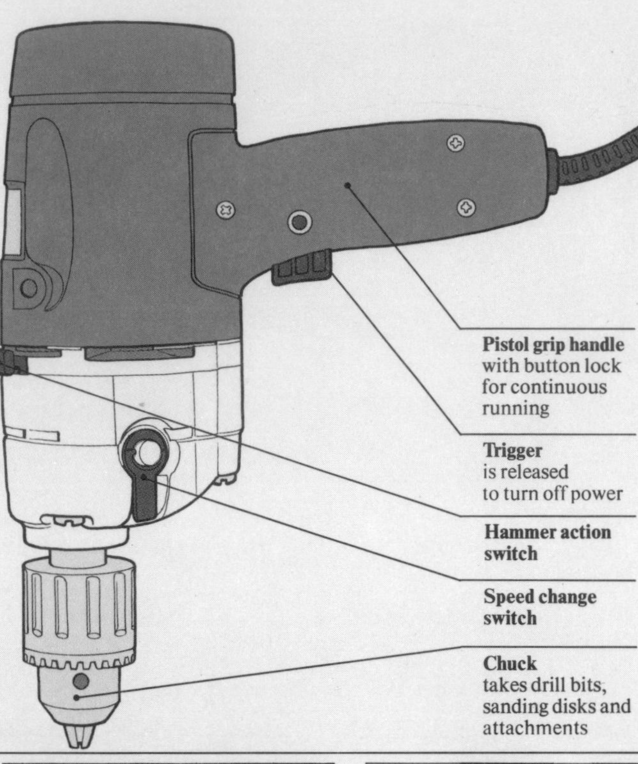

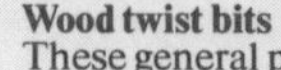

Wood twist bits
These general purpose drills range from 1/16 to 1/4 inch in diameter, and are suitable for most household jobs.

Masonry bits
These have a hardened tip for drilling through plaster, brick and concrete.

Auger bit
This type of bit is handy for drilling dowel holes. Spiral clears shavings from hole.

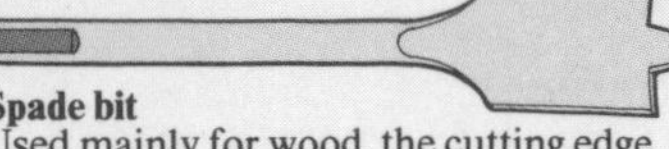

Spade bit
Used mainly for wood, the cutting edge gives a flat bottom to hole.

Drill bits and chucks
Chucks come in three sizes: 5/16, 3/8, and 1/2 inch. Some large drill bits have shafts designed to fit the smaller chucks. Do not fit square shaft brace bits into a power tool.

1 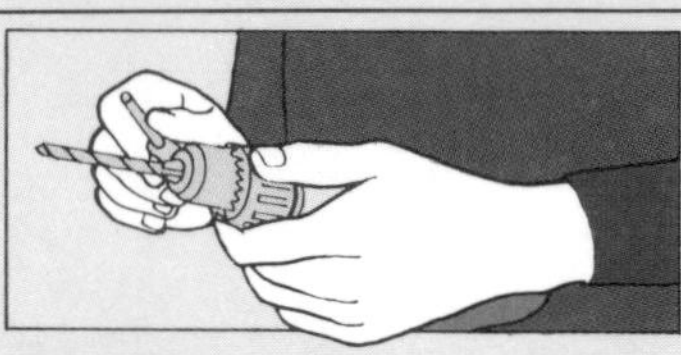

2 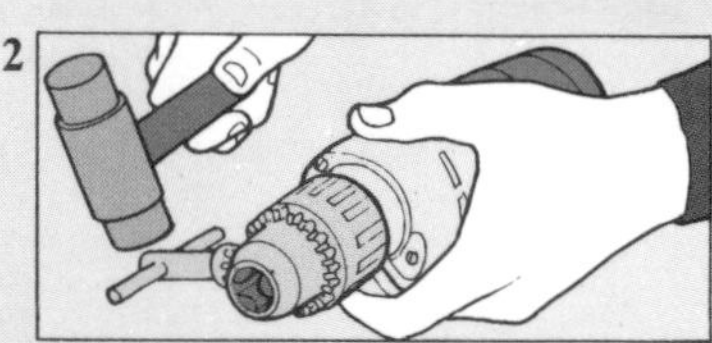

Opening and removing the chuck
*Unplug tool before attending to chuck. **1** Fit key into one of chuck holes and turn to open jaws. **2** To remove chuck from the motor drive, give key a sharp tap with a soft headed hammer, then unscrew chuck by hand.*

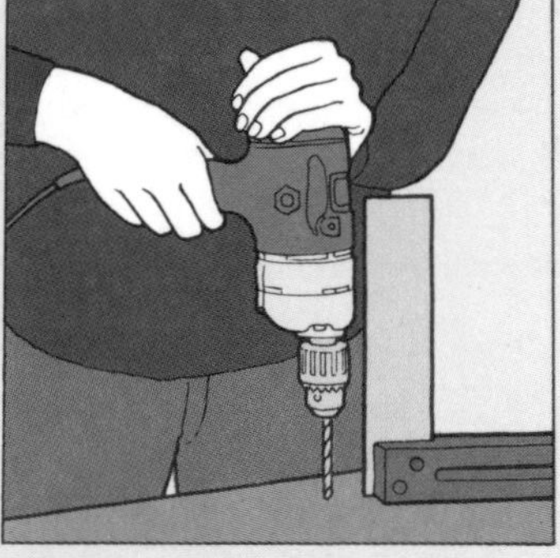

Drilling square
To judge if the hole you are drilling is vertical, use a try square placed up against the drill as a check. Where possible ask a second person to stand back and sight up the drill with the square.

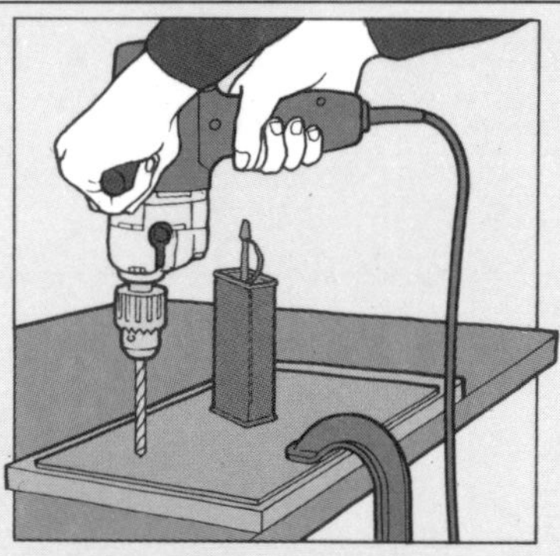

Drilling techniques
Clamp work securely to prevent it spinning, and place a piece of waste wood underneath so that grain does not split out as the drill point emerges. Make sure bits are sharp. Use oil when cutting metal.

1 

2 

Hammer attachment
*Some variable speed drills incorporate a hammer action that can be switched on to make cutting hard masonry easier **2**. Set the drill speed at slow by turning the speed control switch **1**.*

Drill bit sharpener
This machine is designed to grind the bit point to the required angle, which can be set by a control knob according to the bit size. Points are sharpened on a revolving wheel.

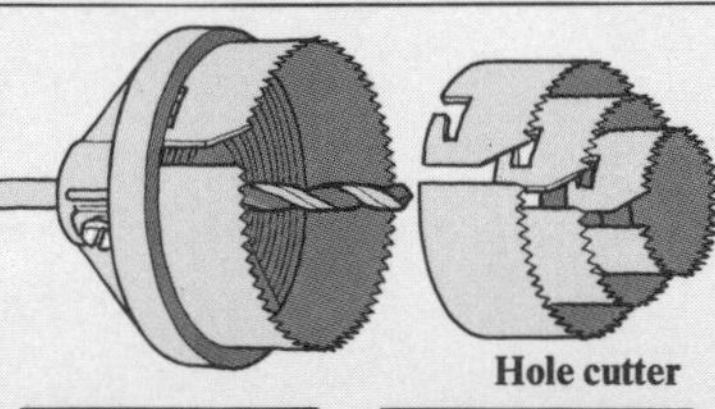

Hole cutter

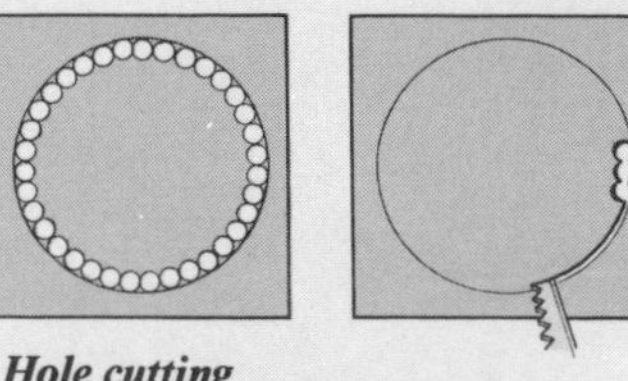

Hole cutting
Cut large holes with a hole saw, which is a central drill surrounded by a cylindrical-shaped saw blade, or else drill small holes around perimeter of the aperture, knock out the center and finish with a half-round file.

Combined drill and countersink

Screw-mate

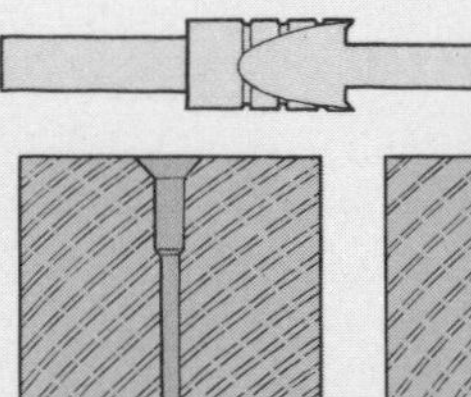

Countersinking
The combined drill and countersink, or screw-mate, allows you to drill a pilot hole, shank clearance hole and countersink all at once. The screw-mate can be fitted with a depth guide for flush fitting or will counterbore the wood.

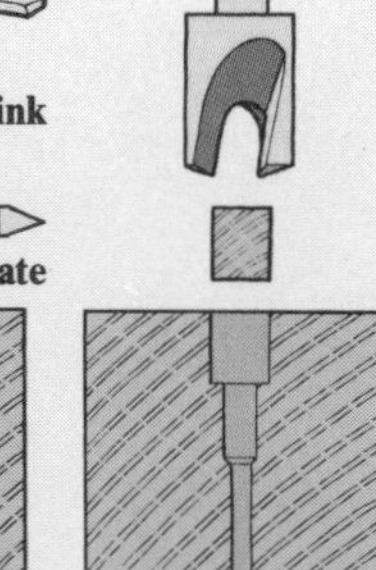

Plug cutting bit
A counterbored screw, where the head is sunk well below the surface of the work, can be covered with a wooden plug. The cutter removes a neat plug from matching wood to glue into the hole. Check the grain direction, which should match the surface of the work. When planed down and finished, the hole should not be apparent.

Bench mountings

Clamping a hand drill on a bench provides a source of power for driving buffers, sanding disks, grinding wheels and for many other attachments. You can set the vertical stand to drill to predetermined depths, a valuable asset for precise repeat work. The horizontal stand leaves your hands free, so that you have a firm grip on the work while grinding or sanding.

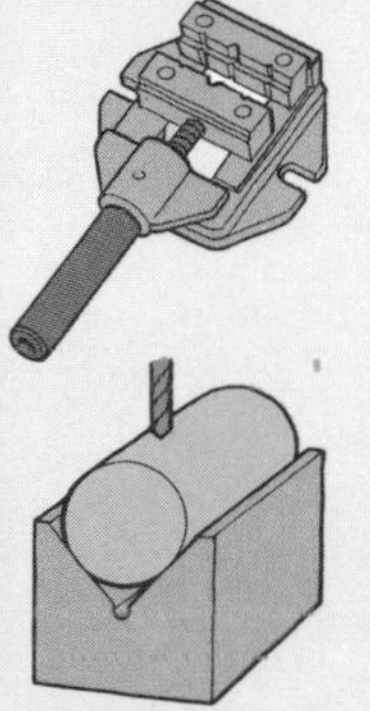

Vise
A small vise which bolts on to the vertical drill stand grips small pieces of work for more accurate drilling.

V block
A simple wooden block can be screwed to the bench or stand, to cradle round wood sections.

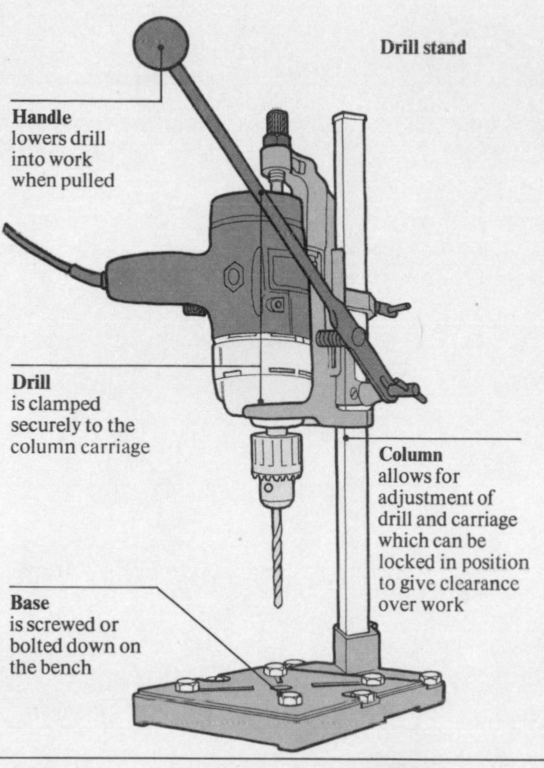

Drill stand

Handle lowers drill into work when pulled

Drill is clamped securely to the column carriage

Column allows for adjustment of drill and carriage which can be locked in position to give clearance over work

Base is screwed or bolted down on the bench

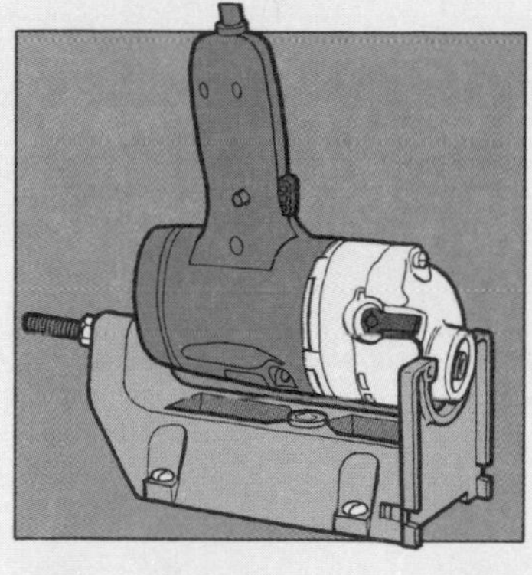

Horizontal stand
The stand enables you to take the work to the drill, which can be set to run continuously. With an adjustable fence attachment, you can work at set angles.

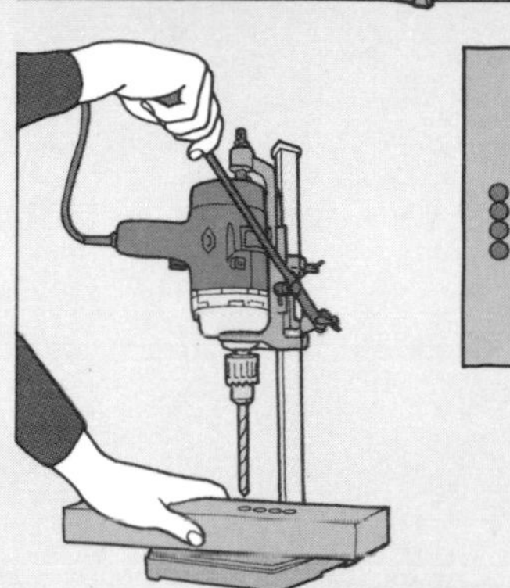

Cutting mortises
You can cut mortises using a vertical column drill stand. Use a bit which matches width of slot, drill a row of holes and clean up edges and corners with a chisel.

Wire brushes

On the right are the two main types of wire brush. **1** The cup-shaped brush can be used freehand for cleaning downpipes, or other fixtures not easily removed. **3** Hold the drill firmly, or the brush action may spin the drill off the work. **2** The wheel-type brush can be mounted on a stand. **4** Hold the work with the wheel turning toward you, and position it on the lower side of the wheel.

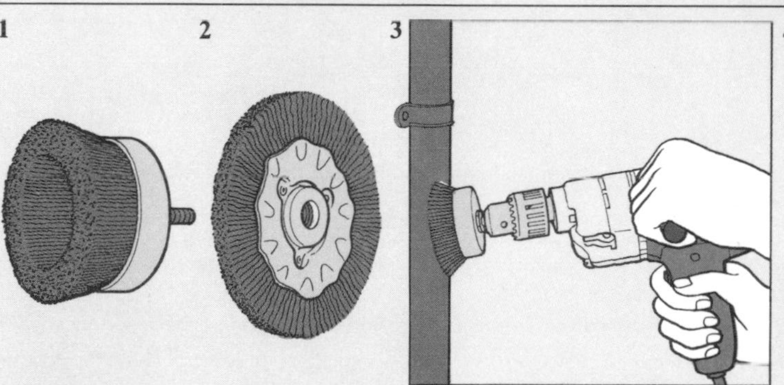

Safety hints

Power tools used correctly can be a great asset to the do-it-yourselfer. Used wrongly they can be very dangerous. Providing certain precautions are observed, power tools can be used safely and with confidence. Always switch off the power and disconnect the plug when making adjustments; the plug should have a grounded outlet. A long cable is very useful, but make sure it is in good condition and does not get caught up in the action, as this may cause accidents or permanently damage the motor. Never use power tools in wet conditions.

At all times use blade guards on circular saws and other similar attachments.

Keep cutting edges sharp: unnecessary force will not produce a clean cut and may cause the cutter to jam. Such rotating force can also snatch the machine from your grip.

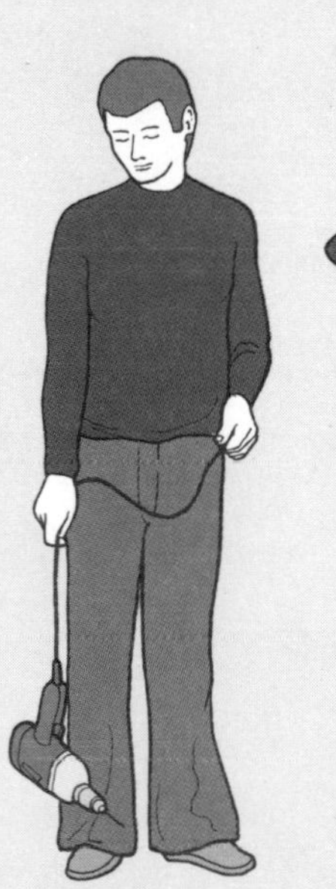

Wrong
Never pick up power tools by the cable.

Right
Pass cable over your shoulder, or hold it clear if your hand is free.

Wrong
Do not wear loose-fitting clothes or a necktie.

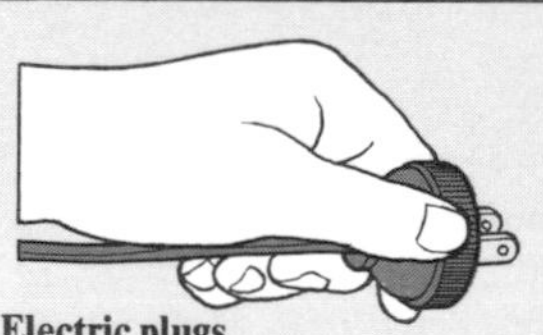

Electric plugs
Plugs should not have slack wiring. Fit all-rubber ones where possible.

Cables
Check regularly in case cable has been accidentally fractured or cut.

Eye protection
If you do not wear glasses, use a pair of goggles when grinding or wire brushing.

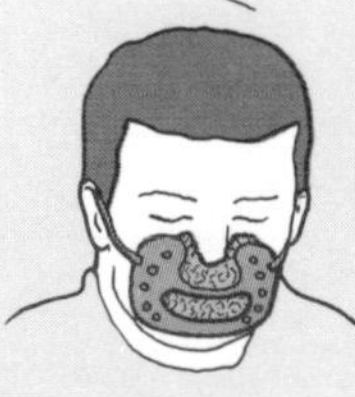

Face mask
Dust is a health hazard in a confined space, where it cannot disperse quickly.

Power Saws

Portable circular saws

Primarily a woodworking tool, the saw cuts a number of different materials accurately and with a minimum of effort on the part of the operator. You can buy a saw attachment for your drill, or choose a complete unit: both take a 5-inch blade. Ideally, a saw should have a $7\frac{1}{2}$ in. diameter blade for more power and deeper cutting. More teeth on a blade mean finer cutting.

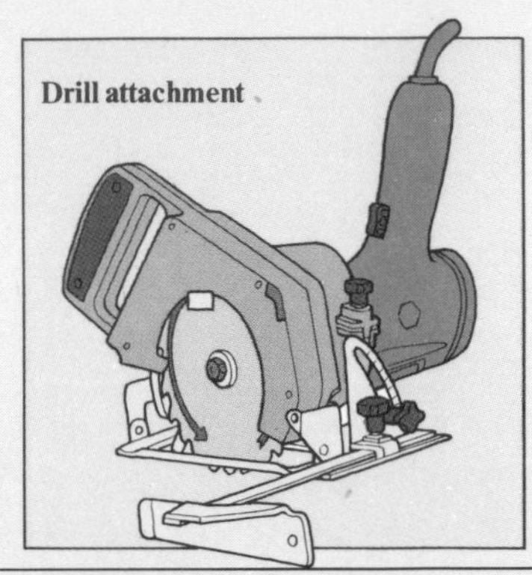

Drill attachment

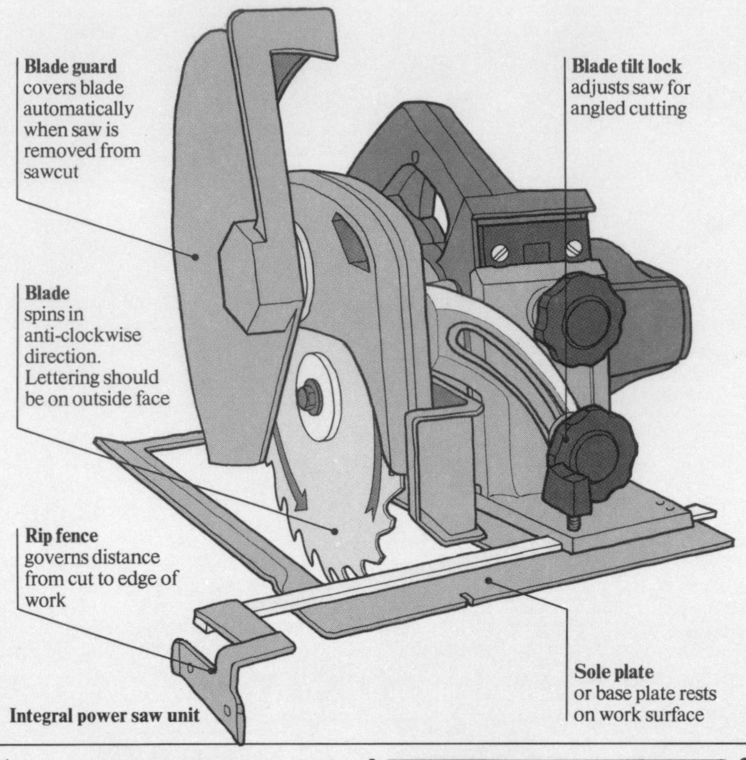

Integral power saw unit

Rip blade cuts with the grain.

Crosscut blade cuts across the grain.

Combination blade cuts with and across the grain.

Carbide-tipped blade cuts both hard and soft materials.

Abrasive blade cuts slate, masonry, plastics and metals.

Changing blades

First disconnect machine's power supply. When fitting blades make sure that the direction of rotation arrow **1** faces you and not the machine. **2** Remove blade by resting teeth against edge of bench, with guard pulled back. Free bolt by tapping bolt wrench. **3** Refit new blade, as indicated on face, passing it through slot in base plate, locating bolt and washer in drive shaft. Finish by tightening bolt with wrench.

1

2

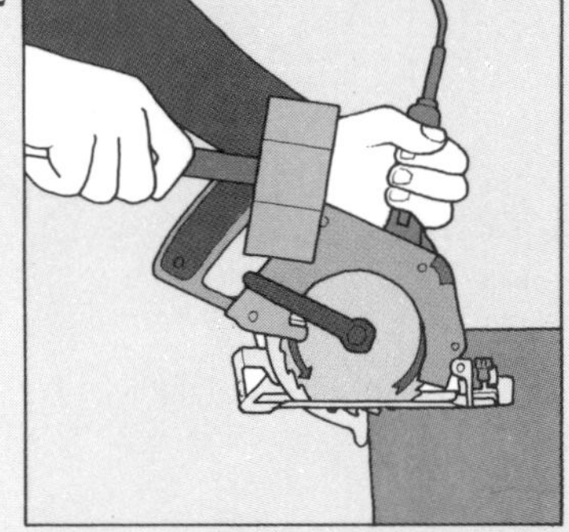

3

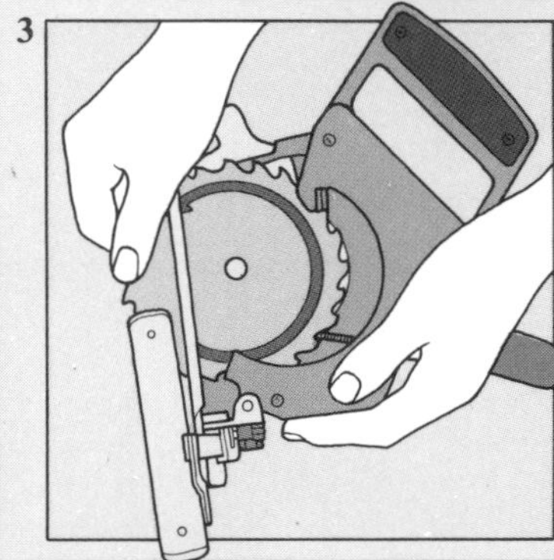

Setting the saw

The depth can be adjusted to cut right through or partly through the work. **1** Adjust by placing the saw on the work, with the blade against the side edge. Release the locknut and swing the body to the required depth. **2** The base plate also tilts for beveled cuts.

1

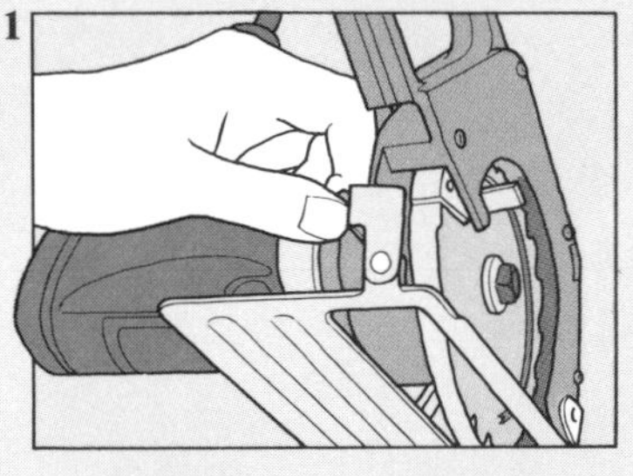

2

Sawing technique

Where the cut is too far away from the edge to enable you to use the rip fence, clamp a batten to the work as a guide. Place the front end of the base plate on the work, switch on and allow the saw to gather maximum speed. Push the saw through the work with a steady even thrust. Do not force the pace, as this can strain the motor, or cause the cut to wander off course. On a long cut the sawcut can close against the blade. Stop the motor, and place a small wedge in the cut before continuing.

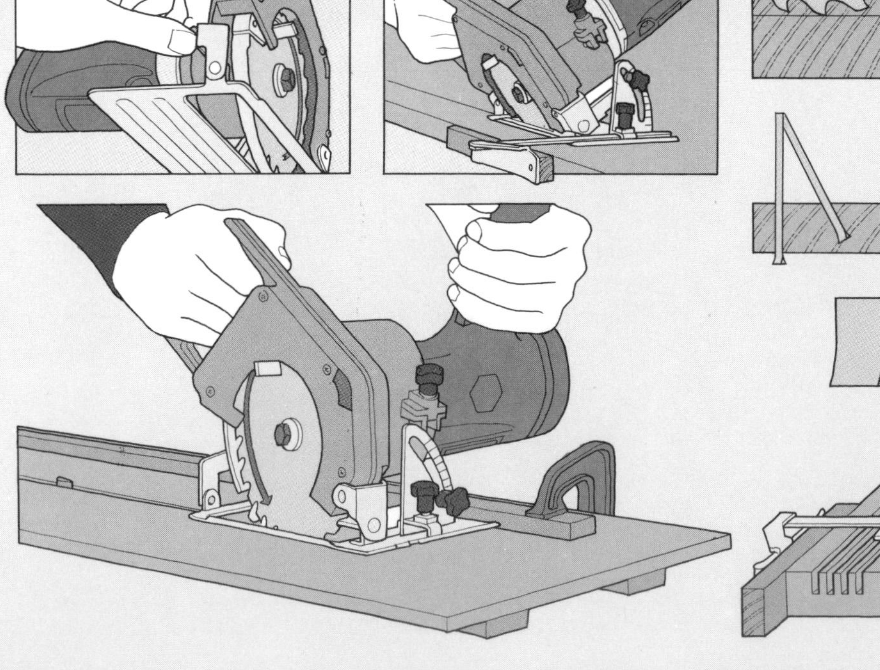

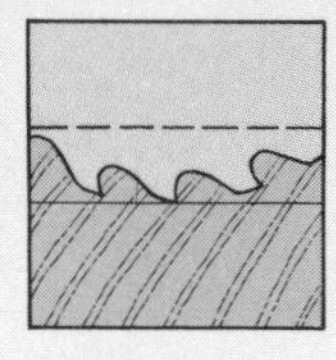

Shallow cuts
Mark depth with line on side edge of work. Set blade so tooth touches line. Test first with spare piece of wood.

Angle cuts
Set the blade to the required angle, using the protractor scale on the base plate. Reset depth of cut accordingly.

Measuring
Take the width of the blade and set into consideration when measuring from the rip fence to the blade.

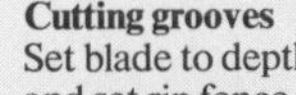

Cutting grooves
Set blade to depth and set rip fence to give a cut for each outer edge. Clean out waste with a chisel.

Saw bench

A saw bench leaves your hands free to guide the work. The bench is a metal table with a wide slot into which the base plate of the hand saw is fitted flush with the bench top, the saw body being slung below. The depth or angle of the blade is adjusted from beneath. The bench is fitted with an adjustable rip fence for straight cutting, and a miter fence for cutting angles, or cross-cutting. The saw bench shown right is fairly simple, and adequate for most domestic workshop jobs; it can be set upon legs, or fitted into a table surface. Circular saws need handling with care and attention, especially when using small pieces of material, or when the guard is off. Always stand to one side of the blade, never in front of it, and feed the end of the work past with the aid of a push stick, a length of batten with a V notch in one end.

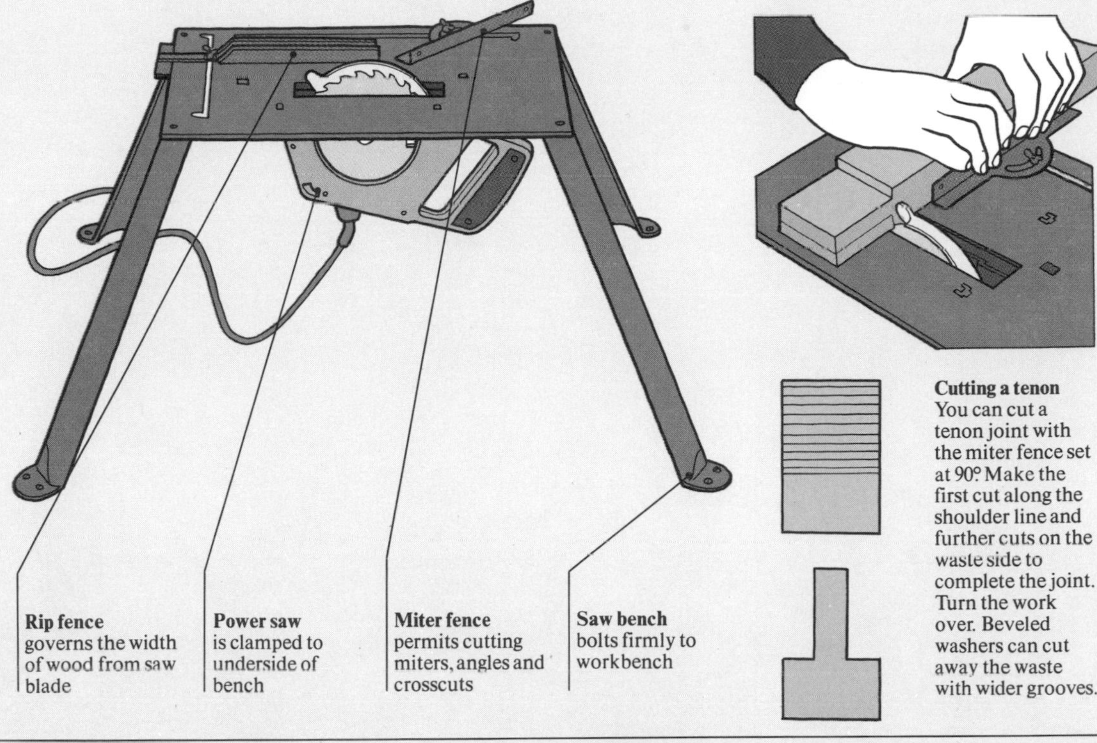

Cutting a tenon
You can cut a tenon joint with the miter fence set at 90° Make the first cut along the shoulder line and further cuts on the waste side to complete the joint. Turn the work over. Beveled washers can cut away the waste with wider grooves.

Using the cutting guides

1 Set the rip fence at the required distance from the blade. Hold the work firmly against the fence, and push it steadily into the saw with a push stick. **2** To cut ends of rails to an angle, set the miter fence to the required angle. Mark the line to be cut on the leading edge of the work and feed to the blade. **3** A rabbet can be cut along a rail using the rip fence. Set the blade depth and make a cut along each adjacent face.

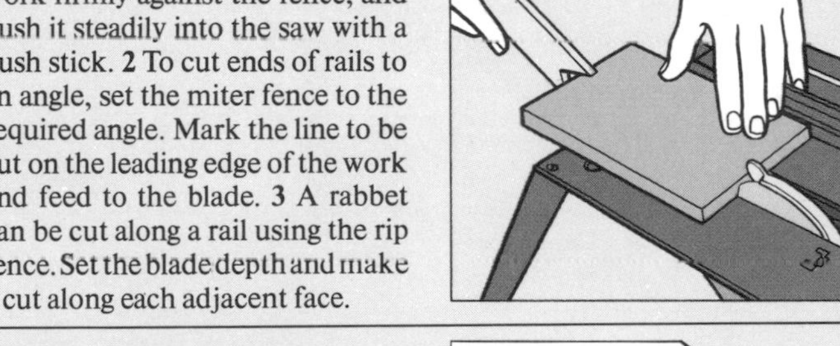

Saber saws or portable jigsaws

A hand-held jigsaw, fitted with the correct blade, can cut softwood up to $1\frac{1}{2}$ in. thick, and hardwood or composition boards up to 1 in. thick; it will also cut metals and plastics. Its main advantage is that it can cut irregular shapes and curves. The blade operates with a reciprocal action, and most blades cut on the upstroke. The work needs to be well secured and to overhang the bench; vibration is avoided by cutting close to the edge of the bench.

Jigsaw blades
Made in a wide range for all materials, blades are fine-toothed so splintering is minimal.

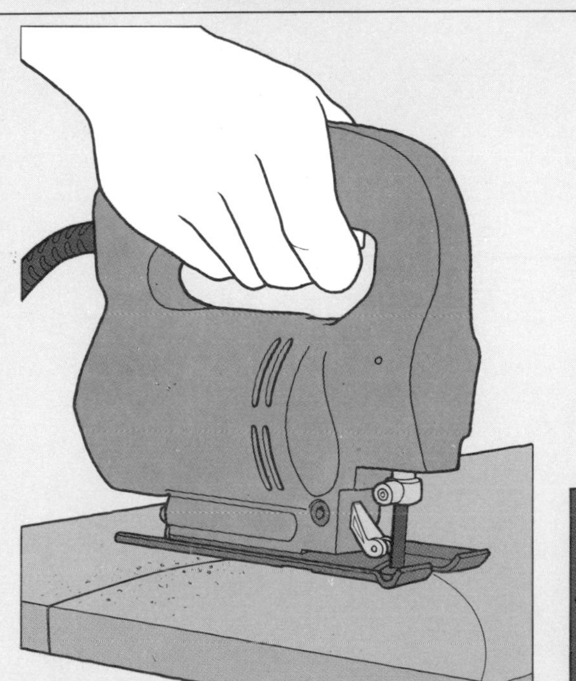

Integral jigsaw

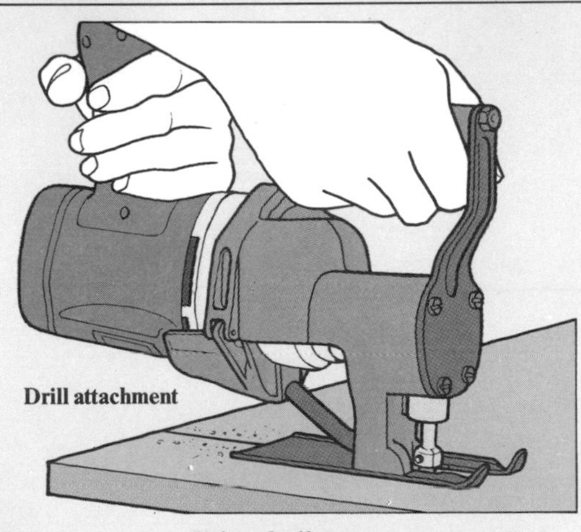

Drill attachment

Using the jigsaw
To start a cut from the edge, rest the tip of the saw shoe on the work. Switch on, and feed blade to the cut. To cut an opening in the face of a board, drill a clearance hole. Cut squares by making a tight turn at each corner, then remove corners by cutting from opposite directions. Because the blade cuts on the upstroke cut veneered boards with the face on the underside.

Sanders

Bench sanders and sanding attachments

Disk sanders, the most usual type of attachment for power drills, have a rubber backing pad up to 6 in. in diameter, generally with a spindle to fit in the chuck. A wide variety of abrasive paper disks are available. The drill can be mounted on a horizontal stand or bolted to the bench in which case the flexible disk is replaced by a flat metal disk, and the abrasive paper is bonded to the disk with adhesive.

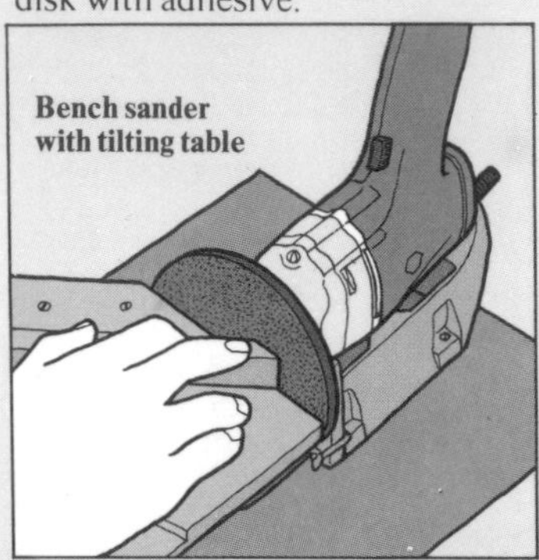
Bench sander with tilting table

Bench sander
When sanding, set the drill at maximum speed. Some work tables have a tilting attachment so that angled surfaces can be accurately finished.

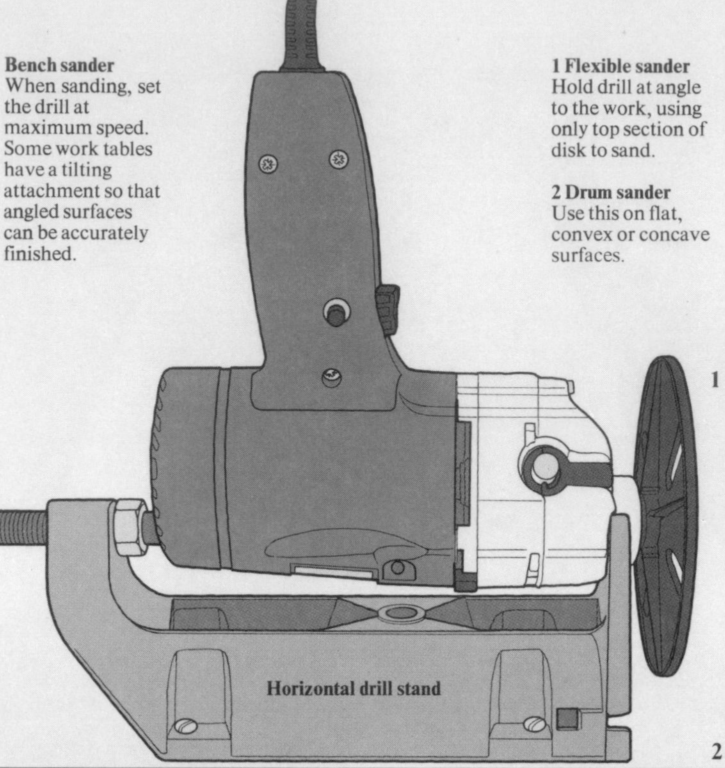
Horizontal drill stand

1 Flexible sander
Hold drill at angle to the work, using only top section of disk to sand.

2 Drum sander
Use this on flat, convex or concave surfaces.

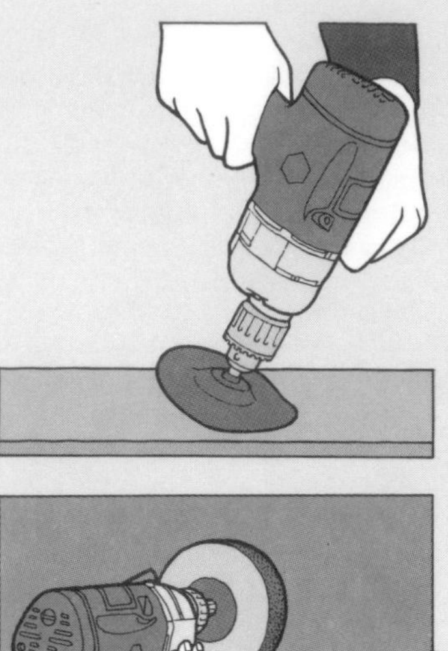
1
2

Changing sanders

1 To apply the abrasive paper to the bench sander, set the disk plate spinning and hold adhesive to the plate. The friction will melt it and coat the surface. Switch off and apply paper. **2** Flexible disks grip the abrasive paper by means of a large, cupped washer and a screw spindle. **3** Drum sander has a foam collar fitted with a band of abrasive paper. When worn, remove from foam and slip on new band.

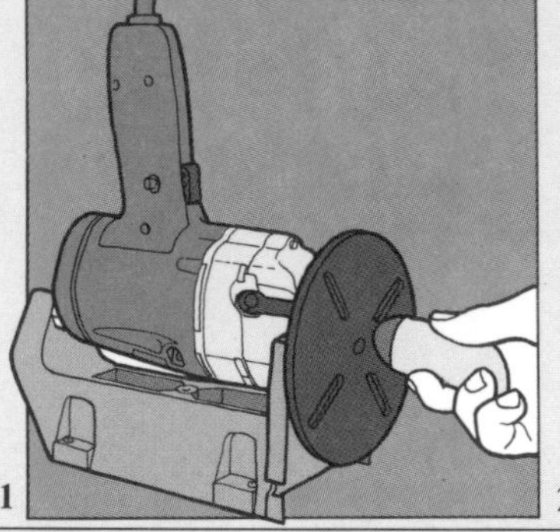
1

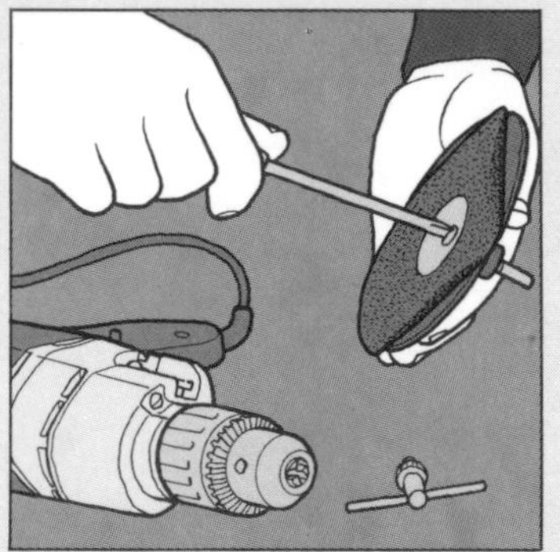
2

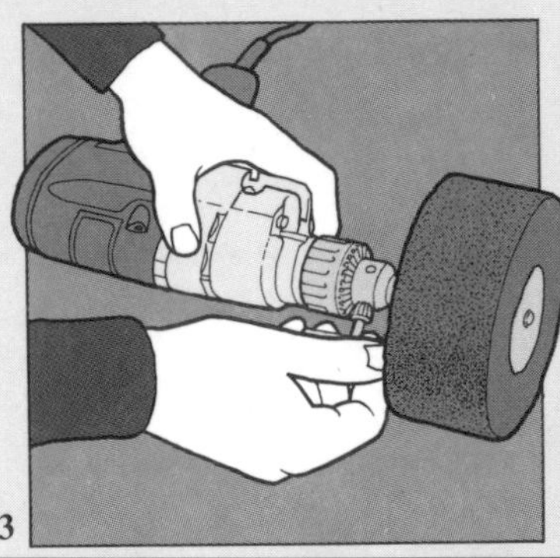
3

Orbital sander

This is only for finishing and can be either an integral unit or a drill attachment. The integral sander performs better: it has a flat, resilient pad that is driven in a fast, oscillating motion producing tiny orbital cuts. The abrasive sheets are fitted across the pad and give a generous sanding area; the various grades work the surface of the wood to a fine finish ready for varnishing.

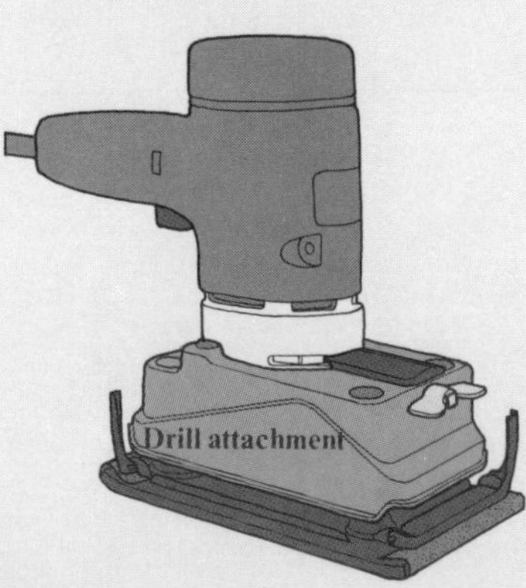
Drill attachment

Integral sander unit

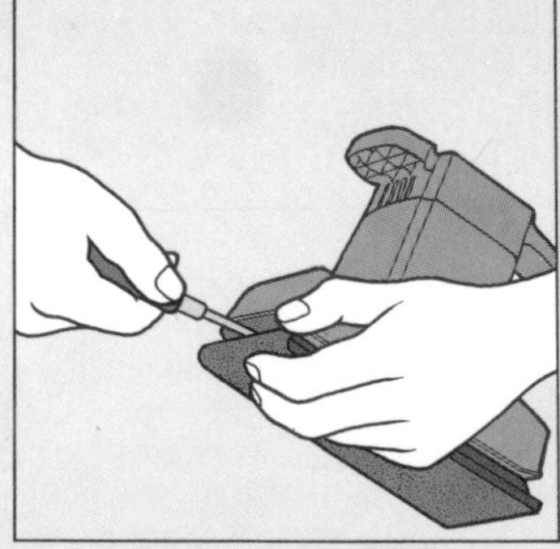

Changing the sanding pad
The paper is fitted over the pad by inserting one end into a clip or toothed shaft with a screwdriver. The other end is similarly fitted, and the paper stretched tight.

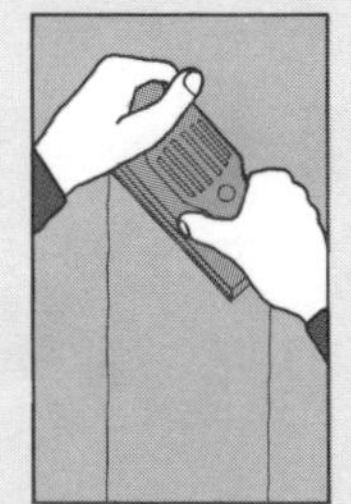
Orbital sander
On wide boards overlap sanded bands as you go.

Grinders & Routers

Bench grindstone
If you anticipate doing much sharpening and grinding work, on workshop and possibly gardening tools, it is worth investing in an integral grinder. This has two grinding wheels, one coarse, the other fine. Alternatively, buy a grinder attachment for your power drill, with the drill mounted on a horizontal bench stand. Both types have wheel guards, with an adjustable tool rest and eye shield. Although the shield is fitted over the guard, wear protective goggles when operating a grinder, to avoid any flying debris. Set the tool rest to clear the wheel by $\frac{1}{8}$ inch at the required angle. This prevents the tool being dragged into the wheel. Have a bowl of cold water by the machine, so that you can cool the work periodically. Finish sharpening fine edged tools on a whetstone. The grinder can also clean and polish metals and remove rust.

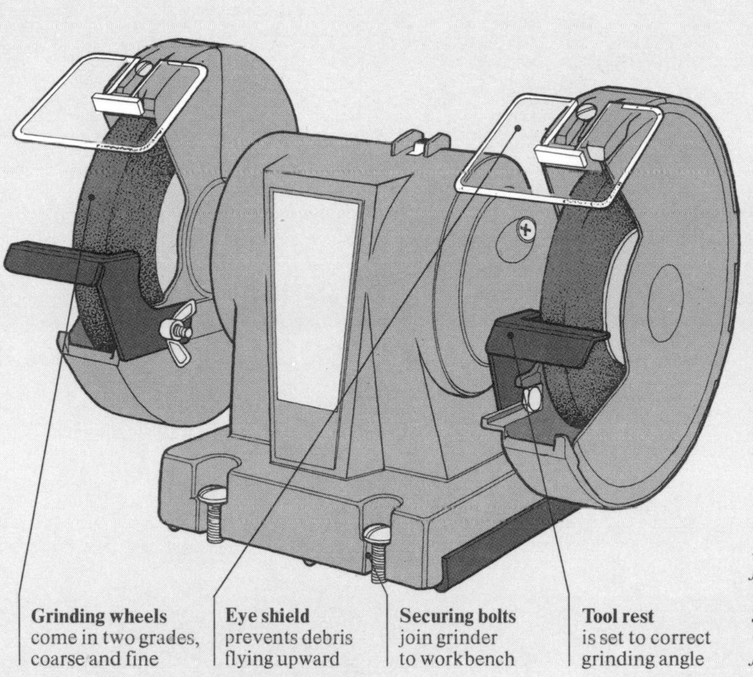

Grinding wheels come in two grades, coarse and fine

Eye shield prevents debris flying upward

Securing bolts join grinder to workbench

Tool rest is set to correct grinding angle

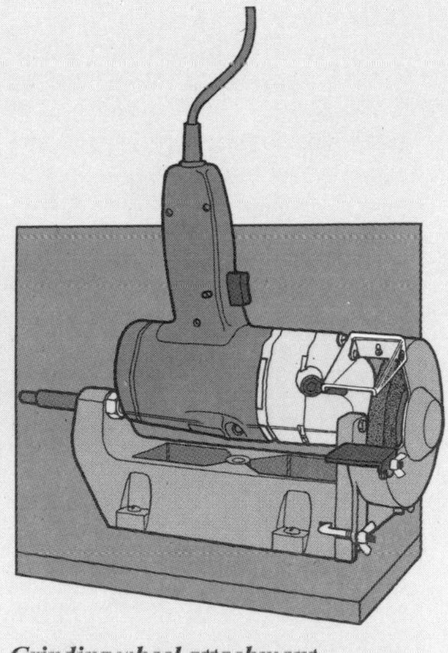

Grinding wheel attachment
A single-wheeled grinder can be fitted to a hand drill which has been bench mounted. Like the integral grinder, the attachment has a guard, eye shield and tool rest. It is handy for sharpening small tools and bits.

Grinding technique
1 Set the grinding angle correctly. **2** Adjust the integral eye shield, which prevents stray pieces of metal flying into your face during the grinding process. **3** Start the machine running and hold the tool flat on the rest. Lightly press the edge into the wheel, working to and fro across the wheel with a sideways movement. Do not hold the tool against the wheel for too long, as this may cause overheating.

1
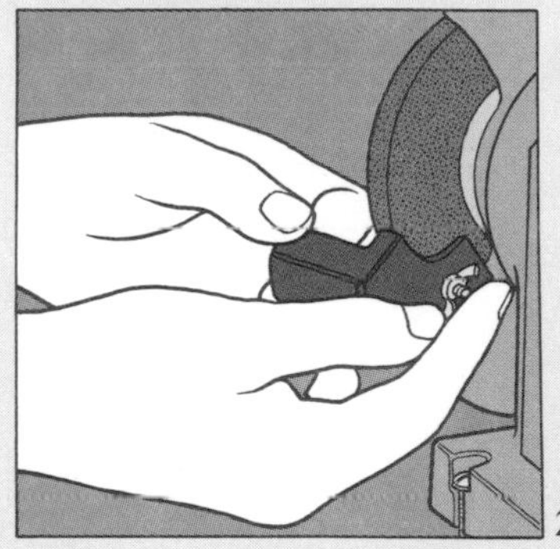

2
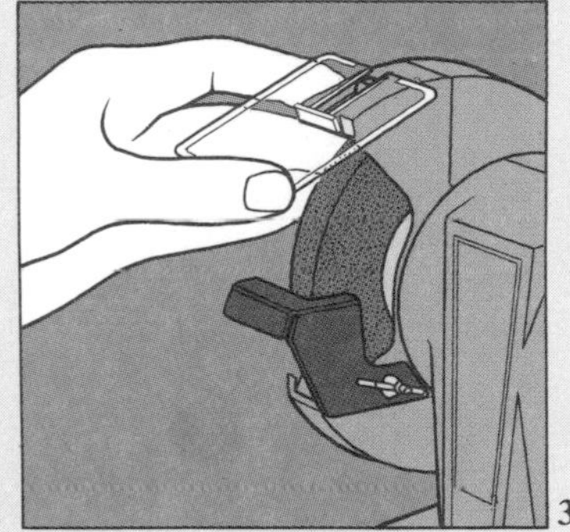

3
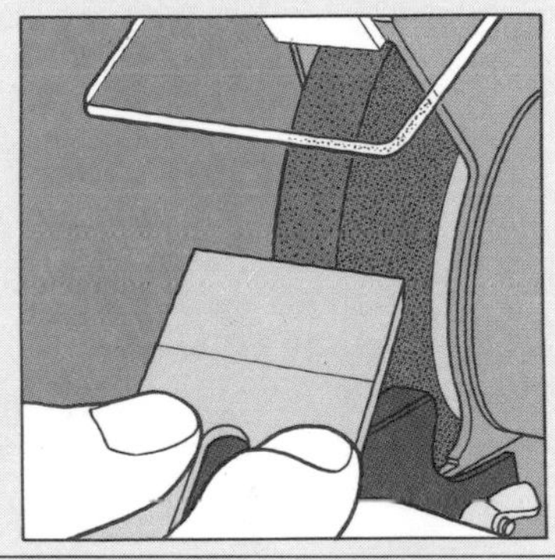

Routers
With a portable router you can cut a considerable variety of shapes, grooves, channels, rabbets, dadoes and other moldings with specially shaped router bits. The bit is locked into the drive shaft of the router, and projects through the center of the face plate. The bit spins in a clockwise direction and should be guided from left to right when making a cut.

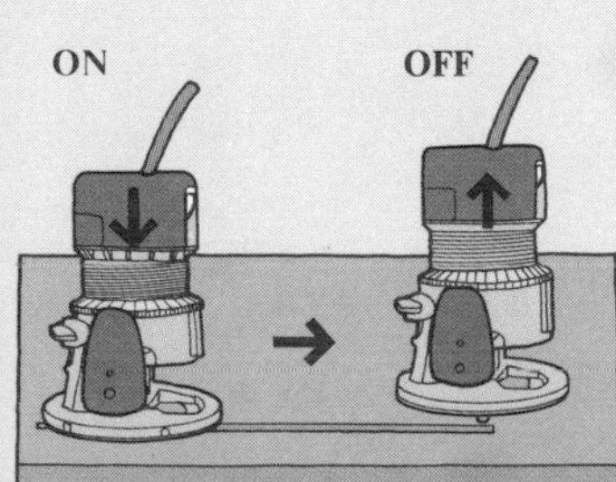

Operating the router
Switch on and lower router into work. Switch off at end of cut and lift clear.

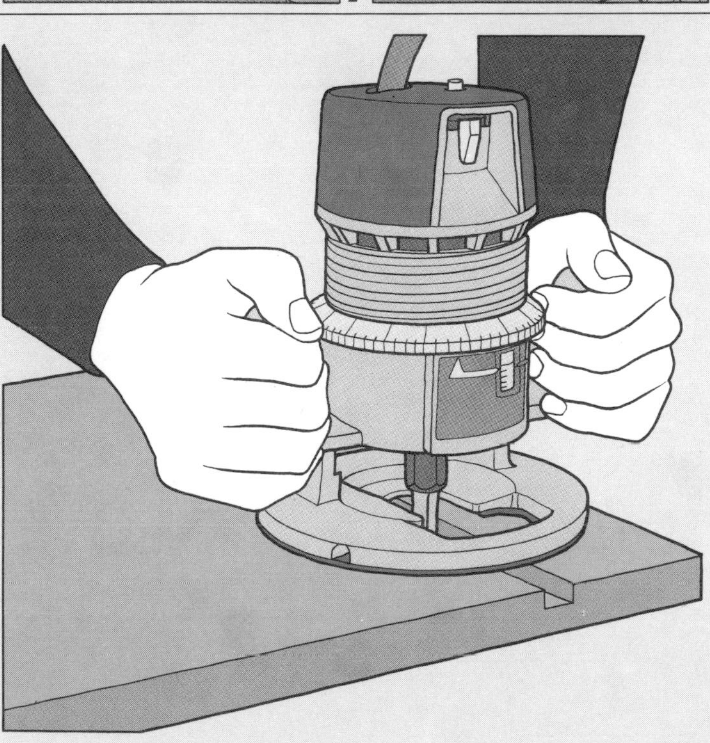

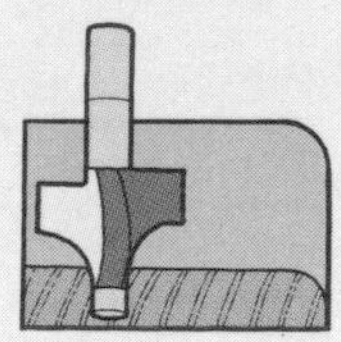

Beading bit is used for rounding off edges, especially of chairs and decorative table tops.

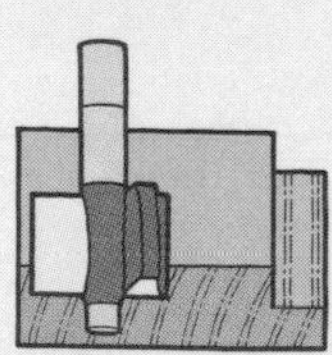

Rabbeting bit makes cutting rabbets quick and easy. The center pin acts as a guide on the wood's edge.

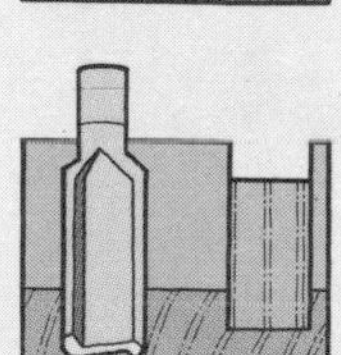

Straight, single flute bit cuts a square sided groove. Make several passes for wide dadoes.

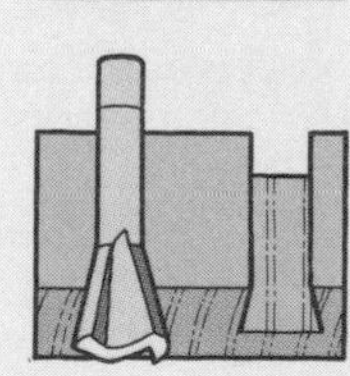

Dovetail bit takes the labor out of dovetail joints. It is useful for drawer making.

Lathes

Lathe attachment
The power drill lathe makes woodturning facilities available to the amateur. You can machine around section parts–either plain cylinders or fancy bulbous turnings–for furniture legs, knobs, children's toys and so on. The lathe consists of a lathe bed fitted with a fixed headstock to carry a power drill and an adjustable tailstock. An adjustable tool rest is bolted to the bed to support the tool. The work is set to revolve, and can then be shaped with a variety of hand tools. The three main types are shown on the right. A face plate can be fitted to the power drill for turning small objects such as bowls, egg cups and container lids. The lathe should be fixed firmly to the bench if it is to be a permanent addition to the workshop; otherwise fix it to a baseboard that can be clamped to a stable support when in use.

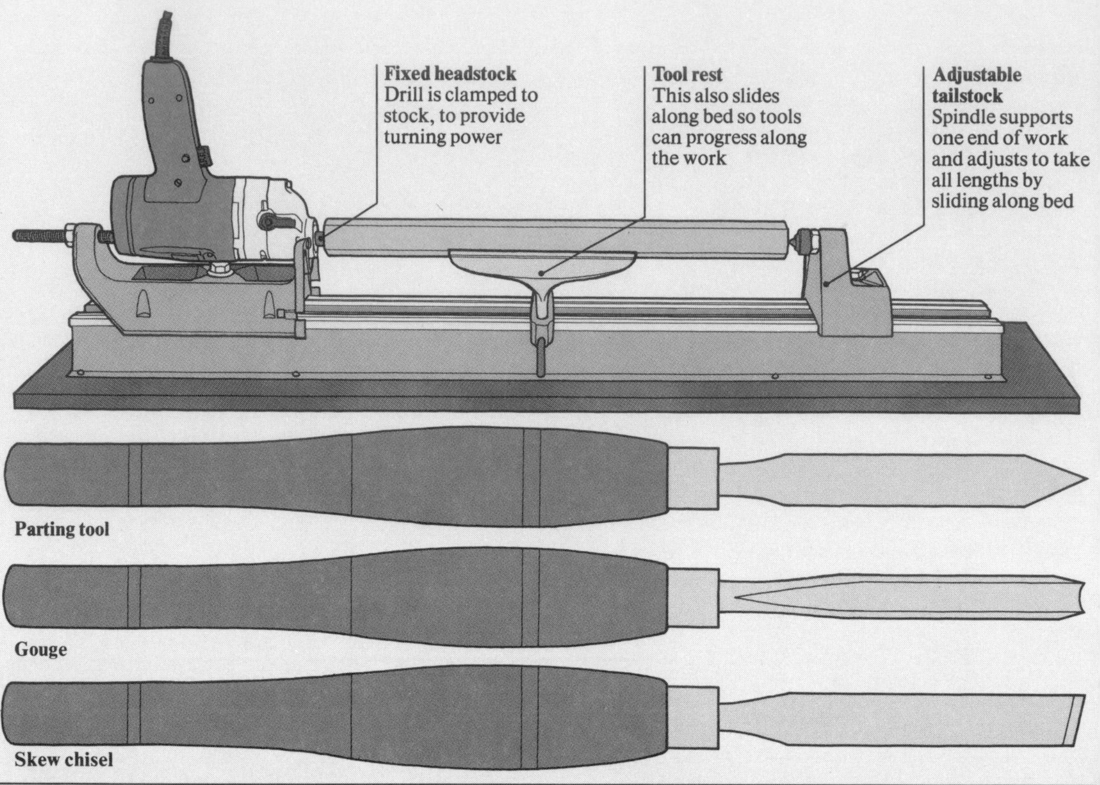

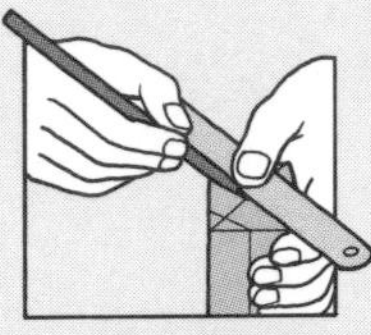

Prepare the wood by cutting to length, allowing some extra at both ends. Check wood is square. Cross mark ends to find center.

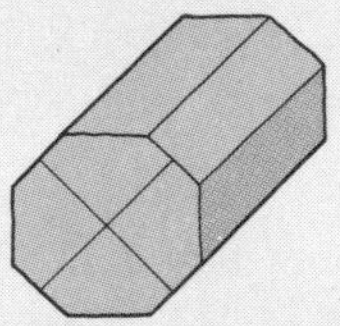

Mark circles at each end with compass, touching sides of square. Plane off corners to make octagon. Indent end centers.

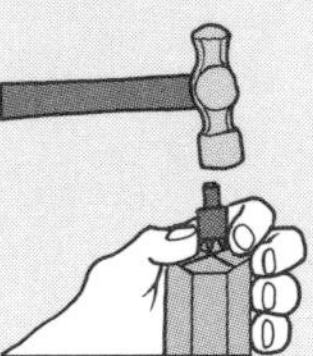

Position the driving center in one end, and drive headstock spindle point and teeth into end grain with a mallet.

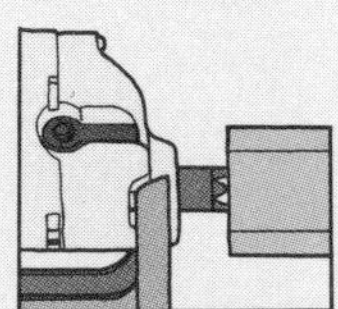

Remove spindle and screw into drill shaft. Position work on drive center and tailstock center.

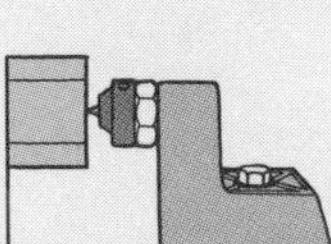

Lock the stock on the bed, and check that work can revolve freely but is not slack between the centers.

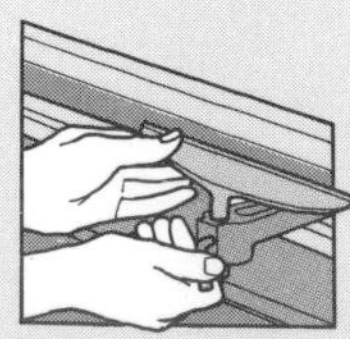

Position the tool rest at the drill end about ⅛ in. from the work and ⅛ in. below axis. Set to run at slow speed.

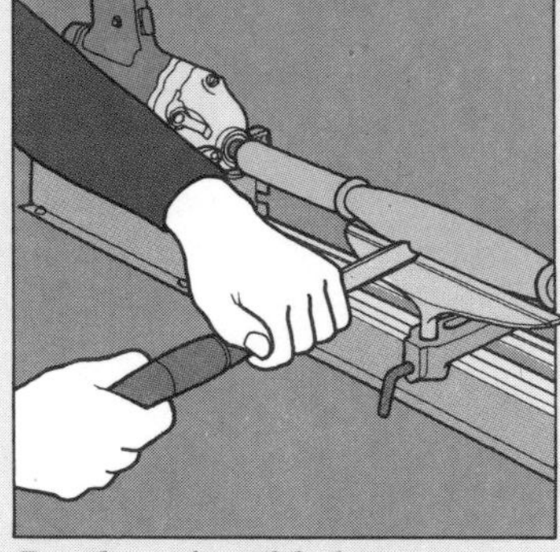

Rough turning with the gouge
Hold gouge firmly on the rest with one hand, the handle in the other hand and steadied against your body. Feed the gouge into the work, using the lower half of the cutting edge. Carefully control the depth of cut. Avoid corner digging into the turned piece.

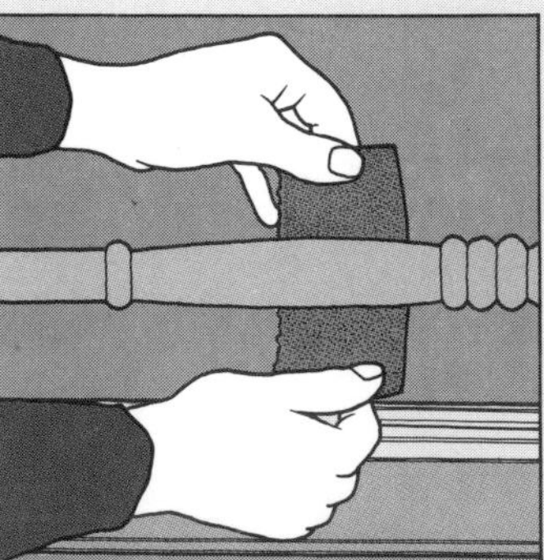

Sanding and finishing
Increase the speed for finishing work. You should only need to sand the surface lightly. Remove the tool rest and hold a strip of abrasive paper against the back of the work while it is turning.

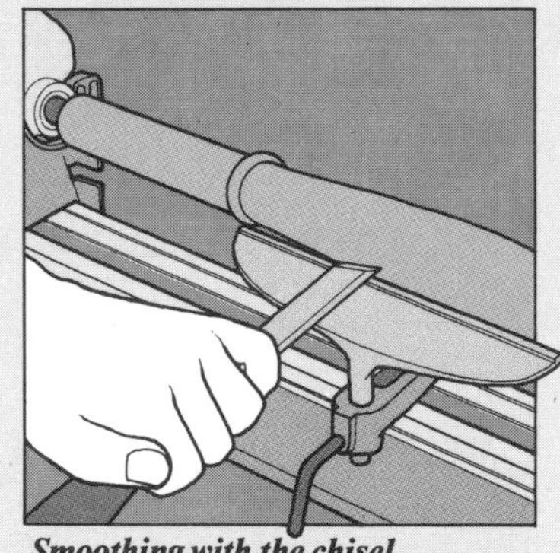

Smoothing with the chisel
Smooth down to finished size with a 1-inch chisel. Tilt chisel on tool rest and use center of cutting edge. Avoid the corner digging into the work, which can damage the job or cause the tool to kick back.

Profile former
For an irregular or complex shape, or for repetition work, make a template cut from cardboard, or use an adjustable needle template. Hold the template against the work repeatedly to check its shape.

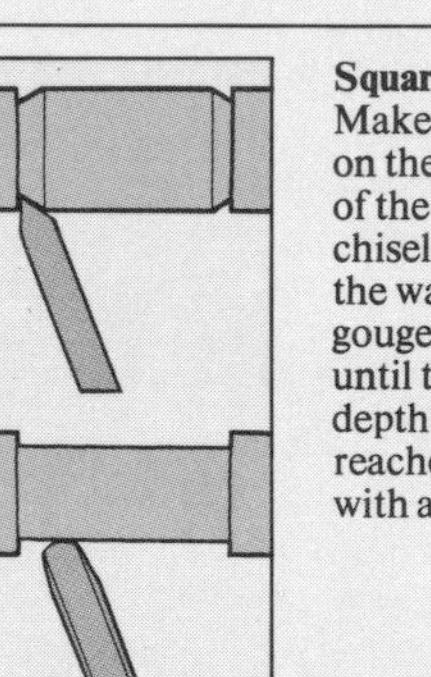

Square cuts
Make two V cuts on the waste side of the lines with a chisel. Remove the waste with a gouge. Repeat until the required depth is almost reached. Finish with a chisel.

Hollows
These are made with smaller gouges. Start at center and swing gouge in an arc to the left then to the right. Continue until required depth and width are reached.

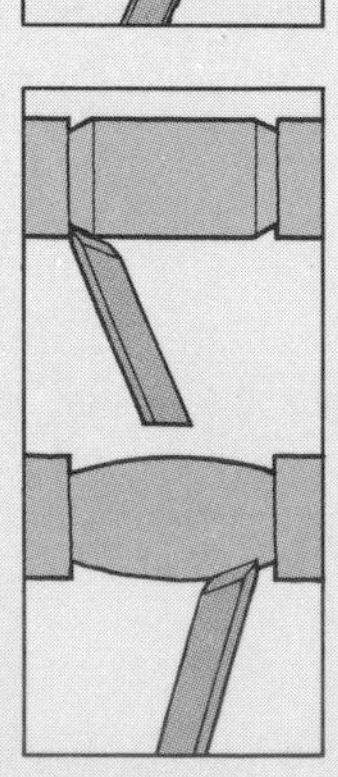

Beads
To cut beads make V grooves as for square cutouts. Round off sides of bead with chisel, cutting in a rolling movement by pivoting chisel on the rest and turning your wrists.

Radial Arm Saw

Radial arm saw
Although this machine is primarily a flexible but non-portable power saw, it performs many other functions as well, including drilling, sanding, polishing and cutting grooves and moldings. As a saw the machine will cut across or with the grain. The motor and saw blade are mounted on an overhead arm which can be pivoted and locked at any angle. This arm is carried by a column at the rear of a fixed worktable. The depth of the cut is adjusted by raising or lowering the column by means of an elevating handle. The motor is carried in a yoke and moves along the arm, an arrangement that allows the blade to be rotated to any angle in the vertical and horizontal plane. The sawing table is fitted with a wooden fence, which can be clamped in two parallel positions for crosscutting or wide ripping. You can make an overlength fence for guiding longer work pieces when ripping. When crosscutting square or at an angle, the saw is pulled across the work by the operator. When ripping, the motor and saw head are locked into position on the arm and the lumber is fed to the saw.

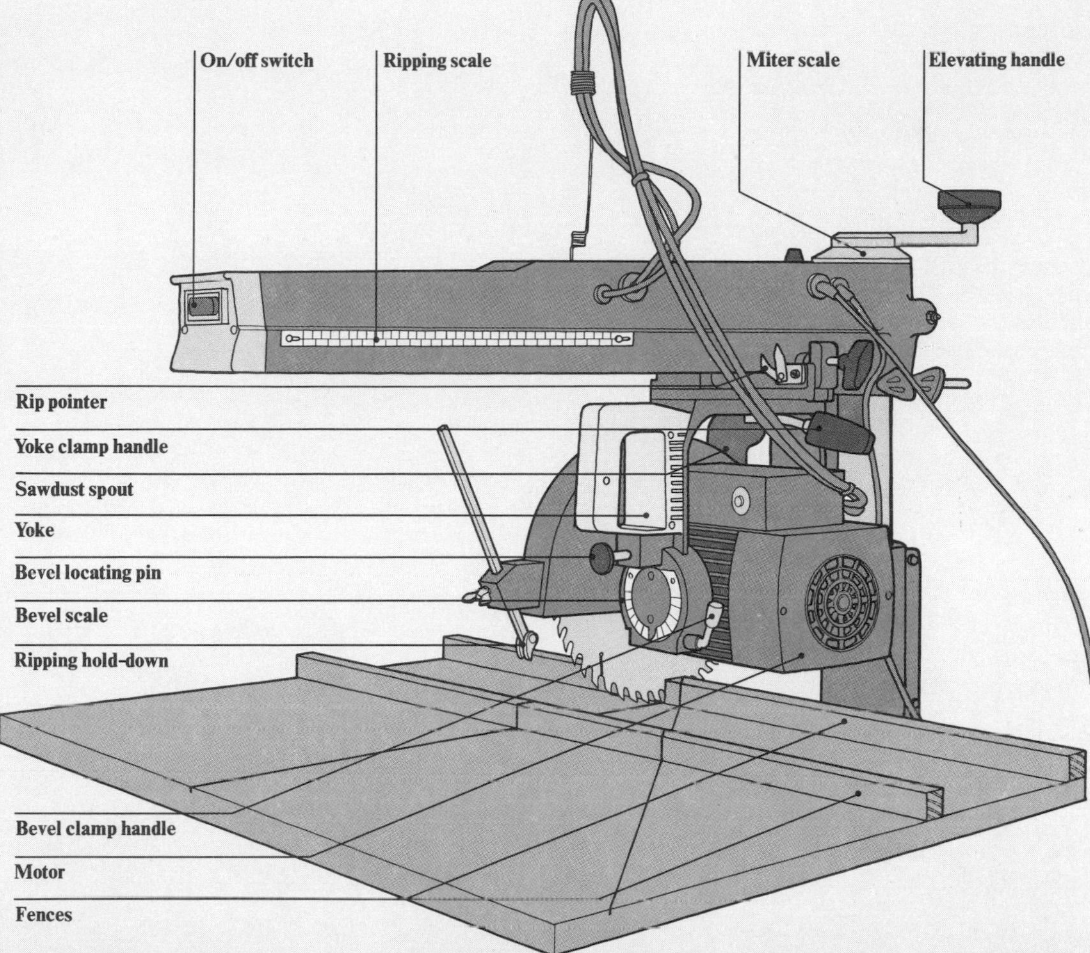

Sawing techniques
Before making a through cut, either for crosscutting or ripping, set the blade so it just breaks through the bottom face of the work. With the blade clear of the sawing table switch on and lower the arm using the elevating handle until the blade is just cutting into the surface; the work can now proceed. Do not set the blade down without running the saw. When crosscutting, hold the work firmly against the guide fence and draw the saw steadily through. Keep the supporting hand well clear of the cut, and control the pace of the cut as it can "run on" and jam the blade. When the cut is complete return the saw to the back of the table then switch off. When ripping, set the blade to run parallel with the fence. Feed the wood from the opposite side to the hold-down assembly on the blade guard, and when cutting a long piece of lumber support the overhang so that it keeps level with the table. Keep the table clear of sawdust to avoid any build-up against the fence; never clear the table with the motor running. Always set the guard according to the work being cut.

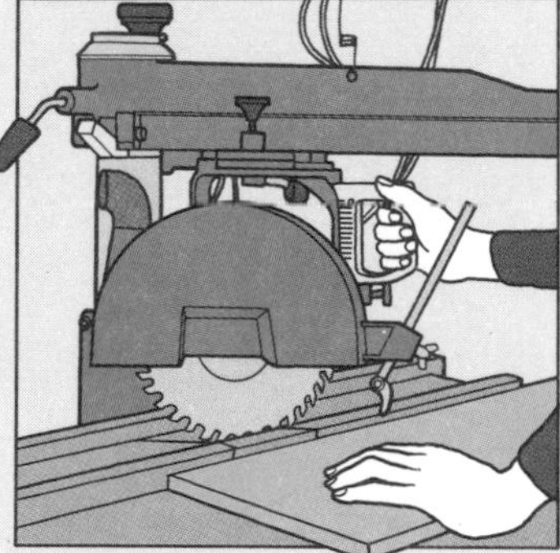

Angled crosscuts
Set required angle on miter scale and hold work firmly against guide fence. Draw saw-motor steadily across work.

Narrow ripping
Blade should be set facing column, and saw head locked into position. Feed work steadily into saw.

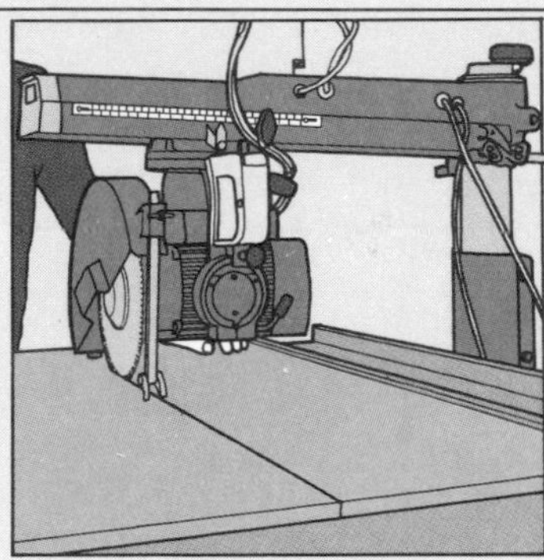

Wide ripping
Turn saw head so it is parallel to guide fence and facing away from column. Reset guide fence to rear. You can cut widths up to 24 inches.

Arm rotation
Release miter clamp handle and lift miter latch. Swing the arm to the required angle and clamp firmly.

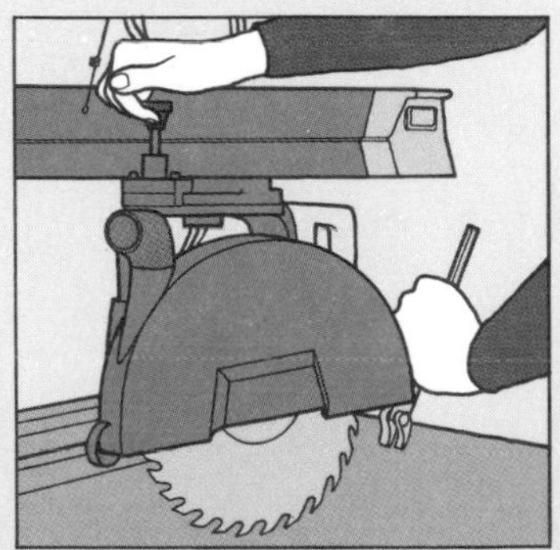

Saw swivel
Release yoke clamp, lift locating pin and swing yoke as required. Yoke is locked by pin at four 90° positions.

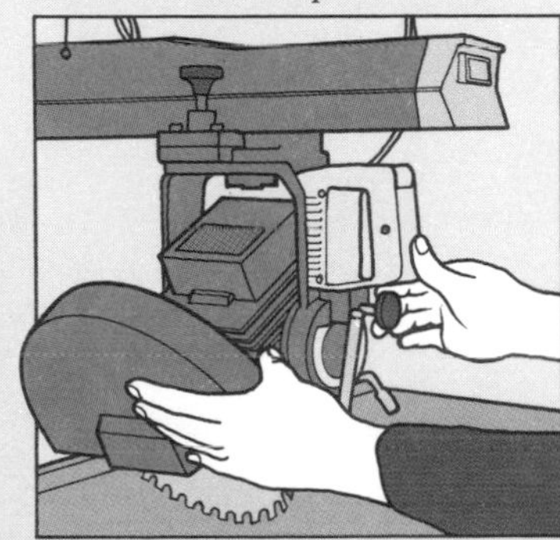

Saw tilt
Elevate arm 20 turns. Release clamp, disengage pin. Set motor to required angle and tighten clamp.

Joining Lumber

Making joints

Accurate, well-fitted joints are not difficult to make if you keep your tools sharp and your saws set correctly to produce a straight cut. Always mark the joint very carefully, using one half as a gauge to mark the other rather than measuring with a rule. Mark the parts to be cut with a marking knife and always cut on the waste side of the line. The parts should fit tightly: never rely on the glue to fill a slack joint.

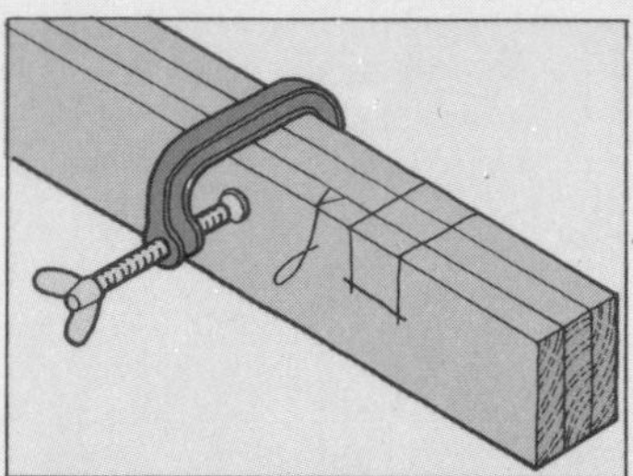

Basic joint making techniques
1 Separate lengths of wood used for the same joint should be marked together while held firm with clamps.

2 The recess or mortise is marked using the piece of wood or tenon which will slot into it; use a square to get accurate right angles.

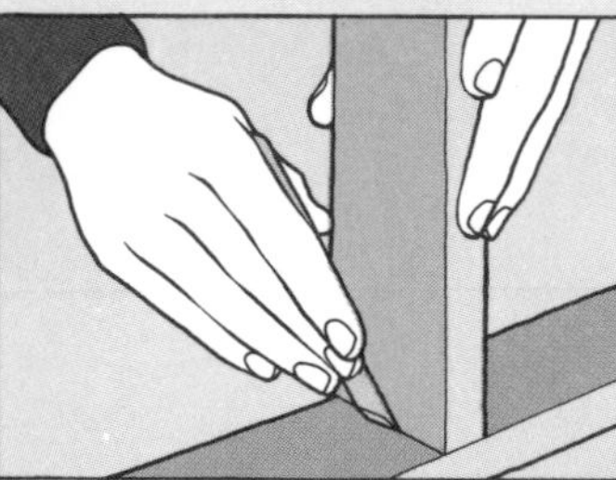

3 Mark the housing, using the rail as an accurate guide, with a sharp marking knife.

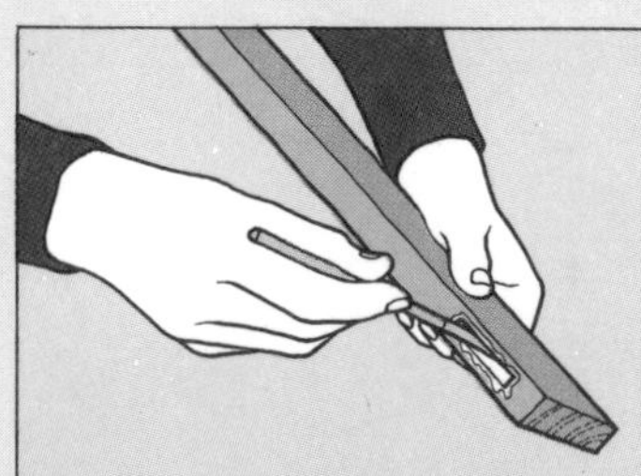

4 Assemble the joint dry to check fit, then put glue into the mortise rather than on the tenon, so as not to force glue clear of the joint.

Right angle joints

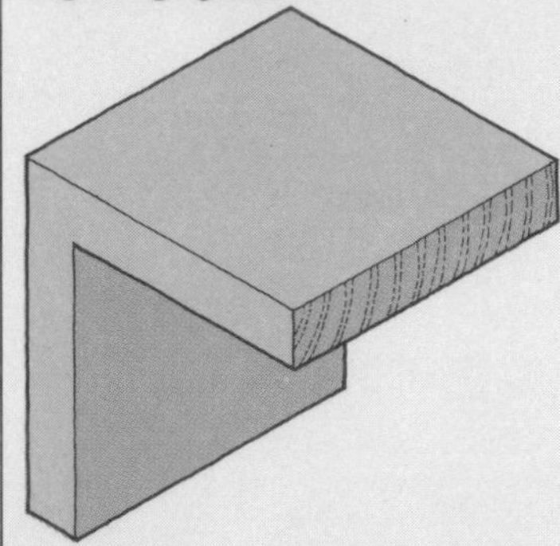

The simplest joint mates together without use of a dado or recess. Instead the ends butt together and are held firm by reinforcements which may be both nailed and glued. The ends should be planed square on a shooting board, although for building work it is acceptable to fit the joint "straight off the saw". Where joints are fixed with nails, avoid splitting by leaving an extra length overlapping on the top member, then plane flush after the joint is secured.

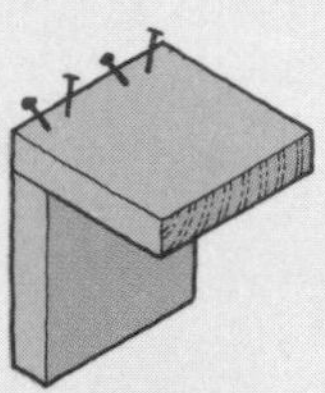

Nailed joint
Nail joint at an angle to make "dovetail" fitting. Set nails firmly in top member before assembling.

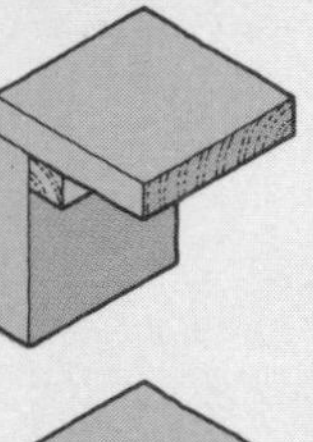

Block reinforced
Corner blocks can be "rub-jointed" into underside of joint. Glue two adjacent sides of block and rub into place.

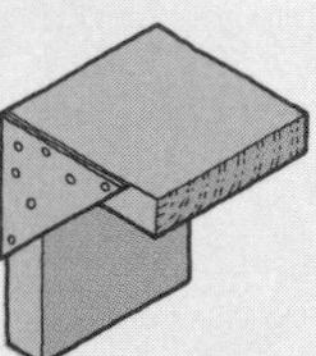

Corner gusset
Nail and glue triangular corner plate of hardboard or plywood to edge of corner assembly.

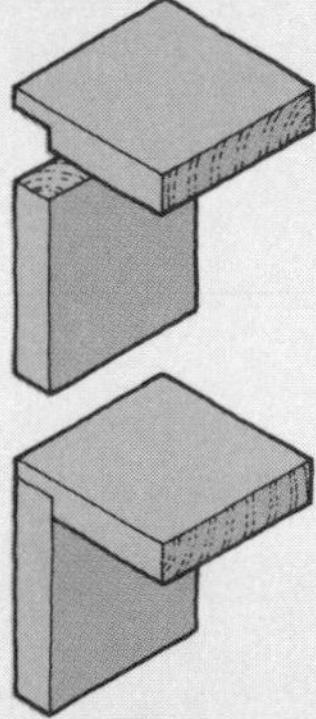

Rabbeted joint
Cut square end of joint first. Mark out rabbet on mating piece at half to three quarters of thickness. Cut rabbet with a tenon or power saw. When cutting, allow extra length on the lap, and trim flush after gluing. Glue and secure with "dovetail" nailing.

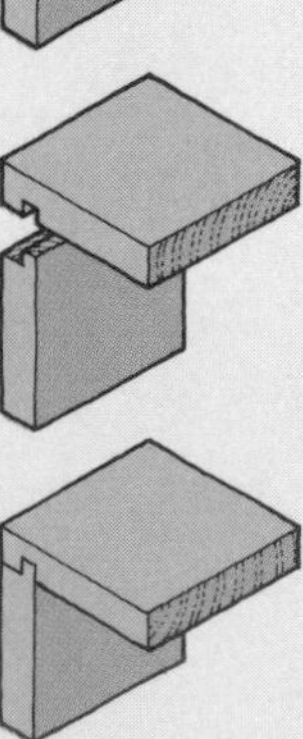

Dado rabbeted joint
Cut a tongue in one half of joint half as thick as wood. Mark out dado recess in other half, using tongue as a guide. Cut dado with tenon saw and chisel out waste. Assemble with glue and secure with sash clamps.

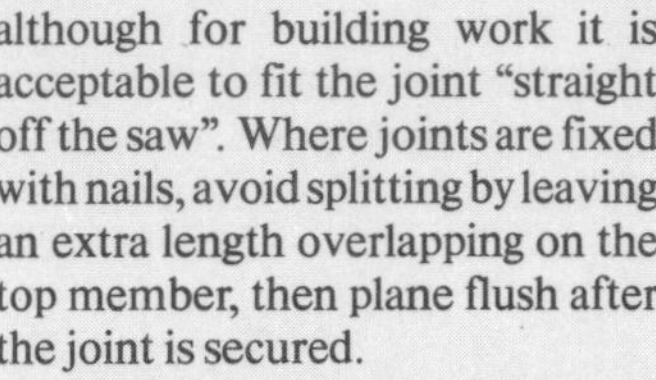

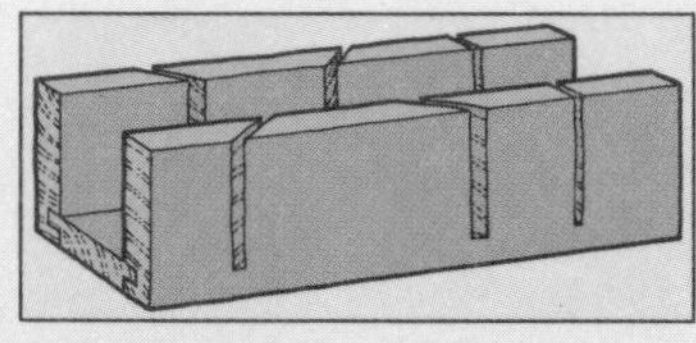

Making a miter
A 90° joint formed by mating two 45° ends is a miter, cut using a miter box and backsaw.

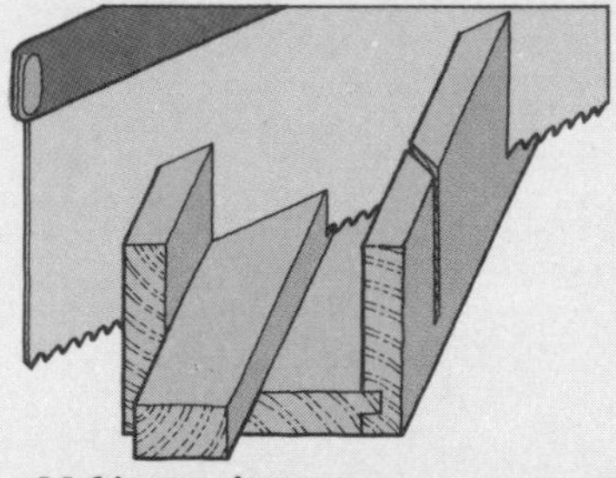

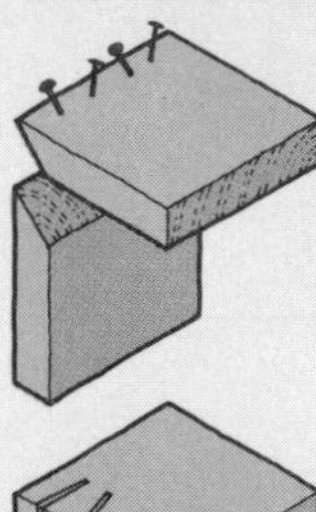

Nailed miter
Establish nails in one half beforehand, in dovetail fashion. Glue ends and clamp joint in a vise while hammering.

Veneered miter
For a stronger bond, cut grooves across outer corner at an angle and insert glued veneer. Plane flush.

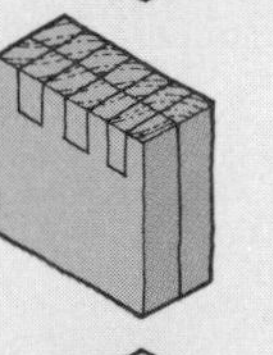

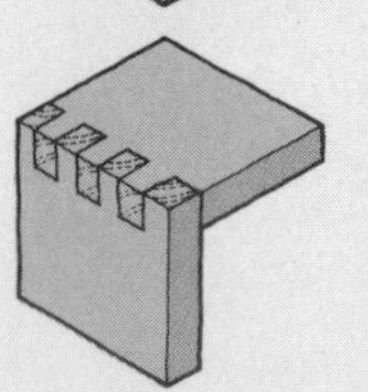

Box joint
Secure both ends of wood together in a vise. Measure and mark fingers a little over length. Saw each finger down to shoulder line, and chisel out waste in between. See joint is not too tight. Glue and clamp, plane finger ends flush.

Right angle joints

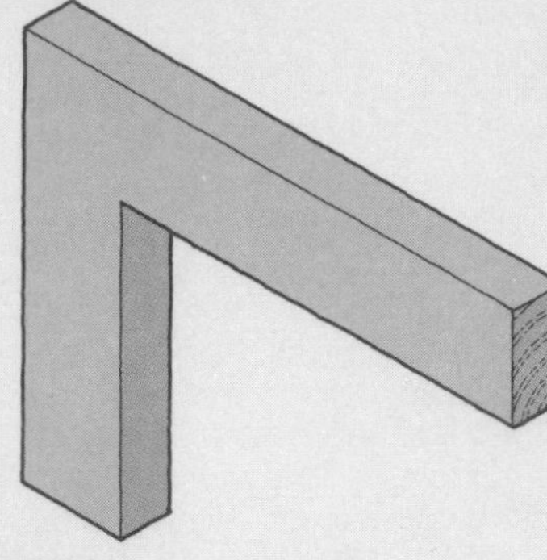

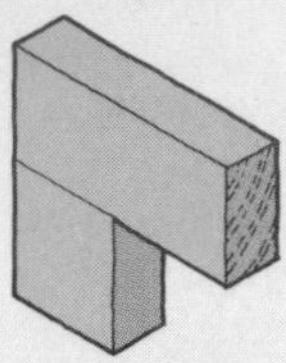

L joint
It is better to cut a miter for this joint than to risk splitting the wood by nailing through larger dimension.

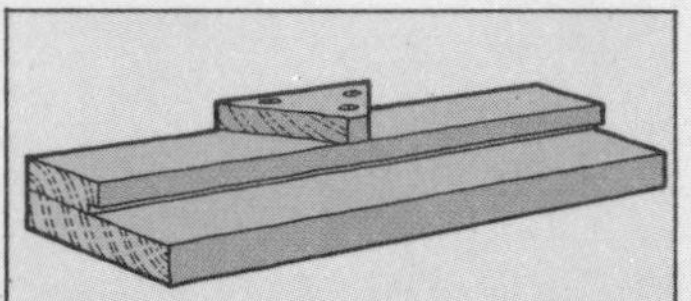

Using the miter shooting board
After using the miter box for cutting your miter, trim on a miter shooting board so that you plane at a correct angle of 45°.

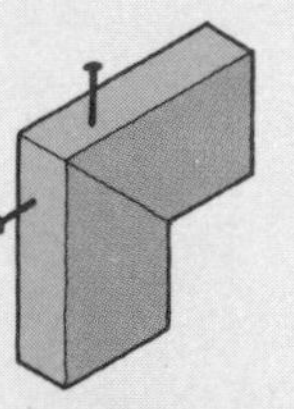

Nailed miter
Secure this with nails, driven in at right angles from both sides.

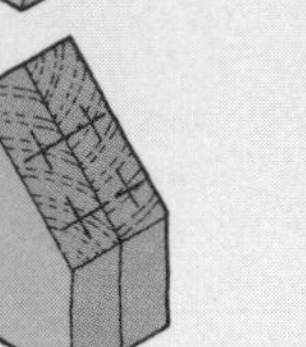

Doweled miter
Place halves side by side and mark positions of dowel holes. Drill holes with a depth gauge on the bit. Holes at inner corner of joint are deeper for added strength. Cut dowel pegs to length. Glue and clamp until set.

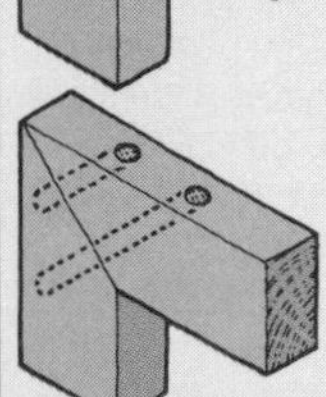

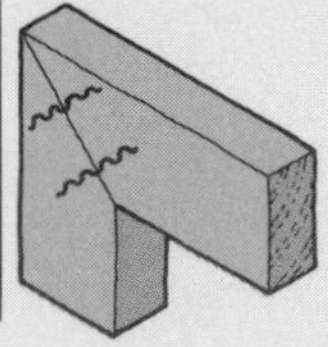

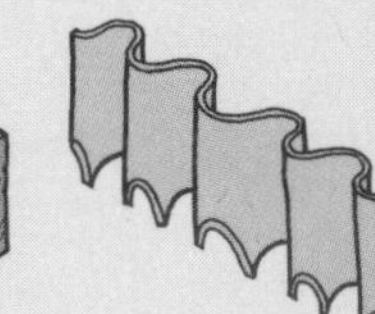

Using fasteners
Secure joint from both sides, using corrugated fasteners one third the thickness of the wood.

Making dowel joints
Mark dowel positions on a center line. Drive brads into marks, snip off the heads with pliers. Make a marking jig with two battens fixed at right angles. Hold upright firmly, then push other half against brads to make exact centers for dowels.

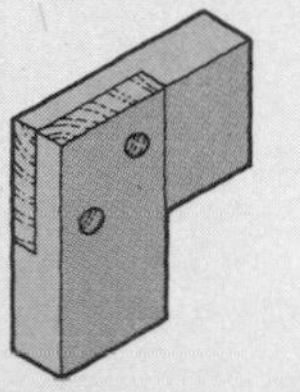

Rabbet joint
This simple joint is formed of two rabbets, each half the thickness of the wood. To make this rabbet joint mark out both halves of joint together, cut them with a backsaw. To cut, hold saw at an angle to work and cut one half down to shoulder. Reverse wood and repeat, leveling up saw as you finish down to shoulder. Fit joint dry, and drill holes to take dowels, staggered to avoid splitting. Cut dowels overlength. Glue join as in top picture and tap in dowels, then trim flush with saw and block plane.

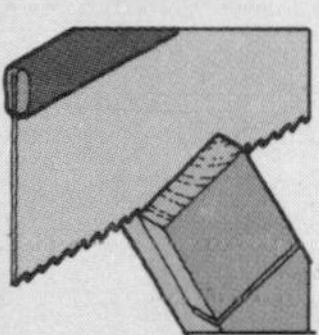

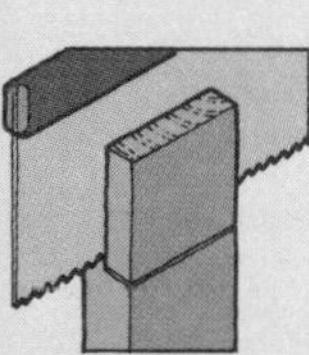

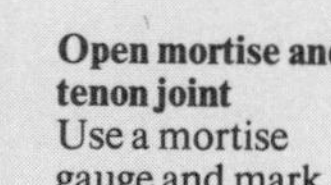

Open mortise and tenon joint
Use a mortise gauge and mark out both halves of joint so that tongues are one third the thickness of wood. Cut and chop out waste with chisel.

Dowel joint
Cut both ends square, leaving extra on upright. Mark position of dowels. Drill holes and tap dowels into place. Glue and clamp until set, then plane off excess on upright.

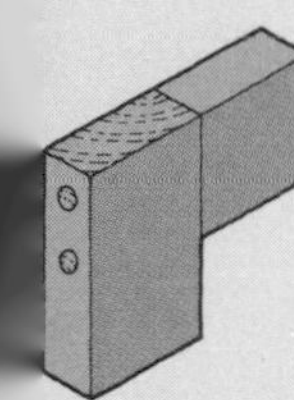

Through dowels
Drill through one half of joint into the other. Tap overlength dowels into holes, plane flush when glue has set.

Haunched tenon
A tenon in a corner joint needs a haunch to prevent the rail twisting out of line. The haunch should be one third as long as the tenon and one quarter as wide. Mark out both halves together. Cut tenon first, using it to mark length of mortise. Drill and chisel out waste from mortise, and cut to receive the haunch, sawing down to the shoulder. Glue and secure with sash clamps, planing flush when glue sets.

Angled haunch
Cut haunch at an angle, as shown, to avoid seeing it through the end grain of the stile.

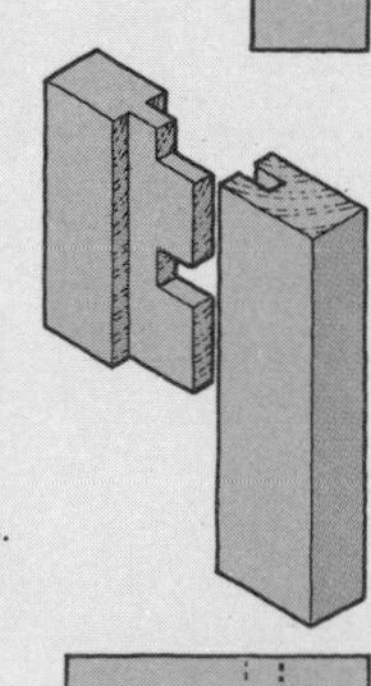

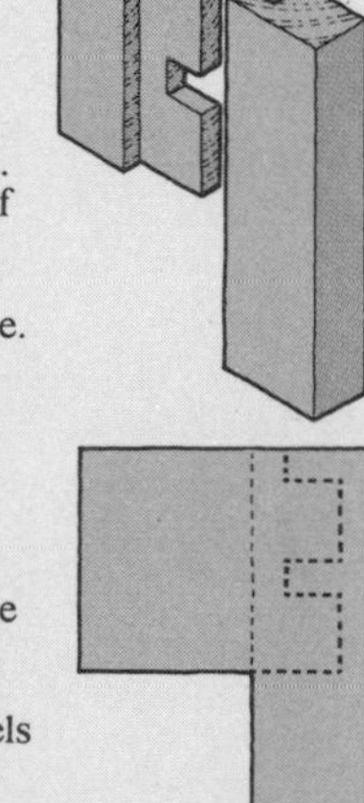

Twin mortise and tenon
Used for rails on door frames, the tenon is divided in two with a haunch running between to prevent the rail twisting. Any mortised joint over 6 in. wide should have twin tenons to avoid weakening the stile. Cut the joint as for a single mortise.

T joints

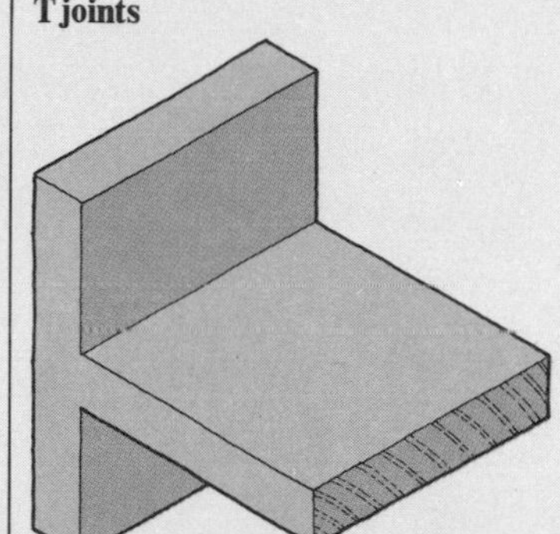

This type of joint is useful for shelving, and may carry a lot of weight. Simple, light joints can be made by nailing and gluing, reinforcing with screwed brackets. For strong joints, use the variety of techniques shown below: doweled, dado and stopped dado (which hides the joint), or the very strong stub and tenon joint. The techniques resemble those described opposite for right angle joints.

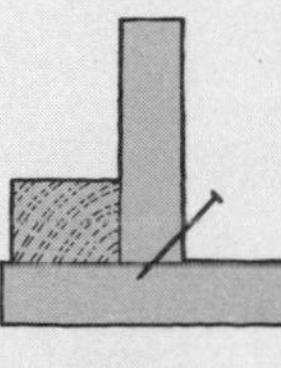

Nailed butt joint
Clamp a block against one side, to keep joint still while driving nails at an angle. Move block to nail the other side.

Dowel joint
At regular intervals set dowels two thirds the thickness of stile.

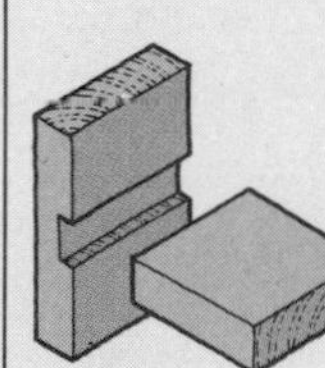

Dado joint
Square up position of rail on stile, and mark out dado with marking knife. Cut dado one quarter to one third thickness of stile. Cut down to depth of shoulders, chop away waste with chisel.

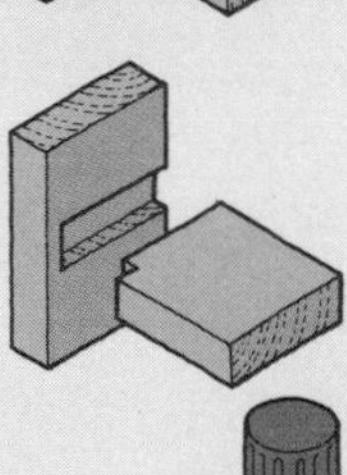

Stopped dado
The dado stops short of front of stile. Notch the rail to fit around the blind end.

Stub tenons
Where possible, make tenons square and equally spaced. This join can be made with a stopped housing or through housing.

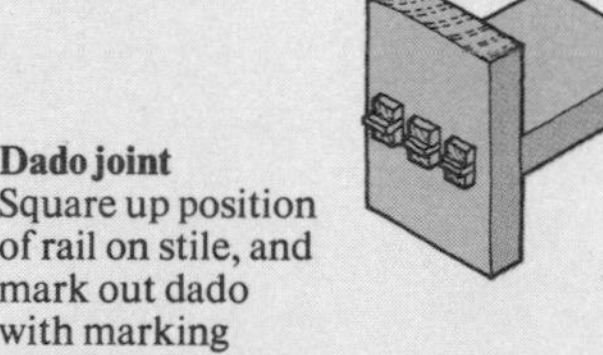

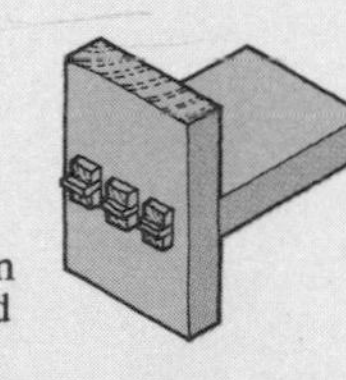

Through tenons
When cutting a through mortise for the tenons, clamp the stile on a waste board, and drill right through to avoid splitting the wood. Chisel waste from both sides.

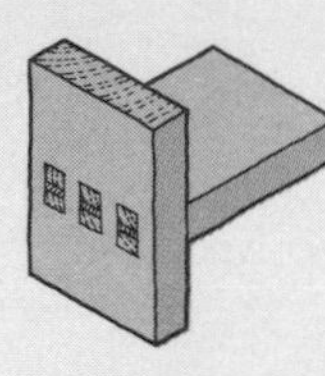

Using wedges
Wedges help secure the tenons. Make a saw cut across tenons before joining. Clamp joint, then glue and tap wedges into cut.

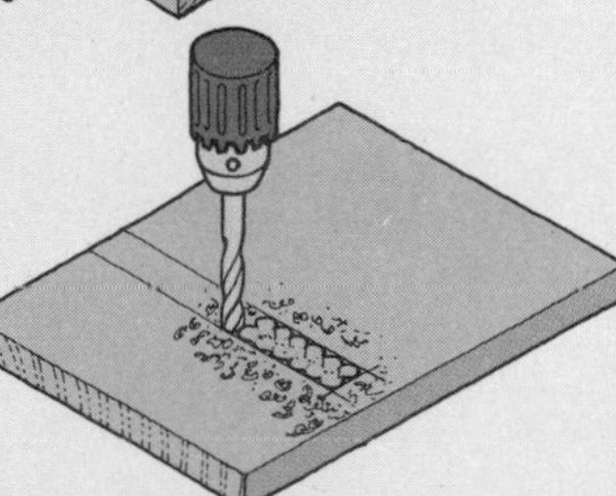

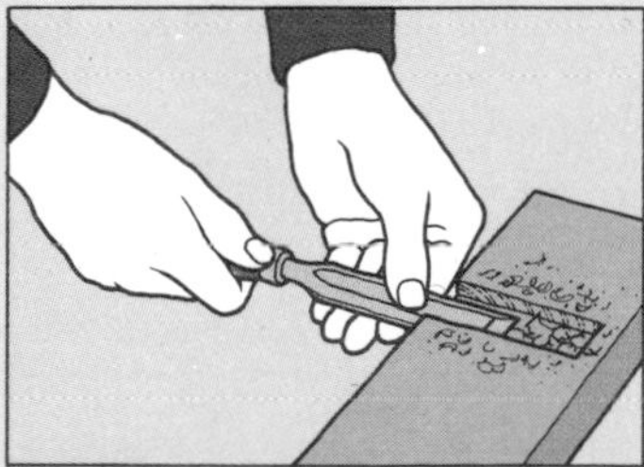

Cutting a stopped dado
The dado should stop about ¾ inch short of the front edge. Drill out a mortise to the depth of the dado at the stopped end and trim with a chisel to give clearance for a backsaw. Make parallel cuts down to the shoulder line. Clear away the waste with a chisel keeping the blade parallel to the bottom of housing.

Joining Lumber

T joints

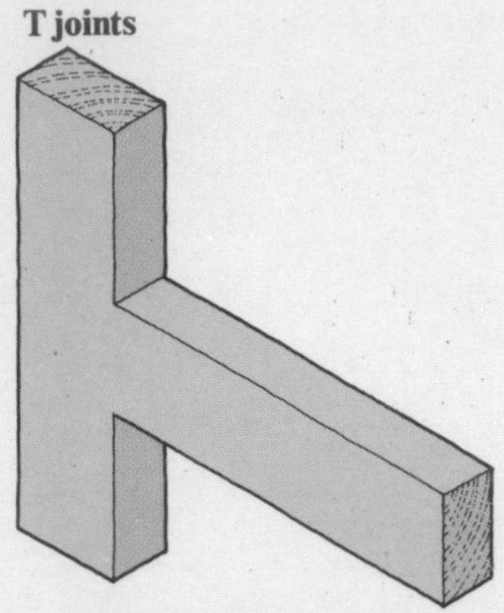

This type of joint is commonly used in all forms of frame construction. For building work use a butt joint secured by dovetail nailing or corrugated fasteners. There are a variety of joints used in furniture making, depending upon the amount of skill or finish required. Bridle joints and tenon joints are by far the strongest and will prevent the frame twisting.

Butt joint
Often secured by nailing or by use of dowels and glue (see pp. 128-129), where finish is not important. This can also be secured by fasteners. Set fasteners at an angle to the joint to prevent rail's grain splitting.

Half lap joint
Mark out width of cutout. Mark depth of housing and thickness of lap – they should be equal. Cut out housing as shown below right, and cut lap as previously described.

Dovetail lap joint
This technique gives added strength to lap. Cut one half of lap to angle of 15°, and use it to mark off matching housing.

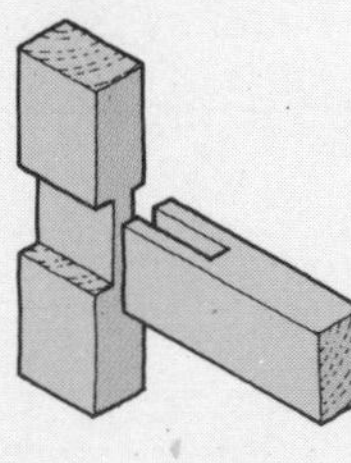

Bridle joint
This is a stronger variation of the lap joint, as the gluing area is nearly doubled. Use a mortise gauge to mark out halves of joint, dividing thickness of wood equally into three parts. Leave extra length on laps. Plane flush after gluing.

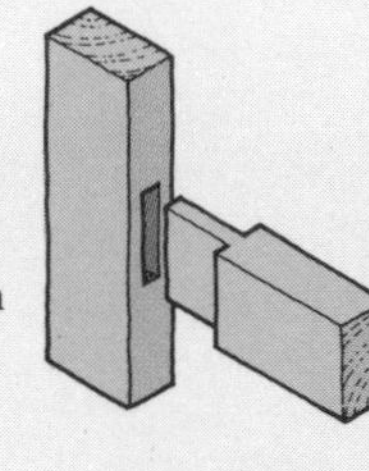

Stopped tenon
The mortise and tenon should be marked and cut out as described on p. 128. If the mortise does not go through the stile, it is a stopped tenon. Put a depth gauge on the bit when drilling out the mortise to ensure an even depth. Cut the tenon a little shorter than this setting.

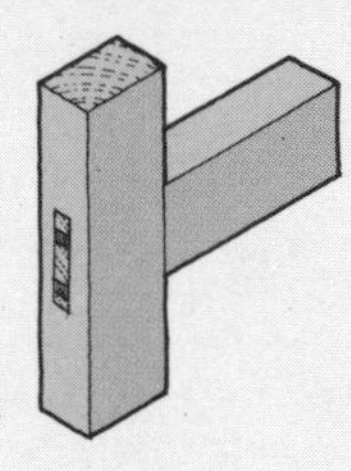

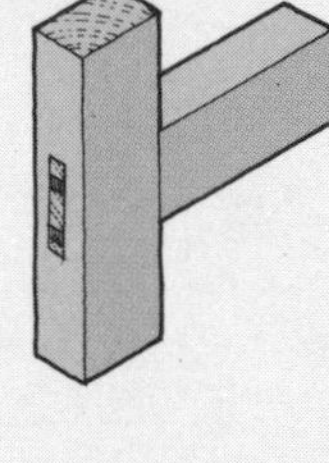

Through tenon
In this joint, the mortise is cut right through the stile. The joint is given added strength with wedges. Cut parallel grooves across end on tenon so that the wedges will spread it when driven home.

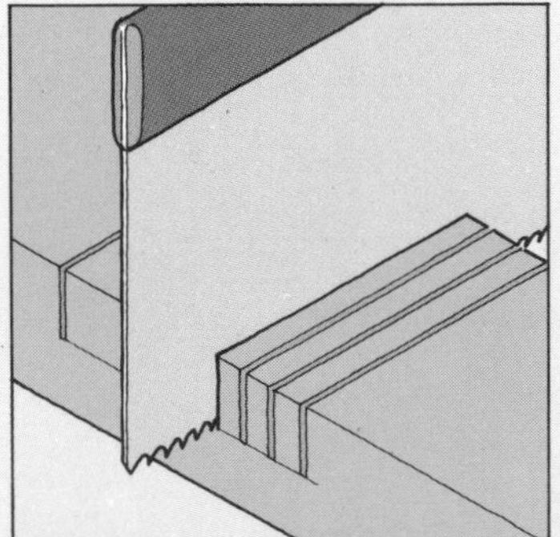

Cutting dadoes
Clearing out the waste material from a wide dado or cutout is easier if you make successive cuts with the saw, and then use a chisel to trim it neatly.

T joints

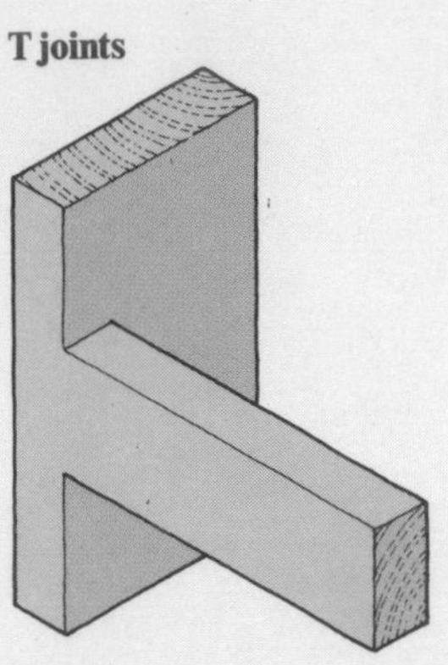

This type of T joint allows you to join different widths or sections of wood. The butt and lap are suitable for rough frame construction, the dovetail for additional strength, and the barefaced for cabinets.

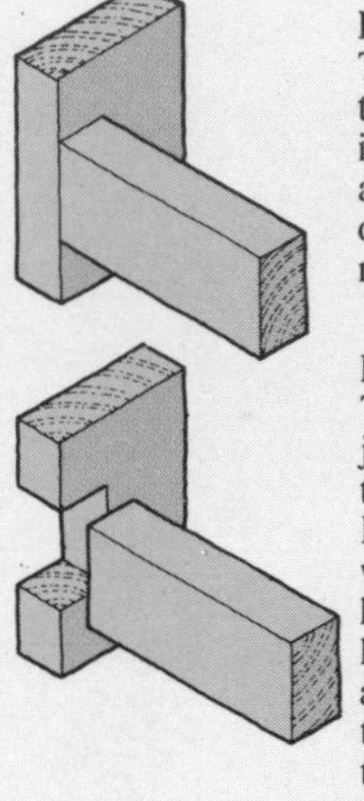

Butt joint
The strongest type of butt joint is fixed by dowels as on p. 129, or by dovetail nailing and gluing.

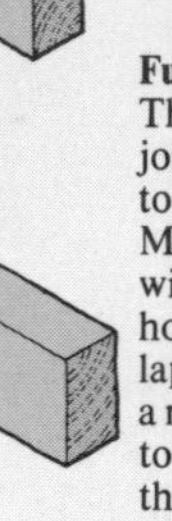

Full lap joint
This is ideal for joining a crossrail to a wider siderail. Mark out the width of the housing, using the lap as a gauge. Use a marking gauge to match thickness of crossrail, and mark out depth of housing on siderail. Secure with dovetail nails, dowels or screws.

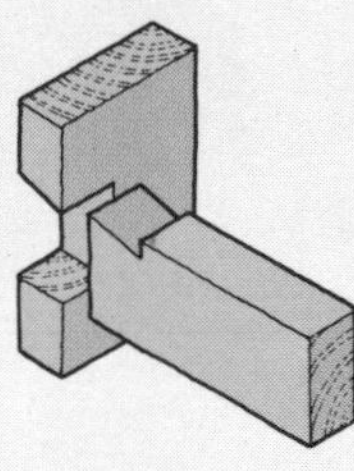

Dovetail lap joint
This can be strengthened by dovetailing the crossrail lap into the siderail. Make the crossrail joint first (see far left) and use it to mark housing. If the crossrail is wide enough, a full dovetail can be cut in the rail.

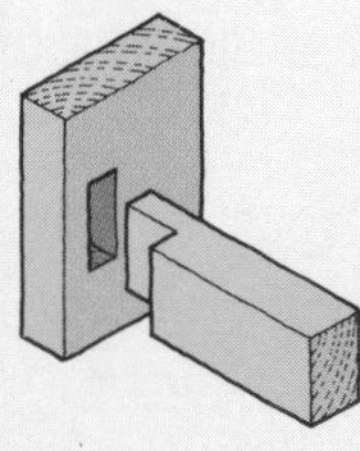

Barefaced tenon
When mating a crossrail into a wider siderail, offset the tenon to one side. Set a mortise gauge to divide the end of the rail in two and use the same measurement to gauge the mortise. Cut out mortise and tenon to make it either a stopped or through joint.

Three-way joints

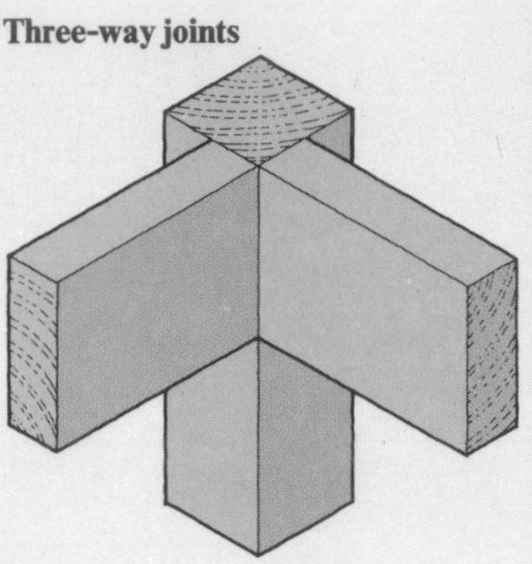

Joining three or more pieces of wood is no harder than joining two: the butt and dowel joints are fairly simple, the mortise and tenon joint needs practice. All are used in making many types of framework.

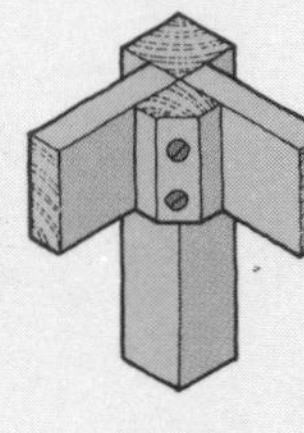

Butt joint
The corner block here gives additional strength and support. Plane off one corner and drill clearance holes for screws. Cut ends of rails square, glue and clamp them to block until glue sets. Screw through block into leg.

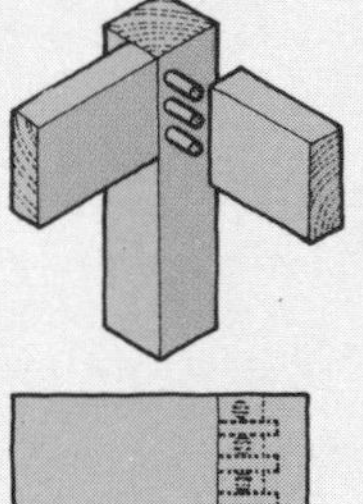

Dowel joint
Follow the previous instructions for dowel joints, but in this case stagger them so that they cross each other inside the leg. This is not difficult if you take careful measurements.

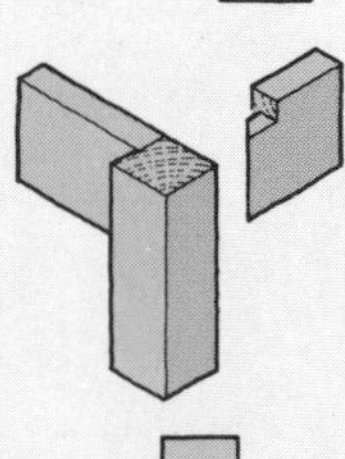

Mortise and tenon
This neat, very strong joint is more complicated than the previous ones. Proceed as for a barefaced tenon (left) but miter the tenon ends to give you sufficient length in the mortise. If the joint is at the end of a leg it should be haunched.

X joints

These occur in furniture making where the dowel joint is often used, in wooden window frames using housing joints, and in building construction, where the cross lap joint is both strong and neat.

Cross lap joint
Clamp the two pieces together and mark out both. The housings should be the same width as the wood's thickness, and half the depth. Cut both housings down to shoulder line, and remove waste with a chisel. Remove clamps, fit and glue the joint.

Dowel joint
Mark dowel positions on upright with brads, hammer brads into upright and snip off heads. Use brads to mark dowel centers on end grain of rail. Clamp both rails in a vise, and mark off second rail from first. Drill holes in rails to take dowels. Remove brads and drill through upright. Glue and pass dowels through into rail ends.

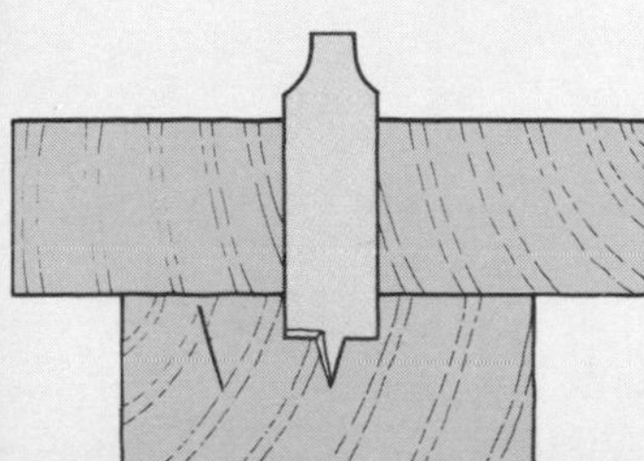

Drilling dowel holes
To avoid splitting the grain as the drill emerges, support the work on waste wood and drill through.

X joints

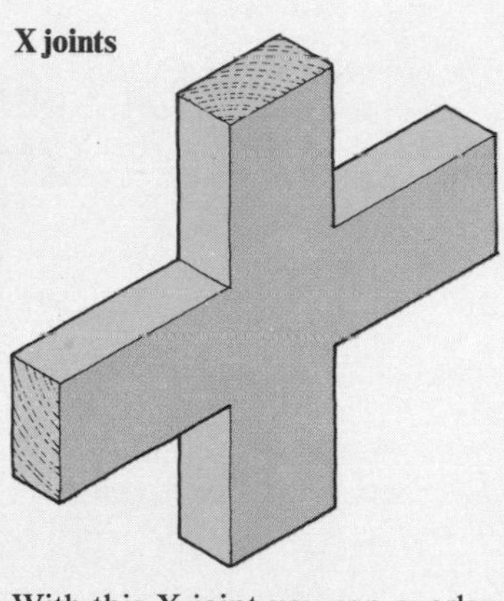

With this X joint you can overlap the two cross-members and screw them together, cut dadoes for a neater cross lap, cut a mortise and tenon or a mitered bridle joint, or use the familiar dowel joint.

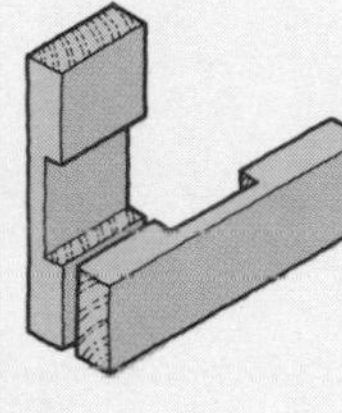

Cross lap joint
Mark out both halves together so that the dadoes are the width of the wood, and half the depth. Saw down to the shoulder line of both halves clamped together, and remove waste –as shown on p. 130. The joint may be glued and nailed or screwed.

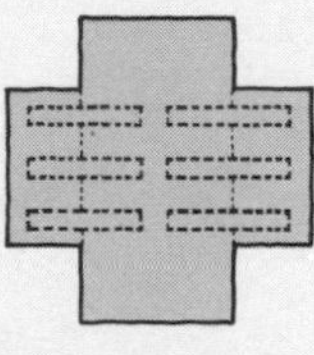

Dowel joint
In this joint the dowels do not go right through the upright. Mark the centers with nails as previously described. Make dowels as shown below.

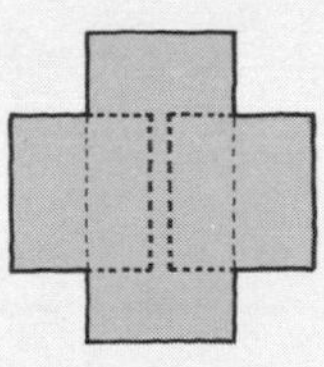

Mortise and tenon
Cut through mortise on the upright member for a neat, strong joint. The tenons should be half the width of the upright. Glue and clamp until joint sets firm.

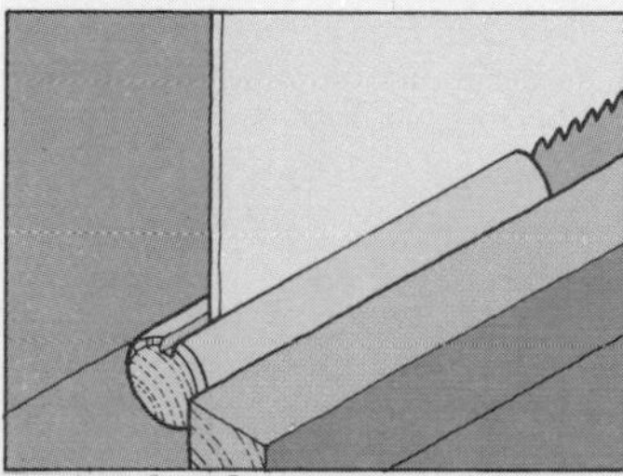

Gluing dowels
Using a backsaw make a shallow cut along dowels for glue to escape; otherwise the wood may split.

End-to-end joints

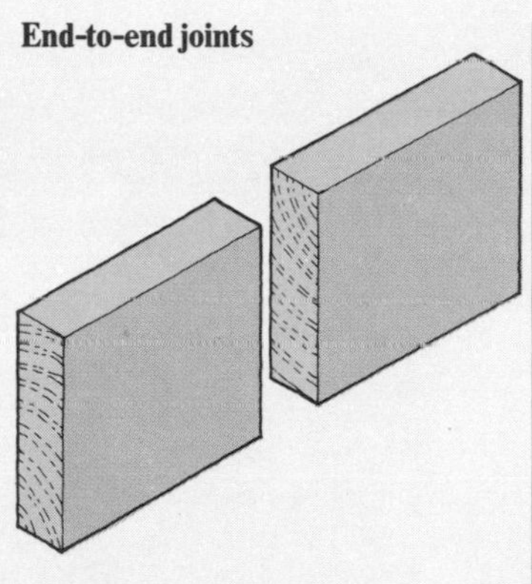

Although you can buy lumber of considerable length, there are occasions when you need to join two lengths end to end, particularly in flooring or roofing repairs, or when building extensions.

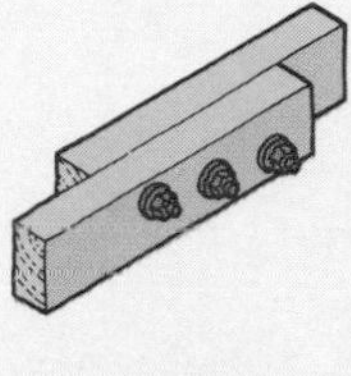

Simple lap joint
This method of joining may be used where a staggered joint is acceptable. Overlap the ends three times the width of lumber. Drill holes and use large carriage bolts with washers and lumber connectors sandwiched in between to increase grip.

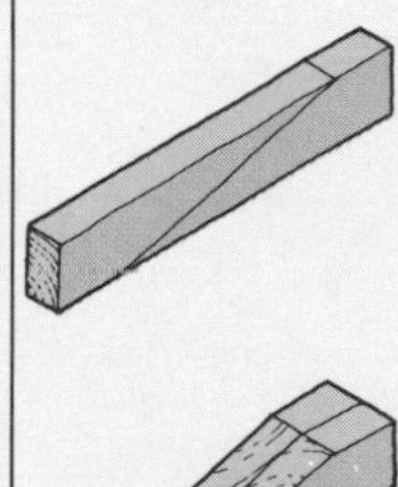

Scarf joint
Plane a matching angle on the ends of the lengths. Clamp the pieces together and cut an angle. The length of the bisecting line should be four times the width of the wood. Reverse one piece, glue and rub joint together. Clamp with battens and C clamps until glue sets hard.

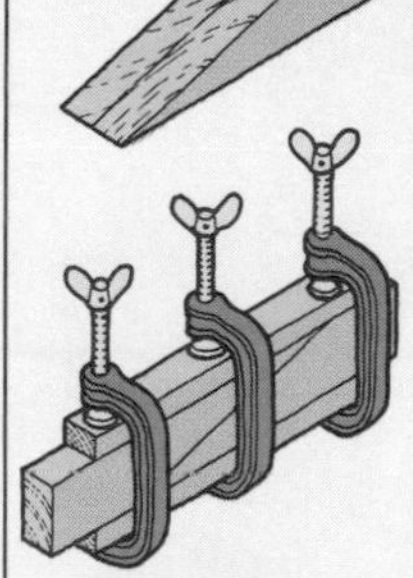

Reinforced butt joint
Fix plywood plates, four times as long as wood is wide, to each side with glue and staggered screws.

Splayed lap joint
Cut shoulders together at an angle of 45°. Cut bisecting line and reverse one to mate with other.

Edge to edge joints

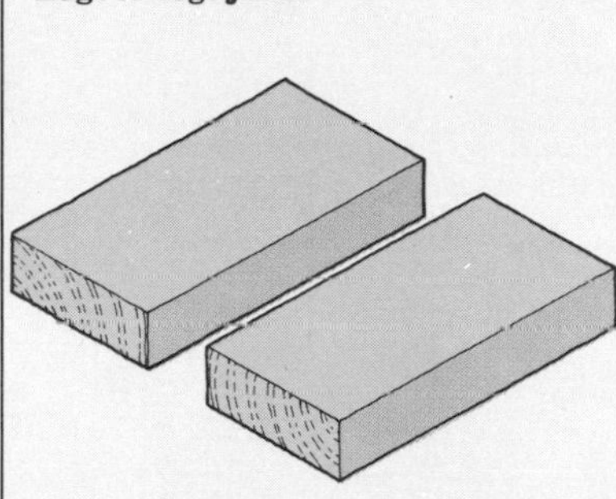

This technique is employed to increase the width of planks or panels. It is not easy, because it requires planing the finished panel flat and square by hand. There are, however, three common joints.

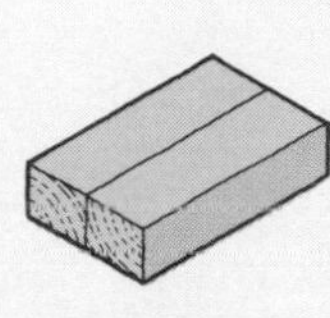

Butt joint
Clamp two pieces in a vise and plane edges square. Place together and hold up to light to check fit. Glue and hold in sash clamps.

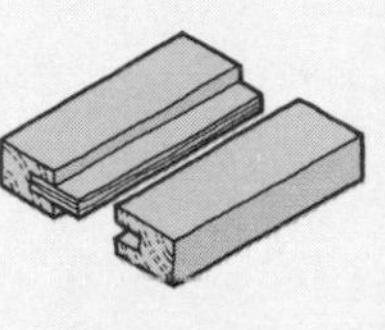

Splined joint
Cut a spline from plywood. Spline should be one third the thickness of boards and 1½ times as wide. Cut a groove in both edges of boards to take half the width of spline. Glue edges and grooves, tap in spline, join edges and secure with clamps.

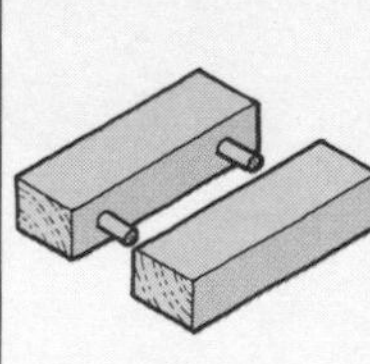

Dowel joint
Plane edges square and mark off dowel positions on both halves, spacing them at 9-inch intervals. Use dowel jig for accurate drilling, each hole as deep as thickness of board being joined. Glue and set dowels, join boards and clamp.

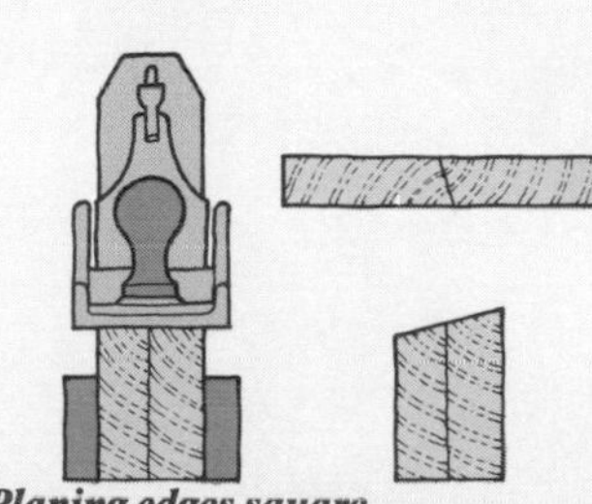

Planing edges square
Even if the edges are not completely square, the boards will still lie flat as long as they are not reversed.

Making Drawers

Drawer making

Drawers can be more or less elaborate according to the skill of the maker. Because of the often complex construction and the need for careful fitting within narrow margins of tolerance, cabinet drawer making is a skilful job, demanding such techniques as dovetail joints – even secret dovetailing – central bearers, stopped running grooves and so on. But drawer making for average domestic use in the kitchen, bathroom or workshop requires only simple techniques, although the final result can still look professional. A drawer, after all, is only a type of box, and box construction is not necessarily complicated. Furthermore drawer making kits in plastic, hardwood or softwood are sold in many hardware stores, and in a wide variety of shapes and sizes to meet most needs. See facing page for how to assemble these. All the joints and means of construction are described elsewhere in this section, as well as a number of details which you can combine to make a drawer that suits your specifications. Do not be put off if you have a limited range of tools or equipment for drawer making: grooves, for instance, can be constructed from molding strips rather than being cut by specialized tools.

Methods of running

All drawers have to run on some type of bearer. Often it is the bottom edges of the drawer sides that rest on the bearers; this is the most hard-wearing system. Alternatively, the drawer can hang on a bearing runner, or else the bearer fits into a long groove in the side of the drawer. In some modern drawer units, metal bearers have superseded the traditional wooden type. The bearer usually acts as a "kicker" for the drawer below, preventing it from tipping forward when pulled out. Traditionally a rail between the drawers masks the runner.

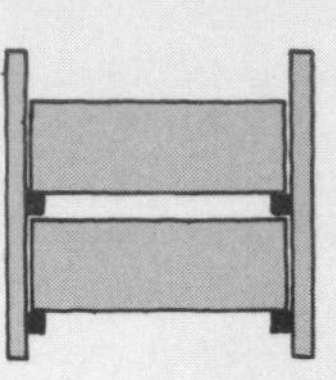

Wooden bearing section

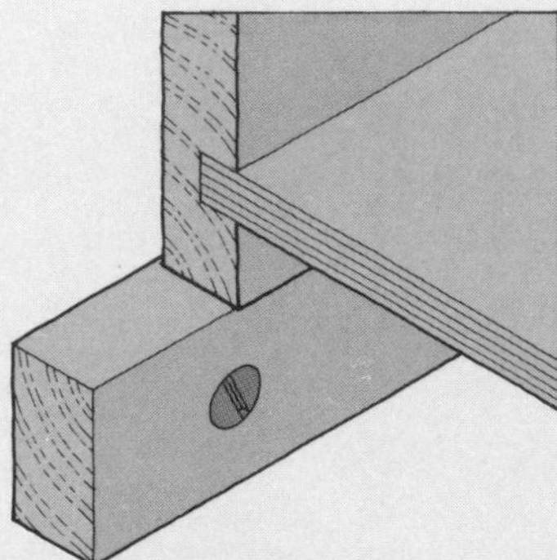

Screw and glue battens to sides of cabinet. Cut slotted screw holes if sides are solid wood to allow for movement. The runner can be hidden from view by overhang on the drawer front when closed.

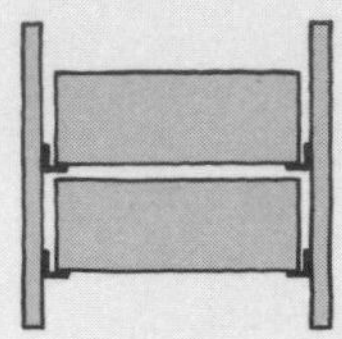

Metal bearing L section

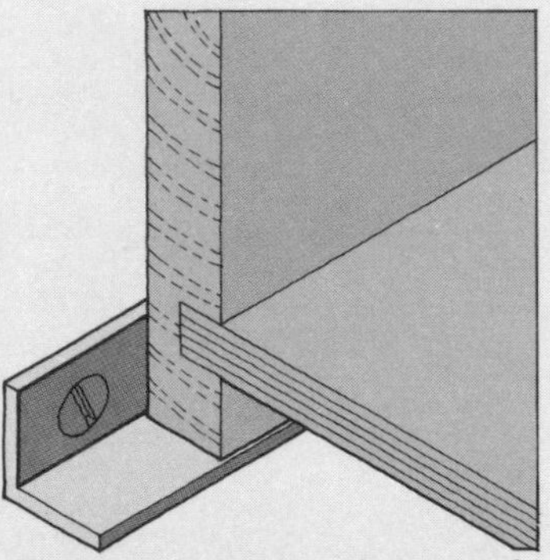

Screw metal section as shown to side of cabinet. Apart from being very hard-wearing, it also takes up less room than a wooden batten. Allow for thickness of metal when measuring width of drawer.

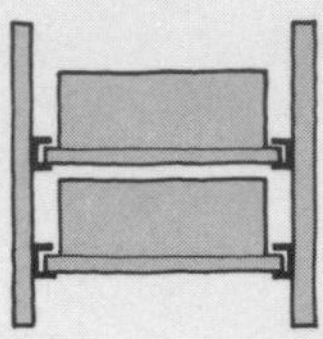

Metal bearing U section

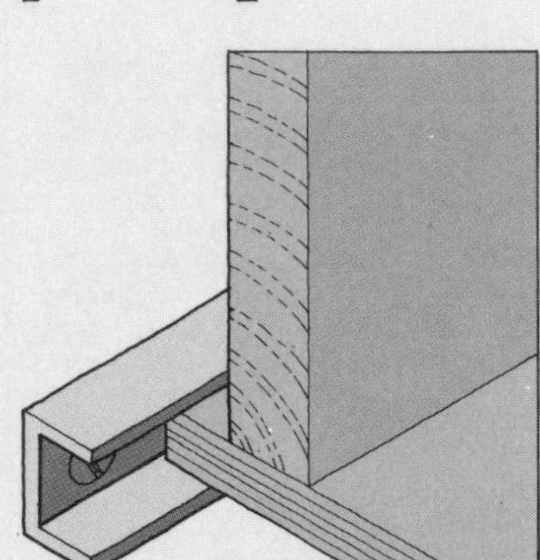

Using this section gives you a combination of side and bottom run, acting as a runner and kicker at the same time. The drawer bottom, made of $\frac{1}{4}$ in. plywood, extends beyond the sides to run smoothly in the U bearing.

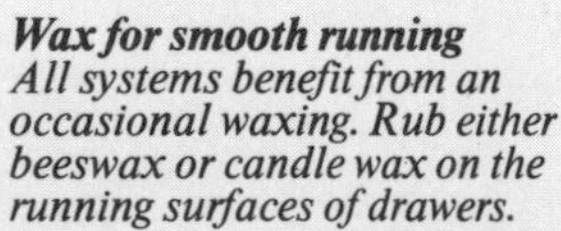

Wax for smooth running

All systems benefit from an occasional waxing. Rub either beeswax or candle wax on the running surfaces of drawers.

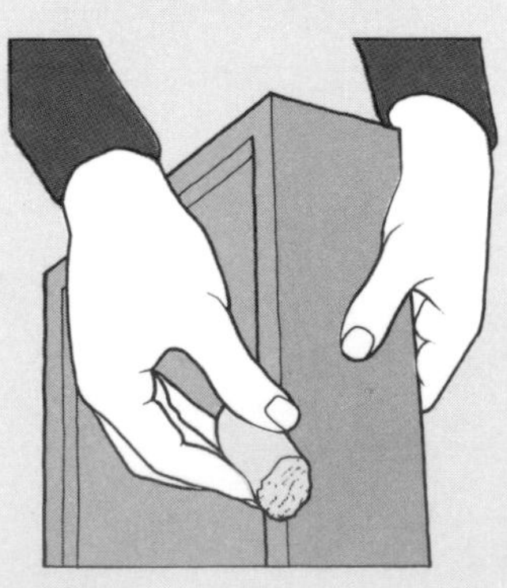

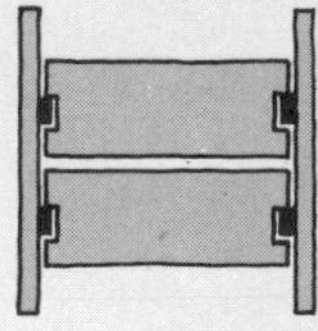

Side running drawer

Screw and glue batten to side of cabinet so it mates with groove, cut in side of drawer and no more than half its thickness. Screws should be well countersunk in bearer.

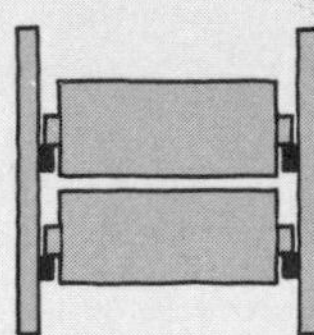

Side hanging bearer

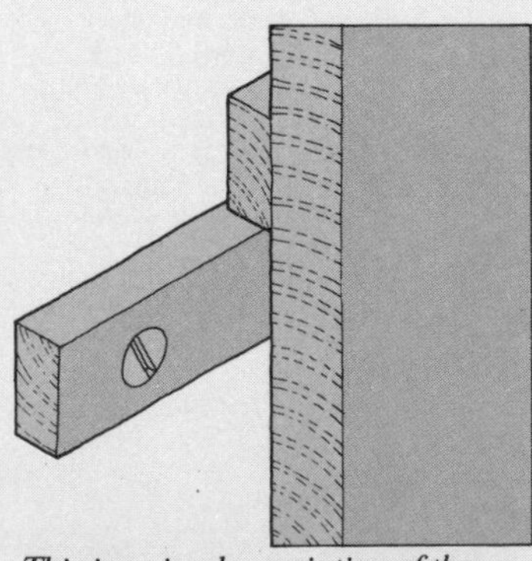

This is a simpler variation of the side run system, eliminating the groove. Screw and glue a batten to drawer side. Hang drawer from this runner on a pair of battens or metal bearers screwed to the cabinet side. Provide a kicker by securing a second batten to the cabinet side.

Top hanging bearer

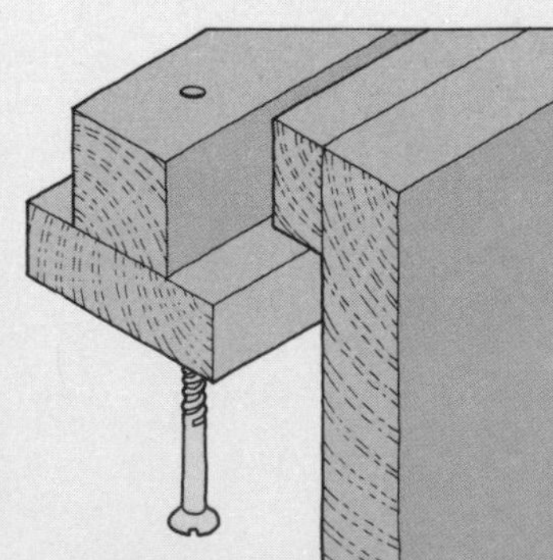

Screw and glue a batten flush with top edge of drawer slides. This runner can hang from a metal or wooden bearer fixed to underside of a work surface instead of cabinet sides supporting bearer.

Drawer bottoms

Most drawers today have hardboard or plywood bottoms, which are still traditionally fitted into the drawer at a final stage of the construction, in order to hold the assembly square and firm. The bottom slides into grooves in the side panels and front, the back stopping short of the grooves to permit the introduction of the drawer bottom, which is then nailed to the underside of the back.

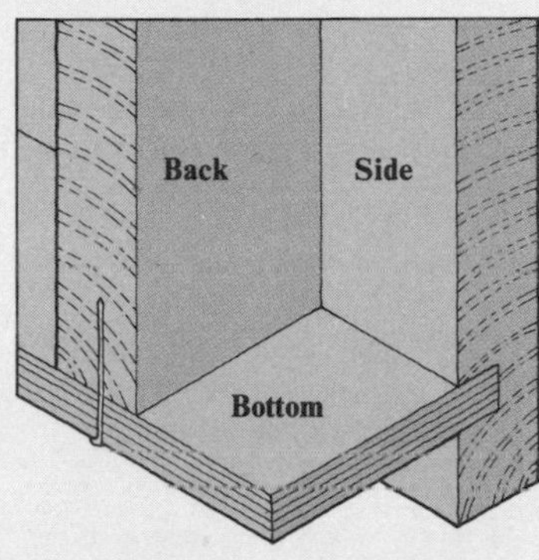

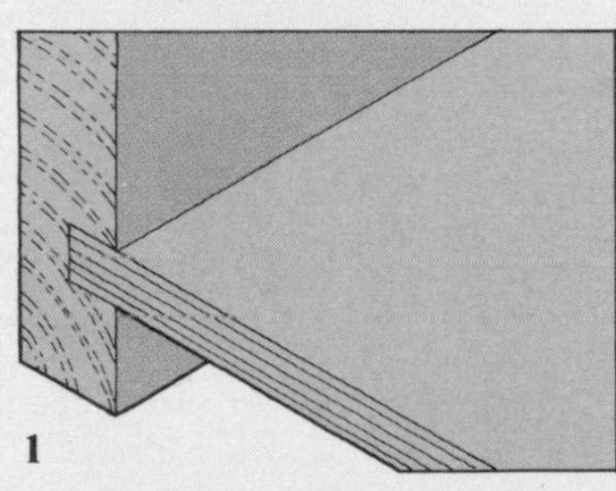
1

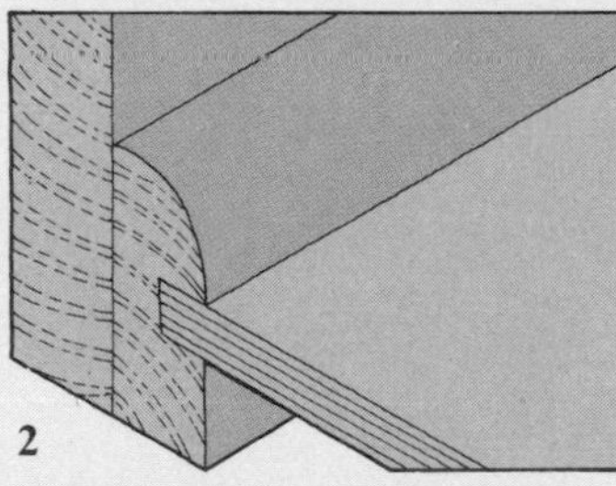
2

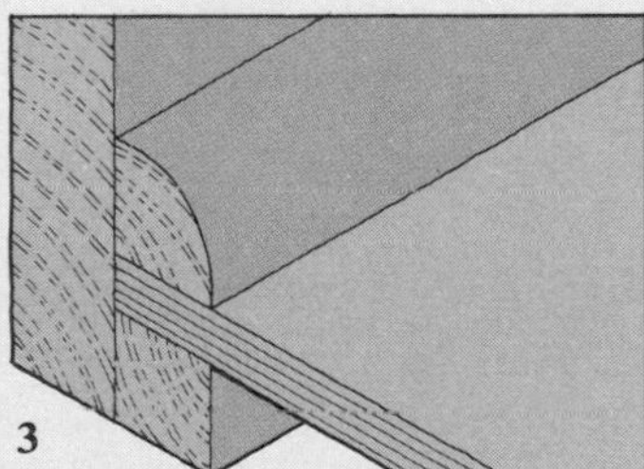
3

Fitting drawer bottoms
1 Slot drawer bottom into a groove cut in drawer sides and front, ⅜ inch from bottom edge.
2 You can buy ready-made drawer slip moldings which should be glued to the inside of the drawer
3 Alternatively make your own by using two simple wooden moldings to support drawer bottom.

Drawer fronts

The overlap drawer front **4** can not only overlap the cabinet sides but also the top or bottom rail, or any combination required (see diagrams right). This is often made with a structural front, using the same material as for the drawer sides. It is then covered with an overlapping false front of show wood, which can be a laminated composite board, screw fixed from the inside.

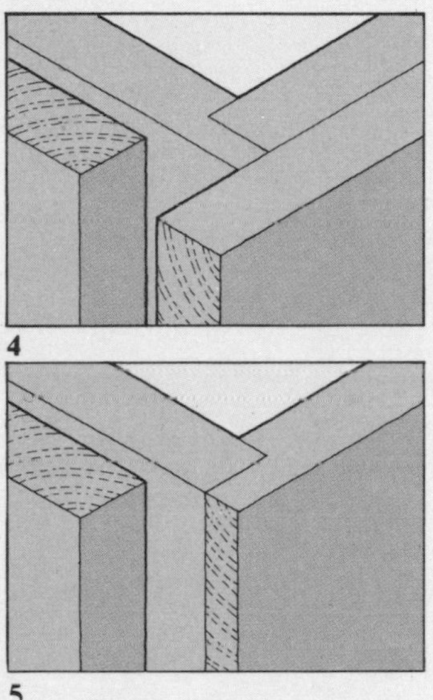
4

5

The inset drawer front **5** lies flush with the cabinet sides. It is usually made from solid wood and is a structural member with the drawer side jointed into it.

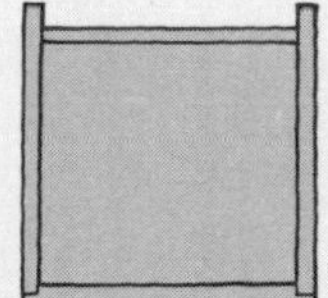

Combining details
Vary drawer construction details to suit your needs. The diagrams on the right show two possible combinations

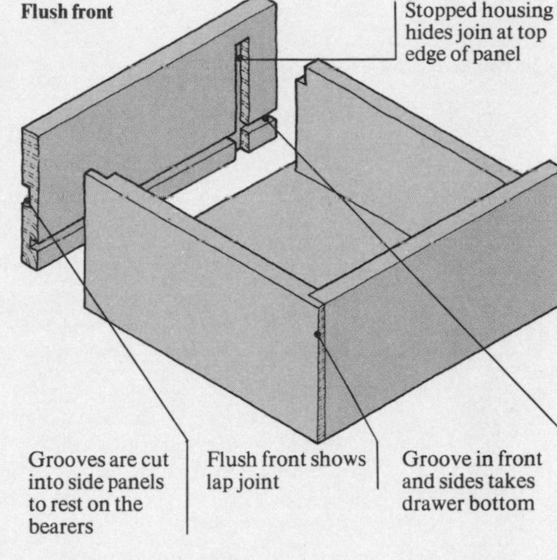

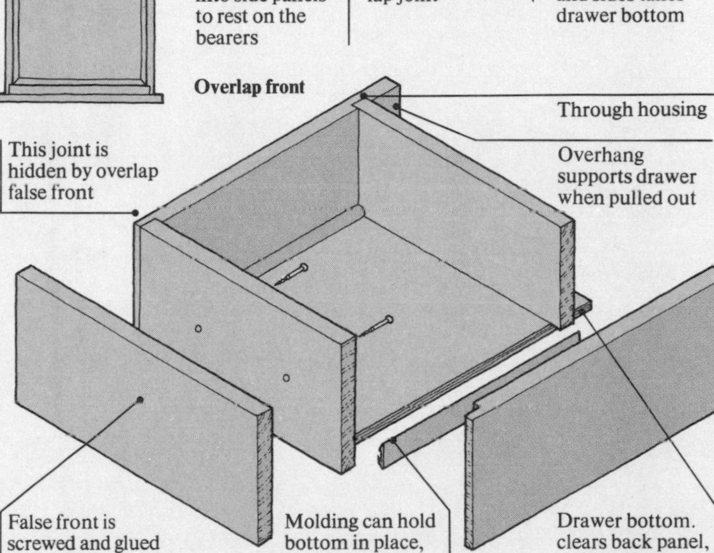

Plastic drawer kits

Using a plastic drawer kit turns drawer making into an extremely simple task, since you merely put the drawer together by hand without the help of adhesive. It consists of a back and sides cut from a molded plank ready grooved for the bottom panel and drawer runners, with plug-in corner joints and front fixing plates. It will run smoothly over a long period without requiring lubrication.

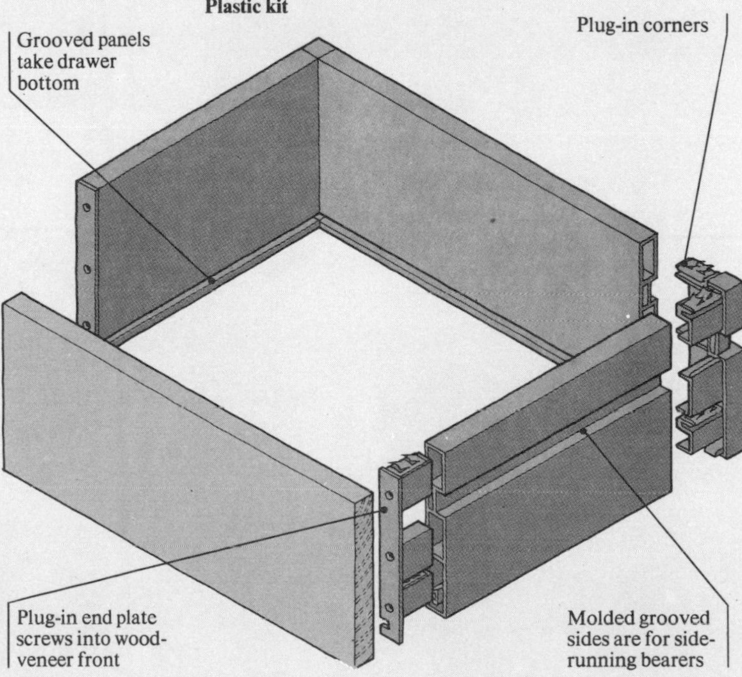

Hardware

Wall Hardware

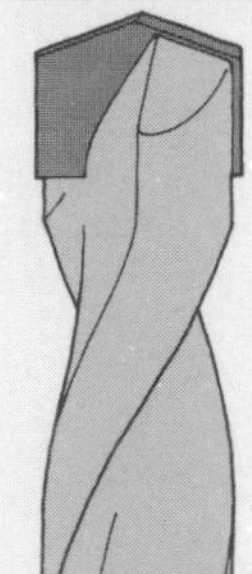

Masonry bits

Fixing attachments to a solid plaster wall needs some type of plug or anchor to hold the screw. In most cases this is a fiber or plastic plug. To make the hole you will need a carbide-tipped drill bit. Use a hand drill, or the low speed on a power drill. Drill sizes are related to plug and screw sizes: choose a no. 10 bit to match a 10 screw and plug.

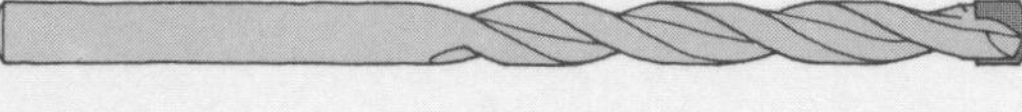

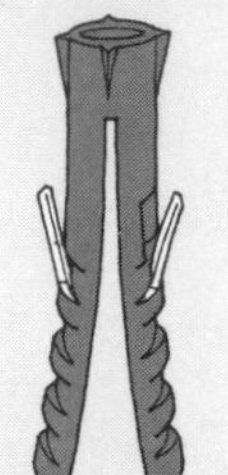

Filling plug

This is an expanding, toothed plug that tightens its grip in the hole as the screw is driven in. Cut a fiber plug just long enough to take the whole length of the thread, otherwise it may start to bind. Start the hole in the plug with the screw before fixing.

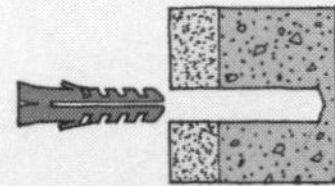
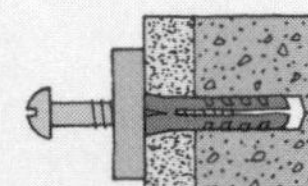
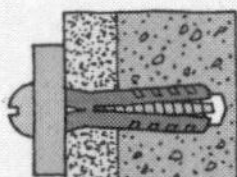

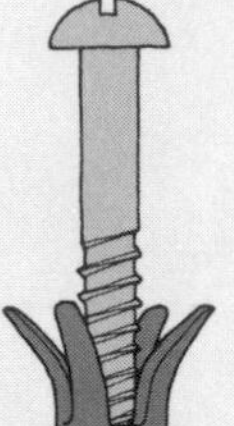

Petal plug

This very economical and efficient anchor is for fixing to a cavity wall. The plug is passed through a drilled hole the same diameter as the plug, the screw engaged in the plug. As the screw is tightened, the petals spread to grip the inside face of the cavity.

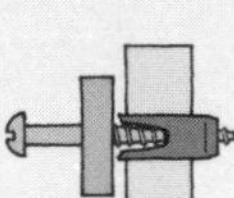
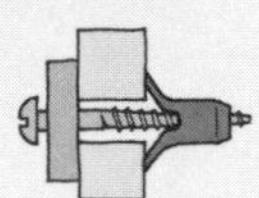
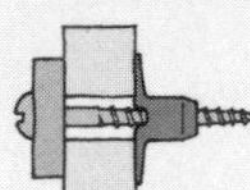

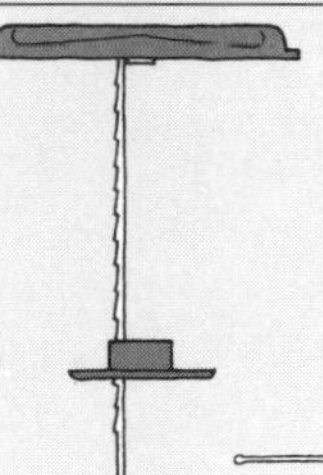

Gravity toggle

This remains a permanent anchor, even when the screw is removed. The anchor goes through the hole in the panel, but retains a plastic strip carrying a plug. The plug is pushed into the hole, ready for the screw. The strip is then cut away.

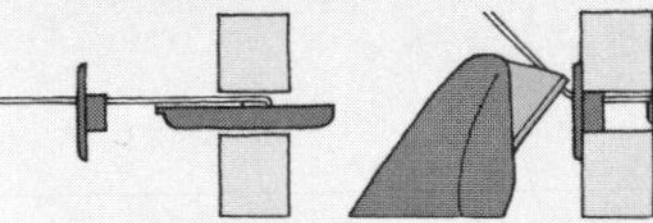
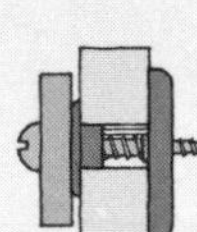

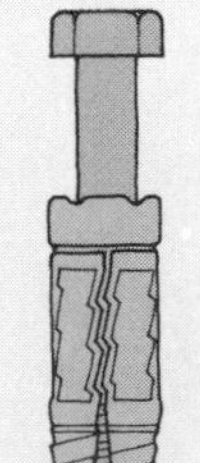

Masonry bolts

Plastic or metal bolts both provide a strong fitting. The bolt is pushed into a hole of matching diameter. The action of tightening the bolt expands the fitting to grip the sides of the hole.

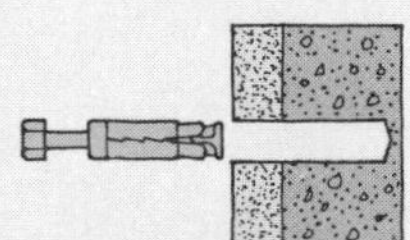
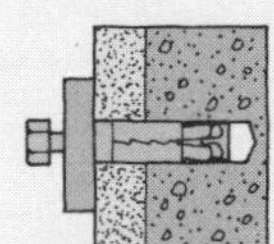
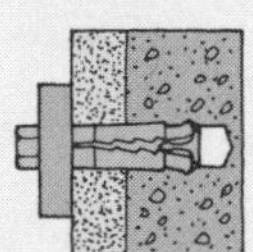

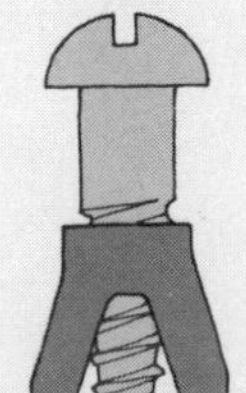

Spreading plug

This joins thin sheets of material. Drill a hole to match the diameter of the plug and engage a machine or wood screw. The screw will rivet the material together.

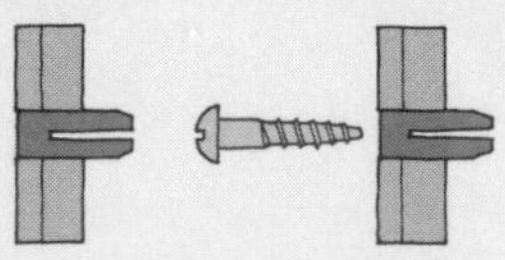
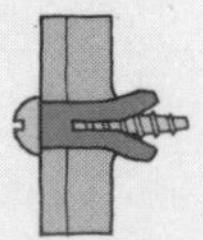

Toggle bolt

This thin bolt is fitted with a special toggle or nut. Swing toggle in line with bolt and pass through cavity hole. Revolve the bolt and pull until toggle grips inside of panel; then tighten to secure.

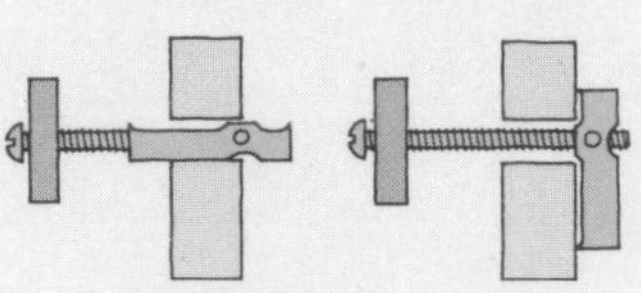
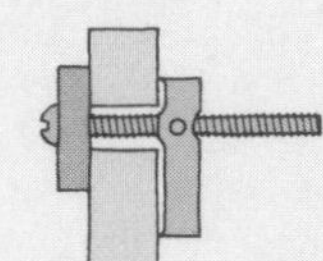

Split-wing toggle

Similar to the above, this toggle has sprung wings which open out inside the cavity. Pull back on bolt and tighten to secure. To install this fitting you need to make a fairly large hole in the panel.

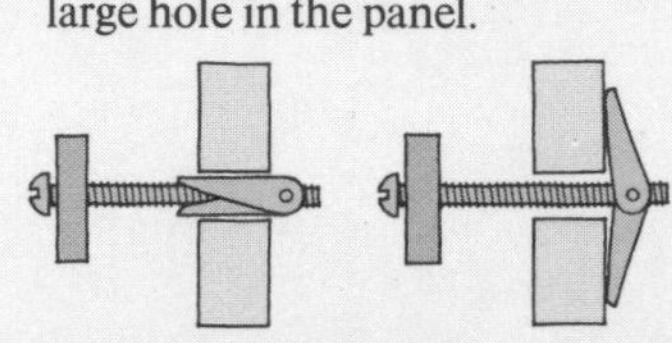
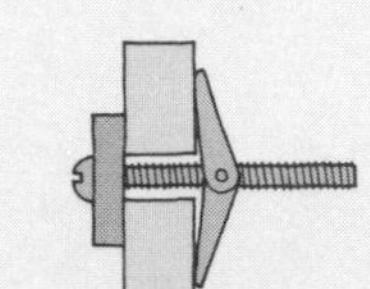

Collapsible anchors

Certain types are made of metal or rubber sleeves. They fit the hole in the panel but also expand behind when the integral bolt is tightened, riveting themselves into place.

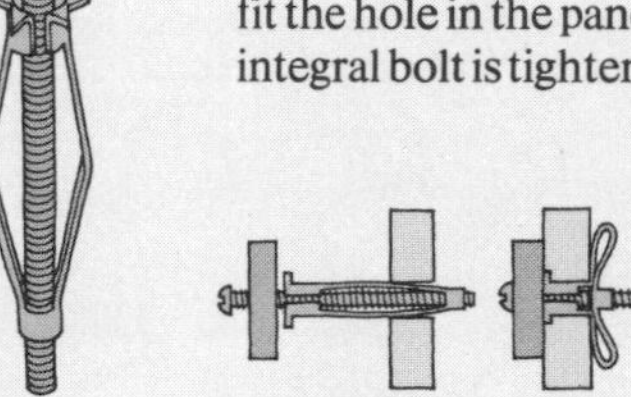
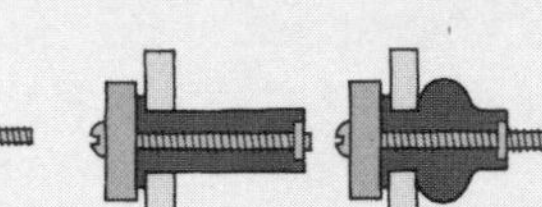

Locks

Mortise lock

The lock is housed in a slot cut into the edge of the door in the manner of a mortise and tenon joint, hence its name. Skill is needed to cut and fit a mortise lock, but the finish and added security are worth the effort. A strike plate is set in flush to the door jamb surface.

Face-mounted lock

This is the easiest type of lock to fit. The mechanism is screwed to the back of the door, flush with the closing edge. The only additional fitting work is cutting a key hole through the door into the lock. This may then be covered with an escutcheon plate. A flush-mounted strike plate is usually screwed to the cabinet to match lock position.

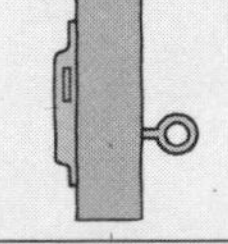

Barrel lock

This type of lock fits snugly into a hole drilled through a door or drawer. When the key is turned, a hooked retainer is ejected from the back and turns through 90° to engage with the strike plate. The face of the lock is usually although not invariably flush-fitting.

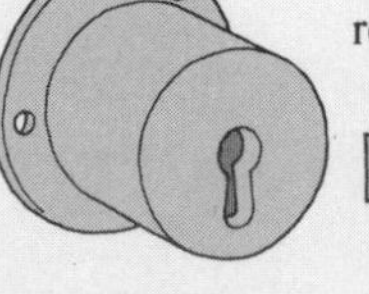
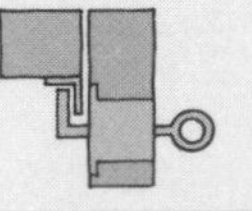

Knockdown Fittings

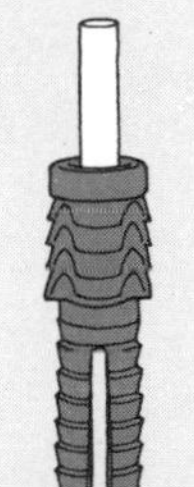

Plastic dowel plugs
One serrated edge of the dowel is fitted into a hole in a panel drilled to size, and a peg is then fitted into the dowel to spread the end tightly. The dowel section still protruding is driven into a matching hole in another panel: in this way both panels are connected.

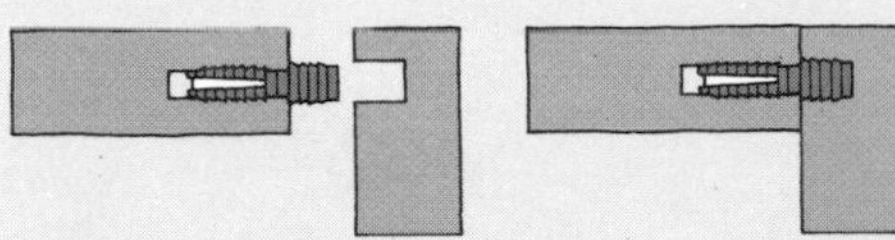

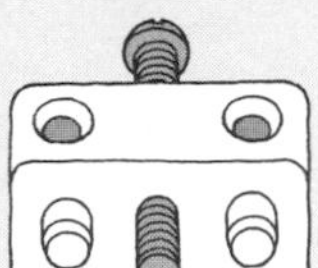

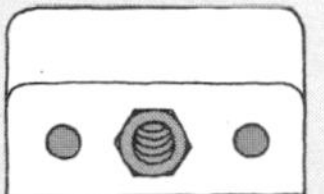

Corner joint
This joins two panels at right angles. The plastic blocks are screwed to the panels, and mate together by tightening an integral nut and bolt. It is usually necessary to have two fittings per joint.

Bolt and barrel nut
This is a method of joining lumber sections to panels. The steel barrel nuts are at right angles to the bolt, which passes through the end of a rail, locating the thread in the nut. The joint is tightened with a key in the bolt head.

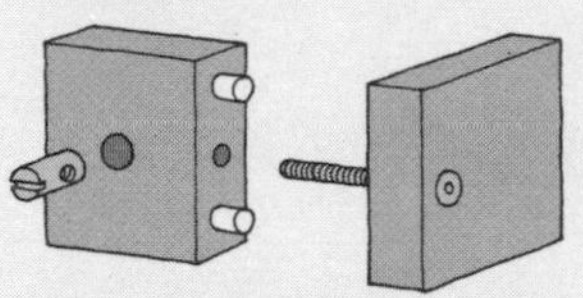

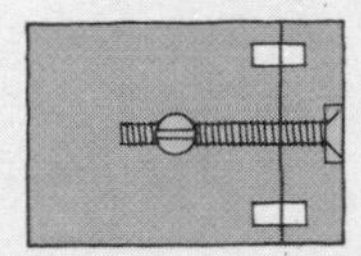

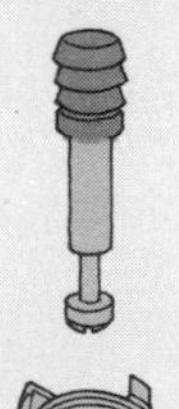

Bolt and cam fitting
This makes neat right angle joins with particle board or lumber panels, but requires a high degree of accuracy. A special purpose bolt locates on a cam, the joint is pulled tight by turning cam with a screwdriver.

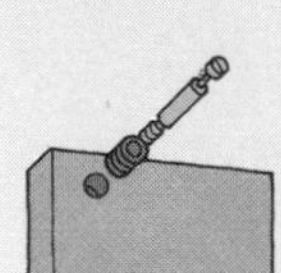

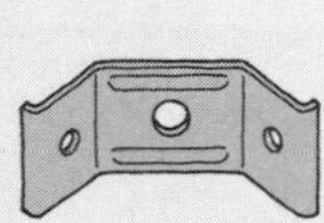

Corner table plate
This provides a strong joint where a table leg meets two rails. A slot is cut in each rail to take the end flanges, but the plate may also be secured with wood screws. A threaded bolt passes through the flange into a threaded insert in the leg and a wing nut pulls the joint tight.

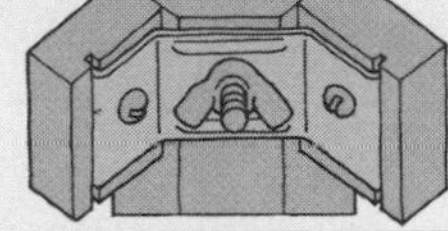

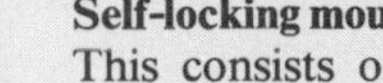

Self-locking mount
This consists of two identical steel fittings: one is screwed to the wall, the other to the back of a lightweight cabinet or mirror. The cabinet or mirror is then sited so that the two plates interlock.

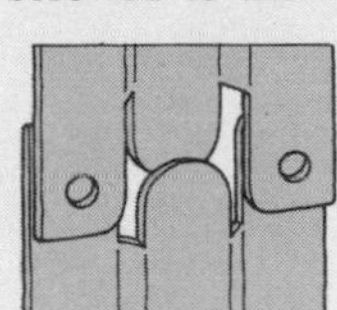

Reinforcing Plates

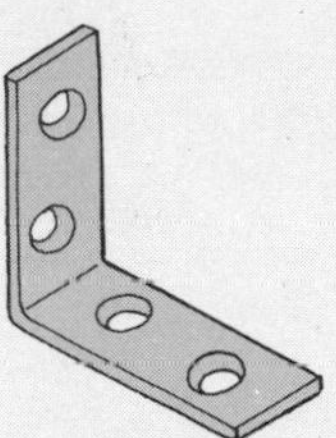

Metal braces and plates
These are used where the finish is unimportant. There are three basic designs and they all help to secure right angle joints and are sold in various sizes. The plates usually have holes for flathead screws.

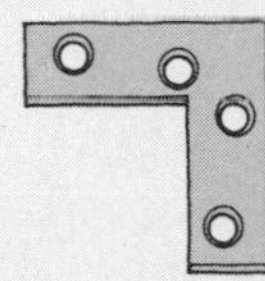

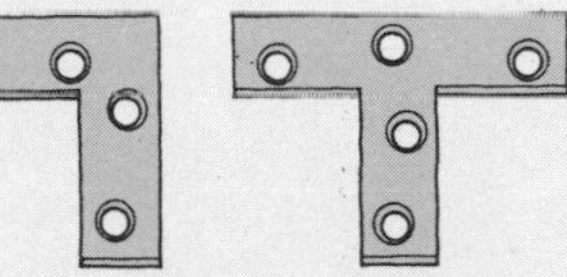

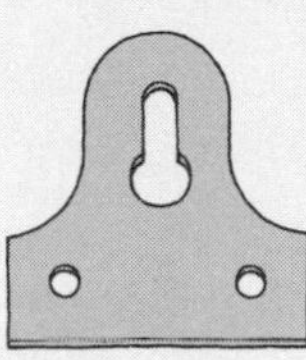

Mirror plates and keyhole plates
These fit snugly on the back of mirrors or lightweight cabinets, to overhang the edge. Keyhole plates are for a concealed fitting. The two plates screwed into the back of the mirror align with the heads of screws driven into the wall. Both types are designed for easy removal.

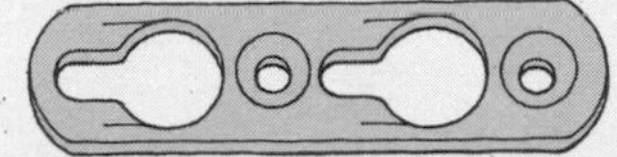

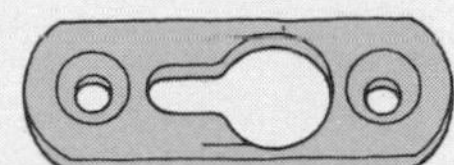

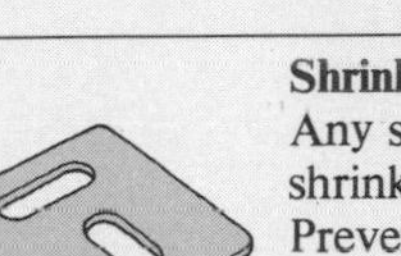

Shrinkage plates
Any solid wooden panel will eventually move due to shrinkage and may split if securely screwed to a frame. Prevent this by fixing a shrinkage plate in place of a rigid bracket. The plates are designed with a slot to take roundhead screws; when movement occurs in the lumber, the screw can move in the slot. Use the slot which lies at right angles to the grain of the wood.

Sliding Door Systems

Cabinet door
Sliding doors fit into grooved glides, which take thin panels of hardboard, plywood or glass. These plastic tracks can be face-mounted, but it is much neater if you groove the cabinet and flush-mount the track. Tracks must be matched so that the top track is deeper than the lower, to facilitate the removal of doors.

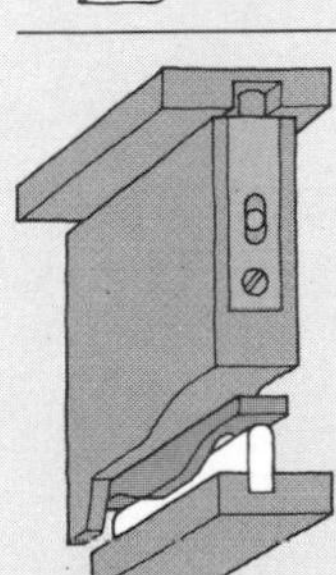

Face-mounted door
For thicker doors cut a groove in the door's lower edge to take a single edge track, set into the cabinet. Reinforce the groove with a special purpose lining. Matching grooves must be cut in the upper section of the cabinet to take retractable bolt fittings, which are screwed to the back of the doors, and set in flush.

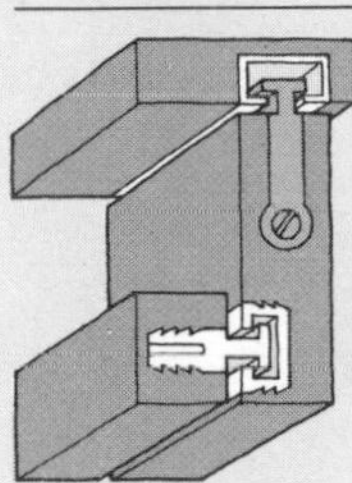

Suspended door
This is the type to choose if you want to avoid the inconvenience of a glide track along the bottom front edge of a cabinet. The track is fitted to the top edge, from which you suspend the doors by means of a special track fitting. A lined groove in the bottom of the door prevents it moving in and out.

Hardware

Hinges

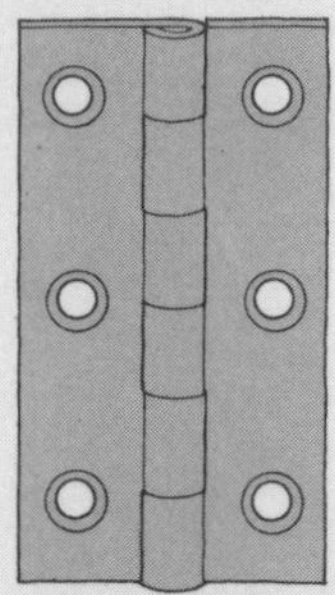

Butt hinge

Available in a range of sizes and finishes, this is used mainly for cabinet and household room doors. The hinge should be cut into the door edge and the jamb to fit flush with both surfaces, with at least half the barrel projecting.

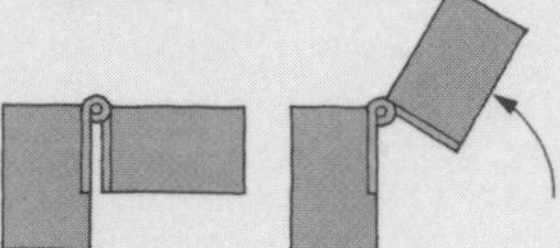

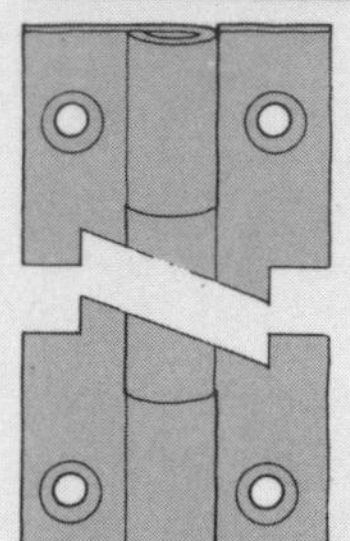

Continuous or piano hinge

Traditionally used to hinge the lids of pianos, this hinge may be fitted to the edge of any cabinet door or lid requiring support along its entire length. The hinge can be cut to length, and is screwed directly on the surface. Piano hinges are available in a range of metals, the most usual brass or aluminum.

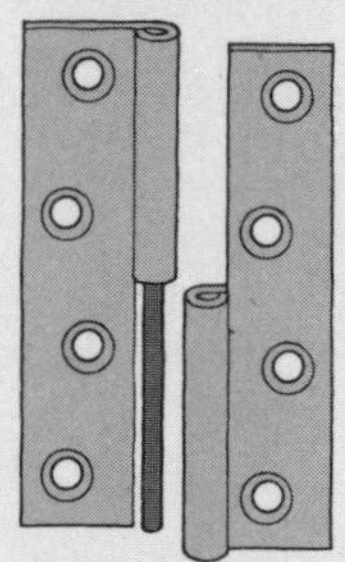

Loose joint hinge

A normal hinge has a fixed pivot pin. A loose joint hinge differs in being a "lift-off" type: this means that it is made in two parts so that one half can be lifted off the pivot pin. It is thus very easy to remove the door.

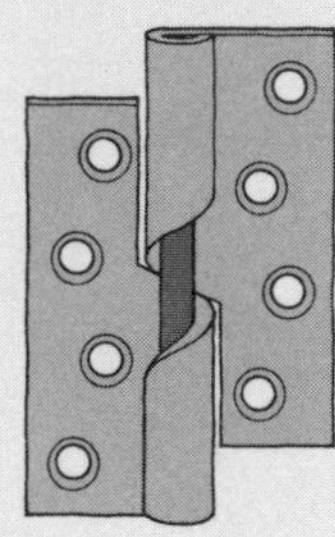

Rising butt

This is a variation on the loose joint hinge. As the door opens, the hinge lifts the door slightly so that it clears the carpet.

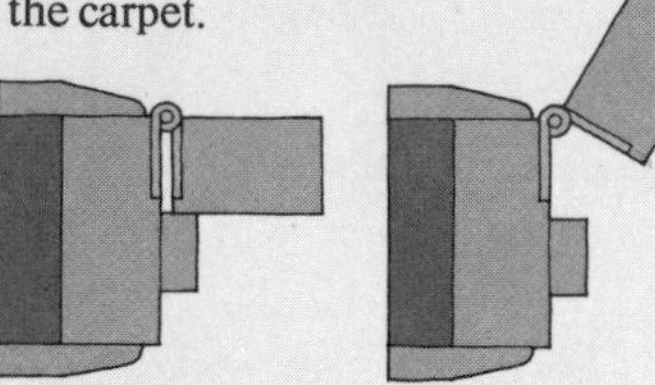

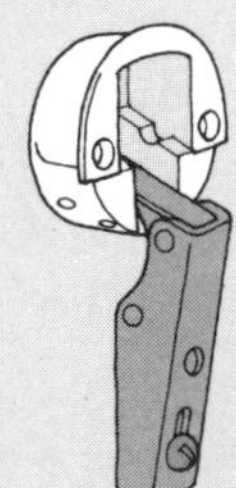

Concealed hinge

Made from a combination of metal and plastic, this is an asset mainly for cabinets in rooms where space is limited. It is designed so that a lay-on door can open to 90° without increasing the cabinet's width. The barrel section of the hinge is set flush with the door.

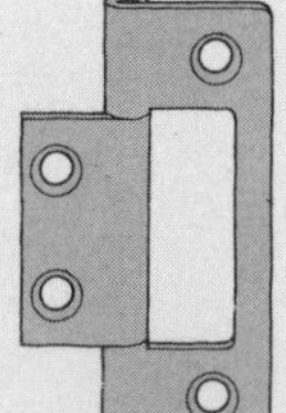

Flush hinge

A lightweight hinge, this is designed to act in the same way as a butt hinge. It has the advantage of not needing to be let into the woodwork.

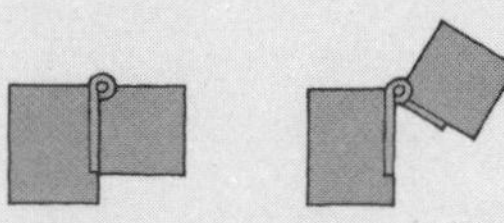

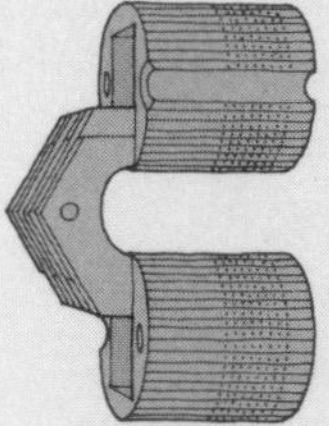

Concealed cylinder hinge

This is particularly useful in bi-fold or concertina doors. Normally made of brass, the hinges are plugged into holes drilled in the door and jamb. They are adjustable and secured by means of small screws, and can be used with flush or lay-on doors.

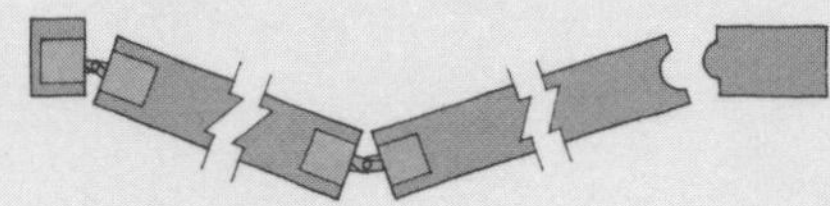

Pivot hinge

Designed to be used on a cabinet with lay-on doors butted against a similar cabinet, this hinge allows the door to clear the adjacent cabinet door. If necessary it can even open flat against it.

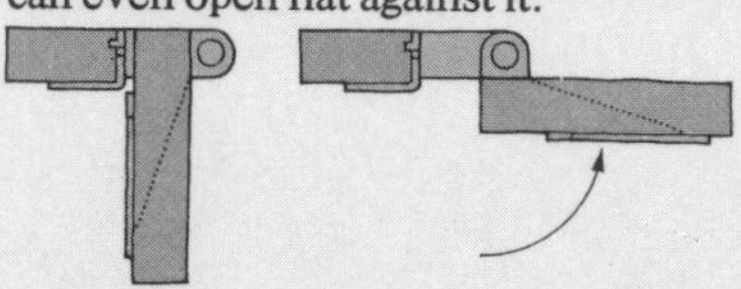

Semi-concealed hinge

Although similar to the pivot hinge, in this case part of the hinge is visible on the outside of the door. It is available as a fixed pin or a loose joint hinge.

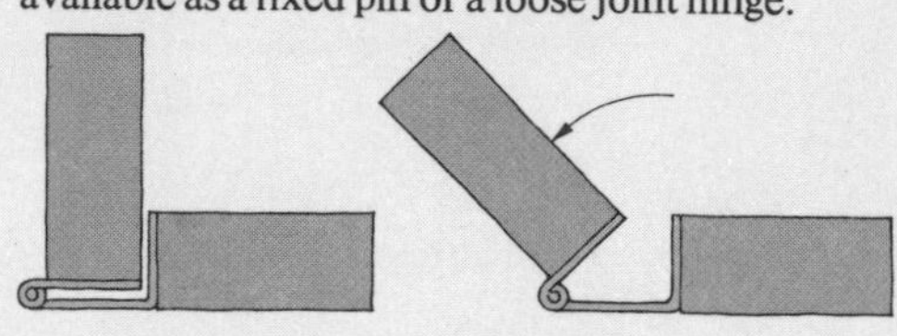

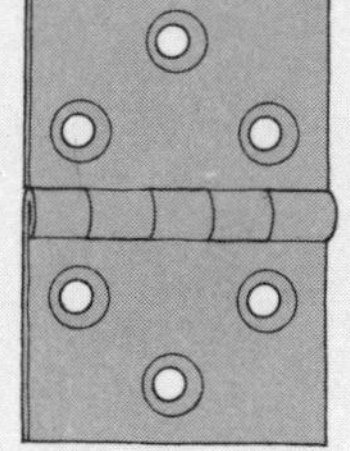

Back flap hinge

This is a butt hinge with larger leaves, so that the screw fixings are away from the edge of the lumber.

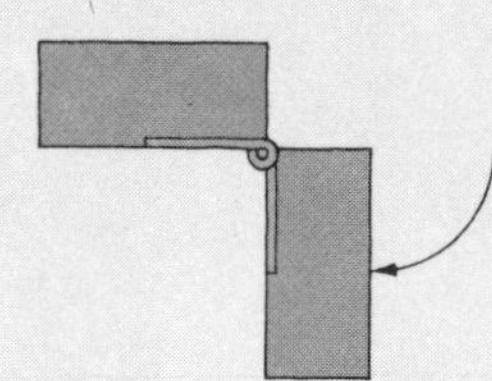

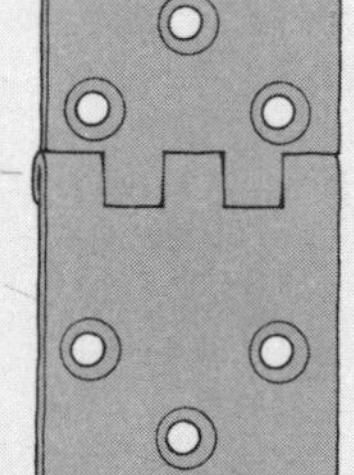

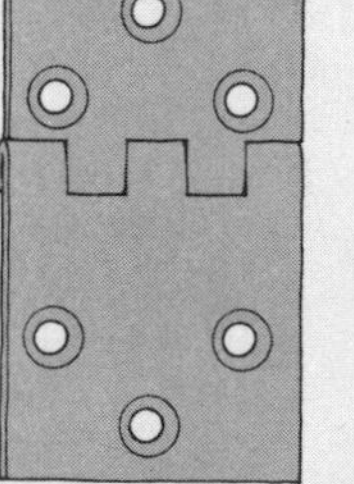

Table hinge

Table tops that are mated to the top with a rule joint need a hinge with one leaf larger than the other, to span the gap made when the flap is lowered.

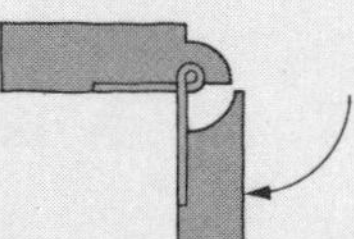

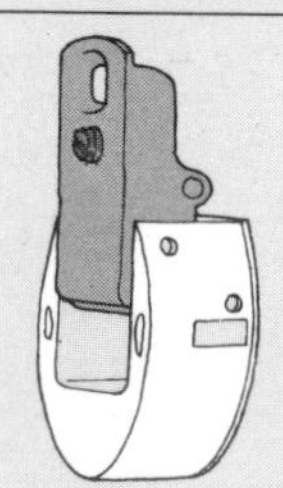

Flush-fitting hinge

This hinge allows a lay-on drop flap to sit flush with the inner surface of a cabinet. It is suitable for a bar-server cabinet or a writing desk.

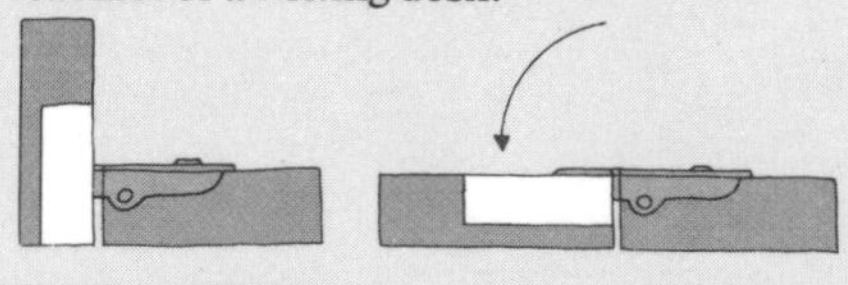

Door Catches

Magnetic door catch

There are many types of magnetic door catch, and they all work on the principle of a cased magnet which is normally fixed to the cabinet, and a metal strike plate fixed to the door. When attracted by the magnet, the plate holds the door closed. There are two main types: one is mounted inside the cabinet, the other is cylindrical, and plugs into a hole bored in the cabinet edge. The latter is common with "lay-on" doors.

Single-roller catch

This is similar to the magnetic catch in that it comes in two parts, a cased mechanism and a fixed stop. There are many variations, but the mechanism usually consists of a sprung peg or roller which aligns with the stop; the stop is fixed and the mechanism is usually adjustable.

Automatic latch

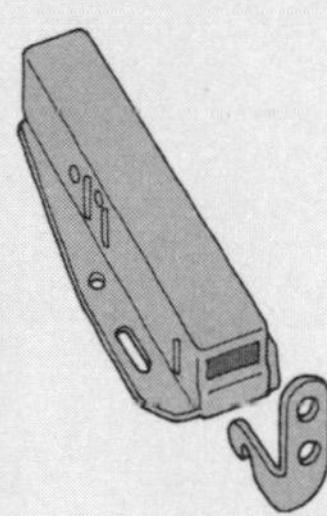

This allows you to open a cabinet door without a handle if your hands are full. By applying pressure on the door you operate a latch which automatically swings the door open. The mechanism is housed in a large metal casing, mounted in the cabinet. The latch hook is fixed to the inside of the door, and must be accurately positioned in relation to the mechanism.

Ball catch

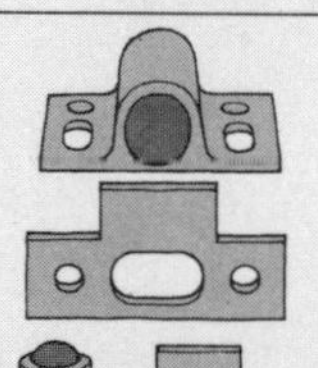

This catch has a spring-loaded ball held in a cylinder. When the door closes the ball aligns with a cup, molded in a strike plate.

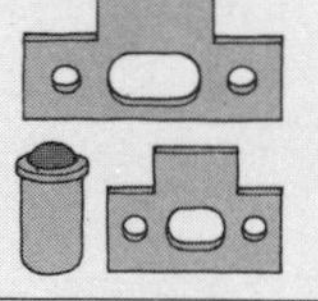

Casters and Glides

Casters

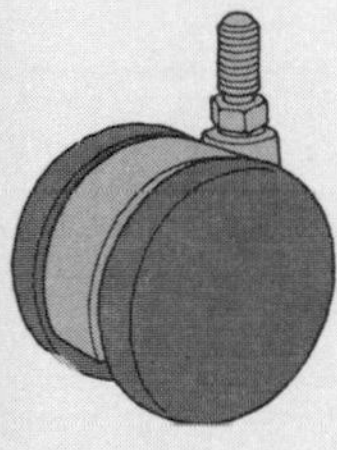

These are plugged or screwed into the bottom of legs, and fitted with a screw plate for fixing to the base of furniture. The type of caster you choose depends on the weight it must carry, and where it is usually sited: as a rule, heavy, movable furniture needs large casters. Casters are made of metal and plastic, and a ball-type caster is less likely to run channels in your carpet than a swivel-wheel one. Use general purpose plate casters for food trolleys, cribs and lightweight beds.

Glides

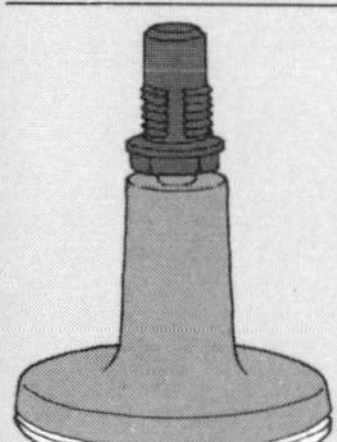

These usually have a shallow, domed base made from highly polished plastic, which reduces the resistance between floor and furniture. They also plug into inserts in the bottom of furniture legs. Glides are suitable for upholstered furniture which is not frequently moved about.

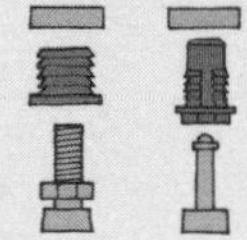

Furniture Bolts

Face and flush bolts

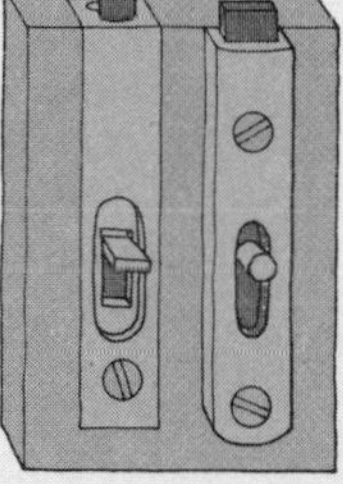

Furniture bolts are usually quite small fittings, either of brass or chromium plate, designed for cabinets and cupboards. The face-mounted bolt is the easiest to fit, as it is merely screwed into the inside of the door. The flush-fitting bolt must be enclosed in the thickness of the door. Both bolts need a separate metal catch plate with which the bolt aligns.

Drop Flap Stays

Folding stay

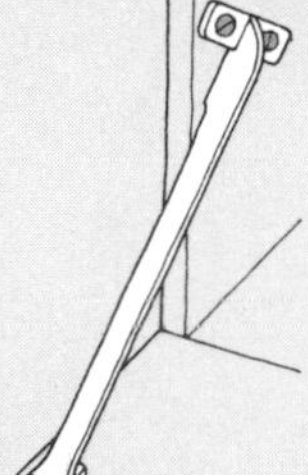

This is suitable for lightweight drop flaps, and is molded in one piece from plastic. Screwed to the cabinet and flap, it folds in half when the flap is closed. A chain will do the same job, but can be noisy or spoil the interior finish.

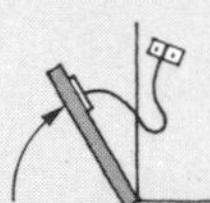

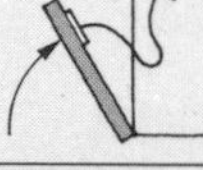

Lift up stay

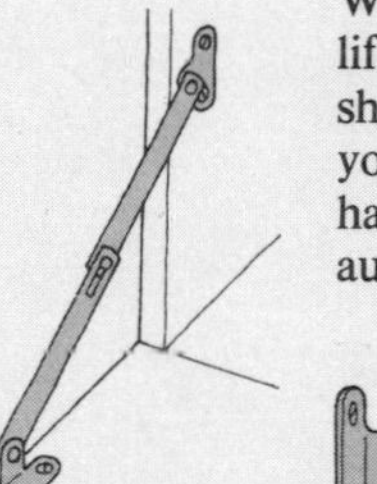

Where you have flaps that are hinged at the top and lift from the bottom-over a closet, for example-you should fit a stay to support it while open. This allows you to remove articles from the cabinet with both hands. Choose the friction stay type (see below) with automatic mechanism.

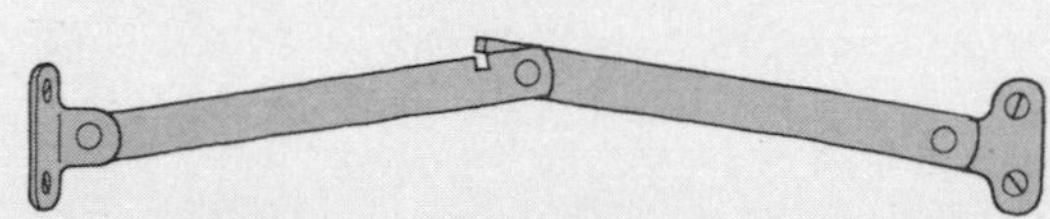

Sliding flap stay

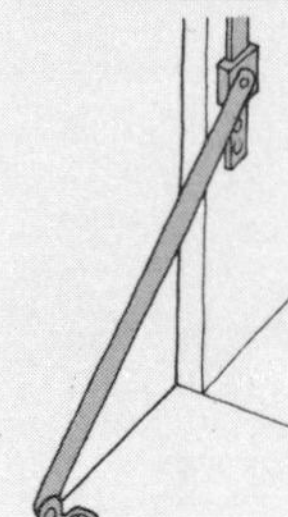

This type of stay does not break into the cabinet when the flap is closed. A channel or flat track is screwed to the cabinet, and can be fitted vertically or horizontally. A supporting arm, screwed to the flap, slides on the track. Various hinged ends to the supporting arm exist and can be screwed or plugged into the flap.

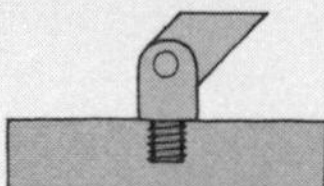

Friction stay

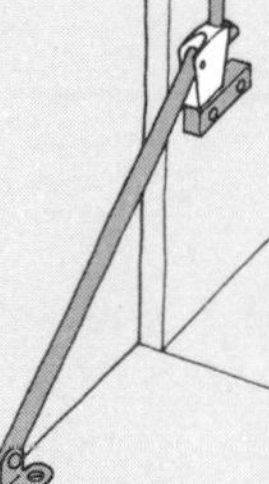

With a very heavy drop flap, you may need to fit a friction stay. This controls the rate at which the flap opens, bringing it to rest at the required height.

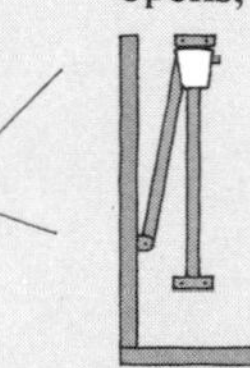

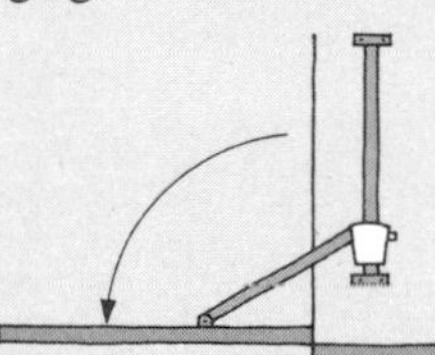

Cranked stay

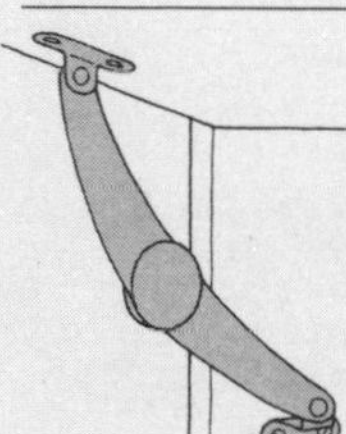

This resembles the folding stay and the lift up stay in that it cranks in the middle, but it is made from two metal arms hinged at the center. When the flap is closed the stay "breaks" and folds into the cabinet.

Measuring & Marking Metal

Tools

Steel ruler
A steel ruler is a better buy than one of wood or plastic, being more accurately graduated and less likely to wear. A 12-in. ruler with both inches and centimeters marked off is the most useful.

Square
A square is used for marking lines at right angles to an edge. An all-steel 4-in. or 6-in. square is good for average jobs; use a woodworking square for larger ones. The T bevel enables you to mark lines at right angles to any edge and to transfer them and other angles to new areas using an adjustable blade.

Dividers
Dividers will mark circles and parallel lines. Choose a size between 6 and 8 inches.

Scriber and center punch
A scriber will mark lines on metal, where the metal is to butt. The center punch establishes centers and marks places for drilling.

Techniques

Accuracy and care are needed for correct measuring and marking of metalwork, so you will have to apply the right techniques, using the tools described above.

Straight lines are measured with the ruler and marked with a scriber along a straight edge, if the line is to be cut. If the marks are for measuring only, use a pencil.

Parallel lines can be established and marked by using the dividers, allowing you to draw a line parallel to an edge, or to another line.

Lines parallel to a surface can be marked with an improvised surface gauge – a scriber mounted on a block of wood, a matchbox or tin can – and a surface table as shown on the right. This technique is useful for marking longitudinal lines on a cylinder, or on objects of an irregular shape.

To establish right angles, use a square. If the blade of the square is not long enough, extend the blade with a steel ruler, and scribe along the edge of the ruler. Odd angles are marked with the bevel, plus a protractor or combination square.

For marking a center or defining a spot for drilling, use a center punch. The mark made by the punch should be deep enough to hold the point of a small twist drill.

To mark a cylinder, or a tapered or irregular shape, see right.

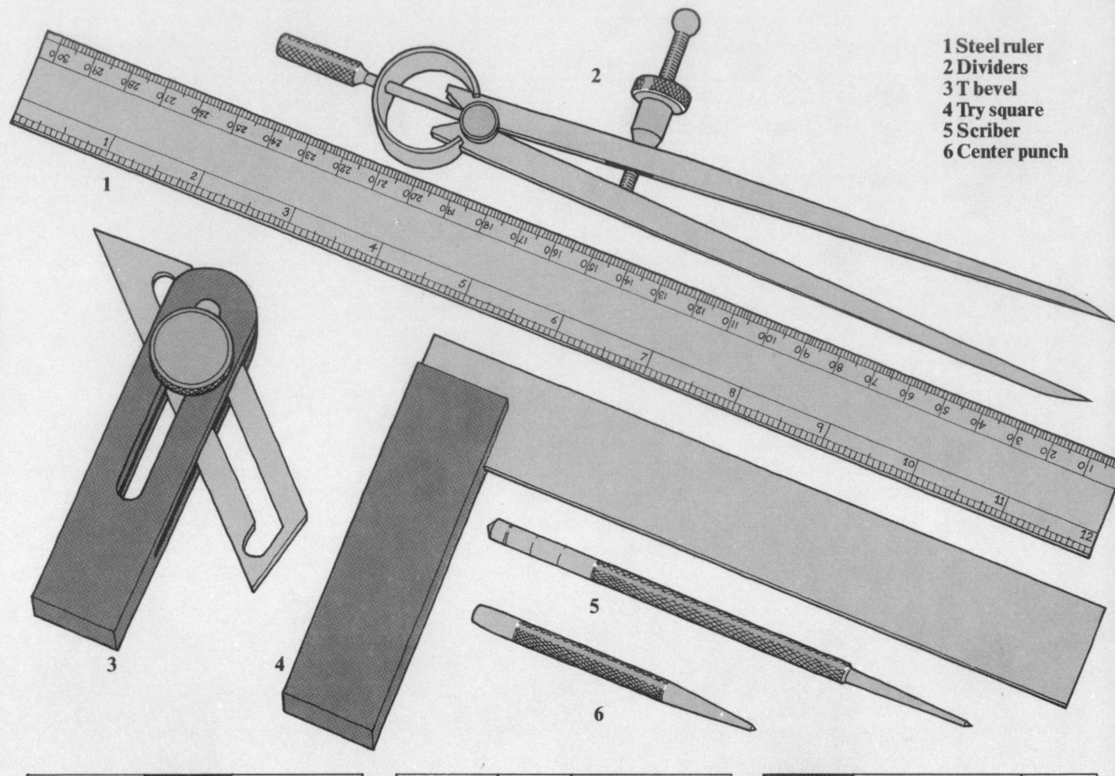

1 Steel ruler
2 Dividers
3 T bevel
4 Try square
5 Scriber
6 Center punch

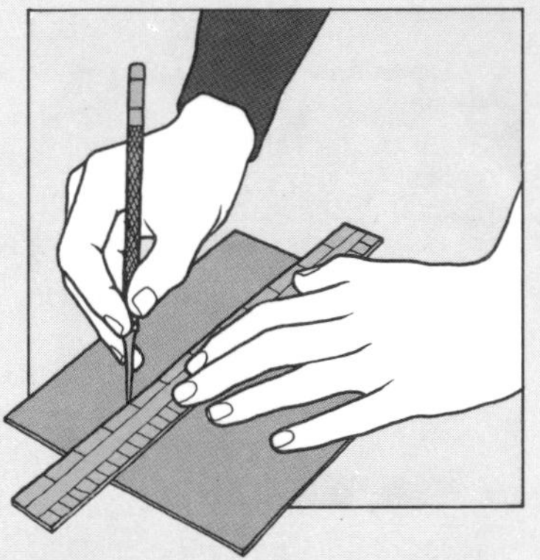

Marking straight lines
Mark each end of the line and align the ruler with the marks. Run the scriber along the edge with a firm stroke. If the point of the scriber becomes blunt, it must be re-ground.

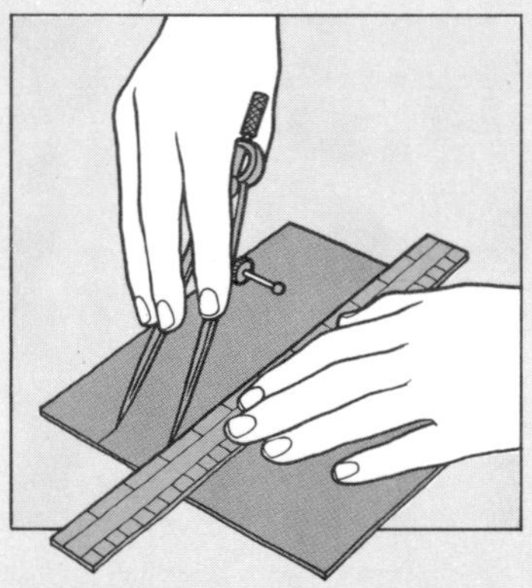

Marking parallel lines
Use the dividers, setting the points apart to correct distance. Use the edge of the ruler as a guide. To transfer measurements, place the points in the appropriate divisions.

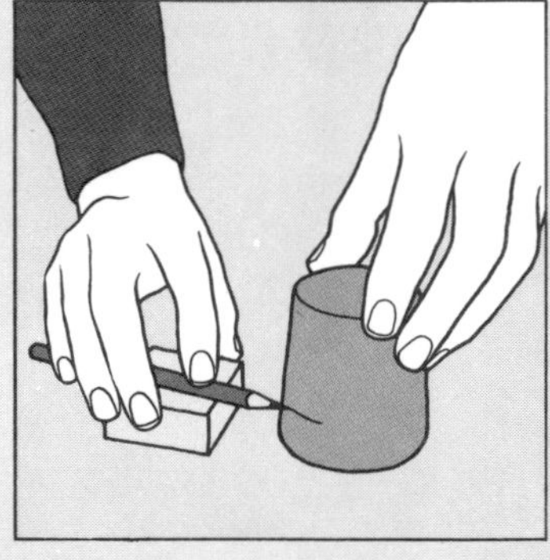

Lines parallel to a surface
Mark with a surface gauge and table. On a flat worktop, mount the scriber on an object of the height required. Align the scriber to the work, hold the gauge firm and rotate work against it.

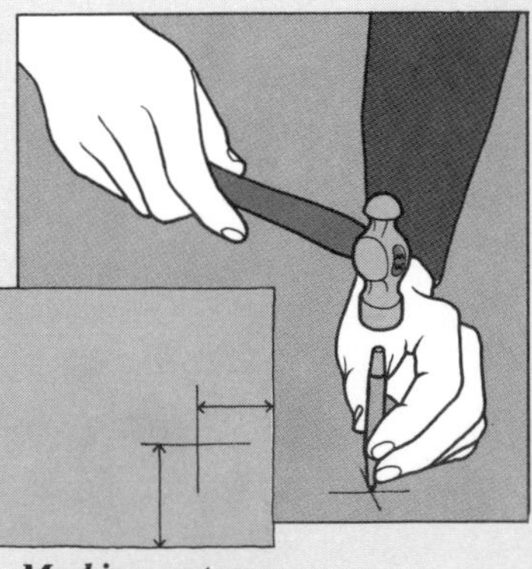

Marking centers
A point can be established by intersecting lines, as shown in the inset above. Mark with the center punch, holding it upright and hitting firmly with a hammer.

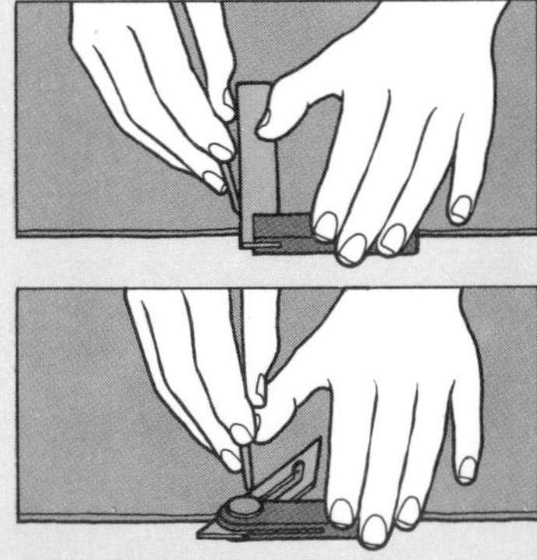

Marking angles
For right angles, place the stock of the try square against the edge of the work, with the blade flat along the surface. Draw a line along the blade. Mark other angles with the bevel.

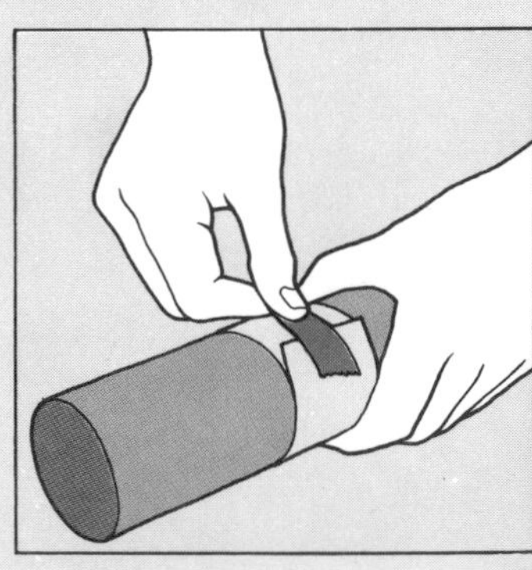

Marking cylinders
To mark a cylinder at right angles to its axis, use a straight-edged piece of paper, taped in position so that the ends overlap and the edge aligns. Mark along this edge.

Gripping Metal

Tools

Swivel-base vise
The most useful vise for nearly all types of metalwork is the bench-mounted swivel-base vise; the size should be related to the average scale of the work. The serrated jaws provide a very firm grip; marks on the metalwork can be avoided by using fiber covers.

Clamp-on vise
The clamp-on vise is a smaller version of the above, fixed to the bench by means of a clamp. The main disadvantage of this vise is its lack of stability.

Pliers
Pliers are invaluable for bending, gripping and manipulating sheet metal and wire. The most useful are lineman's pliers and the long-nosed pliers. To hand-hold work firmly, to clamp pieces of metal together or grip metal while grinding, drilling and cutting, use a plier-wrench.

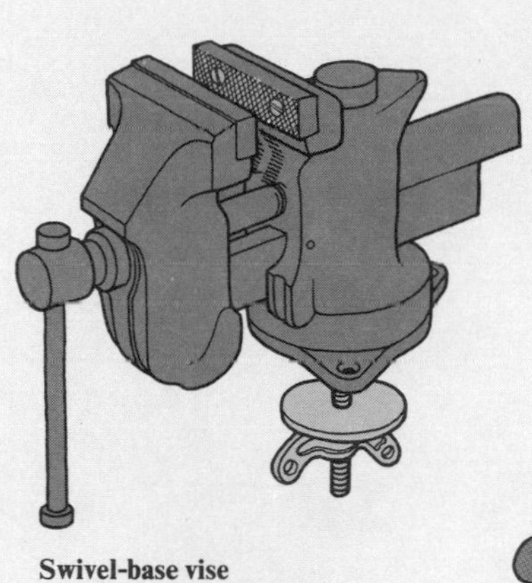
Swivel-base vise

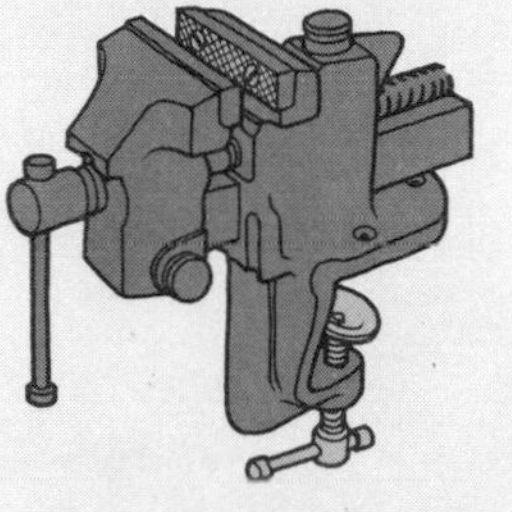
Clamp-on vise

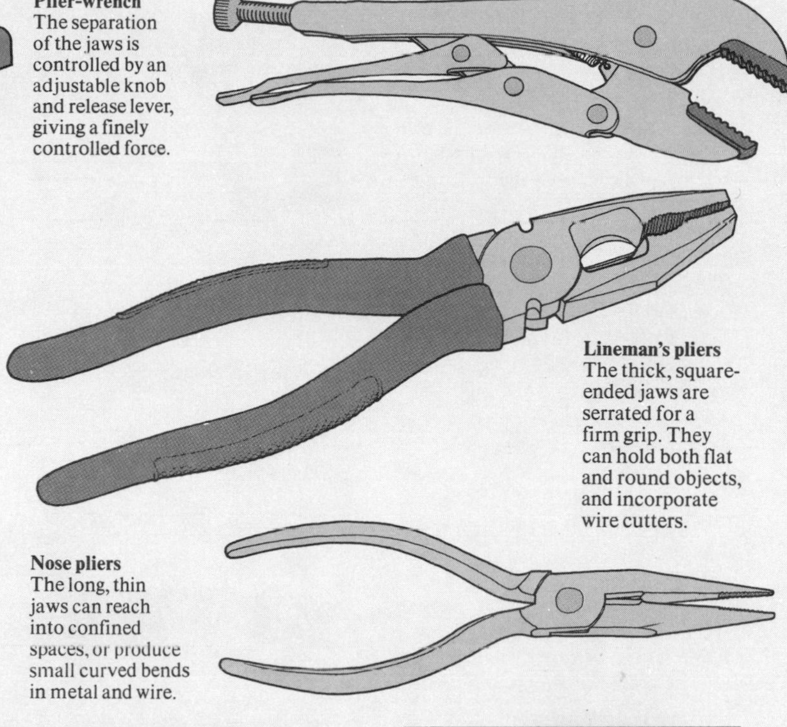
Plier-wrench
The separation of the jaws is controlled by an adjustable knob and release lever, giving a finely controlled force.

Lineman's pliers
The thick, square-ended jaws are serrated for a firm grip. They can hold both flat and round objects, and incorporate wire cutters.

Nose pliers
The long, thin jaws can reach into confined spaces, or produce small curved bends in metal and wire.

Techniques

The choice of the tool depends on the size of the job, also whether the metal has to be worked with a tool for which both hands are likely to be needed.

If you are going to file metal, for example, you will need to grip the work in a vise, in order to apply the file correctly. Remember, though, that a vise is capable of exerting great force; it may not only damage the metal, but can crush hollow objects, such as pieces of tubing. Some vises have grooved jaws so that you can hold rods and tubes securely in position. As we have seen, serrated jaws can damage the surface of metalwork. Make a set of improvised covers by hammering pieces of sheet aluminum to fit snugly over each jaw. Trim off the waste. To grip thin metal for cutting, use blocks of wood to increase the support, and cut as close to the wood as possible.

Choose pliers when you want to cut wire, bend sections of light metal, or grip round or flat sections. Hold pliers in one hand and the work in the other. If you want to avoid marking the work, tape the jaws of the pliers with masking tape. The technique of using the plier-wrench is shown on the extreme right. When cutting short lengths of wire with pliers, use a receptacle to catch any flying remnants: they can be dangerous.

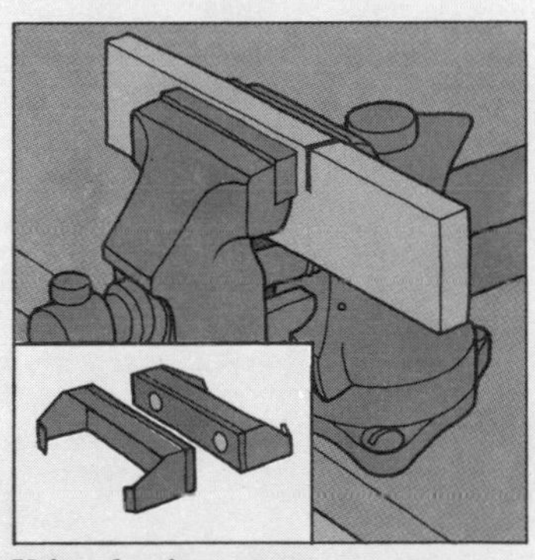
Using the vise
Clamp the work in the vise as close to the jaws as the action will comfortably allow. If filing or sawing produces a high-pitched noise, or the tool slips, the work will need to be more firmly secured.

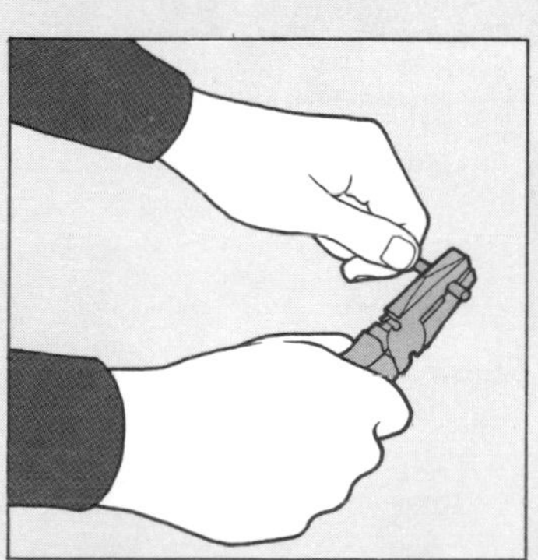
Using pliers
If the work is long enough to provide leverage, hold it in the left hand, and bend with the pliers held in the right hand. With shorter lengths, use two pairs of pliers.

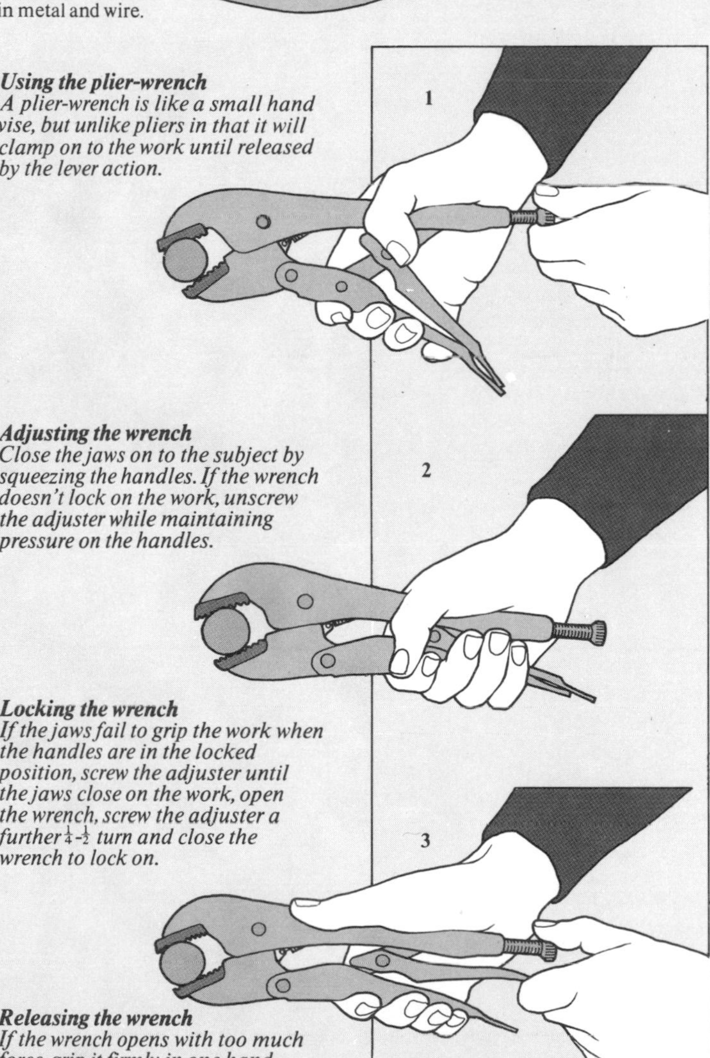

Using the plier-wrench
A plier-wrench is like a small hand vise, but unlike pliers in that it will clamp on to the work until released by the lever action.

Adjusting the wrench
Close the jaws on to the subject by squeezing the handles. If the wrench doesn't lock on the work, unscrew the adjuster while maintaining pressure on the handles.

Locking the wrench
If the jaws fail to grip the work when the handles are in the locked position, screw the adjuster until the jaws close on the work, open the wrench, screw the adjuster a further $\frac{1}{4}$-$\frac{1}{2}$ turn and close the wrench to lock on.

Releasing the wrench
If the wrench opens with too much force, grip it firmly in one hand, and pull the release lever with the other.

Saws

Tools

Hacksaws

The hacksaw is the main tool for cutting metal. The easiest type to use has a pistol-grip handle and will adjust to take different lengths of blade, which are tightened by means of a wing nut. The teeth on all blades face forward, though they vary in number depending on the thickness of the metal to be cut.

The junior hacksaw

The junior hacksaw should be used for finer work. The blade is held in place by the spring of the frame.

The mini-hacksaw

You can use any hacksaw blade in the mini-hacksaw, even a broken one; the blade slots into the handle and is held firm by a screw clamp.

The abrafile

A hacksaw frame can be fitted with an abrafile and secured by special clips. An abrafile is a thin, round blade which cuts in any direction, and is useful for shaped work.

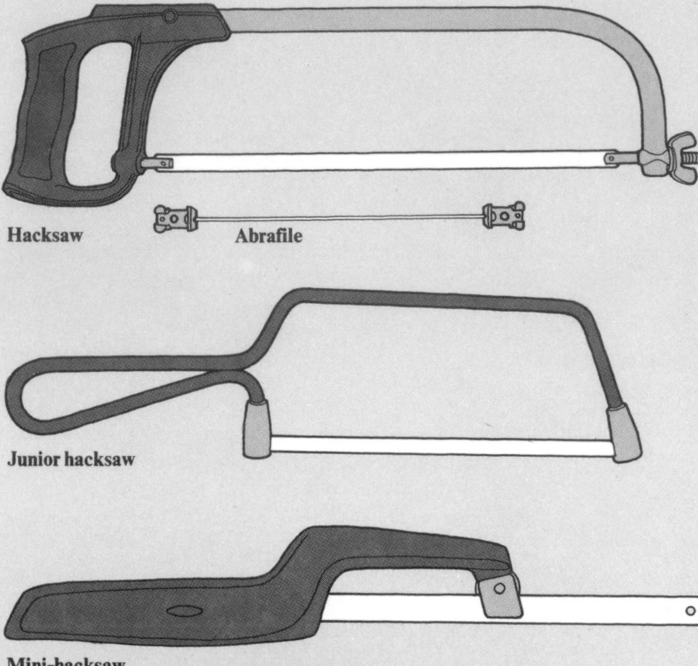

Techniques

Using a hacksaw

Secure the work firmly in a vise. Select the appropriate blade: a coarse one will reduce clogging when sawing soft metals such as aluminum or copper, a fine blade is best for hard metals such as steel. When cutting brass, choose a new blade because a worn one is inclined to slip. Stand at an angle of 45° to the vise jaws, your feet apart. Hold the saw so that the frame is in line with the forearm, and steady the frame with the other hand. Use your thumb as a guide when starting to cut. Short, backward strokes will establish the cut, then saw with the whole length of the blade, releasing pressure on the back stroke, cutting with the forward stroke. If the cut wanders, or the blade jams or breaks, you are probably twisting the frame out of line with the cut.

Cutting thick sections

When cutting thick sections of metal, it is advisable to saw on all sides, working toward the center. First, mark the metal all around to guide the cut, and lubricate with light oil. Saw to the depth of the blade on one side, rotate the work away from you, and saw along the guide line: the first cut will help to establish the second. If you change the blade during cutting, it may jam in the cut, as the old blade will have worn thin, thus making a narrower slot in the metal.

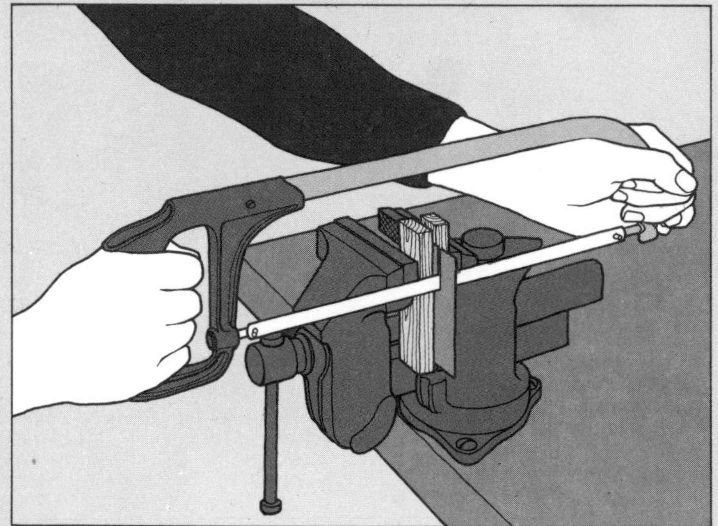

Sawing technique
To prevent vibration, support sheet metal with pieces of wood. Cut with the blade on the waste side of the line. If the frame obstructs the sawing when the cut is deeper than the saw will allow, turn the frame in relation to the blade to give you the maximum freedom of movement.

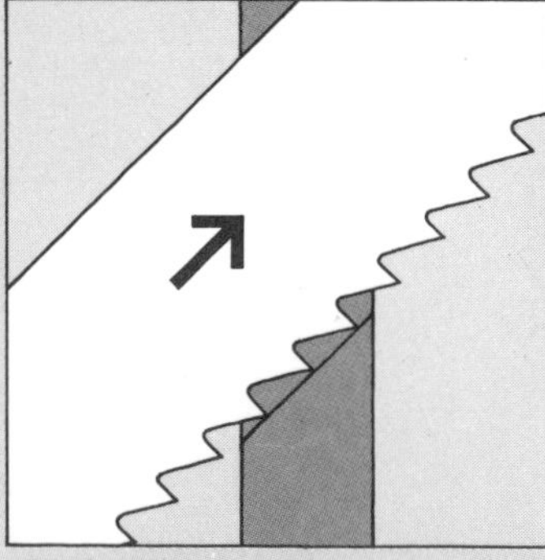

Cutting sheet metal
Saw thin sheet metal at an angle to get at least three teeth into the cut.

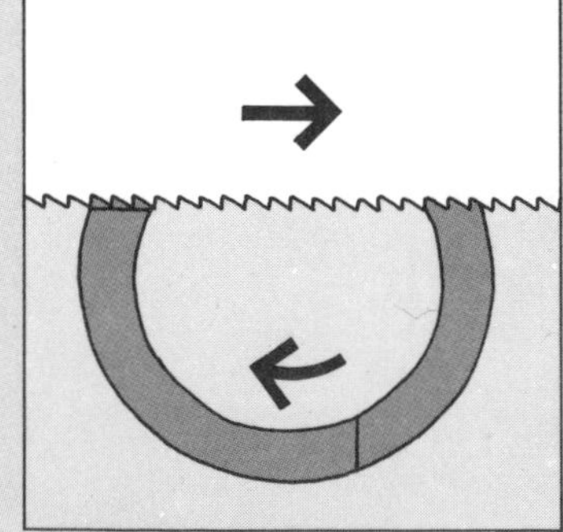

Cutting metal tube
Rotate thin tubes away from the saw during cutting.

Files

Tools

Files are for shaping and smoothing metal. They are made of very hard, brittle steel which cannot be sharpened and breaks easily. There are five basic shapes: flat, half-round, round, square and triangular.

Sizes and grades

Lengths vary between 4 in. and 18 in. and there are five grades: coarse, bastard, second cut, smooth and dead smooth. Ideally, you should have a couple of sizes of each shape in each grade, but in practice far fewer will do. The flat file is designed with a safe edge which is smooth, and is used when working against an unprotected "shoulder." There is a range of special-purpose files, including curved files for large concave and convex areas, used for automobile bodywork and for delicate machine work.

Techniques

Filing

Filing can be hard, slow work, so it is a good idea to begin by removing as much surplus metal as possible with a saw before finishing the shape with a file.

Clamp the metal to be filed securely in a vise. Steady the end of the file with one hand while holding the handle in the other (never use a file without a handle, as the tang might penetrate your hand if the file jams). Stand with your legs apart and with your elbow at the right height to file the material accurately, in full length strokes, employing pressure on the forward one, lifting it on the back one.

When you have finished cross-filing a piece of metal you may want to obtain a final, smooth finish. Draw a smooth or extra smooth file at right angles to the metal, a technique known as draw filing.

To speed up the cutting action of a file, and to get a good, flat surface, change the direction of the cut occasionally. Soft metals will clog the file in the same way as they will clog a hacksaw blade. The debris can be removed by brushing the file with a special, short-bristled wire brush called a "file card." Any really stubborn clogging can be removed with the point of a scriber. Always keep files in a protective cover or in a tool rack as they can be easily damaged or mislaid.

1 Flat file
2 Hand file
3 Square file
4 Round file
5 Triangular file

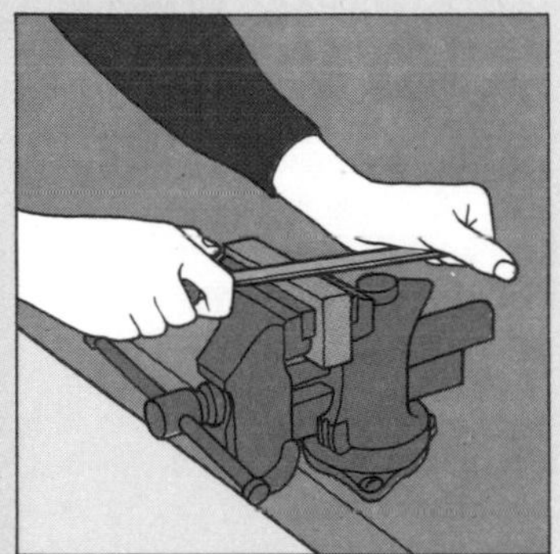

Filing technique
The technique is very similar to the one employed in hacksawing. The work must be firmly held in a vise, the file steadied with both hands.

Draw filing
A final finish can be obtained by drawing a smooth file at right angles across the metal.

Drills

Tools

Drill bits for metalwork are called "twist drills." They are used either in a hand brace or a power drill. Drilling thick sections of metal can be laborious, and here a power drill is desirable; it is also more accurate, steadier and more easily controlled than a hand drill. Drills are made in two grades: carbon steel and high-speed steel. The latter is more expensive, but has greater lasting qualities, and is essential for working with hard steel. Drill bits are available in sets, or singly. To sharpen bits use a power grinder, maintaining the angles of the cutting edges.

To limit or repeat the depth of the hole you are drilling, wrap a thin strip of adhesive tape around the bit, or attach a plastic depth gauge. Make sure you do not drill beyond the measured depth, or you may force the gauge up the bit.

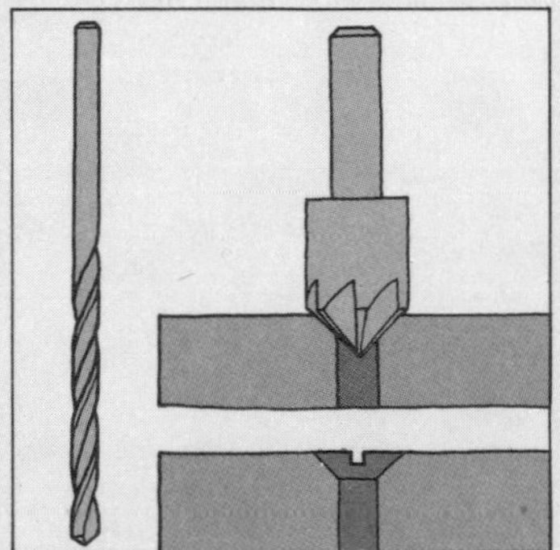

Countersinking
Make a recess in the surface of the metal for the head of a screw by using a countersink bit (right) or a large twist drill (left).

Using a power drill
Clamp the metal, punch center of the hole to take the drill point. Lubricate with light oil.

Snips

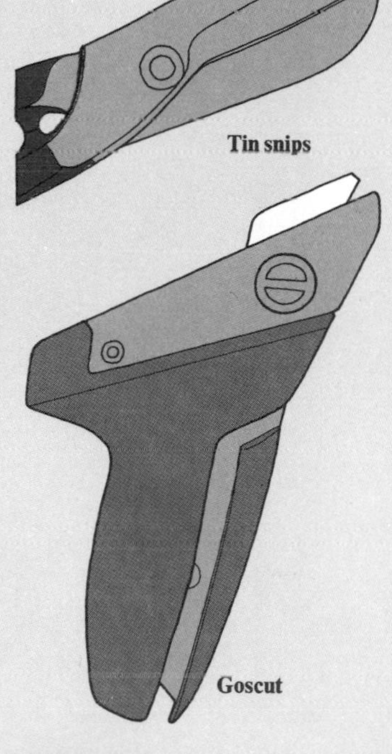

Tools

Tin snips
Tin snips work on the same principle as scissors, and are one of the most useful of sheet metal cutting tools. The thickness of the metal to be cut is limited only by the strength of the user. A pair of straight-sided tin snips 8 in. or 10 in. long is the most convenient kind.

The goscut
This tool shears through sheet metal with a finely-toothed blade: the sheet is supported by the cutter's anvil and thus avoids distortion. Cuts of unlimited lengths can be made, and the goscut has an additional blade for cutting circles and curves. The cutting shears remove a thin strip of waste metal equivalent to the width of the anvil, which must be allowed for when marking out the work. One advantage of this technique is that it avoids distorting metal on either side of the cut.

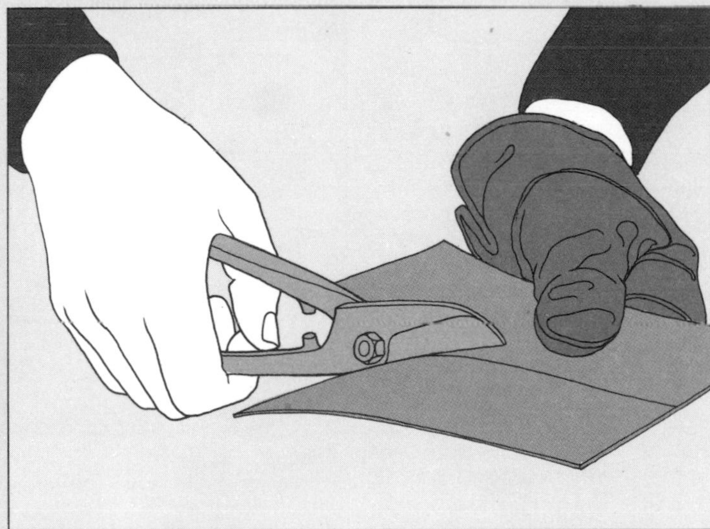
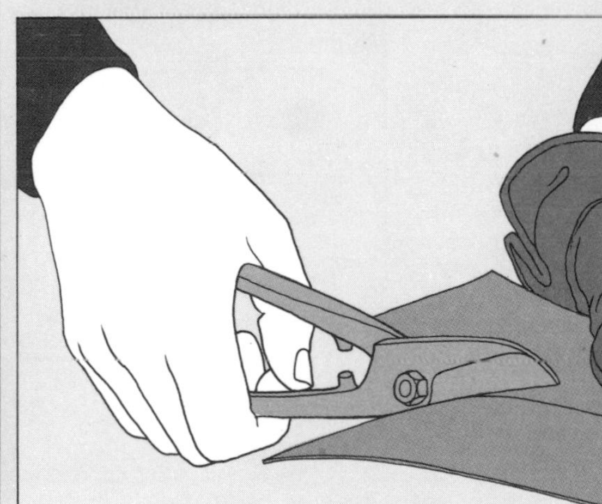

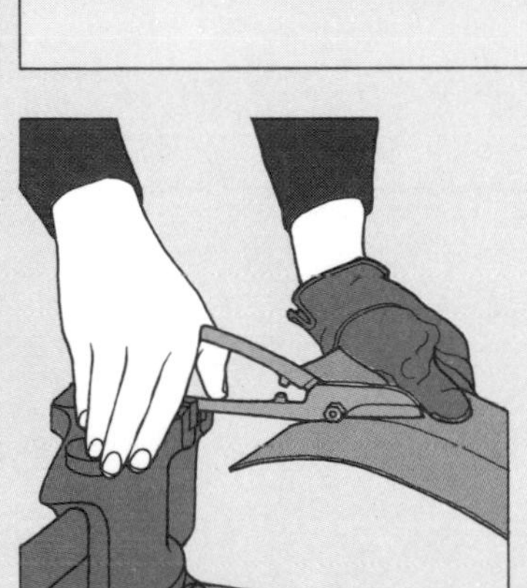

Cutting thick sheets
You can increase the cutting power of tin snips by securing one of the handles in a vise, exerting downward pressure with your hand on the free handle.

How to use tin snips
When cutting sheet metal, first scribe a layout line as a guide. Keep the upper blade of the snips over the line, and use the maximum amount of cutting edge. As a precaution, hold the metal in a gloved hand. You will find it easier to cut shapes and circles by removing as much waste as possible toward the layout line before making the cut. Sheet metal and plastic can also be cut with hawk-billed snips, which exert greater pressure, and have a blade which passes through two anvil blades, giving extra support to the work. These actually cut a fine slot in the material. Like the goscut, or light sheet cutter, cuts of unlimited lengths can be made.

Bending Metal

Tools

Different metals and the forms in which they are found call for varying tools and working techniques.

Hammers and mallets
A conventional wooden mallet can mark metal, so use a softfaced mallet with a rawhide, rubber or plastic head. The ball peen hammer is used for general work: the hemispherical part of the head is designed for riveting.

Pliers and asbestos gloves
To hold hot metal, use pliers or heatproof gloves, but keep them dry as water in the fabric will turn to steam when in contact with hot metal, and can scald your hand.

Coil springs
To bend tubing you may need coil springs. These are available in sizes to fit the standard copper pipes used in plumbing.

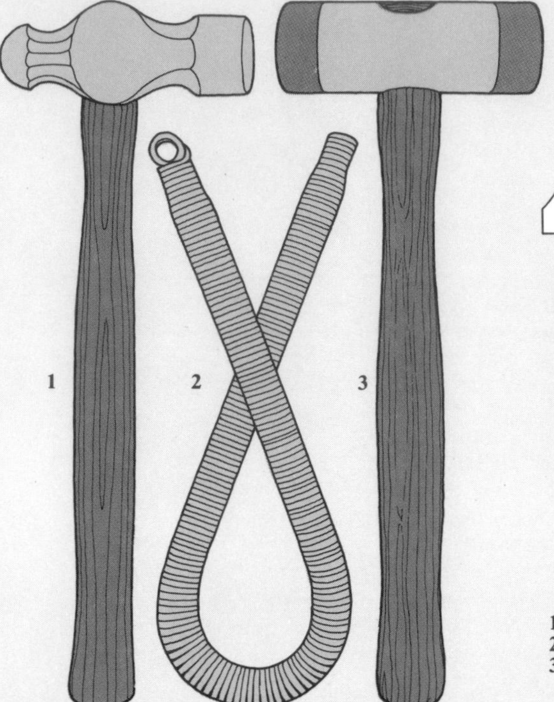

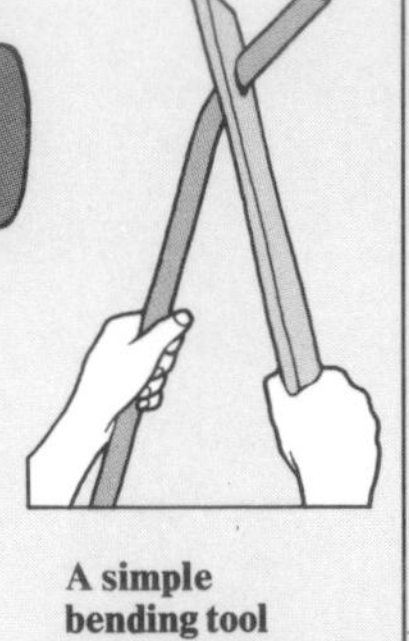

A simple bending tool
A short length of wood, say 2 in. x 1 in. with a hole bored in one end, can improve leverage when bending tubing. It can be used in conjunction with a coil spring, or without a spring if some kinking is acceptable.

1 Ball peen hammer
2 Coil spring
3 Soft faced mallet

Techniques

Sheet metal should be firmly clamped between two pieces of wood held in a vise, or in a vise with soft jaws. Use a mallet to bend the metal, working backward and forward along the length, bending it a few degrees at a time to avoid stretching it. Scribe on the inside of the bend, or use a pencil or tape to avoid causing a crack.

Using a coil spring
When placed over a length of tubing, the spring resists the tendency of the tube to flatten at the point of the bend, and instead forces the metal on the outside of the bend to stretch. The spring should cover the region of the bend, then be bent to the required angle.

Making curves
To bend a strip of metal into a curve, use a steel or hardwood former **1.** Grip the former in a vise **2** and hammer the metal at the point of contact, or just beyond.

Bending by applying heat
It is easier to bend steel if you heat it, then hit it with a heavy hammer on a solid anvil, block or vise **3.** Hold the metal with tongs or gloves. By heating you can make tight bends in heavy lengths of bar, and taper or flatten bar and rod.

Bending rods
Extra leverage can be provided by slipping a larger piece of tube over the work, with a vise or piece of wood as a clamp **4.**

Bending sheet metal
For bending lengths of sheet metal, you will need to support the work between wood blocks held in a vise, and additional C clamps.

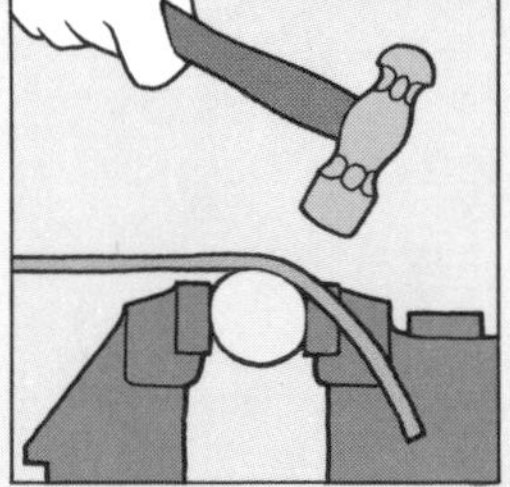

Making a safe edge on sheet metal

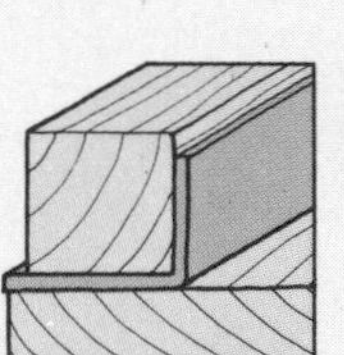

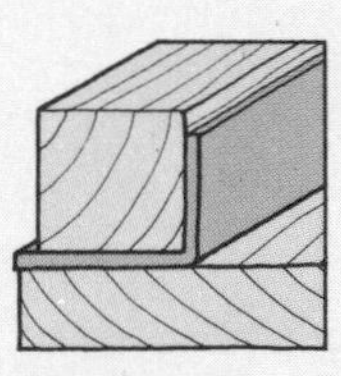

1 Strengthen the edge of sheet metal by folding it over. Use two blocks of wood to make a right angle in the metal.

2 Tap the edge over, using a spacer (a steel ruler will do).

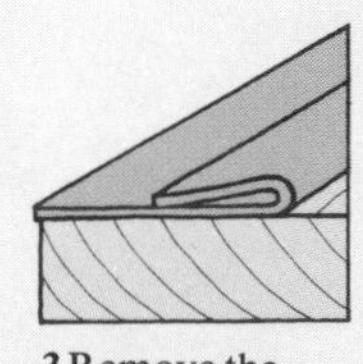

3 Remove the spacer and tap down the edge, but don't flatten it completely.

Joining Metal

Tools

Soldering irons and materials
Soldering irons are used for melting soft solder and applying it to the joint, the most useful and convenient size being a mains electric iron of 125 watts. The solder is usually purchased in the form of bars, or as wire containing a resin core (for electrical work, or where the work cannot afterwards be cleaned), and also in paste form. Flux for solder is applied to the work to dissolve the oxide, and is available in liquid or paste form.

Gas torch
A propane gas torch has an adjustable flame, and uses disposable cylinders. It will give you a high heat to melt hard solder and to braze metal. Solder comes in strip or wire form, brazing flux is usually made as a borax-based powder. Other methods of metal joining include riveting, gluing with epoxy resin, and fixing with nuts and bolts.

Techniques

Metal to be soldered should first be cleaned, and the flux applied while the iron is heating. Dip the iron in the flux and apply solder to both surfaces. Quickly assemble the joint and heat with the iron, applying more solder to form a molten bead along the join; all the solder must melt to form a strong bond. Hard soldering and brazing differ from soft soldering in the alloys used. The former have a higher melting point, so you will need a gas torch to bring the metal up to yellow heat. Make sure that the joint has a good fit, and won't move while soldering; wire together if necessary. Apply the flux and melt it into the joint, then apply the solder by touching the hot metal with the end of the solder bar, or small pieces held in contact with nose pliers. Work from the bottom and let the flux float on the solder.

Contact adhesives
When brazing brass, the brazing material must melt at a lower temperature than the work. The flux must be removed, and if it sets hard, be chipped off with a coarse file. The nature of the work determines the type of joint, and large areas of low stress where some degree of flexibility is expected can be glued with contact adhesives. For stronger joins, use epoxy resins. The setting times of epoxy can be shortened by heating the work.

Finishing Metal

1 Pop riveter and rivet
2 Electric soldering iron
3 Adjustable wrench
4 Gas torch

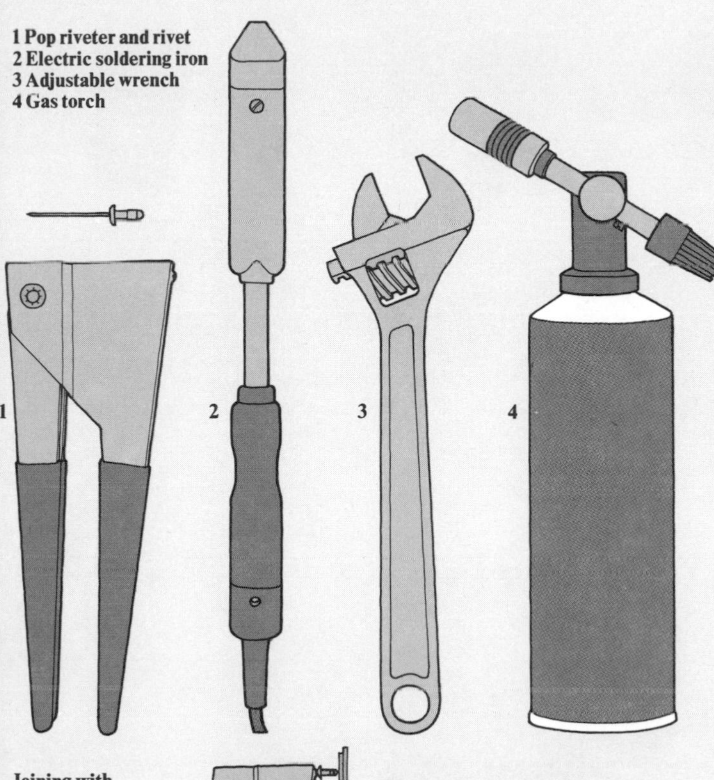

Joining with pop rivets
1 Drill holes of the right size to take the rivets. Fit the rivet's shank into the tool.

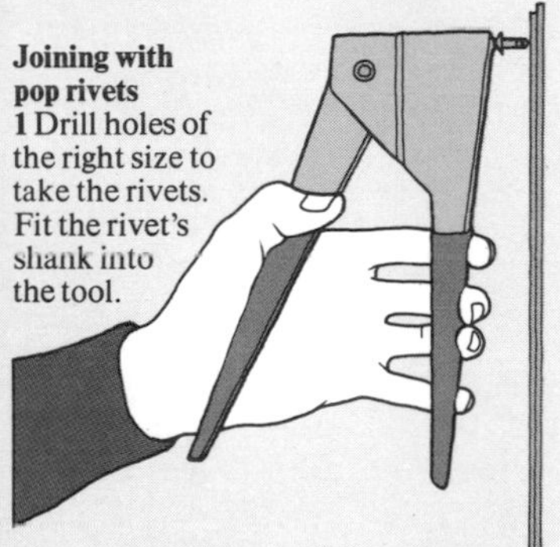

2 Press riveting tool hard against the work to seat the rivet. Squeeze the handle until the shank breaks. If the shank fails to break, move it further into the tool and try again.

3 The top of the shank expands the end of the rivet, and then breaks off, the shank pulling clear. To remove rivets, chisel off the head and punch out, or countersink and punch out.

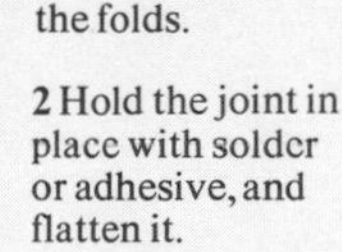

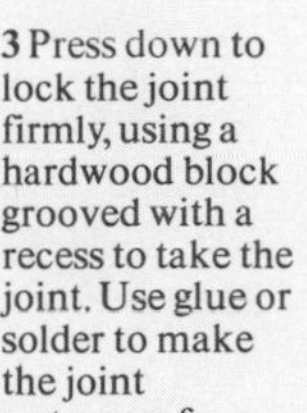

Wrenches and bolting
One or two sizes of adjustable wrench avoid the need for a complete set of fixed ones. They are used with a wide range of nuts and bolts, a simple way of joining metal. The weakest part of an adjustable wrench is the moving jaw. Apply the wrench so that the force is directed to the jaw and not the tip, otherwise the wrench may slip.

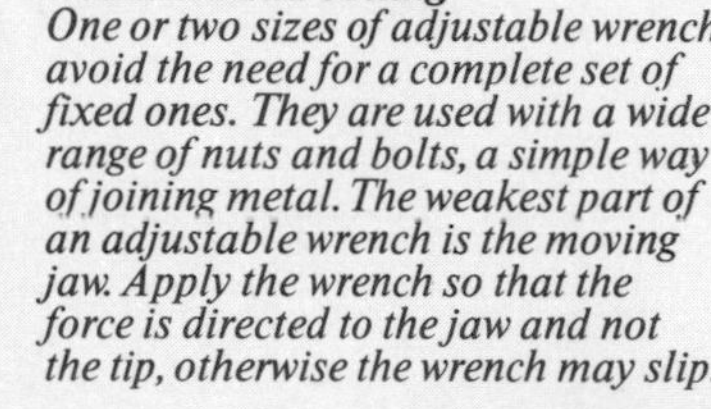

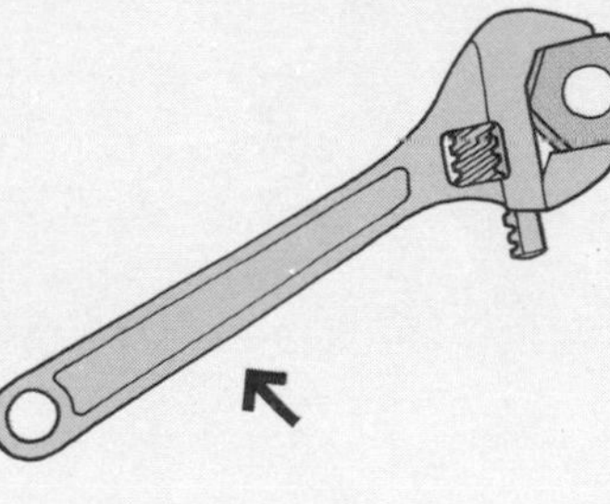

Making a folded joint
1 Sheet metal can be joined by folding, as with a safe edge, then interlocking the folds.

2 Hold the joint in place with solder or adhesive, and flatten it.

3 Press down to lock the joint firmly, using a hardwood block grooved with a recess to take the joint. Use glue or solder to make the joint waterproof.

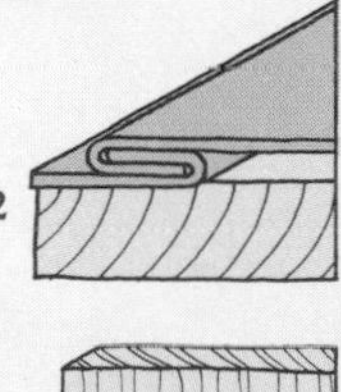

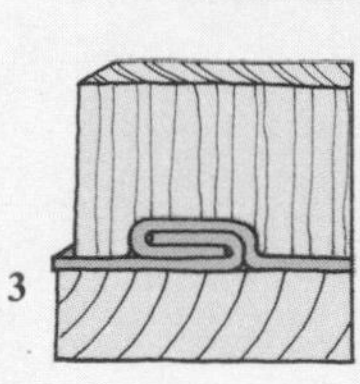

Tools

Wire brushes
A wire brush fixed in the chuck of a power drill, either hand-held or bench-mounted, removes dirt, loose paint and oxide, and can be used to give metals a medium luster finish. Power wire brushes are available in a variety of sizes and degrees of hardness: to remove rust, choose the hardest brush (but remember, a steel brush can cause erosion in soft metals). Protect eyes from flying debris.

Power buff
A power buff is made of cloth disks and should be used with a bench-mounted drill for the rapid polishing of metal; a disk 6 in. in diameter, with the drill running at the highest speed, is ideal. Use an abrasive buffing compound.

Abrasive cloths and paper
Emery cloth and paper, and "wet or dry" paper, are abrasives for finishing metalwork.

1 Wire brush
2 Power wire brush
3 Power buff

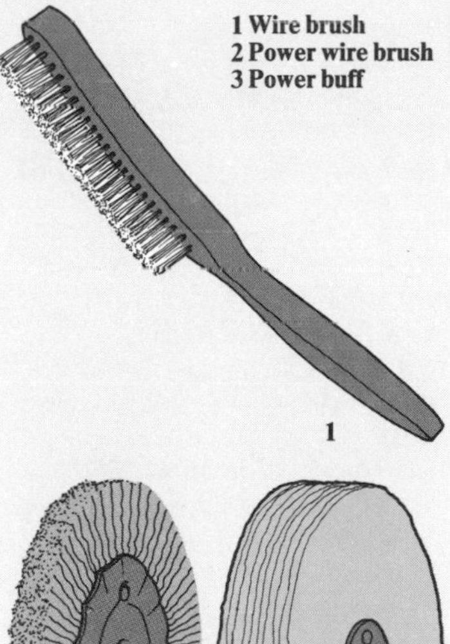

Techniques

If you want to remove file marks, start with the coarsest grade of emery paper. When the marks are erased, change to a finer grade of abrasive, and work at right angles to the previous direction; repeat until the desired surface is obtained. To rub down small, flat surfaces, fix a sheet of abrasive to a flat board and rub the work on this; you can also use a whetstone. For external curves, tear a strip of emery cloth, 1 in. wide or less, and draw this rapidly to and fro across the work. There's quite a technique to using a power buff. To polish metal, start the buff spinning, and apply the abrasive. Press the work firmly against the wheel, but take care that the buff does not grab it. Do not hold a sharp edge against the direction of rotation. The buff will round off sharp edges, and tends to obliterate patterns–in fact it can wear right through thin metal, especially plating. Finish the job with a cloth and metal polish.

You can maintain a polish on most types of metalwork by cleaning with detergent or alcohol, and then applying a clear lacquer. Brass and copper kept indoors may require little protection, but mild steel can be hardened against corrosion. First polish metal, then heat to a red heat with a blowtorch, then quench in light oil.

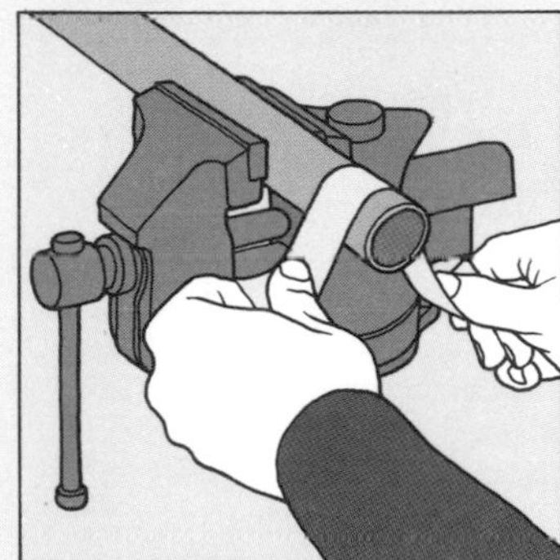

Polishing external curves
Use a strip of emery cloth in preference to paper, which tears easily. Secure the work in a vise, as shown above, and apply the strip briskly across the surface, using both hands.

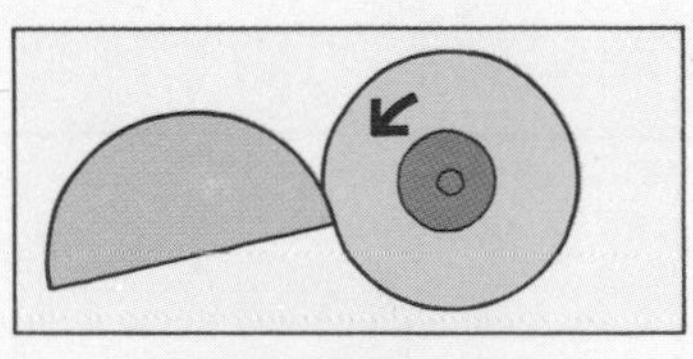

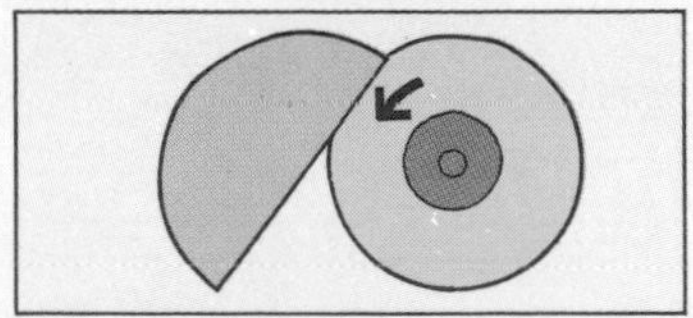

Using the power buff
The top picture shows the right way to apply work to the buff; the bottom picture is the wrong way. As you polish, continue to apply abrasive as needed.

Laminates

Laminate Surfaces

Plastic laminate is an ideal domestic material, both decorative and functional. It is tough, durable and has a good resistance to heat, which is why it is so widely used as a finishing surface for kitchen units and worktops. Laminate is made in two thicknesses: 1/32 in. for vertical, low-wear areas; 1/16 in. for horizontal surfaces. You can choose from a wide range of designs: patterns, woodgrains, plain colors and textured surfaces, with gloss or mat finishes. In spite of its heat-proof qualities, you should not place very hot objects on a plastic surface, as it may blister or scorch.

Cutting laminates
Laminate can be cut with a fine-toothed saw or special knife blade, and worked with a file or drilled with sharp twist drills. Cut the laminate slightly larger than board it is to cover. When it has finally bonded, you can trim the edges with a block plane, and a final finish can be achieved with a hand scraper or with fine sandpaper. It is easier to cut shapes after the bonding process; sharp corner cutouts should be avoided when the laminate is unbacked. Power saws can be used for cutting, with fine toothed blades. The laminate will need to be firmly secured, and cut while face down.

Bonding
Plastic laminates should be treated as veneers, and bonded to a suitable core material such as plywood or particle board; solid wood is not a stable base for laminating because of its natural tendency to movement due to moisture changes. If lumber must be used, you must line the wood with 1/8 in. plywood or hardboard, screwed or nailed down. Laminated panels need a balancing laminate on the reverse side to help prevent the board from bowing caused by the intake of moisture and the pull of the adhesive. Special laminates are made for this purpose, and are cheaper than the finished sheets. While it is possible to laminate one surface only, the panel must be screwed to a solid frame. Before bonding laminate to the core material, both should be allowed to become acclimatized to the surrounding conditions for about 48 hours. When applying adhesives, remember that they often bond on contact, so take care that surfaces are correctly aligned. Absorbent core materials need two coats.

Using a saw
Cut 1/16 in. laminate with a fine backsaw held at an angle to prevent chipping. Support sheet near cut line.

Cutting with a knife
With a special laminate cutting blade, score through the surface to the core layer using a straight edge.

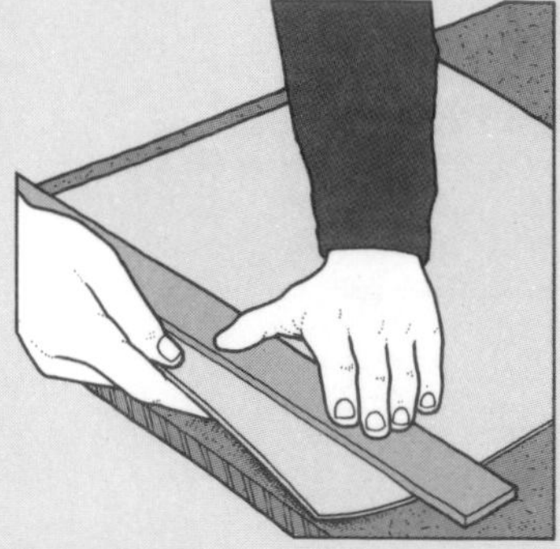

Snapping along the line
Press the straight edge firmly on the cut line and lift up the free edge to snap off the board.

Providing a grippable surface
Before bonding, first roughen the surface of the board with coarse sandpaper around a block of wood.

Spreading adhesive
Apply contact adhesive with a notched spreader to both surfaces and leave until touch-dry.

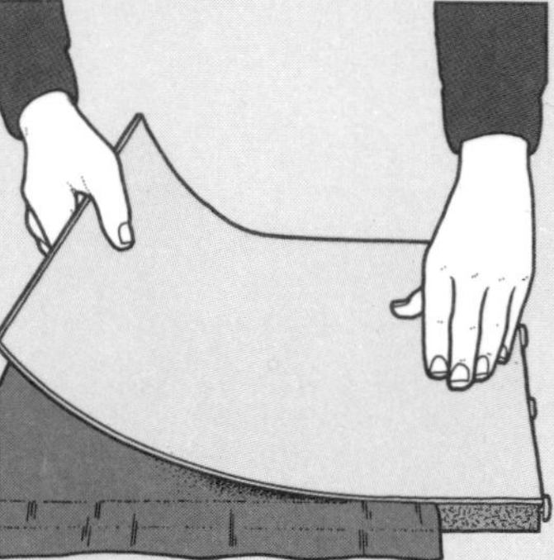

Positioning the laminate
Lay greaseproof paper on board and butt laminate against top of two thumb tacks. Press down and slowly withdraw paper.

An alternative barrier
Over large areas where paper is impractical, thin wooden slats can be laid between the laminate and the board.

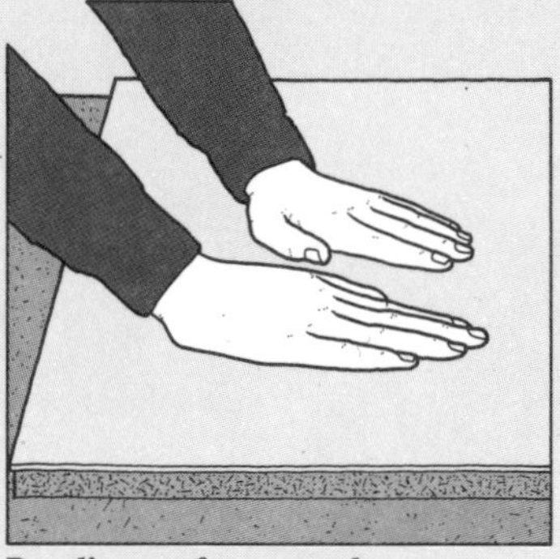

Bonding surfaces together
With the barrier removed, press the laminate down over the entire surface, working from the center outward.

Trimming edges
Edges should now be trimmed with a block plane, then covered with strips of laminate.

Finishing edges
Covered edges need trimming to an angle of 45° to prevent chipping. Trim corners in the same way.

Additional bonding technique
If edges of top sheet fail to adhere, use C clamps and wood as above. Finally finish with a hand scraper.

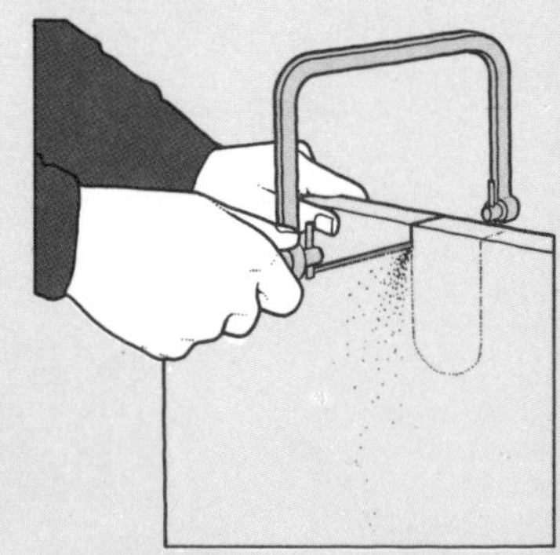

Cutting shapes
These should be done after the bonding process. Use a coping saw and finish with a smooth file.

Acrylics

Acrylic Sheets

Acrylic plastic can be transparent or colored in a wide range of plain shades; it can be smooth or textured. Thicknesses range from 1/32 in. to ½ in. and the most usual thickness is ⅛ in. Clear acrylic is made in sheet form, as well as in tube and rod sections in a variety of sizes. In sheet form it is an excellent substitute for the more brittle glass, an acrylic door panel is less hazardous than a glass one. Acrylic, however, is not as hard as glass and is likely to scratch, though careful polishing will remove all but the deeper marks. Sheets are supplied with a paper covering on both sides to protect the highly-polished surfaces. Leave the paper on as long as possible while the material is being worked; it can provide a useful surface for marking.

Cutting

Acrylic handles very much like plastic laminate (see opposite). It is important to use sharp tools and correctly-set saws, as any build-up of waste may melt the plastic through friction, and result in a rough edge. Drill acrylic with a power drill or hand brace fitted with twist bits; do not force the pace, as heat through friction may damage the hole. Back the plastic with wood when drilling, to prevent a split on the underside.

Polishing

Polish with a power buff, or brand-name liquid polish, graded for bringing the surface up to a high gloss. Wipe surfaces with a clean cloth between coats. Deep scratches may be removed with very fine wet or dry paper, the surface well lubricated with water.

Gluing

Acrylic can be solvent glued to form a welded joint. Mask the faces along the edge of the glue line with tape. Both glued surfaces should be brought together at an angle, then closed up to squeeze out air and excess glue. A strip of masking tape will make this easier: the technique is shown on the right.

Bending

A temperature between 300°F and 340°F will make acrylic pliable. Overheating will cause blistering. If size permits, use an oven for heating. If you do not need to mold the entire piece, apply local heat only, especially when making small bends in thin sheet. Electric heat is preferable to gas, which can scorch the surface.

Clamping to a bench
Acrylic needs to be firmly held for cutting. Use C clamps and wood. Cut line should just cover the edge.

Finishing edges
Trimming can be done with a woodworking router, or a sharp plane with a finely-set blade.

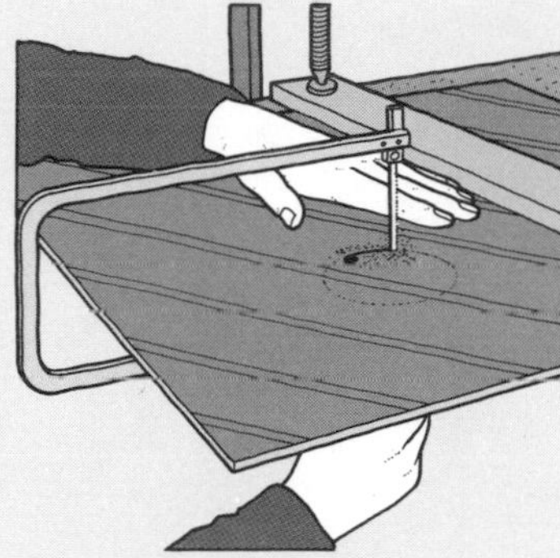

Cutting holes
Clamp the sheet to the bench and use a power drill hole saw. Cut large holes with a fret or coping saw.

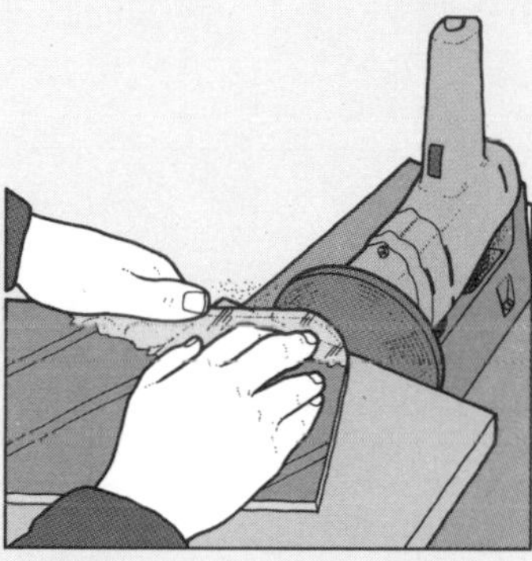

Cutting corners
Disk sanders, mounted on a bench, will shape external corners. Feed material slowly to avoid overheating.

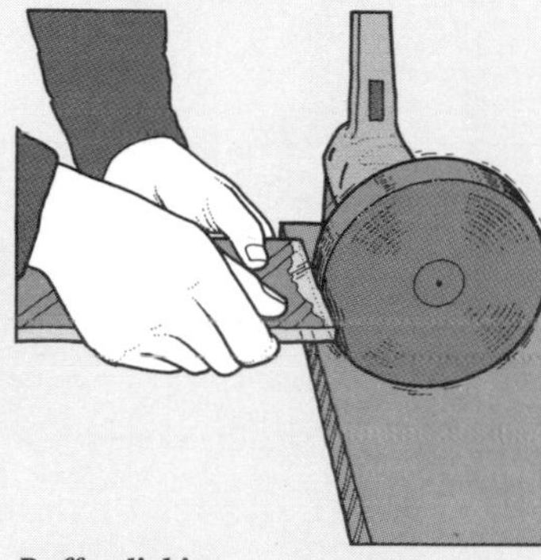

Buff polishing
Use a 6 in. power-driven cloth buff while applying a block of mild abrasive wax which is held against the wheel.

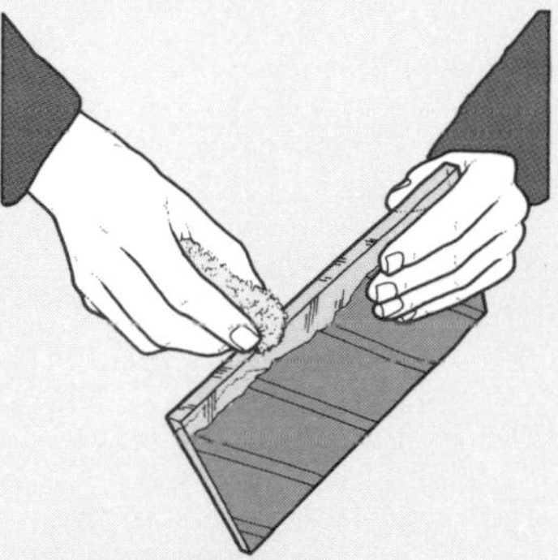

Liquid polishing
Apply polish with a cotton pad, using light pressure. Change pad regularly, and do not allow to dry.

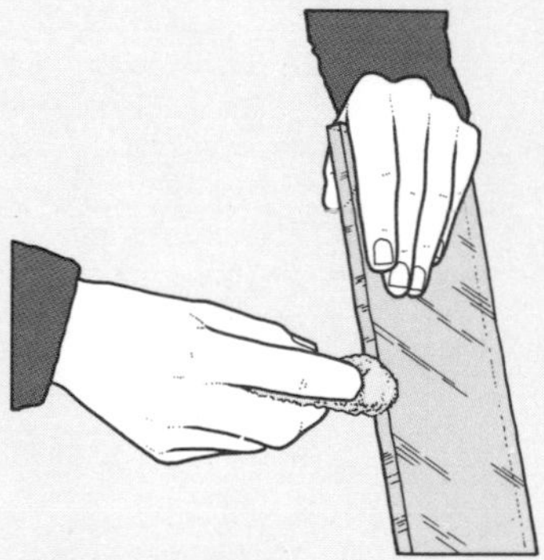

Cleaning surfaces
Air bubbles in glue line may be due to grease or dirt. Wipe edges with lighter fuel before bonding.

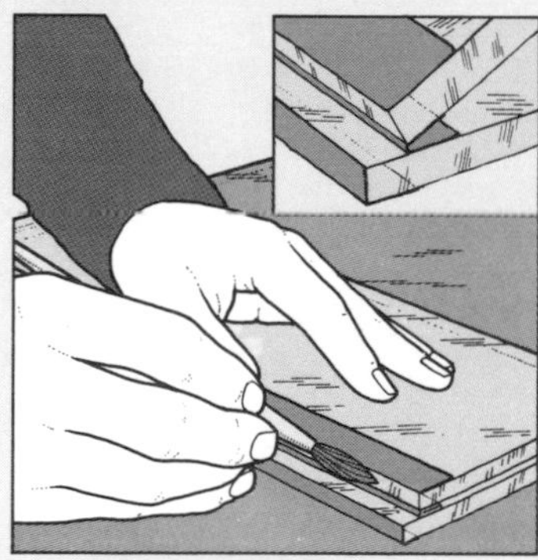

Assembling parts
Position the parts dry and check for square. Protect the edges with masking tape and make hinge as shown inset. Apply liquid adhesive.

Gluing surfaces
After glue has been applied to both surfaces, bring them together after about 30 secs. Remove tape when glue is dry.

Bending acrylic
1 Isolate heated area with aluminum foil. Wrap tightly around plastic with shiny face out. Tape in place.

2 Wear protective gloves, and hold the plastic over the burner of a stove, preferably electric. Keep plastic moving to even out the heat.

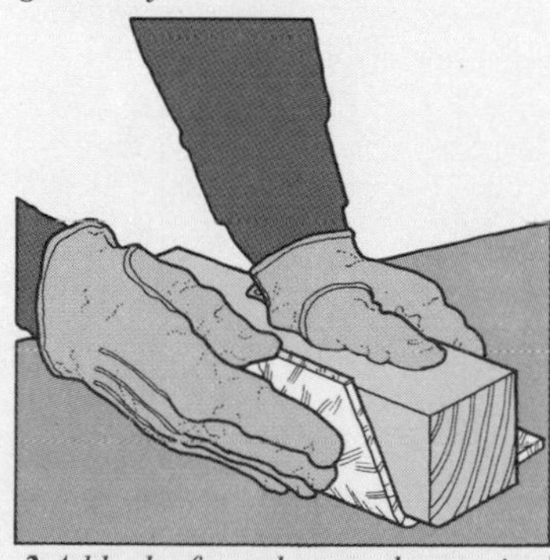

3 A block of wood cut to the required angle, with a slightly rounded corner, will help form bend until plastic cools and hardens.

Materials & Supplies

Basic Principles

The skills needed for upholstering are not beyond the scope of the average non-professional. Along with the right tools and materials an understanding of the basic principles of upholstery will allow you to tackle most jobs successfully. The basic techniques are those of stitching, of stretching materials and fastening them to a frame. Although a well-used chair will probably have to be re-sprung and re-covered, you will rarely be faced with a complete upholstering job. Moreover, in many cases the original stuffing and some of the covering material can be retained.

Tools

You may already possess many of the tools required – screwdriver; pliers; pincers; large scissors; sharp knife; bradawl; medium, half-round file; mallet; joinery hammer; chisel; ruler; tape-measure. In addition, these special tools will be needed for particular jobs: webbing stretcher; tack remover; regulator; needles; skewer pins, and finally, an upholsterer's hammer.

Upholsterer's hammer
The round end should be between $\frac{1}{2}$ in. and $\frac{5}{8}$ in. in diameter, which must be kept smooth and free of grease. The other end is a claw for removing tacks.

Webbing stretcher
This is essential for stretching the traditional, woven webbing. You can make one from a block of wood.

Tack remover
A tack remover will remove all but the most deeply-embedded tacks; for these you will need a screwdriver and mallet.

Scissors and knife
Scissors should be about 9 in. long with broad, strong blades. A knife with replaceable blades is useful for trimming, especially leather and plastic-coated material.

Regulator
This distributes the stuffing evenly through the muslin.

Needles
A mattress needle is for stitching straight through upholstery. It is double pointed with the eye at one end, and should be about 10 in. long. Curved needles are useful where you cannot use a straight one. Dressmaker's needles finish off corners; upholstering pins or skewers are for temporarily holding covering materials in position.

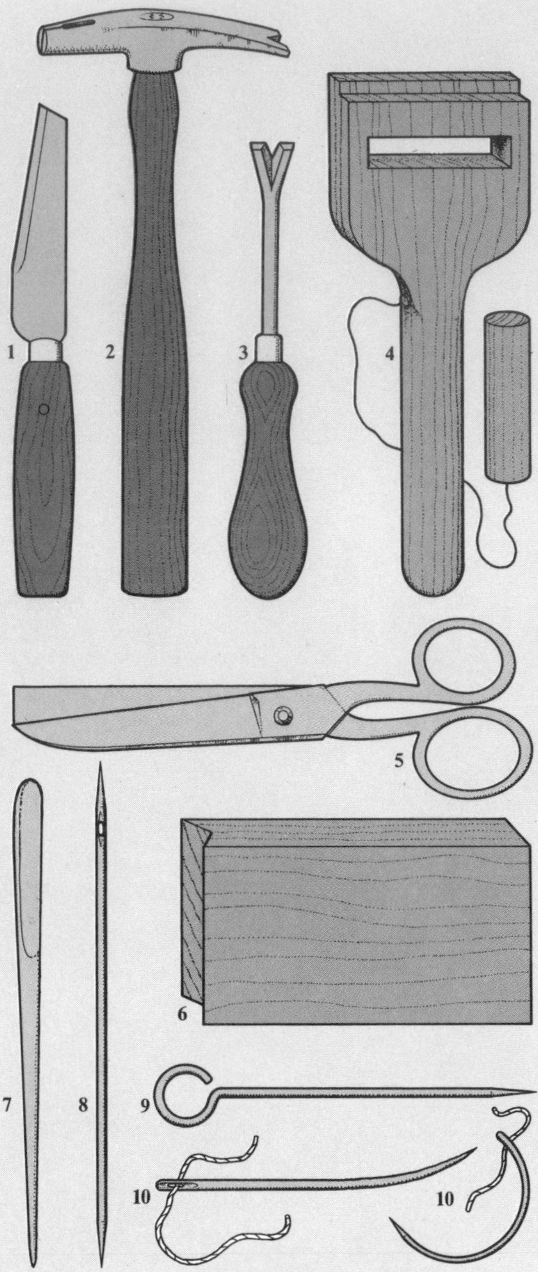

1/5 Knife and scissors
Cutting tools must be sharp and sturdy to use with thick materials.

2 Upholsterer's hammer
The best tool for driving in tacks, although you can use any small-headed hammer.

3 Tack remover
Slips under the tack head to lever tack from the frame. Some people prefer a screwdriver.

4/6 Webbing stretchers
Made in a variety of designs, the notch pivots on the frame to pull the webbing taut.

7 Regulator
A wide, flat tool about 8 in. to 10 in. long, for distributing stuffing through the muslin.

8 Mattress needle
About 10 in. long and double pointed. Used for drawing twine straight through upholstery.

9 Skewers
These can be driven through the material into stuffing, to hold covering in position.

10 Curved needles
A curved needle will more easily draw thread through a flat or fixed surface. It can also be used for drawing twine through webbing to secure coil springs.

1 Traditional webbing
2 Rubber webbing
3 Tension springs
4 Sagless springs
5 Coil springs
6 Piping cord
7 Tacks
8 Button head tacks

Webbing
Webbing is stretched across the frame to support the springs and the stuffing. While a variety of grades and widths are available, the best is made of jute, the $3\frac{1}{2}$ in. width the most suitable. Rubber webbing has also become popular.

Springs
Tension springs are long, closely-coiled springs about $\frac{1}{2}$ in. diameter which are stretched across the frame. Sagless springs, also known as zig-zag or serpentine springs, are made from a single, thick steel wire and tensioned in parallel arcs across the frame. They are obtainable together with fixing clips for repair work. Coil springs are the best known of all steel upholstering springs, and are obtainable from 4 in. to 10 in. high, in various gauges of wire. The higher the gauge number the thinner the wire, and therefore the softer the spring.

Tacks
Cut blue steel tacks are sharper than the cheaper, wire tacks and the heads are larger and less likely to break off. Tacks are made in about 15 sizes, from $\frac{3}{16}$ in. to 1 in. in length. Use $\frac{5}{8}$ in. or $\frac{1}{2}$ in. cut blue for webbing; $\frac{1}{2}$ in. or $\frac{3}{8}$ in. cut blue for burlap and cambric; $\frac{1}{2}$ in. or $\frac{3}{8}$ in. wire tacks for muslin and final cover. Don't bother to use up old tacks, the points are blunted and the heads may break off. Gimp pins are used for fixing gimps and braids, but rubber adhesive has largely superseded them. Button head tacks have domed brass heads or are colored and covered for decorative pinning.

Piping cord
This is obtainable in a variety of thicknesses, stitched inside strips of material to make welts.

Buttons
Tack buttons are for fixing through thin upholstery to a solid base, such as a padded headboard. Buttons covered with a cloth tuft and anchored to the back of the upholstery by means of twine, either through the material or a wire loop on the button are used to give a quilted effect.

Twine and thread
Spring twine is for tying down coil springs, and needs to be strong, so choose the 6-cord grade. Stitching twine is used for general upholstering work; upholstering thread is used for stitching and sewing up covering fabrics.

Fabrics

Burlap
This is closely-woven jute cloth, less stiff than canvas. Burlap is available in widths from 40 in. up to 72 in., and cloth with a weight of 10 oz. per yard is the most useful. Burlap is used over coil springs to support the padding materials, and also to stretch over areas of the frame to support stuffing materials.
Muslin
This is unbleached cotton cloth with many upholstering uses if bought in a heavy enough grade: as a layer over the second stuffing before the final padding; as an inner cover for cushions; as a layer over the top padding before the final covering material. Used in the last way, muslin has many advantages. For example, it allows the stuffing to be pulled down into the shape and degree of firmness needed, since delicate, lightweight cover fabrics do not have sufficient strength. Also, a pile fabric such as velvet is protected from the stuffing by an intermediate layer of muslin; a foam stuffing can draw in the pile and cause the velvet to go bald.
Black cambric
This is an inexpensive cotton fabric which gives a neat finish to the underside of an upholstered seat, when used as a dust panel. Burlap is also used, but is less dustproof.

Stuffings

Traditional stuffings include horse hair, wool, vegetable fibers such as cotton linters, and feathers for loose cushions. Today the range has been increased by the introduction of man-made fibers, rubberized hair, foam rubber and plastic foam. These new materials have brought about many changes in upholstery techniques. Animal fibers are mainly horse hair, which is the finest quality, and cattle and hog hair, used in the cheaper grades. The longer the hair, the longer it remains resilient. If the hair removed from old upholstery is of good quality, it is worth using again after beating out the dust and treating with a moth-proofing solution. Rubberized hair is made in thicknesses from $\frac{3}{4}$ in. up to 4 in. and in sheets to be cut as needed. It can be used in a similar way to foam rubber and plastic foam, but it packs down more quickly. Used over a resilient base, and covered with a layer of cotton felt, it makes an inexpensive stuffing.

Vegetable fibers
Certain vegetable fibers are used as substitutes for hair and they include the following: Spanish moss, from the oak trees of southern USA, the dark brown, top grade of which comes close in quality to that of horse hair; palm fiber, clean and inexpensive but not very resilient; coco fiber from the husk of coconuts, hard wearing but resilient.
Cotton felt
This is made from the short fibers or linters, left over after the long fibers have been removed for spinning into yarn. The most useful thickness is the 1 in., employed as a top padding before the muslin and final cover are fitted. The main function of cotton felt is to take up surface irregularities in the stuffing beneath, and to stop hairs and fibers working up through the top cover.
Polyester fiber felt
Similar to cotton felt, this holds its shape and resilience very much better, and is widely used in the making of loose cushions, often in conjunction with foam rubber or plastic foam as the center core.
Feathers and down
Geese and ducks are the main providers of fillings for cushions and pillows, and a mixture of about 30% feathers to 70% down gives a soft but not too slack cushion. Chicken and turkey feathers are also used, but they are stiffer and tend to pack down. It is important that feathers are contained within a suitable ticking casing to stop them working through the cover.
Foam rubber and foam polyurethane
Man-made foam polyurethane and foam rubber are much easier to use than the traditional stuffings. Used mainly in sheet form, both types can be bought in thicknesses from $\frac{1}{2}$ in. up to 4 in., and in densities ranging from extra soft to extra hard. The softer densities are used for cushions, or for laying over a denser foam. You can build up from two or three layers of foam where you need deep upholstery, with the firmest density at the bottom. The density of foam upholstery should be such that, when sat upon, neither the springs nor the hard base can be felt. When using covering materials for foam cushions on a plywood base, especially materials like leather or plastic-coated cloth, allow adequate ventilation for the foam to compress and return without delay.

Covering Materials

Choosing the right material
The choice of the final covering materials for your upholstery will naturally depend upon your taste, but the amount of wear the material is likely to expect is a very important consideration. A golden rule is to buy only those materials recommended for upholstering – materials that will not fade, or wear badly, and that are color fast.
Leather and plastics
Almost all upholstering leather comes from cow hide, which is split into different qualities. The top layer of the hide is the best, and is about 3⁄64 in. thick; the remaining layers are graded accordingly. Although leather is a strong and very attractive material, some skill is needed in knowing which parts of the skin to use. In principle, the center part of the animal's skin, or back, is used for chair or sofa seats, while the underside parts that tend to stretch are used for the outside areas. The stuffing needs to be firmer for leather work and where shapes are strongly curved you will have to use pleating and buttoning techniques. Edges should be finished off by close nailing with button head tacks, or by matching semi-circular molding.
Plastic-coated materials are easier to use, especially the kind with a knitted back, but unmounted vinyls should be avoided, as they are inclined to tear. Expanded plastic-coated fabrics feel softer and have better wearing properties than other vinyl fabrics. When stitching these fabrics, use the largest needle and the thickest cotton or polyester thread that your machine will take, setting it to give not more than 6 stitches per inch.
Woven materials
Modern upholstering textiles use a variety of fibers, including linen, cotton, wool, silk, rayon and polyester, each having particular properties of strength, texture and so on. The majority of textiles are a combination of two or more.
You can learn a lot about the working qualities of textiles by laying them over a chair seat. Medium-weight textiles are best for most upholstering work. The thicker varieties are difficult to sew and pleat, while the lightweight fabrics may tear away from the tacks. Ideally, you should use an undercover of muslin to hold the padding in shape and to take most of the strain.

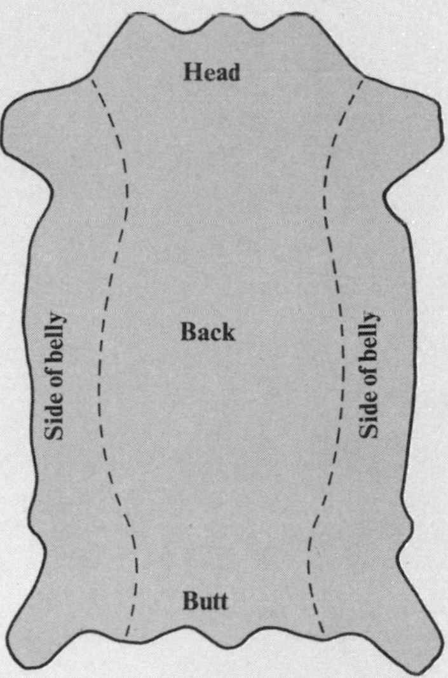

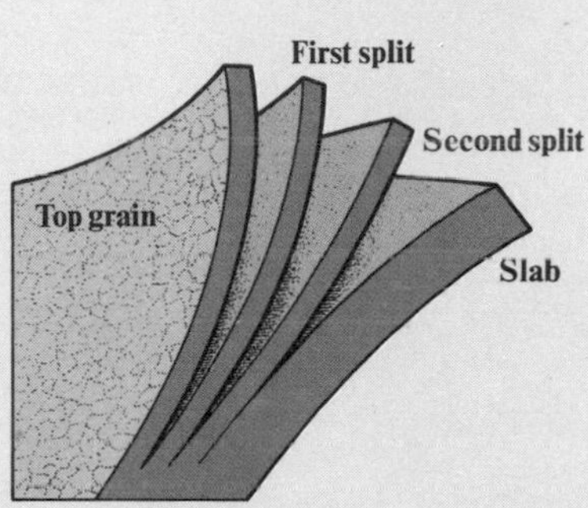

Grades of leather
Cow hide is split into various grades according to the working qualities of each layer. Top grain, where the hair used to be, is best, followed by the first and second splits.

Care and Maintenance

Leather should be cleaned with a mild soap (not detergent) and water solution, rinsed with a damp cloth, then wiped dry. A mixture of 2 parts linseed oil to 1 part vinegar cleans leather and helps to keep it supple. Plastic-coated materials need only be cleaned with a damp cloth, and wiped dry. Great care should be taken in the cleaning of woven upholstery materials. Remove dust with a vacuum cleaner before using a suitable brand name cleaner, following the instructions. Always test out a cleaner on an unnoticeable area. Apart from loose covers and cushions, most upholstering fabrics cannot be removed for laundering. Potential stains must be wiped off immediately with cold water. Alcohol stains may clear after an application of 1 oz. borax to 1 pt water. The same solution can be used to treat burn marks. Other stains may be treated with salt, lemon juice, or carbon tetrachloride.

Upholstering

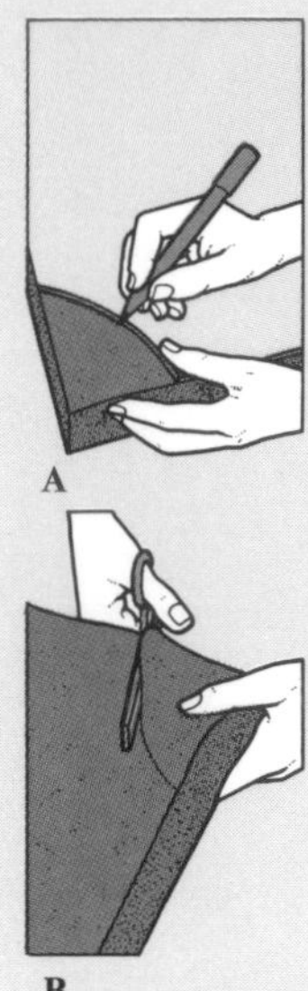
A
B

Techniques

Foam rubber and foam polyurethane
Begin by making a paper or thin cardboard pattern to the shape required. Lay the pattern on the foam and mark around with a ballpoint pen or a piece of tailor's chalk, **A**, pressing lightly. Cut the shapes slightly over size, about 3/16 in. to every 10 in. overall, so that the foam is later used under slight compression, and is not stretched; this also allows the cover to be held snug and in tension. Large scissors and those with serrated blades are useful for cutting foam up to 1½ in. thick, **B**, as well as for trimming. Join foam surfaces with adhesive, the self-vulcanizing type being the simplest to use. Spread a thin layer on both surfaces and leave for a few minutes before bonding. Dust with talcum powder to dry off surplus adhesive; this reduces the friction between foam and covering material. To attach foam to frames or bases, use contact-adhesive muslin tape.

Edge finishes
Edge finishes are used when joining the foam to a frame or base, irrespective of the type of springing. The square edge finish is suitable where the cover is made with a piped border. Line the sides of pincore foam rubber, **A,** or foam polyurethane, **B,** with ½ in. or ¾ in. sheet foam of a firmer density than the piece you are lining. Now stick the muslin tape, cut to size, on the face of the lining. Allow sufficient tape to overhang so that you can stick it to the frame. You can trim back the top edge at an angle, to take the extra thickness of the cover and piping. **C** and **D** show how a feathered edge gives a curved finish to the sides. Cut the foam vertically, allowing an extra ½ in. or more all round, according to the thickness. Now taper back the edges to 45°, in such a way that the top overhangs the bottom. Tape the top surface, leaving sufficient overlap, then pull down and tack to the base, making sure tape is pulled down evenly, using temporary tacks at about 3 in. intervals. Finally, drive in permanent tacks at 1 in. intervals, removing the temporary tacks as you proceed. If you are edging a seat, start at the back, then the front, and finish on the sides. A cushioned edge, **E** and **F,** is similar to the above, except that the sides are left vertical. This gives a firmer edge for heavyweight covers.

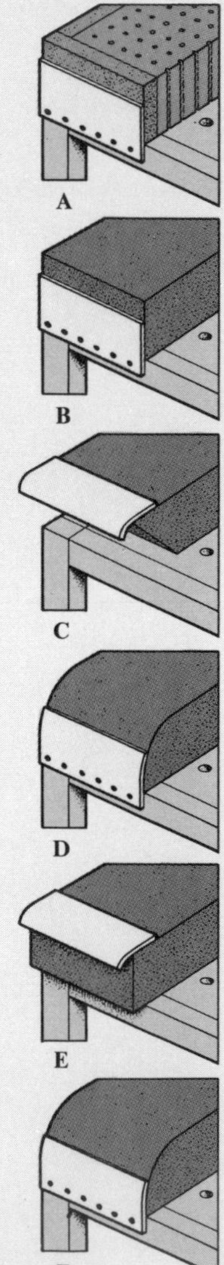
A
B
C
D
E
F

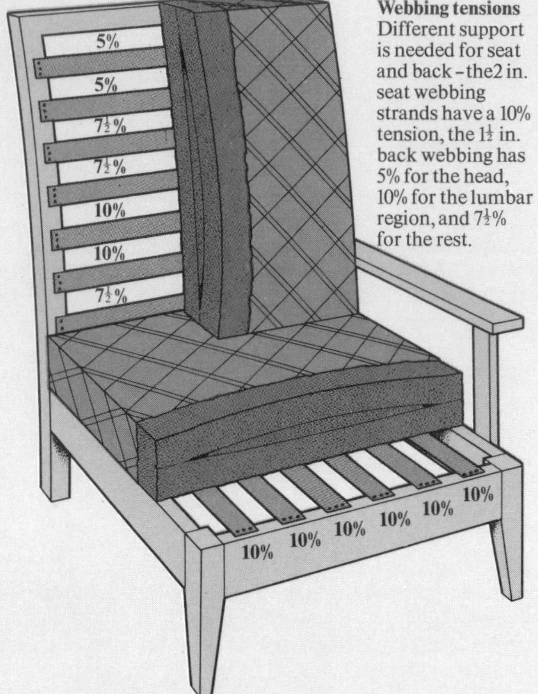

Webbing tensions
Different support is needed for seat and back – the 2 in. seat webbing strands have a 10% tension, the 1½ in. back webbing has 5% for the head, 10% for the lumbar region, and 7½% for the rest.

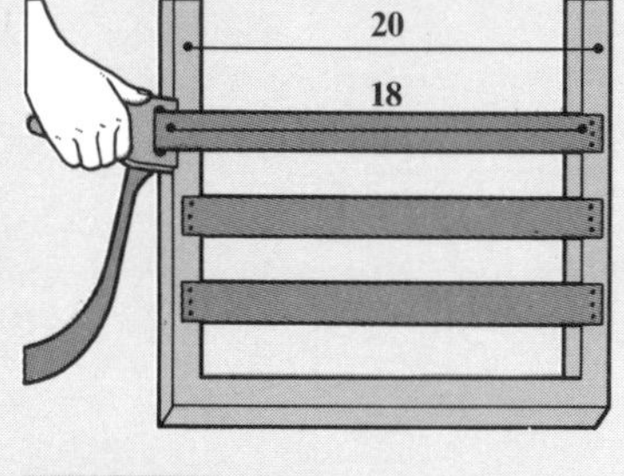

Stretching the webbing
To obtain a 10% tension for a 20 in. seat, fix webbing to back and mark a pencil line 18 in. from this point. Pull webbing over front rail and tack at line; cut webbing leaving a ¼ in. trim. Work from roll only.

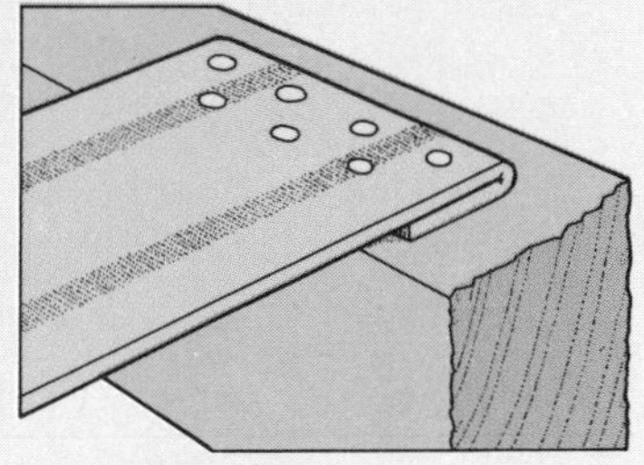

Tacking to the frame
Fold 1½ in. of end under to double thickness. Use seven ⅝ in. tacks to fix to frame, ½ in. from outside edge of rail.

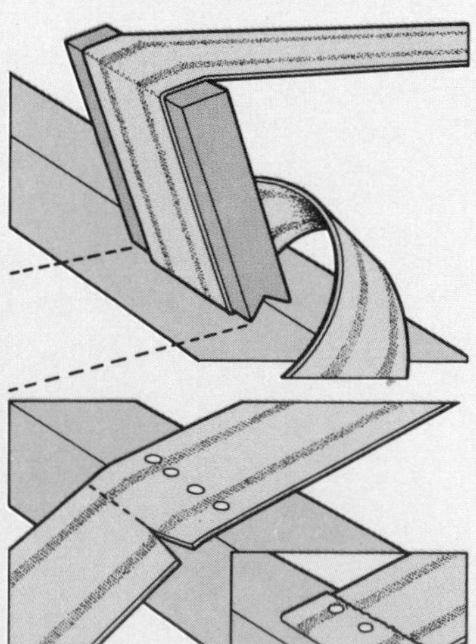

Using the stretcher
Pull webbing tight across the frame. Press down until webbing is flat on the rail.

Tacking off the web
Drive four equally spaced tacks to secure webbing. Cut 1½ in. beyond tacks. Fold over and drive three tacks between first four.

Rubber webbing
Rubber webbing is usually mounted on the frame in parallel bands. Interlacing should only be used to provide a very firm base, or to give extra tension in a particular area, the lumbar region, for example. Fix your webbing with tacks or nails, using either ⅝ in. blue steel, large head tacks, or ½ in. wide nails. 2 in. width webbing needs three fasteners at each end. Before nailing, see that the inside edges of all rails are beveled or rounded – a sharp edge can chafe rubber webbing. Various tensions will need to be applied to the webbing, according to the positioning. The amount of tension applied to the webbing when fixing regulates the degree of support: a minimum of 5% stretch gives a soft support and a 10% gives a firm support. Obviously, the seat takes the greatest strain and the webbing must be stretched to a 10% tension. For example, in a 20 in. wide seat, strands will need to be stretched 2 in. to obtain a 10% tension. If a 5% tension is required, the webbing must be stretched 1 in. For 7½% tension, stretch 1½ in. The degrees of tension needed for an armchair seat and back are illustrated left. Use 2 in. wide webbing for the seat, and 1½ in. for the back. Strands should never be more than 1¼ times the width of the webbing apart.

Traditional webbing
Mark where the webs are to be positioned, allowing between ½ to 1 in. space between. Allow wider intervals for backs and arms of chairs. The usual sequence when webbing a chair is to begin with the arms and the back, tacking to the bottom rail then stretching and tacking to the top rail. The horizontal cross webs are then interlaced, stretched and tacked in position. For the seat, work in a similar fashion, tacking webs to the back rail then stretching and tacking to the front rail. Where the width of the rail will allow, the ends of the webs should be set about ½ in. from the outside edge. Use a bat-type stretcher, or make your own from a piece of softwood. The stretcher needs to be the width of the webbing, and about 6 in. long, with a 1 in. groove cut at one end. Wrap the webbing across the end of the stretcher, locate the notch on the edge of the rail, and lever down until the webbing is flat on the rail. The underside of the tack head holds the webbing in place, so drive the tacks in straight.

Coil sprung upholstery
Although coil springs are used to give a wide variety of upholstering effects, there are several basic principles of installation which remain more or less constant.

Webbing
You will need interlacing webbing to support coil springs. Having decided the positioning of the springs, you should attach the webbing to the frame so that cross-over points are sited under each spring. A piece of burlap can be tacked over the webbing before tying down the springs. This gives additional strength to the base and a firmer effect to the upholstery.

Springing
Springs must be stitched to the webbing with spring twine, using a curved needle, making three or four fixing ties to each spring. Start with a slip knot for the first tie, then continue with a series of half-hitch knots, and use a double-hitch for the final tie. Knots and securing technique are shown right. The next stage is to secure the tops of the springs so that they are held in place, and under compression. Springs should be no more than a maximum of 2 in. below their non-compressed height, otherwise the upholstery will feel hard and uneven, and the webbing will be under excess strain. Try and arrange the springs so that they are evenly spaced in straight lines in both directions. Tie the tops of the springs with strong yet soft twine, starting with the center row. Drive a $\frac{5}{8}$ in. tack halfway into the top of the back seat rail. Tie twine around it and hammer home the tack. Work toward the front of the chair, and make two ties at the top of each spring, using a secure knot. Finish by securing twine to front rail with a tack. Continue with remaining rows and then cross-tie: the sequence is described on the right. Cover with burlap, first tacking to the top edges of the frame, with an excess of 1 in. all round. Fold over and tack down along the lines of the other tacks. Sew the tops of the springs to the burlap.

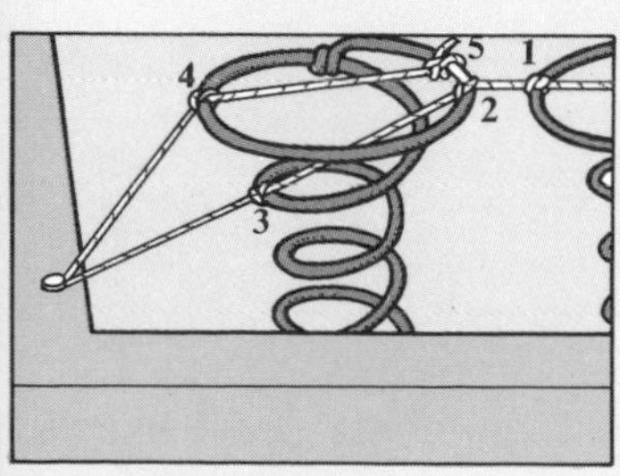

Flat top stitching detail

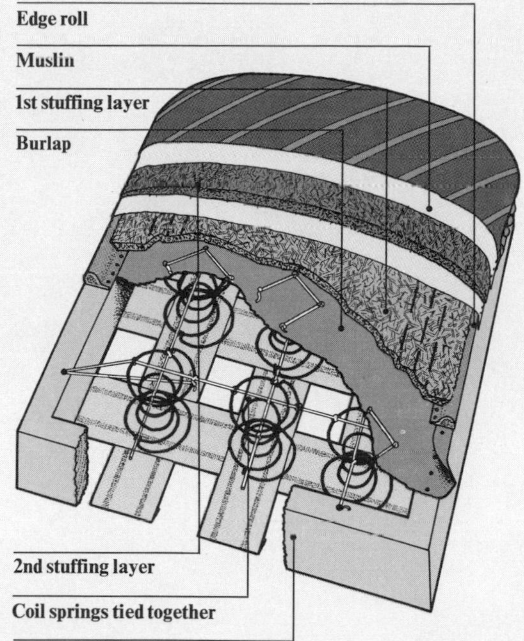

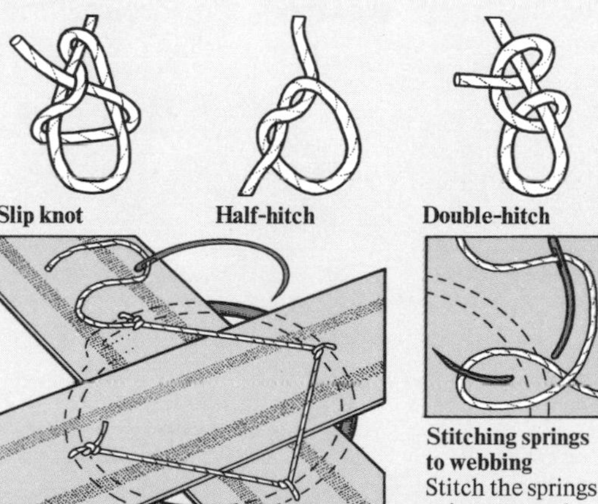

Stitching springs to webbing
Stitch the springs using a curved needle, making a slip knot, two half-hitches and a double-hitch, as shown.

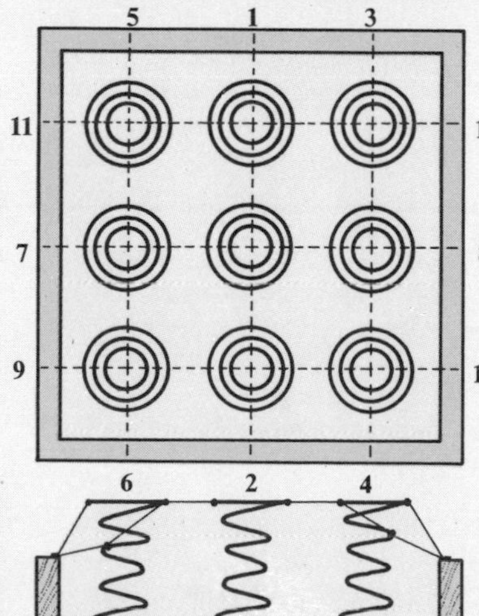

Tying sequence
Begin in the middle row, work from front to back, then do flanking rows. Now work across from side rail to side rail using same sequence.

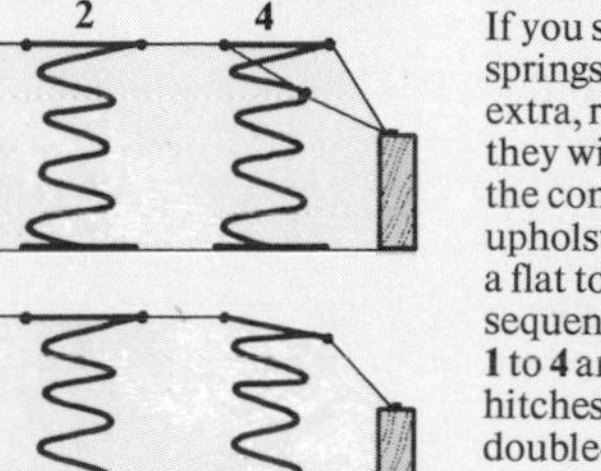

Round top

Contour springs
If you secure coil springs with an extra, return tie, they will alter the contour of the upholstery, giving a flat top. Tying sequence is shown: **1** to **4** are half-hitches, **5** is a double-hitch.

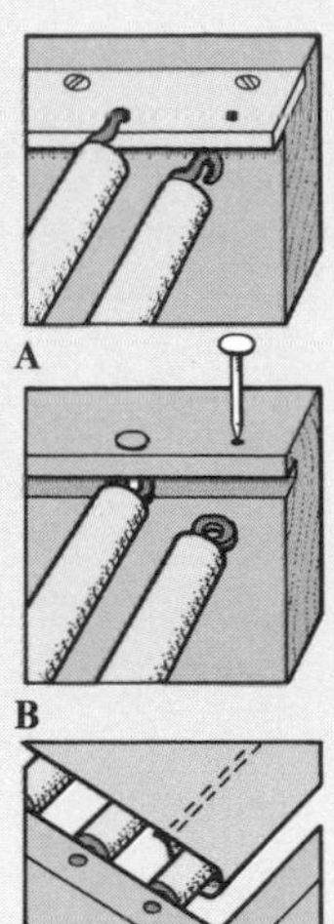

Spring cover
These springs require a fabric cover to reduce the wear on the underside of the cushion.

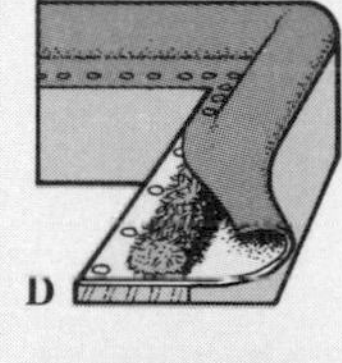

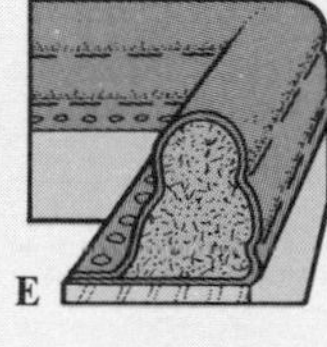

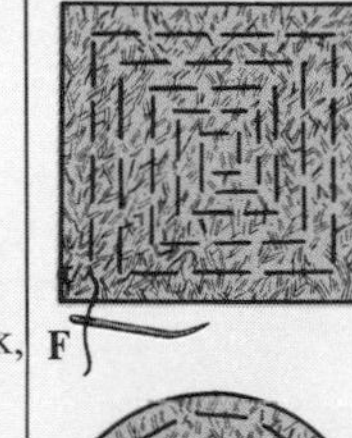

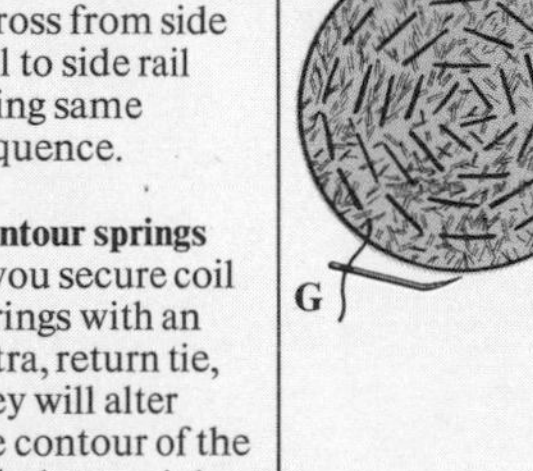

Tension springing
Cable springs of $\frac{3}{8}$ in. diameter can be used for chair backs, and $\frac{1}{2}$ in. for the seats. The springs are often sold with woven or plastic covers; if they are not, you will have to fit a panel of burlap or black muslin over them, to reduce wear on the upholstered cushions. Make the panel with a hem down the sides, and a 2 in. wide slot at each end, through which the front and back springs are passed. Springs can be anchored to a steel strip fixed to the frame **A,** or by pins that locate through a rebate **B.**

Sagless springing
It is important to choose springs of the correct gauge and length, and with the right type of clip fixing. They are usually set with centers 4 or 5 in. apart, and their length should be such that there is an arc height of $1\frac{1}{2}$ in. for firm support, and $2\frac{1}{4}$ in. for greater softness. To fix clips to the frame use $\frac{3}{4}$ in. or 1 in. hammer-screws, or large-headed nails with ridge stems.

Edge rolls
These provide a firm, controlling edge for a loose fiber stuffing and give a softer surface to frame edges. They can be bought in diameters from about $\frac{1}{2}$ in. to $1\frac{1}{2}$ in. To make your own, tack a strip of burlap to the edge of the rail, lay an even thickness of fiber over the tacks. Fold the burlap over the fiber, working from the center toward the ends until it is a firm rounded shape of the required diameter. Tack down the burlap with a line of tacks driven between the first line of tacks, using a regulator to even out the fiber **D.** For edge rolls of a large diameter the fiber will have to be both stitched and tacked **E.**

Stuffing
When foam is to be laid over springs, an intermediate stuffing of fiber will help provide even support. Use small well-teased quantities, gradually building up to the required thickness. Blend layers together carefully, making sure that the thickness around the sides is only slightly above that of edge rolls. Use twine and a mattress needle to fix stuffing and make your stitches about 3 in. long over the stuffing, but only about $\frac{1}{2}$ in. long in the burlap over the springs. A round seat **G** is stitched in more of a spiral than a square seat **F.** Fix muslin over the intermediate stuffing before applying the top stuffing, which should slightly overhang the edge rolls.

Upholstering

Techniques

Reupholstering a dining chair

You can replace the old stuffing in a dining chair and renew the webbing. This also gives you the opportunity to replace the top covering as well, with perhaps a different material or pattern. The quantity of covering material needed varies according to the size of the pattern and the length of the repeat. Plain material, or one with a small pattern, is easier to use and has the least wastage. In any event you should measure very carefully before cutting, especially with large patterns, where you may have to centralize a motif on the seat. Check that the design is the right way up and that it is properly aligned. Full size paper patterns are invaluable. Position covering material by cutting a V notch in the front and back edge, and align with marks made in the centers of front and back rails.

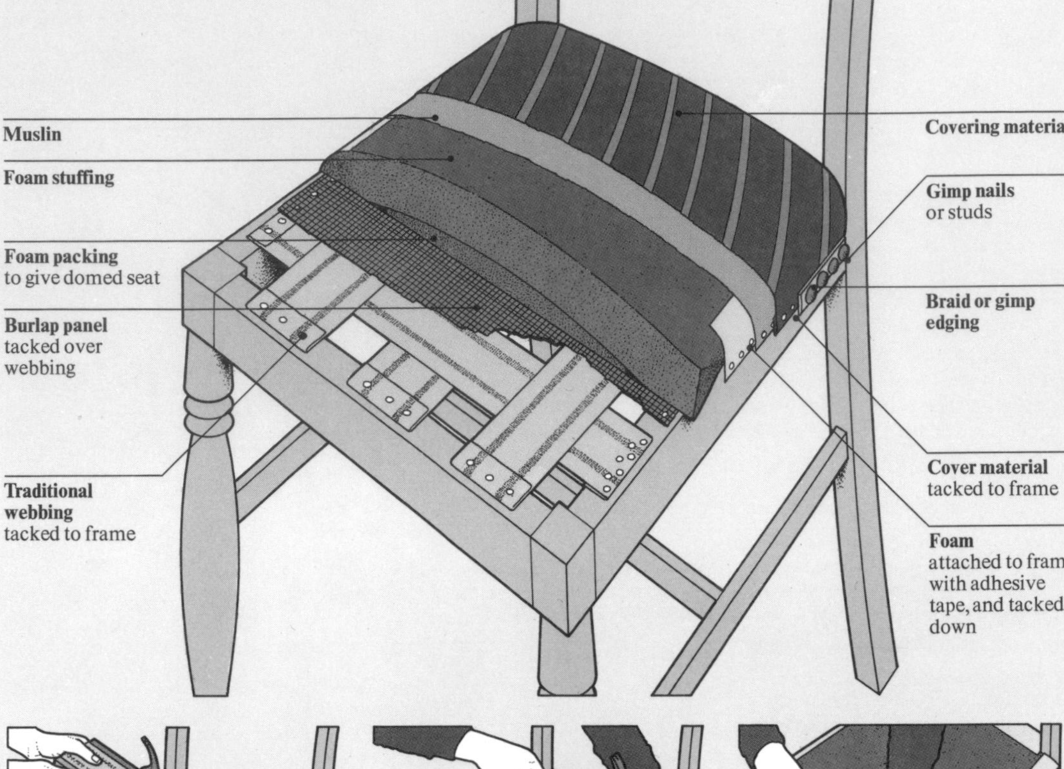

Stripping off old webbing
Use a tack remover or screwdriver to pry off tacks and webbing. Check frame for any damage, loose joints or broken rails. On some old chairs, the front legs extend some $\frac{3}{8}$ in. above top and side rails, and should be sawn off flush.

Fitting new webbing
Use traditional webbing material and fit the new webbing as described on the previous pages. Tack the webs to the back rail first, then to the front, and then fit the interlaced cross webs.

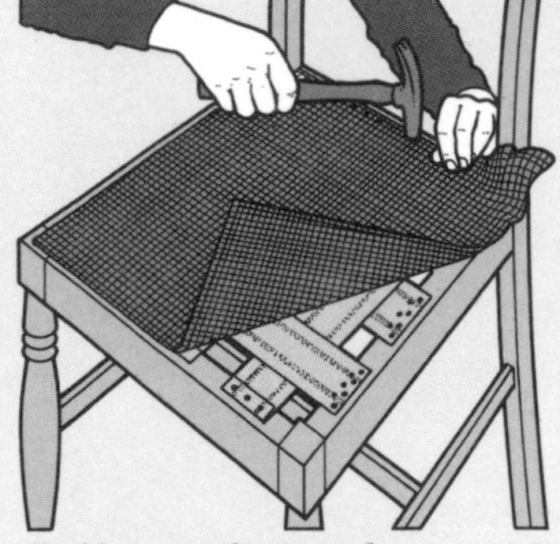

Tacking on a dust panel
Cut a piece of burlap or cambric to the shape of the seat, allowing an excess of about 1 in. all around. Fold under to leave $\frac{1}{2}$ in. from the outer edge of the frame rails, and tack down.

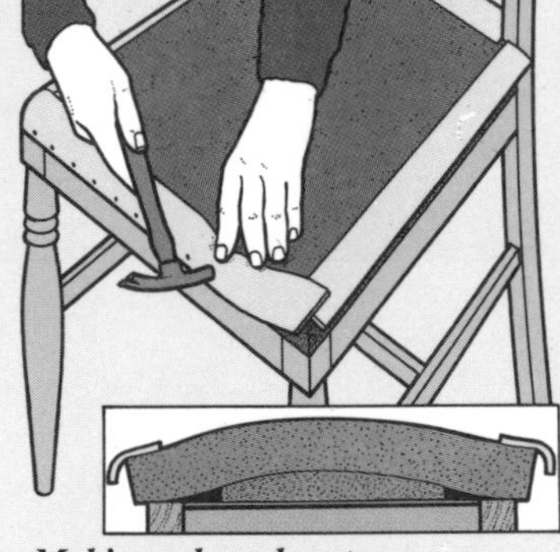

Making a domed seat
Mark and cut foam to shape of seat leaving a $\frac{3}{4}$ in. border. Use a medium-firm foam $1\frac{1}{2}$ in. to 2 in. thick. For the domed top, cut another piece of slightly firmer foam (1 in. to $1\frac{1}{2}$ in. thick) which is $2\frac{1}{2}$ in. to 3 in. smaller overall. Taper edges, and glue to underside of main piece.

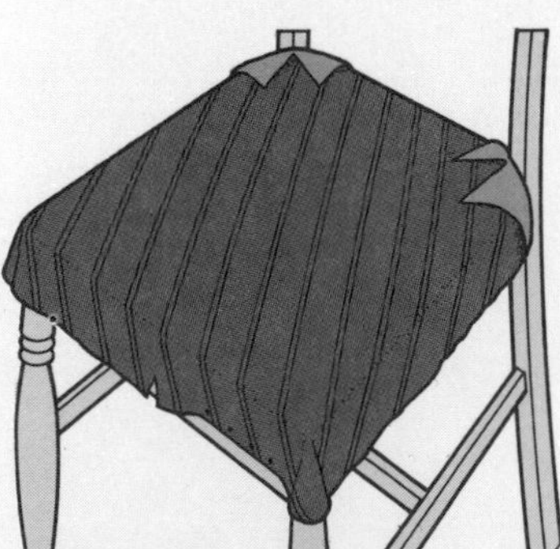

Fixing material with temporary tacks
Place covering material on seat and temporarily tack from center working outward. Start at back, then do front and finally side rails, smoothing cover gently. Stop 2 in. from ends on all sides.

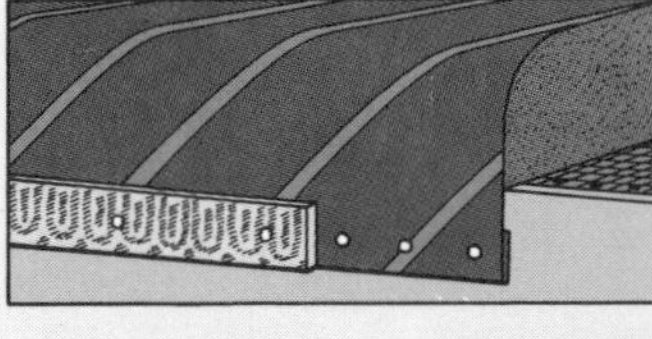

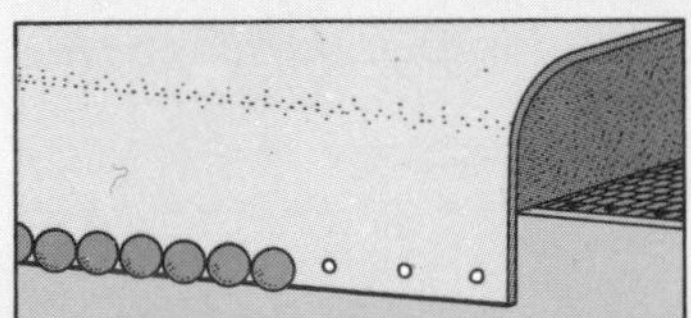

Edge finishes
Thin material covers should be folded under and tacked, the tacks covered with gimp, fixed with gimp nails or adhesive. Thick covers are trimmed after tacking with a sharp knife, then close nailed or finished with gimp or braid.

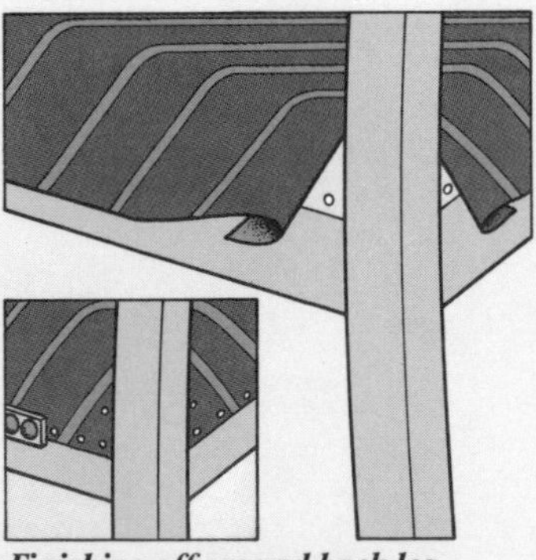

Finishing off around back leg
Turn two back corners forward, make a short diagonal cut so you can fit the cover around the back leg, tucking down between front edges of leg and upholstery, and so there are no wrinkles. Drive in temporary tacks.

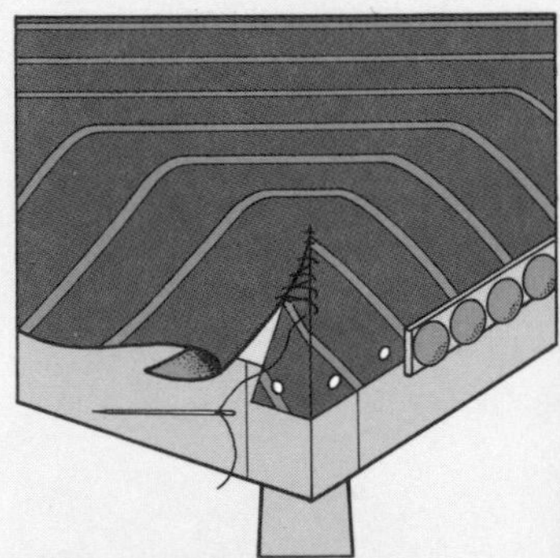

Finishing front cover
Cut away some of the surplus material inside the pleats. Tack down as shown above, fold front piece under, and slip stitch if needed to make a seam. Finish edge as previously described.

Reupholstering loose seats

A new, loose seat for a dining chair is an easy upholstering job. If the frame is in good condition after stripping, re-web with interlaced, traditional webbing and cover with a burlap panel. If the frame is in poor condition, replace it with a plywood panel, about $\frac{3}{8}$ in. thick, with overall dimensions slightly smaller than the frame recess, so as to leave room for the covering material. You may also have to plane down the original frame slightly if adding a thicker cover. If the plywood is too thin to rest flush with the top of the seat rails, glue and nail strips of wood to the rabbets. To ensure adequate ventilation for the foam, bore $\frac{1}{2}$ in. holes 4 in. apart through the plywood base. Choose foam of a really firm density, and about 1 in. thick. A slight dome to the seat often improves the appearance, and gives a smooth line to the covering material. To achieve this, cut a piece of $\frac{1}{2}$ in. thick, firm-density foam, to about $2\frac{1}{2}$ in. smaller overall than the seat size. Taper off the edges and stick it centrally to the underside of the main foam slab. The larger piece should be about $\frac{1}{4}$ to $\frac{3}{8}$ in. larger overall than the seat. Taper back the edges, and fix with adhesive tape and tacks (see p. 148) to the sides of the frame. Cover with muslin and cut the covering material to size. Tack to the frame or plywood and finish the corners as shown right.

Marking out seat shape
Lay the frame on a suitable piece of rubber pin-core or polyurethane foam. Mark around with a ball-point pen.

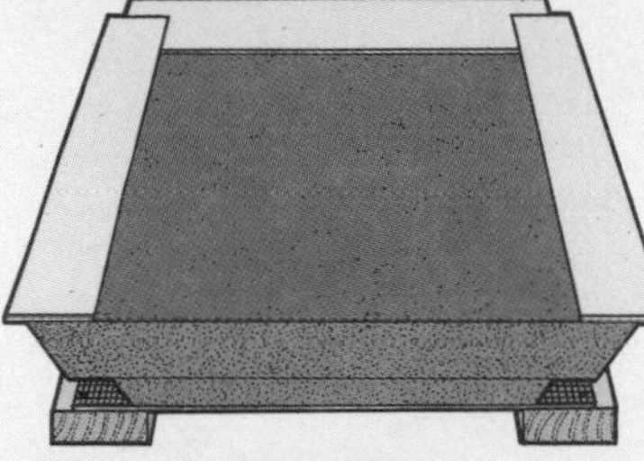

Taping down the seat
Make a slightly domed seat with two layers of foam (see p. 150) feathered back and taped to seat frame.

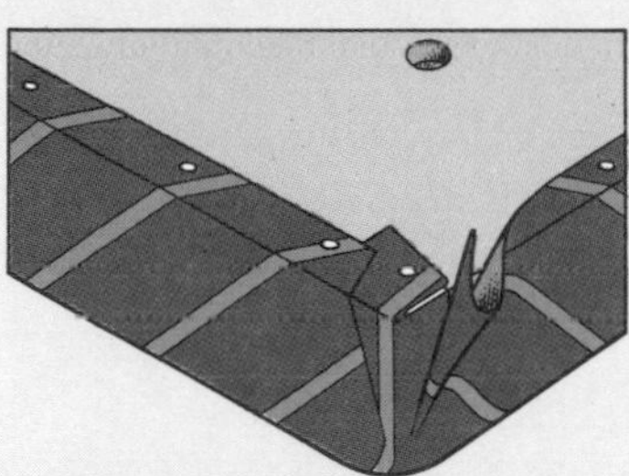

Finishing corners
Fold material under, if needed cut away some surplus, and tack to the underside of the frame as shown.

Repairing an easy chair

When the seat of a chair sags, the webbing has become stretched or torn and affected the coil springs. Remove the webbing and old tacks and then cut the twine ties to the springs. If the springs have forced their way through the burlap and the fiber stuffing, the chair will need complete reupholstering. But if the seat is otherwise repairable, simply re-web (see p. 149), and tie the springs back into position with a curved needle and strong twine. This is the tricky part of an otherwise easy job. You may have to sort out the springs and unlock them from each other, then stretch and tack the front crossways webs, fitting the springs in position as you go, and tying them down. Cut a new burlap or cambric dust panel and tack into place as previously described (see opposite page).

Reversible foam cushion and cover

To make an 18 in. square by 4 in. high cushion, cut two pieces of foam to 18x18 in. and 2 in. thick, and one piece 12x12 in. and $1\frac{1}{2}$ in. thick. Lightly fix the three pieces together with adhesive. Cut four firm foam strips 4 in. wide and $\frac{1}{2}$ in. thick. Two pieces should measure 18 in. the other two 19 in. Bond walls to sides. Cut cover material 18 in. square, plus $\frac{1}{2}$ in. for seams. Cut four strips 4 in. wide and 18 in. long for borders plus $\frac{1}{2}$ in. all around. Stitch all seams except the bottom back one, which you slip stitch together after the cushion has been inserted.

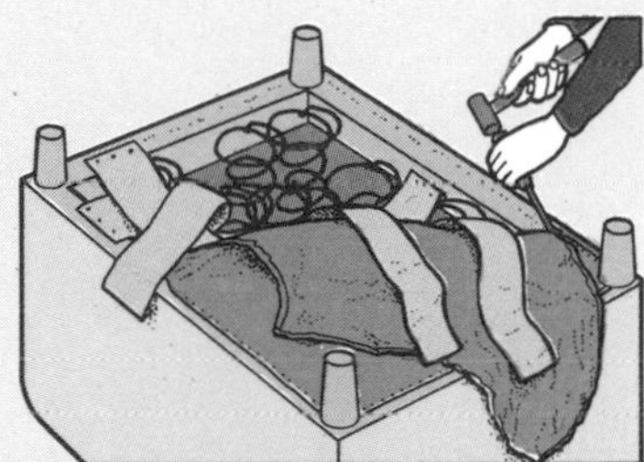

Stripping off old webbing
Remove the black cambric dust panel. Pry tacks from old webbing with a screwdriver and mallet, or tack remover.

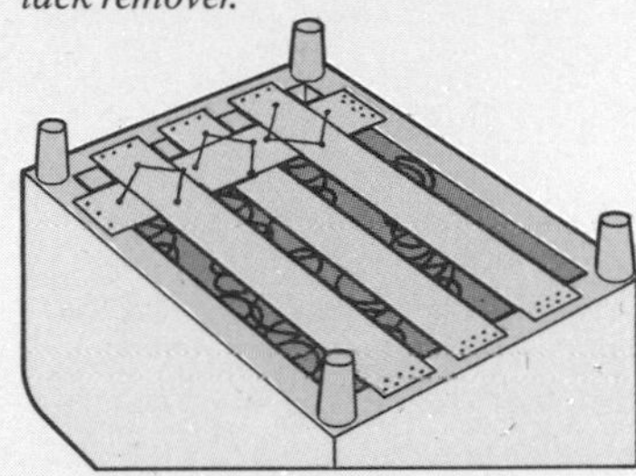

Renewing webbing, fitting springs
Cut springs free of ties. Re-web as previously described, with interlaced webs. Tie springs to webbing with twine.

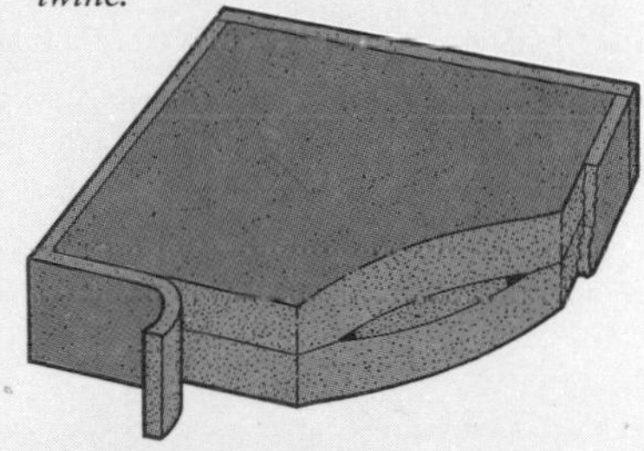

Reversible foam cushion
This domed cushion is made with a thin piece of foam sandwiched between two larger pieces.

Piping

Piping is used to cover seams in upholstery. Cut strips of material $1\frac{1}{4}$ to $1\frac{3}{4}$ in. wide, to cover the internal cording. If possible, cut the strips on the bias – that is, at 45° across the material. Use a piece of chalk to mark the position of the cord on the right side of the material **A.** Fold material right side out along the chalk line and press lightly. Pre-shrink the piping cord, then lay it along the crease **B.** Fold material over and pin into position Use a zipper foot and sew close to the cord, **C.**

To join two pieces with piping, such as sides and fronts, make a strip of piping the length of the edges to be joined. Lay pieces edge to edge with right sides together, and place corded strip between. Pin as close to the cord as possible and then machine-stitch together, **D.** Open the seam and press flat.

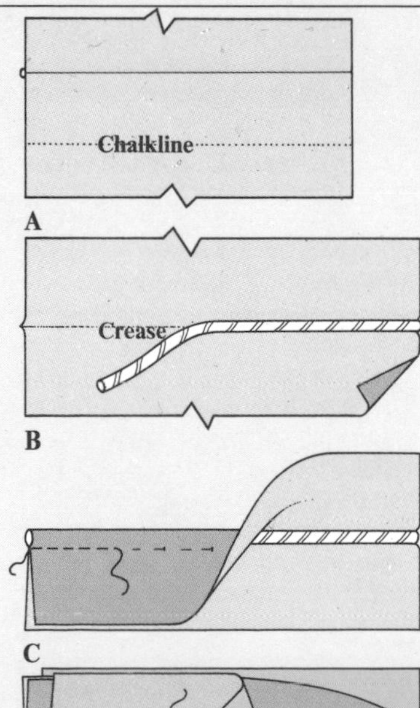

Piping an edge

Make a corded strip of required length. Lay the strip edge to edge on the face side of the material, pin into position, and sew as close as possible to the stitch line of the corded strip **E** using the zipper foot of the machine. Turn raw edges back to the reverse side of the material, so that the cording is on the edge. Press and hem edges into place **F.**

Binding an edge

Cut a strip on the straight grain of the material, $1\frac{1}{2}$ in. wide, and the length of the edge to be bound, plus $\frac{3}{4}$ in. With right sides together sew the binding to material turning under $\frac{3}{8}$ in. at each end, **G.** Fold the binding over the raw edge, turn under $\frac{1}{4}$ in. and hem along the stitch line, **H.**

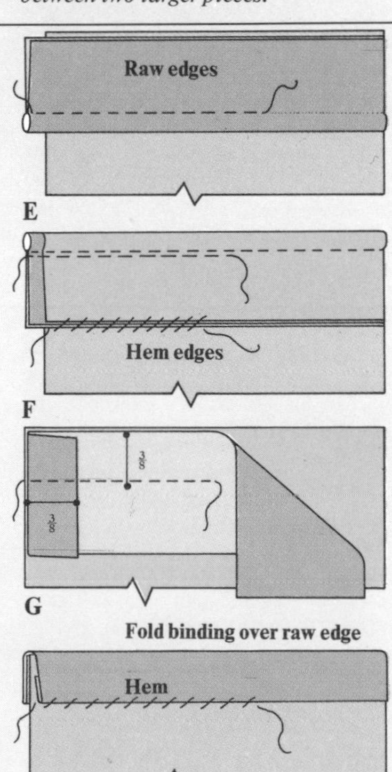

Electrical Equipment

Tools

With a limited selection of special tools and a simple understanding of wiring and fittings, a non-professional can tackle most domestic electrical jobs. All fittings are standardized to make installation and identification easy. Terminals and wires are color-coded, so that there will be no confusion when connecting one to the other. Electrical work, therefore, should be safe if you follow the correct procedures: always switch off the power before starting work, and check with a tester; use the correct tools for the particular job in hand – for example, use only a fuse puller for removing cartridge fuses; make proper connections and check them with a tester; fit grounding wires to those fittings and appliances that need them; periodically inspect wires for damage, and plugs for fractures. However, if there is a job that you are not sure about, call in a professional electrician.

The following selection of special tools will make D-I-Y work easier:

Voltage tester has a neon bulb connected to two wires with metal probes. Use it to check that the power is off before starting work, and whether the ground is functioning when the power is on.

Continuity tester is a pen-shaped unit containing a small battery. You use it when the power is off to check for breaks in circuits of fittings. The clip is attached to one point of the fitting, the probe makes contact with the other – if the bulb lights the circuit is working.

Pliers can be long-nosed pliers for manipulating wires in awkward spaces and for making loops, or else lineman's pliers for heavier work.

Multi-purpose tool is designed to cope with a variety of jobs; it can cut wire close to a wall as well as stripping wires of different gauges of their insulation in the calibrated holes. By means of crimping jaws it can fit solderless terminals to wires and can clean crop small bolts.

Utility knife is useful for cutting through thick insulation on cables.

Electrical screwdrivers have insulated handles and the longer shafts reach into tight spaces. Have two sizes of the slotted type and two sizes for cross-head screws.

Fuse puller or plastic pliers are used for pulling cartridge fuses.

Flashlight with a swivel-head can be stood or hung with the beam directed on the work.

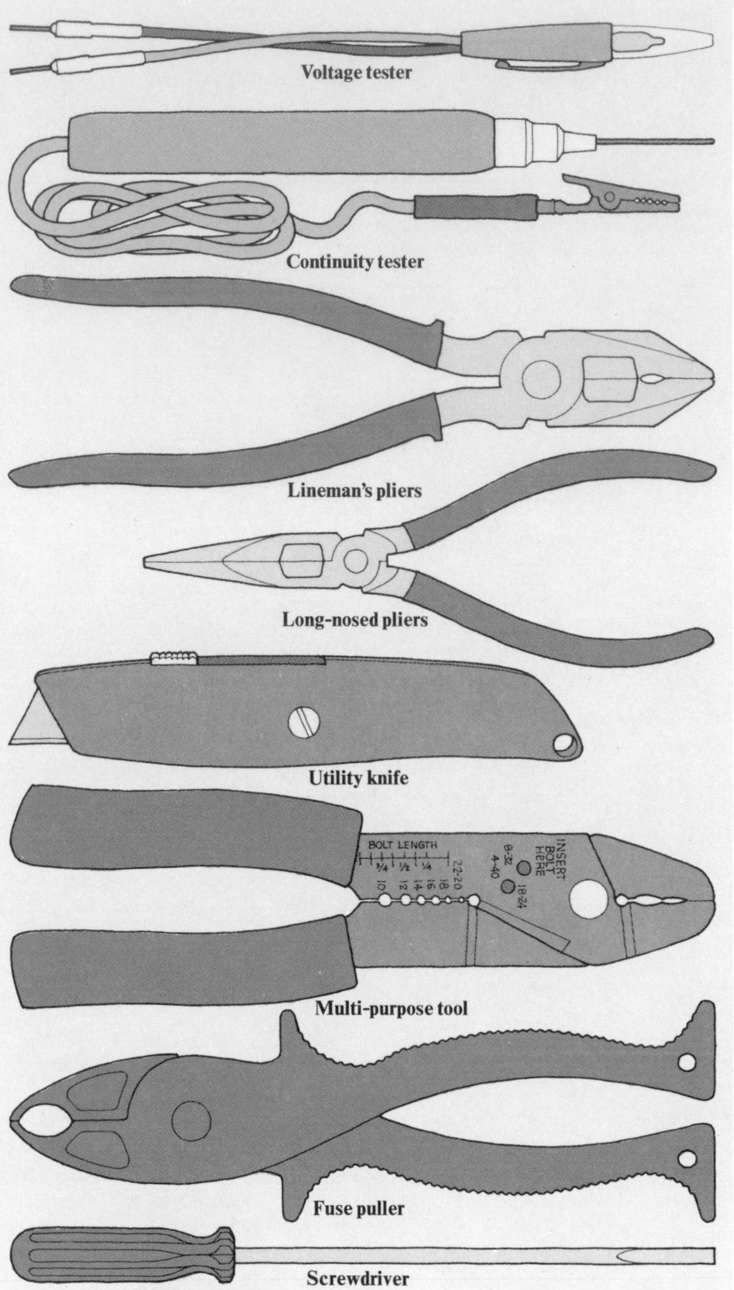

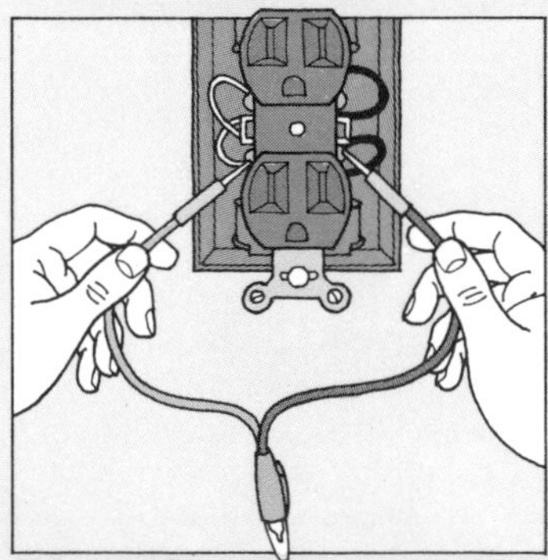

Using a voltage tester
To check whether power to a receptacle is off, place probes on bare ends of black and white wires at terminals. Test both sets of wires. Bulb should not light. If it does, remove fuse or switch off circuit breaker immediately.

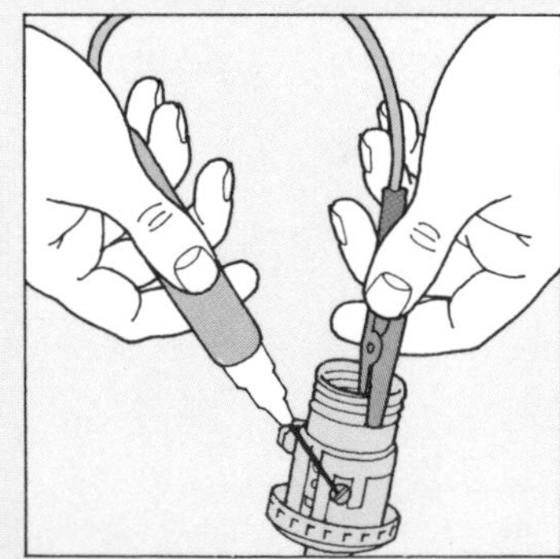

Using a continuity tester
To check whether a socket is faulty, clamp the alligator clip of continuity tester to the socket and place probe on terminal. Tester should light. If it does not, the socket has an open circuit and should be replaced.

Switching off the power
Before starting work, shut off the electricity at the service panel, either by pulling out the relevant fuse, or by switching off the circuit breaker. These are identified by the chart on the panel door.

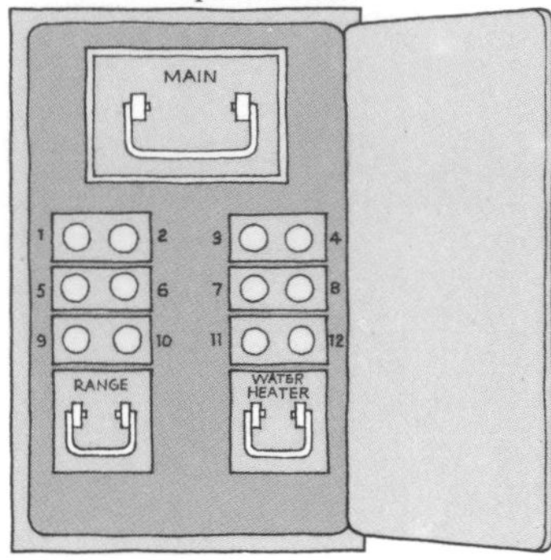

Main fuse box
Power is controlled through knife-blade fuses that protect the circuits. Removing the MAIN block shuts off all the power. Plug-type fuses below protect the individual circuits. The smaller blocks contain cartridge fuses for large appliances.

Circuit breaker box
The double switch at the top is the mains cut-off. Linked double breakers protect the heavy appliance circuits. Single switches protect the individual, 120 volt circuits.

Safety precautions
When identifying a fuse circuit, check by switching on the light and test the receptacles – they should not be live. By extracting one fuse only, the others can remain in use. If in doubt, extract the main cartridge to shut off power. When extracting fuses, grip the glass rim only, and do not touch anything with the other hand. Use the fuse puller for cartridge fuses. Wear rubber-soled shoes and stand on a dry floor.

Circuit breakers and fuses

Each circuit consists of a flow of electricity from the main supply. A device fitted in the circuit controls the flow, so that when the circuit is broken, the appliance shuts off. This safety device, a fuse or circuit breaker, protects against shock or fire, and automatically stops the flow of electricity when the current exceeds the circuit rating. The fuse burns out or "blows" when power becomes excessive. Fuses have to be replaced to renew the circuit; modern systems now have switches instead which are designed to open when overloaded and can be reset when the fault has been located. Amperage is marked on the fuse; never fit a higher rated fuse to overcome overloading.

Identifying faults

Trouble may be caused either by an overloaded circuit, which results if you use it to supply too many appliances at the same time, or by a short circuit brought about by damaged insulation or a loose terminal connection. In the latter case the hot wire comes in contact with the neutral wire, or a grounded box, and results in a sudden surge of power. A faulty circuit can be easily identified at the service panel. Plug fuses have a mica window showing a metal bar, if this is intact the circuit is in working order. If it is broken, a fault is present. A clear mica window indicates an overloaded circuit in which case the number of appliances on the circuit must be reduced. A charred mica window indicates a short circuit and the fault must be traced and corrected. With the circuit breaker system, a fault will throw the switch into an "off" position.

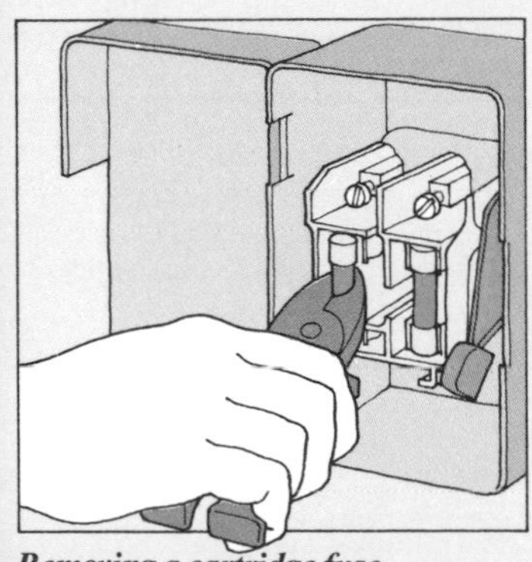

Removing a cartridge fuse
As cartridge fuses are often used for higher rated circuits, they should only be removed with the all-plastic fuse puller.

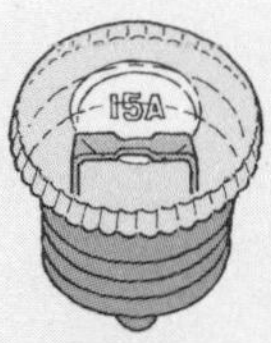

Plug fuses
are threaded for screw fixing. Grip only the knurled edge when removing. Faults are shown below a normal fuse.

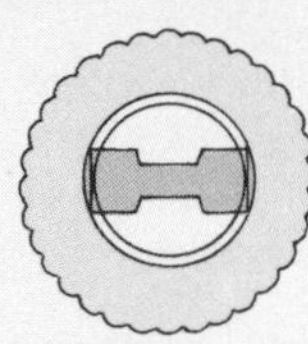

Normal

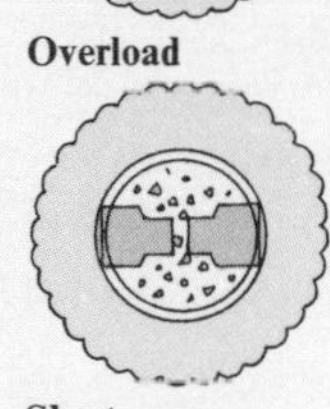

Overload

Short

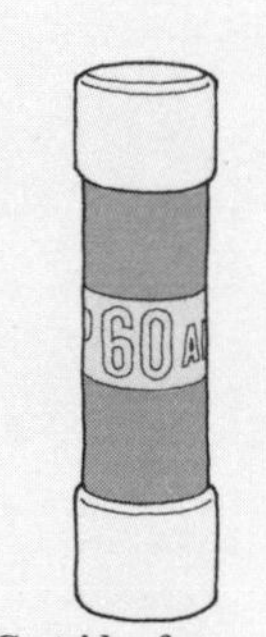

Cartridge fuses
are used to connect to the main supply and for higher rated circuits. Capped type carries up to 60 amps, knife-edge 60 and above.

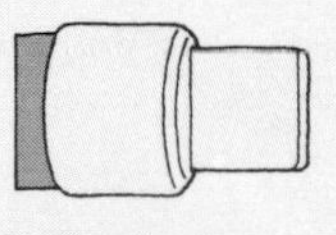

Knife-edge fuse

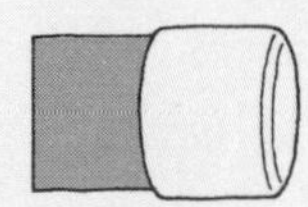

Capped fuse

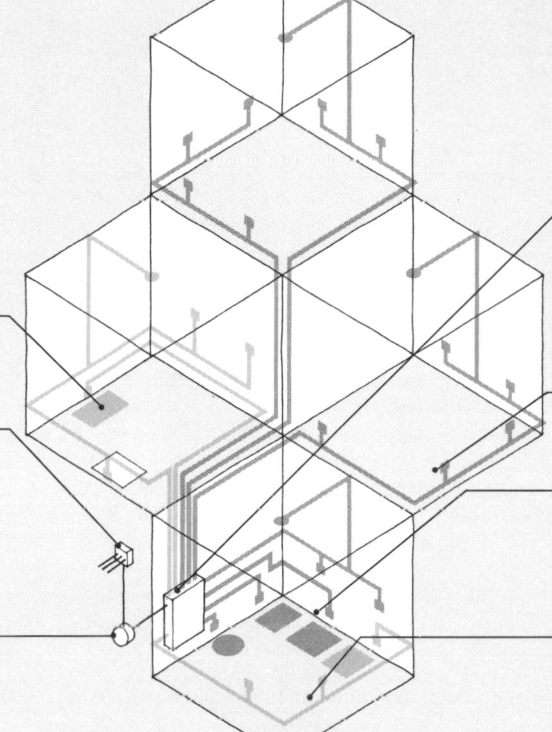

Separate circuits
Outlets in each room are ideally shared between two circuits to provide power while one is turned off.

Distribution
Not more than eight outlets should be fitted to one circuit, to prevent overloading.

240 volts, 50 amps
for electric range

Entrance head
receives supply from power plant. Modern systems have two 120V supplies to produce 240V

Electricity meter
measures the quantity of power consumed by the household

Service panel
receives the main supply and distributes it through individual circuits, which are protected by a fuse

120 volts, 15 amps
is for lamps, TV and other small appliances

240 volts, 30 amps
is for large appliances such as a water heater, air conditioner, clothes dryer

120 volts, 20 amps
takes medium-rated appliances such as a toaster or refrigerator

Wiring

Under the color-coded system the black wire, or "hot" color carries current under pressure; the white, or neutral wire completes the circuit. Wiring systems may carry currents of separate voltages. 120V circuits have a hot wire and a neutral wire, grounded at the service panel. Switches must not be fitted in the white wire of the circuit. 240V circuits have a cable carrying two 120V hot wires, one black the other red, plus a bare copper ground wire. Neutral is not used, the return flow alternates between the two hot wires. The ground wire is a safety measure.

Circuit wires are plastic covered; the size number relates to the diameter–the lower the number the greater the current carrying capacity. Do not exceed the maximum current rating expressed in amperes. Wire can be aluminum or copper. Use fixtures designed for aluminum circuits if your house is so wired. Cables combine from two to four wires in a tough outer casing. Armored BX cable is only suitable for indoor circuits under dry conditions; plastic cable is made in three types: NM, for dry indoor conditions; NMC, for damp indoor or above ground outdoor; UF, for below ground outdoors. Cords are flexible wires made of thin strands, insulated by plastic.

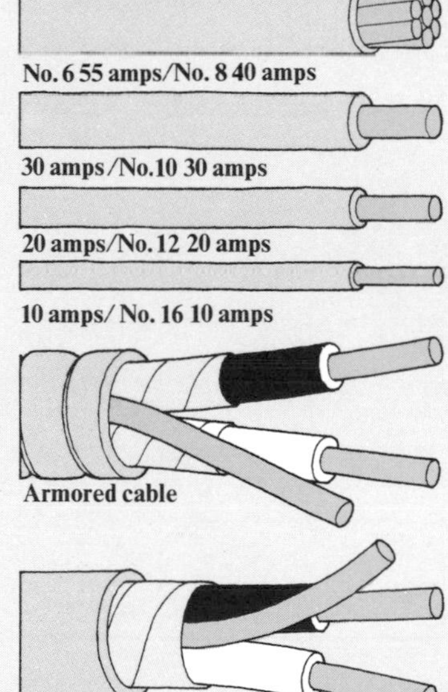

No. 6 55 amps/No. 8 40 amps

30 amps/No. 10 30 amps

20 amps/No. 12 20 amps

10 amps/ No. 16 10 amps

Armored cable

Plastic cable

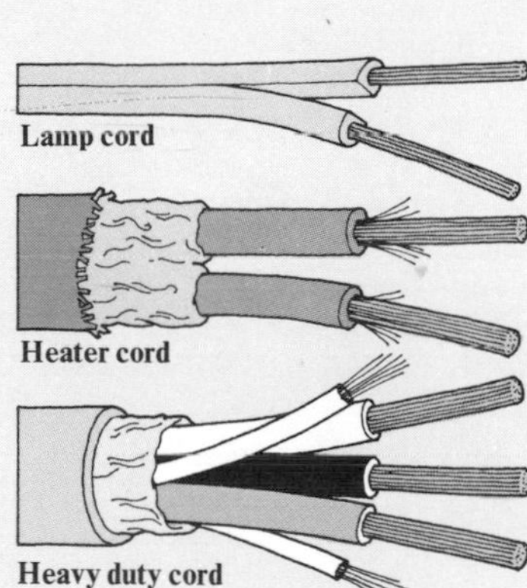

Lamp cord

Heater cord

Heavy duty cord

Wires
55-60 amps supply stoves and central air conditioners. 30 amps are for large appliances, dishwashers, etc. 20-15 amps for lighting, TV, and 10-7 amps for door bells.

Cables
Flexible armored BX cable has plastic-coated wires wrapped in paper, contained in metal spiral-wound sheathing. Plastic sheathed cables are cheaper and more flexible. Paper wrapping protects inner wires from abrasion. Both types have a bare ground wire.

Cords
Twin wire plastic cord is for lamps, radios and clocks; heater cord has wires embedded in asbestos sheath and braided fabric for toasters and irons. Heavy duty cord has a plastic covering and is used for power tools.

Electrical Repairs

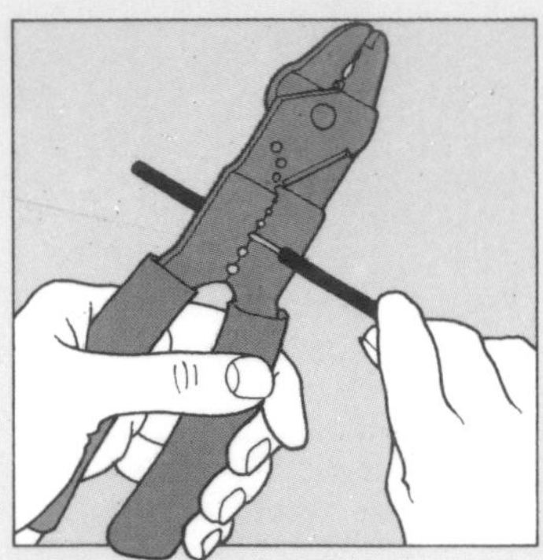

Stripping wires
Strip a cable by first removing the outer covering, according to the length of inner wire you wish to expose. Hold the cable on a steady surface, and cut along the center with a utility knife, taking care not to cut into the core insulation. Peel back the sheathing to the beginning of the cut, slice off the loose end and tear off the wrapping paper around the wires. Use a wire stripper to bare ends. Place the wire in the appropriate calibrated hole, close the tool over the wire and twist to make the cut. Now pull the wire through the tool to remove the insulation. Do not use a knife to cut the insulation, as this can damage the wire, and may cause an electrical fault as well.

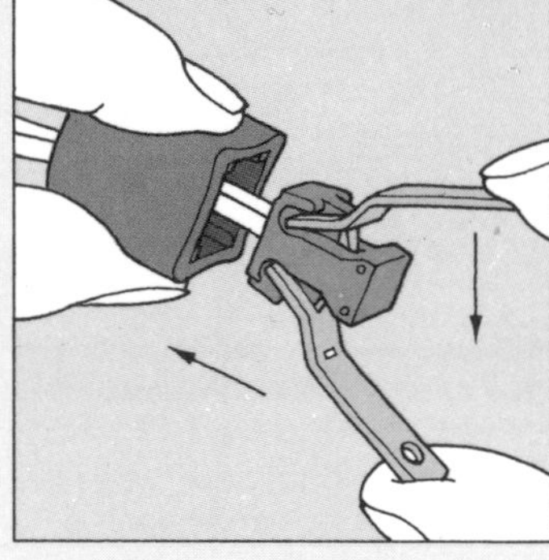

Fitting a quick clamp plug
With the quick clamp plug there is no need to strip the cord ends to bare the wire, you merely cut the end square with wire cutters; the wire should not project beyond the insulation. Push the end into the fitting as far as it will go, then close the clamp. This forces the wire on to spiked terminals that pierce the insulation. The type of plug illustrated above has hinged prongs that each puncture a wire. The outer casing, fitted over the cord first, is slid back over the plug body holding the prongs in place. These quick clamps are light-duty fittings, and should only be used with no. 18 cord. Never pull the plug from an outlet by the cord.

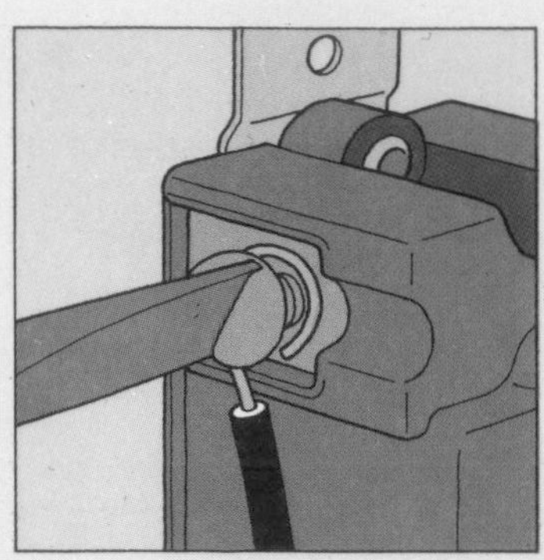

Connecting wires
Wire connections can be either fitted to terminals or spliced together. For screw terminals, bare sufficient wire to loop ¾ of the way around the terminal. Use nose pliers to grip the end. Loosen a terminal screw, hook the loop clockwise over the screw and tighten up – the turning action will close the loop.

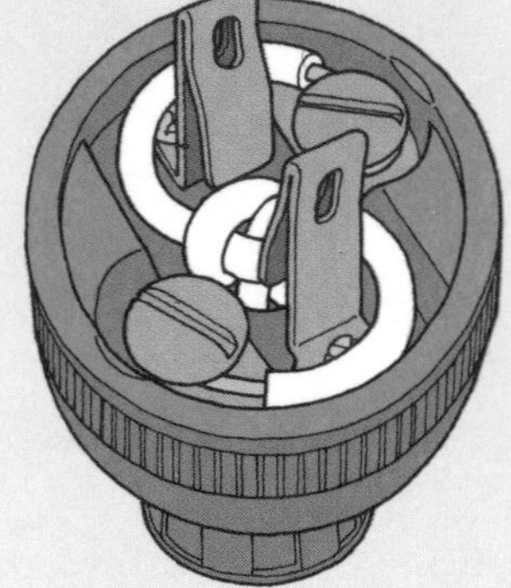

Wiring a plug
There is a wide variety of patterns for plugs and connectors taking two and three-core wire cords. Wires can be fitted to screw terminals or held by a quick clamp fitting where the terminals make contact by piercing the insulation. This type is only suitable for flat, twin-wire cords, where the plug is not regularly removed from the receptacle. To fit wires to screw terminals, pass the cord through the neck of the plug, and tie an underwriter's knot, as shown on the far right. Bare the ends, pull the cord back until the knot rests in the neck of the plug. Turn each wire around a prong, loop the ends clockwise around the screw terminal next to the prong, and tighten screws. The wires can be fitted to either terminal – wires and terminals are interchangeable. Fit the insulating disk over the prongs, if supplied, and press into the front of the plug. To fit heavy-duty cords, attach the coded wires to matching terminal screws. Press the insulation disk into place, then tighten the clamp on the cord.

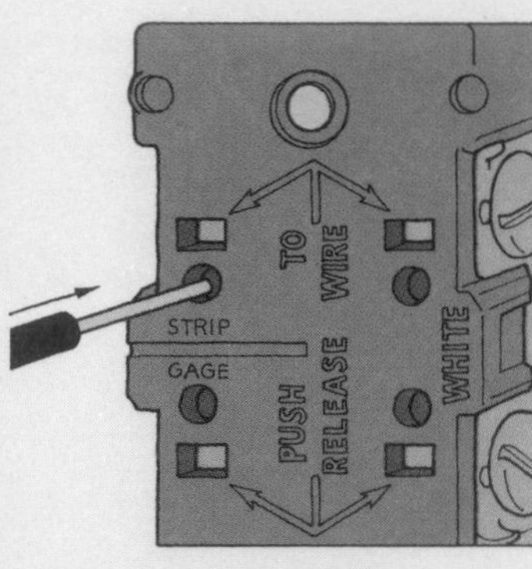

Wiring a plug-in terminal
Some switches and receptacles are made with two methods of attaching wires, either with conventional screw terminals, or holes in the back for inserting bare wires. To fit wires using this plug-in method, strip off the insulation to the length indicated by the strip gauge on the back of the receptacle – about ⅝ in. Push the wire into the round hole, up to the insulation; a built-in gripper will hold the wire in place.

Rewiring a lamp socket
Damaged lamp cords should be replaced with either a no. 16 or no. 18 twin-channel lamp cord; the length should be sufficient to reach the lamp without slack that will trail over the floor. Before starting, disconnect the plug from the outlet and remove the bulb. Release the outer shell from the socket. Press on the mark printed on the side, using a screwdriver to release the shell from the socket cap, pull it clear and lift off the insulating sleeve. Remove the socket by releasing the cord wires from the screw terminals. Untie the knot in the socket cap and pull the cord through – the cord may also be knotted in the lamp base. If the socket is faulty, it can now be replaced. A bent socket cap can be removed by releasing the set screw that secures it to the center pipe. To refit the socket and rewire the lamp, simply reverse the procedure using an underwriter's knot.

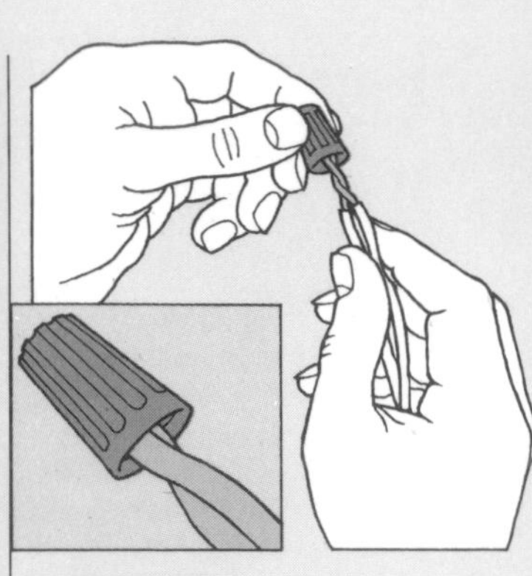

Splicing wires
Spliced wires should only be fitted in a metal junction box. Strip off about ¾ in. of insulation from the ends of wires. Place them side by side with their ends level, and twist them together with a pair of pliers. Fit a wire nut over the twisted end, turning in a clockwise direction to cover the bare ends completely. The copper spiral housed in the plastic cover binds the ends tightly. Wire nuts are made in various sizes to suit wire gauges.

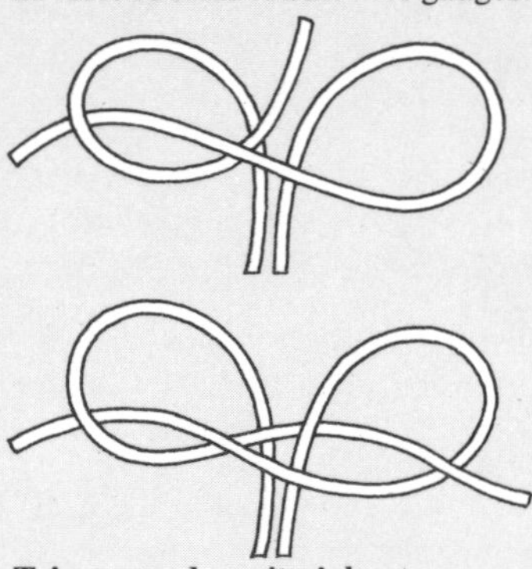

Tying an underwriter's knot
An underwriter's knot is necessary to protect wires from strain in case a plug is pulled from a socket by its cord. This knot should always be firmly pulled into the plug casing between the prongs.
First separate the two wires down the center seam about 2 in. Then tie them as shown above making two loops with each wire exiting through its partner's loop. Strip ½ in. of the insulation from each end and twist the strands together. Loop the ends and fix to the terminals. Pull the cord back until the knot nestles in the center of the socket.

Switches

Fitting a new switch
It is important that replacement switches are rated the same as the old ones. Check against the data stamped on the mounting strap which should carry the safety approval marks, having been tested by the Underwriter's Laboratories, Inc., shown as UND. LAB. INC. LIST., or the Canadian Standards Association (CSA) symbol. The maximum voltage and amperage the switch can control, such as 10 amps at 125 volts, is also shown. If your house has aluminum wires, be sure to use switches that carry an additional stamp CO. ALR.

Dismantling the switch
Turn off the power supply to the switch by removing the fuse or circuit breaker at the main electrical service panel and remove the cover plate. Single-pole switches are the most common type and are always fitted to the hot (black) side. On occasion it will be found that a white wire has been used which should be recorded as hot and marked with black tape at the end. Use a voltage tester to check the power is off. Place one probe on the grounded box and the other on each of the brass terminals in sequence. The tester should not glow in either case. If it does, the correct circuit will have to be identified at the service panel and shut off. Check again. Now unscrew the fixing screws holding the switch in the box. Pull the switch out, **A**, and locate the brass terminal screws. Loosen these and unhook the wire loops, using nose pliers if necessary, **B**.

Wiring systems
With the switch removed, you will be able to see the method of wiring. If there is only one cable entering the box, with one black wire and one white, both connected to the switch, this is known as a switch loop, **C**. In this case the white wire is hot and should be marked with black. The ground wire is fixed to the box screw. If two cables enter the box, it is known as middle-of-the-run wiring, **D**. This has two hot wires going to each terminal. The two white wires are neutral, connected with a wire nut. The two bare ones are ground wires, similarly connected but with the addition of a green insulated ground jumper wire, attached to the box grounding screw. Connect the hot wires to the new switch and replace by reversing disassembly procedure.

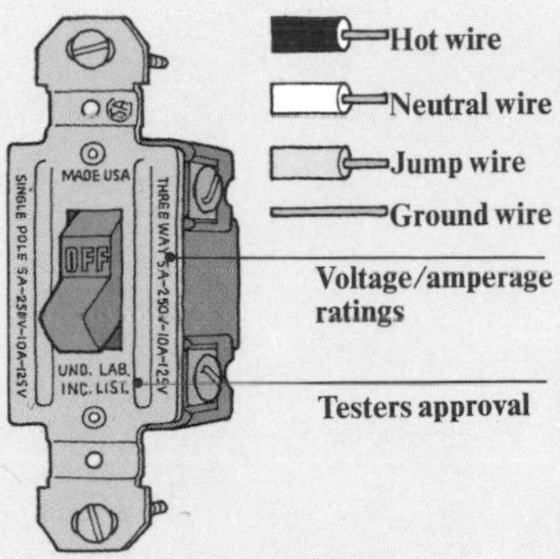

A

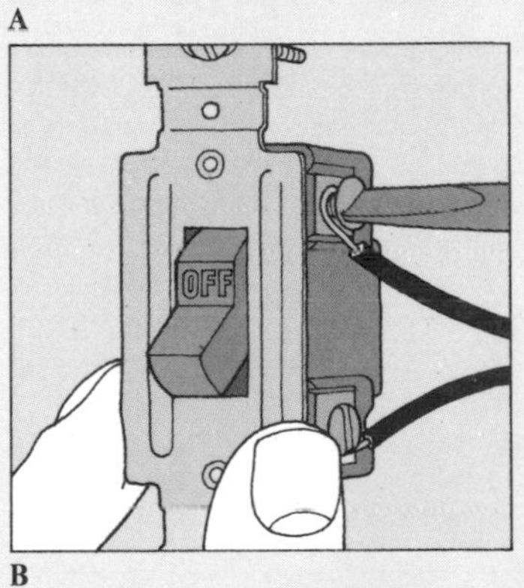

B

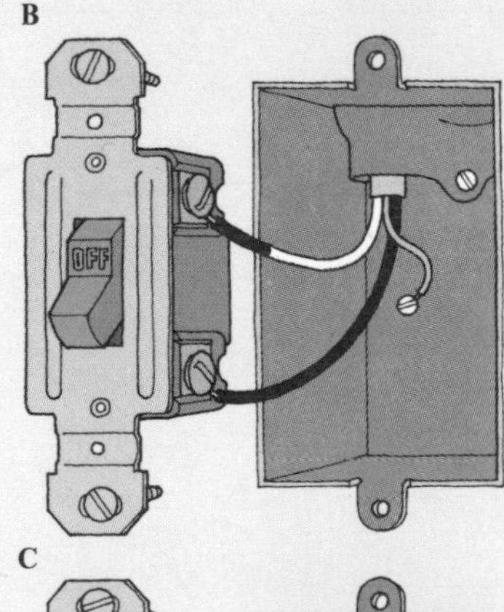

C

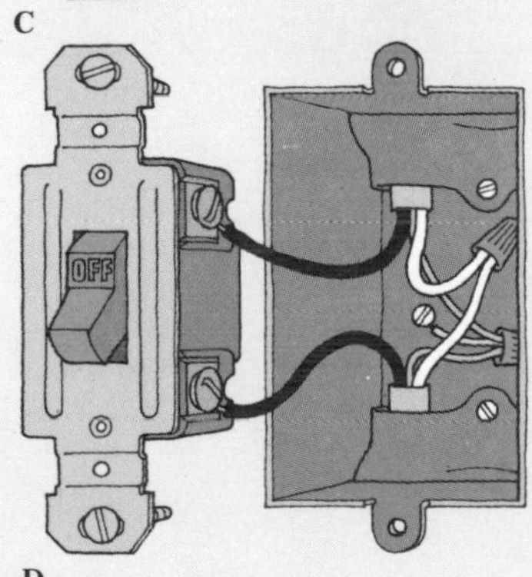

D

Outlets

Replacing a 120 volt outlet
A damaged outlet, or one that does not hold a plug firmly, should be replaced. If the problem is a slack plug, check this first, as it is less trouble to replace than a socket. Fitting a new receptacle is a straightforward job; in most cases it is a matter of connecting the existing wires to new terminals. Some old fixtures may be inadequately grounded – or not grounded at all – in which case you must fit insulated ground wires, known as "jumpers." Always use a three slot grounded receptacle as a replacement, and see that it conforms to the same voltage and amperage, marked on the body. The size and wire type may also be marked. This may be abbreviated CU or CU Clad only, meaning that copper or copper clad are suitable wires. For solid aluminum wire, the marks should read CO-ALR, CU-AL, or AL-CU.

Fitting
Shut off the power at the service panel. Remove the cover plate **A**, and check with a voltage tester. Unscrew the fixing screws attaching the receptacle to the box, and pull it clear. Slacken the terminal screws and remove the wires.

Middle-of-the-run-receptacles
These fall between the start and end of a circuit run. You will see a cable bringing power into the box, and another carrying it out **B**. Connect each black wire to a brass terminal, and each white wire to a silver terminal. A green insulated ground jumper wire should be attached to the green ground terminal, and one fitted to the back of the box; both should be fitted to the bare ground wires and capped with a wire nut. Circuits made with armored cable, but with no ground wire, have the black and white wires fitted in the same way, but it will be necessary to attach a green jumper wire directly between the back of the box and the ground terminal on the receptacle, for both middle-of-the-run, **C**, and end-of-the-run methods.

End-of-the-run receptacles
These have one cable only entering the box, **D**. If it is the plastic, three-wire cable, attach the single black wire to a brass terminal, and the white wire to a silver terminal. Green jumper wires about 4 in. long should be fitted to the back of the box, and the green terminal screw, joined to the bare ground wire with a nut.

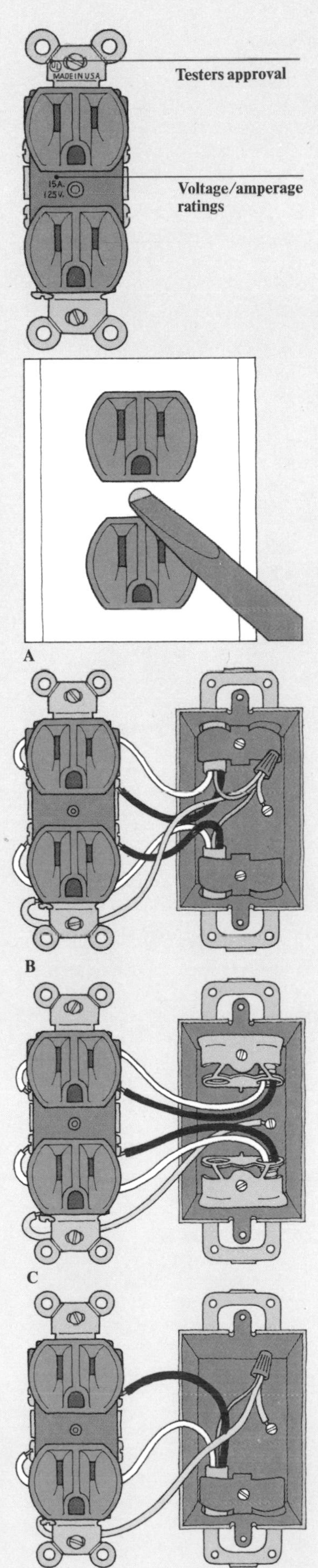

A
B
C
D

Plumbing Equipment

Plumbing Systems

The only work likely to be done by the home-owner is the care and maintenance of faucets, emergency repairs to pipes, and the unclogging of drains. Before attempting any work, you should familiarize yourself with the plumbing system in your home. The drawing on the right shows a typical system for a two-storey house with basement. The system can be divided in two parts: the incoming fresh water, and the outgoing waste water. The cold mains supply feeds water under pressure through small bore pipes to every fixture or appliance in the house. Similarly, the heated water is circulated to outlets, usually in parallel with cold supply. Drainage is kept separate to prevent contamination. Traps are fitted in the pipe runs, and have removable plugs for cleaning. The system should also have plugs at the elbows, between the branch wastes and the horizontal runs, so that you can remove blockages from pipes.

Pipes and tubing

Pipe runs can be made of galvanized steel, copper or plastic. Galvanized steel is found mostly in older homes in sizes $\frac{1}{2}$ in., $\frac{3}{4}$ in. or 1 in. It is tough and durable. Because it is very rigid it must be threaded for jointing. Copper tubing is made in three types – soft, flexible and hard. It has thinner walls than steel and the most common sizes are $\frac{3}{8}$ in., $\frac{1}{2}$ in. and $\frac{3}{4}$ in. One inch or larger hard grade is used for underground work. Plastic piping is relatively new and popular due to its lightweight and easy cutting qualities, but check local building codes before using. It is simple to install and will not corrode. It is made from PVC and CPVC although only the latter takes hot water.

Tools

A 12-in. pipe wrench, with jaws that open to about $1\frac{1}{2}$ in. is useful for gripping all square and hexagonal nuts. A strap wrench has a heavy webbing strap to loop around pipe, for gripping and turning the pipe. Basin wrenches have a head that swings through 180° for reaching joints under sinks. A hand-held tube cutter cuts pipes and a flaring tool is necessary for making solderless compression joints. Add to this basic selection of tools a soldering iron, wire brushes, emery paper, screwdrivers and a hacksaw.

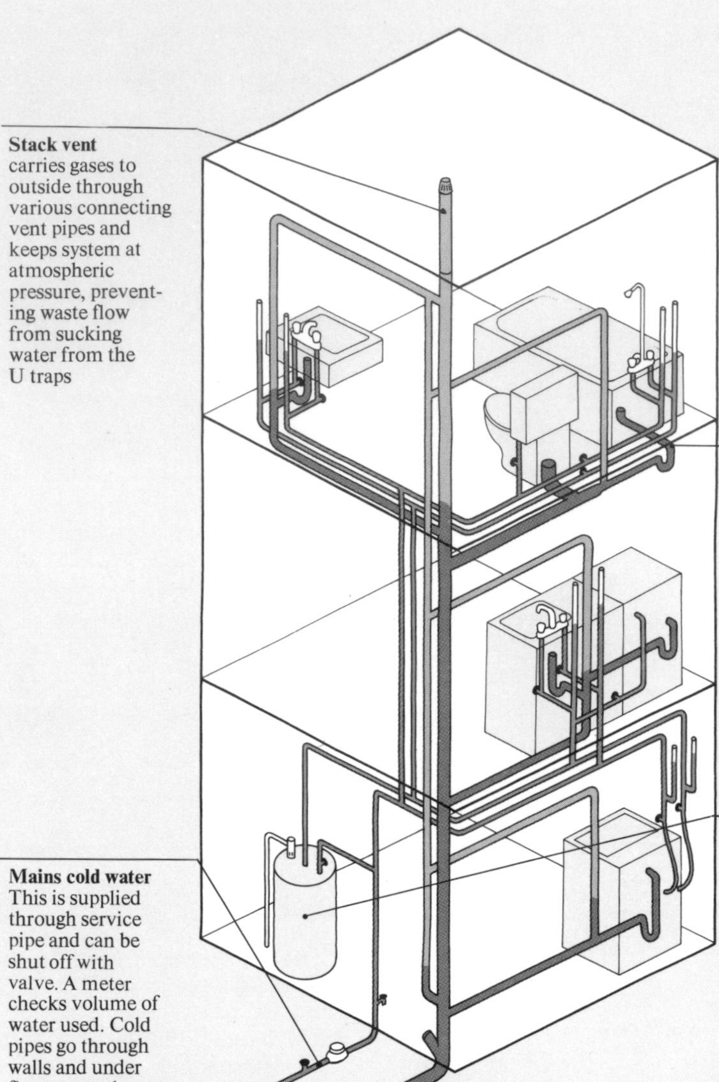

Stack vent carries gases to outside through various connecting vent pipes and keeps system at atmospheric pressure, preventing waste flow from sucking water from the U traps

Mains cold water This is supplied through service pipe and can be shut off with valve. A meter checks volume of water used. Cold pipes go through walls and under floors to outlets

Shower trap Drain system has U traps at each fixture to contain a water seal, preventing sewer gases entering house. Drain pipes slope to let water run off

Water heater Cold water is fed through water heater. Hot water runs parallel with cold supply. Water under pressure goes through small bore pipes, connected to faucets. Pipe runs usually have right angle or T joints

Turning off water The system should have supplementary shutoff valves to the main one. Keep a chart handy, so you can locate the appropriate valve

Main shutoff valve

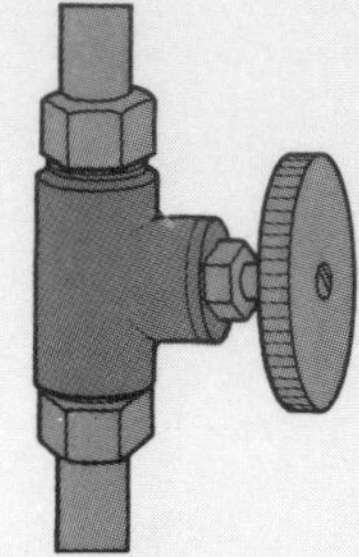

Turn handles clockwise to stop the flow.

Lavatory valves

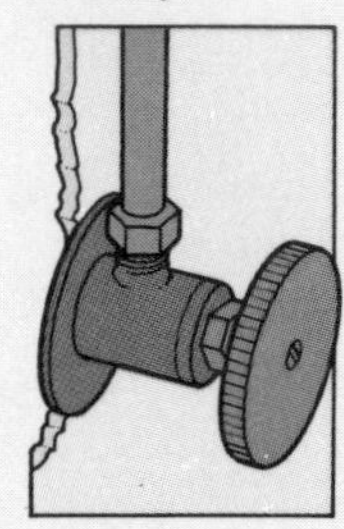

Your sink probably has valves controlling the faucets, which are located underneath. Turn these off before repairing a faucet.

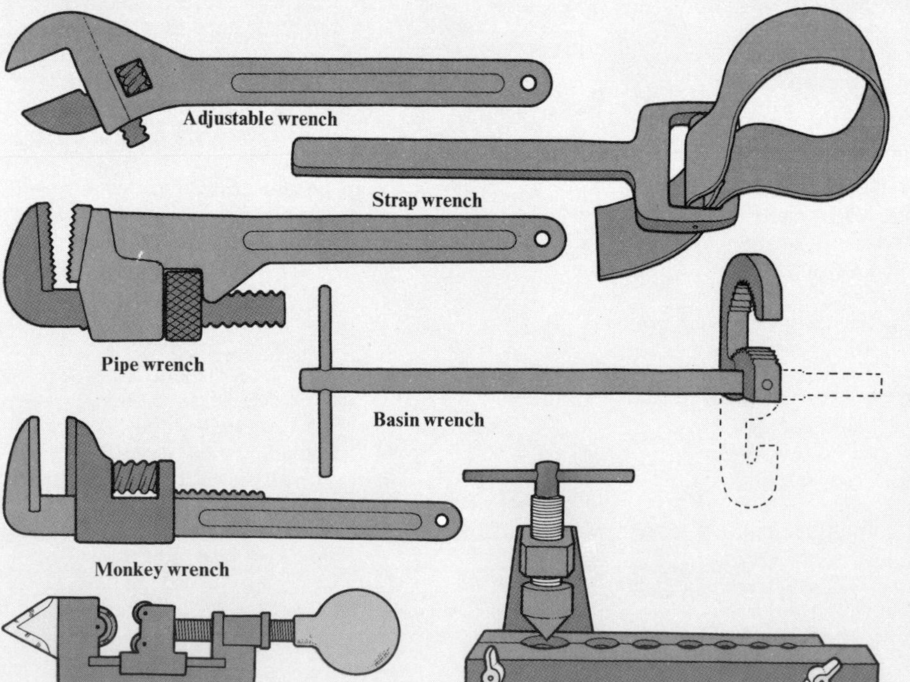

Wrenches The pipe wrench has adjustable, toothed jaws to grip a round section. Monkey and adjustable wrenches have smooth jaws for gripping nuts on fixtures. Strap wrench is used for gripping easily-damaged pipes, such as brass tubing. Basin wrench removes fixture nuts in awkward places.

Cutting tool Tube cutters have a cutting wheel and rollers to cradle pipes, these are adjustable to take different sizes.

Flaring tool Split die block with holes flares pipe ends to take tapered fittings.

Repairs

Fittings

Pipes are joined together with fittings. Special insulating fittings are made for joining steel pipe to lead or copper pipe. Adaptors connect pipes of different size and type.

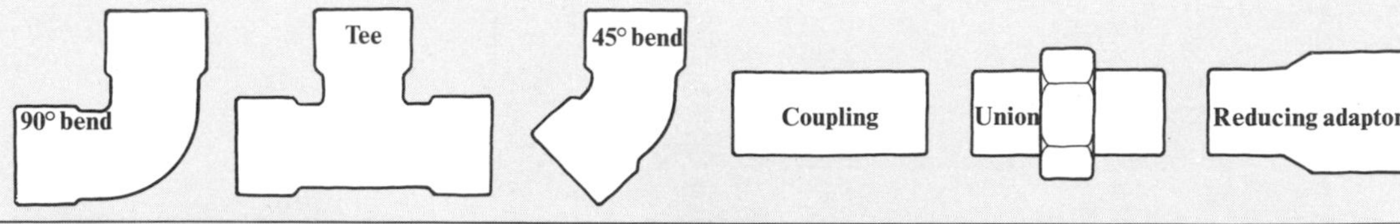

Connecting galvanized steel pipe

If you need to replace a length of pipe, first cut off the supply at the nearest valve. Your plumbing supplier will match up the parts for the new length, consisting of two pipes and a union joint. Before fitting together, apply oakum rope or pipe-joint sealing compound or tape around threads. Screw fittings together with pipe wrenches. If there is a slight gap, screw pipes out slightly to bring joint together.

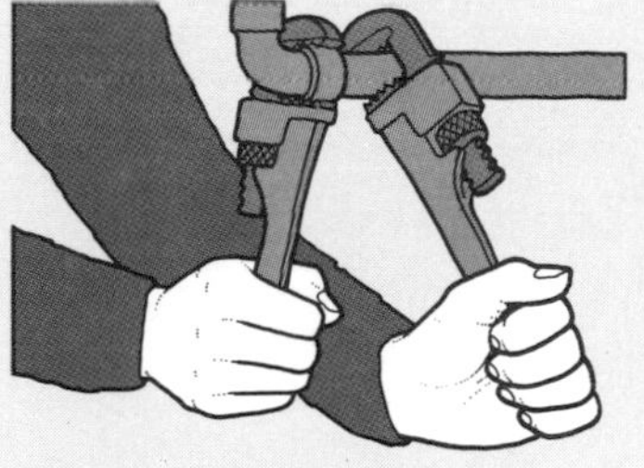

Disconnecting threaded pipe
Cut through the pipe with a hacksaw. Unscrew each half, using two wrenches, for pipe and fitting.

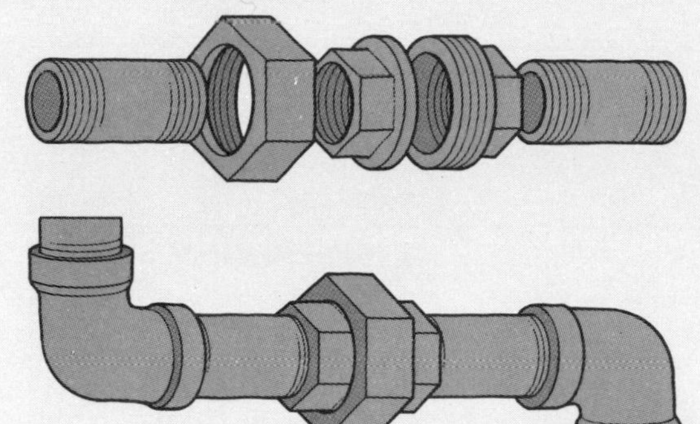

Assembling a new section
Two new pipes, the same metal and length as the old pipe, are joined by a union.

Connecting up
Pipes are threaded on to old fittings, then joined with new union fittings and ring nut. Seal before assembling.

Soldering joints

Neat permanent joints are easy to make, using solder-type fittings for both rigid and flexible tubing. The key to a good joint is the thorough cleaning of parts to be soldered. Follow the steps shown right for the correct procedure. Always heat the work to melt the solder, never melt the solder with the flame. Test the temperature of the solder by removing flame and touching joint with solder; when it melts it is hot enough. Use plumber's solder, and hold it to the hot joint. The solder will fill the joint to make a complete seal. Solder all joints while fitting is still hot (reheating will soften the joint already made, and weaken the seal).

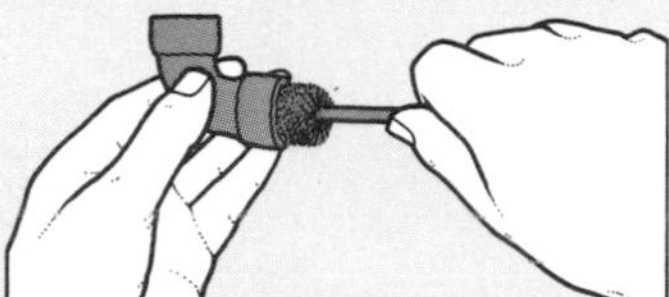

Cleaning the fitting
Use a wire brush to clean joints before applying flux and solder to ensure a watertight fit.

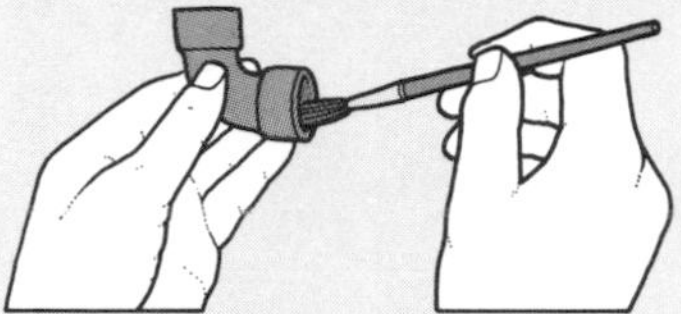

Applying flux
Immediately after cleaning, apply a thin film of paste flux with a brush, working well into fitting.

Cleaning the tube
Use fine emery cloth or steel wool to produce a shiny surface. See that no burrs remain from cutting.

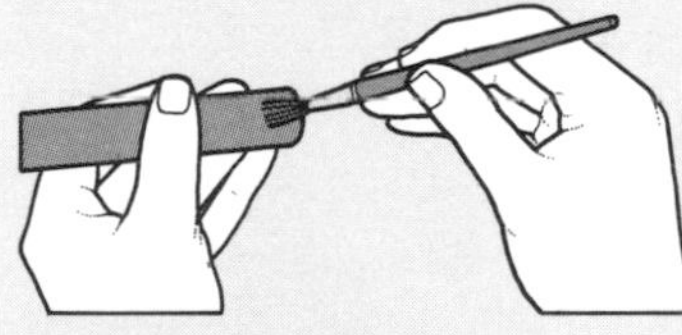

Applying flux to tube
Brush flux on tube. Slot tube and fitting together, and twist to spread flux evenly. Wipe off excess with rag.

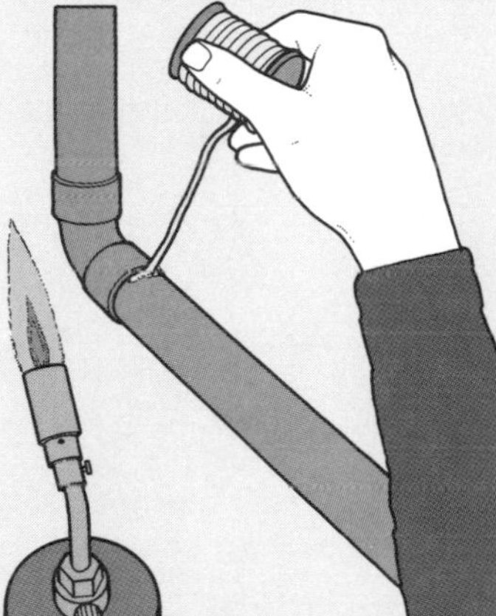

Soldering the joint
Heat fitting with propane torch, moving flame evenly over the surface. Apply solder to the joint when hot.

Making non-soldered joints

Flexible copper tube can be joined with soldered, flare, or compression joints. When cutting tube, take care not to dent or distort the end. Make the flare as shown right. Compression joints are made by different means: fit the flange nut on the tube, followed by a compression ring. Push the tube into the fitting, and hand-tighten the nut on to the thread. Then tighten with wrenches to compress ring.

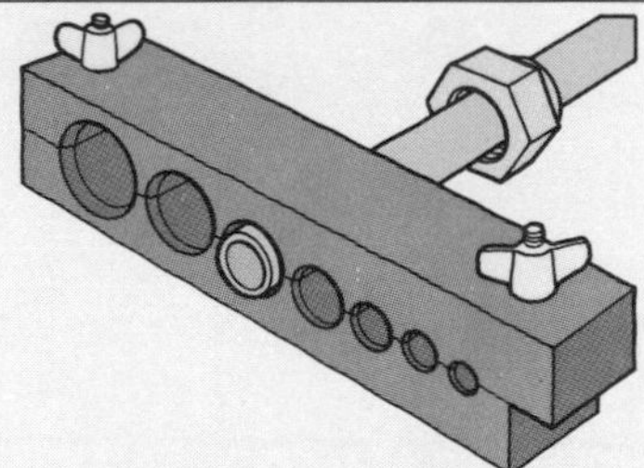

Choosing correct die
Place fitting flange nut over tube. Clamp tube in correct size hole in die block.

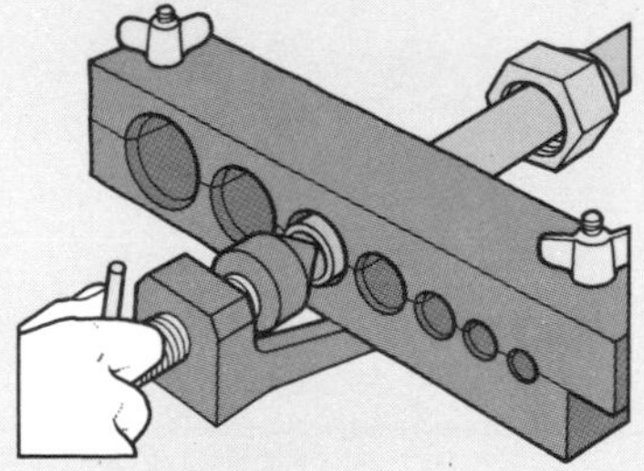

Flaring the end
Fit yoke assembly to end of tube, and tighten down the screw. This will spread the tube end to a flare.

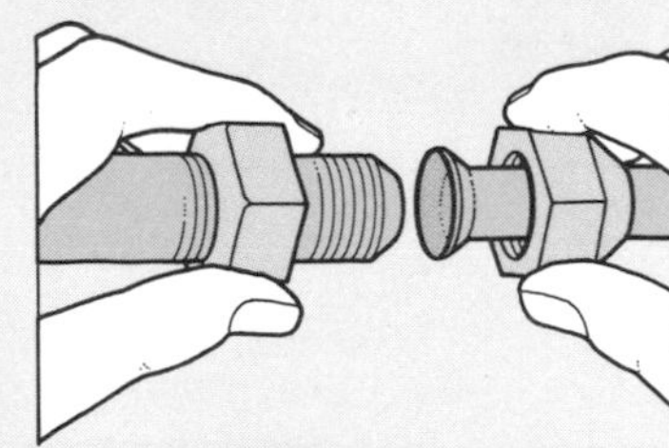

Assembling the joint
Remove the die, and fit the tapered end of the fitting into the flare. Screw nut on to fitting and tighten.

Joining plastic pipes

Plastic pipes are joined to fittings using a solvent cement. Cut the tube with a hacksaw. Remove burrs with sandpaper, and trim to a bevel around the outside edge, so the tube slips into the fitting to make a snug join. Apply the cement as shown, and assemble the parts. Leave the joint to set at least an hour, or preferably overnight, before running the water.

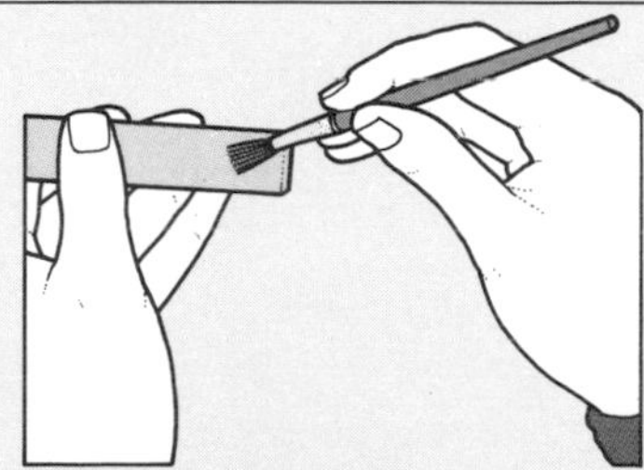

Cementing pipe
See that pipe and fitting are a snug fit. Apply cement to the end of the pipe with a brush.

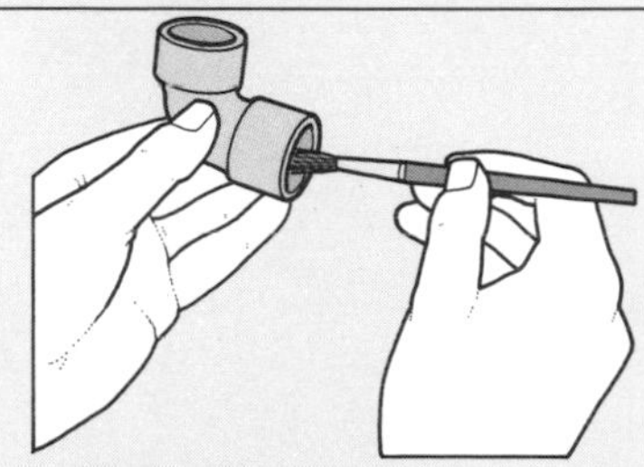

Applying cement to elbow
Quickly apply solvent cement to the elbow fitting; the cement dries rapidly.

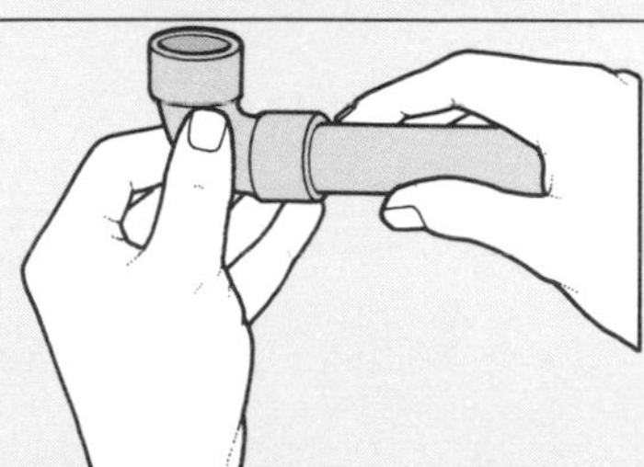

Fitting parts together
Twist pipe in the fitting to ensure an even spread of cement. Line of cement should show around the joint.

Plumbing Repairs

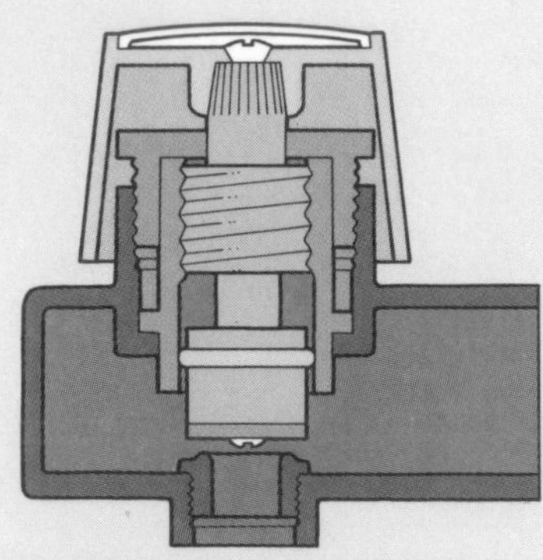

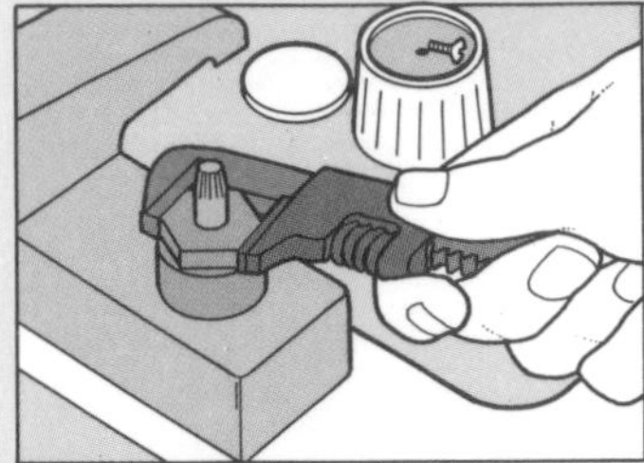

Dismantling a faucet
Use an open-jaw wrench to remove the locking nut or packing nut, located under the handle or bonnet.

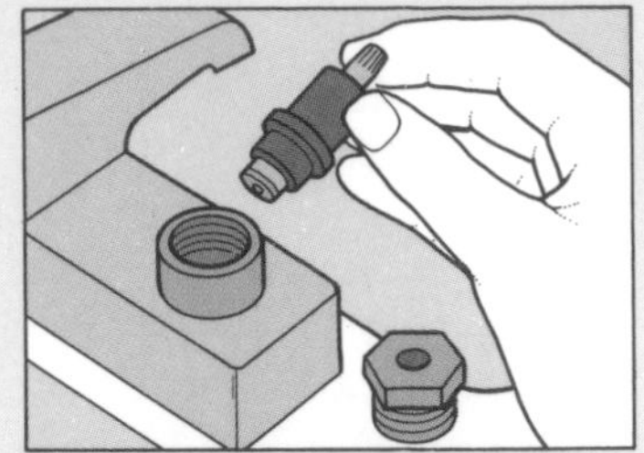

Removing stem assembly
Take out the stem and unscrew the washer retaining screw or nut.

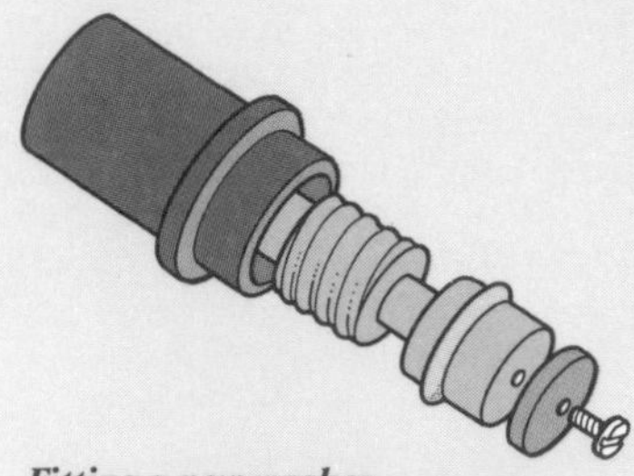

Fitting a new washer
Fit a new washer of the correct size, then re-assemble the faucet. Keep a supply of spare washers.

Leaking stem faucet
If a rubber washer wears out, you will have to replace it with a new washer of the same size. Begin by removing the handle or bonnet and follow the diagrams, above right. If the faucet leak is due to a packing washer or "O" ring, the water will creep up the stem and escape by the handle. Remedy the fault by tightening the washer, or replacing it. If the "O" ring is worn, fit a new one, first smearing grease on the stem.

Inspecting the faucet seat
Check the seat. If it has worn it can be smoothed down or fitted with a replacement part.

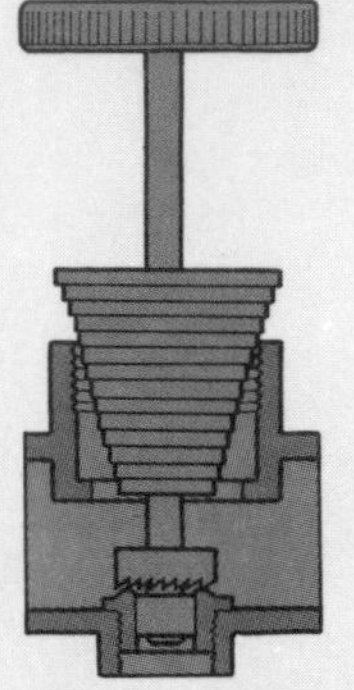

Seat dressing tool
Fit an appropriate cutter for the seat. Screw cone until secure and the tool is vertical. Now turn the knob with a few firm strokes. Do not press too hard. When the action is smooth, remove the tool and check the seat with your finger. Repeat if necessary.

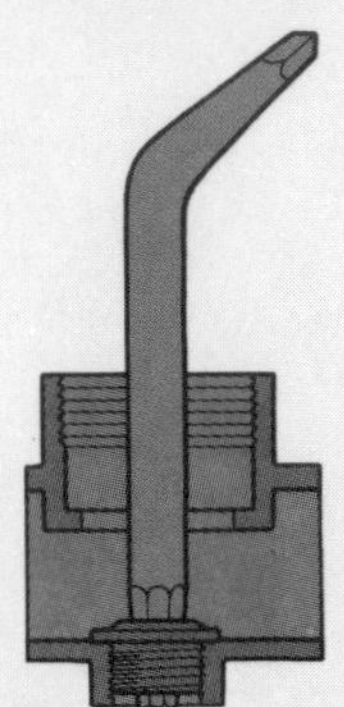

Seat replacement
You will need a seat wrench that matches your faucet opening. Plug into the seat and unscrew to remove it. If you cannot fish it out with the wrench, use a thin pair of pliers. Give the new seat a wipe with joint compound before fitting.

Leaking pipes
If a pipe springs a leak, turn off the supply at the nearest valve. Determine the type of leak - split pipe, a hole, or leaking joint. A split requires the use of a pipe clamp of appropriate size while a small hole needs a hose clip. Epoxy paste is used for slow leaks around fittings although the joint must be completely dry before the paste can be applied to it.

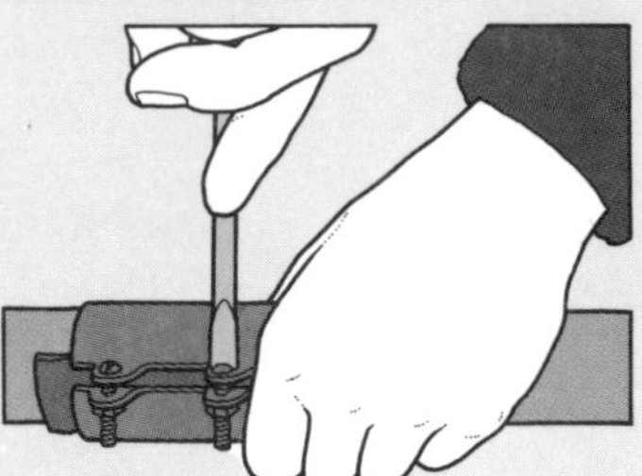

Fitting a pipe clamp
If a pipe is split, apply a pipe clamp tightly, trapping the rubber pad to seal the leak.

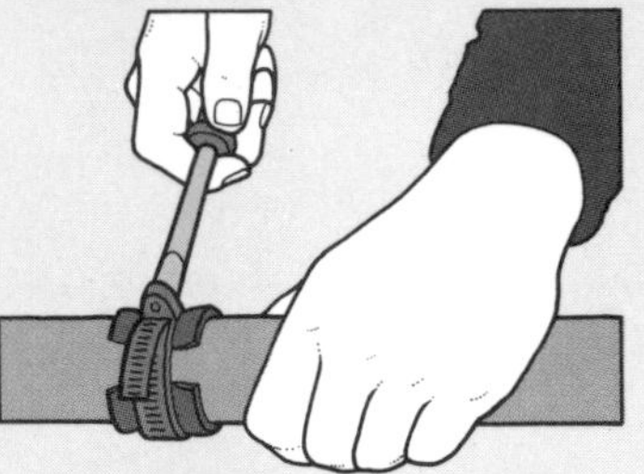

Using a hose clip
To repair a small hole in a pipe, use a hose clip around a rubber pad. Screw clip tightly to compress pad.

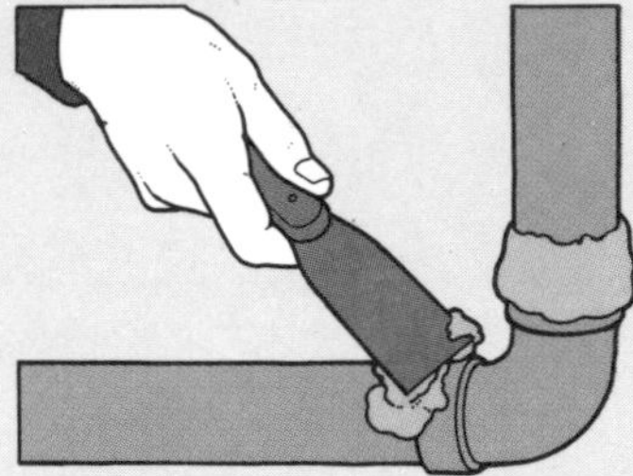

Sealing with epoxy paste
Slow leaks around fittings in a low-pressure system can be sealed with epoxy paste when dry.

Frozen pipes
Pipes often freeze in cold weather and methods of thawing include boiling water poured over rags, heating the pipe with an appliance such as a hair dryer, or using a propane torch. Keep faucet open to allow water to escape. Place a protective sheet of asbestos behind the pipe, and pass the torch flame over the pipe. The safest method is to use electric heating cables which plug into a normal outlet.

Thawing a pipe
Wrap old cloth or rags around the frozen pipe and pour boiling water over them.

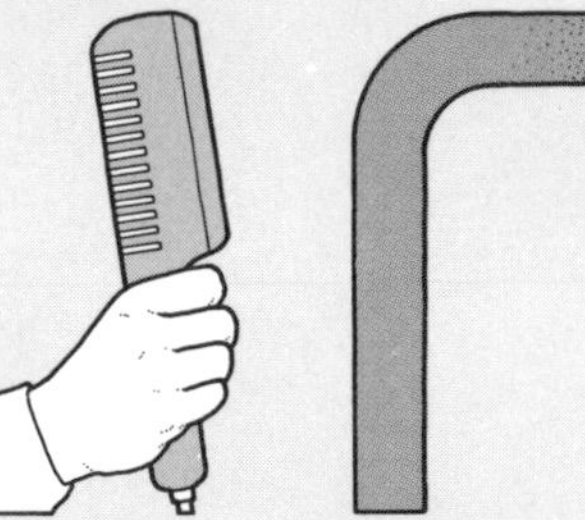

Heating with an appliance
If the pipe is in a recess and boiling water can't be used try a hair dryer or an iron.

Preventive electric cables
Pipes likely to freeze should be wrapped with electric heating cable and covered in insulation.

Blockages
Clogged drains may be cleaned with a brand name drain cleaner, a rubber plunger or a drain and trap auger. To operate the auger, remove the trap plug and push the flexible cable with the auger tip into the pipe. Turn the handle clockwise while alternately pushing and retarding the auger. As the handle reaches the mouth of the pipe, fasten it further back along the cable.

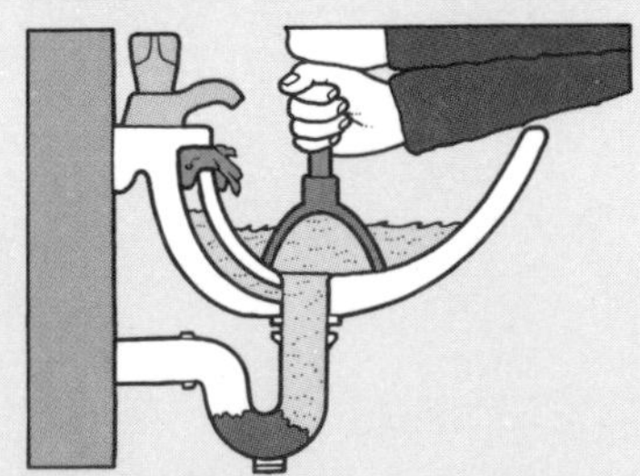

Using a plunger
Fill bowl to cover plunger cup. Block overflow opening with rag. Work plunger with a pumping action.

Clearing the trap
If blockage persists, remove the plug under the U bend of the trap and clear out debris.

Using an auger
If blockage is lower in the pipe, insert an auger. Crank the handle and push until blockage shifts.

Heating Systems

Convection
Currents of air rise carrying heat.

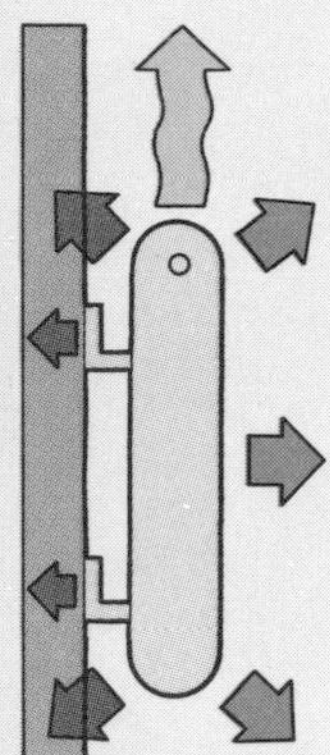

Conduction
Transmission of heat is by contact.

Radiation
Heat rays from one source are transmitted into space.

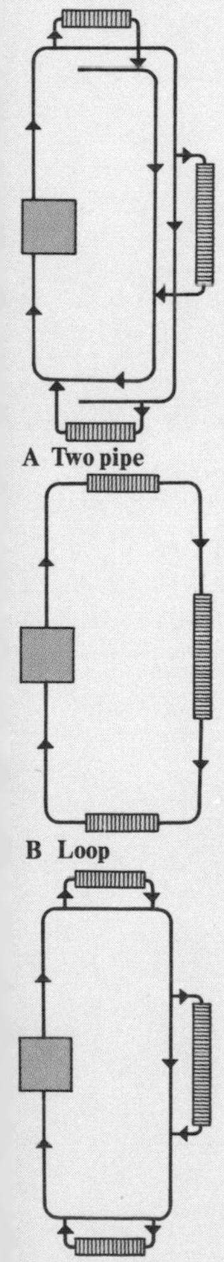

Home Heating

Heat is transmitted in three ways: *radiation* is the flow of heat rays from a heater out into the room. The warmth you feel when standing in front of a fire is known as radiant heat; *convection* is the effect caused when air is heated; warmed air rises and bears the heat with it. On meeting cooler surfaces or cool air, it gives up its heat, cools and settles; *conduction* is the transference of heat by contact. Hot water running through a water jacket or radiator transmits its heat through the metal by conduction – the heat then passes out into the air. The actual source of heat can be generated by three different systems: hot water, warm air, or electricity.

Hot water system

Heating is provided by hot water circulated through pipe runs in the floor and dispersed in the rooms by radiators or convectors. The area remains warm even after the thermostat has automatically shut down the boiler. Mains water is supplied to a central boiler, where it is passed through boiler sections, which are then heated so that the water temperature is between 180° and 240°. Some systems work on the gravity principle: water expands when heated, takes up more space in relation to its weight, and so becomes lighter. This heated water rises to flow into radiators, giving off a percentage of its heat. The water then returns to the boiler. The system relies on the difference in temperature for the rate of flow. A forced hot water system has a circulator pump that forces water through the pipes – also known as a hydronic system. One version has a pipe to carry the water from the boiler, and another to return it, **A**. This two pipe system is recommended for large houses, as the water flow is then more efficient. An economical installation for small houses is the loop system, **B**, where the flow is in one continuous circuit. The disadvantage is that you shut off the whole system if one radiator is closed. With the one pipe system, **C**, this problem is avoided, as the radiators are connected by branch supply pipes to the main supply pipe; shutting off one radiator will not affect the others. A further refinement is the zone system, where zone circuits are controlled by a thermostat, so that different areas can run at different temperatures.

Warm air systems

Warm air systems which utilize air ducts below the floor to circulate warm air about the house are of two types. Gravity-type systems work on the principle that hot air rises while cold air sinks, thus bringing about a circulation of air. The forced air system uses a blower to push the air around. The latter requires a lower furnace temperature and therefore uses less fuel. The central furnace can be fired by gas, oil, coal or electricity. The blown air is directed over a heated jacket or exchanger, where it is warmed by hot gases from the burner passing through on the inside. These gases are carried away through the stack to the chimney. The flow then goes through a warm air plenum connected to a series of supply ducts fitted in the floors and walls, entering the room through wall-mounted grilles called registers. The rate of flow can be controlled either by louvers in the ducts, or at the registers. The registers for most warm air systems are placed in or just above the baseboards, while others may be fitted to the floor. In both cases you must keep them free from dust, otherwise the flow will be restricted. Furnaces usually have a filter in the ducting; replace the disposable type when needed, and clean the washable type. The efficiency of your heating system may also be impaired by heavy drapes or furniture placed across the registers.

Electric systems

Electricity can be used to power a water heater for a hydronic system or a warm air furnace. Electric boilers are usually more compact than other fueled types, and do not need a flue, which means that installation is easier as the boiler can be positioned in any convenient space and at less expense. Another form of electric powered heating is the radiant type fitted in ceilings. Here, the principle is that a low-resistance cable becomes hot when a current is passed through it. Cables are embedded in the plaster or sandwiched between plaster boards to form a large, radiant heater. Ceiling units containing the cables can be installed in your home, the panels being fixed over the ceilings; embedded cables are usually installed only in new buildings. With an electrical system, little in the way of maintenance is needed, and it is economical to install but it is expensive to run.

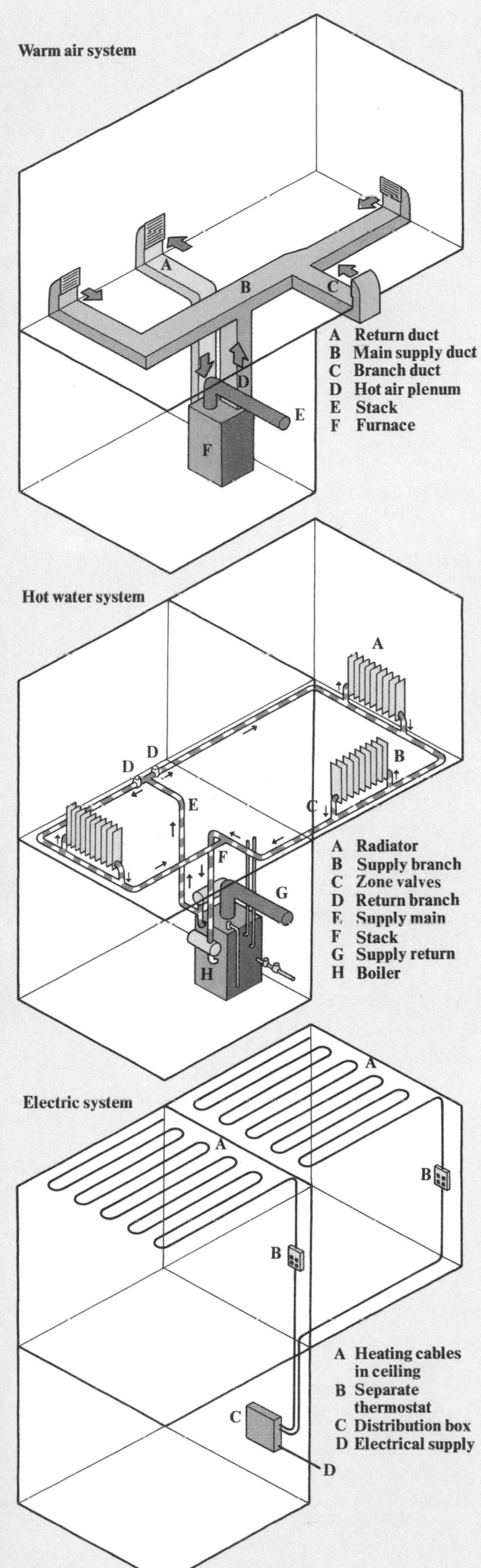

Insulation & Air Conditioning

Insulation

A heated interior needs insulation in order to maintain a consistent atmosphere. Insulating materials are available in four basic types: flexible, rigid, loose-fill, or foil. They all act as heat barriers. The first three work by preventing the passage of heat by means of a thick layer of material containing tiny air pockets. The foil type works by reflecting the heat rays; some insulation products use both types.

Flexible insulation

Most flexible materials contain fiberglass in the form of blankets or batts. Blankets are made as continuous rolls, in widths to fit the standard stud and joist spaces, and in thicknesses of 1 in. to 3 in. The fiberglass is usually faced with paper on one or both sides, or with one side of foil. Batt insulation is made in sections from 15 in. to 23 in. wide, and from 24 in. to 48 in. long. Thickness varies from 2 in. to 6 in. Both types usually have a flange of about 1 in. width along the long edges, for stapling to joists or studs.

Rigid types

These may be constructed of shredded, reconstituted wood, or of foamed polystyrene plastic. The wood type is a lightweight or low density panel made in small tile size, or in large 4ft x 10ft sheets, and in thicknesses of $\frac{1}{2}$ in. to 1 in. Foamed polystyrene is rigid but very light and easily worked. Thin sheets can be cut with a knife, thick sheets with a saw. It is ideal for the insulation of ducting – just bond with suitable adhesive.

Loose-fill and reflective insulation

A barrier can be formed by loose particles of various materials, such as mineral wool, polystyrene beads or vermiculite. These can be spread over surfaces to any required thickness, or injected into wall cavities with a blower, a method suitable for older buildings. Reflective insulation, in corrugated paper backed form or sheets, depends on the reflective quality of aluminum foil when used as a heat or vapor barrier.

Vapor barriers

These prevent the moist warm air penetrating the insulation; it may be an integral part of the material or can be a separate film stapled over the surface. The barrier should always face the warm side and should be carefully fitted as a continuous membrane around plumbing, heat ducts or electrical fittings.

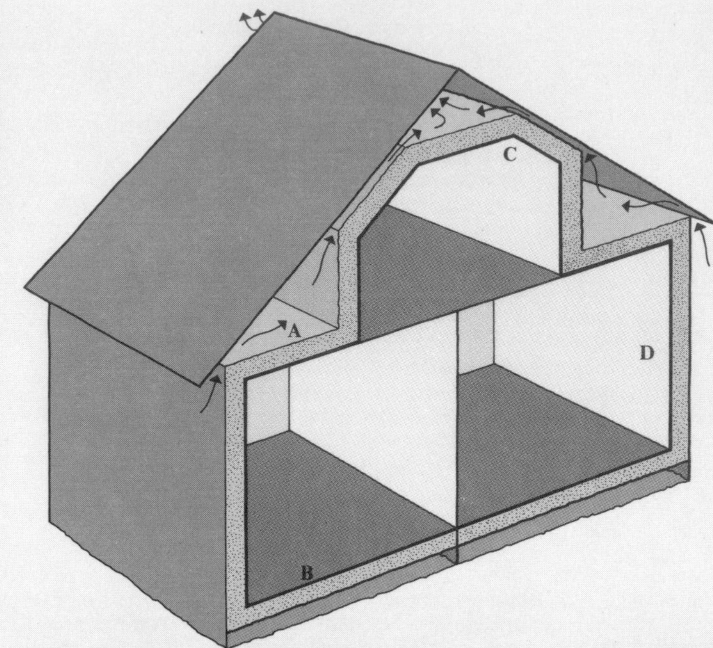

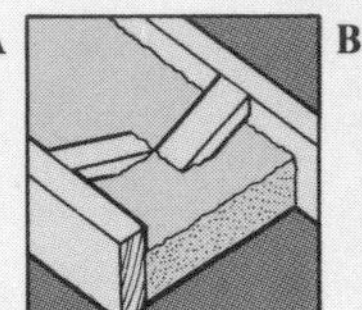

A Vapor barrier faces down
Use loose-fill 6 in. deep.

B Vapor barrier faces up
Use $3\frac{1}{2}$ in. with wire mesh.

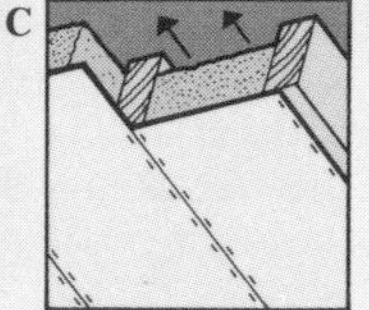

C Vapor barrier faces inside
Use $3\frac{1}{2}$ in. blanket fixed front or side.

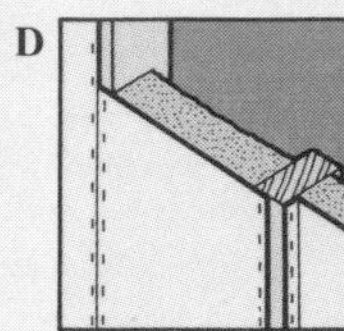

D Vapor barrier faces outside
Use 6 in. batts and leave air gap.

Air Conditioning

Air conditioning units are of two kinds: integral, ducted units built into the central heating system, and individual units. Simply described they work by cooling warm room air with a refrigerant carried in evaporator coils, and then return recycled air back into the room, via blower fans. In this process air conditioners not only cool the air, they dehumidify it too. Water vapor condenses on the evaporator coils to drain down through the machine, where a fan disperses it through the condenser coils. Diagrams of both unit types are shown, right.

Installation

Individual units can be fitted in a window opening, or through a wall. Small units can be bought with a self-assembly installation kit. These generally have a frame that fixes the front of the unit in the window opening while the remainder is cantilevered out over the sill. The unit is centered in the opening, the gap each side fitted with screw-on panels. The sash has a seal, closed on the unit assembly, and all other gaps are sealed with gaskets. The service cord is connected to a grounded receptacle. The wall-fitted type of unit is contained in a sleeve, inserted into the wall. Central air conditioners can be linked to a central heating furnace, utilizing existing ducting, or it can be a separate unit with its own ducts. Central installations are usually more efficient and less costly to run than individual units and they are quieter. They are, however, initially more expensive to buy and install when no existing ducting is available. The work should only be done by an expert.

Operation and maintenance

Individual units are simple to operate, and most have a temperature control, dual-speed fan and adjustable air flow. Check the filters regularly – these are located behind the front of the unit. Remove the front panel, check with the handbook, then vacuum and wash the plastic or metal type filter in warm water. Renew the disposable type. While the grille is off, vacuum the coils to remove any debris. Central air conditioners should also have their filters inspected at monthly intervals.

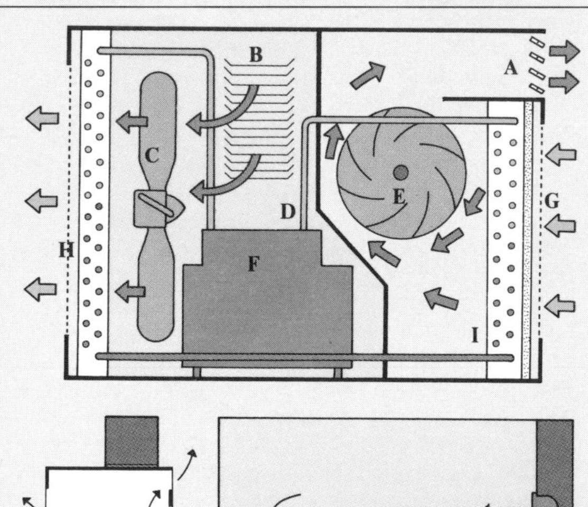

Individual units

A Adjustable louvers
B Side vents
C Fan
D Refrigerant tube
E Blower
F Compressor
G Air filter
H Condenser coils
I Evaporator coils

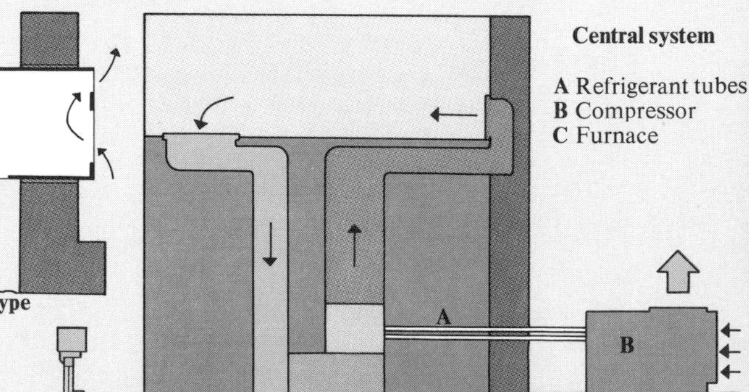

Central system

A Refrigerant tubes
B Compressor
C Furnace

Cooking & Eating Areas

Planning Your Kitchen

Basic considerations

The average domestic kitchen is the busiest area in most homes. It is the most frequently occupied, frequently used room. Because a modern kitchen can be expensive to equip, it is wise to give a great deal of care and thought to its planning and the siting of appliances. The main advantage of labor-saving devices is that they free you to do other things, and an initial expense can prove very economical in the future; freezers, garbage disposal units and dishwashers all have an important place in the well-run modern kitchen.

The first thing to do in planning a kitchen is to consider the position of the basic elements: sink, stove and refrigerator. Much depends on the shape and size of the room, of course. This, and the ground you have to cover between the elements as you work dictates their place in relation to cabinets, worktops and other domestic appliances. As we shall see, these elements are the main features of the "work triangle", where various areas of activity are grouped together in such a way as to form the most sensible and convenient arrangement possible.

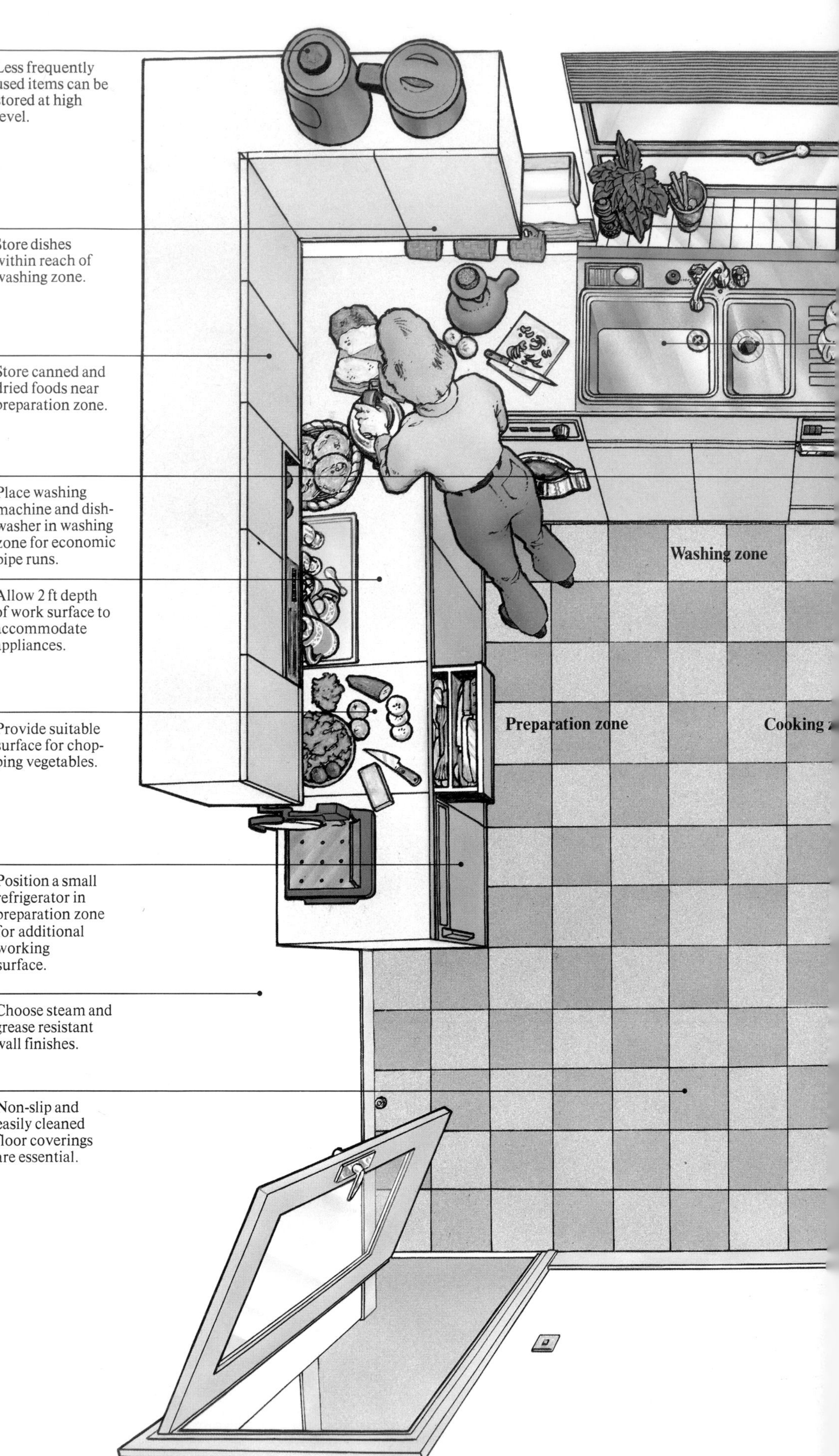

A carefully-planned, U-shaped kitchen. The sink, in its traditional place under the window, where it is supplied with good natural light and is economical to plumb, forms the apex of the "work triangle". The preparation zone and cooking zone are evenly positioned at each corner, in order to reduce fatigue and the risk of accidents.

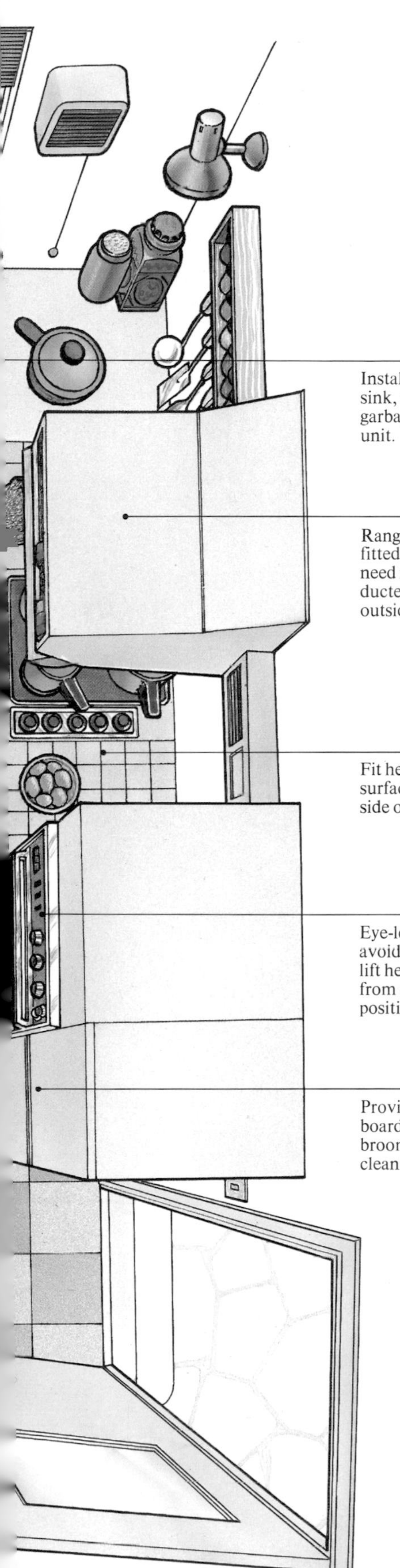

Install double sink, one with garbage disposal unit.

Range hoods fitted with filters need not be ducted to the outside.

Fit heatproof surface either side of range.

Eye-level oven avoids having to lift heavy dishes from crouched position.

Provide tall cupboard for storing brooms and cleaning materials.

1

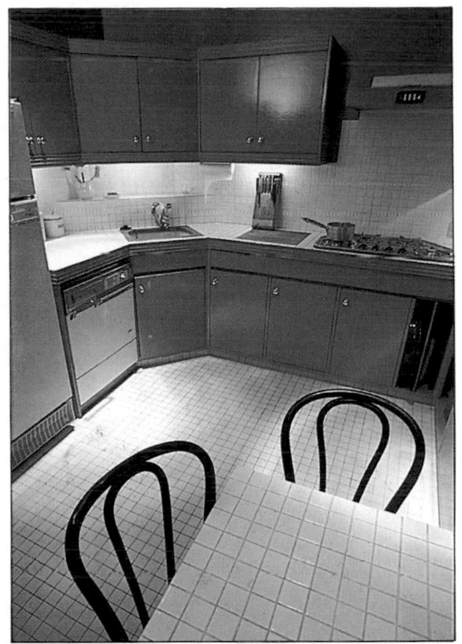

2

3

4

1 Galley kitchen
A narrow room is usually fitted out as a "galley" kitchen to make the best use of space. Avoid through traffic in the work area to reduce the risk of accidents.

2 L-shaped kitchen
Deep cabinets formed by corner units are a common problem. In this "L" section kitchen, the corner has been filled in and tiled to form a shelf and reduce the depth of the cabinets.

3 Work oasis
In a large kitchen, a central unit can be fitted out with additional appliances and work surfaces. The interaction of "work triangles" needs to be carefully considered.

4 Open plan kitchen
If you spend a lot of time in the kitchen, an open plan scheme will allow you to supervise activities in other parts of the house. Efficient ventilation is essential with this type of layout.

Planning Your Kitchen

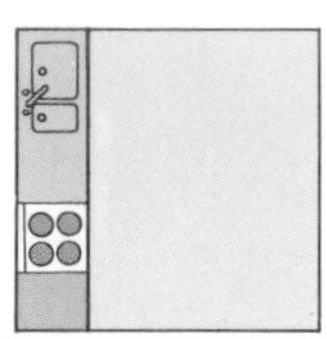
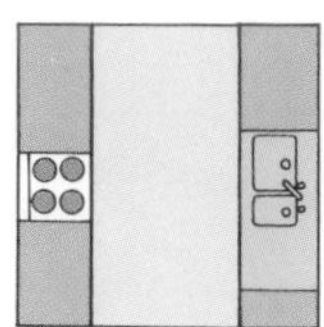
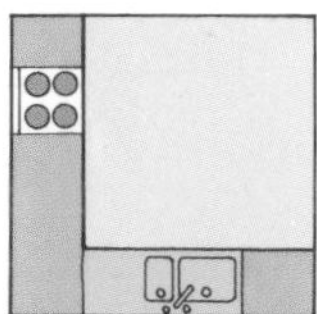
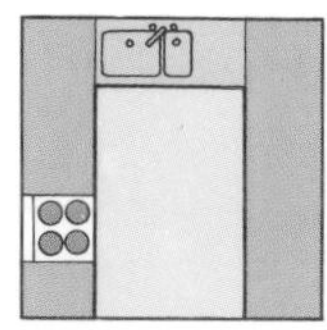

Kitchen layout
The room's shape and the position of the doors and windows determine the work area. The final layout may depend on one of four standard plans: the straight line, the galley, the L-shape and U-shape.

Work zones
All kitchens contain at least three main working areas: washing, cooking, preparation. The washing zone includes an area for cleaning vegetables, for disposal of waste and dishwashing. The cooking zone is where oven, grill and range are located. The preparation zone is for chopping, mixing, and so on, and includes the refrigerator.
Make a sketch plan of your kitchen and arrange each of these zones to form a triangle. Measure your kitchen to see if the total length of the sides of the "work triangle" exceeds 20 ft. If so, the zones are too far apart, and work may prove tiring. If the total is less than 15 ft, space is cramped.

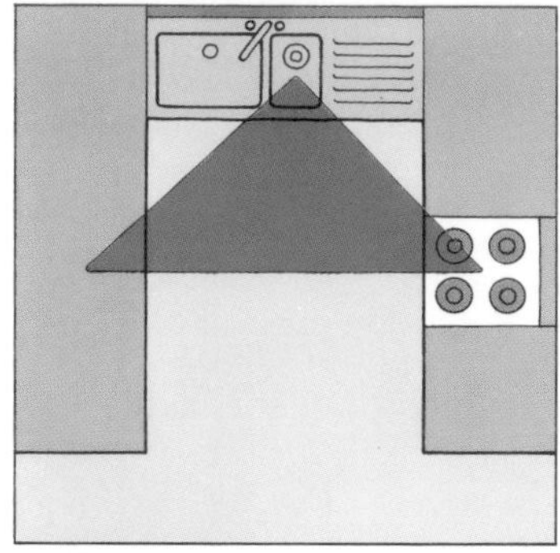

Work triangle
This diagram of a U-shaped kitchen shows the three basic areas of activity, arranged to form a "work triangle." The washing area is located at the apex which is often the most practical position for it.

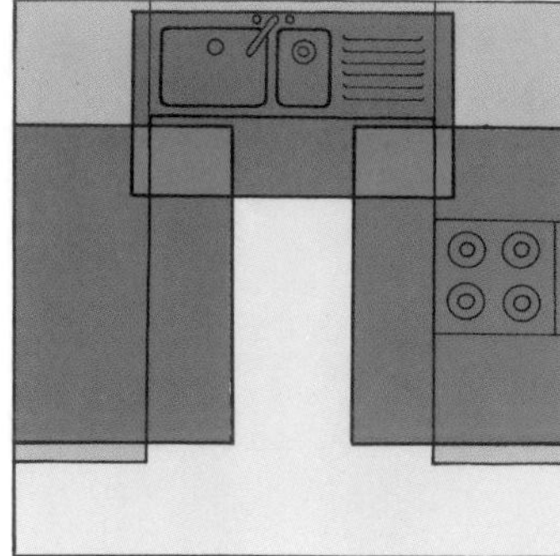

Zones of activity
These will be arranged to suit your particular needs, of course, but placing the sink under the main window is common in many kitchens, and the other zones can then be placed accordingly.

Optimum heights
An average person standing in front of a 2 ft deep work surface has safe and easy access to a top shelf 5 ft 8 in. from the ground. Below the level of the work surface accessibility is not so critical.

Dimensions of kitchen units
It is in the vertical dimensions of a kitchen that the individual requirements are most likely to vary. Work surfaces should be at a comfortable height to avoid unnecessary strain and accidents – most ready-made systems provide worktops 2 ft deep and about 3 ft from the floor, though sinks may be 38 in. when measured from floor to rim. Position your wall units about 18 in. above the work surface if the standard 36 in. height suits you. If you are not of average height it is possible to obtain some kitchen base units which are also fully wall-mounted; this means that the counter top heights can be adjusted. Most ordinary kitchen systems are fitted with an inbuilt recess about 6 in. high and 3 in. deep for your toes, so that you can stand close to the work surface in comfort; the gap between a wall-mounted base unit and the floor serves exactly the same purpose.

Allowing for appliances
A wall cabinet should not be less than 18 inches above the work surface; any smaller gap than this does not allow enough room to keep most of the common kitchen appliances.

Depth of wall cabinets
Wall cabinets should be set back far enough not to obscure your view as you make use of the work surface; you should also be in no danger of bumping your head. A maximum depth of 12 in. is suggested.

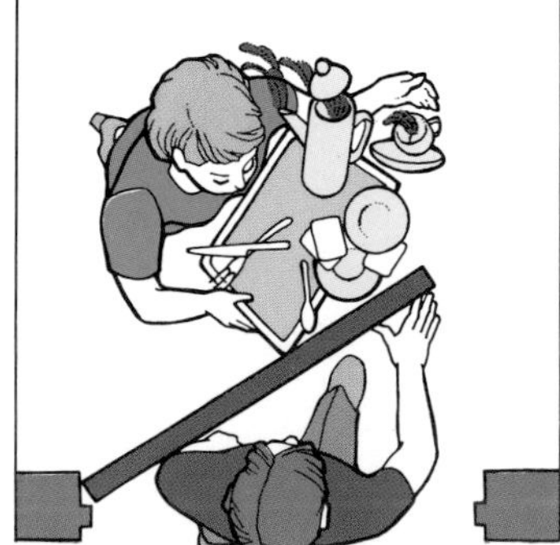

Door safety
Try to avoid placing a stove near a door. Kitchen doors should be glassed-in, so a person approaching can be seen. They should also be hinged in such a way as to reduce accidents.

Circulation space
When you design the work triangle for your kitchen, try to avoid through traffic impeding any of your movements to and fro, particularly if the traffic is likely to consist of children. You can install safety gates to define the circulation and work area, and if you have adequate ventilation, you may be able to dispense with a door entirely, and rely on a safety gate instead. Where two people may have to pass, allow a space of about 4 ft – this measurement will also permit safe access to cabinets or appliances situated beneath the work surface.

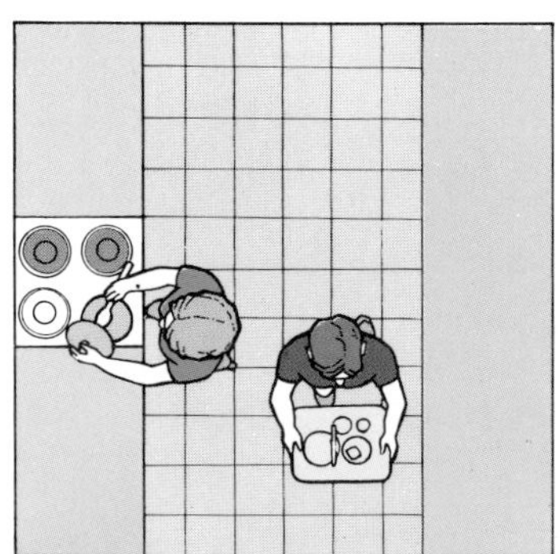

Passing space
Make sure that there is at least 3 ft of space behind you as you stand at your worktop, especially if there is regular through traffic in your kitchen.

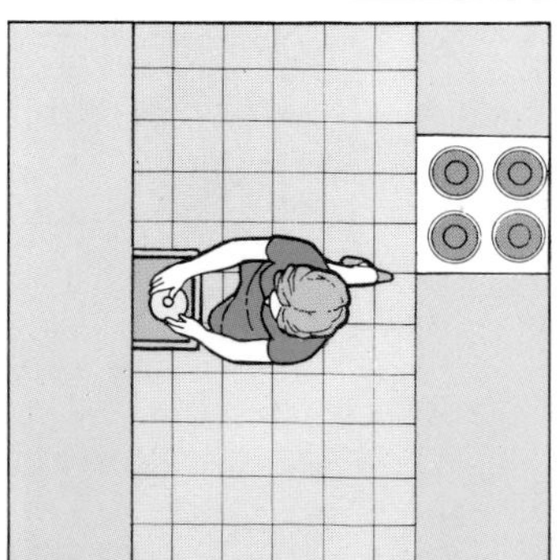

Access space
The same amount of space should also allow comfortable and safe access to objects placed below the level of the worktop.

Safety precautions
The kitchen is potentially the most dangerous area of the home, as it is equipped with electrical appliances. To minimize risks, the control of these appliances – the switch of the garbage disposal unit, for example – should be well out of the reach of children. Many types of traditional all-in-one stoves are not ideal in safety terms. A better system is the separate range set into the worktop (preferably rear of center) with perhaps a deep-frying unit recessed alongside. Saucepan clamps, a further safeguard, can be fitted to the range. The grill and oven units should be installed at eye level, and positioned at the very end of a series of cabinets.

Safety with storage
Do not position food storage cabinets above or too near a cooking unit, the rising heat may damage the cabinets and spoil the contents. There is also an increased possibility of accidents occurring when you reach across the range.

Safety with windows
Do not position your range in front of, or adjacent to a window, where you might be obliged to lean over the burners in order to open or close it. There is a danger that drafts could blow out a pilot light where a gas range is used.

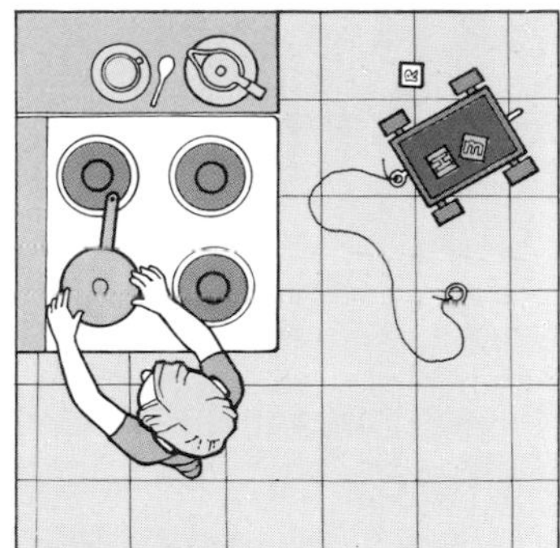

Safety with children
Avoid placing your range at the end of a series of units. Quite apart from the fact that you need heat-proof surfaces on either side, on which to place hot dishes, such a position makes it too easy for a child to reach the handles of pans.

Lighting
Good lighting is essential to any well-designed kitchen, and there should be lights of sufficient intensity to provide overall illumination. A central ceiling light can be rather harsh, a point to consider if your kitchen is also to be a dining area. Although a central light is convenient, it is better employed in conjunction with indirect lighting, such as a light track carrying a number of spotlights. This system will give you a degree of flexibility, with which you can illuminate almost every part of the room. Other types of lighting are shown on the right, but your final choice will depend on the location of your range and work surfaces.

Incorrect lighting
A single, central light is unsatisfactory as it will throw your shadow on to any local work surface, and also on to wall cabinets. Either dispense with it altogether, or use it in conjunction with other lighting.

Correct lighting
Keep your central light if you want to provide a general background illumination, and place additional lights above the work surface. Fluorescent tubes, located under the wall units, are ideal.

Alternative lighting
An alternative plan is to install ceiling lights, positioned above the front edge of your work surface. If possible, have them recessed into a false ceiling. Recessed lights are neater and stay cleaner than other forms of lighting.

Ventilation
So persistent are some types of kitchen odors that it is quite difficult to ventilate an average domestic kitchen adequately. Opening a window never really clears the air of grease, smoke and odors, but merely forces the atmosphere back into the room. There are two methods by which you can ventilate your kitchen – either by an electric fan vented straight through an external wall, and perhaps incorporating a ducted hood, or by means of a filter hood fitted directly above the range. Filters will absorb grease and smoke, but are less efficient in dispersing odors. The filters are made of charcoal or carbon granules, and must be regularly cleaned or changed. If you install an electric fan, it should relate to the size of the kitchen: the more powerful the fan, the better chance you have of really clearing the air.

Electricity
Your kitchen plan should allow not only for the appliances you possess at the moment, but also for those that you may acquire in the future. You will need outlet boxes for large appliances which are not built-in, like dishwashers. Portable appliances need sets of double outlets to the rear and just above the worktops. The switch for a garbage disposal unit should be located more than 3 ft away from the sink, and high enough to be out of the reach of children. All appliances have a cable from appliance to outlet, and you should aim to keep the length of these cables to a minimum; they should not trail across worktops or over the floor. An electric stove should never be connected to a ring circuit, but needs its own subcircuit. Ideally, the lighting circuit should be separate from all heavy-duty circuits.

Location of electrical outlets and/or switches

Appliance	Area	Position	
Stove	Cooking zone	High level	●●●
Refrigerator	Preparation zone	Low level	●●●
Dishwasher	Washing zone	Low level	●●
Deep freeze	Need not be in kitchen	Low level	●●●
Waste disposal	Washing zone	High level	●●
Exhaust fan	Cooking zone	High level	●●
Range hood	Cooking zone	High level	●●
Coffeemaker	Preparation zone/Eating area	Work level	●
Rotisserie	Preparation zone/Eating area	Work level	●
Blender	Preparation zone	Work level	●
Toaster	Preparation zone/Eating area	Work level	●
Can opener	Preparation zone	Work level	●●
Frying pan	Cooking zone/Eating area	Work level	●
Carving knife	Preparation zone	Work level	●
Hot plate	Eating area	Work level	●

key	
●●●	Appliance should be permanently connected to supply
●●	Not essential but convenient if appliance is permanently connected
●	Unnecessary for appliance to be permanently connected

Unit Design

Kitchen layouts
The two most functional arrangements of kitchen units are the L-shaped layout and the U-shaped layout. The range of units shown here is based on a 12-inch module, and includes wall and base cabinets 12 and 24 inches wide, corner cabinets 24 and 36 inches wide, a base drawer unit and tall ventilated cabinet 24 inches wide and a 48-inch wide sink unit.

The base units will give you ample storage for all kitchen items, at a comfortable height. The bottom of the cabinet space has been raised to avoid any need for the user to crouch down; the ample plinth gives clearance for when you stand at the worktop and facilitates floor cleaning. The plinth area and the space behind it can incorporate a drawer for additional storage. Or with a flexible floor covering such as vinyl or linoleum you can run the material up the face of the plinth (see pp. 168-169).

Some special features
All the upper cabinets are fitted with adjustable shelves and 12-inch wide doors. The narrow width of the doors takes a safety factor into account: they do not project beyond the front edge of the countertop. The 24-inch units can be fitted with strip lights to illuminate the work surface. The countertops are faced with plastic and are provided with a drip-groove on the underside. Handles are recessed and are less likely to catch on clothing.

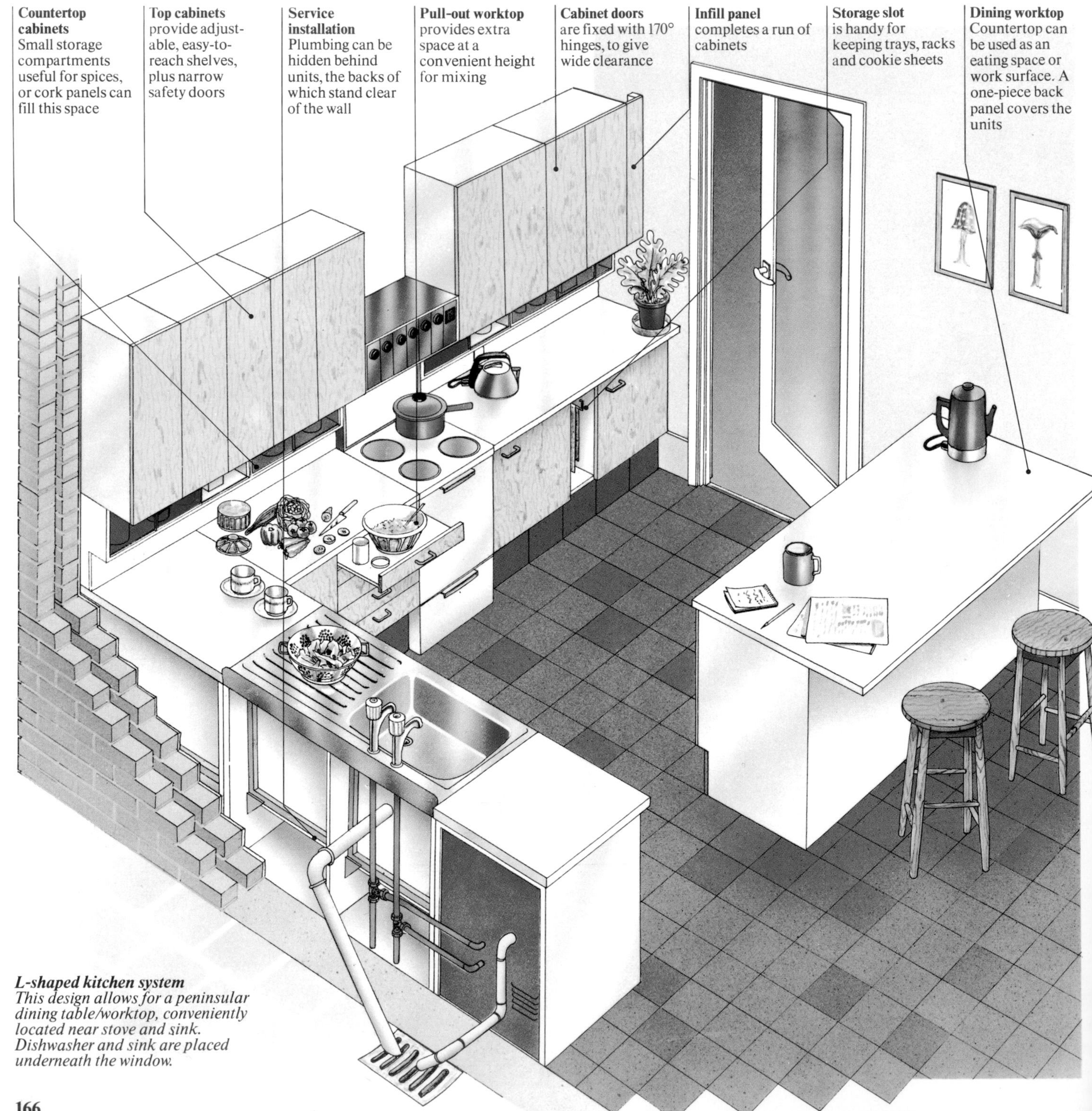

L-shaped kitchen system
This design allows for a peninsular dining table/worktop, conveniently located near stove and sink. Dishwasher and sink are placed underneath the window.

The range of fittings

The basic 24-inch unit can be provided with the following features: adjustable shelves with doors hung so that they can swing clear; a bank of drawers with an additional pull-out worktop for lower level mixing purposes; a complete pull-out interior with easier access to heavy items. The tall ventilated unit provides long-term food storage, the upper door being fitted with shallow shelves for small goods. The bottom can be fitted as a conventional cabinet or with a pull-out interior. The corner base units have double-hinged doors to give a pillarless opening into the cabinet.

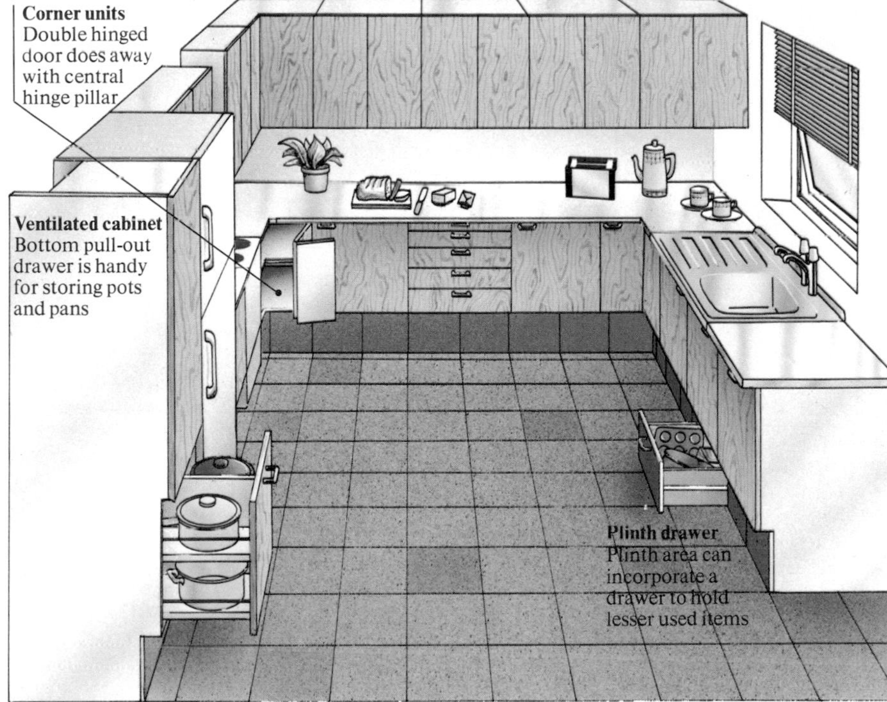

U-shaped kitchen system
This design incorporates a tall ventilated cabinet for foods that do not need storing in the refrigerator. The bottom space can have a pull-out interior. Units are conveniently grouped for maximum efficiency. For information about the "work triangle" and activity areas, refer to pp. 162-163.

1 Tall ventilated cabinet
The upper door of the cabinet can be fitted with a shallow storage rack. The shelves are adjustable to accommodate various items.

4

4 Pull-out worktop
A pull-out worktop fitted in the drawer unit provides a surface at a lower level, suitable for hand mixing.

2 Drawer fronts
Cut all the drawer fronts from one piece of board to ensure that the wood grain matches.

5

5 Pull-out interior
Pull-out interiors fitted in place of cabinet doors provide easy access to stored objects.

3 Chopping board
The pine chopping board shown here is made from 1 in. lengths of 3 in. x 3 in. lumber glued side by side. Sand down the end grain surfaces with an orbital sander.

1

2

3

6

6 Plinth drawer
Optional deep drawers housed in the plinth, and faced to match the floor finish, can store less frequently used items.

Kitchen Units

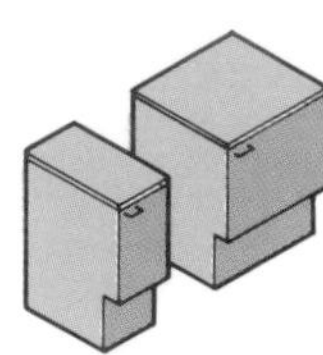

Base unit

Cut away from bottom front corner of sides **1** a piece 2¼ in. wide and 12 in. high. Face cut edges with iron-on plastic veneer. Drill two lines of 1/16 in. pilot holes for shelf supports 4 in. and 14 in. from front edge. Space rows 2 in. apart starting 16½ in. from bottom edge. Fit bottom panel **2** with corner joints (see p. 135) to the sides, front edges flush. With corner joints fit top rails **3** level with top edge, the front rail flush with front edges of sides, the back rail set 4 in. from back edge. Screw back battens **4** to sides and bottom with 1¼ in. no. 8 screws so they are flush with top rail. Paint the hardboard back panel **5.** Contact glue hardboard to face of battens and top rail. Screw and glue 4 in. right angle triangular plates to back edge of bottom shelf to brace sides. Edge veneer door panel, **6.** Drill 1¼ in. diameter holes ½ in. deep for hinges in back face, centered 4 in. from top edge and 3 in. from bottom left or right side (see **A** left). Fit the back plates to the sides to correspond with hinges. Mount the hinges on the plates and adjust set screw to level the door as necessary. Drill clearance holes for handle screws 1¼ in. from top edge and 2 in. from side edge. Fix handle. Edge shelf **8** with iron-on plastic veneer. Screw chrome screw eyes at required height and fit shelf. Finish exposed edges of plinth fascia **7** with iron-on plastic veneer before fixing to front edges of side panels. Where a corner unit is fitted overlap one board on the other and fix a softwood batten to longer board and screw the other fascia to the batten **B.**

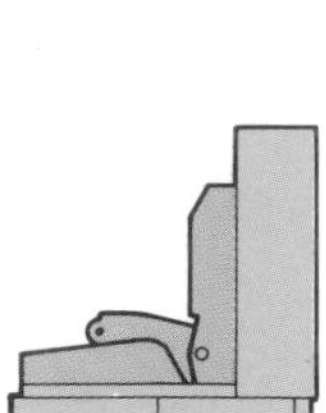

A

Plinth drawer

Cut a storage drawer 21¾ in. wide and 16 in. long with sides 8 in. wide from ⅜ in. plywood (see pp. 132-133). Cut a fascia panel 24 in. wide and 11⅞ in. high from ⅝ in. particle board. Finish face and edges as fixed plinth. Screw the fascia with ¾ in. no. 8 screws through the front of the drawer which extends downwards ¾ in. Screw a drawer slide to each side panel 3 in. up from bottom edge. Screw the mating runners to each side of drawer 1¾ in. up from bottom edge to screw centers. Fit drawer as **C.** Where two drawers are side by side and sharing a single side panel, the overlapping fascias will have to be reduced by ⅜ in. as in **D.** If a continuation of fixed panels and plinth drawers is used the panel ends will have to be screwed to a batten fixed to the cabinet sides, **E.**

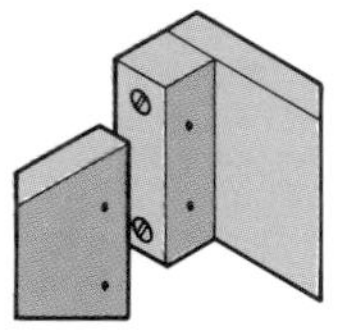

B

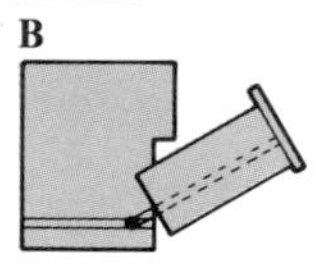

C

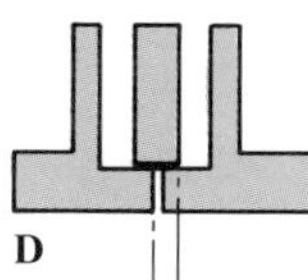

D

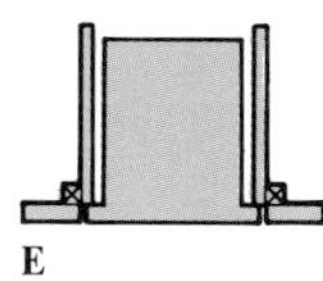

E

Drawer unit and pull out worktop

Make the drawers with lay-on fronts to match door panels. Top drawer sides measure 4 in. wide, the lower three drawers have sides 4¾ in. wide (see pp. 132-133). The bottom drawer front extends downwards ⅝ in. to mask the frame. Fit handles at center 1¼ in. down from top edges. For a pull out worktop, cut a ⅝ in. particle board panel **1** 21¾ in. long x 18 in. wide and laminate surfaces with plastic. Dowel joint the long side to a 24 in. x 3 in. wide drawer front **2** flush with bottom edge. Fit the handle as drawers. Fit board on 20 in. long drawer slides.

Countertops

Countertops are 24 in. wide and can be cut from ¾ in. particle board. After cutting to size, laminate the board with plastic (see p. 144). Cut ¾ in. particle board battens 4 in. wide to length and width of top; miter ends and screw flush with top edges using 1¼ in. no. 8 screws. Edge with matching laminate. Cut a ¼ in. wide groove ⅛ in. deep, ½ in. from front edge in underside of top. Lacquer with polyurethane. Fix the top to the cabinet with screws counterbored through the top rails. When making a top to fit a run of cabinets, it is wiser to measure directly from the cabinets when in position than to calculate the length. Diagram **F** shows method of corner fittings.

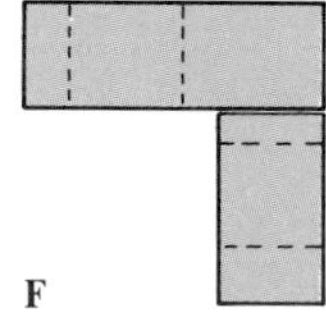

F

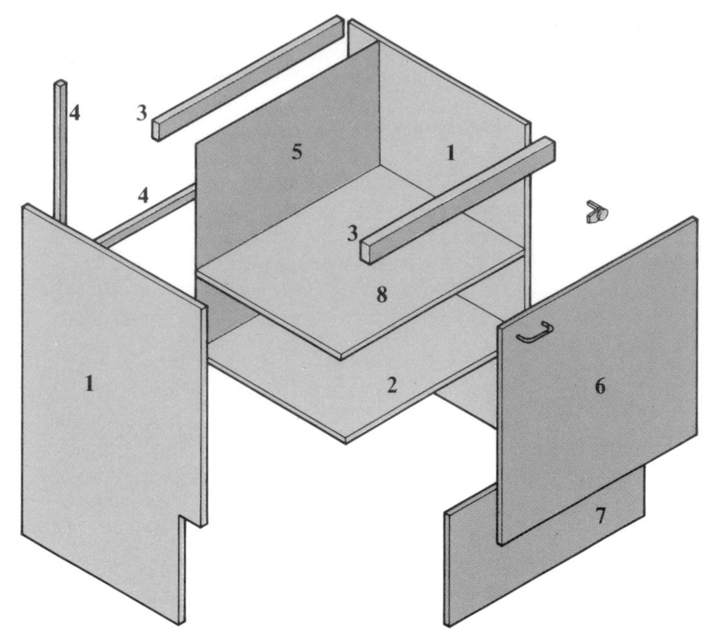

No	Part	Quantity	Length	Width	Th	Material
1	Side	2	34½	22⅛	⅝	Veneered particle board
2	Fixed shelf	1	22¾	19	⅝	Veneered particle board
3	Top rail	2	22¾	2	1	Softwood
4	Back battens	3	19¾	1	1	Softwood
5	Back panel	1	21¼	22¾	⅛	Hardboard
6	Door	1	22⅞	24	¾	Pine plywood
7	Plinth	1	As required	12	⅝	Veneered particle board
8	Shelf	1	22⅝	17¼	⅝	Veneered particle board

Hardware: 2, 170° opening concealed hinge. 1, 3¾ 'D' handle. 4, ⅞ x 2 screw eyes.
N.B. Softwood dimensions are nominal. All dimensions are shown in inches.

Pull out worktop

Countertop

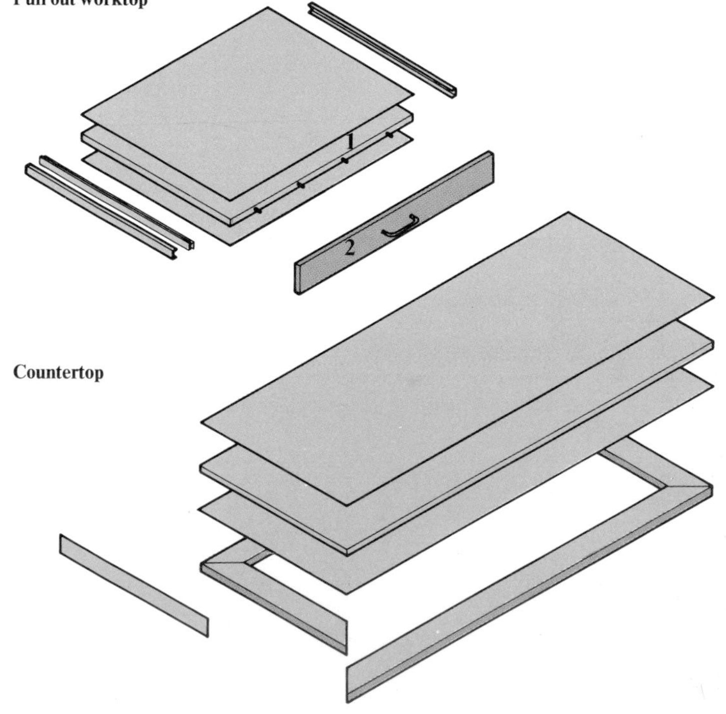

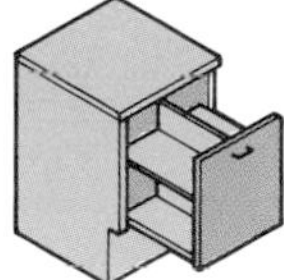

Pull out interiors

Finish the exposed edges of all panels with iron-on plastic veneer. Screw the bottom shelf **1** to the center partition **2** with 1½ in. no. 6 screws. Drill four rows of 1/16 in. pilot holes in back **3** and front **4** for shelf support screw eyes. The rows are ¾ in. and 8½ in. from each side respectively in back panel, 1⅞ in. and 9¾ in. from each side in front. Fix the back to the bottom shelf and center partition with 1½ in. no. 6 screws. Fit the inner slides to bottom shelf flush at front ends. Measure the width between end brackets of slides and screw the locating brackets **5** to the back face of front to correspond, 1½ in. up from the bottom edge. Locate front on slide and fix to center partition with a corner joint. Screw in shelf supports and fit shelf. Fit one extra screw eye in front and back panels to carry plastic covered wire fitted with screw hooks to form barrier. Fit the handle at center of front 1¼ in. down from the top edge.

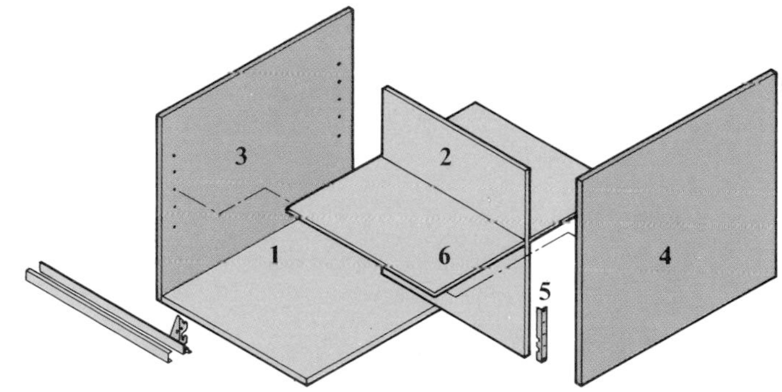

No	Part	Quantity	Length	Width	Th	Material
1	Bottom shelf	1	21⅝	17¼	⅝	Veneered particle board
2	Partition	1	18⅝	17¼	⅝	Veneered particle board
3	Back	1	19¼	21⅝	⅝	Veneered particle board
4	Front	1	22⅜	24	¾	Pine plywood
6	Shelf	2	17⅛	9¾	⅝	Veneered particle board

Hardware: 2, 17¾ telescopic cabinet slide. 1, corner joint K.D. fitting. 1, 3¾ 'D' handle. 4, 16 plastic coated wire. 4, ⅞ x 2 screw eyes. 8, ¾ x 3 plain cup screws.
N.B. All dimensions are shown in inches.

Countertop storage

Cut away a piece from bottom front corner of sides **1** 6 in. long x 2 in. wide. Finish cut edges. Drill 1/16 in. pilot holes in two lines 1 in. from front and back edges. The holes are spaced 2 in. apart starting 4 in. up from notch. Dowel joint top and bottom **2** into sides (see pp. 129-131). Nail and glue back to back edges. Finish edges of shelf **3** and support on screw eyes in sides. The fascia panel **5** can be cut to fit the length of one unit or, where a number of units are fitted, be one continuous board. Fix the panel with wood screws to the front edges of sides. Fit the screws with white plastic cover caps. To fit power outlets into fascia, cut a clearance hole for electric box which is fixed flush with face. The cable runs can be passed through a 1 in. diameter hole cut through the lower section of sides. The open shelf unit can be enclosed by sliding doors which can be of clear glass, plexiglass, smoked plexiglass or plastic laminated hardboard. Contact glue top and bottom track flush with front edges. Locate doors in track.

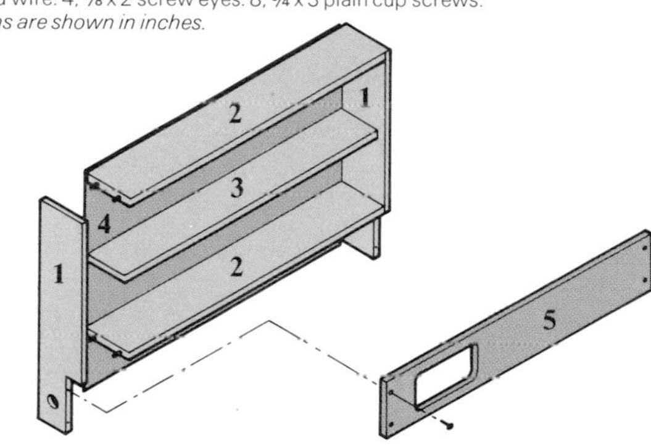

No	Part	Quantity	Length	Width	Th	Material
1	Side	2	18	4	⅝	Veneered particle board
2	Top and bottom	2	22¾	4	⅝	Veneered particle board
3	Shelf	1	22¾	3¼	⅝	Veneered particle board
4	Back panel	1	24	13¼	⅛	Hardboard
5	Fascia	1	24	4¾	⅝	Veneered particle board

Hardware: 4, 1¼ x 6 woodscrews. 4, white plastic screw caps. 4, ⅞ x 2 screw eyes (optional). 2, 11¾ x 11½ x ⅛ glass. 22¾ long top & bottom sliding door track with ⅛ groove. *N.B. All dimensions are shown in inches.*

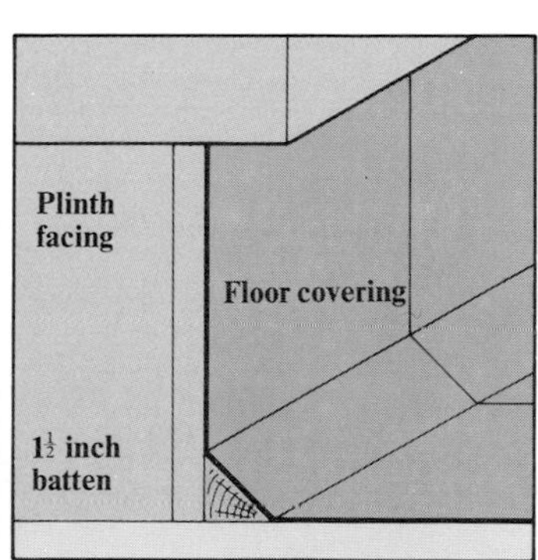

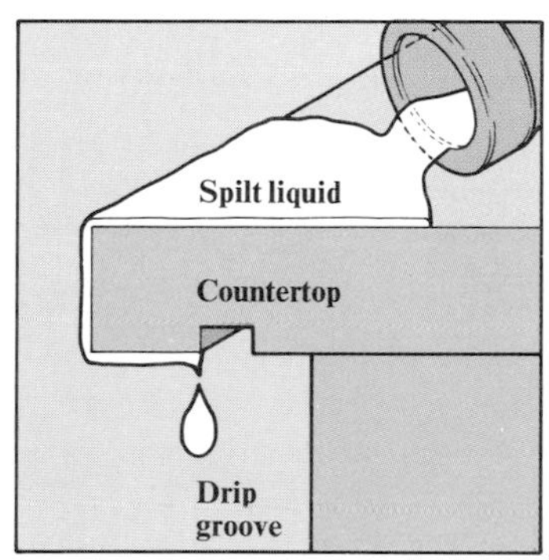

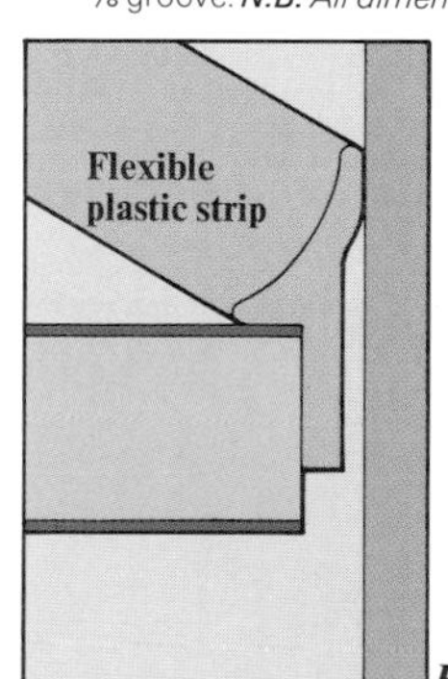

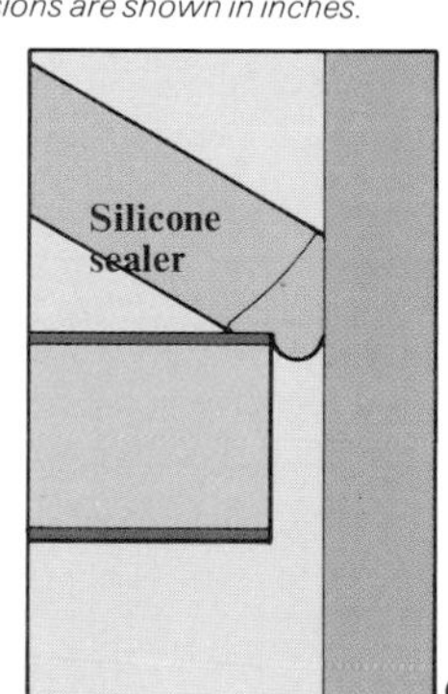

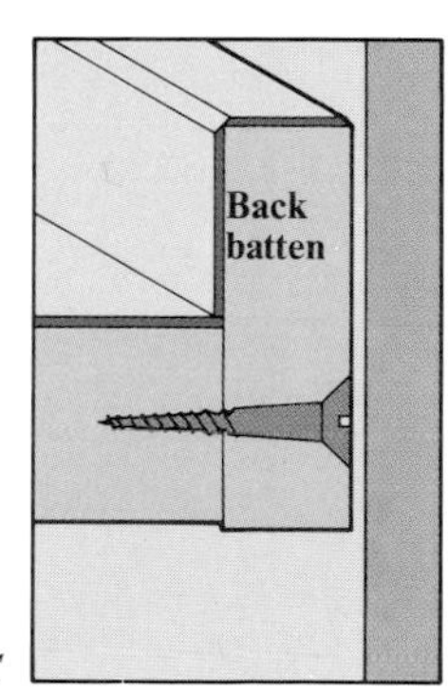

Continuing floor surface
The junction between the floor and the plinth can be finished at a right angle, butting the floor finishing material to the plinth fascia. Otherwise the floor and plinth can be joined by a length of 1½ in. right angle triangle batten, in which case the floor covering can be carried across the batten and on to the plinth, linking the unit with the floor. This is only suitable for a fixed plinth.

Containing spilt liquids
Instructions for making the countertop include a groove, cut into the underside of the front edge. This "drip groove" acts as a barrier, preventing spilt liquids running down the cabinet fronts. The laminate on the countertop can be continued around the front edge and right up to the groove on the underside.

Filling spaces between countertop and wall
The gap between countertop and wall can be sealed with a flexible plastic strip, cut to length and glued to the back edge of the top, the upper part following the contour of the wall, ***A*** *above. As an alternative, you can seal the gap with a silicone sealer. The sealer is applied by squeezing the contents from a tube into the gap. This material is particularly suitable for glazed ceramic tiled walls,* ***B*** *above. Where an uneven wall creates gaps between wall and unit that cannot easily be filled, fit a batten to match the finish of the worktop,* ***C*** *above. The width of the top will have to be reduced according to the thickness of the batten, in order to maintain the correct worktop width.*

Kitchen Units

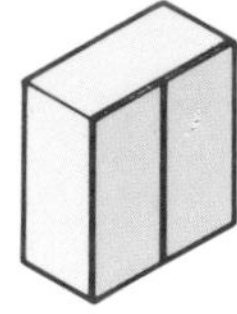

Top cabinet

Lip cut edges of sides **1**. Drill two lines of 1/16 in. pilot holes in sides, 2 in. and 8 in. from front edge, starting 6 in. from bottom edge, rows 2 in. apart. Counterbore and screw front rail **2** to underside of bottom shelf **3**, 1 in. from front edge. Screw top batten **4** through top **5** flush with back edge, using 1½ in. no. 8 screws. Fit bottom and top to sides with corner joints (see p. 135), front edges flush. Make top flush with top edge of sides, bottom rail flush with bottom edge. Paint back panel **7** and glue to back battens **6** which are screwed to sides and bottom flush with top batten. Lip edges of doors **8** and fit lay-on hinges 4 in. from top edge and 6 in. from

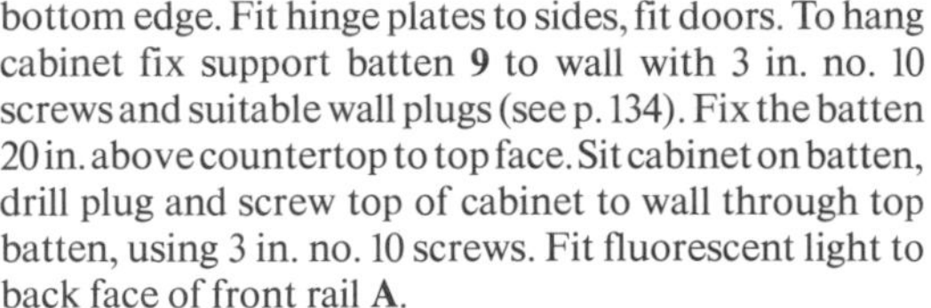

bottom edge. Fit hinge plates to sides, fit doors. To hang cabinet fix support batten **9** to wall with 3 in. no. 10 screws and suitable wall plugs (see p. 134). Fix the batten 20 in. above countertop to top face. Sit cabinet on batten, drill plug and screw top of cabinet to wall through top batten, using 3 in. no. 10 screws. Fit fluorescent light to back face of front rail **A**.

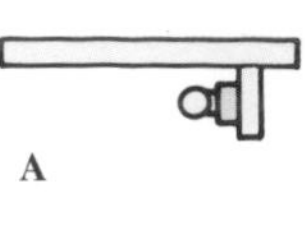

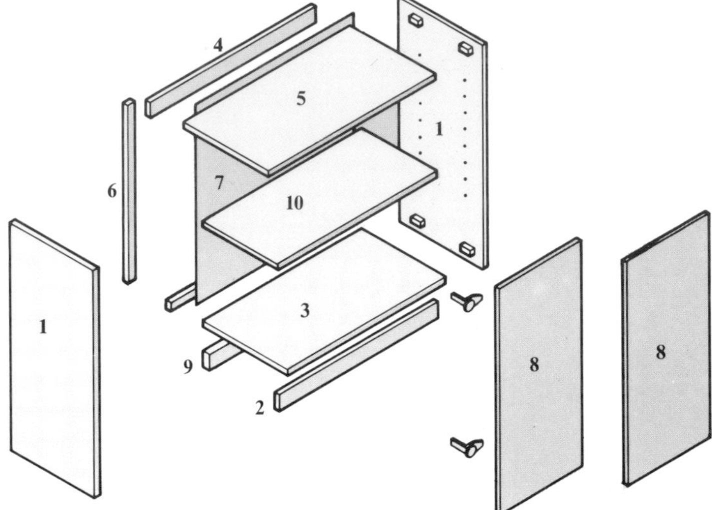

No	Part	Quantity	Length	Width	Th	Material
1	Side	2	28	12	⅝	Veneered particle board
2	Front rail	1	22¾	2¼	⅝	Veneered particle board
3	Fixed shelf	1	22¾	12	⅝	Veneered particle board
4	Top batten	1	22¾	2	1	Softwood
5	Top	1	22¾	12	⅝	Veneered particle board
6	Back battens	3	19¾	1	1	Softwood
7	Back panel	1	24½	22¾	⅛	Hardboard
8	Doors	2	28	12	¾	Pine plywood
9	Support batten	1	22⅝	2	1	Softwood
10	Shelf	1	22⅝	10⅞	⅝	Veneered particle board

Hardware: 4, 170° opening concealed hinge. 8, corner joint K.D. fittings. 4, ⅞ x 2 screw eyes. ***N.B.** All dimensions are shown in inches.*

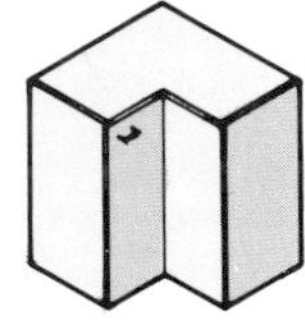

Top corner cabinet

Make sides **1** as for to cabinet. Cut shelves **2** to shape **A**. Notch back corner to take post **3** made from two lengths of softwood, beveled on one long edge and glued together. Edge front of top and bottom with veneer. Counterbore and screw front rails **4** and **5** to underside of bottom shelf 1 in. from front edge. Screw top battens **6** through top, flush with back edges. Fix top and bottom to one side with corner joints (see p. 135). Screw and glue back post flush with top and bottom. Fit three back battens **7** to fixed side and bottom, flush with top battens. Paint back panels **8** and contact glue to back battens. Cut adjustable shelf **9** to shape **B**, and finish edges. Fit remaining back batten to side panel and back. Fit door panels **10** and **11** as for base corner unit. Drill 1/16 in. pilot holes for shelf supports through back panel, into one side of back post, 1 in. from corner. Hang with support battens **12**.

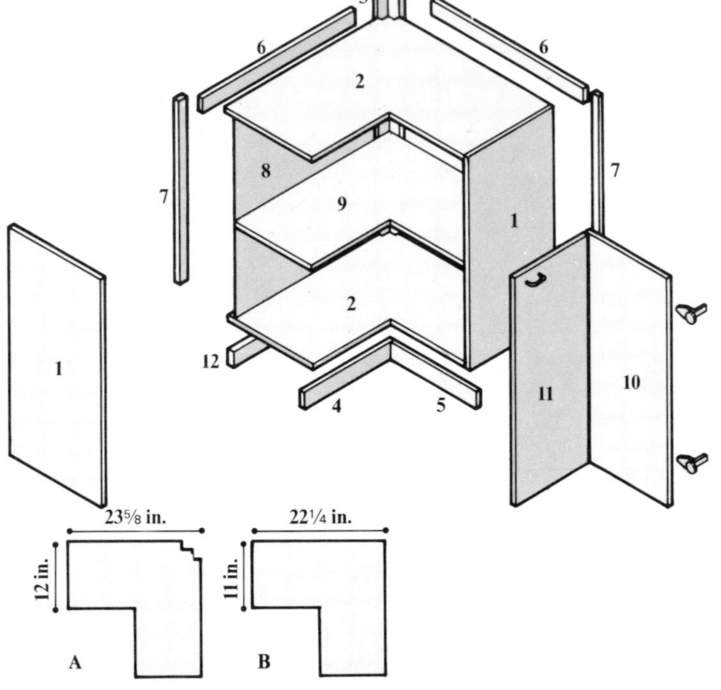

No	Part	Quantity	Length	Width	Th	Material
1	Side	2	28	12	⅝	Veneered particle board
2	Top/bottom shelves	2	23⅜	23⅜	⅝	Veneered particle board
3	Post	2	25¾	2	1	Softwood
4	Front rail	1	13	2¼	⅝	Veneered particle board
5	Front rail	1	12⅜	2¼	⅝	Veneered particle board
6	Top batten	2	21⅜	2	1	Softwood
7	Back batten	4	19¾	1	1	Softwood
8	Back panel	2	24½	22⅜	⅛	Hardboard
9	Shelf	1	22¼	22¼	⅝	Veneered particle board
10	Door	1	28	12	¾	Pine plywood
11	Door	1	28	11⅛	¾	Pine plywood
12	Support batten	2	22⅜	2	1	Softwood

Hardware: 2, 170° opening concealed hinges. 1, 28 long x 1¼ piano hinge. 8, corner joint K.D. fittings. 4, ⅞ x 2 screw eyes. ***N.B.** All dimensions are shown in inches.*

1 Natural look
In this kitchen the peninsular storage unit creates a galley kitchen layout and is also a room divider. The breakfast bar is convenient and its top is visually linked to the interior fitments by the use of a functional wood grained laminate.

2 Glass infill unit
Pictures 2, 3 and 4 all fill the space between top and bottom cabinets. A shelving unit with sliding glass doors stores the small bottles or jars that so easily get lost behind the larger objects on open shelves. Making instructions are given on p. 169.

3 Magnetized infill panel
A ferrous metal panel makes space for hanging recipes or letters. Thin gauge steel sheet, painted on both sides, can be fixed with screws or mastic adhesive. The thickness of the paper being held is determined by the strength of the magnets.

4 Cork infill panel
If you are finishing your floor with cork tiles, you can use up the spare ones on an infill panel. A unified look is achieved if the tiles are matched with the interior scheme in this way. If the tiles are not pre-finished apply a couple of coats of sealer.

1

2

3

4

Kitchen Units

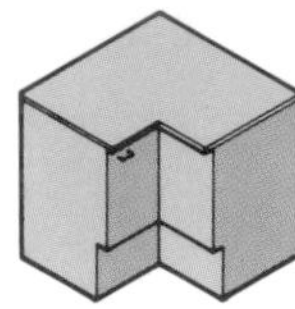

Corner base unit

Cut and finish sides **1** as for base unit. Join back legs **2** into a right angle with triangular plates **3,** one flush with top, the other 20¾ in. down. Cut shelf **4,** edge front with veneer and notch back corner to fit around back leg, **A.** Fix shelf **4** to sides, front edges flush. Sit corner of shelf on lower plate and fix with 1 in. no. 8 screws. Fit one end of rails **5** to sides with corner joints (see p. 133), the other is glued and screwed down to top of back leg. Cut and glue a cross lap joint in rails **6** 13¼ in. from front end. Fit rails to sides with corner joints and screw through back rails. Screw battens **7** and **8** to sides and bottom shelf flush with top rails. Cut notches in top edges of back panels **9**. Paint board. Using contact adhesive glue backs in place. Drill two lines of 1/16 in. pilot holes for shelf supports in sides and through back panels into back leg, 2 in. from back corner. Space holes 2 in. apart. Fit screw eyes at required height. Cut shelves **10** from one board, **B**. Place cut edges together to form a right-angled shelf. Screw half a ¼ in. plywood strip **11** to one half of shelf. Position shelves on supports, screw both halves together through strip. Fit door panel **12** with lay-on hinges. Hinge door panel **13** to face of other door with 1¼ in. wide piano hinge, **C**. Fit handle. For plinth see p. 168. Make countertops as described. Run one top into corner, butt adjacent top up to it, **D**.

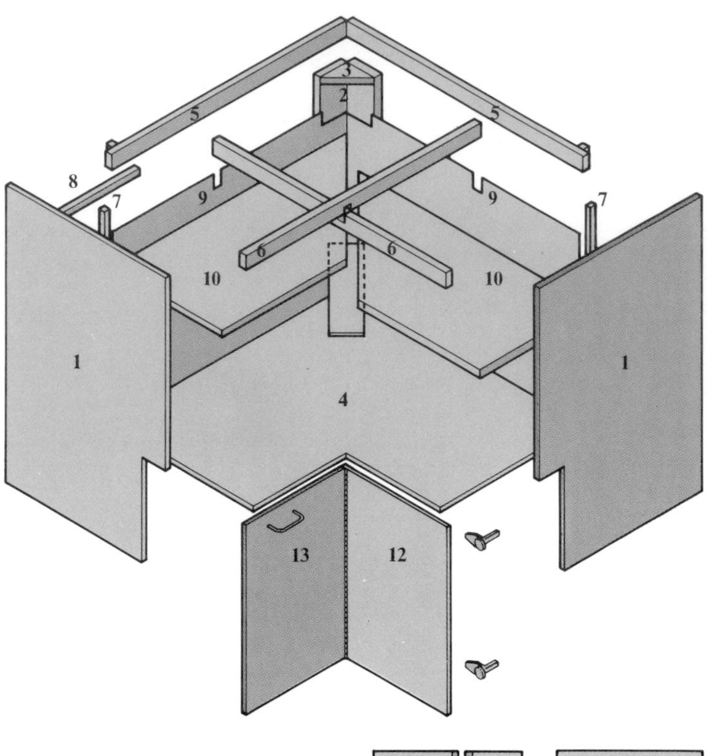

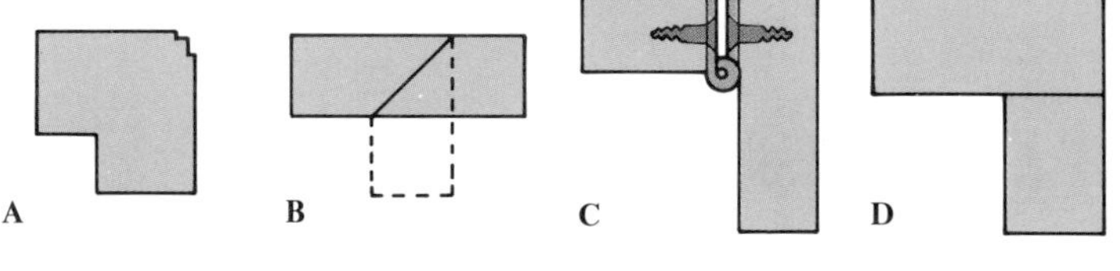

No	Part	Quantity	Length	Width	Th	Material
1	Side	2	34½	22⅛	⅝	Veneered particle board
2	Back legs	2	34½	4	1	Softwood
3	Triangular plates	2	4	4	½	Plywood
4	Fixed shelf	1	32⅞	32⅞	⅝	Veneered particle board
5	Back rails	2	31⅞	2	1	Softwood
6	Front rails	2	31⅞	2	1	Softwood
7	Back battens	2	19¾	1	1	Softwood
8	Back battens	2	26½	1	1	Softwood
9	Back	2	31¼	21¼	⅛	Hardboard
10	Shelf	1	48¼	15	⅝	Veneered particle board
11	Strip	1	14	4	¼	Plywood
12	Door	1	22⅜	13⅞	¾	Pine plywood
13	Door	1	22⅜	13	¾	Pine plywood

Hardware: 2, 170° opening concealed hinges. 1, 22⅜ x 1¼ piano hinge. 8, corner joint K.D. fittings. 1, 3¾ 'D' handle. 4, ⅞ x 2 screw eyes. *N.B. All dimensions are shown in inches.*

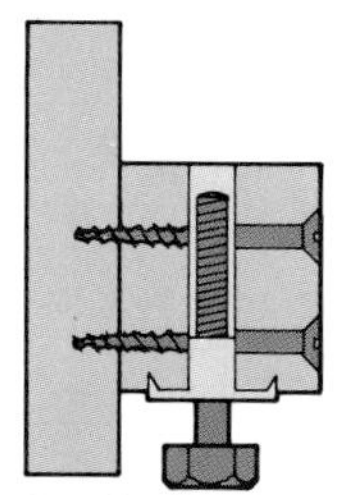

Level units
If floor is uneven make an adjustable leveler. Drill a clearance hole through a block of wood and fit a tee nut in the underside to take a bolt. Screw blocks to sides ¾ in. from bottom. Jack up units by turning bolt head. If units are joined you will need fewer levelers.

Tall ventilated cabinet

Cut away lower front edge of sides **1A**. Drill two lines of seven 1/16 in. pilot holes for bottom cabinet shelf supports, 4 in. and 13¾ in. from front edge, spacing rows 2 in. apart, starting 16¼ in. from bottom edge. Drill pilot holes in upper cabinet area 7 in. and 16¾ in. from front edge, rows spaced 2 in. apart, starting 39½ in. from bottom edge. Fit top **2** and bottom **3** to sides with corner joints (see p. 133), front edges flush. Screw back battens **4** and **5** to sides, top and bottom flush with back edges of cabinet top and bottom. Cut a rectangular hole 4 in. x 12 in. through back panel **6,** 2 in. from top edge, and 16½ in. from bottom. Glue a perforated zinc sheet 6 in. x 14 in. to the back face of panel across the hole. After painting, glue the back to face of battens. Screw front rail **7** to underside of fixed shelf **8,** flush with front edge. Face rail and edge with plastic laminate. Fix shelf to sides with corner joints, 36 in. up from the bottom edge of sides to top face of shelf. Edge veneer bottom door **9** and add lay-on hinges as with base unit. Fit handle. Veneer top and side edges of door **10**, bevel bottom edge to 45° starting and finishing 2 in. from ends **B**. Fit door to cabinet by three lay-on hinges set

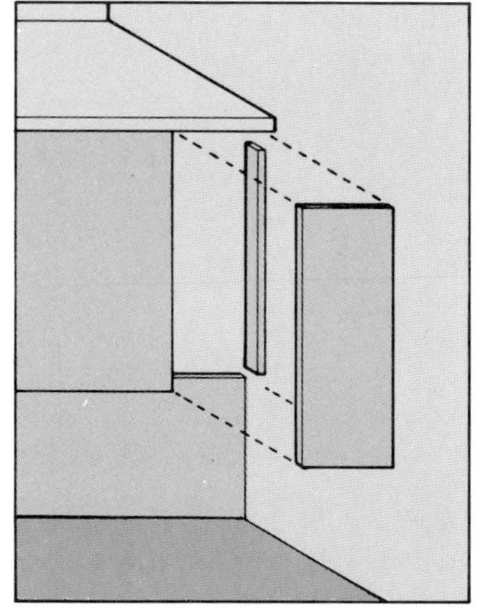

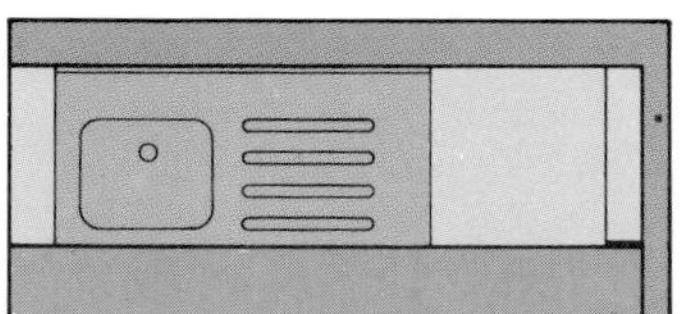

Concealing corner gaps
Fit infill panel covered by countertop to bridge short corner gaps. Extend plinth fascia scribing end to wall. Screw a 2 in. x 1 in. batten to wall and cabinet end, so as to bring panel flush with doors. Glue panel to battens.

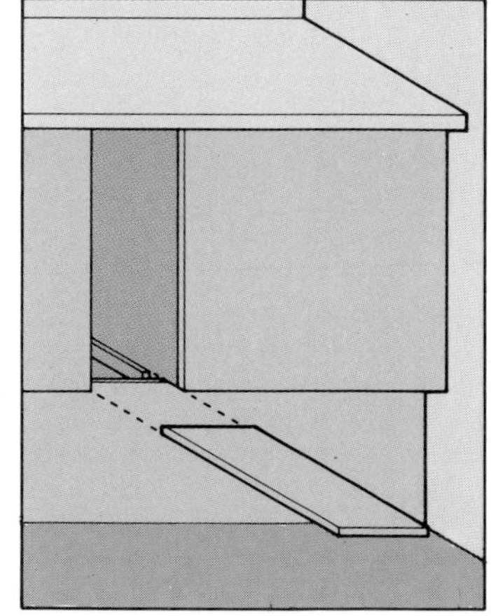

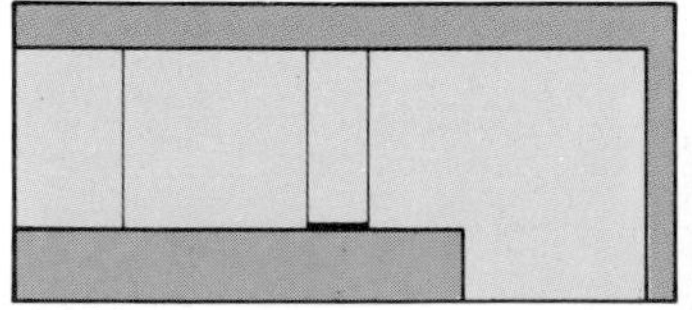

Making a tray recess
If a gap of less than 12 in. between cabinets is calculated, additional storage space can be created by continuing the countertop and plinth fascia across, and fitting a bottom shelf on battens screwed on each side, level with plinth.

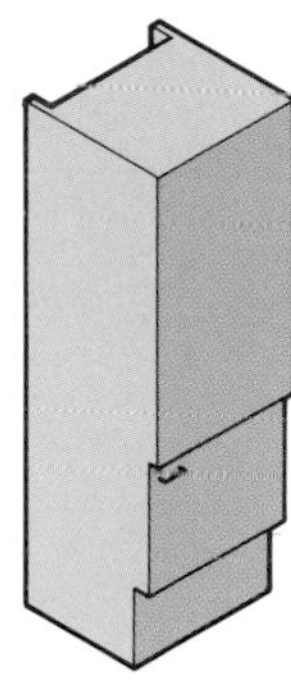

Tall ventilated cabinet: continued
at center and 8 in. from top and bottom edges. Fit adjustable shelves **11** and **12** on supports. Drill pilot holes in storage rack sides **13,** 2 in. apart and ¾ in. from each edge. Stop-dowel joint sides to top and bottom **14.** Screw corner plates in each corner flush with back edge. Hang frame centrally on back of door. Screw in supports and fit shelves. Fit screw hooks in ends of expanding wire, and attach to a screw eye in front row of each side to form a barrier **C.**

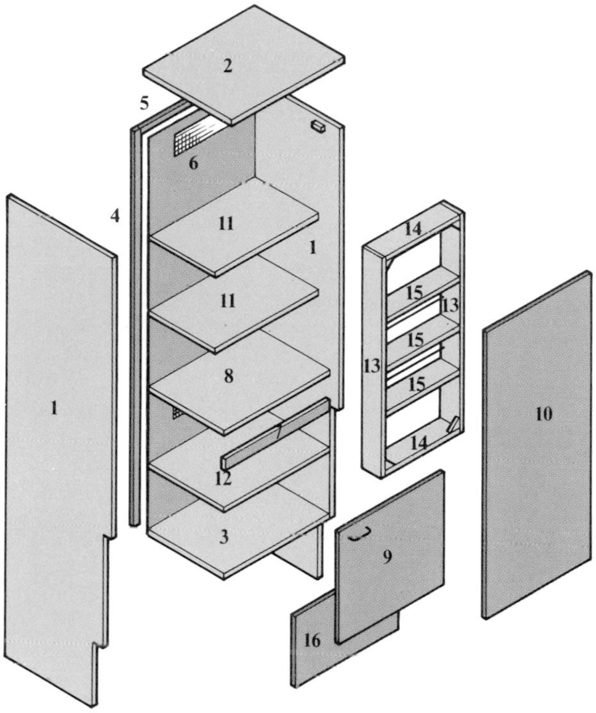

No	Part	Quantity	Length	Width	Th	Material
1	Side	2	82	23¼	⅝	Veneered particle board
2	Top	1	22¾	20⅛	⅝	Veneered particle board
3	Bottom	1	22¾	19	⅝	Veneered particle board
4	Back batten	2	68¾	1	1	Softwood
5	Back batten	2	20¾	1	1	Softwood
6	Back	1	68¾	22¾	⅛	Hardboard
7	Front rail	1	22¾	2	1	Softwood
8	Fixed shelf	1	22¾	18	⅝	Veneered particle board
9	Bottom door	1	22⅜	24	¾	Pine plywood
10	Top door	1	47½	24	¾	Pine plywood
11	Shelves	2	22⅝	14	⅝	Veneered particle board
12	Shelf	1	22⅝	17¼	⅝	Veneered particle board
13	Rack sides	2	39	4	⅝	Veneered particle board
14	Rack top/bottom	2	16½	4	⅝	Veneered particle board
15	Rack shelves	3	16⅜	4	⅝	Veneered particle board
16	Plinth	1	as required	12	⅝	Veneered particle board

Hardware: 4, 170° opening concealed hinges. 1, 3¾'D' handle. 24, ⅞x2 screw eyes. 4, 16 plastic coated wire. 2, 14x16 perforated zinc. 12, corner joint K.D. fittings. *N.B. All dimensions are shown in inches.*

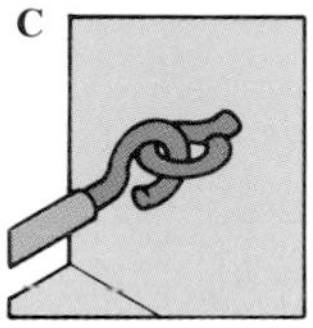

Sink unit

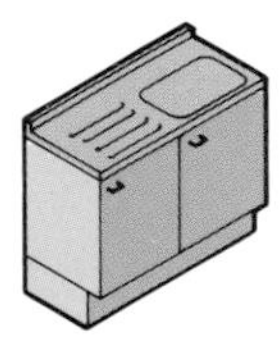

Finish and assemble parts **1-5** as for base unit. Make extension side **6** as side **1** but omit the 1/16 in. holes for shelf supports. Fit bottom panel **7** with corner joints (see p. 133), the front edge should be flush with front edge of sides. The bottom can be fixed to either side of completed cabinet to accommodate a left or a right handed sink top, **A.** Fit top rail **8** with corner joints 6 in. from top edge of side and 4 in. from back edge to face of rail. Finish exposed edge of packing batten **9** with iron-on plastic edging, and screw to side **1**, front edges flush. Fit fascia rail **10** to packing batten and side, with corner joints flush with front edges. Screw back battens **11** to sides and bottom, flush with top rail. Fix back panel **12** as for base unit. Screw and glue four 4 in. right angle triangular plates to back edges of bottoms, to brace sides. Fit the doors **13** with 170° lay-on hinges as for base unit, except that the top hinge on sink side door must be centered 8 in. from top edge. Fit shelf and plinth **14** as for base unit.

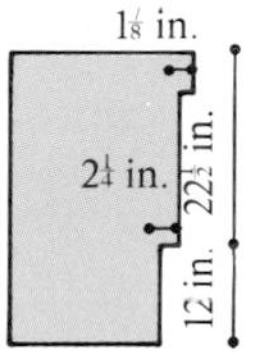

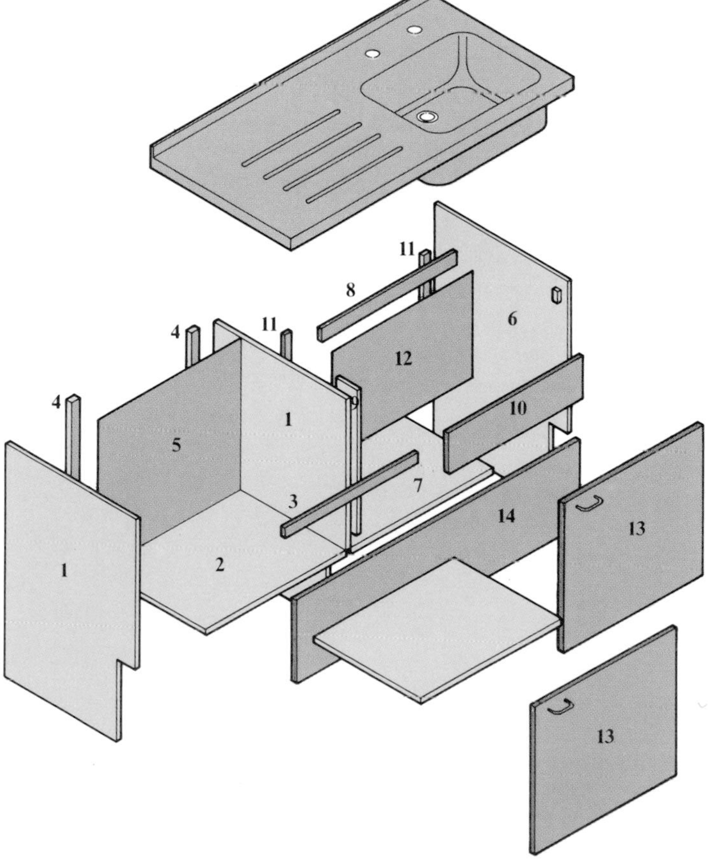

No	Part	Quantity	Length	Width	Th	Material
1	Side	2	34½	22⅛	⅝	Veneered particle board
2	Fixed shelf	1	22¾	19	⅝	Veneered particle board
3	Top rail	2	22¾	2	1	Softwood
4	Back battens	3	19¾	1	1	Softwood
5	Back panel	1	21¼	22¾	⅛	Hardboard
6	Extension side	1	34½	22⅛	⅝	Veneered particle board
7	Fixed shelf	1	23⅜	19	⅝	Veneered particle board
8	Top rail	1	23⅜	2	1	Softwood
9	Packing batten	1	21¾	4	⅝	Veneered particle board
10	Fascia rail	1	22¾	6	⅝	Veneered particle board
11	Back battens	3	19¾	1	1	Softwood
12	Back panel	1	23⅜	15¾	⅛	Hardboard
13	Doors	2	22⅜	24	¾	Pine plywood
14	Plinth	1	As required	12	⅝	Veneered plywood

Hardware: 4, 170° opening concealed hinge. 16, corner joint K.D. fittings. 2, 3¾'D' handle. 48 x 24 sink top. 4, ⅞ x 2 screw eyes. *N.B. All dimensions are shown in inches.*

2
5
6
4
11
1
14
11
15
13
15
8
13
15
1
10
14
12
3
9
16
A
1⅛ in.
2¼ in.
22¼ in.
12 in.
B
C
11
8
6
4
11
12
4
1
10
5
7
3
14
13
1
2
13

Tables & Accessories

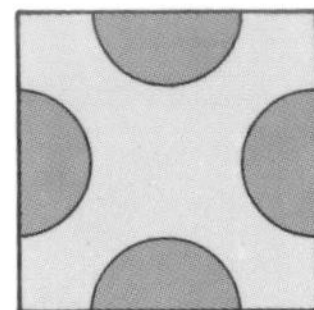
A

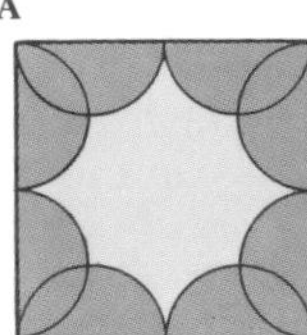
B

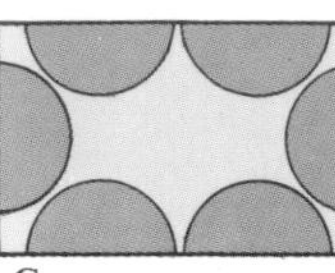
C

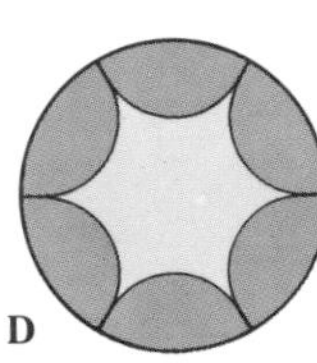
D

Dining tables
Each person sitting at the table will need about two feet of space and sufficient leg room under the table. A square table will take four people comfortably as **A,** depending on its size, and can accommodate eight, but with less elbow room, **B.** Because the leg spaces overlap, the corners cannot be fully used. Placing only one seat on each side avoids this but makes this shape uneconomical in terms of seating capacity. A rectangular shape, which could be a square table with an extension, provides greater seating capacity without being bigger in area than the square, **C.** As with a square shape, the legs are best placed at each corner. This eliminates uncomfortable leg straddling. Extension leaves added to the end **E** make for more comfortable seating than if placed in the middle, **F.** A round table is perhaps the most sociable shape, but not the easiest to construct. A three foot diameter top will accommodate four people while six can sit comfortably around a four foot diameter, **D.** An oval table combines the best qualities of both round and rectangular tables, especially if it, like the round table, is mounted on a pedestal base, thus providing generous leg room. The height of a table top should be about 30 in.

E

F

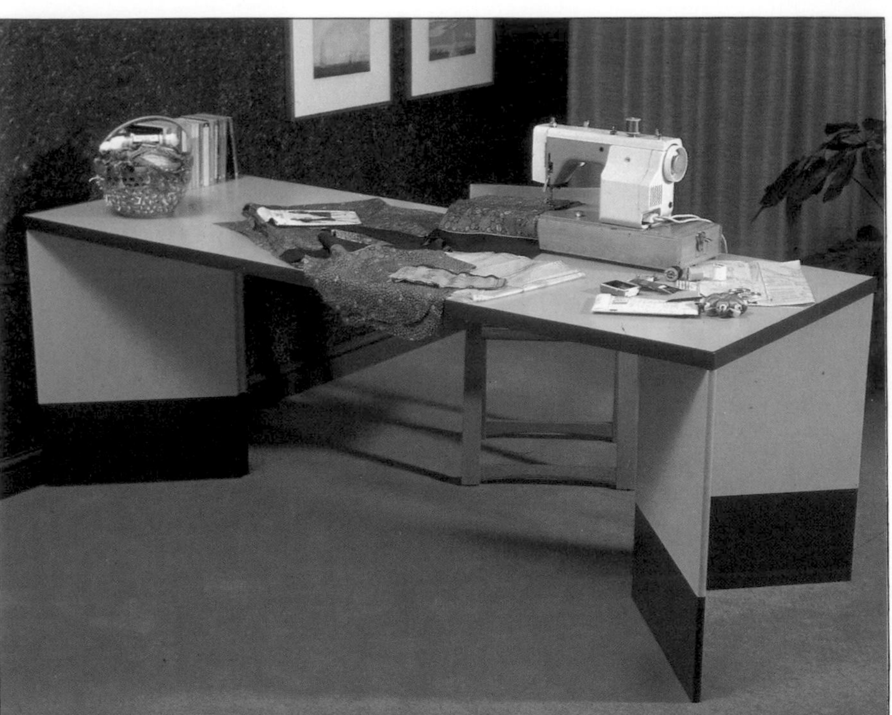
1

2

1 Folding table
Provides an additional work surface when not used for dining, see p. 176 for making instructions.

2 Round table
This shape is perhaps the most sociable and best suited for conversation. See p. 176 for details.

3 Candle holder
Various lengths of chromed metal tube make a decorative candle holder as shown on p. 176.

4 Glass vase
Vases, both square and rectangular can be made of $\frac{1}{4}$ in. glass as described on facing page.

5 Salad servers
Acrylic sheet made pliable by heat can be shaped to form these salad servers, see facing page.

6 Napkin rings
Simple shapes, useful as napkin rings, are easily cut from acrylic sheet, as described on page 175.

7 Mats and coasters
A cork tile can be cut to produce a table mat and 3 coasters. See p. 176 for making instructions.

3

4

5

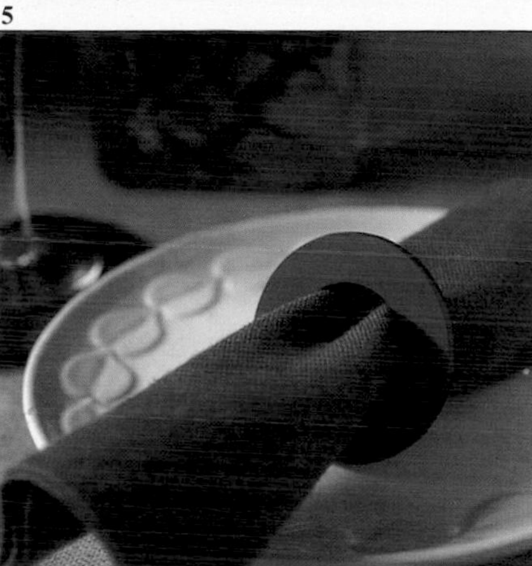

6

7

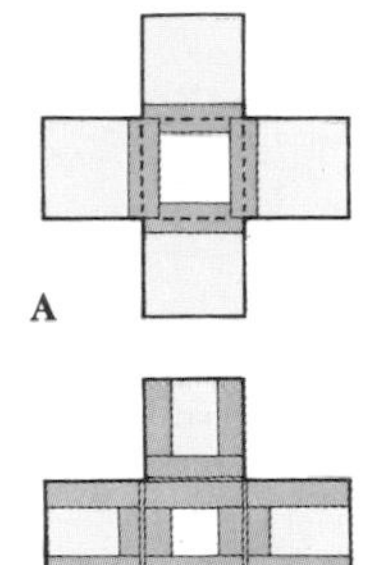

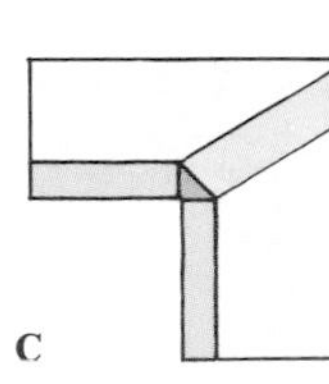

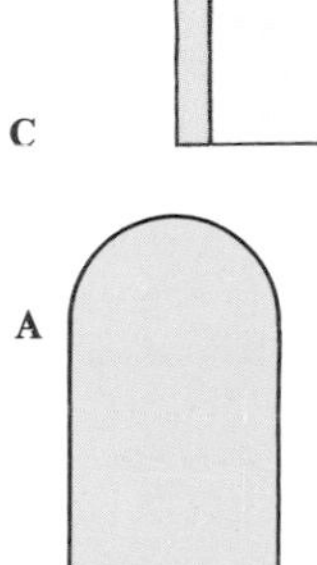

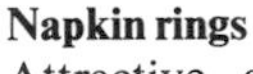

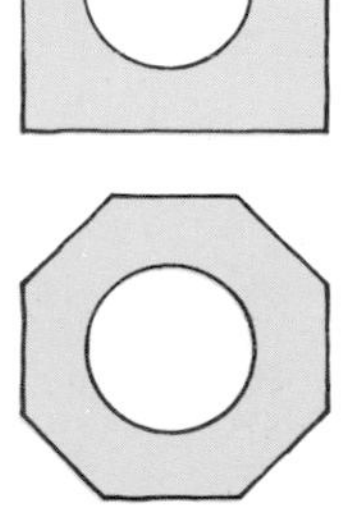

Glass vase

A rectangular or square-shaped vase can be made of ¼ in. glass. Decide the width of your vase (say 4 in.) and cut a 4 in. square base. Cut the sides to length and smooth down the edges with wet and dry paper, lubricated with water. Use masking tape to join the bottom ends of the four sides to the base, **A.** Apply masking tape flush with edges of base and sides, on the reverse side **B.** Support the base on a wooden block, cut to the same height as the sides. The sides will hang down, the tape acting as a hinge. Check for alignment and apply silicone rubber sealant in the angles formed by sides and base, filling to excess. When set (about 24 hrs) stand assembly on the base. Crease four strips of tape and press into the inside angles of sides. Apply sealant to the side edges as for base and allow to set. Remove tape, and with a sharp knife trim off excess sealant to give a 45° angled joint **C.**

Salad servers

Cut the shape for each spoon from ⅛ in. acrylic sheet, making a shallow saw cut in one face stopping 4½ in. from the curved end **A.** Heat the handle over a flame to within 2 in. of the curved end, until the plastic is pliable, taking care not to scorch it (see pp. 144-145). Use protective gloves and fold along the scored line, then place between battens in a vise, with the curved end projecting 4 in. Tighten the vise to flatten the sides together. When set, remove from vise and trim any misalignment between the two edges. Cut end off handle to make an overall length of 11 in. Sand and polish the cut edges. Seal the crease at spoon end with solvent adhesive.

Napkin rings

Attractive and colorful napkin rings can be simply made from ⅛ in. acrylic sheet cut into a variety of geometric shapes. First mark out the design on the protective paper which usually covers acrylic sheeting and then cut out the shapes with a fine-toothed saw. A round shaped napkin ring can be cut with a hole saw in a power drill, using the 2½ in. cutter for the outside, and the 1¼ in. for the inside. The 1¼ in. cutter is also used for the hole in square and octagonal rings. Finish the edges with a fine abrasive paper and polish (see pp. 144-145).

Tables & Accessories

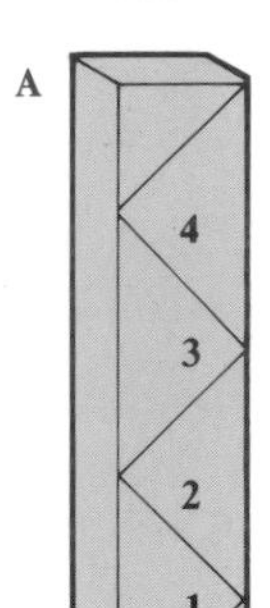

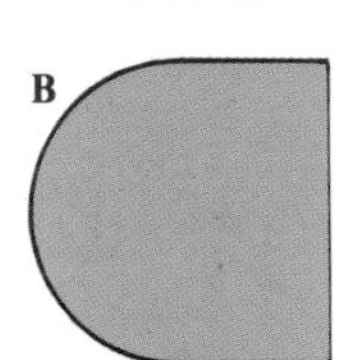

Round table

Cut the four particle board panels to size; these form the central column **1.** Nail and glue them together, lapping each panel on one edge to its neighbor. Mark and cut the four softwood blocks as shown in **A,** from a length of 2 in. x $1\frac{1}{2}$ in. These triangular blocks fit flush in the top and bottom four corners of the column. Mark and cut two disks **2** from 1 in. particle board, cutting around the edge of the bottom base disk and shaping it into a full circle, **B.** Fill the open grain of disk edges with epoxy filler, and sand smooth when dry. Measure and mark for screw holes, drill pilot holes in the corner blocks, and screw through the disks so that they fit centrally to the top and bottom of the column. To make the top, cut a square particle board panel as follows: mark diagonals from corner to corner to determine center, then draw a circle to whatever diameter you may need. Cut with a power jigsaw or a compass saw with the board held in a vise, trim the edge square with a spokeshave or block plane. Now lay the board flat on the bench, clamp, and curve the edge with a power router, using the appropriate bit. Alternatively, work around the perimeter with plane or spokeshave to form a circle. Finish with a sanding block, fill any chips or holes with filler paste, sand again. Smooth off top before painting. To attach to the base, center on top disk, and screw through the disk into the underside of the top.

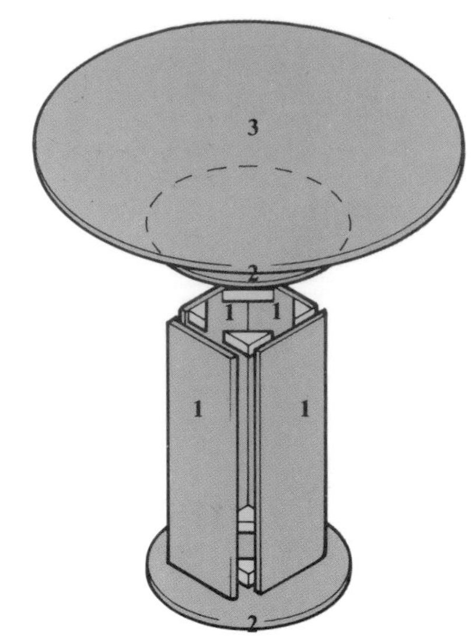

No	Part	Quantity	Length	Width	Th	Material
1	Column sides	4	26½	9¼	¾	Particle board
2	Column disks	2	23½ dia		1	Particle board
3	Top	1	47 dia		1	Particle board

N.B. All dimensions are shown in inches.

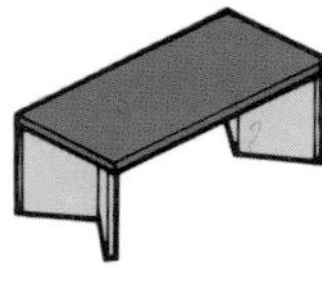

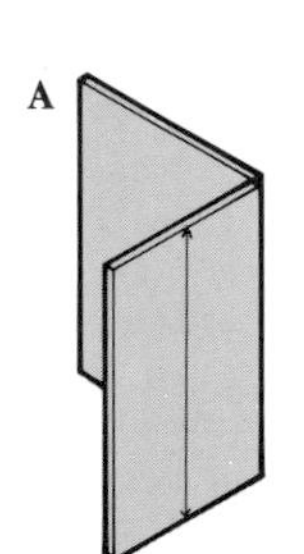

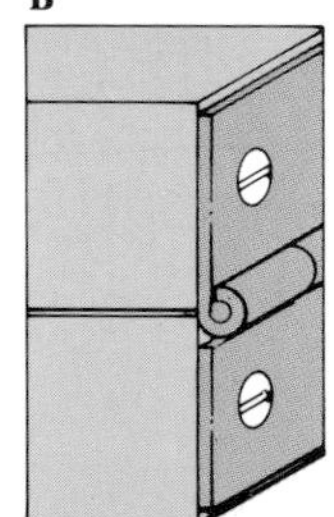

Folding table

An extremely useful idea for a small apartment or where the dining room is used for other purposes, is a dining table that can be folded and stored away.

Cut out leg panels **1** from lumber core plywood making sure the grain of the core runs vertically on both panels as in **A,** so that hinge screws will go into side grain and not end grain of wood. Drill a hole $\frac{3}{8}$ in. diameter and $\frac{3}{4}$ in. deep in the top edge of both leg panels, $1\frac{3}{8}$ in. from one corner – these holes take the pegs that locate into the table top. Cut a $1\frac{1}{2}$ in. length of dowel $\frac{3}{8}$ in. diameter, and glue into the hole. Glue lippings to front edges of panels **2.** Sand all surfaces for painting. Lay each pair of panels together with their edges flush. Mark and screw a piano hinge to the back edges of each pair, **B.** Paint leg panels throughout. Drive $\frac{1}{2}$ in. diameter rubber-headed nails in the bottom edges 1 in. from side edges, or fit rubber pads. Lip, face and balance top **3** with plastic laminate. Finish all edges with a $\frac{1}{16}$ in. chamfer. Alternatively, nail and glue a wooden lipping that matches the side lipping to each end. Sand the wood all around and paint the top throughout. Drill clearance holes $\frac{3}{8}$ in. diameter and $\frac{7}{8}$ in. deep in underside of table top, $1\frac{3}{8}$ in. from side and ends at the corners. Set up the leg panels and fit the top on the pegs. If the pegs are a tight fit, reduce them slightly with a file and dome the ends.

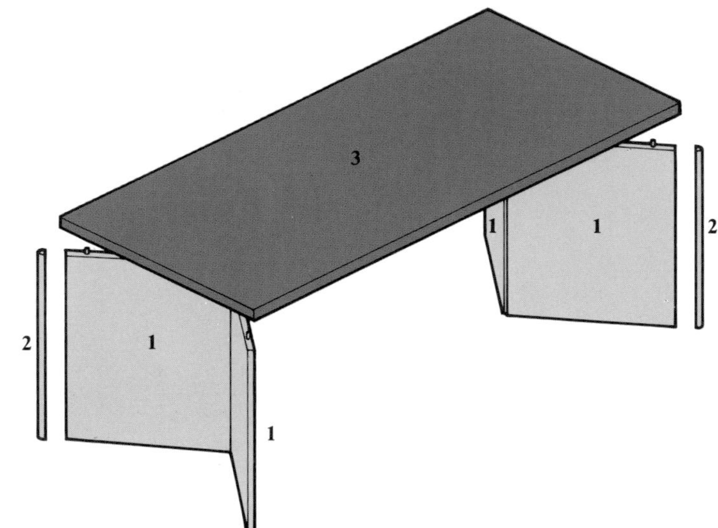

No	Part	Quantity	Length	Width	Th	Material
1	Leg panel	4	27½	22	¾	Lumber core plywood
2	Lipping	4	27½	¾		Half round molding
3	Top	1	78	33	1½	Hardboard flush door

Hardware: 2, 27½ long piano hinges. 8, ½ rubber headed nails. ***N.B.*** *All dimensions are shown in inches.*

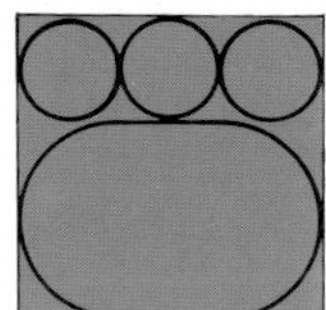

Table mat and coasters

One oval table mat and three circular coasters can be cut from one 12 in. x 12 in. cork floor tile. Set a compass to a 4 in. radius, and mark two semicircular arcs, with centers 4 in. apart on a line 8 in. from top. Set the compass to a 2 in. radius and mark three circles on the remaining 4 in. strip. Using a metal ruler as a guide, cut out the shapes with a sharp knife. First cut the tile into a rectangle and three squares. Make the curves by taking successive tangential cuts from the corners. Finish the edges with fine abrasive paper, and seal with a clear polyurethane lacquer.

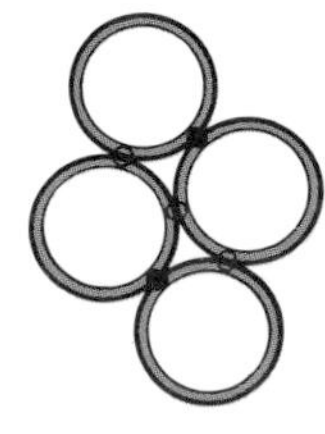

Candle holder

Cut length of 1 in. diameter chromed brass tube into pieces of 3, 4, 5 and 6 inches. Finish the cut edges and remove burr with fine emery cloth. Cut four disks from thin gauge brass sheeting to fit inside diameter of tube. Soft solder disks inside the bases (see pp. 142-143). Prepare tubes for gluing by cleaning surfaces with a lighter fluid. Apply epoxy resin adhesive to the side of 3 in. tube and glue to 4 in. tube, bottom ends flush. Repeat for 5 in. and 6 in. tubes. When glue has set, position tubes together and note where they touch. Apply bands of glue on shorter pair and bond to remaining pair.

Leisure Areas

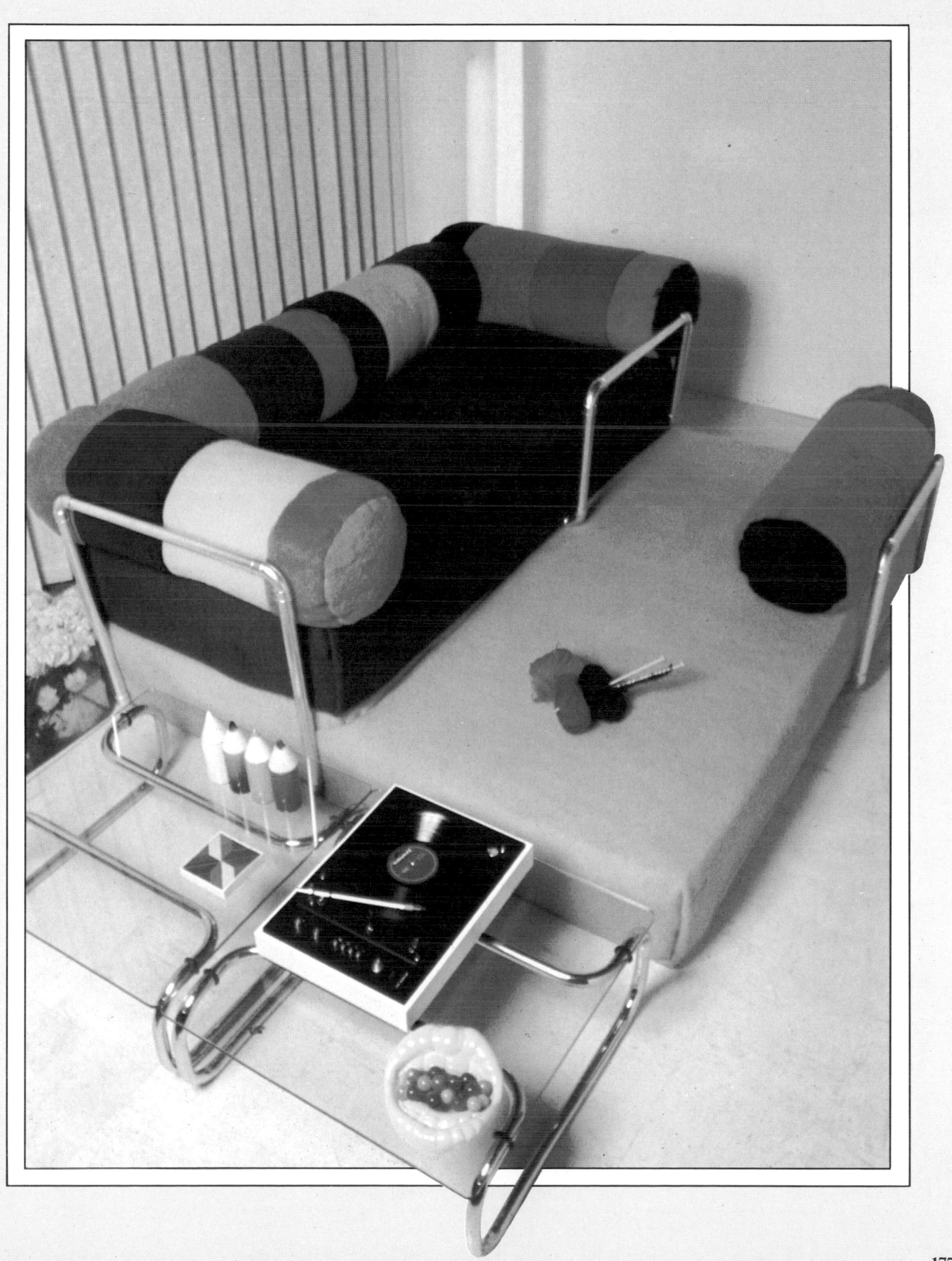

Choosing Chairs

Chair design
Our modern preoccupation with backache has led scientists to examine carefully the effects of stress on the human body, and in particular the way we sit. Many designers have not seriously considered the facts of posture and implemented them in chair designs. A "comfortable" chair was one that was heavily upholstered and bulky; the majority of chairs are utilitarian or rather severe. Deck chairs, for example. are so constructed that they can be easily stacked, or moved from one place to another; they are flexible enough not to rock on an uneven surface, and they are quite comfortable for short periods. Yet for the human body, adaptable though it is, deck chairs are badly designed. The curved nature of the seat fails to support the spinal column, and can thus produce backache. It also pushes your head forward, restricting the rib cage, and unless you sit with your knees drawn up, the front rail presses on the back of your legs. If deck chairs are difficult to sit in, they can be formidable to get out of, although they still remain a popular means of relaxed, informal seating, and we are prepared to ignore most of their bad points.

Comfortable seating
Let's now look at the main characteristics of a comfortable chair. Firstly, the seat should slope from front to back, at such an angle that your entire body is in a relaxed position. The front part of the seat must be at a height that allows you to relax without applying pressure on the back of your legs; a similar restriction is caused by the seat being too deep. A low-back chair must be high enough to support your back from seat to shoulder level. A high-back chair should be designed to give support in the form of a gentle "S" shape. This will most closely follow the natural curve of the spine, supporting the small of the back, the shoulders and the head. A chair with a footstool enables you to achieve a semi-reclining position, and many manufacturers produce a matching chair and footstool. Of a similar nature are lounging chairs, which usually have a more ample length of seat, combined with a back angle for a reclined position. This type of chair, if well-designed, is extremely comfortable, but may take up more space.

Elementary comfort
Deck chairs are lightweight, easy to stack, cheap to produce, but the design distorts posture. A well-designed chair (below) incorporates these qualities: the seat should slope from front to back, it should not be too deep, and it should be at a comfortable height. The chair must be stable, and not threaten to tip over in any direction.

High enough to support head and neck

Correct slope relaxes body. Gentle S-shape supports back

Chair wide enough not to topple sideways

Length and height of seat allows freedom for legs

Low back chair must at least reach shoulder level if it is to provide adequate support.

High back chair gives additional support to the lumbar region as well as to the head and shoulders.

Lounging chair combines a back rest with a long seat for a comfortable reclining posture.

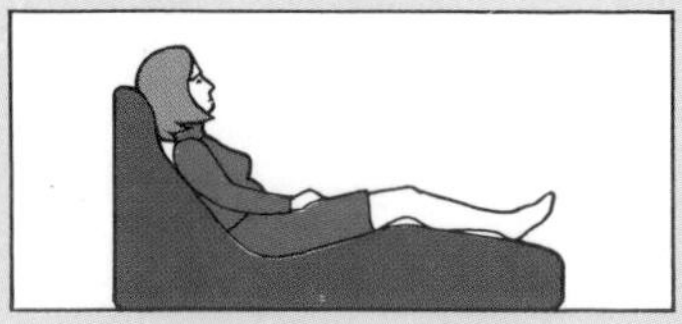

Chair and footstool provide an alternative way of achieving similar relaxed seating.

Seating

A Two-seater sofas placed opposite each other allow occupants to converse and observe a focal point outside the area. There is also room for a low table.

B This arrangement can fit the corner of a room, but it restricts use of table and the adjacent seat.

C Introduction of a three-seater gives more freedom of access, and use of tables, but naturally demands more space.

D A simple, compact arrangement, but it excludes a focal point.

E A three-seater and two single chairs offer great flexibility, but they occupy more space.

F Similar to layout C, but more expensive because of the specially-designed seating.

Planning layouts

Seats should be arranged so that the occupants can easily relate to each other, and also to the surrounding area. Taking a living room as an example, you will need to provide a comfortable area in which to relax, and one that allows communication between people, and where everyone can relate to some focal point within, or just outside the area – a TV set or a fireplace. There must, of course, be adequate leg room for the occupants of the chairs, room enough to allow you to get up and move around, and for others to pass by without inconvenience. The basic methods of planning seating layouts are illustrated on the left.

Relating to a focal point

Perhaps the simplest layout of all is the two-seater sofa, shown in figure **A.** The occupants are seated side by side, the layout is economical in terms of space, providing good access to the seating. The occupants can also relate to a focal point, although the two-seater arrangement somewhat limits its position, which has to be precisely located to be appreciated by both. In fact, this positioning is true of all seating arrangements, but some are more flexible than others. Two-seater sofas set at right angles, figure **B,** with a table at the corner, are marginally better where the focal point is concerned, and the occupants are able to share the table, but leg room is restricted in the corner seats.

Greater flexibility

In figure **C,** the layout provides an excellent area of communication, creating a cosy atmosphere for conversation. Ideally, the arrangement requires the addition of a three-seater to provide sufficient access and leg room, and the focal point is more or less limited to a central position. The arrangement in figure **D** also provides good communication, and the sharing of a side table, although it is difficult to include a communal focal point. The traditional sofa and two chairs in figure **E** demand a larger area of space, but are more flexible since the seating can be easily moved around. Some manufacturers construct versatile seating units designed to fit together in continuous curves. This arrangement in figure **F** avoids cramped space at corners, as in figures **B** and **C,** but being of an unconventional design is likely to prove expensive.

Space between seating

1 Where two sofas are sited opposite each other, each with one end placed against a wall, they should be sufficiently apart to provide plenty of leg room, and also include enough space for access.

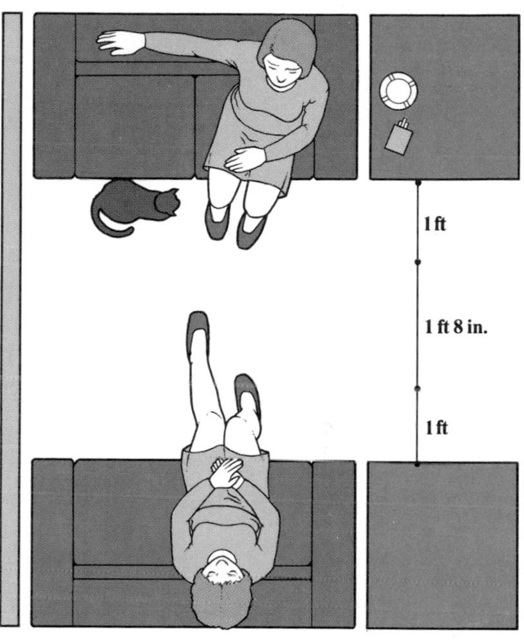

2 Where the opposite sofas are sited away from the wall, there is room for access at either end. The position also allows space for a small table. The area around the sofas should provide at least 2 ft of passing space. This type of arrangement is more suitable in a larger room, with perhaps a central fireplace.

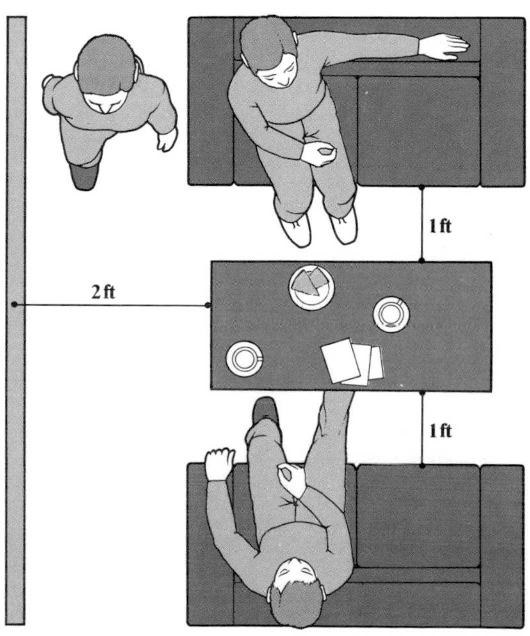

Upholstered Seating

Upholstered range

Individual units offer the greatest flexibility for seating arrangements. Three corner units and two chair units have been grouped together in **1** to form an "L" shaped arrangement. The overall length of the seating is determined by the number of chair units placed in between. Similarly the layout can be altered to a "U" shape with the addition of another corner unit and the appropriate number of chair sections.

The arrangement below, **2**, used left and right hand corner units only, placed together to make two-seater sofas. Here again, the length can be increased with the addition of chair sections.

Apart from the flexibility and scale of arrangements, the individual sections allow the units to be easily moved for changing needs. This might be for a permanent rearrangement or for a temporary move while decorating or cleaning. In the latter case the seat cushions can be removed and the base and back or arm assemblies stacked together. Unlike those sofas with leg frames the flat base panels avoid the indentations in floors and carpets caused by the point loads on the legs. The flat base panels also allow the sections to be slid over the carpet with comparative ease when necessary. If the units slide too readily, fit rubber pads. Cut four two inch squares from ribbed rubber sheeting not thicker than $\frac{1}{8}$ in., and glue them to the underside, one inset from each corner. This is recommended for rooms with polished wood or other hard floor finishes. In the case of uneven hard floors such as stone slabs the pads may have to be made thicker to accommodate the different levels.

Full making instructions for the upholstered range are given on pp. 182-183.

1

2

Occasional Tables

1

1 Mirror top table
The side panels of the mirror top table have been finished with a rich dark stain to contrast with the silver top. Bright colors can also be used according to the interior scheme.

2 Games table
The checkerboard is etched into the surface of the laminate. When the game is not in progress the permanent finish provides an attractive geometric design for the top. To clean the top use a liquid detergent solution and rub dry with a cloth, do not apply polish.

3 Table base
The base of the table houses the games pieces in a felt lined compartment.

2

3

Upholstered Seating

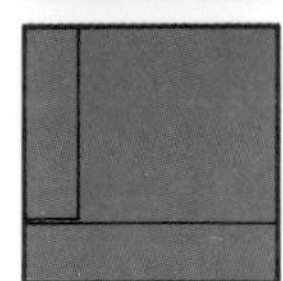

A

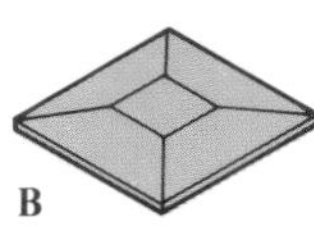

B

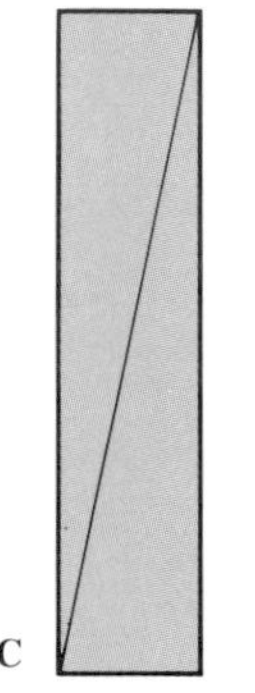

C

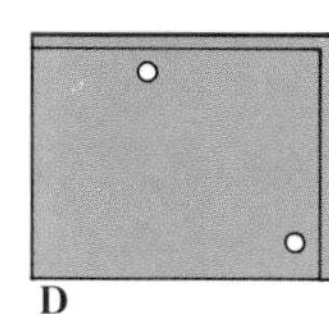

D

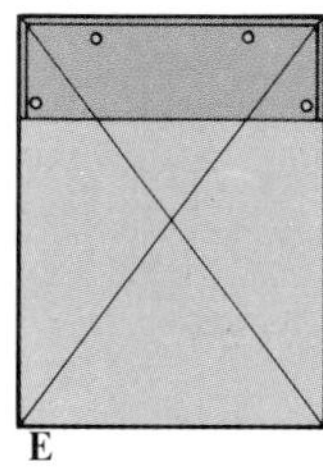

E

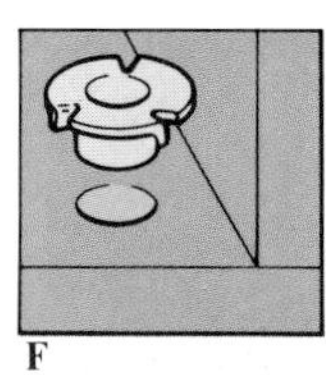

F

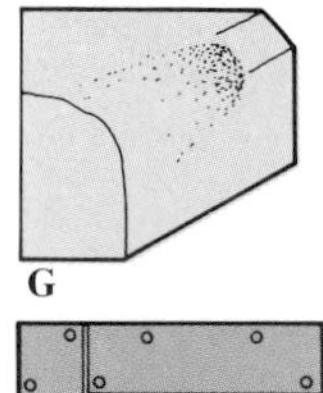

G

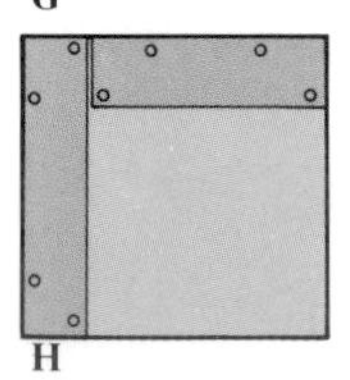

H

The basic range
This wide seating unit is based on a 26 in. wide module which offers plenty of scope for the layout of the seating. There is a basic chair with a seat, back and bolster cushion, and this can be fitted with a side section to create a corner or an end unit. The height of the back provides ample support for the shoulders, while the top of the cushion comfortably supports the head. A great advantage of this upholstered range is that while the design has been based on a traditional style and cushioned comfort, you do not need to be an expert in upholstery to make it. The construction of the units is very simple: sandwiches of foam (providing simple springing) and butt-jointed wood paneling. The seat back and sides are made as individual units to simplify the upholstery and are fixed to a base panel by means of bolts. Your upholstery supplier should be able to cut the foam to your measurements, and to supply the correct adhesive for bonding.

Base panel
The base panel is made in two sizes – 32½ in. x 32½ in., and 32½ in. x 25 in. The larger size carries the side unit (see **A**). Finish the edges with iron-on lipping and stain the lipping to blend with the upholstery; the panel will be drilled for bolt fixings when you make the back unit.

Base and seat cushions
Apply adhesive to one side of medium foam base cushion **2**, and bond to the firm reconstituted foam nosing **3**, flush all around. For the seat cushion, trim the top surface of tapered layer **5** down to ⅜ in. on the outside edges over a 6 in. wide band all around as in **B**. Bond the pad to the center of the top surface bottom layer **4**. Bond top layer **6** over the pad, to the lower layer, flush all around.

Back unit frame
Screw and glue back panel **7** to back edge of base board **8**. Cut triangular end panels **9** to shape, and screw and glue to inside faces of back and base board, flush with edges. Two pieces can be cut from one 7 in. wide board, see **C**. Drill four clearance holes for tee nut connectors in base board 1 in. from edges **D**. Clamp assembled back frame to the base panel **1** flush with the three sides, **E**. Drill clearance holes for ¼ in. diameter bolts in the base panel, using holes in the frame as a guide for their position. Countersink the holes on the underside, to receive flat head bolts. Fit tee nuts in frame **F**. Number the board and underside of back frames.

Back unit cushion
Bond soft outer layer **11** to medium density foam inner layer, **10**. Bond capping **12** to top edge of block, with one long edge flush with the front face of inner layer. The other edges should overlap. Apply adhesive to inside of back frame and press cushion assembly into place. Cut foam ½ in. deep along diagonal edge of end panels, so foam will spring out flush with face of panels. Apply adhesive to outer face of back panel and under edge of capping overlap. Glue back skin flush all round. Bond end skins to both ends. Trim away ½ in. strip from corners of top capping with scissors, on long edges only. Use coarse sandpaper to rub edges into a smooth curve, **G**.

Side unit
Make this in the same way as the back unit, using parts **15-22**. The side unit is bolted to the base panel in the same way as the previously described back. However, the back unit, when fitted with the arm, will be flush on two sides only; there should be a ½ in. gap between arm and back, when both are positioned on the base. When clamping the frame to the base for drilling, remember that the corner units are either right or left handed, **H**.

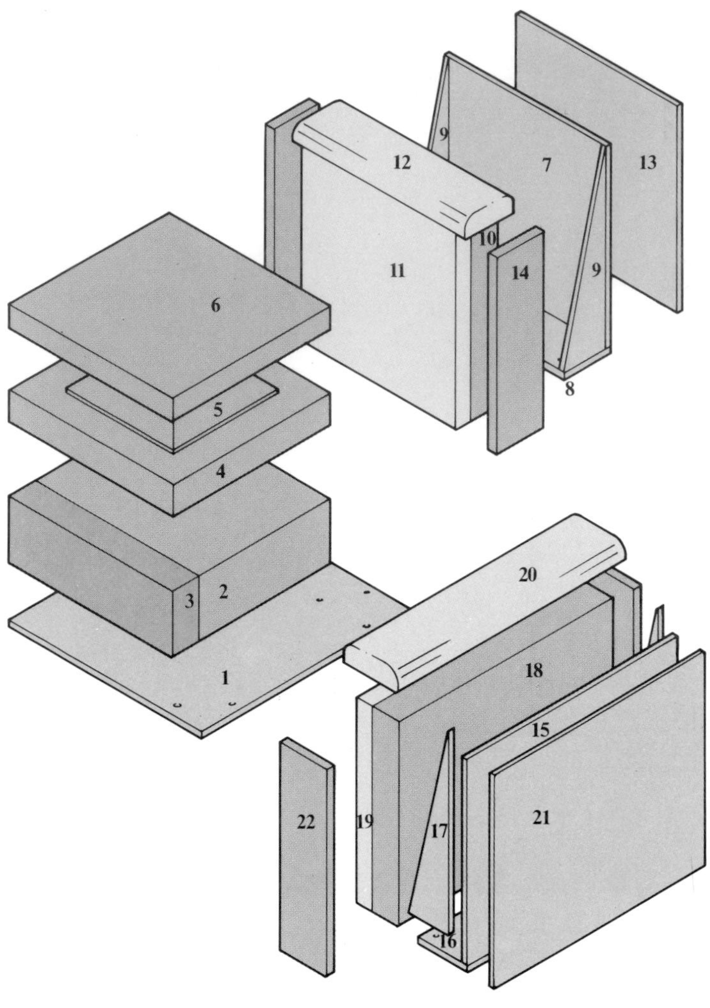

No	Part	Quantity	Length	Width	Th	Material
	Seat base					
1	Base panel	1	32½	32½	¾	Plywood
2	Base cushion	1	26	22	8	Medium density foam
3	Nosing	1	26	8	4	Firm reconstituted foam
	Seat cushion					
4	Bottom layer	1	26	26	3	Medium density foam
5	Tapered layer	1	18	18	1	Medium density foam
6	Top layer	1	26	26	2	Medium density foam
	Back unit					
7	Back panel	1	27½	25	½	Particle board
8	Back base board	1	25	7	¾	Particle board
9	Back end panels	2	26¾	7	½	Particle board
10	Inner layer	1	26¾	25	4	Medium density foam
11	Outer layer	1	26¾	25	3	Soft density foam
12	Capping	1	25	8	2	Soft density foam
13	Back skin	1	27½	25	½	Medium density foam
14	End skins	2	27½	8	1	Medium density foam
	Side unit					
15	Arm panel	1	32½	27½	½	Particle board
16	Arm base board	1	32½	7	¾	Particle board
17	Arm end panels	2	26¾	7	½	Particle board
18	Inner layer	1	32½	26¾	4	Medium density foam
19	Outer layer	1	32½	26¾	3	Soft density foam
20	Capping	1	34½	8	2	Soft density foam
21	Side skin	1	32½	27½	1	Medium density foam
22	End skins	2	27½	8	1	Medium density foam

Hardware: 4 tee nuts with 4 1½" countersunk bolts to fit. Foam adhesive.
N.B. *All dimensions are shown in inches.*

Upholstery
The seating can be covered with any upholstery fabric you choose. Remember with patterned fabrics to cut the pieces, using the paper patterns, with the design or repeat matching at the seams. If it is a large repeat pattern this can mean a considerable amount of wastage. Large designs that form a repeat should be cut so that the shape is central on the fabric panel when made up.
All velvets and velvet-type materials have a light and dark shade which depends on the direction of the light.

Seat base
Cut four sides, using the pattern for the top cover, and stitch together across ends and diagonal corners, on the top face only and with right sides together, I. Turn it inside out. Cut one square inner panel, fold over hem and press flat. Top stitch over center hole in top face. Fit the cover over the foam base and slip stitch the remaining diagonal corners on the underside.

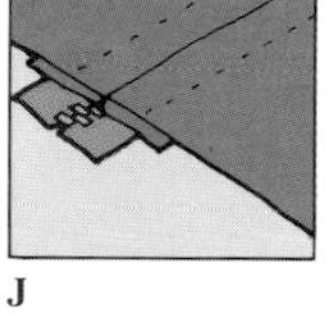
I

Seat cushion
Cut out three borders and two half borders for the back, using the patterns. Fit a 24 in. zipper to back borders. With the right sides together, baste ⅝ in. from one long edge, **J**. Press seams open. Pin closed zipper along seam line. Machine stitch ⅜ in. on each side of the center, using a zipper foot. Oversew the ends for extra strength. Remove basting. Stitch completed back border to sides and the sides to front border, right sides together, **K**. Stitch borders to top and bottom panels, right sides together. Clip corners to achieve a sharp corner. Open zipper and turn cushion cover inside out. Fold foam pad in two and slip into cover. Fasten zipper.

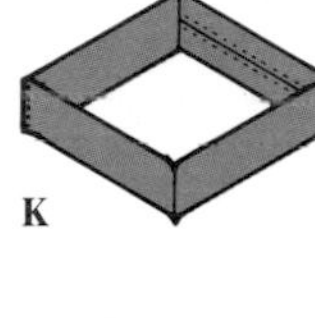
J

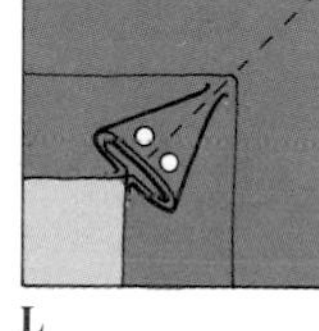
K

Back and sides
Cut out two end panels and one back or side panel and notch the edges on the center line. Pin the seams with right sides together, aligning the notches. Work away from the center around both sides. Machine stitch. Slip the cover over the foam and fix with tacks to the underside of the framing. Take care to avoid distorting the foam by getting the tension evenly distributed. Turn the corners under and fix with tacks, **L**.

L

Bolster
There are two patterns for the bolster, one for the straight seat unit and the other for a corner unit where a mitered end will be needed. For the straight bolster lining, cut out two narrow end panels and make a cut in the front edge to mark the bottom of the curve. Cut out the front panel and notch the side edges to mark the bottom of the curve. With right sides together, stitch the back seam to form a tube. Align notches in the end and front panels and pin seams. Taking care to follow the curve **M**, stitch the seams, leaving the bottom edge of one end open, so that you can turn the cover inside out and fill with loose foam stuffing. Clip the curved hem, then slip stitch to close after filling. Use a long needle to make a row of stitching through the center – this helps to hold the bolster in shape and prevents the filling falling to the bottom **N**. For the top cover use the same patterns and make up in a similar way to the lining, but only baste the back seam and stitch the ends in completely. Remove the basting to insert the filled bag. Close the back seam with slip stitching; it is not necessary to stitch through the top cover. Make the mitered corner bolster in the same way, using one narrow end panel pattern, one wide panel and the cut-away front panel patterns. To make a pair of corner bolsters, fit the mitered panel in the left or right hand end. The cut-away front panel patterns will have to be turned over when cutting a left or right handed cover.

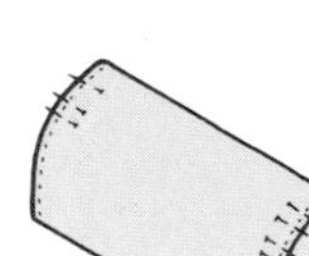
M

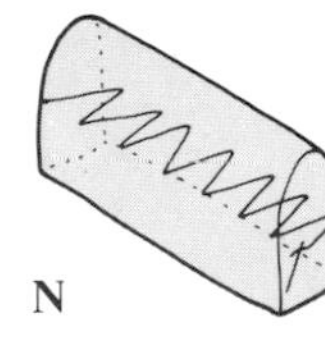
N

Pattern pieces

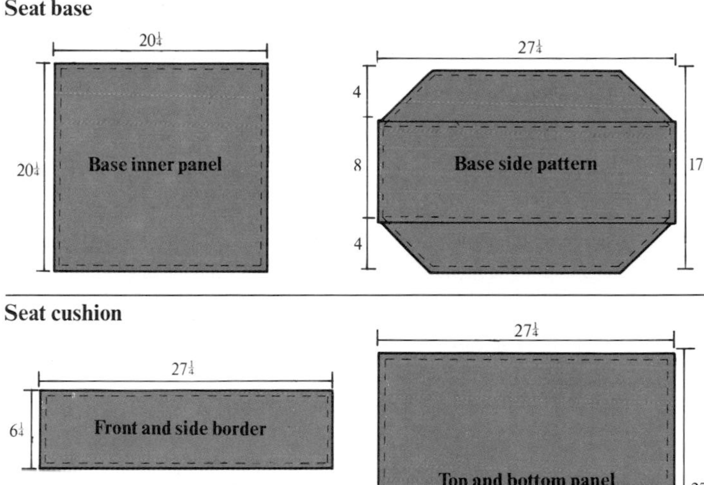

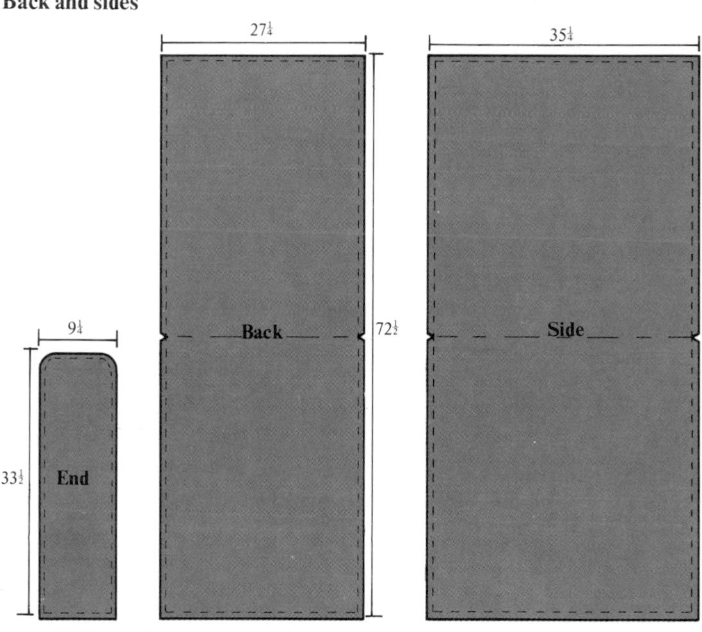

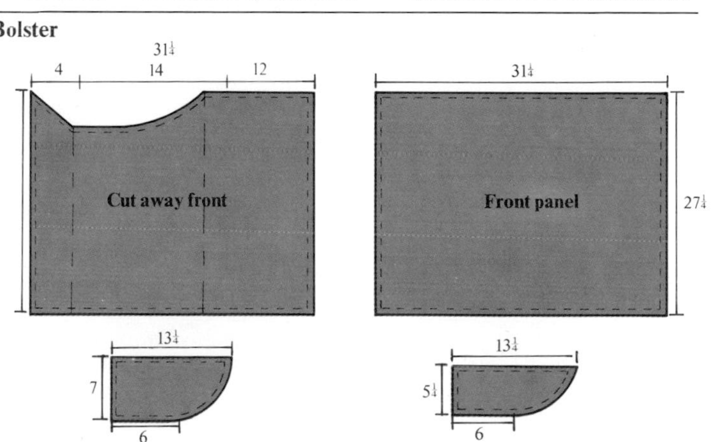

Cushions

Cushions and throw pillows

Cushions are the simplest and most versatile form of seating. They can readily adapt to form "day beds" at will. They are an excellent source of inexpensive additional seating and, with the proper covering, are also useful outdoors in the garden or patio. Very popular with children, cushions are ideal in the playroom, safe in even the most boisterous of games. Throw pillows and cushions are an inexpensive way of adding unexpected color to an interior. Given different front and back covers they can completely change the tone and emphasis of a room. Cushions can be made quite easily and stuffed with a variety of materials including hard and soft foam, left-over yarn or ready-made pillow forms. Use the instructions on p. 186 to make the covers shown right. The dimensions are for large floor cushions, but any of the designs would look good on smaller throw pillows.

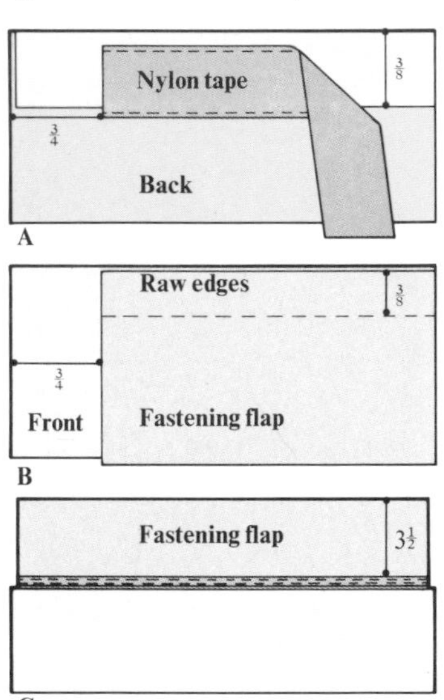

Basic cushion plans

Cut front and back pieces, each $35\frac{1}{2}$ in. square. Cut fastening flap, $7\frac{3}{4}$ in. x $35\frac{1}{2}$ in. Cut a strip of nylon tape fastener 34 in. long. With wrong side of one of the squares facing you, turn back a hem of $\frac{3}{8}$ in. Place one side of the nylon tape over the raw edge and stitch down **A.** Fold flap lengthways with right sides together, and stitch at each end with a $\frac{3}{4}$ in. seam. Turn right side out and sew to the front of the cover with a $\frac{3}{8}$ in. seam **B**. Sew the other side of the nylon tape to the fastening flap, $\frac{3}{16}$ in. from the seam joining the flap and the front **C**. With right sides together, sew the back and front along the three raw edges with a seam of $\frac{3}{8}$ in.

Quilted square

Folded square

Woven square

Patchwork square

1 A new life for material
Cushion covers can be made from almost any material which has perhaps out-worn its original use. Old bedcovers, curtains, even rugs can be used to make comfortable seating at almost no cost. The variety of materials only adds to a colorful interior.

1

2 Patchwork pillows
Even fabric scraps can be used to make patchwork cushion covers. Strips and squares are the easiest to handle, but you can also use triangular and octagonal shaped patches.

3 Round cushions
When making a round cushion cover try to choose a patterned fabric which reflects the shape of the cushion.

4 Handworked pillows
There are many kits available which enable you to design and make your own cushion covers, by using techniques such as embroidery, weaving, appliqué or crochet.

2

3

4

Cushions

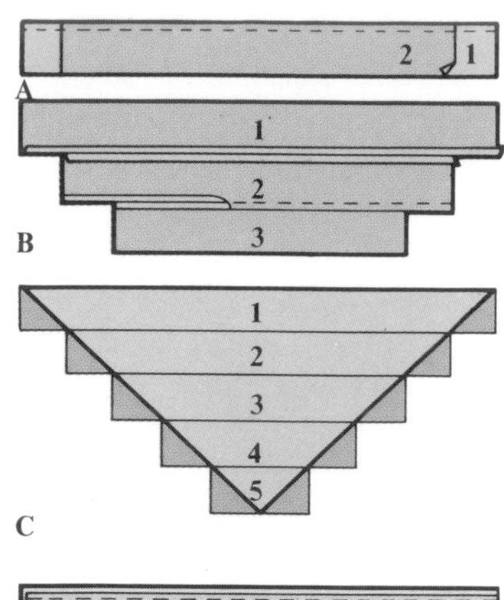

A B C

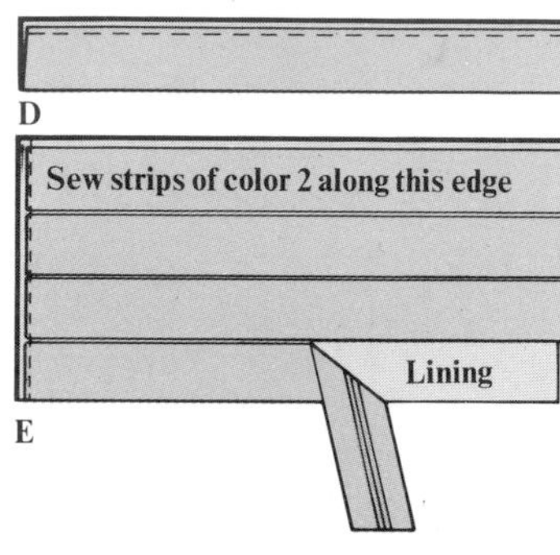

D E

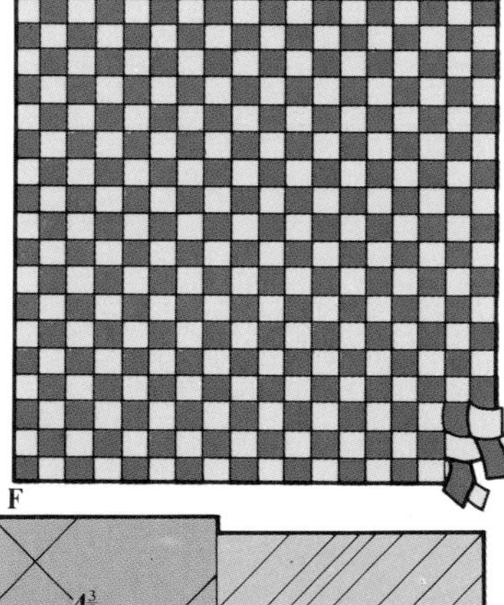

F

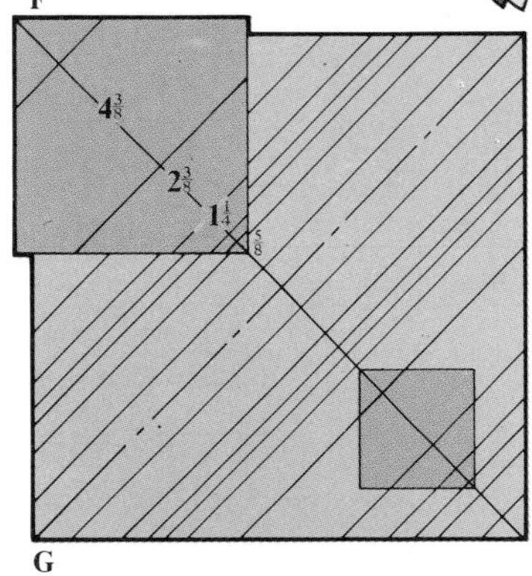

G

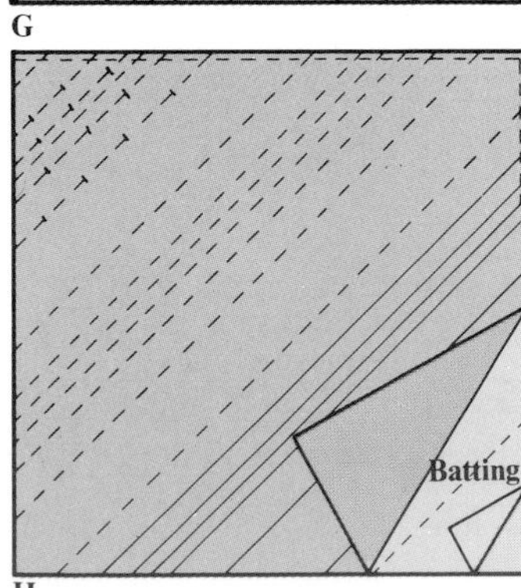

H

Patchwork square
Mark all centers with tailor's chalk. With right sides together and center marks aligned, stitch a piece of color **1** to one of color **2** with a ⅜ in. seam as shown in **A**. Open out and press the seam flat. Align center mark of color piece **2** with the center of color piece **3**. Sew together and press seams open as in **B**. Repeat for colors **4** and **5** until a shape is formed as shown in **C**. Draw lines with the chalk from the center bottom edge of color piece **5** to the top corners of **1**, trimming off excess fabric, **C**.
Repeat **A** to **C** to make four triangles. Align the colors carefully and sew the triangles together to form a square. Finish the cushion cover following the instructions for the basic cover on p. 184.

Woven square
Fold and sew all 36 strips into tubes using a 3/16 in. seam as in **D**. Press each piece flat with seam open. Pin and sew all 18 strips of color **1**, edge to edge, along one side of the lining, making sure that seams are to the back as in **E**. Repeat with all strips of color **2** joining them to the top edge of the lining. Lay the lining with its attached strips flat on a large non-slip surface. Weave the two colors together, pinning each strip firmly to the lining once it has been placed in its correct position. When all strips have been pinned down, stitch along the two remaining edges, **F**. Some basting may be necessary to hold the strips in place. Finish the cover as on p. 184.

Quilted square
Mark the right side of front as shown in **G**. Place the front over the lining, right sides facing out and stitch along one of the central chalk lines through the front and lining as in small diagram. Lift back the front and place a piece of cotton batting close to the stitches. Always cut the batting strips slightly narrower in width than the panel to be quilted. Cover the batting so that the front curves over it and stitch the front to the lining, close to the other edge of the batting as in **H**. Continue quilting using the method described and working from the central panel outward to the corners. Do not quilt the ⅝ in. panels. Sew front to lining along all four edges trimming away excess batting with stitch line ⅜ in. from the raw edge. To finish the cushion cover follow the instructions for the basic cover on p. 184, using the quilted square instead of the front.

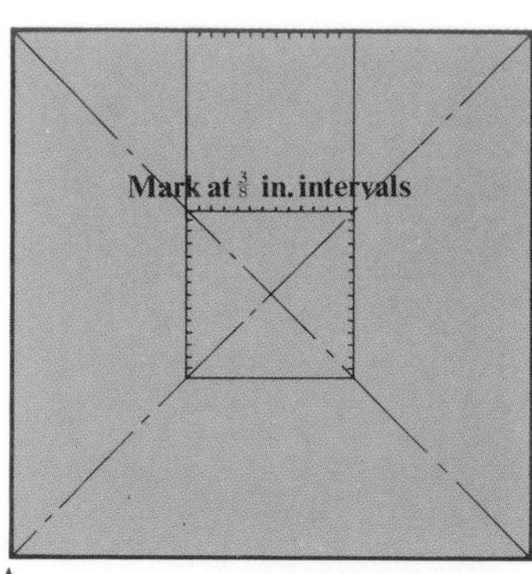

A

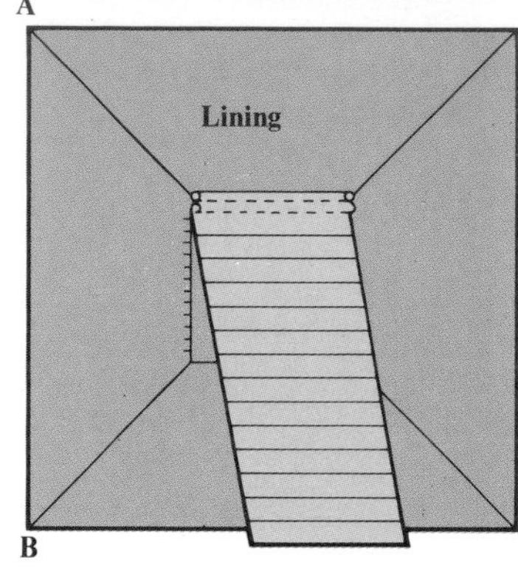

B

Folded square
Mark diagonals on the lining with tailor's chalk to find the center. Draw a rectangle 11⅜ in. x 11¼ in. in the center and mark stitch lines for the folds at ⅜ in. intervals, **A**. Hem the long edges of the nine 11¾ x 56 in. pieces, turning over 3/16 in. of material each side. With chalk mark off ⅜ in. at each end of the 9 pieces and then mark 30 divisions at 2 in. intervals to show where stitch lines will be placed. Position first piece, right side up over lining. Fold raw edge under ⅜ in. aligning with the top edge of the square, and top stitch close to the lining's edge, **B**. Line up first stitch line with first mark on lining, pin into position along the chalk line, allowing material to fold upwards. Sew to the lining, tacking at ends. Continue aligning the chalk marks on the first piece and the lining then sew into position. The raw edge of last fold should be turned under ⅜ in. and top stitched. Repeat for the other 8 squares. Finish as p. 184.

Patchwork square

No	Part	Quantity	Length	Width	Material
	Color 1	Total	60¼	36	Any non-stretch fabric i.e., cotton, cord, velvet, canvas or similar material.
1	Back	1	35½	35½	
2	Patchwork pieces	4	4⅜	35½	
3	Fastening flap	1	7¾	35½	
	Color 2	Total	17½	36	
4	Patchwork pieces	4	4⅜	29¼	
	Color 3	Total	17½	36	
5	Patchwork pieces	4	4⅜	21¼	
	Color 4	Total	9	36	
6	Patchwork pieces	4	4⅜	14¼	
	Color 5	Total	7¼	36	
7	Patchwork pieces	4	4¾	7¼	

Woven square

No	Part	Quantity	Length	Width	Material
	Color 1	Total	163	36	Any non-stretch upholstery or firm dress fabric e.g. cotton, cord, cotton mixtures or similar materials.
1	Back	1	35½	35½	
2	Lining	1	35½	35½	
3	Fastening flap	1	7¾	35½	
4	Weaving pieces	18	35½	4⅜	
	Color 2	Total	78	36	
5	Weaving pieces	18	35½	4⅜	

Quilted square

No	Part	Quantity	Length	Width	Material
	Cover and lining	Total	125	36	Cotton stretch fabric such as velvet or similar material
1	Front	1	35½	35½	
2	Back	1	35½	35½	
3	Lining	1	35½	35½	
4	Fastening flap	1	7¾	35½	
	Quilting	Total	78	18	Washable cotton
5	Quilting	2	35½	18	Batting

Folded square

No	Part	Quantity	Length	Width	Material
	Cover	Total	257½	36	Thin cotton or jersey.
1	Back	1	35½	35½	
2	Lining	1	35½	35½	
3	Fastening flap	1	7¾	35½	
4	Folded square	9	11¾	56	

Hardware: Nylon tape 34 long. ***N.B.*** *All dimensions are shown in inches.*

Occasional Tables

Games table

A good example of an occasional table, so-called because it has no specific purpose other than to provide a low table surface in the living room, is the checkerboard table. This particular table can be decorated with other designs following the instructions given for the checkerboard covering or can be left plain.

To make the basic table miter the ends of the framing boards **2** and glue to the underside of top **1,** making sure top is flush with the edges. Paint the underside surface when glue is dry. Lip and veneer the top with plastic laminate. Nail and glue one side **3** to shelf **4** with the top surface 6 in. from bottom edge and one edge flush. Nail and glue the remaining sides around the shelf with one edge lapping its neighbor. Finish the outside faces of box with plastic laminate. Line the box with felt: cut and bond a square piece to the bottom, cut side pieces to size and shape and bond to the inside faces and top edge. Trim the edge flush with the outside face, then locate top over the box.

A

To make the checkerboard top, construct a mask to cover the top out of a sheet of self-sticking plastic film. Mark out the squares working from two sides, **A.** Cut through the acetate with a sharp knife keeping to the squared area. Peel off alternate squares, **B.** Rub over the exposed squares of laminate evenly with fine steel wool to mat down the surface. When finished, remove the remaining mask and dust the top to remove any debris still left.

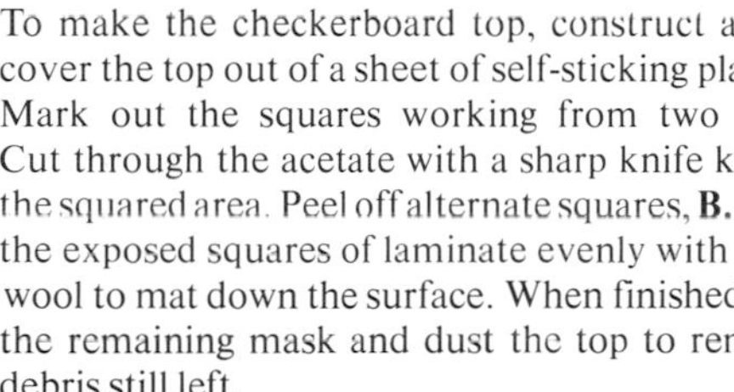

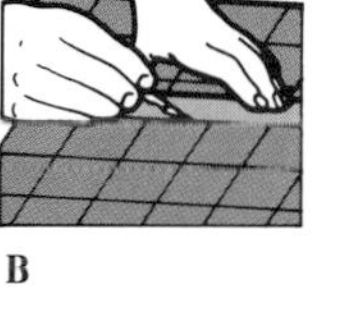

B

No	Part	Quantity	Length	Width	Th	Material
1	Top	1	24	24	¾	Particle board
2	Framing	4	24	6	¾	Particle board
3	Sides	4	11⅛	11⅛	¾	Particle board
4	Shelf	1	10⅜	10⅜	¾	Particle board

N.B. All dimensions are shown in inches.

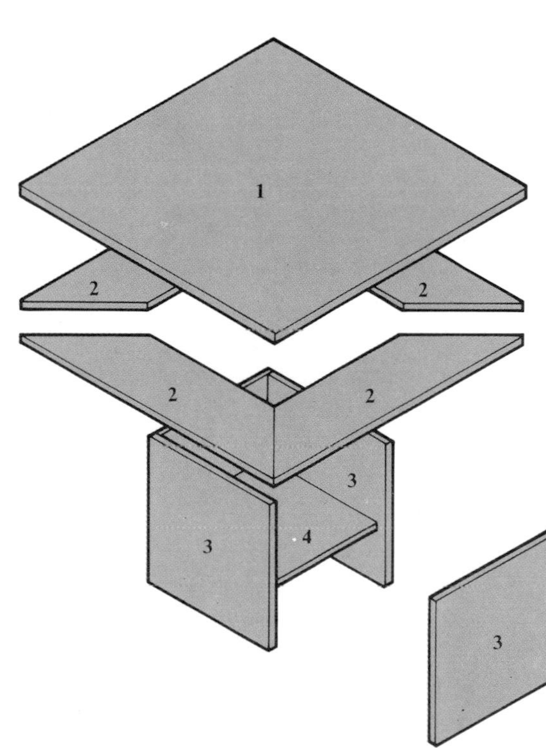

Mirror top table

This occasional table would be especially suitable for a corner seating arrangement and its mirrored top would display art objects or plants to their best advantage. Naturally it would not be suitable for regular use or around children. A smoked plexiglass top could be substituted for the mirror.

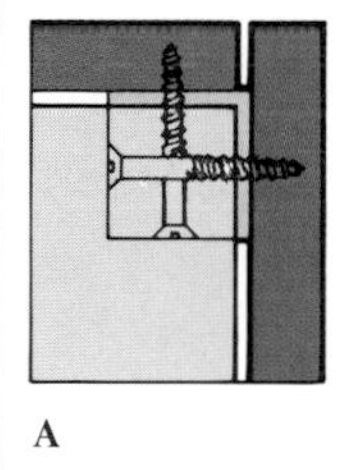

A

Cut sides **1** to size, finish cut edges with iron-on wood veneer to match required finish. Drill clearance holes for socket casters in the center of one end of the corner battens **2.** Drill and countersink two clearance holes for fixing screws in two adjacent sides of the battens. Stagger the holes so that the screws are clear of themselves and the caster spindle. Screw and glue one batten to each side on the inside face, flush with the bottom edge, and inset ⅝ in. from left hand end. Screw and glue sides together through corner battens, allowing a ⅛ in. gap between the end of one side, and the inside face of the other – a ⅛ in. packing piece will make this easier, see **A.** Check the diagonals for square. Finish all around with a suitable wood stain. Edge top board **3** with iron-on matching veneer. Finish edges to match sides and seal both surfaces. Sit the top on the corner battens, with an equal gap between its edges and the side faces. Drill a pilot hole and countersunk clearance hole through each corner, for screw fixing into the battens. Fix the top with 1½ in. no. 8 screws. Fit the casters. Have the mirror top **4** cut to size, ground and polished. Bond the glass to the top board with contact adhesive, fitting flush all around.

No	Part	Quantity	Length	Width	Th	Material
1	Sides	4	30¾	8	⅝	Veneered Particle board
2	Corner batten	4	7⅛	1½	1½	Softwood
3	Top board	1	30⅛	30⅛	¾	Lumber core plywood
4	Top	1	30⅛	30⅛	⅛	Mirror glass

N.B. All dimensions are shown in inches

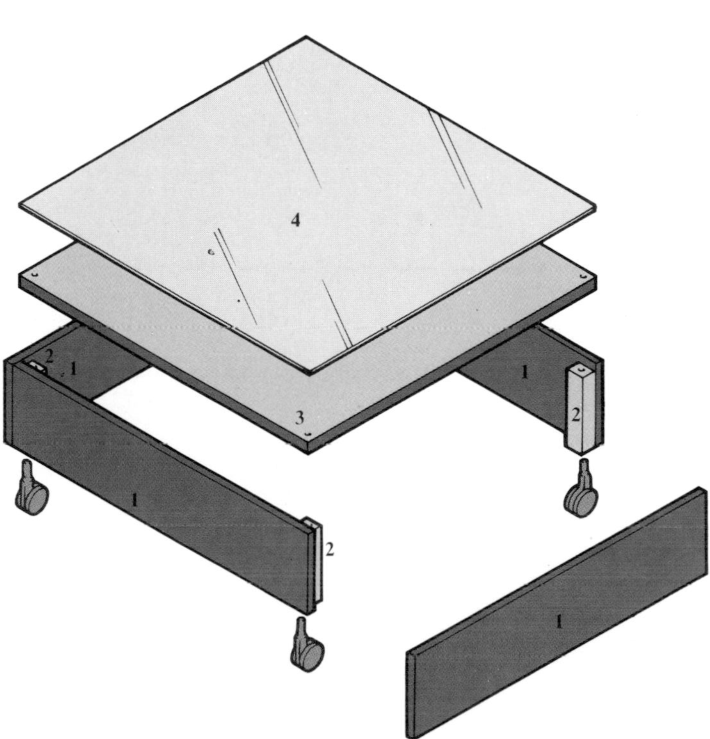

Picture Frames & Lamps

Choosing lamps and frames
Carefully chosen lamps and picture frames can transform an interior. Ideally they should offset or bring out the room's major features or characteristics. There are traditional designs associated with both lamps and frames, but modern materials have brought many changes. Today's lamps are made of chrome, acrylic and glass fiber on flexible mounts. Today's picture frames also make use of aluminum, chrome and acrylic. In general, match the fittings to their surroundings: a traditional lamp shade may be out of place in a modern interior, and a modern frame will probably not suit an old, deep-colored oil painting.

Making lamps
Nearly all forms of lighting are expensive to buy, but often the techniques perfected by manufacturers are too refined to imitate at home. The solution is to combine bought and home-made fittings. In **3** right, acrylic sheets were bought whole, then cut up, joined, and fitted with a lamp holder. In **4** right, a manufacturer's spot light fitting, originally a table lamp, has been converted by the addition of an aluminum tube and some simple wiring. The results in both cases are simple but effective.

Making frames
Some art supply stores sell frame sections by the foot. Often you can find old frames in antique shops. Or choose frames that you can cut down to size. The problem in cutting a frame lies in cutting the miter to make the right angle. If you do a lot of framing, invest in a miter box and a miter shooting board (see p. 128) to help you cut a precise miter, and a miter clamp to secure the corners while nailing and gluing. Nail and glue the miters together, using the clamp. Fill the nailholes afterwards, and paint them to match the finish.
Having made the frame, fit a piece of glass 1/16 inch thick (see **9**, right), 1/8 inch smaller than the rabbet. Sandwich both print and mount between the glass and some form of stiff backing. Fix in place with framing nails. Seal the back with brown paper edged with gummed paper strip. Fit picture hanging wire or cord through screw eyes, or through picture rings screwed into the frame. Full instructions for making these lamps and frames are to be found on page 190.

1

2

1/2 Display areas
A glass topped table can be made into a display surface if a small table lamp is installed under the top. Use textured glass to diffuse the light. Three dimensional objects can be displayed in a shelving niche fitted with an overhead fluorescent light. A baffle should mask the fitting from view.

3 Pendant lamp
A simple pendant lampshade can be made by bonding square acrylic panels. A cord is passed through a hole in the corner of the shade.

4 Adjustable spots
A simple light fitting can be made by clamping spotlights to a tube which slides on a suspended wire cable. Friction on the cable holds the tube at any required height.

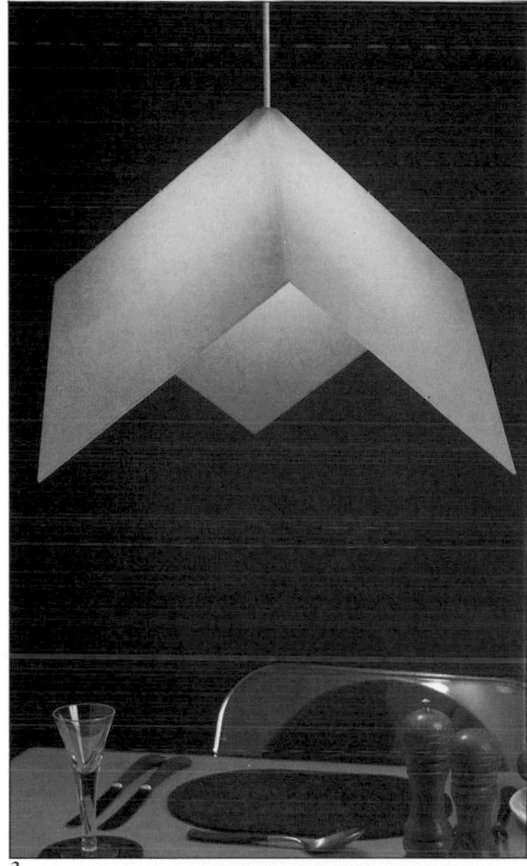
3

4

5

6

5 Adjustable frame
This suspended frame is designed to display "batik" and other printed artwork which look best when viewed against the light.

6 Metal frame
A simple picture frame is made by gluing two L-shaped aluminum sections together.

7
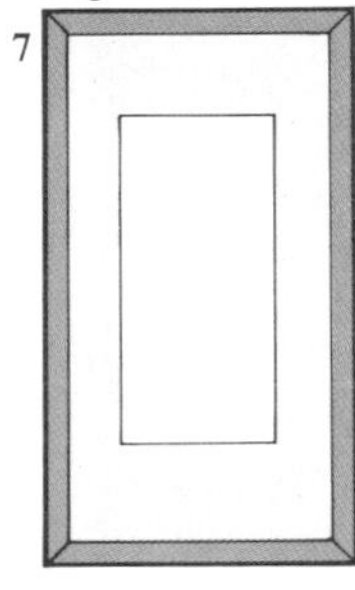

7 Mount proportions
Mounts vary but bottom should be deeper than sides.

8 Picture size
Make all measurements on the rabbet, not on the outside edges.

8
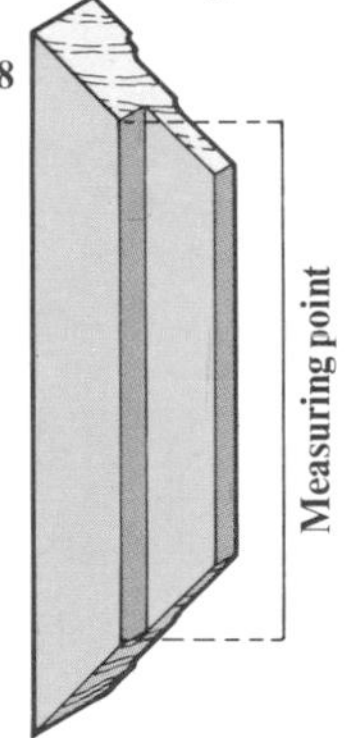

9
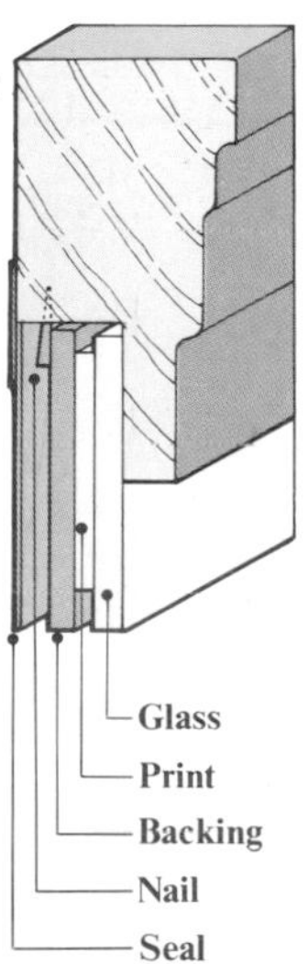

Picture Frames & Lamps

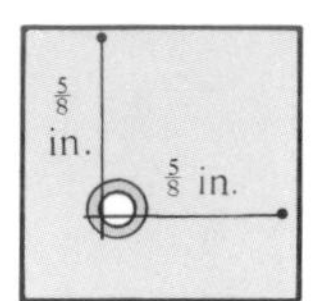

1 Corner clearance position

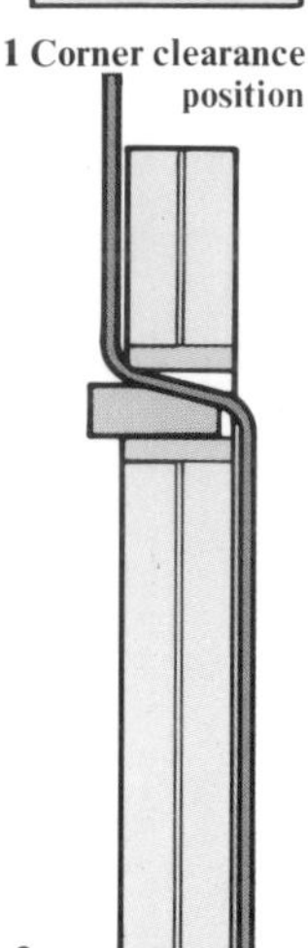

2

Acrylic picture frame

To make this ceiling-suspended frame, cut two pieces of clear ⅛ in. acrylic sheet to artwork's size, allowing at least a 2 in. border. Prepare the two pieces as follows: peel off protective paper from one side of each sheet; stick both sheets together with double-sided tape. Use a fine saw to prevent chipping edges, then smooth down with a block plane, and polish. Drill a clearance hole **1** in each corner ⅝ in. from edges, to take a ¼ in. length of ⅛ in. bore acrylic tube. Make a registration mark across both sheets at one corner. Separate sheets. Bond the tubes to one sheet using solvent adhesive, keeping the ends flush. Cut two 4 in. weights from 1 in. diameter chromed brass tube. Plug one end with a ½ in. length of 1 in. dowel, glued with epoxy adhesive, and sand flat with abrasive paper. Drill a 1⁄16 in. hole through center of the plug, seal wood with clear varnish. Thread one end of a length of fine wire cable through the hole and loop around a short nail. Pull wire through to lock nail under plug. Pack the tube with plasticine to add weight. Match sheets together, thread the wires through holes in the corners, and fix to the ceiling as for a suspended light fitting (bottom right). To frame artwork, lift weights to slacken the wires and sandwich item between sheets. Slide frame up the wire and lock into place with a ⅜ in. diameter rod, tapering on one side **2**. Fit a peg into each top hole.

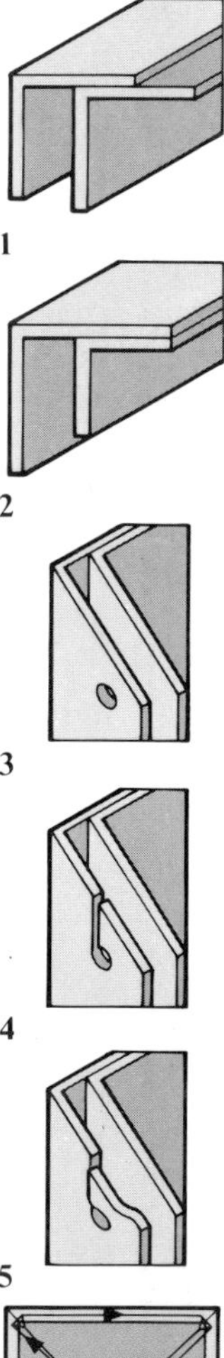

1, 2, 3, 4, 5, 6

Aluminum picture frame

Picture frames can be made from lengths of standard right-angle aluminum. Two lengths of the same section give a stepped detail on the outside face **1**, or one section larger than the other gives a flush face, as shown in **2.** Fix the two sections together with quick-drying epoxy resin, or double-sided tape for an instant bond – the tape method is only suitable for smaller pictures. With a ½ in. equal angle, you bond one to the other, leaving a 3⁄16 in. gap; if your picture is mounted on card, and you need a wider groove, use a larger section, such as ¾ in. Bear in mind that whatever the size of the metal frame used, the gap must be wide enough to take the picture, the glass and the backing board. Strips of softwood of the necessary thickness, spaced at intervals between the aluminum angles will help to set the gap while the epoxy hardens. When the aluminum lengths have bonded hard, cut them to size, mitering the ends as follows: mark miter with a combination square on back face of channel, continue the line vertically on the side face. Grip side face in a vise, cut miter with a hacksaw, finish with a smooth file. Now mark and drill a 3⁄32 in. hole in the back face of each corner **3**. Make a saw cut with a small hacksaw on the hole side of the vertical center line **4**. Remove the sharp edges with a needle file or rattail file. Using a pair of nose pliers, make a double bend in the corner tabs **5**. Polish the aluminum. Cut a backing board from a piece of cardboard to the exact size, measured from the bottom of the groove in the framing. The card must fit snugly into the grooves of all four sides. Have a piece of picture glass cut to the size of the backing board, but less ⅛ in. all around. Sandwich the picture between the board and glass, and slot it into the frame grooves. If it does not fill the width of the groove, pack it out with strips of card. Now, using strong fishing line, make a loop at one end and hook it over the top left-hand corner tab. Wind it diagonally around the lower right-hand corner tab and then complete as indicated, tying off on the top right-hand corner tab **6**. This cord not only holds the frame together but provides a hanging thread.

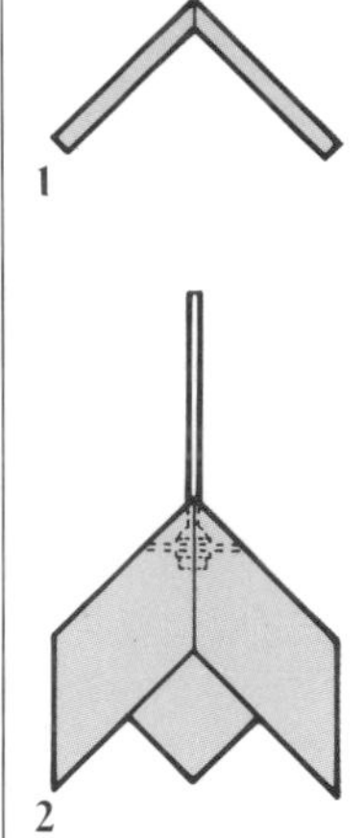

1, 2

Acrylic lampshade

Cut three 12 in. x 12 in. squares from ⅛ in. acrylic sheet. Cut a chamfer on two adjacent edges and remove the corner from the chamfered sides **1.** Polish the exposed edges. Bond the chamfered edges with a suitable adhesive; strips of masking tape will help to hold the edges secure. When bonded, remove the sharp edges with fine abrasive paper and polish. To install the lamp socket, cut a 4¾ in. equilateral triangle from acrylic sheet. Drill a clearance hole in the center to take the lamp socket, and drill three ¾ in. holes around it for ventilation. Wire up the lamp socket and attach it to the triangular plate. Pass the cable through the corner hole in the shade, and fix to the ceiling outlet **2**; the shade should sit level on the plate. Remember that opaque colored acrylics will give a colored light so use a plain or textured opal acrylic for white light.

1, 2, 3

Suspended spotlight

A suspended floor-to-ceiling adjustable light can be made from a hooded spotlight with a clamp attachment such as the Concord Babystar. The lamp housing is clamped to a 2 ft length of ⅜ in. aluminum tube. Before fitting the lamp, drill two 1⁄16 in. holes in one side of the aluminum tube, ⅜ in. apart and ⅜ in. from one end. Drill one hole, same size, ⅜ in. from the opposite end, in line with the other two. Angle the holes as in **1.** Thread a length of fine wire cable through the holes **2**, the wire being a few inches longer than the distance from floor to ceiling. Pass the wire and tube through the clamp fitting on the lamp, and lock it on to the tube. Attach the bottom end of the cable to a base plate, made as follows: cut a 9 in. diameter base from ½ in. particle board; drill a ½ in. hole through center and glue a 1 in. length of aluminum tube flush with the bottom face. Then form a mound between base and tube with a resin filler paste, and trim its outside top edge to a ½ in. radius. Use filler to cover the grain on cut outer edge of base, then rub down and color with a polyurethane paint. Cut an 8 in. diameter disk from 1⁄16 in. mild steel. Fix underneath to base plate with flathead screws, trapping the end of the cable passed through central hole. Attach wire to a light tension spring, fitted to a hook in the ceiling **3**.

Bedrooms

Choosing Beds

Mattresses and bases

People spend a third of their lives sleeping so much thought should go into choosing a bed. The size of the bedroom as well as your own sleeping preferences will determine whether you choose single beds or a double bed which can be of several sizes. Some brand name mattresses are made with a zipper down the center, to turn two singles into a double, or vice versa. This makes it possible for two individuals with different support needs to share a bed. Mattresses usually consist of a number of individual springs covered with ticking and padded with hair or fiber stuffing, or of foam rubber of various densities, but at least 4 in. thick. The mattress should provide firm support yet should "give" in the right places. A sprung mattress should be used with a box spring base unit for most comfort while the foam mattress rests on a firm base. This base needs to be well ventilated by a series of $\frac{3}{4}$ in. holes, 4 in. apart, then topped by an additional layer of $1\frac{1}{2}$ in. fabric-covered profiled foam for extra softness and comfort.

Bed bases can be of two types: the sprung-edge one has a flat top and a soft edge and is the best base for a sprung-interior mattress. The soft edge makes it unsatisfactory for use as a sofa. The firm-edge type has a deep wooden frame all around and has a slightly convex top. This is better for sitting on, especially when combined with a foam mattress to make a sofa.

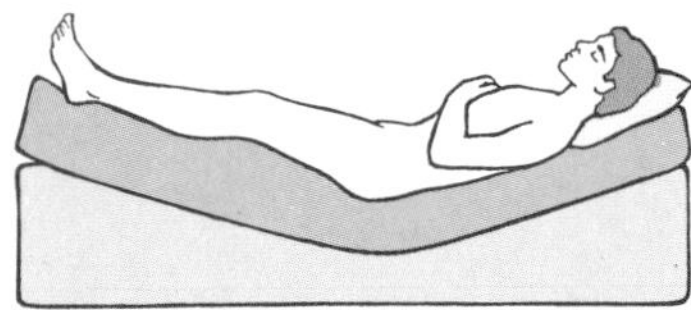

Poor body support
A mattress that is too soft may sag in the middle and can cause backache. A breakdown in the springing in either the base or the mattress itself is the likely cause and the damaged item should be replaced with a new one.

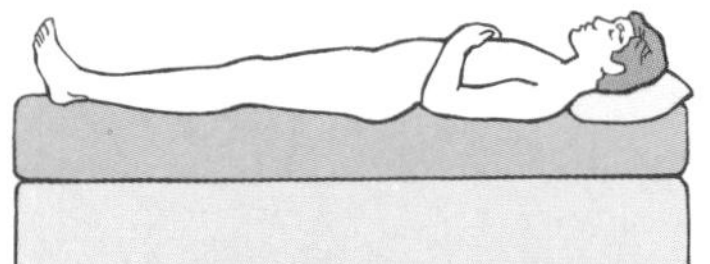

Proper body support
The best foundation for a sleeper is one that provides comfortable, non-distorting support, while maintaining a firm, horizontal base. The mattress should cushion the body while providing firm support.

1

2

3

1 Easy-to-make single beds
These beds are extremely simple in construction and are fitted with storage boxes which can be used as tables, storage, or even to support a television set for the late night movie. Construction details for all beds are given on pp. 194-195.

2 Storage boxes
These boxes used for bedside tables have a two-part lid to provide access to the interior without having to remove everything first. Storage boxes at the foot of the bed are ideal for spare bed linen.

3 Larger double
The two single beds can be pushed together to form a generous double bed. This is a useful arrangement for furnishing a guest room where double or single beds can be supplied at will.

4 Platform bed
Make your bed the focal point of a room by placing it on a raised platform. The lower tier can be used for additional seating or a storage table.

5 Co-ordinated cover and headboard
A simple bed is made more decorative by a floor length bedspread and matching headboard. Instructions for making these are on p. 196.

4

5

Circulation space
Space around a bed must allow for the proper maintenance of the room as well as ordinary daily activities. There must be sufficient space to make the bed, turn the mattress and clean around the bed. If space is limited, casters fitted to the bed make cleaning easier. The rest of the bedroom furnishings should not intrude on this space. Fitted sheets and quilted coverlets can reduce the space needed for bed making.

Space around a double bed
About 2 ft 6 in. is needed on all three sides of the bed, if head is against a wall, to produce enough room for ordinary activities.

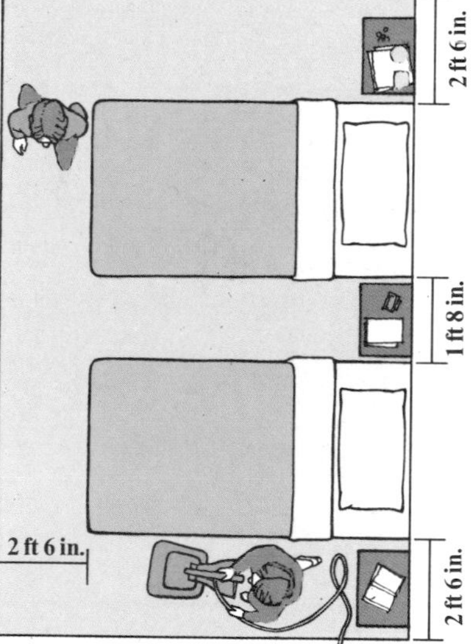

Space around twin beds
Single beds set apart with a table between them need an intervening space of at least 1 ft 8 in.

Space around a single bed
Allow just over 2ft 6 in. at the side and foot if placed against two walls. The bed should be movable.

Beds

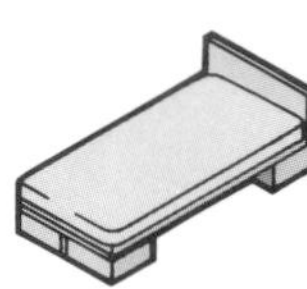

Single bed with storage boxes

Cut open mortise and tenon joints at ends of inner frame rails **1** and **2** (see p. 129). Cut a ¼ in. deep x ¾ in. wide dado on inner face and underside of rails, 15 in. from each end of side rails and center on end rails. Notch each end of leg panel **3** and one end of panel **4** to slot into dadoes, as in **A** left. Cut away top edge of leg panels to 3 in. deep, running out to corner notches at 45°. Glue and screw panels **4** to center of panels **3**. Glue inner frame corner joints and assemble; check diagonals for square. Glue leg assembly into dadoes and screw into frame. Screw and glue from inside outer end rails **5** and side rails **6** to inner frame. Set top edge ¾ in. above top edge of inner frame. Drill two holes for 3 in. carriage bolts through one end, each 6 in. from inner corner. Cut headboard **7** to size and finish edges with iron-on veneer. Hold board level with bottom edge of outer rail and mark hole centers before drilling. Sand and fill surfaces for painting, sand edges and round off corners of slats **8**. Finish with polyurethane. Fix slats to chair webbing 2 in. apart, using tacks. Set webbing 4 in. from slat ends. Cut a 1¼ in. block from scrap piece of slat, wrap one end of webbing around block and screw to top edge of inner frame, using 1½ in. wood-screws in washers. Tension webbing on frame and fix. Screw small casters to bottom panel **11**, 2 in. from corners. Nail and glue sides **9** to panel to give ¾ in. clearance over floor. Nail and glue sides **10** to base and fixed sides, and battens **12** to long sides, 5/16 in. from top edge on inside face. Cut off 2 in. of one corner of top **13** at 45°.

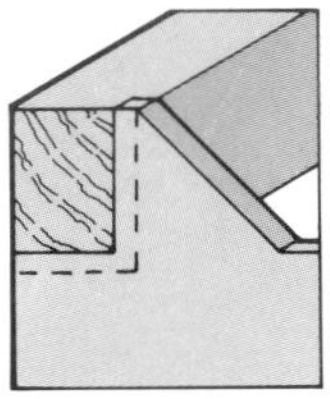

A

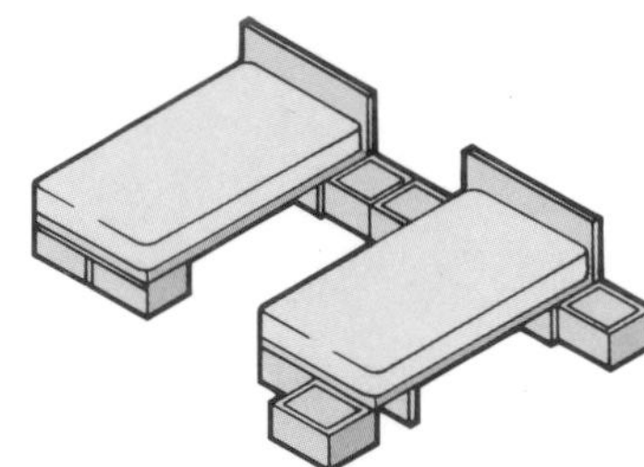

Single bed arrangement
The two beds can be arranged as separate units. The storage boxes at the head can be pulled out and used as bedside tables.

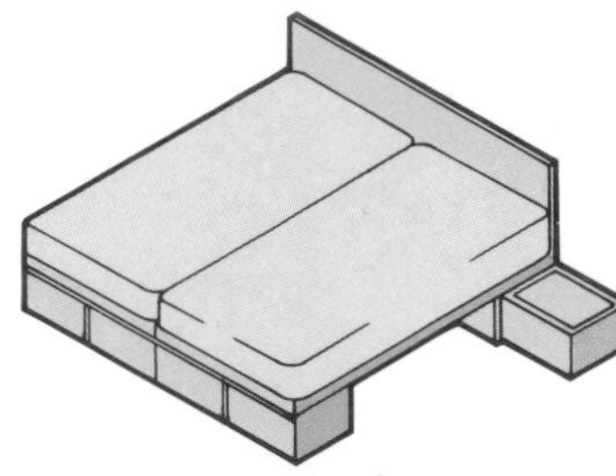

Double bed combination
When the two frames are placed next to each other to form a double bed, the storage boxes at the top of the bed can be stored underneath it.

No	Part	Quantity	Length	Width	Th	Material
1	Inner side rail	2	76½	3	2	Softwood
2	Inner end rail	2	37½	3	2	Softwood
3	Leg panel	2	37½	12	¾	Particle board
4	Leg panel	2	15	12	¾	Particle board
5	Outer end rail	2	37½	3	1	Softwood
6	Outer side rail	2	78	3	1	Softwood
7	Headboard	1	39	20	¾	Particle board
8	Slats	18	37	2	⅜	Birch plywood
9	Long side	2	17½	8¼	¾	Particle board
10	Short side	2	15¾	8¼	¾	Particle board
11	Base	1	17½	14¼	¾	Particle board
12	Batten	2	17½	½	½	Hardwood molding
13	Top	1	17⅜	14⅛	¼	Birch plywood

Hardware: 2, 3 carriage bolts, 4 small casters per box. ***N.B.*** *All dimensions are shown in inches.*

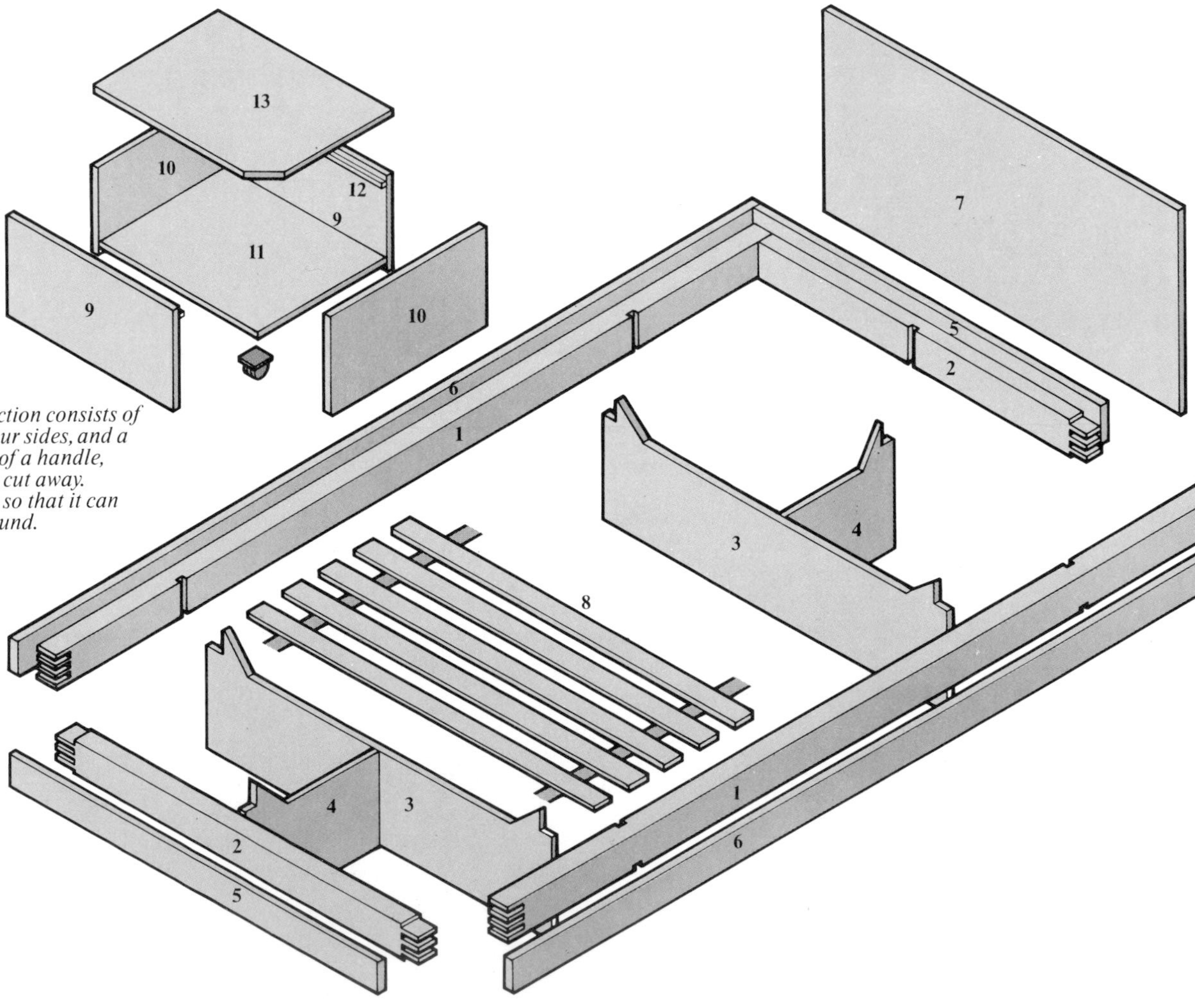

Storage box
This simple construction consists of a base panel with four sides, and a drop-in lid. Instead of a handle, a corner of the lid is cut away. The box has casters so that it can easily be moved around.

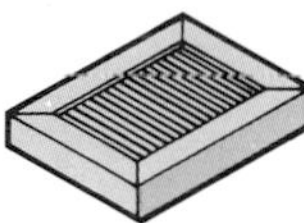

Platform bed

Cut ¾ in. particle board, 9 in. wide, for side and cross panels **1** and **2**. Each end must project 9 in. beyond mattress. Cut cross lap joints (see p. 131) on edge of both, 12 in. from each end and at center of side panels. Glue panels together and check for square. Cut a ¾ in. particle board plinth fascia **3**, same size as side panel. Screw and glue to ends of cross panels. Cut plinth fascia **4**, same size as cross panel, plus the thickness of fascia on the length. Screw and glue to ends of side panels and fascia, flush with outside face. Measure overall length and width of platform, and cut top panels **5** and **6** to these lengths. Measure the width from the inside face of panels **1** and **2** to the outside face of fascia **3** and **4** and cut tops to match. Miter the ends and screw and glue to top edges of panels. Cut sixteen 2 in. x 1 in. softwood slats **7** to fit between side panels. Support the slats on 2 in. x 2 in. battens **8**, screwed and glued to the inside of side panels, to bring the slats flush with the top boards. Space the slats evenly and screw them down. The platform may either be covered with a matching carpet up to the slats, or else it may be painted or varnished. If you want to make the unit free standing for placing in the middle of a room, for example, add an extra side and end fascia. The length of the end fascia should be increased by a further ¾ in. For a double platform, make a second plinth, repeating the previous instructions except for the slats, but making the parts 18 in. longer than the original measurements. Place the first platform centrally on the second and screw both platforms together securely.

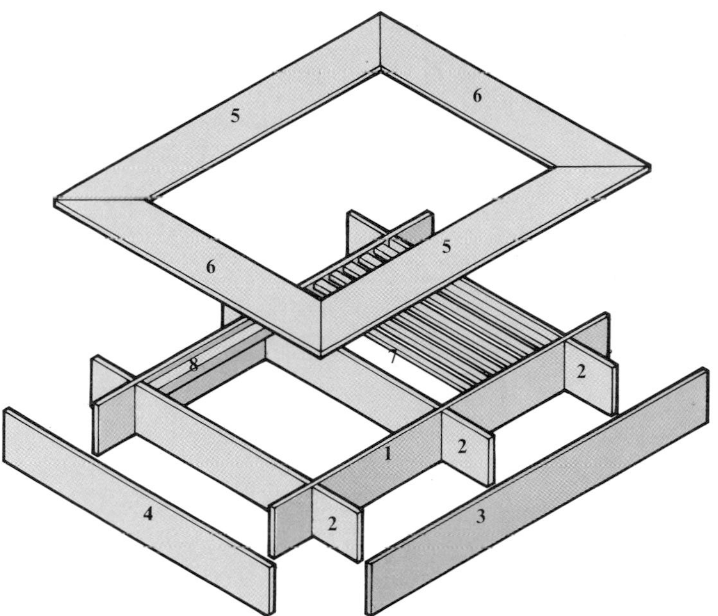

No	Part	Quantity	Length	Width	Th	Material
1	Side panel	2	As required	9	¾	Particle board
2	Cross panel	3	As required	9	¾	Particle board
3	Long plinth fascia	1	As required	9	¾	Particle board
4	Short plinth fascia	1	As required	9	¾	Particle board
5	Long top panel	2	As required	13½	¾	Particle board
6	Short top panel	2	As required	13½	¾	Particle board
7	Slats	16	As required	2	1	Softwood
8	Battens	4	As required	2	2	Softwood

N.B. All dimensions are shown in inches.

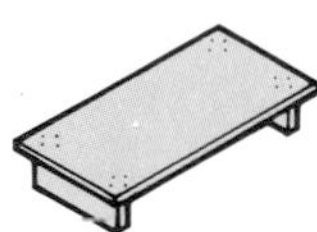

Simple bed

Cut cross lap joints (see p. 131) on the edge of long rails **2** and short rails **3**, 4 in. from the ends as in **A**. Sand down and finish with paint or varnish. Drill ½ in. diameter holes for ventilation at intervals of 4 in. through base panel **1**, starting 2 in. from the edges. Round off the corners and all edges and sand to a smooth finish. Seal the board with clear polyurethane. Assemble frame and check for square by measuring across the diagonals. Position the base panel centrally on the rails, and screw down with four 1½ in. no. 12 screws at each cross lap. Do not glue the joint: the frame can then easily be dismantled and transported. If the bed is to be pushed against a wall to save space in the room, fit a set of casters in the bottom edge of the short rail. This will allow you to move the bed more easily when it is being made. To fit the casters drill the socket hole to the required depth 1½ in. from the ends.

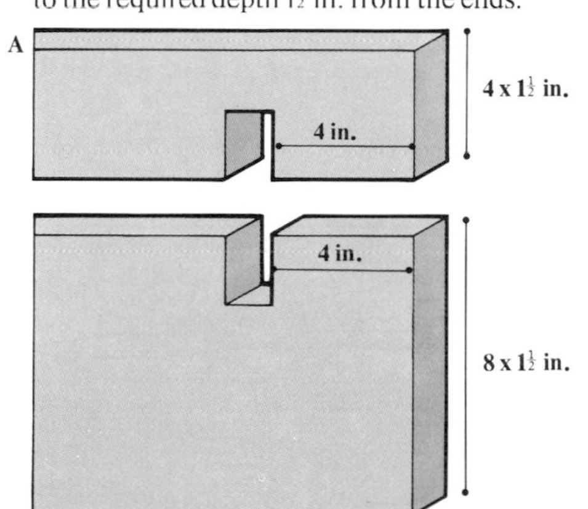

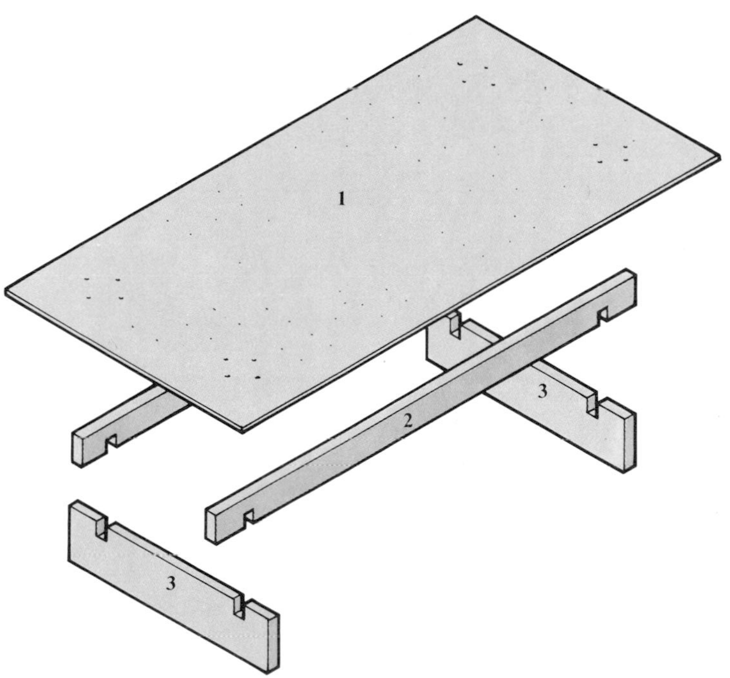

No	Part	Quantity	Length	Width	Th	Material
1	Baseboard	1	78	39	½	Exterior plywood
2	Long rail	2	70	4	1½	Softwood
3	Short rail	2	31	8	1½	Softwood

The dimensions given are for a mattress 39 x 78. For other sizes change dimensions to fit.
N.B. All dimensions are shown in inches.

Bedspread & Headboard

Bind edge
Bind edge
Cord
4 4 4 4
A

Bind edge
Bind edge
Cord
8 8
B

Bedspread

Cut material according to layout; the center panel should have piping (see p. 151) applied crossways at 8 in. intervals, with an allowance at one end of $\frac{3}{4}$ in. for the seam joining center to end panel. The piping should be $1\frac{1}{2}$ in. shorter than the width of the panel, so that the side seams of $\frac{3}{4}$ in. can be sewn easily, see **A**. Apply piping to the side panels at 4 in. intervals, allowing $\frac{3}{4}$ in. at one end for the seam joining the sides to the end panel. The cord should be $1\frac{1}{8}$ in. shorter than the width of the panels, so that the $\frac{3}{4}$ in. seams and the $\frac{3}{8}$ in. bound edges can be sewn easily, **B**. Join the sides and the center panel with piping, aligning alternate cords at the sides with those at the center. Apply $19\frac{1}{2}$ in. lengths of piping to end panel at 4 in. intervals so there is a flat edge for the $\frac{3}{8}$ in. binding and $\frac{3}{4}$ in. seam at sides and center panel. Using piping, join end panel to the center and sides, **C**. Bind all four edges and press.

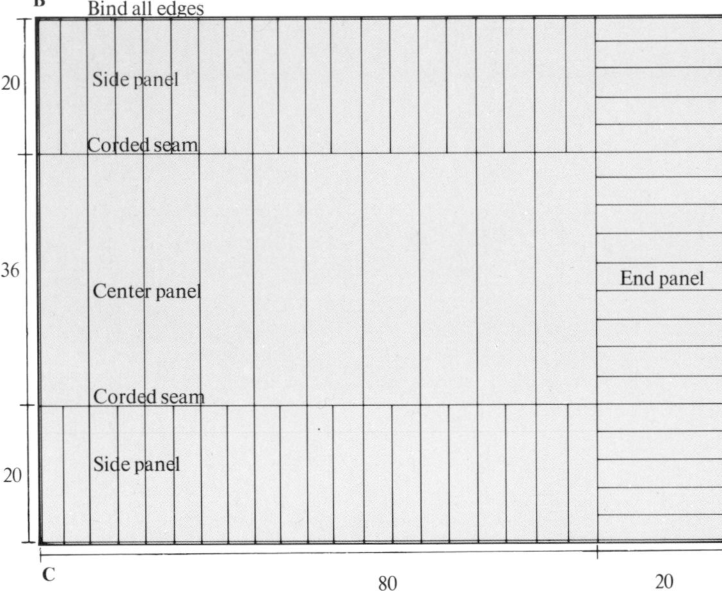

Cutting layout and dimensions

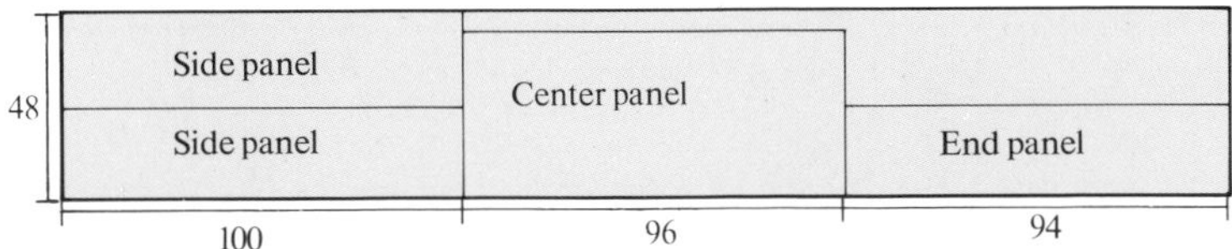

No	Part	Quantity	Length	Width	Material
	Bedspread	Total	21½ft	48	Any medium or lightweight furnishing fabric.
1	Center panel	1	96	37½	
2	End panel	1	94	20¾	
3	Side panels	2	100	20¾	

Hardware: 162ft cotton piping. ***N.B.** All dimensions are shown in inches.*

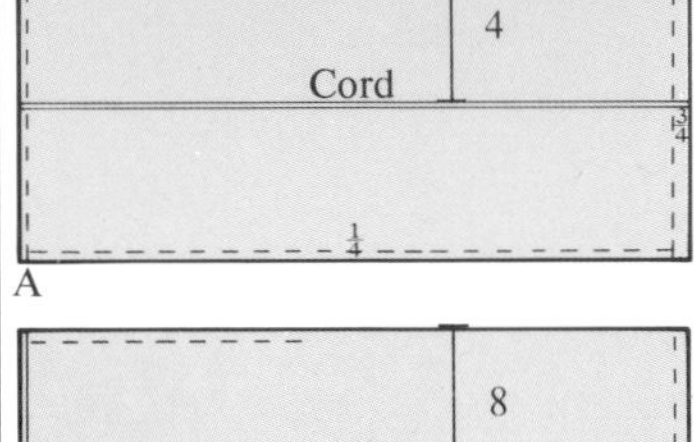

Corded edge
Cord
Cord
8
8
8
Gather line
B

Headboard

As shown in the list below, cut six pieces of fabric $9\frac{1}{2}$ in. x $20\frac{3}{4}$ in. for the two top panels, two middle pockets and the two bottom pockets. Cut one piece $26\frac{3}{4}$ in. x $37\frac{1}{2}$ in. for the padded center panel and one piece $24\frac{3}{4}$ in. x 76 in. to cover the rod from which to hang the headboard. Apply piping to the back and sew all six side pieces, starting with the top pocket, **A**. Add piping to the center panel at $8\frac{1}{4}$ in. intervals to allow for the curve of the material over the padding. Gather and apply piping to the two sides. Sew to the back, leaving the sides open. Fill the three sections with kapok stuffing and sew up the sides, **B**. Join the top of the headboard and the cover for the hanging rod with piping. Bind the sides and the bottom. Turn the edge of the rod cover under by $\frac{3}{8}$ in., pin and baste in position to the back. Machine stitch on the right side, as close to the piping as possible. Finally, tack down top of each of the pockets to keep them in position, **C**.

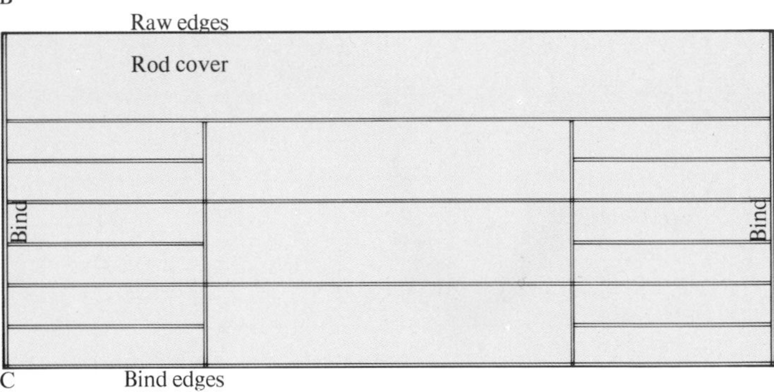

Cutting layout and dimensions

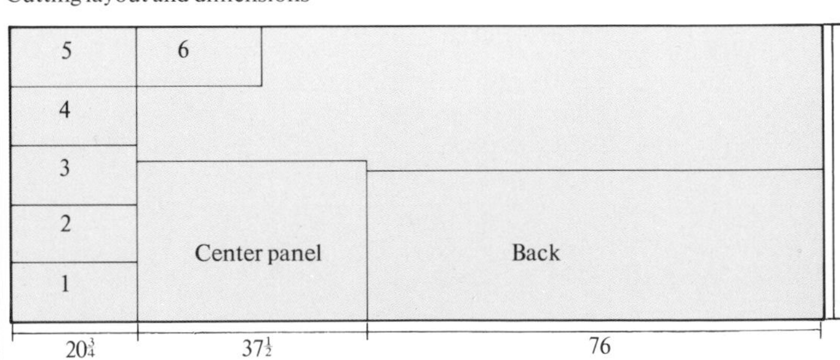

No	Part	Quantity	Length	Width	Material
	Headboard	Total	15ft	48	Any medium or lightweight furnishing fabric.
1	Center panel	1	37½	26¾	
2	Back	1	76	24¾	
3	Top panels	2	20¾	9½	
4	Middle pockets	2	20¾	9½	
5	Bottom pockets	2	20¾	9½	
6	Rod cover	1	76	8	

Hardware: 54ft of cotton piping cord, kapok. ***N.B.** All dimensions are shown in inches.*

Bathrooms

Planning Your Bathroom

Bathroom fixtures

If you intend to install a new bathroom, or simply alter an existing one, plan the positioning of any new fixtures as carefully as you would plan appliances in a kitchen.

If it is the only bathroom in the house, think about the needs of the various members of the family who use it. If there are children, or perhaps someone elderly, consider their requirements when planning and siting the fittings. Is a bathtub a better choice than a shower, or do you have space for both? If not, you can convert your bathtub to provide a shower area.

All these decisions should take precedence over the actual color and shape of your new bathroom fittings, but bear in mind that there is an impressive selection of fittings and appliances now available; many are designed for use in restricted spaces, few are expensive.

The bathtub

The dimensions of the standard tub are 60 in. x 27 in. wide, though there are several variations, and if you or other members of the family are tall, you may want a longer one. The only critical factor with a standard size of bathtub is the height of the rim, which is usually between 20-24 in. but if the tub is going to be used by children, or the elderly, choose one that is lower.

Many tubs are available with a handle that runs parallel to the rim, a precaution against accidents that can happen when getting in or out of the tub. As an extra aid, fit a wall-mounted handle where most convenient, and have a non-slip surface installed on the bottom of the tub. Also, see that the tub you like has a bottom as flat as possible. The majority of tubs are usually made of cast-iron or pressed steel, but the modern trend is for plastic. These have the advantage of being both lightweight and chip-proof. The only disadvantages are that they must be framed securely in order to avoid twisting, and scouring powders must not be used for cleaning. The framing can be concealed by paneling, which will also hide plumbing details.

If you have a choice, consider siting the faucets across a corner or alongside a wall, though this is not necessarily a good position for all members of the family, since it means having to stretch across the tub to operate the faucets.

The bathroom sink

These are made of plastic, pressed steel or vitreous china, the latter being the most attractive and hardwearing. There is a sometimes confusing variety of sink basin designs available. To help you in your choice, here are some practical points to bear in mind. The sink should have a large enough capacity for washing, so that you can put your hands in without the water overflowing. Avoid wide, shallow sinks as these are slow to empty and mean extra cleaning. A sink with an overflow is better than one without, for although the latter are stylish, they are very impractical. Check when you choose a sink that the faucets can be conveniently placed – will you hit them with your head if you want to use the sink for hairwashing? Don't forget to provide a safe stool in the bathroom, to allow smaller members of the family to reach the sink.

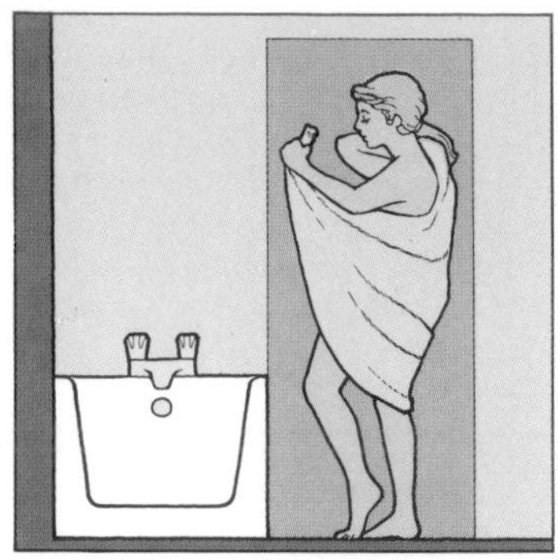

Activity area
The space by the tub should allow sufficient room to get in and out comfortably and safely.

Dressing and drying
The area must have enough space so that you can dry yourself, and so an adult can wash and dress a child.

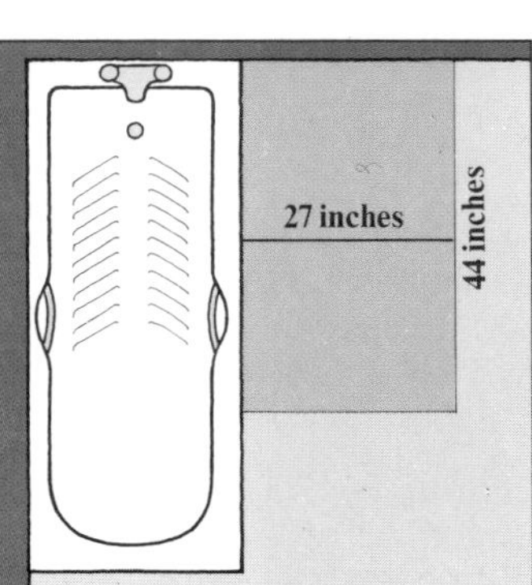

Dimensions
The ideal dimensions along the side of the tub, and convenient to the faucets, should measure 27 in. x 44 in.

Safety precautions
For children and the elderly, fix a vertical pole from floor to ceiling, and a handle to the wall.

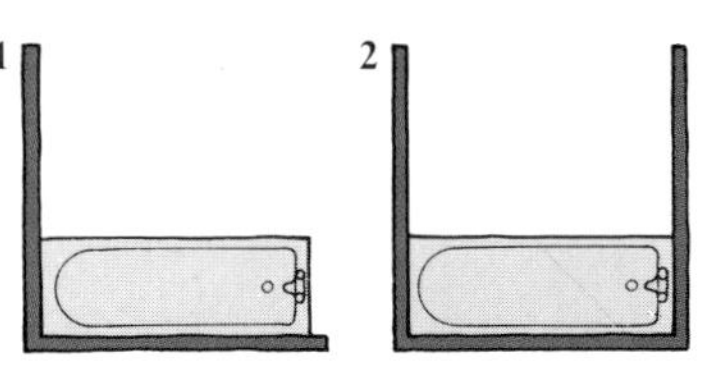

Right
Main positions for siting a bathtub
1 Corner location
2 In a recess
3 Alongside wall
4 One end at wall

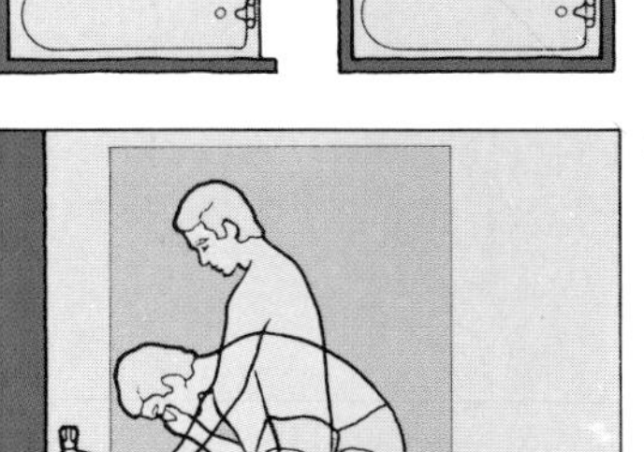

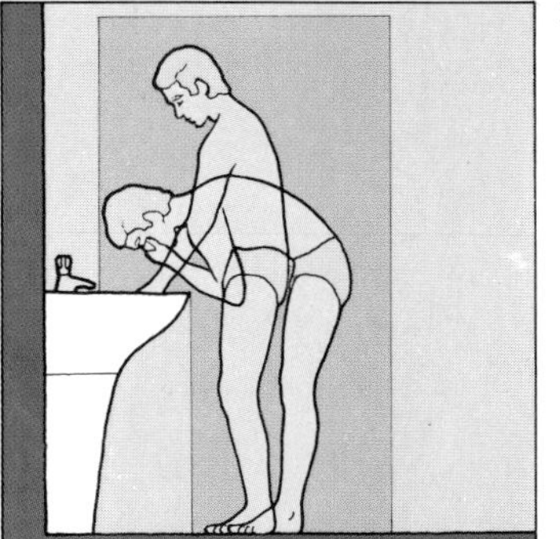

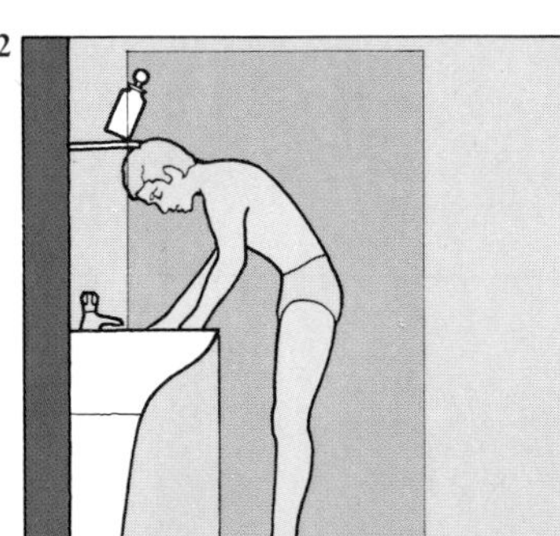

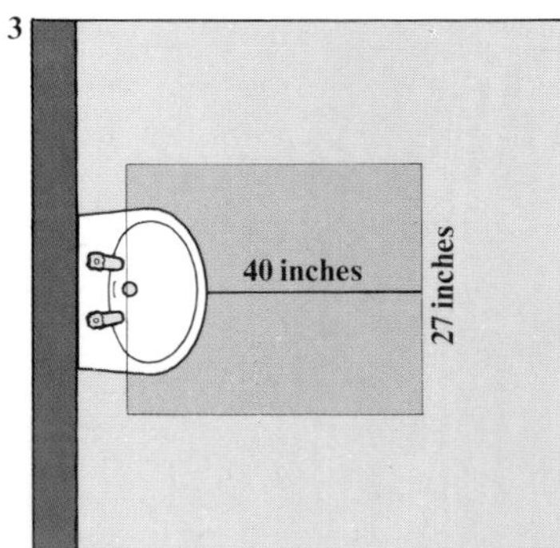

The bathroom sink
1 *The bathroom sink should be large enough to be used for hairwashing. The ideal height from floor to rim is 31 in.*
2 *Never position shelves, soap-holders etc., over the sink, where they could result in an injury, particularly if your vision is obscured by hairwashing.*
3 *The activity area in front of a sink should be about 27 in. x 40 in.*

Bracketed sink
Most bathroom sinks are sold with a means of attaching to a wall, many with brackets.

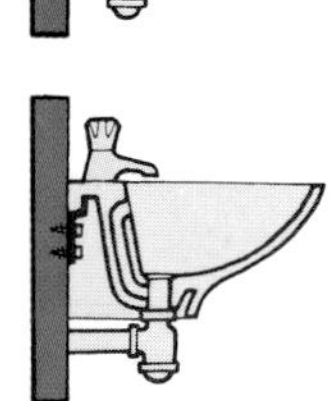

Bolted fixing
An increasing number of modern sinks have "secret" fittings at the back, for bolting to the wall.

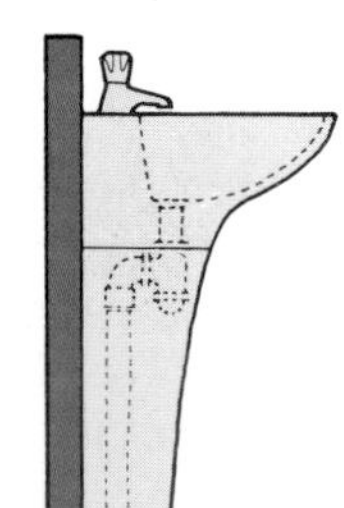

Pedestal sinks
An alternative is the pedestal support which conceals pipes. It can be removed for servicing.

The shower
A shower provides one of the most compact bathing areas, and has considerable advantages in space-saving; showers also use less water than bathtubs. Position your shower so that there is a reasonable amount of adjacent space for drying, and perhaps for dressing. The shower bottom in which you stand may be made of either enameled steel, ceramic or acrylic. The average height for this is about 6 in. If you are installing a new bathroom, you might consider having the bottom recessed into the floor, with a framing of ceramic tiles. A handle in the wall of the shower area is useful for elderly users, also a soap dish recessed into the wall. Make sure that the shower head is at a convenient height, and the shower has a flow control. If a hinged or sliding glass door is impractical, substitute a plastic or waterproofed screen, just long enough to be tucked inside the bottom rim.

Bathroom layout
The shape of the room and the position of the doors and windows will, as in your kitchen, determine the siting of fixtures. Remember, though, that it is generally more economical to place plumbed fittings along one wall; they are also easier to conceal. Re-siting a toilet from one part of the room to another may present problems, especially if the floor is concrete. Activity areas can be designed to overlap one another (see diagram, right), as it is unlikely that several fixtures will be used simultaneously; a sink may overlap the rim of a bathtub, for example. A combined tub and shower is another practical way of having the best of both worlds.

Allow for additional fittings, those that you may wish to incorporate at a later stage, when you plan the room. You will need a small storage cabinet for toilet articles and drugs, a mirror, a toilet paper holder, towel rails, soap dishes for both sink and shower or tub, a sturdy bathroom stool, perhaps a scale, a waste paper basket and possibly a laundry hamper as well.

The particular layout of a bathroom can also influence your choice of wall and floor coverings – whether you should have ceramic tiles, or a waterproof wallpaper, or wallboards to hide unsightly pipework. A large mirror is convenient, and creates the illusion of extra space.

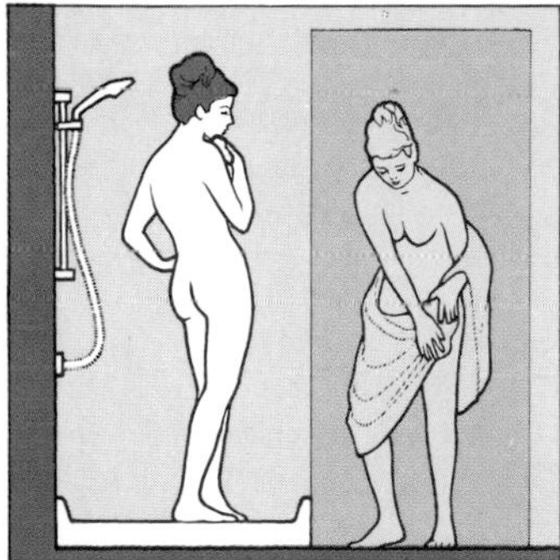

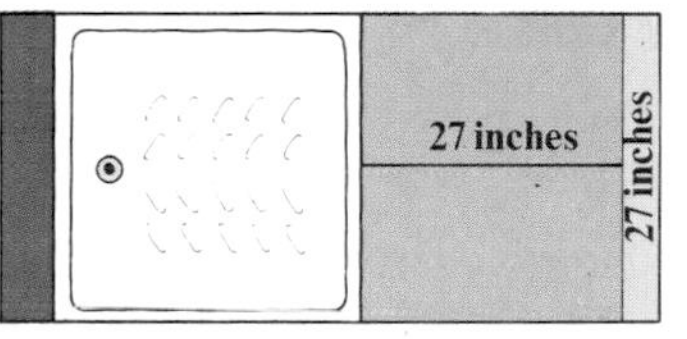

The shower
Standard dimensions of a shower are 36 in. x 36 in. square. It should be enclosed on two or three sides, a door or shower curtain on remaining sides. A slightly smaller space than the shower itself, say 27 in. square, will allow room for access and drying.

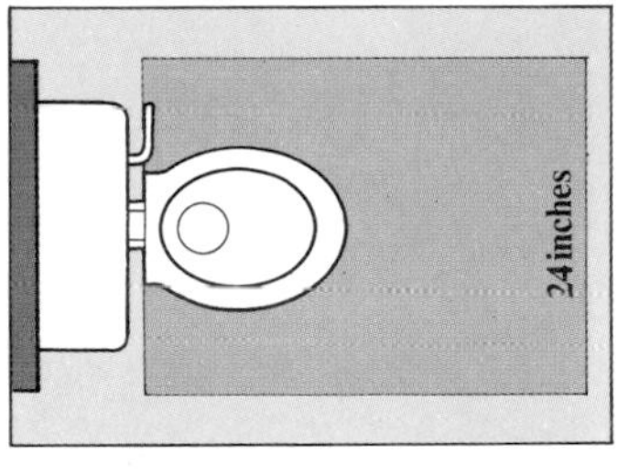

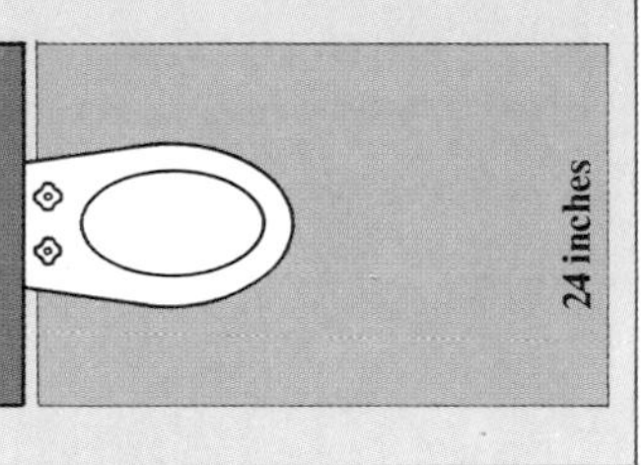

The toilet and bidet
For adequate access to the toilet allow an area 24 in. across. The space between a toilet and fitted bidet can be less than this as it is unlikely both these fixtures will be in use at the same time.

The toilet and bidet
Almost all toilets are washed down by water from a tank. The older type has a separate, wall-mounted tank, which provides a good flushing action. Close-coupled toilets are those in which both tank and bowl are designed to fit together as a unit. The low-level toilet is also popular because the tank is always mounted just above the bowl, connected by a short supply pipe. Narrow tanks of this type can be concealed behind a false wall panel. Toilets are usually made of vitreous china, and are able to withstand the use of powerful cleaners. (Tanks can be either plastic or ceramic.) The standard height is 15 in. and is considered ideal as an optimum height. In terms of height and area, these factors also apply for a bidet. Plumbing regulations in certain places demand that a bidet should have its own supply, and should be connected to the soil pipe.

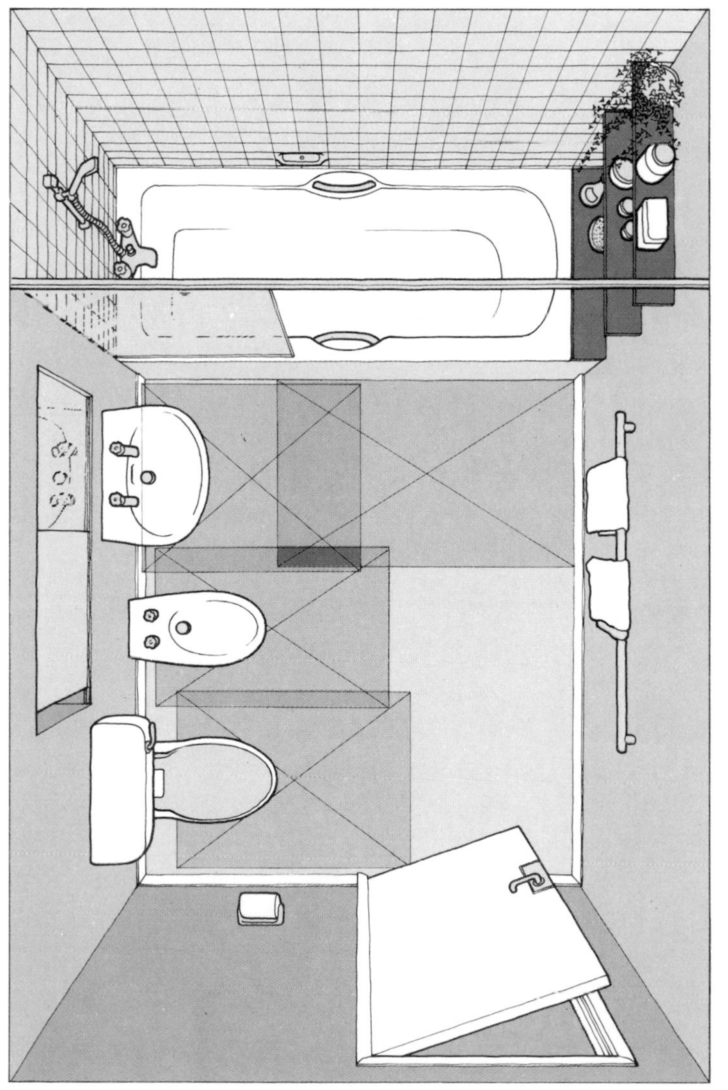

The ideal bathroom
In planning a bathroom, you should attempt to combine the qualities of spaciousness, light, warmth and good ventilation; it should also be easy to keep clean. Most bathrooms possess at least two or three of these qualities, though space is usually a problem. Ventilation will help toward keeping a bathroom odorless and clean. An evenly-heated bathroom will cut down considerably on condensation. A radiator that is part of the central heating system is perhaps the best way of heating a bathroom, especially one of the type incorporating a towel rail. If you intend to use another form of heating, it must be one specifically designed for bathrooms, operated either from the outside, or inside by means of a pull cord. Anything else may be extremely dangerous. To change the air in a bathroom, make sure that the window is easy to open and close, or that you have a fitted grille as part of the room's ventilation plan; a window will produce condensed moisture unless you insulate it. The most effective system of all is an exhaust fan mounted to an external wall, preferably in combination with a through draft from an opposite window. Some fans can be made to operate with the action of the toilet flush, a bathroom light, or by a pull cord adjacent to the door.

Bathroom Design

Designing for comfort

Bathrooms are no longer treated merely as functional washrooms and most people today want to create an attractive and comfortable room as well as a practical one. White tiled walls and non-absorbent floor coverings are not only old-fashioned in appearance but make an interior appear cold and noisy.

The bathroom shown right was designed around the needs of a family with small children. The deep pile carpet is laid over a sealed floor sheeting and is made in easily removable sections which can be cleaned in a washing machine. The sunken bath is readily accessible from the raised floor and the faucets are located within convenient reach of all family members. The medicine cabinet, which is fixed to the ceiling, however, can only be reached by adults on the upper level. It contains an integral lighting unit which illuminates the sink beneath it. The sink is fitted into a streamlined, easy-to-clean, cabinet which has a pull-out drawer for storing towels. The wide step access to the upper level allows children to reach into the sink comfortably. Additional storage can be built into the window recess and screened by a translucent shade.

Lighting unit
is integral to ceiling-fixed cabinet and lights sink below

Bathtub rim
is adjusted to the height of the steps which should not exceed 8 in.

Economical plumbing
results from close proximity of faucets and drains

Platform
should be large enough to allow for drying space

Medicine cabinet
is well out of reach of children

Lower step
provides a platform for children using the sink

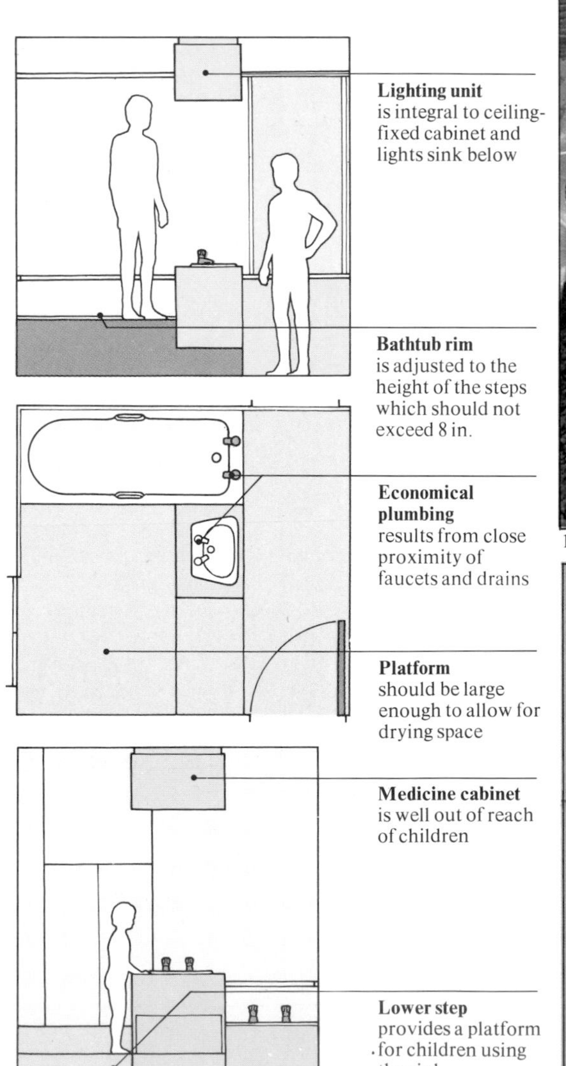

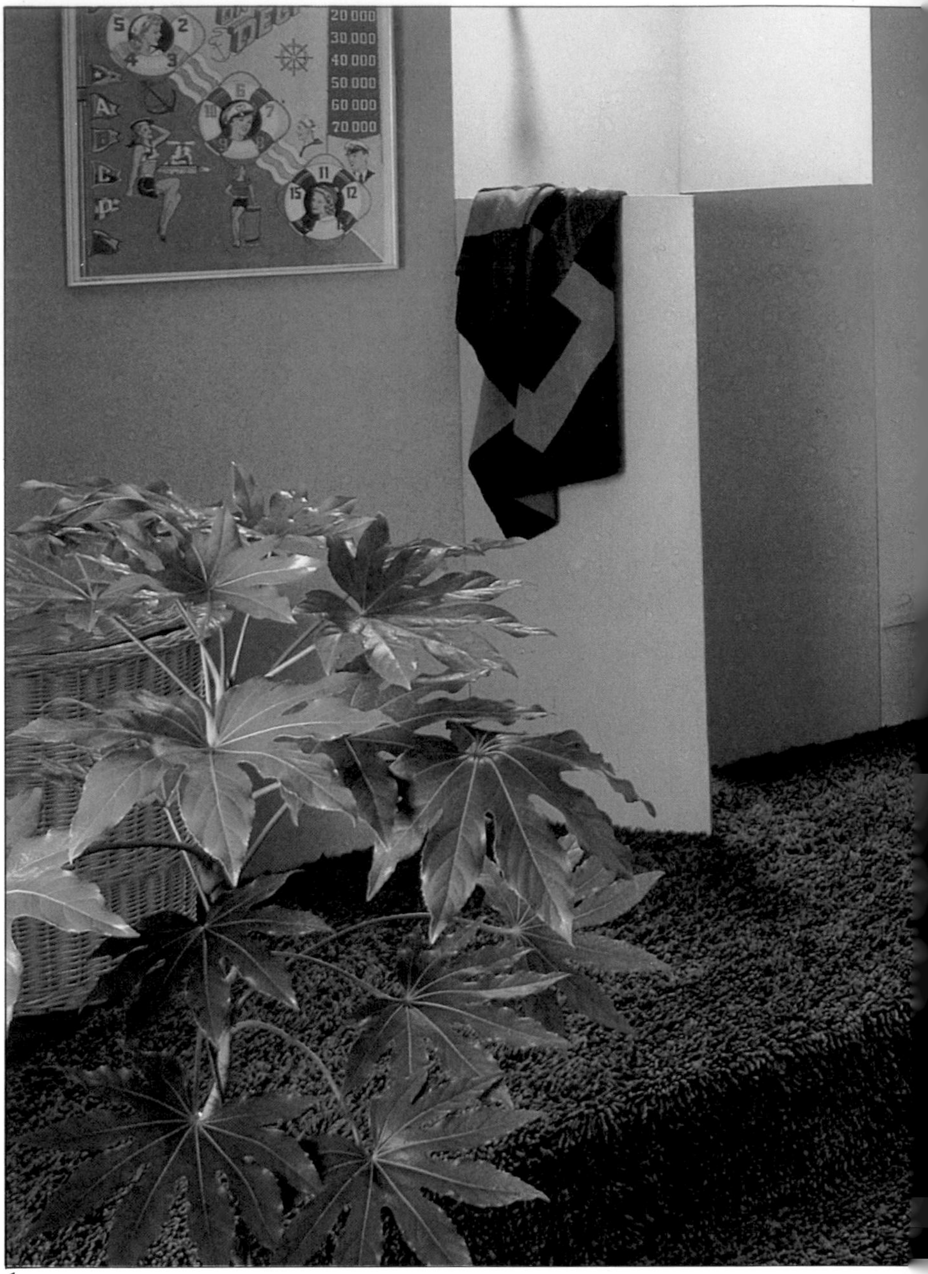

1

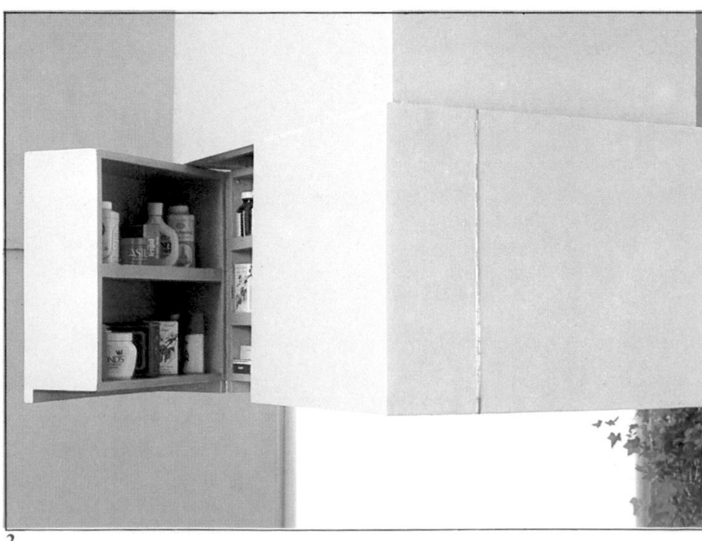

2

2 Medicine cabinet
The suspended medicine cabinet has storage doors providing shallow shelves for clear display of the contents.

1 Purpose-designed bathroom
The features in this bathroom have been designed to meet the needs of a growing family. The split level floor provides comfortable access to the units and fixtures for all ages.

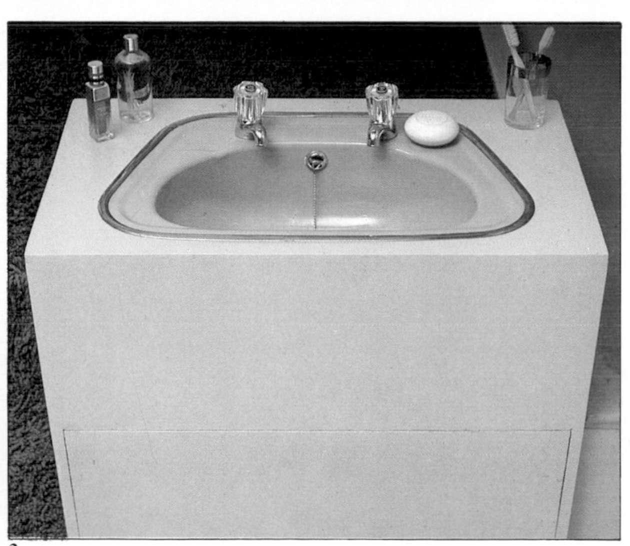

3

4

3 Bathroom sink
The wide ledge around the inset sink provides a useful surface for toiletries in use. Access to the plumbing is through a removable panel at the rear.

4 Window screen
A sliding acrylic panel is used to screen glass storage shelves in the window opening.

Raised Floor

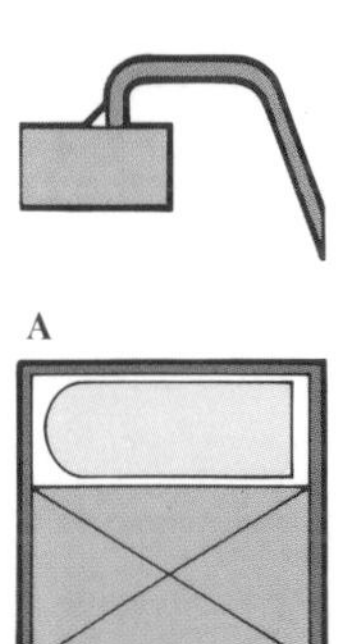

A

B

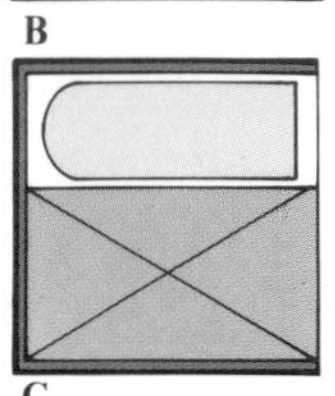

C

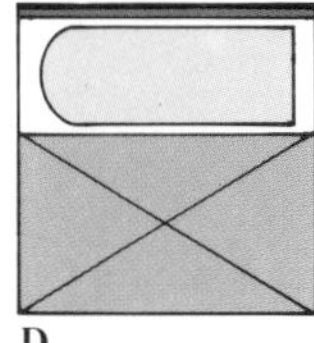

D

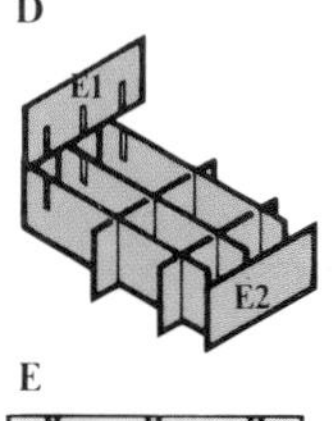

E

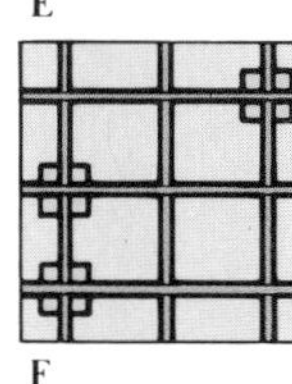

F

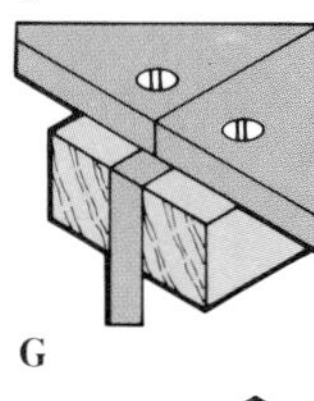

G

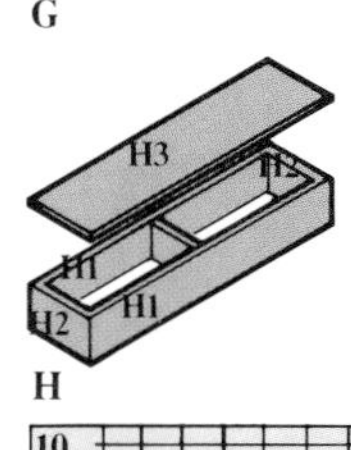

H

One way of achieving a sunken bathtub and well within the scope of the non-professional is to raise the floor to lie level with the rim of a regular bathtub. The height of the floor will be determined by the rim height of the bathtub; the rim edge should lap the floor surface to give a waterproof seal, **A.** The junction should be sealed with a flexible sealant, such as silicone rubber.

Where the bath spans the room as in **B,** a simple method is to fit the ends of the floor joists to wall plates, which are lengths of joist lumber screwed securely to the wall with lap joints. The open front can be paneled across with a sheet of $\frac{3}{4}$ in. particle board, fixed to the front joist and to a 2x2 in. floor batten. To calculate the approximate section of 2 in. thick softwood joists for a given span, see graph below. For spans where the section would be very large, install intermediate props of 3 x 2 in. lumber, bolted to the sides of the joists, thus reducing the span and therefore the section. The joists should be spaced 12 or 16 in. apart between centers. This allows for the edges of $\frac{3}{4}$ in. particle board to share a joist. When working from a wall, take the first measurement from the wall face, and subsequent widths from the center of the joists.

When the floor cannot be supported by walls, as in **C** and **D,** you can have an alternative structure, one that could also suit **B.** Make this structure from panels of $\frac{3}{4}$ in. particle board slotted together with cross lap joints, and glued, see **E.** The distance between joints should not exceed 24 in. to center. Cut the panels **E1** to equal the height of the underside of bathtub rim, less the thickness of the floor sheeting, say $\frac{3}{4}$ in. Measure length for panels in both directions, allowing about 2 in. extra on panels that run under bathtub rim. Mark and cut cross lap joints 6 in. from each end and at equal spaces in between. Glue together and check edges are level. Position unit and check level: if floor is uneven, place 6 in. squares of thin plywood under center of joints to carry weight in both directions, see **F.** Cut and scribe fascia panels **E2** to the wall and floor to finish flush with top edge. Screw fascia to edges of panels with 2 in. particle board screws. Finally, fit $\frac{3}{4}$ in. particle board flooring to top of framework with $1\frac{1}{2}$ in. screws; where two boards share an edge **G,** glue $1\frac{1}{2}$ in. square battens to each side of support member, and drive screws into these.

Make the steps as a series of boxes from $\frac{3}{4}$ in. particle board **H,** the height not to exceed 8 in., the tread not less than 9 in. Cut front and back panels **H1** and cross members **H2** to length and height you need. Glue and screw together, spacing cross members not more than 24 in. apart. Screw the completed frame to the fascia of the raised floor through the back panel. Screw and glue the tread board **H3** to the frame, flush all around. Finish outer surfaces with a waterproof seal if carpeted, or cover with linoleum tiles or rubber matting.

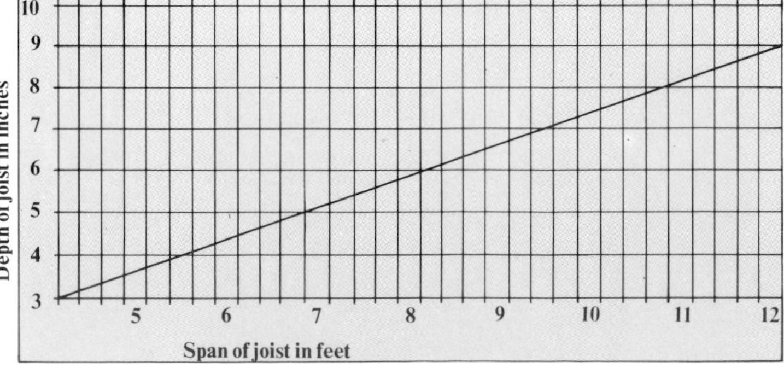

Window Screens

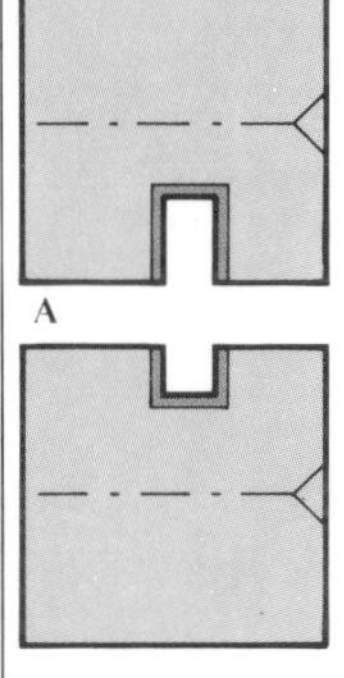

To make a useful storage area for small items in a window recess not less than 3 in. deep, measure width and depth of opening and have $\frac{1}{4}$ in. glass shelves cut to fit, with edges ground. If width is over 30 in. use pine boards, sealed or painted. Support shelves on studs fitted to each side of recess. Screw two battens, grooved to take a single door track **A,** to the wall 2 in. above and below opening. Paint to match the wall. Buy an acrylic sheet to fit between sliding tracks, and 4 in. wider than width of opening. Cut and bond two lengths of $\frac{1}{2}$ in. x $\frac{1}{2}$ in. aluminum angle to the face of the screen, flush with edges, for handles.

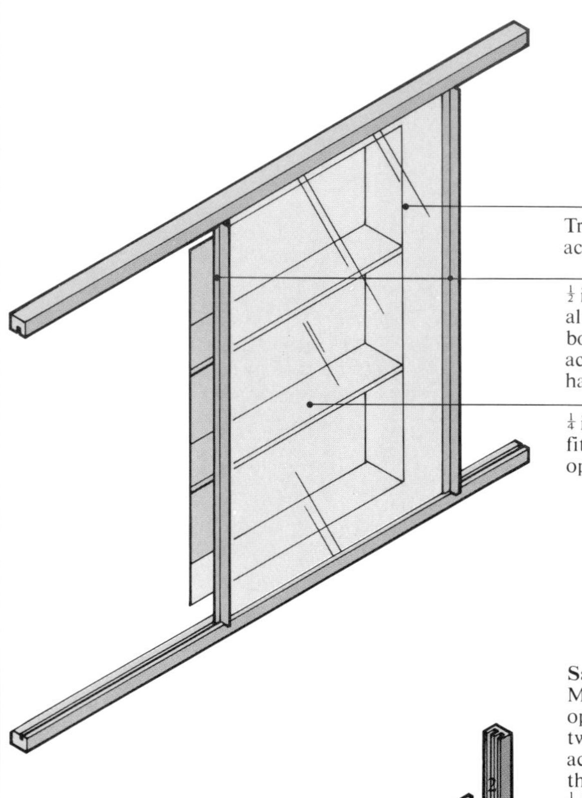

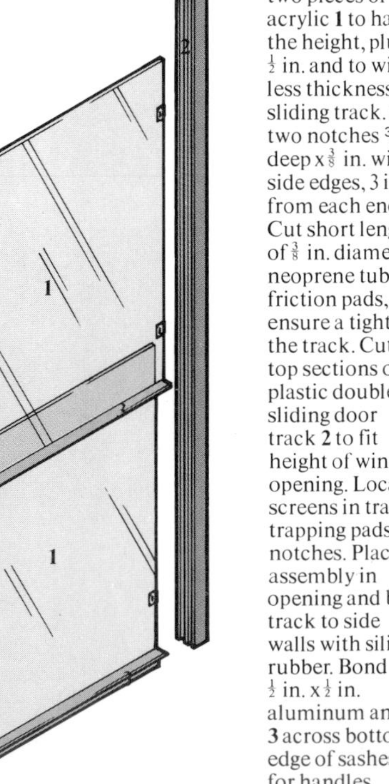

Sash-type screen
Measure window opening, and cut two pieces of acrylic **1** to half the height, plus $\frac{1}{2}$ in. and to width less thickness of sliding track. Cut two notches $\frac{3}{16}$ in. deep x $\frac{3}{8}$ in. wide in side edges, 3 in. from each end **A.** Cut short lengths of $\frac{3}{8}$ in. diameter neoprene tube for friction pads, to ensure a tight fit in the track. Cut two top sections of plastic double sliding door track **2** to fit height of window opening. Locate screens in track, trapping pads in notches. Place assembly in opening and bond track to side walls with silicone rubber. Bond $\frac{1}{2}$ in. x $\frac{1}{2}$ in. aluminum angle **3** across bottom edge of sashes for handles.

Medicine Cabinet

Glue and nail partition **1** flush to shelf **2.** Glue and nail top **3** to top edge of partition, 4¼ in. from one long edge. Drill two rows of 1/16 in. pilot holes, spaced 3 in. apart at 2 in. centers on inside faces of end panels **4,** ⅝ in. from side edge and ¾ in. from bottom edge. Nail and glue end panels to assembly, flush with top edges. Glue and nail back panel **5** flush to top and ends. Drill a 1 in. hole in top to take lighting cord.
Drill pilot holes in door sides **6** as for ends. Glue and nail sides to top and bottom **7,** flush at top and overlapping bottom by 1 in. Nail and glue front panels **8,** flush to door frames. Cut 1 x ¼ in. molding to length of shelves **9** and **10**, and secure to front edges, flush at bottom. Paint all surfaces. Screw angles **11** to back face of partition, flush with bottom edge, and to inside of back at the same level. Cut acrylic diffuser **12** to size. Install fluorescent fitting batten to partition, 3 in. from bottom. Install doors to front edges of sides, piano hinges level at bottom edge. Cut lap joints in frame front rails **13** and nail and glue to side rails **14** to make a frame 26 x 18¼ in. Install corner blocks to strengthen joints. Locate ceiling joists where required (see p. 91). and screw frame to these. Check level, and pack out if necessary. Fill any gaps, and paint to match ceiling. Remove doors and screw carcass to frame through top panel, overlapping at sides and back by ¾ in. Feed lighting cord through hole. Support shelves on studs in pilot holes. Wire light fitting and lamp socket, pass diffuser into light box and support it on angles.

No	Part	Quantity	Length	Width	Th	Material
1	Partition	1	26	14½	¾	Particle board
2	Bottom shelf	1	26	4¼	¾	Particle board
3	Top panel	1	26	14	¾	Particle board
4	End panel	2	16¼	14	¾	Particle board
5	Back panel	1	27½	16¼	¾	Particle board
6	Door sides	4	16 3/16	4¼	¾	Particle board
7	Top/bottom	4	12⅜	4¼	¾	Particle board
8	Front panel	2	16 3/16	13 11/16	¾	Particle board
9	Short shelf	4	12⅛	3⅞	¾	Particle board
10	Long shelf	2	25⅞	3⅞	¾	Particle board
11	Angle bracket	2	26	½	½	Aluminum angle
12	Diffuser	1	25¾	9	⅛	Translucent acrylic
13	Front rail	2	26	1½	1	Softwood
14	Side rail	2	17¾	1½	1	Softwood

Hardware: 2, 16 3/16 piano hinges. 1, 24 fluorescent light. ***N.B.*** *All dimensions are shown in inches*

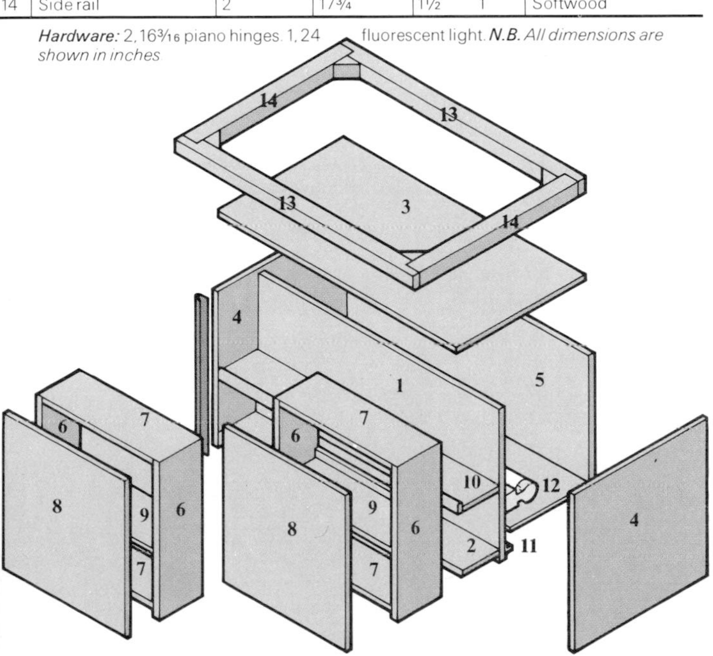

Vanity Unit

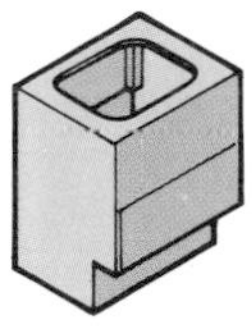

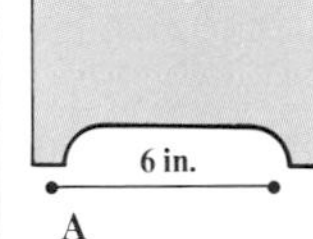

Cut away bottom front corner of sides **1**, to make a recess 4 in. deep by 7½ in. high. Make a cutout in front edge of bottom panel **2** for drawer pull, see **A.** Nail and glue sides to bottom panel, front panel **3,** fixed back panel **4,** and plinth panel **5,** so that all the edges are flush. Cut a clearance hole in top panel **6** for sink (refer to the manufacturer's instructions). Screw and glue battens **7** to inside face of sides, ¾ in. from back edge and level with top. Screw service panel **8** to battens using flat head chrome screws in countersunk washers set 2 in. from top and bottom edges. Fill all nail holes and cut edges in preparation for painting, or finish with plastic laminate (see p. 144). Nail and glue drawer sides **9** to front and back **10.** Nail and glue bottom **11** to bottom edges. Finish false drawer front **12** to match unit and screw through front, overlapping ¾ in. on bottom edge. Fit with drawer slides.

No	Part	Quantity	Length	Width	Th	Material
1	Sides	2	30¾	19¾	¾	Particle board
2	Bottom panel	1	26	19	¾	Particle board
3	Front panel	1	26	11¼	¾	Particle board
4	Back panel	1	26	19¾	¾	Particle board
5	Plinth panel	1	26	7½	¾	Particle board
6	Top panel	1	27½	19¾	¾	Particle board
7	Battens	2	26	1	1	Softwood
8	Service panel	1	26	11	¾	Particle board
9	Drawer sides	2	17½	8	⅜	Plywood
10	Drawer front/back	2	24¼	8	⅜	Plywood
11	Drawer bottom	1	25	17½	⅛	Hardboard
12	False drawer front	1	25 15/16	12	¾	Particle board

Hardware: 2, 17¾ drawer slides. ***N.B.*** *All dimensions are shown in inches.*

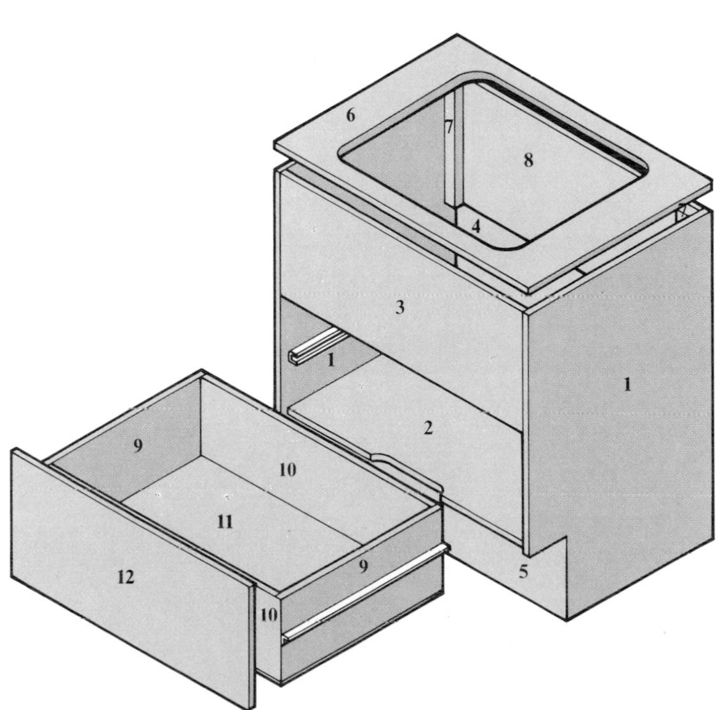

Screens & Rails

1

2

3

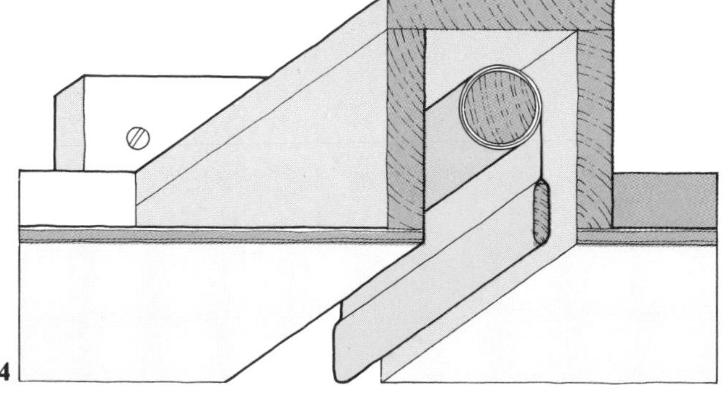
4

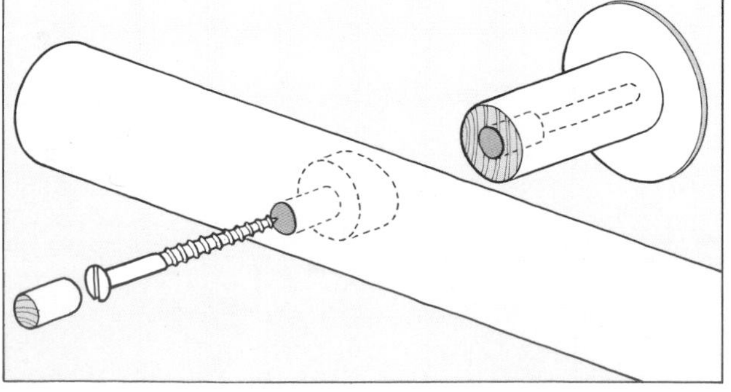
5

1 Window screen
Vertical sliding translucent acrylic screen provides privacy while bathing and reduces drafts and condensation. It will stay in any position; full making instructions are given on p. 202.

2 Shower screen
If you have a combined tub and shower, a fixed screen may reduce access to faucets. A retractable nylon or pvc shade is one answer. Use a shade kit with plastic fittings or lacquer a wooden roller. Do not retract shade until dry.

3 Towel rail
Use $1\frac{1}{2}$ in. diameter dowel, cut to length. It should be supported at least every 48 in. Finish with paint or clear lacquer.

4 Shade fitting
Screw brackets to ceiling joists or use cavity fittings. The roller can be hidden within a lowered ceiling as shown, or behind a fixed valence across the ceiling from wall to wall.

5 Rail fitting
Glue $2\frac{3}{4}$ in. x 1 in. diameter spacers into $\frac{3}{4}$ in. deep location holes in rail with waterproof glue. Drill and counterbore through rail and spacers for 4 no. 10 screws. Cut $2\frac{1}{2}$ in. plastic disks to spread load on wall. Screw to wall and plug hole.

Children's Rooms

Planning A Child's Room

A changing environment
A room for children should be designed for the future as well as the present. A baby's room can reflect its relatively simple needs. There should be a crib or small bed with protective rails and a chest to store clothes, diapers and bed linen. The play pen, for instance, should be put where the parents can supervise. As the baby outgrows its early environment, a more permanent interior can be considered. If space permits the ideal room should contain sleeping, working and playing areas as well as adequate storage for toys and clothes.
Flexible and inexpensive furniture can protect against items becoming obsolete as the child grows up. As far as sleeping goes, a full-sized bed is a better investment than a junior one since it can be used by the child at all times. As it is one of the larger objects in the room, a good deal of thought should be given to its position. Where children share a room, bunk beds or a double-riser provide greater play space. In a small room especially, a bed supported on storage units as shown below, gives a greater amount of floor space. The niche created underneath can be used as a work area or play house. Flexible

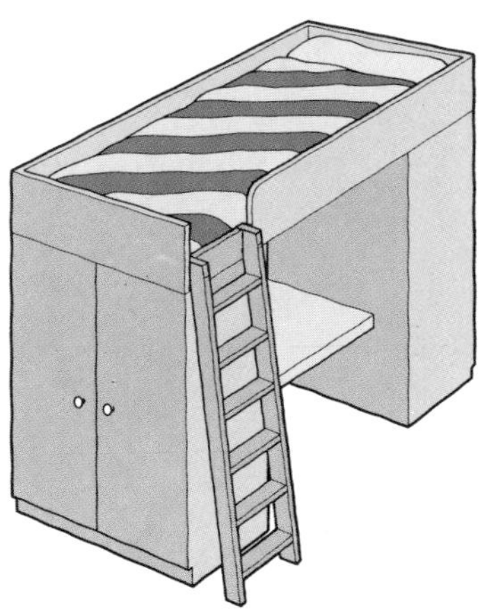

storage space is also necessary for varied collections. A row of units with interchangeable interiors can fulfil most eventual needs. It is worth making the units as tall as possible; the children may not be able to reach the upper limits, but it could be an advantage for the parents. The full height can be utilized if two hanging rails are installed, one above the other. The lower rail can be removed later. Units should be sufficiently flexible to provide drawer storage for toys–the drawers can be of plastic, wood, or in the form of wire baskets.

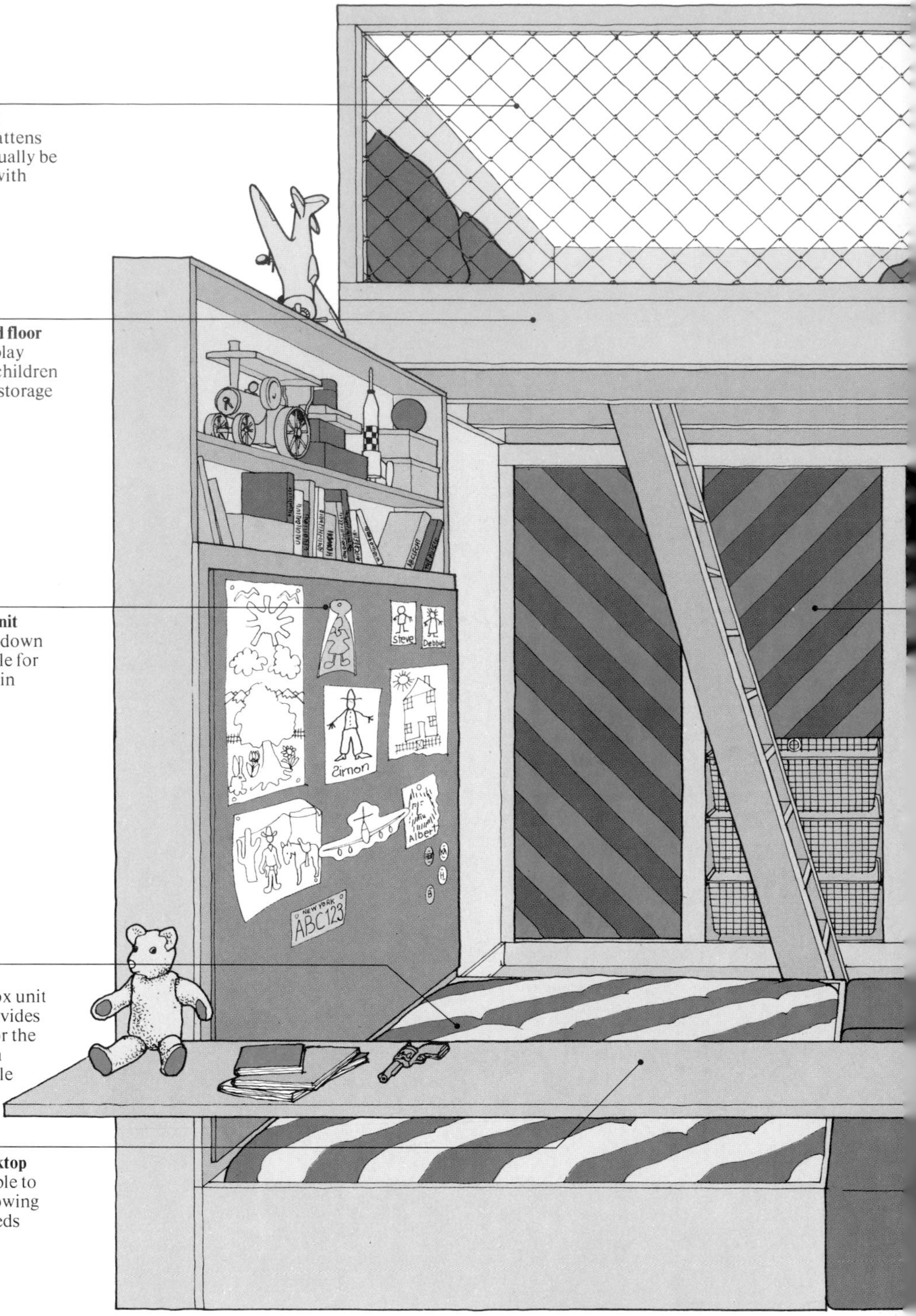

Safety net
fixed to battens can eventually be replaced with boarding

Suspended floor
provides play space for children and extra storage for adults

Hobbies unit
has a fold-down layout table for games, train sets, etc.

Bed
is set in box unit which provides support for the fold-down layout table

Shelf worktop
is adjustable to meet a growing child's needs

Hobbies unit
Make fold-down table the same size as bed frame, plus 1 in. on long side. Fix to wall unit with piano hinge. Glue and screw a 2 in. x 1 in. batten to inside face, 1 in. from each end. Fix large screw eye into center of batten. Fix a batten to underside of shelf in wall unit and fix screw eyes 2 in. from sides. Tie cord to flap ring, pass end through other ring and attach weight.

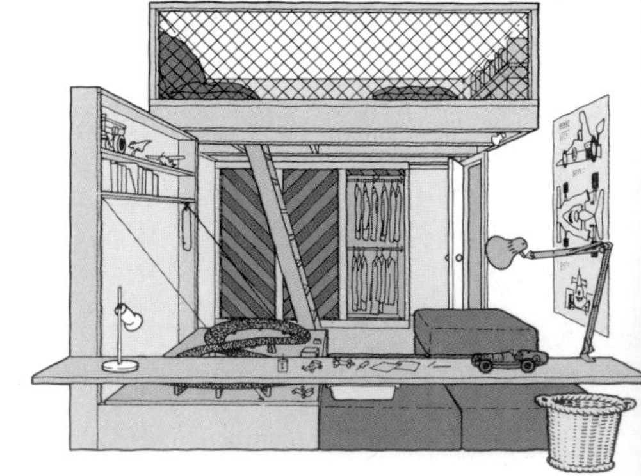

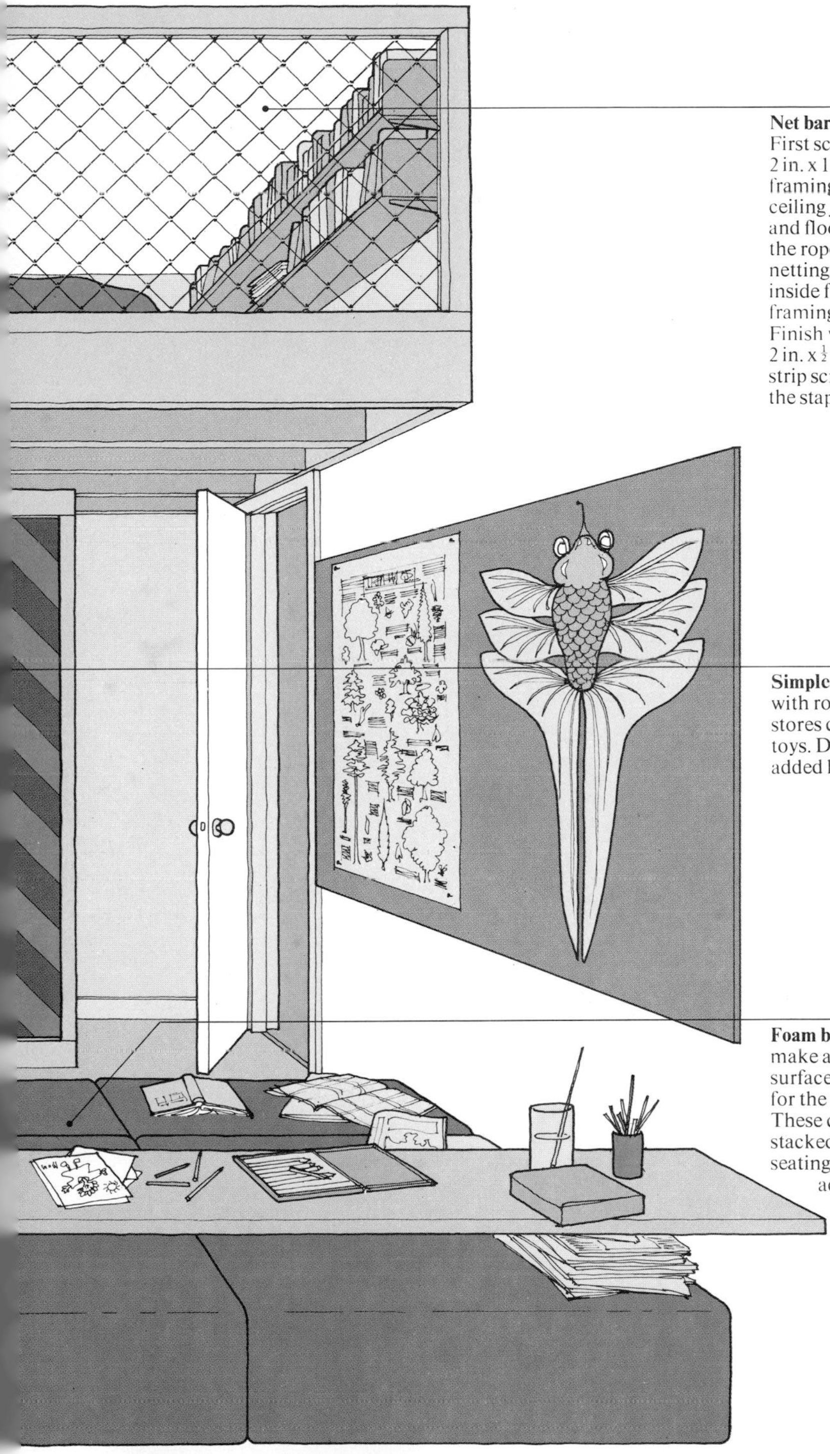

Net barrier
First screw 2 in. x $1\frac{1}{2}$ in. framing to the ceiling joists, walls and floor. Staple the rope or plastic netting firmly to inside face of the framing all around. Finish with a 2 in. x $\frac{1}{2}$ in. cover strip screwed over the staples

Simple closet
with roller shade stores clothes and toys. Doors can be added later

Foam blocks
make a safe play surface and seats for the worktop. These can be stacked to form a seating unit for adults

Study
As the child grows up, the suspended floor play area can be converted for general storage with access by step ladder stored elsewhere. The fold-down table can be removed, the space behind becoming a bookcase. The adjustable shelf/worktop is now arranged for writing: the height should be between 24 in. and 27 in. for children between the ages of 12 to 17. The adjustable chair will suit both growing child and adult.

Storage unit
Cut side panels **1** from $\frac{3}{4}$ in. particle board, 24 in. wide and to the required height. Nail and glue 3 in. x $\frac{3}{4}$ in. vertical battens **2** to the side panels and 2 in. x $\frac{3}{4}$ in. battens **3** to end panels **4** as below. The length of the battens should be equal to the sides less the width of a 3 in. rail at the top and bottom. Cut $\frac{1}{4}$ in. deep rabbets 24 in. apart in four 3 in. x 1 in. rails **5** to receive side panels and then secure with angle brackets and $\frac{5}{8}$ in. screws. Cut base shelf to fit on front and back rails. If the unit falls short of ceiling, fit a hardboard panel

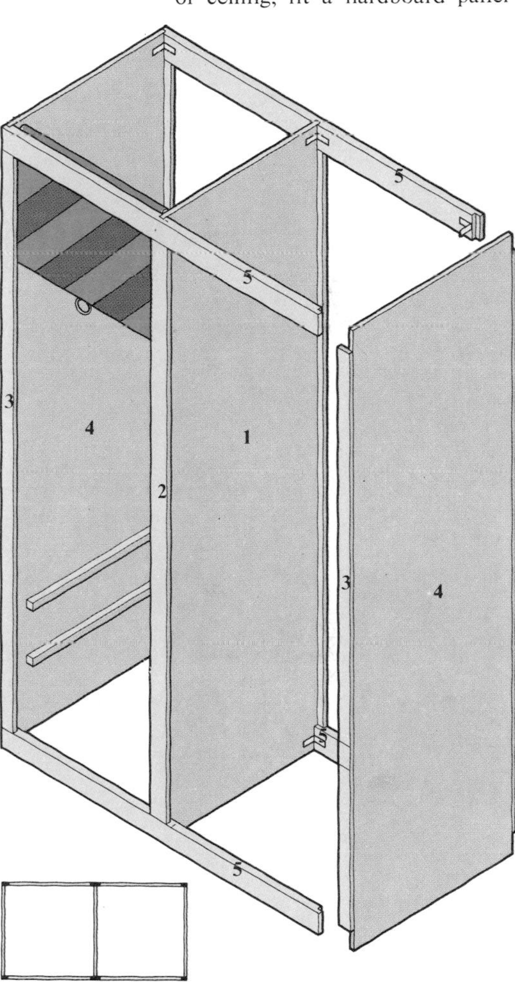

across top. Cut roller shade to width and fix brackets to back face of top rail – the fabric should clear both sides by $\frac{1}{2}$ in. Drawer runners should be fitted on spacer battens to bring them clear of the front, and give clearance for the shade. Face-fixed panel doors 24 in. wide can also be fitted to the unit.

Children's Furniture

1

2

1 High chair
Rounded corners, a sturdy base and easily removable tray make this a safe and efficient feeding chair.

2 Clothes stand
An easily accessible object for hanging both toys and clothes, the stand is made from PVC pipe.

3 Play table and chair
Once the child has outgrown the feeding chair it can convert to a play table and chair.

4 Safety gate
A colorful, easy-to-make barrier prevents children getting into dangerous areas.

3

4

Clothes Stand & Safety Gate

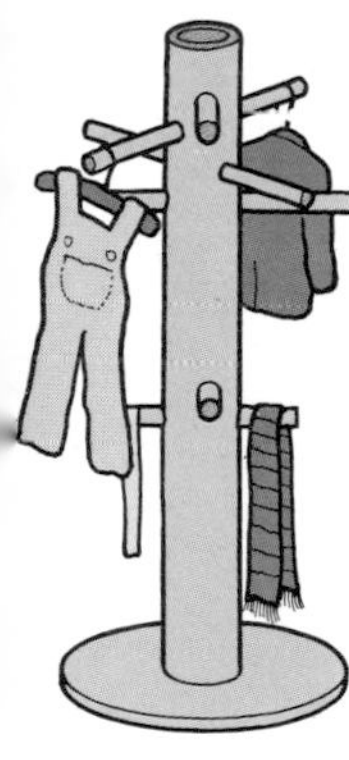

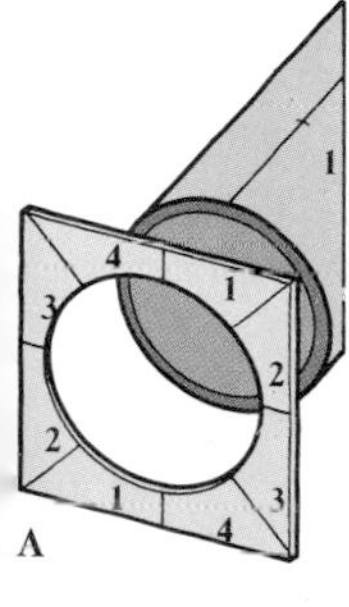

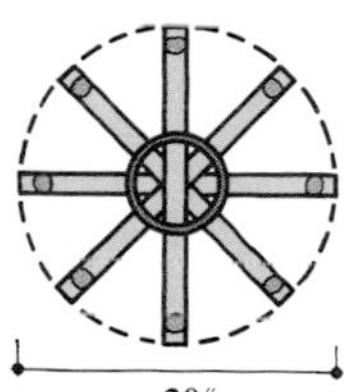

Clothes stand

The column of this stand can be made from a 60 in. length of 6 in. diameter PVC piping, as supplied to plumbers. Mark and cut the tube to length, using a hack-saw and a miter box, smoothing the edges with a file and abrasive paper. Draw a center line down the length of the tube. Make a cardboard template to mark the hole centers for the hanger tubes. Cut a hole in the card to fit over the column, **A.** Keeping one line marked on the card, level with the center line, slide the template down the tube and mark off the four positions for the hanger tubes. Space them 4 in. apart around the column beginning 3 in. from the top. The lower pair, set 24 in. from the bottom, should be marked off in a similar way and placed at right angles to each other. Use a hole saw in a power drill, and cut out the holes to size – if the exact size cannot be made, try the nearest smaller size cutter, then enlarge the opening with a smooth, half-round file. Cut the hanger tubes to length, make a notch $\frac{3}{8}$ in. from each end, with a 1 in. wide half-round file. Position the hanger tubes through the column with the notch side up. Apply PVC solvent adhesive to the joins on the inside of the column using a brush. Cut a 20 in. diameter disk for the base, using $\frac{3}{4}$ in. particle board, with two plug pieces to fit the inside diameter of the column tube. Glue the two smaller disks together, and then to the center of the large disk. Fill the cut edges and make good where necessary with epoxy filler. Glue the column to the base over the center plug, with resin adhesive, and roughen the inside of the tube to provide a better grip for the glue, before assembling. Finish with a PVC paint.

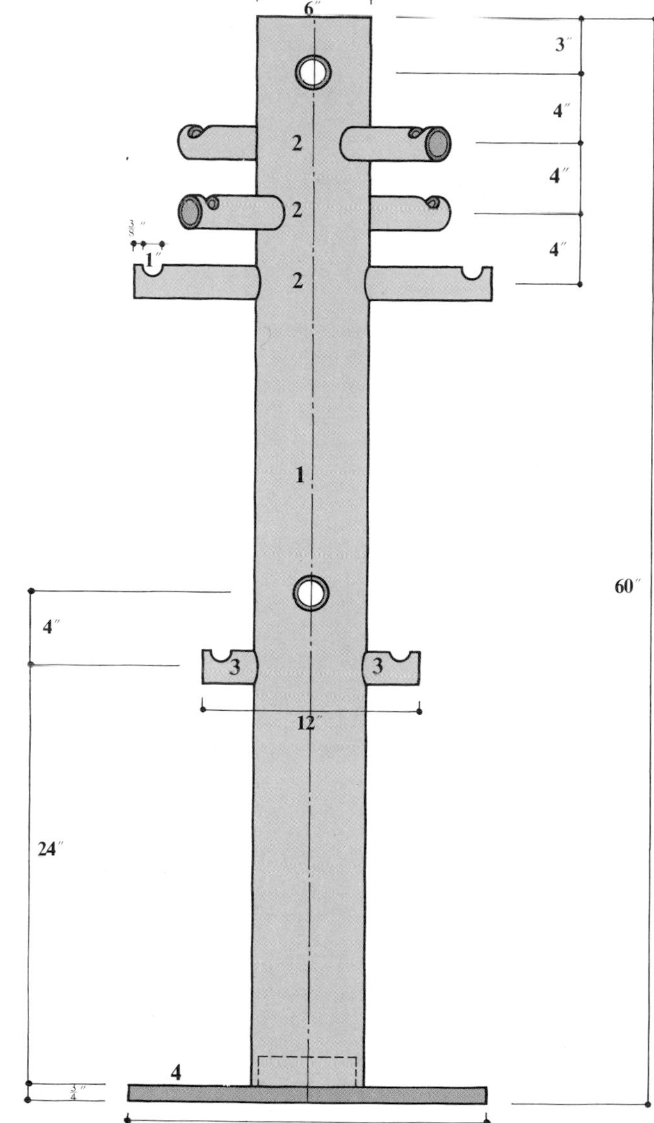

No	Part	Quantity	Length	Width	Th	Material
1	Column	1	60	6		PVC piping
2	Hangers	4	20	1½		PVC piping
3	Hangers	2	12	1½		PVC piping
4	Disk base	1	20 dia.		¾	Particle board
5	Plug pieces	2	To fit inner dia. of col		¾	Particle board

Hardware: PVC solvent adhesive. PVC paint. *N.B. All dimensions are shown in inches.*

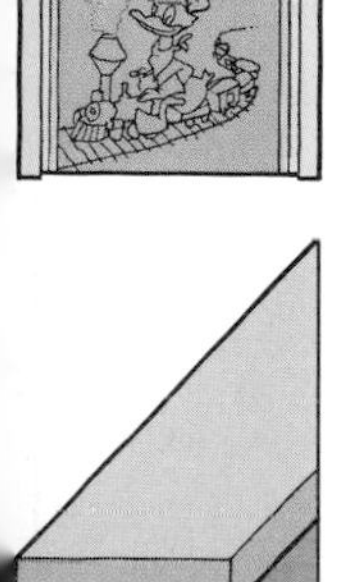

Safety gate

A drop-in safety gate, too high and too heavy for a child to lift, can be a decorative safety measure, especially near access to a steep flight of stairs, or near a kitchen. First measure the width of the opening. Deduct $\frac{1}{2}$ in. from this measurement to take the metal channels. The height of the gate should be not less than 24 in. Buy a colorful poster making sure that it is large enough for the gate panel; it may be necessary to buy more than one, and join them together to make up the size. Try and find a poster that has figures or objects that can be cut around to form the decorative edge of the gate. Cut the poster to shape and lay it on the panel, draw around it and cut to this line. Round off the bottom corners to a $\frac{1}{4}$ in. curve. Sand all edges and faces and paint all around. Glue the poster to one face of the finished board, and seal it with a clear varnish. Cut two lengths of aluminum channel $\frac{5}{8}$ in. wide and deep, to the height of each side of the panel. Drill and countersink three holes to take no. 8 screws in the back face of the channel, and screw to the door frame or wall, then slide the door panel into the two channels.

Cutting out the shape
Use a sharp knife or scissors to cut around poster. Transfer outline to the $\frac{1}{2}$ in. plywood panel. Secure the panel in a vise and cut around the outline with a coping or a power fret saw. Glue poster to panel and varnish with polyurethane lacquer.

Fitting the gate
Make sure that the two aluminum channels align, and that they are the same height as the sides of the panel. Screw them to each side of the opening, then slide the panel gently into place.

High Chair

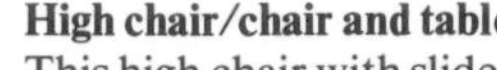

High chair/chair and table

This high chair with slide-on tray is designed to convert into a separate chair and play table after the child has outgrown its feeding chair. Flat shaped parts have been used to avoid internal corners and crevices which are hard to keep clean. The tray has a shallow rim to prevent accidentally spilt liquids dripping on to the floor and a simple child-proof locking system which enables the parent to remove the tray easily for cleaning. To convert the high chair, the top section simply lifts off from the base section which is inverted to make a table.

Making instructions

Nail and glue seat **1** to one long edge of both front and back panels **2,** so that edges lie flush. Punch nails below the surface and plane a 3/16 in. curve along the front and back edge. Cut a ⅛ in. deep stopped dado, 3 in. long and ⅜ in. wide on both inside faces of the sides **3.** Inset this dado 1 in. from the back corner, and at a 10° angle as in **A,** left. Round off the top corners of sides **3** to a 1 in. radius. Drill holes in the sides for two ¾ in. long dowels ⅜ in. in diameter centered 2⅜ in. from the side edges and 7/16 in. down from the top edge, see **B** left. Cut dowels to length, and glue into sides flush on inner face.

Cut the chair back **4** to shape, **C.** Nail and glue sides to seat with bottom edges flush; fit back panel into dadoes. Nail and glue front and back of frame **5** to frame sides **6.** Screw frame into seat so that 3 in. are visible below, **D** left. Fit washers between the sides of the frame and the seat, to fill the gap.

Nail and glue base sides **7** to base front and back panels **8.** Nail and glue base board **9** to base, with an equal overlap all around. Cut a 10¼ in. square hole in foot board **10,** see **E** left. Plane the corners to a curve. Cut the table **11** to shape as in **F.** Nail and glue table top **12** to underside of table frame, with smooth side up. Cut locating battens **14** to shape as in **G.** Nail both battens together and cut out as one piece, using a drill and a compass saw. Separate the parts, and nail and glue one as a left hand face and one as a right hand face to the side battens **13** flush with one end. Nail and glue the assembly to the underside of the table frame, level with the back end and smooth fitting so that it slides in easily across the width of the seat side panels. Shape the ends by following the top frame.

Remove the debris from all the edges, and sand the surface for painting. Paint the high chair to your choice of color. Fit screw eyes into each side below the line of the back panel, to take a child's harness, if desired.

A

B

C

D

E

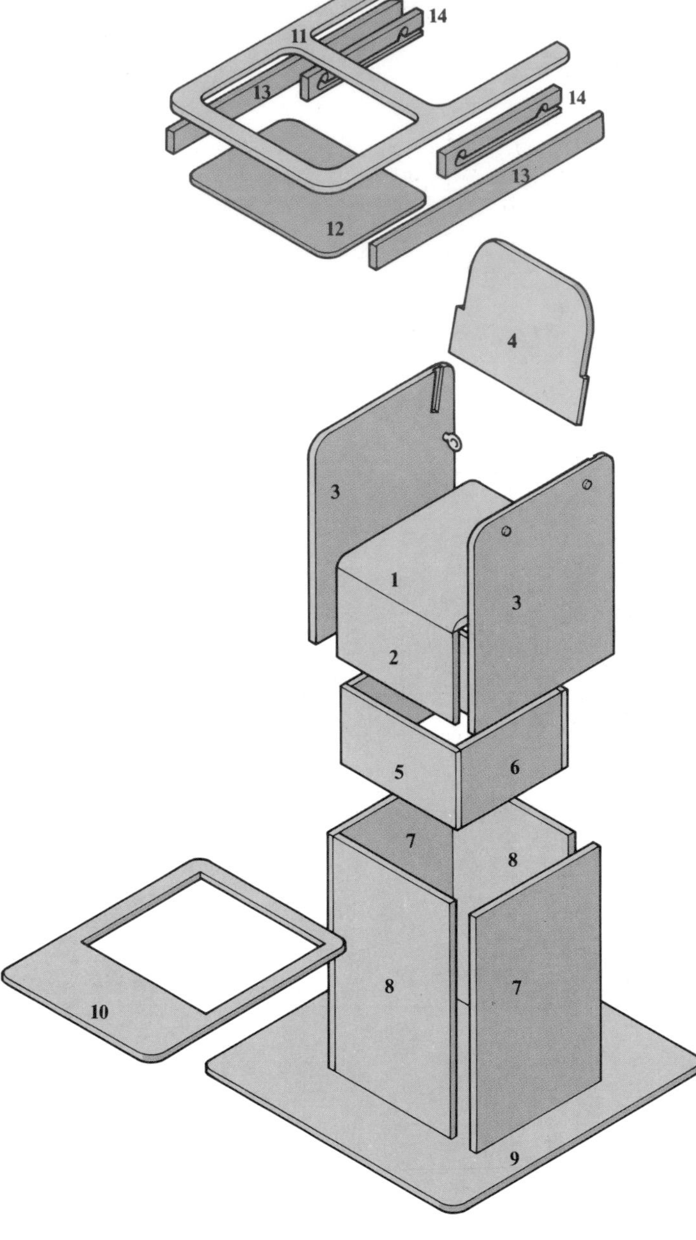

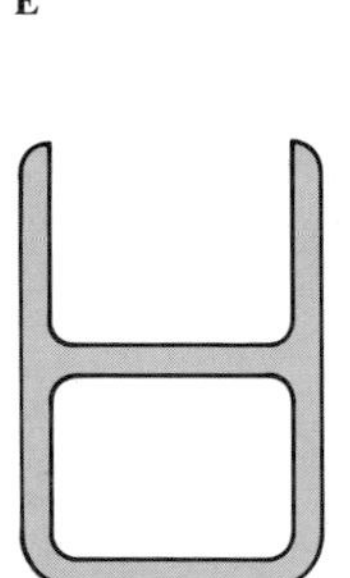

F

No	Part	Quantity	Length	Width	Th	Material
1	Seat	1	11	10¼	⅜	Plywood
2	Front/back panel	2	10¼	6½	⅜	Plywood
3	Seat sides	2	13¾	11	⅜	Plywood
4	Back	1	10½	8	⅜	Plywood
5	Frame front/back	2	10 3/16	5	⅜	Plywood
6	Frame sides	2	9 7/16	5	⅜	Plywood
7	Base sides	2	16	11	⅜	Plywood
8	Base front/back	2	16	10¾	⅜	Plywood
9	Base board	1	20	20	⅜	Plywood
10	Foot rest	1	16	12¾	⅜	Plywood
11	Table frame	1	19¼	13	⅜	Plywood
12	Table top	1	11¼	8½	⅛	Hardboard
13	Side batten	2	17¾	1⅜	⅜	Plywood
14	Locating batten	2	9	1⅜	⅜	Plywood

Hardware: *8, ¾ x 8 C/S woodscrews.* ***N.B.*** *All dimensions are shown in inches.*

G

Storage

Planning Storage

Protecting the contents

Most household goods are stored away to be protected from exposure to sunlight or dust, or perhaps to be kept out of the reach of children and pets. Storage helps to cut down on clutter and to keep floor area free. The type of unit you choose largely depends on its function, and there is an extensive range of basic designs, giving various means of storage and access.

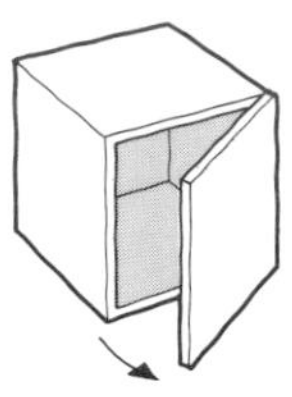

Hinged door
Probably the most common, it is simple to operate and provides access to the entire interior.

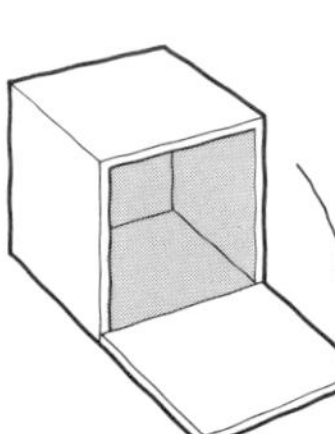

Drop flap door
With the appropriate hinge, the flap can be made to lie flush with the bottom of the unit, forming a continuous surface.

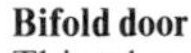

Bifold door
This takes up half the opening space of a regular hinged door, yet still provides a very good access to the interior.

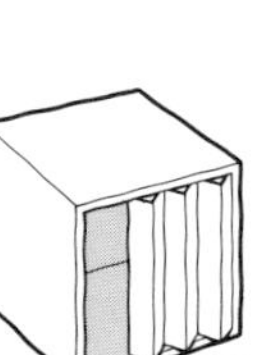

Concertina door
This takes up even less space than a bifold. The combined thickness of the sections means that they have to be made of thinner material.

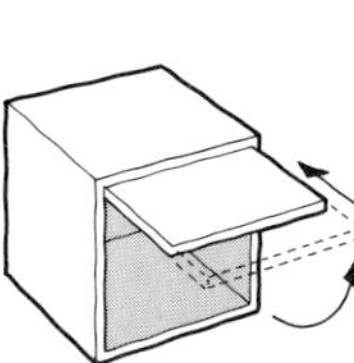

"Up and over" door
Door slides into the cabinet on a track, giving ideal access, while leaving both hands free to remove objects.

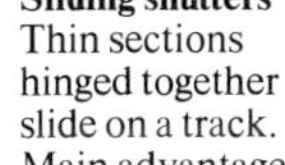

Sliding shutters
Thin sections hinged together slide on a track. Main advantage is that door does not occupy any opening space.

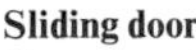

Sliding door
Door occupies no opening space, but limits access to the interior. Some systems have a method of hanging the doors from a top running track.

Flexibility and versatility

Domestic storage systems should be both flexible and versatile, and should not be limited to any particular room. Where possible, choose a system to which you can add supplementary units either extended along the wall, or upward to the ceiling. In this way, you can accommodate extra storage in the existing system. Flexibility within the system is also important, adjustable shelves are better than fixed ones, and drawers or trays are very useful. A combined unit not only gives a room a more spacious appearance, but it also makes it easier to keep clean. Choose a modular system which can be combined to fill any width to within a maximum gap of 2 in. at either end of a row of units; these gaps can then be filled by scribing a batten to the wall. A full fitted unit will provide good insulation against cold and sound and makes better use of existing walls, floor and ceiling as well.

Living room storage

Books, magazines and records may be stored on open shelves, although expensive or fragile books are best kept behind glass to protect them from dust and careless handling. Magazines should be kept flat, or between rigid divisions that prevent their slipping down. Records may be similarly displayed, and a large collection should have a divider between every batch of 50 records. This will enable you to flick through a section without the entire row collapsing. Have the record deck conveniently close to the records, and secure it to a wall-mounted shelf in preference to a floor-mounted unit which is more susceptible to vibration. Choose a shelving system that is finely adjustable, to obtain a level surface. A drinks cabinet can be handy in the living area and bottles should be placed preferably at eye level. To reduce accidental breakages, store glasses on narrow shelves, the depth of a single glass. You will find a drop flap unit handy for both pouring and mixing drinks, and there should be at least one adjacent drawer to hold table napkins, corkscrews and bar equipment.

Toy storage

Children's toys and games need a simple type of storage, easily managed by the children themselves. Narrow cabinets with sliding doors and easily moved wheeled boxes are the most useful.

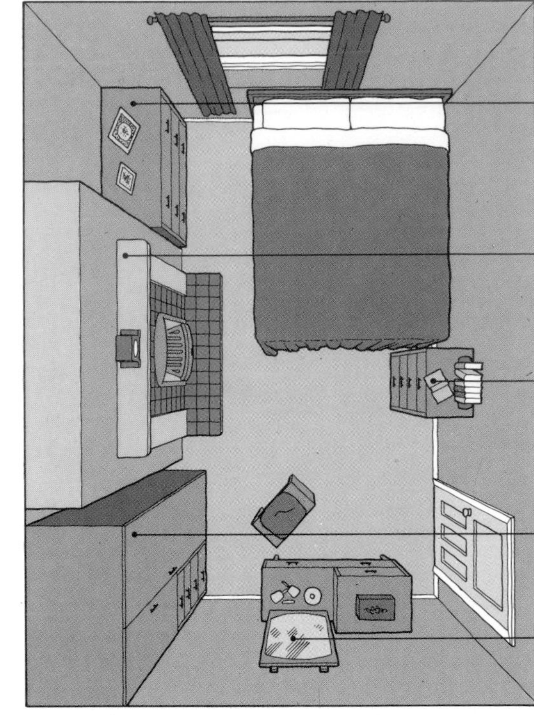

Traditional furniture can restrict space

Low chest wastes storage space above

Fireplace projects into room

Bedside cabinet cannot be positioned at bedhead

Large wardrobe does not fit into alcove

Dressing table impairs door opening and access to wardrobe

Space saving furniture and layout

Drop flap unit containing make up mirror

Convenient units on either side of bed

Fireplace removed to allow circulation around bed

Fitted closets provide ample hanging space for clothes storage

Extra storage space above door

Drop flap dressing table
The dressing table in the top scheme is replaced by a unit which provides much more storage space.

Wire baskets
Wire baskets incorporated in the fitted units, replace the chest of drawers for storing sweaters.

Living room storage

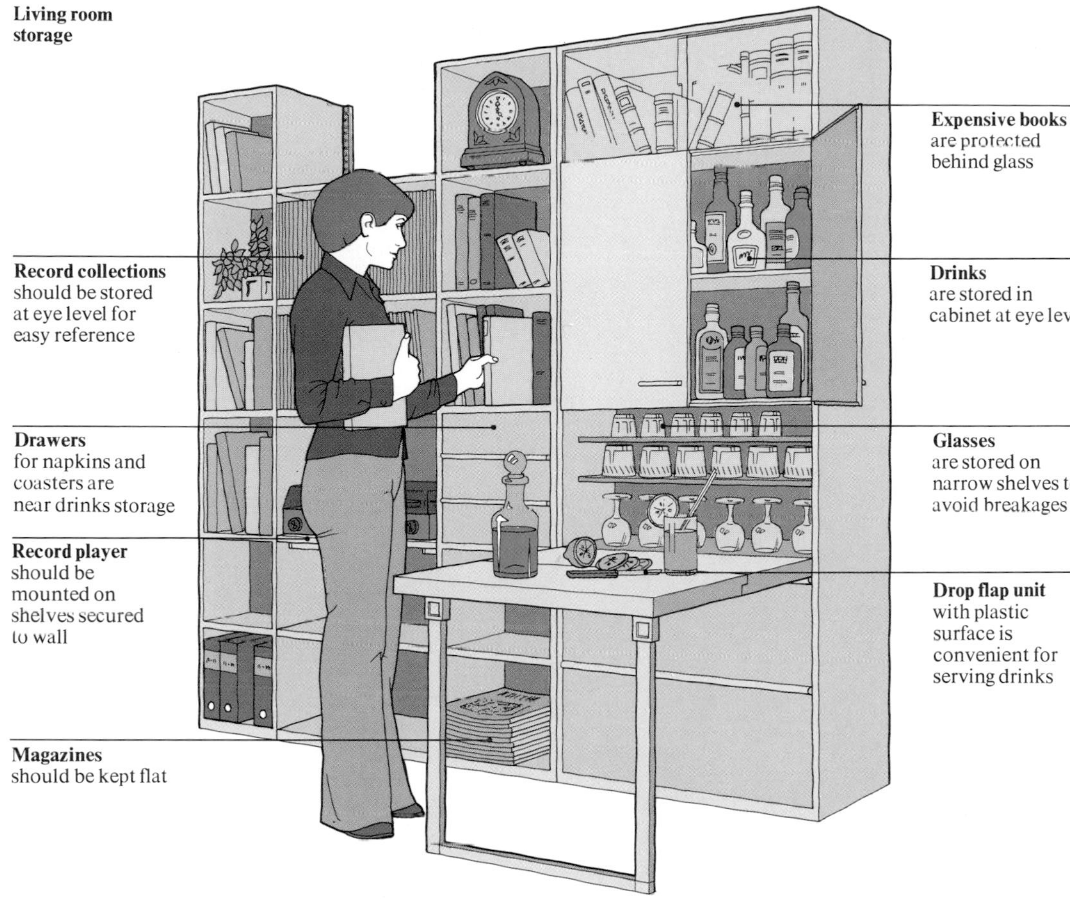

Access to the interior

The interiors of well-designed storage units are usually fitted out in a number of ways so that space is divided economically, and so that contents to the rear of deep units are easily accessible. Interiors can be made to pull out, or to swivel on a hinge or pivot. Trays or drawers can be included, set behind a hinged or flap door. Examples of space-saving devices are shown below.

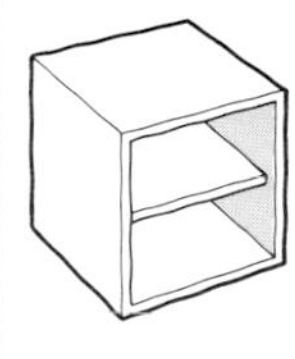

Shelves
These should have vertical adjustments, placed about 2in. apart. Access to back of shelf may mean you have to remove objects from the front first.

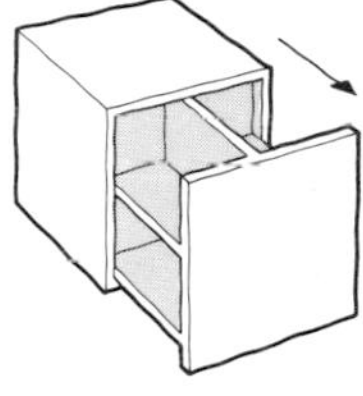

Pull-out interior
Used mainly in kitchen base units, the entire interior slides out for easy access to contents.

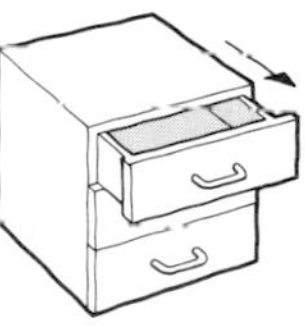

Drawer unit
Drawers divide the interior space into convenient, smaller units, which can be pulled out for access to contents.

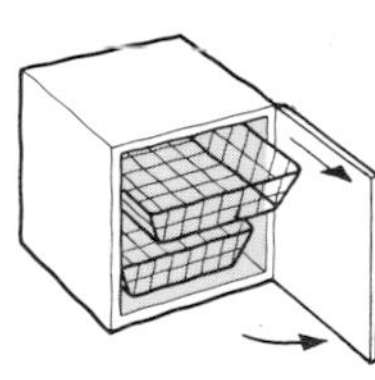

Trays
Although they do the same job as drawers, trays are of lighter construction, being made of plastic-coated wire.

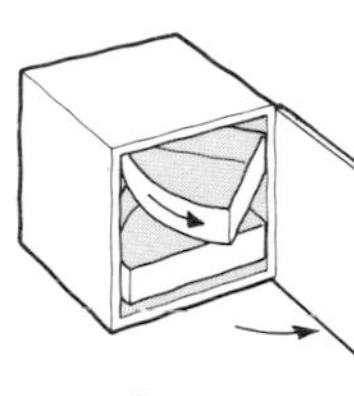

Pivoting trays
These are designed to pivot from one corner, so that they can be swung out for access to contents.

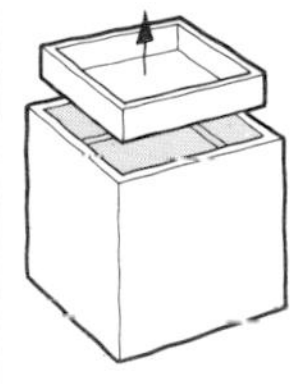

Lift-out trays
Units that open at the top utilize the space best if fitted with stacking trays.

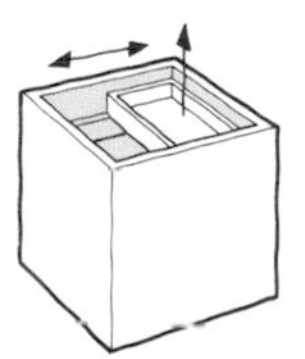

Sliding trays
A sliding tray, half the width of the unit, allows access to contents below, without removing the tray.

Bedroom storage

Clothes usually take up the greatest amount of storage space in a bedroom. The ideal solution is a separate dressing room situated, if possible, between bedroom and bathroom. Most of us, however, have to make the best use of the available space in the bedroom itself. Clothes closets need to be about 24 in. deep to take the width of a coat hanger. The alternative is to have the hanging rail across the depth of the closet, and to provide a pull-out rail. Save space by building the storage units up to ceiling level, and use the upper section for storing things used only occasionally or to install an additional hanging rail. Some systems have a counter-balanced upper rail which can be easily lowered to remove a garment. Shirts and blouses should be kept on hangers, while woolen garments should be folded and stored in drawers. Cosmetics are a problem to store, because of the different shapes and sizes of containers and bottles. Small items might fit in a convenient tray or drawer, but large things are best kept in a deep bin with a lift-up or sliding lid.

1 Pull-out rail
A pull-out rail is essential in a closet less than 24 inches deep in order to locate and remove clothing.

2 Second hanging rail
Utilize the full height of a closet to store out of season clothing. Alternatively hang shorter garments on the upper rail to give clearance for long coats or dresses below.

3 Pull-down rail
Special hardware is available, which allows convenient access to the upper rail.

1 2

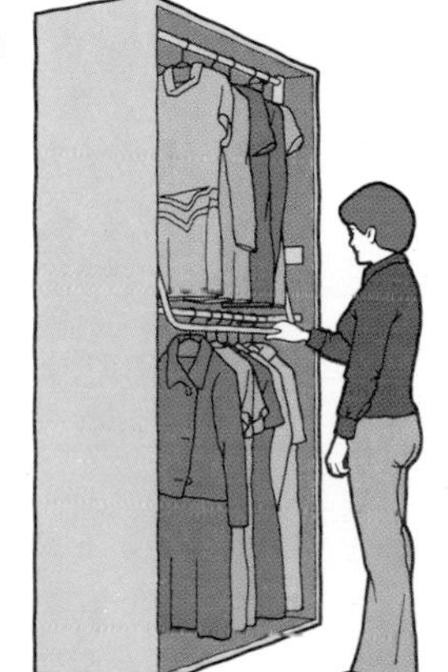

3

Storage Units

1 Room divider
This room divider is made up from four units and is 6 ft 6⅝ in. in length. The lower doors and drawers have been dark stained to contrast with the light colored veneered board and solid lumber used to make up the complete unit. The surfaces have been finished with a clear sealer. All compartments except the drawer unit on the lower level can be made accessible from both sides. Optional glass doors can be fitted to seal off the open shelving as shown here on the two left hand sections. Complete making instructions are on p. 216.

1

2 Wall fitted storage
The versatility of this range is demonstrated here in the wall fitted storage. The elements and the possible combinations are, from left to right, panel doors fitted above and below, a panel door above with drawers below, and a similar combination but with glass doors on the next two units. The unit on the right is a special matching cabinet housing a drop flap writing desk with a small cabinet at the top and two drawers at the bottom.

2

3

5

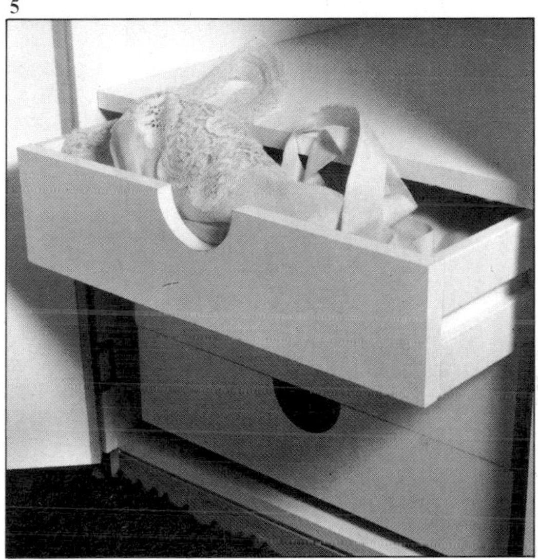

6

3 Writing desk
The cantilevered drop flap writing desk is shown here in the open position displaying three shallow trays and open shelving for writing equipment. It is necessary to screw this unit to a wall through the top back rail; see p. 217.

4 Fitted wardrobes
The bedroom storage system can make use of multiple modules to line a wall. Alternatively smaller groupings could be made, say two units wide, and spaced apart with a worktop fitted in between to make a dressing table. The table can be constructed in the same way as the bottom frame but be twice as wide and fixed between the units 30 in. from the floor. Making instructions are on p. 216.

5 Sliding hangers
Coat hangers can be simply removed or slid apart when hooked into the rings of a sliding track system screwed to the underside of the top panel or shelf.

6 Storage drawers
Banks of drawers can be fitted into the lower section of the wardrobe; the number is determined by the length of the garments hung on the track above.

4

Unit Design

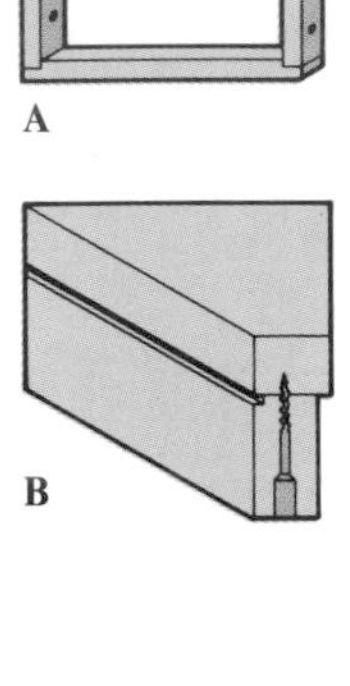

A

B

C

Cabinet/room divider units

Cut a $1\frac{7}{8}$ in. x $\frac{5}{8}$ in. notch in the bottom front and back corners of sides **1**. Finish the edges with iron-on veneer. Drill two lines of $\frac{1}{16}$ in. pilot holes in sides for shelf studs, $2\frac{1}{2}$ in. from front and back edges, rows spaced 2 in. apart, measured $4\frac{1}{4}$ in. from bottom edge for lower cabinet and $31\frac{1}{2}$ in. for upper cabinet. Drill ten pairs in lower section and eighteen in upper. Cut a $\frac{1}{8}$ in. x $\frac{1}{8}$ in. groove $\frac{1}{2}$ in. from the back edge on inside face. Cut lap joints in front and back rails **2**. Nail and glue side rails **3** into joints to form a frame $18\frac{7}{8}$ x $13\frac{3}{4}$ in. Cut a $\frac{1}{8}$ x $\frac{1}{8}$ in. rabbet or chamfer on front top edge. Make up three frames. Drill clearance holes for three $1\frac{1}{4}$ in. no. 10 screws in side rails, staggered on each side, **A**. Screw two frames to two shelves **4** flush all around, **B**. Glue $\frac{1}{2}$ in. dowel pegs in underside of bottom shelf to locate inside corners of bottom frame. Finish all parts with stain and/or clear varnish. Assemble a single unit by screwing the bottom, middle and top frames to the sides, back edges flush with back panel grooves. Fix middle frame $31\frac{1}{2}$ in. up from bottom edge of sides to top face of the shelf. Lay unit face down on the floor and slide in back panel **5** and nail in place to frames. Stand unit upright to fit bottom shelf on the frame. To add extra units, fix three more frames to additional side panel and join to one side of completed unit, locating the back panel in the grooves, and fix as before, **C**. When a side panel is used as a partition in a run of units, cut a groove for the back panels and holes for shelf studs in the outer face. Sit adjustable shelves **4** on screw eyes. The room divider is similar to the cabinet, but it is minus a back panel. The lower cabinet can be fitted with a door on each side for two-way access. Drawers can be fitted; in this case make a back closure panel as for a door, but do not fit a handle. The panel is glued to the middle and bottom section; the upper section can be used with open shelving, glass or panel doors.

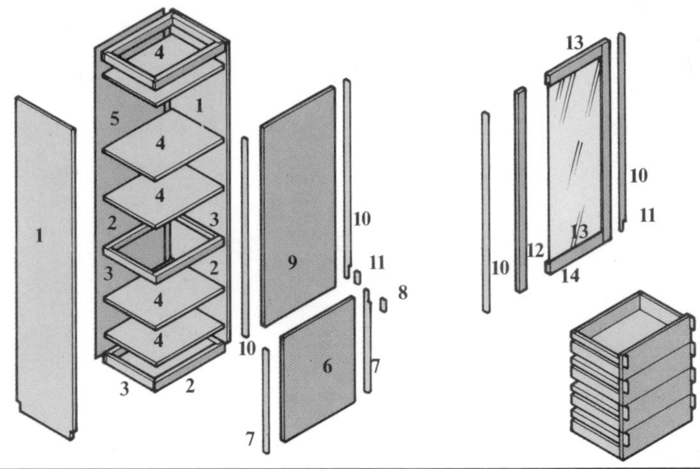

No	Part	Quantity	Length	Width	Th	Material
1	Sides	2	72	15	$\frac{5}{8}$	Veneered particle board
2	Front/back rails	6	$18\frac{7}{8}$	2	1	Softwood
3	Side rails	6	13	2	1	Softwood
4	Shelves	5	$18\frac{7}{8}$	$13\frac{3}{4}$	$\frac{5}{8}$	Veneered particle board
5	Back panel	1	70	$19\frac{1}{8}$	$\frac{1}{8}$	Hardboard
6	Bottom door	1	24	18	$\frac{5}{8}$	Veneered particle board
7	Bottom door lipping	2	24	$\frac{7}{8}$	$\frac{3}{8}$	Small molding
8	Handle	1	3	$\frac{7}{8}$	$\frac{3}{8}$	Small molding
9	Top door	1	46	18	$\frac{5}{8}$	Veneered particle board
10	Top door lipping	2	46	$\frac{7}{8}$	$\frac{3}{8}$	Small molding
11	Handle	1	3	$\frac{7}{8}$	$\frac{3}{8}$	Small molding
12	Stiles	2	46	2	$\frac{3}{4}$	Softwood
13	Top/Bottom rails	2	$14\frac{1}{4}$	3	$\frac{3}{4}$	Softwood
14	Beading	1	114	$\frac{3}{8}$	$\frac{1}{4}$	Hardwood

Hardware: 18, $1\frac{1}{2}$x8 woodscrews. 8, $\frac{7}{8}$x2 screw eyes. 2, magnetic catches. 1, 41x15x$\frac{1}{8}$ glass. 4, 2 flush hinges. ***N.B.*** *All dimensions are shown in inches.*

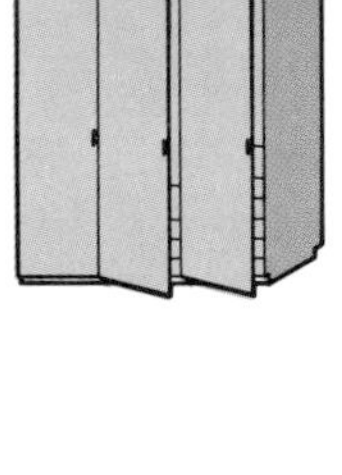

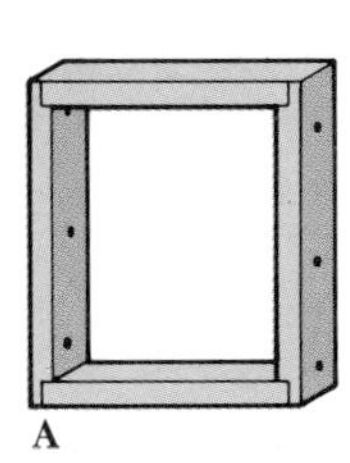

A

Wardrobe unit

A useful storage unit is this free-standing wardrobe which augments built-in closets. The construction of the wardrobe is similar to the cabinet/room divider unit above except that it is deeper from front to back, does not have a middle frame, and is not drilled for fully adjustable shelves.

Make the top and bottom frames $22\frac{3}{4}$ in. long and $18\frac{7}{8}$ in. wide. Drill clearance holes for three $1\frac{1}{4}$ in. no. 10 screws in the side rails **A**. Make and finish the door as for panel doors (see p. 215), but fit the handle $30\frac{3}{4}$ in. up from the bottom edge, on either the right or the left hand side, depending on which way you want the door to open. Screw a glide rail across the center of the top panel, to carry coat hangers. The lower section of the interior can be fitted with drawers, or left to accommodate long garments, **B**. A full length evening dress will need a long drop. A man's overcoat allows room for three drawers below, while suits and skirts allow room for six drawers. Make the drawers $16\frac{1}{2}$ in. wide and 22 in. long, from a 4 in. plastic drawer profile (see p. 133). The drawers should be inset to clear the door and run on $1\frac{1}{4}$ x $\frac{5}{8}$ in. hardwood runners. Cut a $1\frac{1}{2}$ in. deep semi-circular cut-out in the top edges of the drawer fronts and finish with iron-on lipping, **C**. This wardrobe works very well when other units are added for additional storage. After making the first unit, fix additional units consisting of frames and one side panel to the completed unit, locating the back panels in the grooves and fixing.

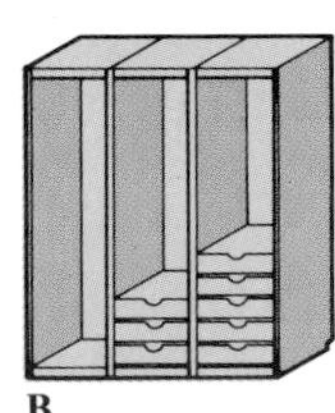

B

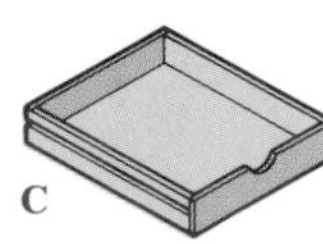

C

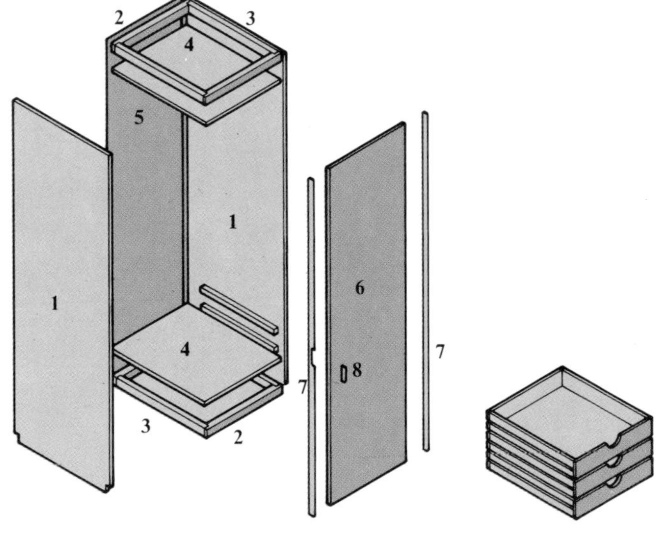

No	Part	Quantity	Length	Width	Th	Material
1	Sides	2	72	24	$\frac{5}{8}$	Veneered particle board
2	Front rails	4	$18\frac{7}{8}$	2	1	Softwood
3	Side rails	4	22	2	1	Softwood
4	Shelves	2	$22\frac{3}{4}$	$18\frac{7}{8}$	$\frac{5}{8}$	Veneered particle board
5	Back panel	1	70	$19\frac{1}{8}$	$\frac{1}{8}$	Hardboard
6	Door	1	70	18	$\frac{5}{8}$	Veneered particle board
7	Lipping	2	70	$\frac{7}{8}$	$\frac{3}{8}$	Hardwood molding
8	Handle	1	3	$\frac{7}{8}$	$\frac{3}{8}$	Hardwood molding

Hardware: 12, $1\frac{1}{2}$x8 woodscrews. 1, magnetic catch. 3, 2 flush hinges. 1, $18\frac{7}{8}$ slide rail. ***N.B.*** *All dimensions are shown in inches.*

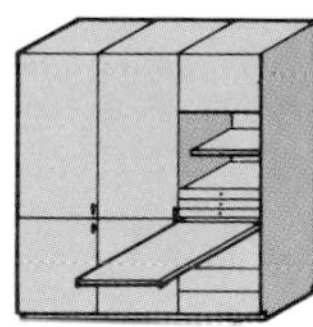

Writing desk unit

Cut the sides **1** as described for the cabinet unit, but omit the pilot holes. Drill instead two lines of holes, ten to each line, starting 14¾ in. from the top end. The rows must be 2 in. apart and the lines are 2½ in. and 10½ in. from the back edge. Make the top and bottom frames, **2**, **3** and **4** as for the cabinet unit. Cut lap joints in ends of center frame front rails **2**. Nail and glue side rails **5** into joints to form a 18⅞ in. x 12 in. frame. Hinge fixed panel **7** to drop flap **8** with an 18 in. piano hinge. Lay the hinged panels flat, with the knuckle uppermost. Place side lippings **10** against the panels and mark and cut them in two, at an angle of 60°, ⅜ in. from the hinge on the fixed panel side, **A**. Finish the panels and glue lippings to the edges, the angled ends butting with a 1/32 in. gap. Cut a ⅝ x ⅛ in. rabbet in the back face of the fixed panel on each side, to house angle bracket **9**. Drill and countersink the bracket for screwing into the rabbet. Cut rabbet joints in side rails **11**. Nail and glue end rails **12** in joints to make a 42¾ x 18 in. frame. Nail and glue center rail **13** between end rails. Screw and glue frame to back face of drop flap only, level with the lipping on sides, and ⅝ in. from top end. Glue remnants of rails to the back of the flap between rails to support top **14**. Nail and glue top to the frame with edges flush. Finish sides and top surface with plastic laminate. Fit handles, one on each side, at the top of the flap as for doors. Fit fixed shelf **15** on screw eye shelf studs in top pilot holes, and screw through ring, **B**. Screw drop flap assembly through bracket **9** into the carcass with the bottom edge of fixed panel **7**, 12 in. from the bottom notch, **C**. Support the worktop at 90° to the unit and mark the line of the top surface on the side panel. Screw the middle frame into the carcass, the bottom edge level with the line, the back edge flush with the back groove. Slide in the back panel **6** from one end and nail to top, middle and bottom frames. Make three 18½ in. x 12 in. x 1¾ in. trays. Drill a 1 in. diameter hole through center of fronts to form pulls. Fit the trays on aluminum runners screwed to the sides, bottom runner sitting on middle frame. Fix shelf **16** on a runner reversed to form a kicker **D**. Fit adjustable shelf on screw eye studs. Fit strong magnetic catch to underside of fixed shelf **15** at center and fix strike plate to drop flap. Make and fit top door **17** as for other panel doors. Make and fit two drawers as described. Screw unit to wall through top frame.

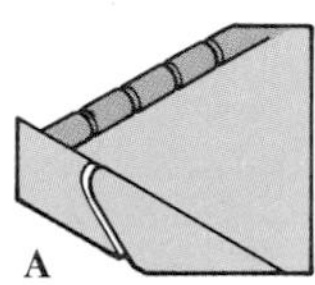

A

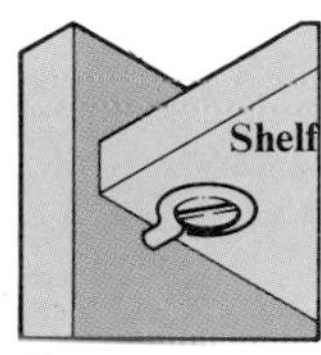

B

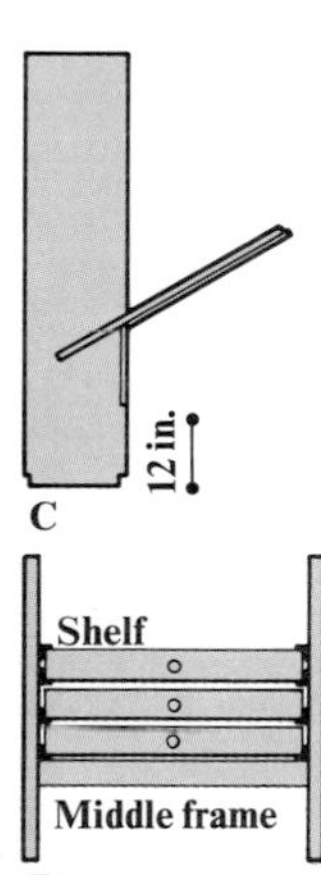

C

D

Door and drawers for cabinet/room divider units

Cut doors from one piece so that grain matches. Finish door panel **6** with stain and/or varnish, omitting side edges. Glue small molding **7** to edges, back edges flush with back face. Fit handle as on right and finish molding to contrast with panel. Make upper door in the same way, fitting handle in the bottom right or left corner – handle fixture is shown on the right. Fit doors on two 2 in. brass flush hinges, 3 in. from each end. Secure doors with face mounted magnetic catches fitted behind handles. To make glass doors, cut a ⅜ in. x ⅜ in. stopped rabbet in back face of stiles **12**, matching rabbet in top and bottom rails **13**. Dowel joint rails into stiles, as shown far right. Finish frame to match unit and fit molding and handle as described for upper door panel. Fit glass. Make a set of four drawers to fit width and depth of the unit, with sides 4¾ in. high (see pp. 132-133). Cut four fronts 18 in. long x 6 in. wide from one panel with grain running vertically. Lip top edges with iron-on veneer, finishing as for doors. Glue molding to side edges, fitting handles as described for doors.

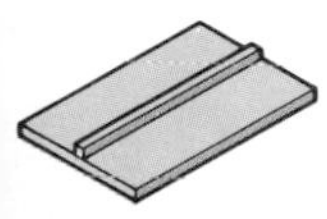

Divider shelf
When unit is made accessible from both sides, glue a 18⅞ in. x 2 in. stop batten across center to prevent books sliding through.

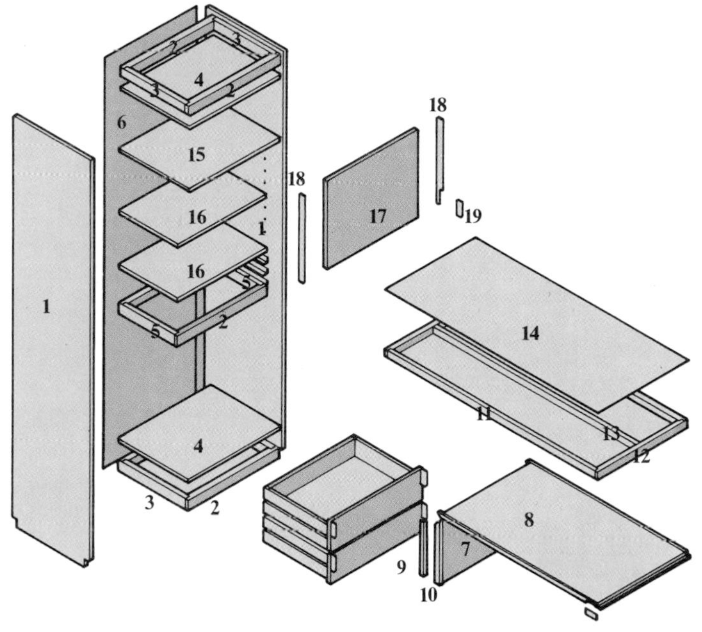

No	Part	Quantity	Length	Width	Th	Material
1	Sides	2	72	15	⅝	Veneered particle board
2	Front/back rails	6	18⅞	2	1	Softwood
3	Side rails	4	13	2	1	Softwood
4	Top/bottom shelves	2	18⅞	13¾	⅝	Veneered particle board
5	Center frame side rails	2	11¼	2	1	Softwood
6	Back panel	1	70	19⅛	⅛	Hardboard
7	Fixed panel	1	18	12	⅝	Veneered particle board
8	Drop flap	1	31½	18	⅝	Veneered particle board
9	Angle bracket	2	11	⅝	⅝	Aluminum angle
10	Side lippings	2	43⅝	⅞	⅜	Small molding
11	Flap side rails	2	42⅞	1½	1	Softwood
12	End rails	2	17¼	1½	1	Softwood
13	Center rail	1	41⅛	1½	1	Softwood
14	Top	1	42⅞	18	¼	Plywood
15	Fixed shelf	1	18⅞	13¾	⅝	Veneered particle board
16	Shelf	2	18⅞	12	⅝	Veneered particle board
17	Top door	1	18	14⅜	⅝	Veneered particle board
18	Lipping	2	14⅜	⅞	⅜	Small molding
19	Handles	3	3	⅞	⅜	Small molding

Hardware: 18, 1½x8 woodscrews. 4, 12x½x½x1/16 ali angle. 2, magnetic catches. 1, 18x1¼ piano hinge. 2, 2 flush hinges. ***N.B.*** *All dimensions are shown in inches.*

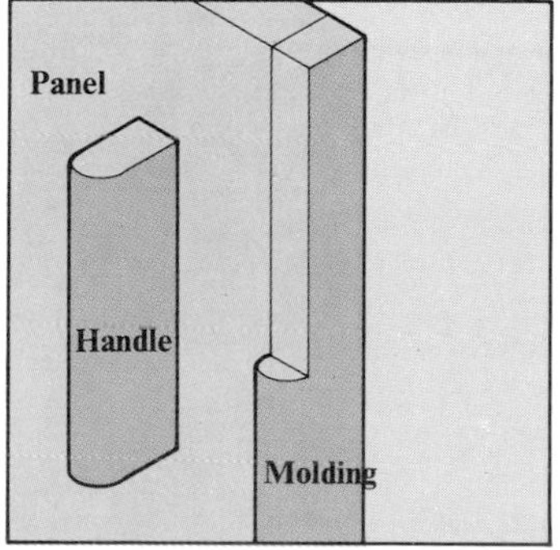

Door handles
*Cut a 3 in. long notch in the front edge of the molding, in the top right or left corner, and flush with door face. Glue handle **8** into notch.*

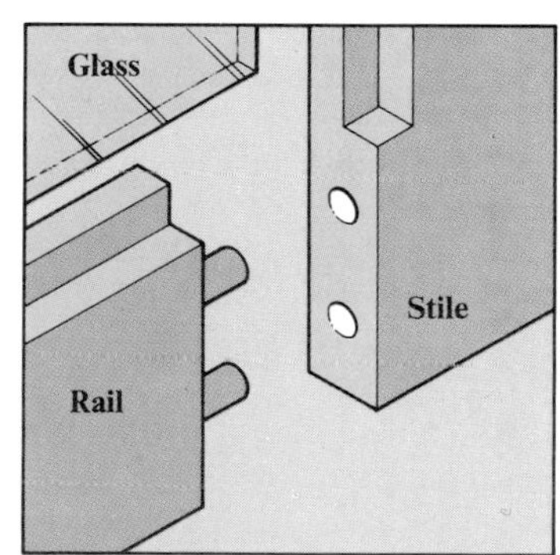

Glass doors
Fit glass into the rabbet of stiles and rails. Fix with pre-finished ⅜ in. x ¼ in. molding, mitered and nailed to frame. Fit the doors on 2 in. flush hinges.

Storage in Unused Areas

Finding extra space
Unused areas are those that tend to be out of comfortable reach, or those odd spaces not used for access and circulation. Both the physical features of a room and the positioning of furniture within it dictate the areas of such unused space. Nearly every room has "dead spots" such as corners and behind doors which are rarely utilized to their full potential and "spare" spaces such as occur against or around walls and ceilings. While these areas may be unsuitable for free standing furniture, they may take purpose-built furnishings. For instance, the area behind a door in an entrance hall might easily take a built-in closet.
If you intend to buy or build storage units, it is sensible to have them the full height of the room. Items needed daily can be contained in the readily accessible part while the out of reach areas will store rarely used items – a small lightweight step ladder can be stored on a hook inside a closet. In any event, before you contemplate additional units, make sure that you are using the available storage to its best advantage. For example, many kinds of clothing traditionally stored on hangers might just as well be folded and put away in drawers, especially seasonal things. Can the additional space in the wardrobe now be used to store other items, say a collection of books that are not in current use, which may be taking up shelf space elsewhere? Can all clothing be stored more economically, so that entire areas are made available for extra storage? By regarding the problem in this way, a lot more space might become available.

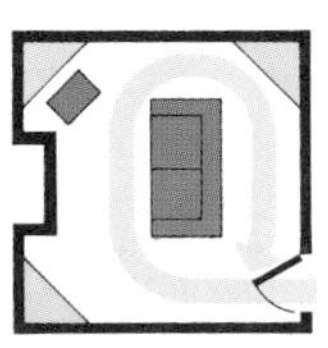

Circulation space
Dead spots are created when access is to a central point only.

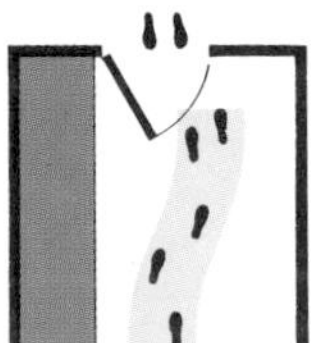

Unused space
Approach to a door is usually by one side only, so area behind it can be used for storage.

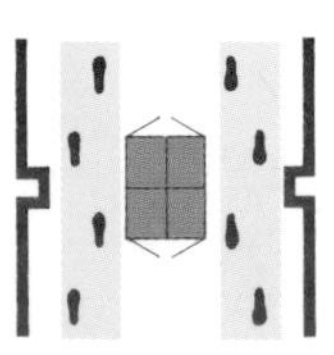

Spare space
With large floor areas two central units placed back to back can supply both halves of a room or hallway.

Using the corners
A room used specifically for one purpose, such as a small dining room where the focus of activity is centered, can make full use of corner storage. If the purpose of the room is unlikely to change, the interior can be treated as a complete unit with built-in fittings which can even improve the shape of the room.

Table
is set to align with the cupboards, in order to harmonize with the room's shape

Built-in cupboard
is set at an angle of 45°. Books can be stored on the adjustable shelves, less used items are on the top

Over bed storage
Suspended storage units take advantage of unused space, especially where they do not intrude on the working or standing space below, as over a bed. Storage can be made more accessible if the floor level is raised to bring it within reach – a platform bed is a good example.

Suspended unit
with sliding doors, could hold additional bed linen, pillows, or blankets

Unit
has built-in recessed lighting, or can house a solarium unit

Top surfaces
of platform can be used as bedside bookshelves

Double platforms
can be covered with matching floor carpets

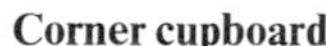

Corner cupboard

First choose the style of doors – these can be panel or louver type, or flush faced so that you can paint or paper them to match the surrounding wall. The doors **1** should be between 18 to 24 in. wide. Measure the height of the room and cut two stiles **2**, 1 in. shorter than the room height, from 2 in. x 1½ in. softwood lengths. Make the doors long enough to give 1 in. clearance at the top, and level with the top of the baseboard at the bottom. Fit doors to the stiles with butt hinges so they are level with the top. Measure overall width of assembly to determine length of bottom and top crossrails **3**. Cut top rails from 2 in. x 1 in. softwood, cut bottom from 1 in. thick wood, 1 in. wider than baseboard height. Cut a 45° miter at the ends. Screw and glue the crossrails to the back face of the stiles, flush at the ends. Check that frame is square. Screw and glue a 1½ in. x 1½ in. fixing batten **4** to the back face of the bottom rails. Position the complete fascia assembly across the corner at 45° with the frame touching the baseboard. Screw the batten to the floor. With the frame set vertically, fix the top to the ceiling with a 2 in. x 1½ in. batten **5** mitered at the ends. Make 2 in. wide scribing strips from hardboard or thin plywood. Hold strips against the wall on inside face of stiles. Mark and cut scribed edge. Glue the shaped strip to inside face of the frame, **A**. Screw triangular blocks to back of stiles and wall about halfway up to support the frame. Make triangular shelves to fit the corner, and support the front edge with a batten. Fix shelves on battens screwed to the walls (see p. 224). This fascia can also be fitted into an alcove, square to the wall if desired.

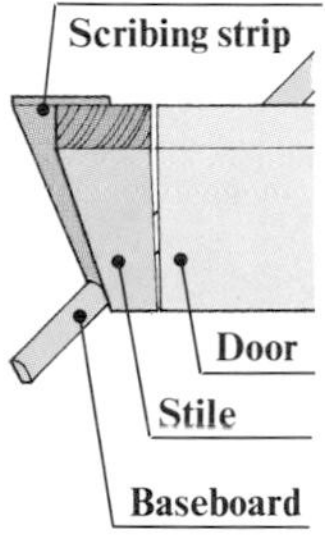

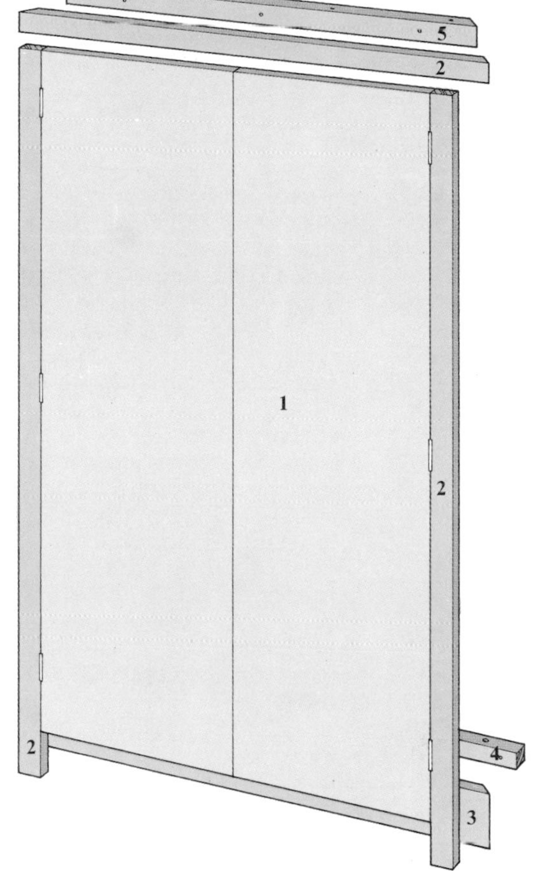

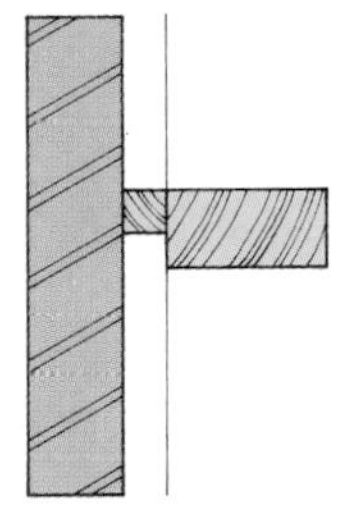

Small molding
A rabbet joint should be made between the frame and the wall.
A small molding set back from the frame can fill gap.

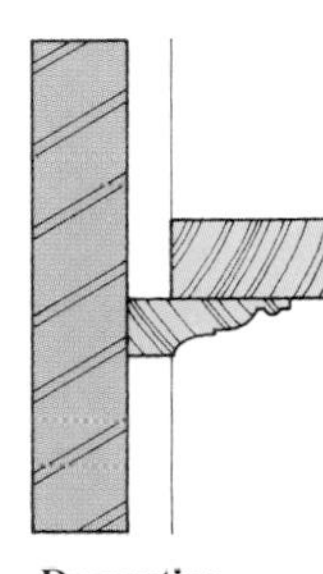

Decorative molding
A face fixed decorative molding can also be used to mask the gap between wall and frame.

Suspended storage unit

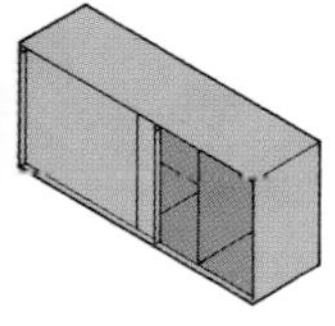

Make the bed and plinth as described on pp. 194-195, so that the top tier is 24 in. wider than the mattress, and 12 in. longer at one end. The lower tier should be 18 in. wider than the top tier and 9 in. longer. If the bed is free standing, make tiers symmetrical. Make three suspended units, the end one the same width as mattress, the sides 12 in. shorter. Cut panels **1** to the required length, from ⅝ in. x 12 in. wide veneered board. Cut end panels **2** from the same style board, 20 in. long. Finish the exposed cut edges. Cut partitions **3**, 18¾ in. long and 11 in. wide. Drill 1/16 in. pilot holes for shelf supports 2 in. apart, 1½ in. from front and back edges of partitions, and 2½ in. from front edges on ends. Glue and dowel joint the partitions to top and bottom panels with back edges flush. The middle partition is placed at the center and the two intermediate partitions are aligned between the middle and the end of the panel. Similarly, joint end panel to top and bottom ends. Cut back panel **4** from ⅛ in. plywood, ⅛ in. smaller all around than unit, and nail and glue to back edges. Glue top and bottom plastic sliding door track to take ⅛ in. thick doors, flush with front edge of top and bottom panel. Cut doors **5** from ⅛ in. plywood or acrylic sheet to required dimensions. Glue ½ in. x ½ in. aluminum angle flush with ends of doors to make handles. Cut out and screw spacer battens securely through ceiling into joists. Set them out as shown in the diagram on the left. Battens should be 2 in. thick if they are to bring the bottom of the cabinet between 55 in. and 60 in. above the top platform of the bed. Fix cabinets to spacer battens, using 2 in. no. 10 roundhead screws with large washers. Fit shelves and locate sliding doors in the track.

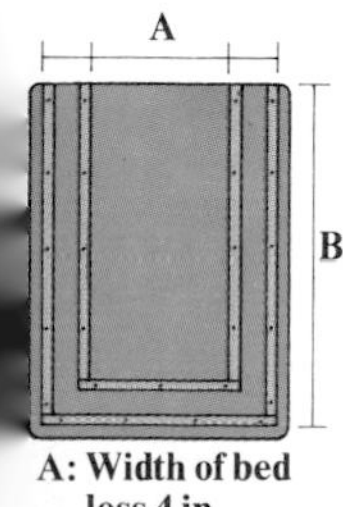

A: Width of bed less 4 in.
B: Length of bed less 2 in.

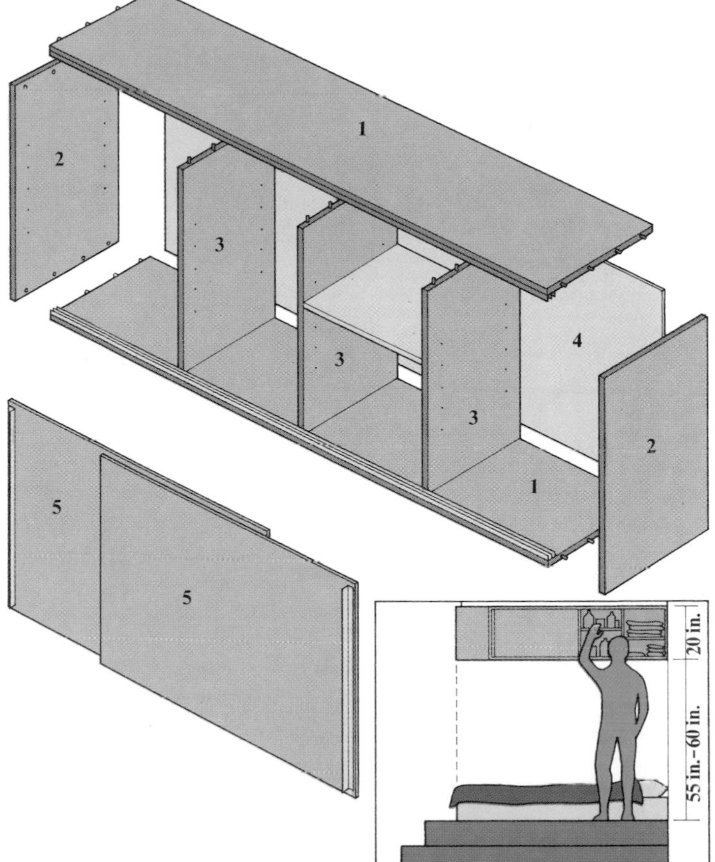

Small Storage Items

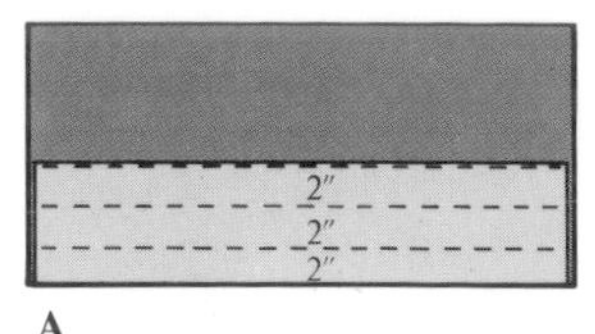

A

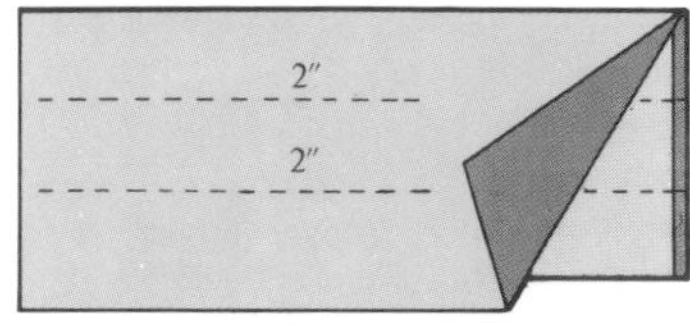

B

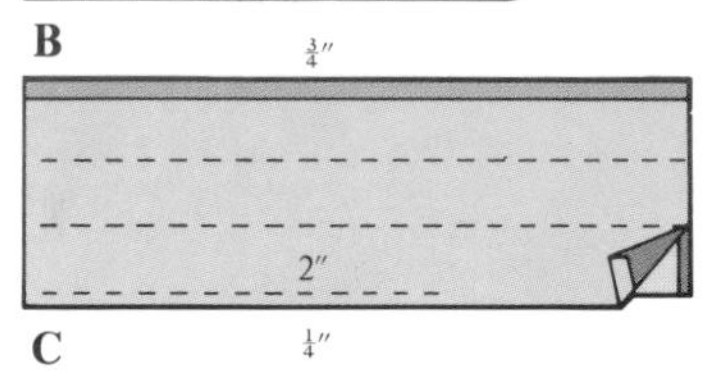

C

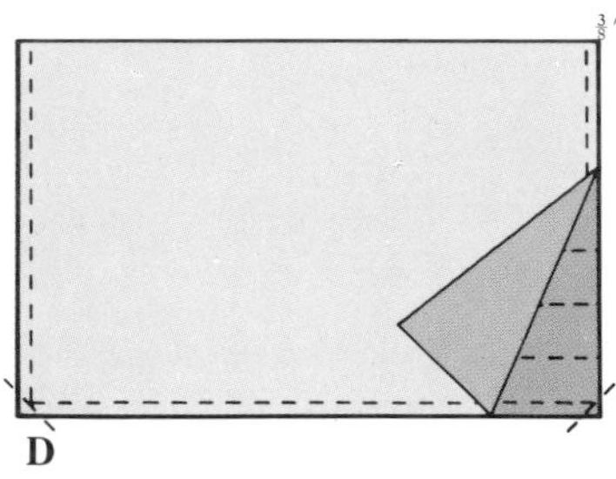
D

Quilted pockets

These storage pockets are useful for many small items like needles, jewelry and accessories. Cut out two pieces of fabric 23½ x 35½ in. for back and lining, two pieces 13 x 23½ in. for small pockets, and two pieces 26 x 23½ in. for deep pockets. Cut two pieces of batting 6 x 22¾ in. and another two 12 x 22¾ in. Stitch batting to inside of pocket by machine **A.** Fold fabric over batting, and top stitch at 2 in. intervals **B.** Turn in outside bottom edge of pocket and stitch to back **C.** Repeat for all but bottom pockets which you stitch flat on to the back. Overlap top of each pocket to cover bottom stitch line of the pocket above. Next, top stitch vertical divisions, and with right sides facing stitch lining along three sides over pockets **D.** Trim corners and turn lining to the back. Turn in top edges of back and lining, and overstitch. Finally, fit four eyelets along top edge of inside pockets.

No	Part	Quantity	Length	Width	Material
	Fabric	Total	126	36	Cotton or canvas fabric
1	Back	1	35½	23½	
2	Lining	1	35½	23½	
3	Small pockets	2	13	23½	
4	Deep pockets	2	26	23½	
	Quilting	Total	54	18	Batting
1	Small pockets	2	6	22¾	
2	Deep pockets	2	12	22¾	

Hardware: 4 eyelets. *N.B. All dimensions are shown in inches.*

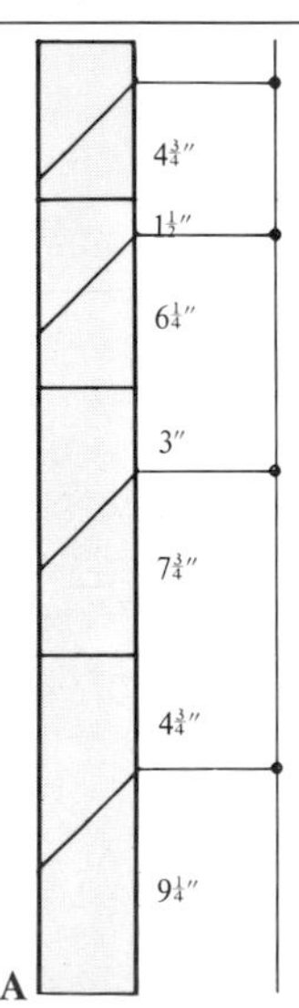

A

Desk tidy

This practical group of containers is made from a length of PVC piping. The sections are joined together as a convenient way of keeping small items handy. To make the tidy, saw the pipe into lengths as shown in **A.** Glue the cut sections along their touching surfaces with PVC adhesive. Spray the assembled pipes with PVC paint, when the adhesive has dried. Cut seven circular bases from plywood to fit the inner diameter of the pipes. Prime and spray bases, then glue them into the bottom orifices of the pipes so that they fit flush.

No	Part	Quantity	Length	Width	Th	Material
1	Pipe	1	40	4 dia		PVC waste pipe
2	Base	7	Diameter as required		⅛	Plywood

Hardware: PVC spray paint. *N.B. All dimensions are shown in inches.*

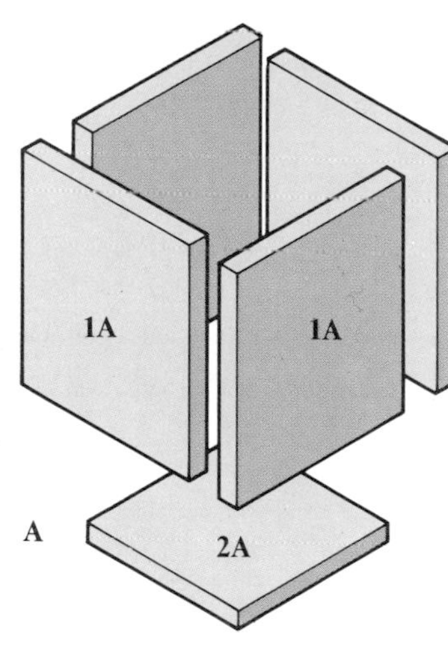

Foam box

A useful, lightweight and attractive container can be made from squares of foam covered by fabric. Cut five pieces of foam as shown in cutting list and glue together as shown in **A** using foam adhesive. Transfer pattern shown in **D** on to paper and cut out fabric according to instructions on the cutting plan. Stitch side edges of pieces **1** together first as in **B,** then sew bottom **2** into narrower end of pieces **1** as indicated in **C** by matching edge marks. Cut out cover panel **4** and hem edges all around. Pinch in the corners along the diagonal dotted line and machine stitch. Cut away corner fold ⅜ in. from the seam line **D.** Glue outer bottom **3** to underside of foam cube. Press seams open before fitting. With cover inside out put narrow end inside cube and pull the rest of the cover over the foam box so it faces right side out. It will be necessary to squash the foam while fitting the bottom of the cover but care should be taken not to damage the edges of the foam.

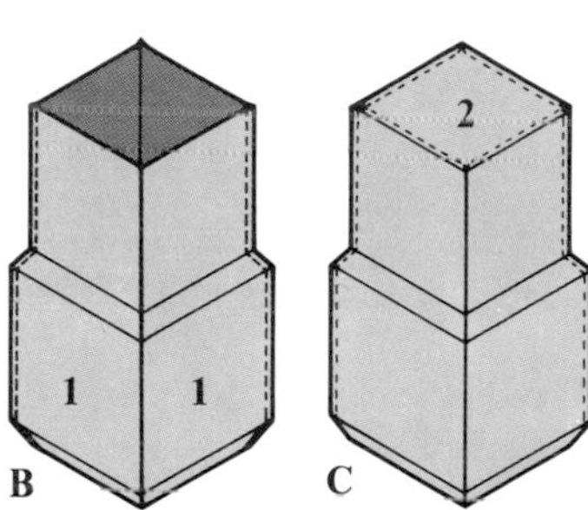

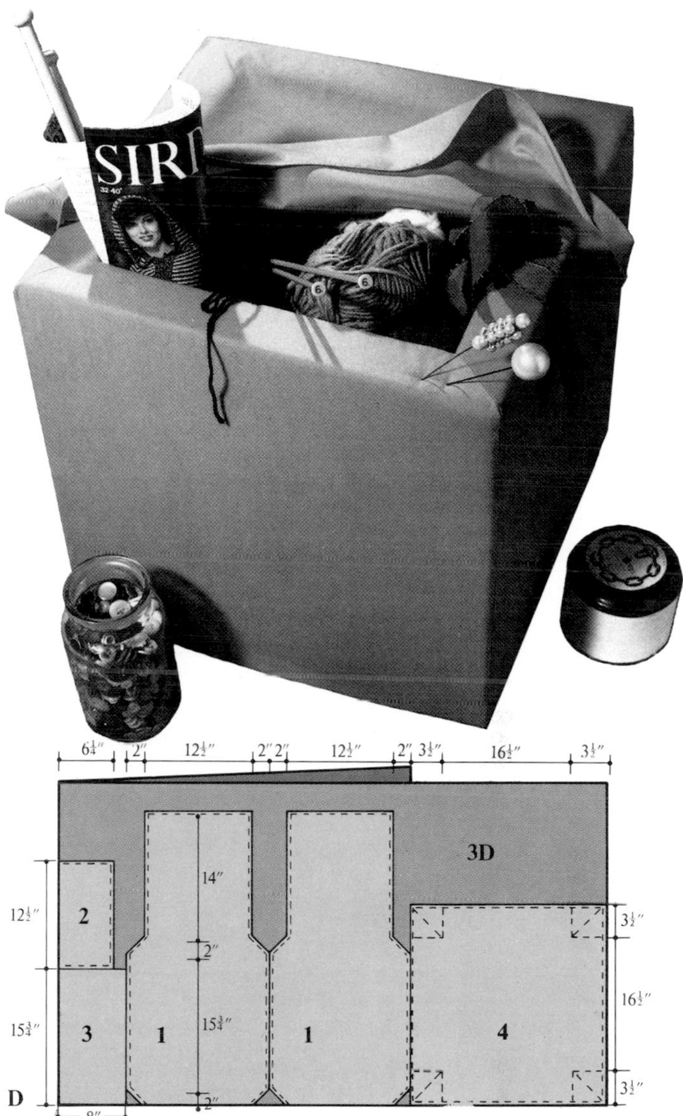

No	Part	Quantity	Length	Width	Th	Material
1A	Side	4	15¾	13¾	2	Polyfoam
2A	Bottom	1	11¾	11¾	2	Polyfoam
3D	Cover	1	92	36		Canvas or cotton fabric

N.B. All dimensions are shown in inches.

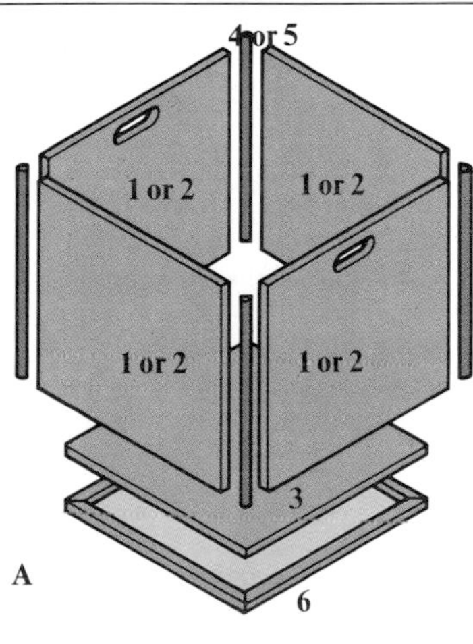

Stacking boxes

Stacking boxes which are useful in limited spaces can be made in two different depths: the cutting list gives dimensions for the separate sides and corner battens. The other parts on the list are common to both. Cut holes for handles in two sides **1** or **2** as in **A** left. Glue corner battens **4** or **5** to each side edge. Glue all sides and bottom panel **3** together, the bottom flush with the side edges. Miter the ends of battens **6** and nail and glue to bottom panel. Fit one box to the other, trimming the battens if necessary. Paint or stain.

No	Part	Quantity	Length	Width	Th	Material
1	Side	4	13	13	⅜	Plywood
2	Side	4	13	8⅝	⅜	Plywood
3	Bottom	2	13	13	⅜	Plywood
4	Corner battens	4	13		⅜	Hardwood molding
5	Corner battens	4	8⅝		⅜	Hardwood molding
6	Battens	8	13	⅜	⅜	Hardwood molding

N.B. All dimensions are shown in inches.

Storing Problem Items

Large toys
Go karts or tricycles that take up a lot of floor space can be safely stored by being suspended on a wall. Use a pair of shelf brackets passed under the axle just inside the wheels.

Making instructions
To make these cushioned brackets which will not mar paint work or cause injury, cut battens to fit tops of the brackets from $1\frac{1}{2}$ in. x $\frac{1}{2}$ in. softwood. Secure with screws. Glue and nail $\frac{1}{2}$-round molding across top at end, and round off bottom edge **A**. Now glue a strip of carpet over the wood **B**. Hang the kart so brackets pass under front axle. If you make the brackets longer, they will support a tricycle.

Wet clothing
A rack near an entrance provides a place to hang wet clothes, hats and umbrellas. It consists of a plastic laminated board with projecting dowels to provide hangers. Water runs into a plastic gutter.

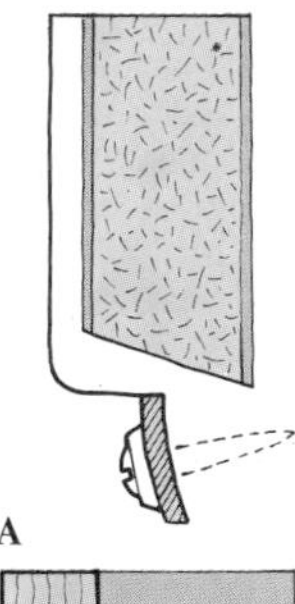

Making instructions
Cut a 4 ft x 6 ft panel of $\frac{3}{4}$ in. laminated particle board, and bevel the bottom edge **A**. Fill and then paint edge. Glue and screw the end panels in place and seal them. Screw gutter in place, using raised-head screws in screwcups. Trim the ends of the gutter flush with the end panels. Caulk inside join with bathtub sealant, **B**. Drill dowel holes for $\frac{1}{2}$ in. dowels and glue the dowels in place, and then seal them, **C**. Use waterproof glues throughout. Now fix the rack to the wall at three points using $\frac{3}{8}$ in. spacers, **D**, and brass countersunk screws in screwcups.

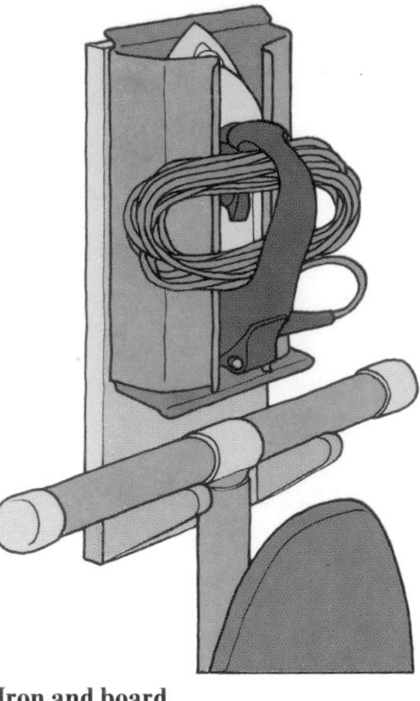

Iron and board
This rack holds the ironing board close to the wall and clear of the floor, while allowing easy removal. The clip which holds the iron is heat resistant, so that the iron can be replaced while still hot.

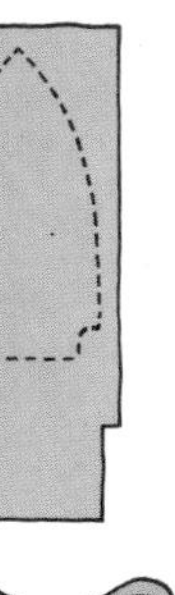

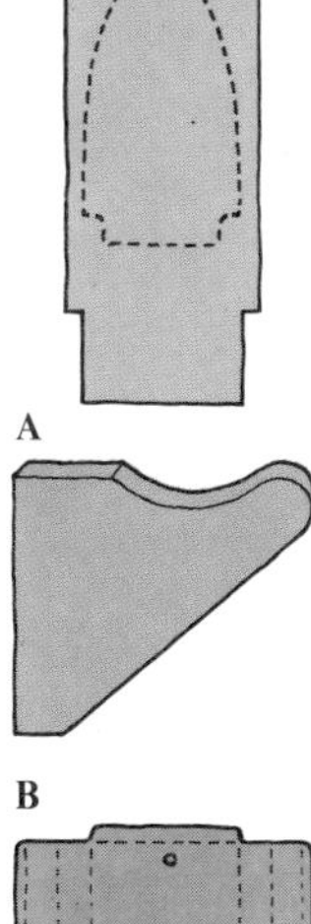

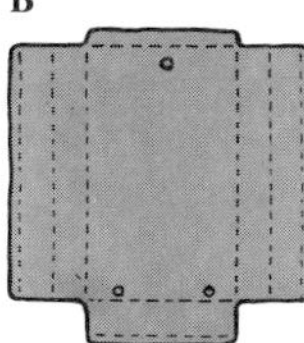

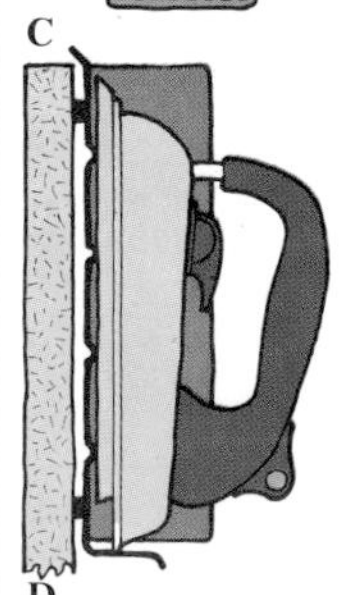

Section showing air gap between iron and clip.

Making instructions
Cut back from plastic laminated board, **A**, and apply edging strip, except to cutouts for hooks. Make two hooks from $\frac{1}{2}$ in. plywood as in **B**, and screw and glue them to back board. Paint with polyurethane to resist chipping. Make clip from 16g aluminum. Cut out the blank and drill three fixing holes. Mark fold lines. Before folding, dimple back part of blank by placing face down and striking with a ball peen hammer **C**. These dimples hold iron clear of rest of the metal, **D**. Fix clip to back board with hardboard spacers. These have countersunk holes, so that when the screws are driven through the aluminum the metal is pulled down into the countersink. Adjust clip to suit your own iron. Fit the rack so the board just clears the floor. Fix back board to the wall before fitting the clip.

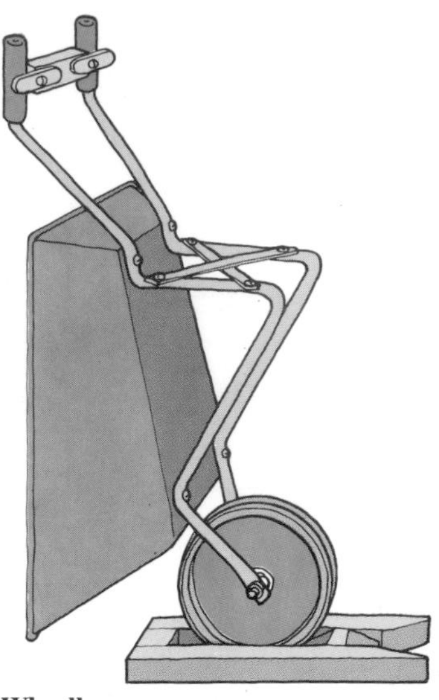

Wheelbarrow
This type of support saves space, and also prevents the wheelbarrow from filling with water. The wall batten with turn buttons holds handles in place, while the trap stays the wheel.

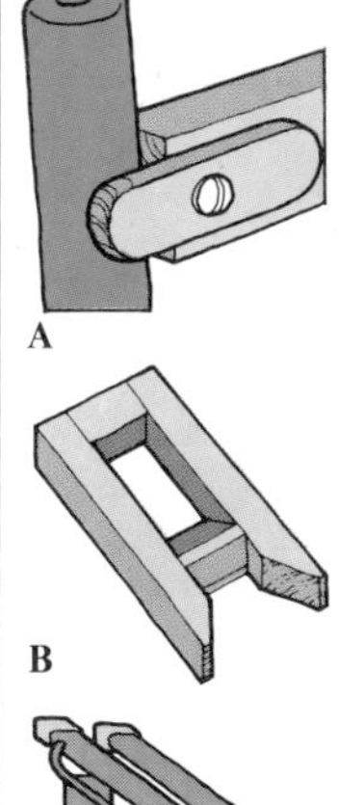

Making instructions
Make batten from 2 in. x 2 in. softwood, the turn buttons from 2 in. x 1 in. Use brass roundhead screws for the pivots with brass or nylon washers, **A**. Ground-fixed wheeltrap is made from 2 in. x 2 in. and 2 in. x 4 in. softwood **B**. Cut drainage slots in side members.

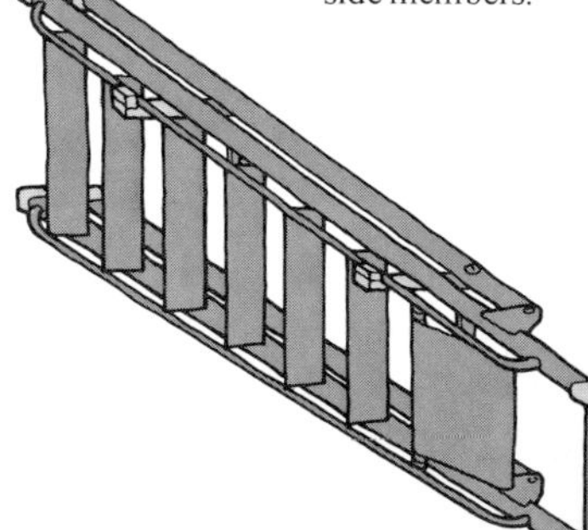

Wall hung stepladder
Hang the ladder on wall brackets at either shoulder or hand height, one or two rungs in at each end. The brackets, which are 2 in. longer than ladder's thickness have wooden top pieces and end stops to reduce the risk of dislodging the ladder.

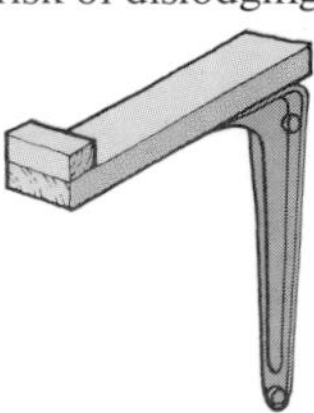

Making instructions
Make battens from wood $1\frac{1}{2}$ in. x $\frac{1}{2}$ in. with $\frac{1}{2}$ in. square molding across end. Place one or two rungs in at each end.

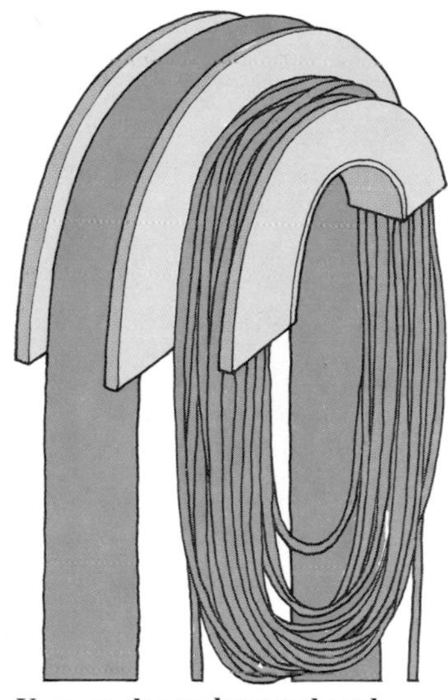

Vacuum cleaner hose and cord

This rack carries the hose on the rear semicircle and the cord on the small one in the front. It is made from $\frac{3}{8}$ in. and $\frac{1}{8}$ in. plywood and is then screwed to the inside of a broom closet.

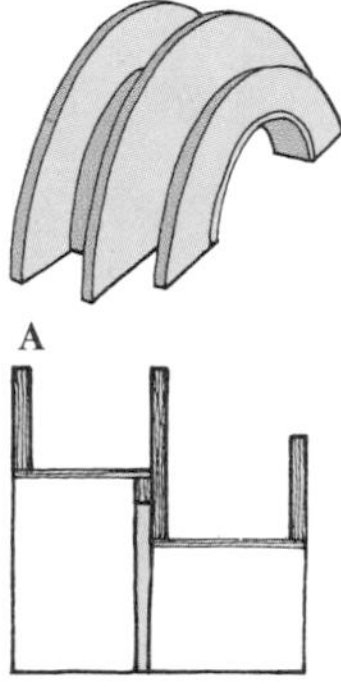

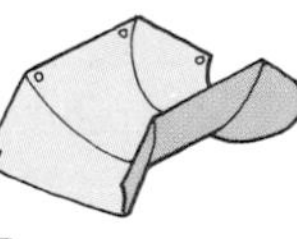

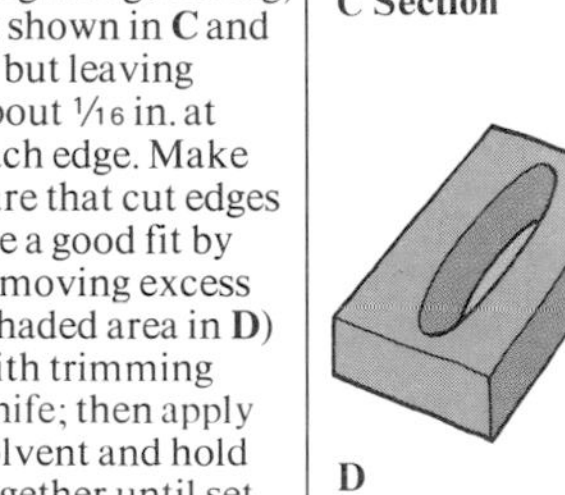

Making instructions

Cut half rings from $\frac{3}{8}$ in. plywood and nail and glue strips of $\frac{1}{8}$ in. plywood in place, **A** – the depth depends on the amount of hose and cord you need to store. Cut the strips with the grain of the surface veneers running across the strips.

Garden hose

To make plastic rack **B** cut segments from a length of guttering, as shown in **C** and **D** but leaving about 1/16 in. at each edge. Make sure that cut edges are a good fit by removing excess (shaded area in **D**) with trimming knife; then apply solvent and hold together until set.

Bicycles

Bicycles can be supported in a stand. Several machines can be stored together racked side by side. A wooden stand that can hold either wheel is probably best, and it can be made as a single or a multiple unit. As a single unit it is easier to move around and pack away. The multiple version is more stable, and the amount of work involved is little more. The rack is designed to be free standing, but can be nailed or screwed to the floor if needed.

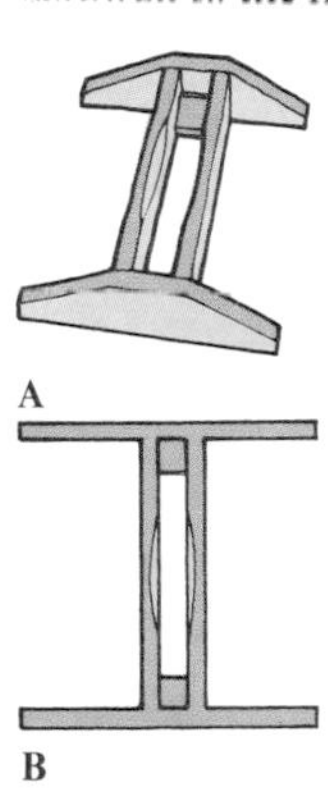

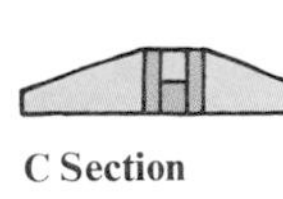

Wooden rack

Use 4 x 1 in. softwood and 2 x 2 in. spacers to make as in **A**, **B** and **C**. The slot should not grip the wheel, but it should be a good fit. It may be necessary to cut away the inside edges to clear the spokes. Taper the cross members to reduce weight and so that you do not trip over them. When making a multiple unit, intervals between individual stands should be kept to the minimum needed to get the cycles in and out easily.

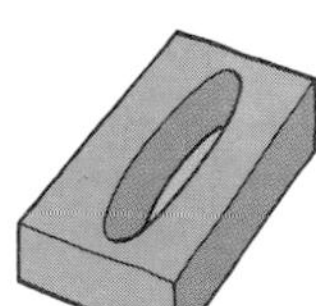

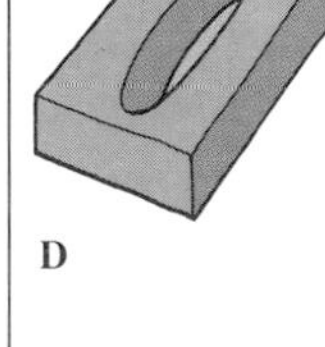

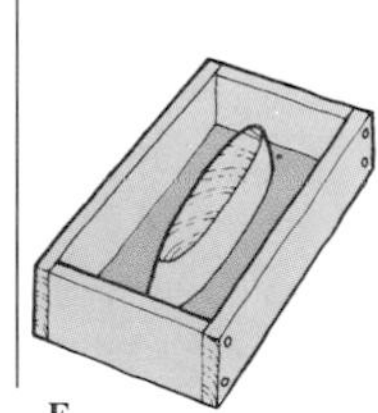

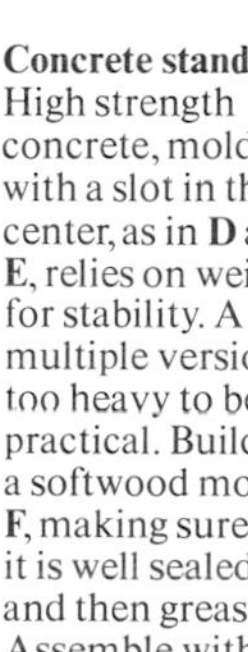

Concrete stand

High strength concrete, molded with a slot in the center, as in **D** and **E**, relies on weight for stability. A multiple version is too heavy to be practical. Build a softwood mold, **F**, making sure it is well sealed and then greased. Assemble with screws to make cast removal easier. At least 2 in. should be allowed between slot and edges of slab. Fill mold, tamping down continuously.

Bicycle hoist

Where headroom permits, a hoist allows a cycle to be raised above shoulder level, freeing the space below for access. It is particularly suitable for narrow corridors or hallways. Choose locations on the cycle where hooks can be attached – rear and front carriers, cross bar, saddle and handle bars, or handlebar extension. Decide where you want the cycle to hang, and check that it can be safely hoisted into that position.

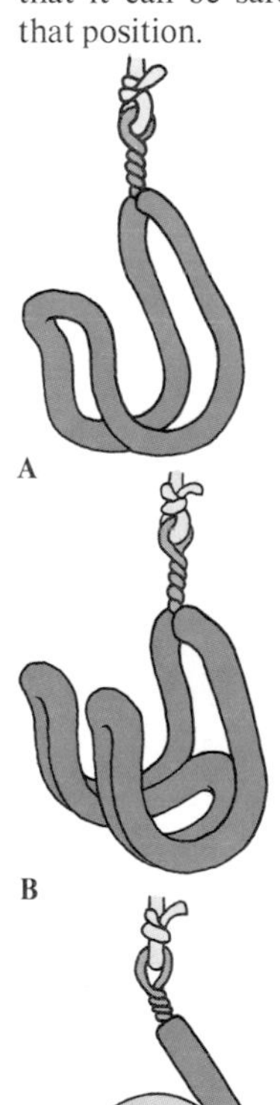

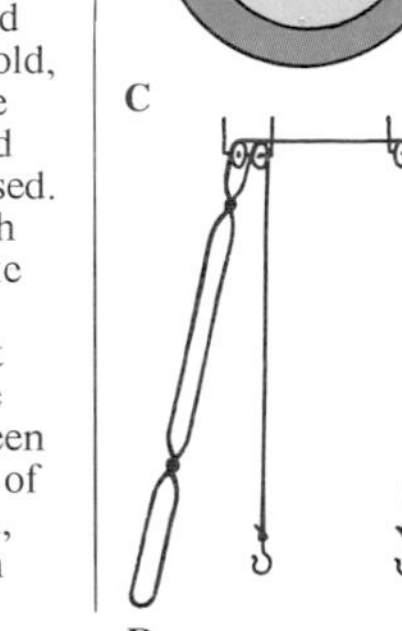

Making instructions

Make up hooks from galvanized wire, covered with plastic or rubber tube to avoid scratching the paint, **A**. A double hook, **B**, is suitable for handlebars. The hooks should be made to grip the machine so that they stay put while cords are tightened **C**. Work out where the pulleys are to go, and where the cord will be tied to the wall. Fit a double pulley nearest this point and a single one at the opposite location. Fit a substantial hook on the wall. Run the cord through the pulleys in a continuous length. The double section should run from the double pulley to the wall fixing, **D**. This section should be knotted in two places – one to stop the hooks descending too far and the other to go over the wall hook to hold the cycle at the right height. Tie hooks in place and do not cut cord until all knots are fixed.

Ceiling mounted ladders

Long ladders are best stored by being suspended from ceiling hooks although this is really only suitable where joists are exposed, as in a garage, for example. The various types of support are illustrated below, including metal hooks for rungs, or wooden ones to take ladder sides.

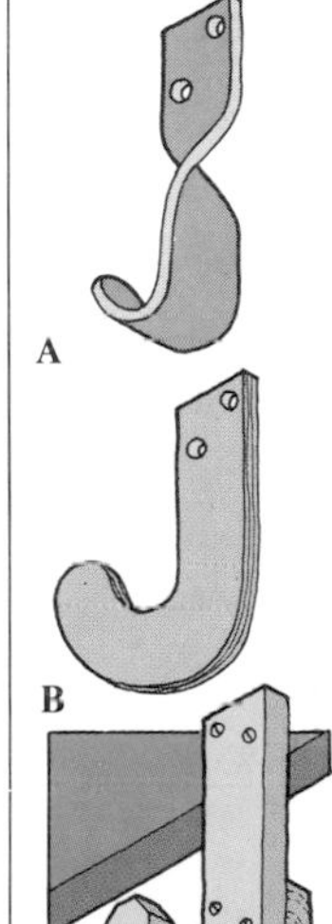

Exposed joist brackets

Where joists are exposed and close together, make hooks of steel, softwood or plywood and screw to sides of joists. Metal hooks can be of the type shown in **A**. Wooden hooks should resemble those in **B** and **C**.

Widely spaced joist brackets

Where space between joists is too great, screw a batten across, and fit steel hooks as in **D**, or hang a double softwood hook from one joist as shown in **E**.

Transverse joist bracket

This is similar to the above and is shown in **F**.

Unexposed joist brackets

To fix a steel hook where there are unexposed joists, screw through ceiling as in **G**. To take a wooden hook as in **H**, screw or nail a 2 in. x 2 in. batten across the two nearest joists.

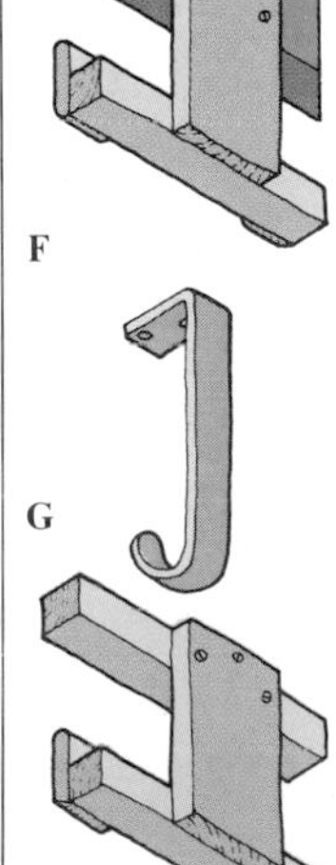

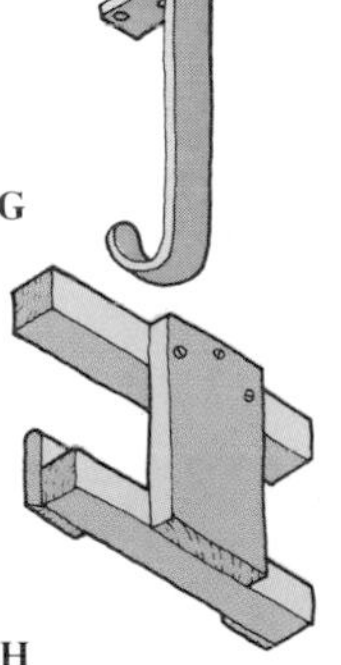

Shelving

Supporting the front edge
Greater loads can be carried on a shelf if you provide support for the front edge. The support may be of wood, or of a metal section screwed to the underside. The various methods are shown below.

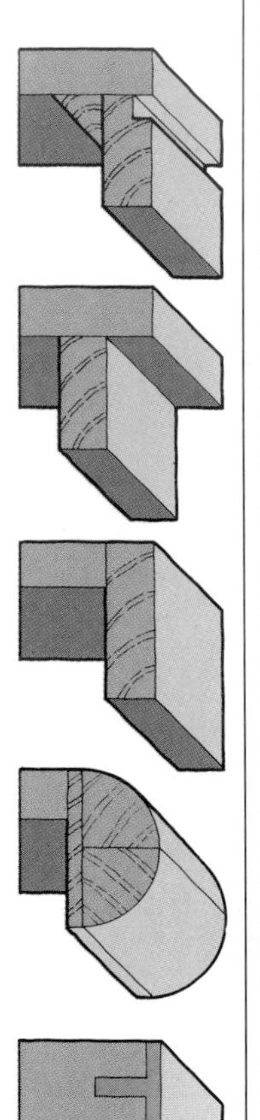

Shelves and supports

Making and erecting shelving is the quickest and cheapest method of providing domestic storage (see pp. 212-213). The shelves must be sufficiently sturdy to take the weight of objects – books especially – without sagging while the supports must be securely constructed and fitted so they do not fall forward. The thickness of the shelf depends on the intended load – although it is wise to assume that this will eventually be greater than originally intended – and on the material itself. The strongest type of shelf is made from solid wood, or lumber core plywood, with the grain running in the direction of the shelf length. Plywood and particle board, although more flexible than solid wood, are also suitable for shelving; particle board is made faced and edged with veneers. Ideally, bookshelves should not be more than 2$\frac{1}{2}$ ft long between supports, with a thickness of $\frac{3}{4}$ in. to 1 in., although you can use a thinner material if the front edge is supported, as shown on the left. Shelves 9 in. wide, with an interval of 9-10 in. between them are suitable for most books. Plate glass can be used for lighter loads, especially in bathrooms. Beveled and smooth-edge glass can be purchased in standard sizes for most shelves.

Cantilevered systems

Shelving is often supported by metal brackets cantilevered from the wall. There are many well-designed systems that can take considerable weight, but which are only as strong as the wall fixing employed. Check the construction and condition of the wall before deciding on the type of fixing (see p. 134). Most types employ a metal track, slotted to take brackets at any level. When fixing the track to the wall, make sure that the surface is vertical, and pack out with wedges where necessary so that brackets line up. Simple pressed metal brackets that need to be screwed to the wall, must be fixed with wall plugs. If this is impractical, screw an upright batten to the wall, and fix the brackets to the batten. This will reduce the number of plugs needed.

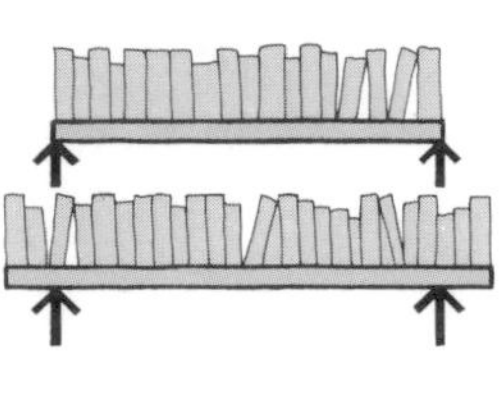

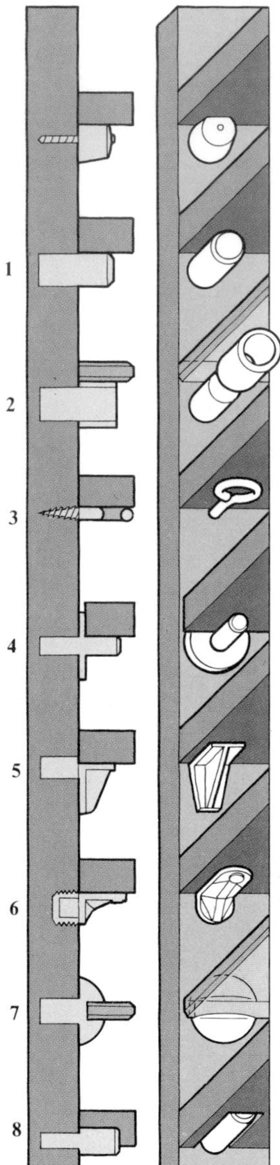

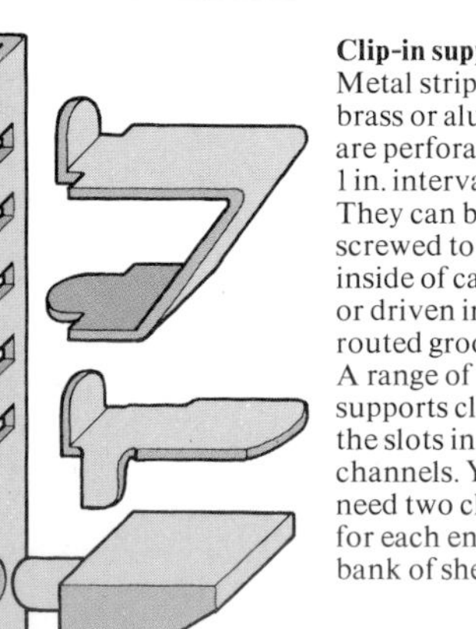

Spacing brackets
Supporting brackets should be 2$\frac{1}{2}$ ft apart, if shelf bears heavy objects. Inset brackets from ends where shelf is longer.

Drive-in studs
Shelf studs with an integral nail can be driven into cabinet sides to support shelves.

Plug-in studs
There are various types of adjustable support in the form of plugs, to be fitted into holes drilled every 2 in. up the length of cabinet sides. The stud can be plugged directly into the hole, which can be strengthened by an insert sleeve or collar. Allow at least four studs per shelf.
1 $1\frac{1}{4}$ in. dowel cut to length and tapped into hole.
2 Plastic or rubber sleeve slips over dowel to support glass shelf.
3 Screw eye shelf studs are easy to remove.
4 Molded plastic dowels plug into holes in cabinet.
5 Molded plastic bracket stud.
6 Plastic sleeves fit into hole and take a wide variety of plugs.
7 Transparent, slotted studs take glass shelves.
8 Dowels can be let into underside of shelf for concealed support.

Clip-in supports
Metal strips of brass or aluminum are perforated at 1 in. intervals. They can be screwed to the inside of cabinet or driven into a routed groove. A range of shelf supports clip into the slots in the channels. You will need two channels for each end of a bank of shelving.

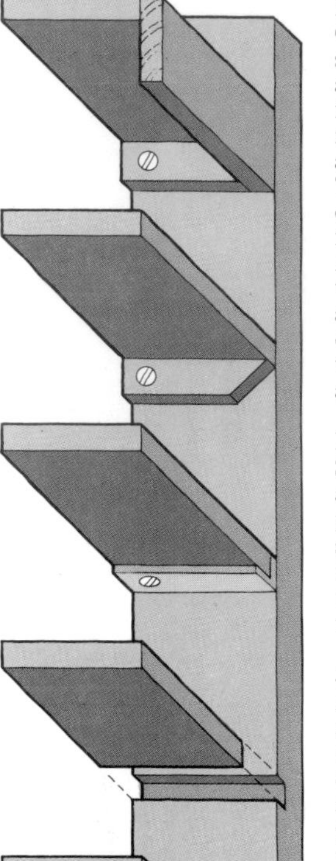

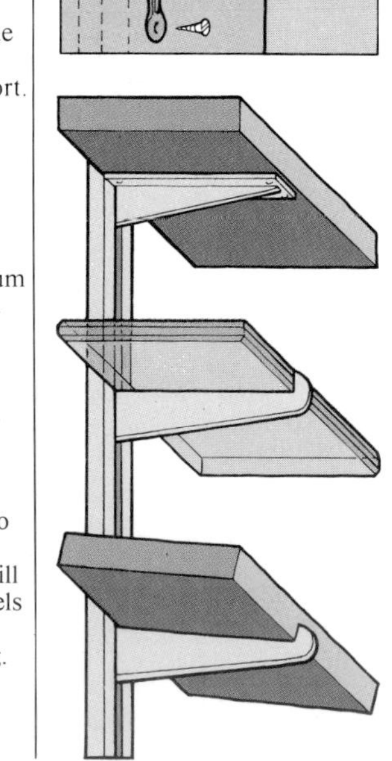

Battens
One of the simplest shelf supports is a batten, either fixed to a wall or into the sides of a cabinet or frame. The battens can be concealed by a front edge support. An alternative is to cut a mitered angle in the front end of the batten to give a neater appearance.

Metal angle
Screw a metal angle to the side panels. Match the size of the angle to the thickness of the shelf to hide the screw fixings.

Joints
A very strong supporting joint can be made by cutting a dado, or a stopped dado, into the side panels. A stopped dado hides the joint (see p. 129). Accurate cutting is essential, so that shelf edges are flush with the upright edges.

Brackets
The simplest type of shelf bracket is the pressed metal angle, with an eye at each end for screw fixing. Use these in places where finish is not important, such as a workshop. They lack the advantage of adjustability. Metal cantilevered brackets fit into slotted uprights screwed to the wall. Of the three types shown on the left, the first has screws to secure the shelf. The bracket with the upturned "nose" takes glass shelves, to hold them secure. Finally, the angled bracket is designed mainly for display systems in stores, but can be used in the home to display objects in a collection.

Work Areas

Workshop

The workshop
There is rarely sufficient space in the average home to provide for a separate workshop, so most people resolve the problem of limited space by combining several activities in one area. Where you site your work area depends on a number of factors. You will need space in which to store tools and materials, as well as conveniently placed outlets for power tools. Safety is an important consideration: woodworking produces dust and shavings which can be a fire hazard, so make sure your workshop contains an extinguisher. The floor must be firm, level and free from obstruction: store tote-boxes and sawhorses under the bench. Provide a large bin to take any waste material, remnants of wood, shavings and dust; you can avoid dust accumulating by running a base board around the workshop which can be easily cleaned. Long pieces of lumber such as planks and doweling, or metal sections such as tubing and rods, can be stored horizontally, on a wall-mounted shelf-system; smaller pieces can be stored in bins. Sheet material is best kept vertically against a wall, supported on softwood battens fixed to the floor and with a front rail to prevent it from slipping off.

Light tracks provide a flexible system for both lighting and power tools.

Workshops must be clearly lit for safety and efficiency. Floodlights provide overall illumination, yet can be adjusted to pick out specific areas.

Store long wooden planks and boards, moldings and battens, on wall shelving. Be careful not to overload any one row of brackets.

Storage for small items
Store heavy objects in tin cans with the contents clearly labeled. Glass jars have the advantage that their contents are immediately visible. To save space you can fix lids of screw-top jars to underside of shelf with two screws.

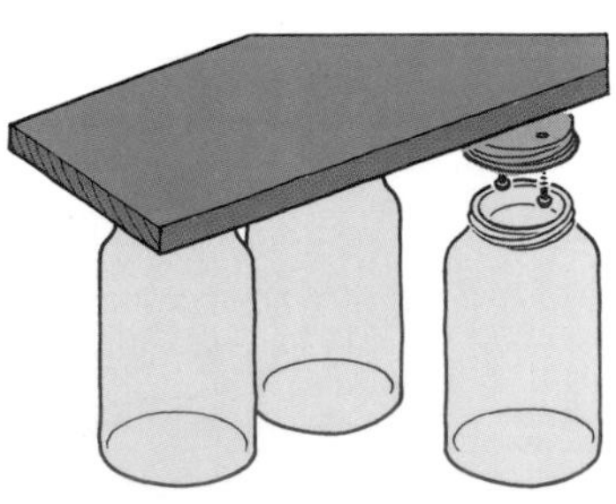

The ideal workshop
Space restrictions in most domestic workshops often mean that several activities have to be combined. In this drawing the ideal conditions of a spacious home workshop are shown. There is room for an L-shaped bench, plus a central work table; good natural lighting is supplemented by light tracks in the ceiling, which also supply electrical outlets for power tools. Storage space is ample, both for sheet material and for items kept away under the bench.

Place sheet material up against a wall; wood panels are likely to become distorted if they are not properly stacked.

Provide storage bins for short lengths of usable lumber and also for the collection of waste material.

A workbench in the center of the workshop allows you to approach a job from all angles. Ideally you should be able to dismantle it easily so that you can make use of the floor space when necessary.

Fit machines not in use with covers, to prevent dust from drying out the oil in bearings or clogging moving parts.

Always keep a first aid kit in a handy position, clearly visible even to a visitor.

Lighting fitted over the window provides light from a constant angle day and night.

Store small items – screws, nails, bolts – in suspended screw-top glass jars.

A pegboard holds odd-shaped tools such as a brace and clamps. Screw it securely to the wall.

The tool rack located at the rear of the bench takes assorted chisels, screwdrivers and punches.

Fit a hinged lid in the worktop so that you can sweep dust and waste directly into a bin underneath.

Use a strong, rigid workbench. To make this one see p. 229.

Tool board

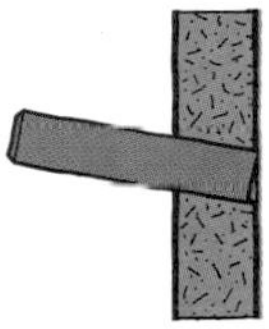

Some woodworking tools such as sash clamps and C clamps are irregularly shaped and difficult to store in compact areas. They are best stored on wall-mounted pegs. You can make a tool board by drilling $\frac{1}{2}$-inch holes in a $\frac{3}{4}$-inch panel of particle board and inserting a $\frac{1}{2}$-inch dowel. Suspend tools from this.

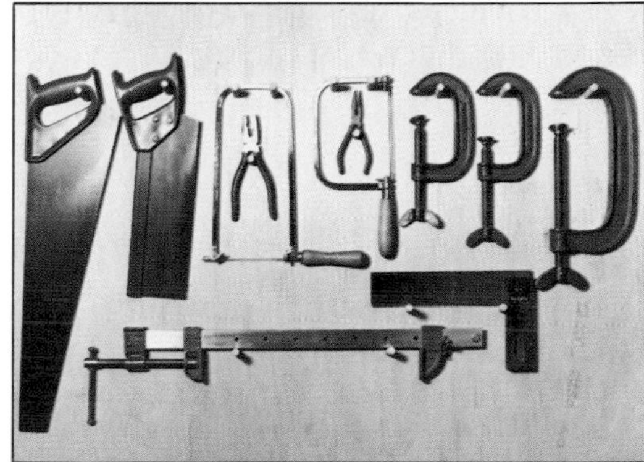

Tool rack

Make a rack with two lengths of $\frac{1}{4}$-inch x $\frac{3}{4}$-inch softwood battens, held in parallel position by spacers. Nail and glue spacers every 18 inches; the rack should then be counterbored through the spacers and screwed to the wall. In addition, have a cover panel fixed to the front. For small punches and screwdrivers, drill the appropriate size holes in a length of plywood and pin it to the top edge of the rack.

Blade guard

Sharp tool blades should be protected by screwing a transparent plastic blade guard to the front of the tool rack. This allows for easy selection of chisels.

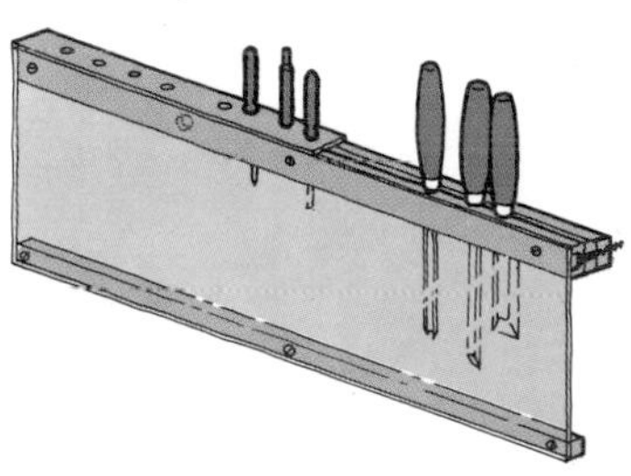

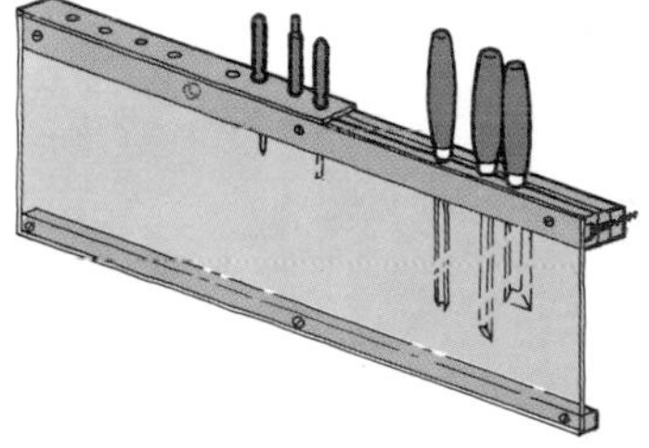

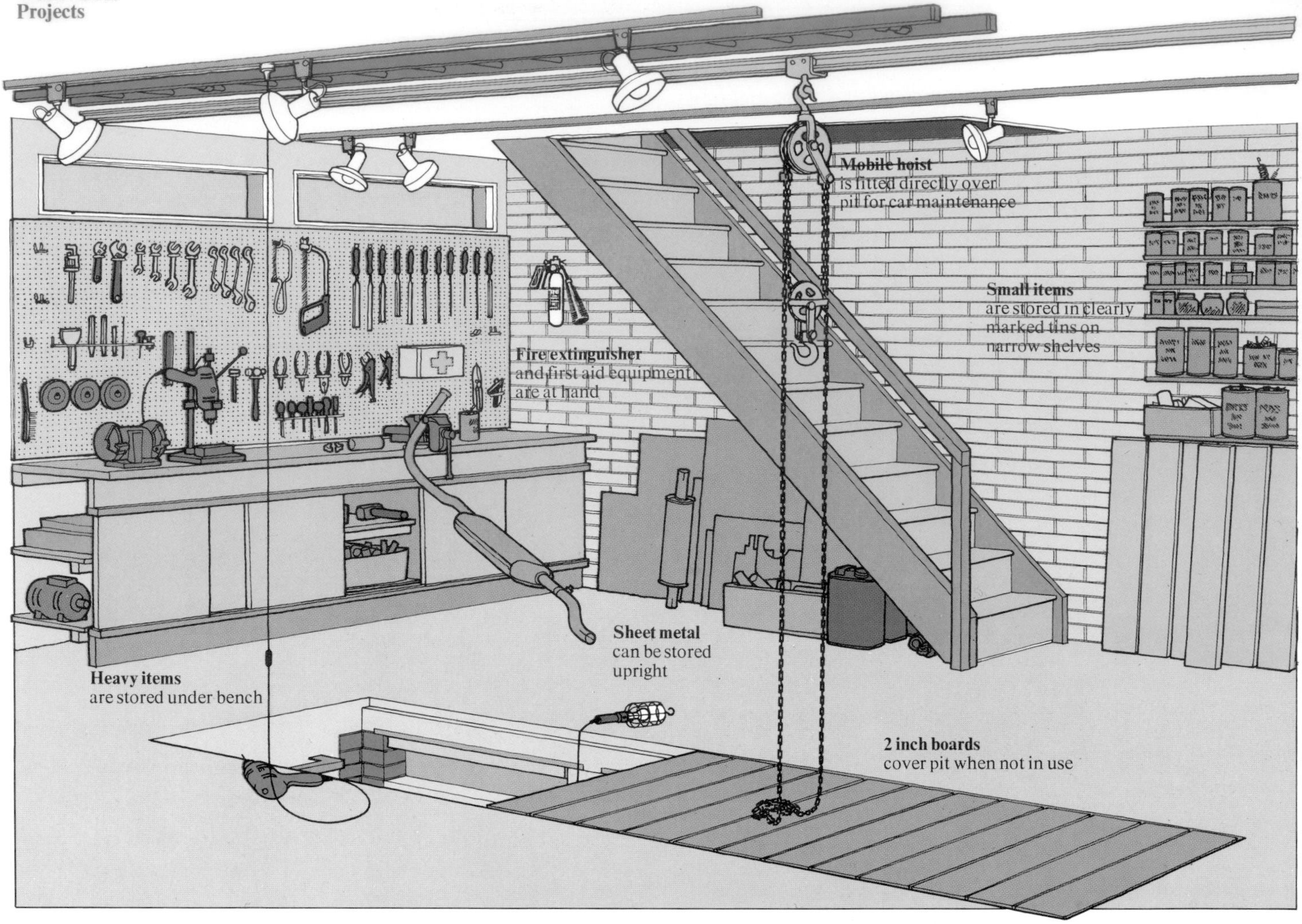

Building an inspection pit

If you plan on doing your own car maintenance, an inspection pit is essential for gaining access to the car's underside. The pit can be sited in the floor of your garage; add a waterproofer to the concrete, and install a vapor proof membrane. The pit should be the between-wheels width of your car, less 4 in. The length should be 3 ft longer than the car, although it can be shorter if necessary. Do not extend the pit into the standing area of the workbench. Mark out the pit in a convenient position; the hole should be 1 ft longer and 2 ft wider than the finished pit and 6 in. deeper. Your eyes should be level with the garage floor when the pit is finished. Follow construction diagrams on the right. The forms (3x1 in. softwood) should be set level 6 in. above bottom of pit. The electric cable conduit can bend around corners by notching. Brick piers are built at 36 in. centers to allow for a 2 ft fluorescent tube in each niche. The spaces between piers are packed with mortar. The top of the concreting forms niches for lamps, power sockets, shelving and supports. Ladder rungs should protrude about 4 in. from surface.

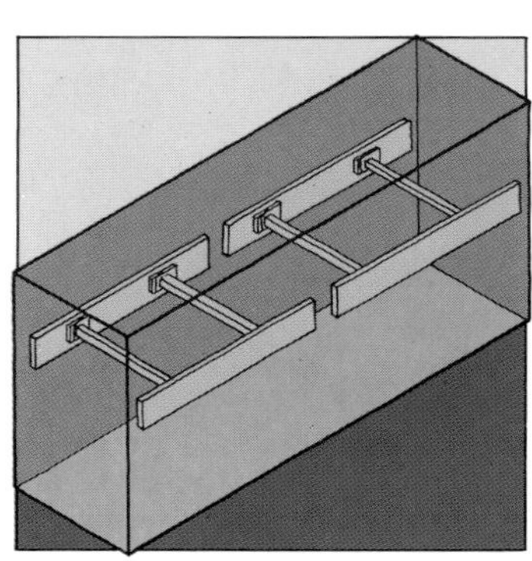

1 Digging and shoring up
Dig evenly over area of pit. If soil is loose, shore up with 2x2 in. cross pieces and double wedges.

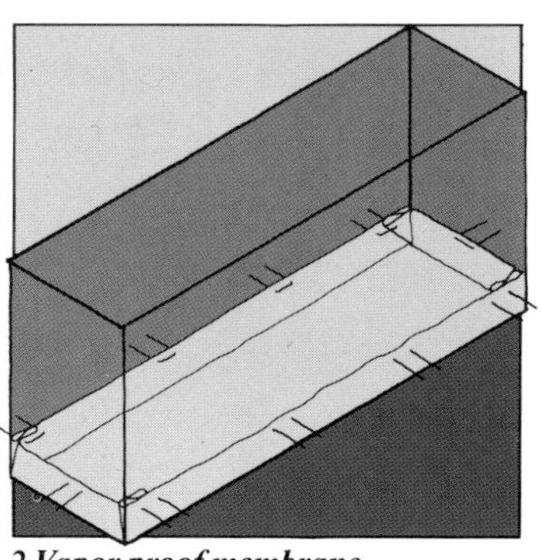

2 Vapor proof membrane
Level floor removing sharp stones. Lay heavy duty polyethylene and turn up sides 6 in. Pin if needed.

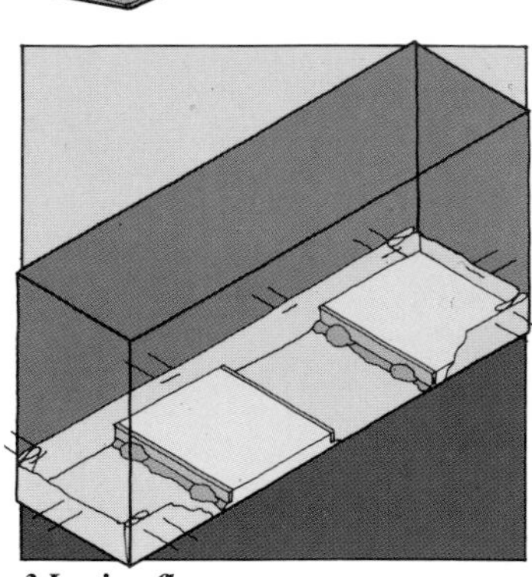

3 Laying floor
Fix forms in waterproof mortar. When dry, lay a bed of waterproof concrete on the floor.

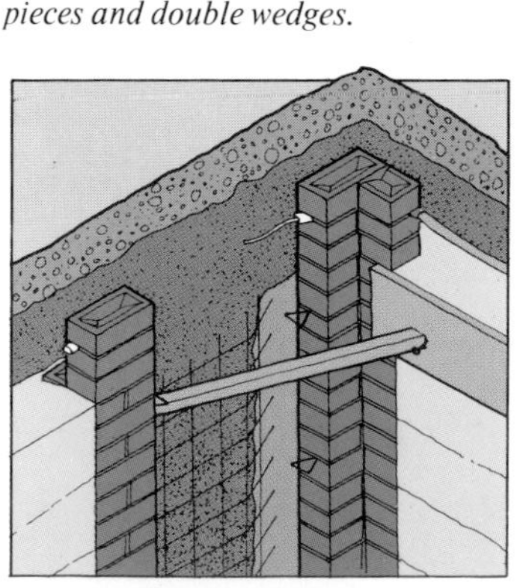

5 Filling in between piers
Use waterproof concrete to fill in between piers and begin progressive forming and concreting.

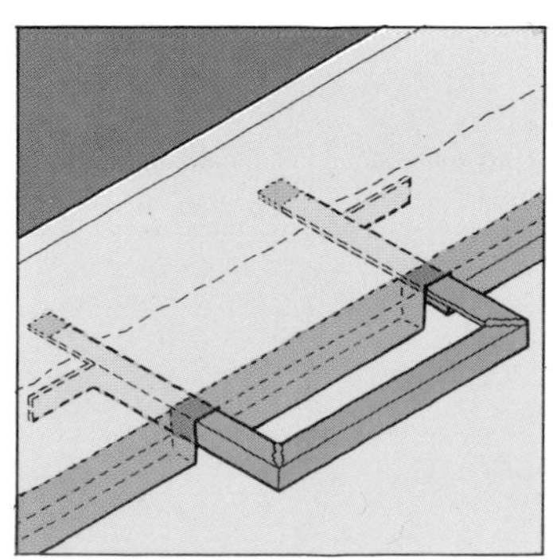

6 Fitting ladder rungs
Cut and bend 3 ft of 1 in. angle iron, welding corners for maximum strength. Position between forms.

7 Shelf and lighting recess
To form lighting/shelf recess, position permanent forms on top of piers and secure with concrete.

Inspection Pit & Workbench

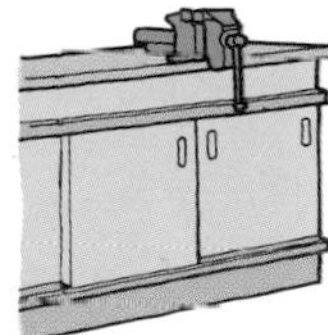

Building a workbench

A workbench should be strong and rigid. The slightest flexibility can cause vibration and spoil your work; this is why a workbench should ideally be fixed to a wall. Securely fix the softwood batten **1** to the wall with screws, so that the top of the bench is about 3 ft from the floor, or at the height that suits you best. Screw legs **2** to front edge of dividing panels **3**. Notch back corner of panel to receive wall batten. Make up plinth and front rail by screwing batten **4** to rail **5**, and **6** to **7**. Position the dividing panels every 2 ft by screwing the plinth rail and front rail to the legs, and screw through the top edge of the panel into the wall batten for location. This panel should be screwed or bolted to the floor. Off-cuts of angle iron make ideal brackets. Make worktop by gluing two boards **8** together. Screw it to front rail, wall batten and dividing panels. Fit one shelf per section, flush with top edge of plinth, the others fitted as needed. Notch shelves to fit around legs. All shelves should be supported on battens **10** screwed to dividing panels, and strengthened by screwing and gluing battens **11** under front edge. If you want to protect contents from dust, install sliding doors **12** between front rail and plinth. A replaceable lining **13** should be fixed to the worktop surface. If the bench is to be used for woodworking, edge front with batten **14** (see small diagram right above); if used for metalwork, edge it with an angled section of steel **15** (see small diagram right below). Edgings should be screwed on so that they can be replaced. Small tools can be stored in plastic or wire trays, supported by the shelves. If you want the shelves to hold heavy objects, increase the size of the shelf batten **11.**

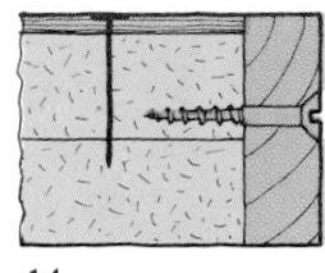

14

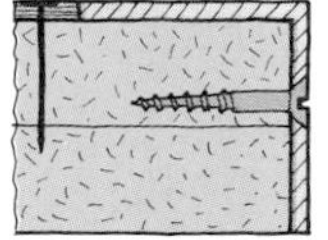

15

No	Part	Quantity	Length	Width	Th	Material
1	Wall batten	1	as required	3	2	Softwood
2	Legs	every 24 in.	34	2	2	Softwood
3	Dividing panels	every 24 in	34	18	3/4	Particle board
4	Plinth batten	1	as required	2	1	Softwood
5	Plinth rail	1	as required	6	1	Softwood
6	Front batten	1	as required	2	1	Softwood
7	Front rail	1	as required	5	1	Softwood
8	Countertop boards	2	as required	24	3/4	Particle board
9	Shelf	as required	23	20	3/4	Particle board
10	Support batten	as required	18	1	3/4	Softwood
11	Strengthening batten	as required	22	2	1	Softwood
12	Doors	as required	25	22	3/4	Particle board
13	Countertop lining	1	as required	24	1/8	Hardboard
14	Lipping (wood)	1	as required	2	1/2	Softwood
15	Lipping (metal)	1	as required	1 x 1	1/8	Steel angle

Hardware: Angle iron floor brackets NB. All dimensions are shown in inches

4 Constructing piers with cabling
Build pier with wire ties every 6 courses to 6 in. from floor. Place electrical cabling under top brick.

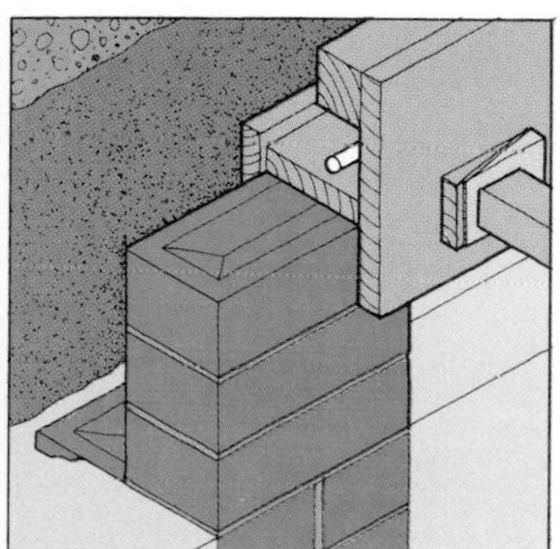

8 Niche for plank covering
Nail 2 in. x 2 in. softwood to 9 in. form board. Insert ½ in. reinforcing rod in concrete.

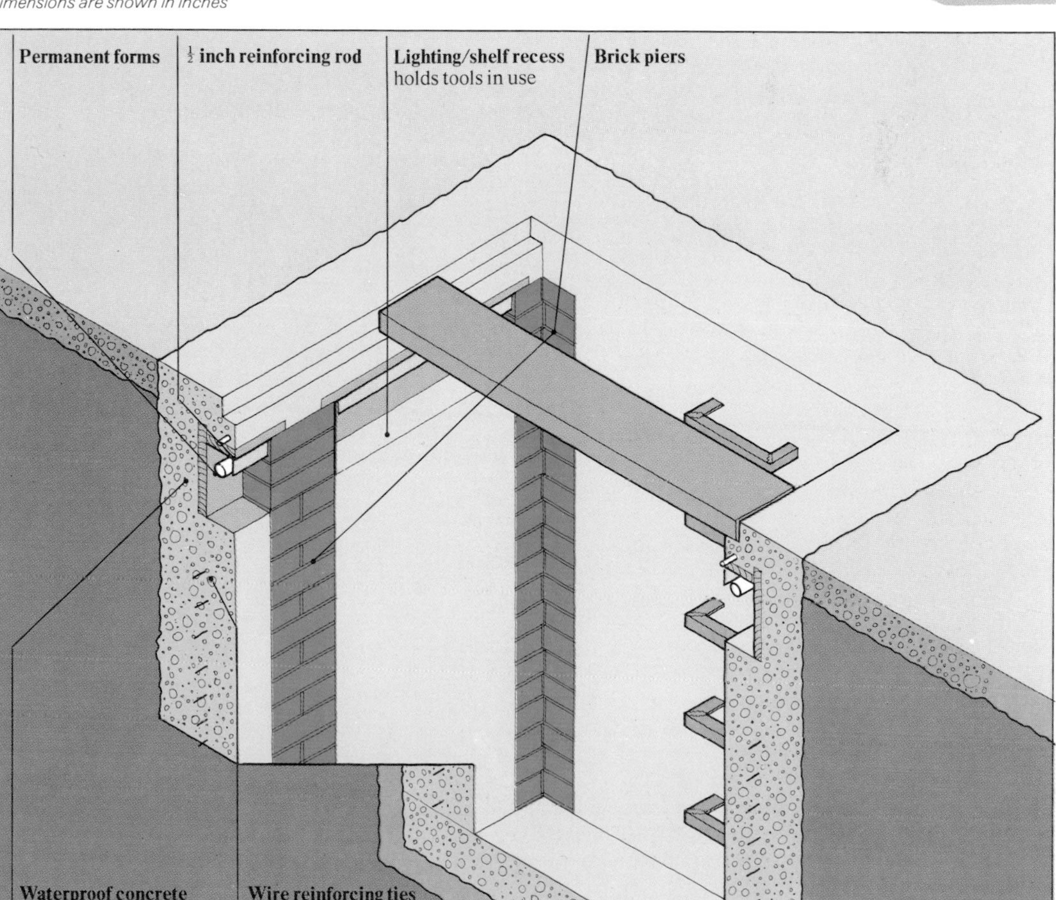

Greenhouse

An artificial climate

The greenhouse is a protected and nourishing environment for plants which traps the sun's rays and keeps off wind and rain. Although it is possible to provide a completely artificial climate by a combination of indoor light and warmth, it is more economical to use the natural light and heat from the sun – hence the traditional glass greenhouse. Even so, a certain amount of supplementary heating may be necessary to grow some types of plant, according to the local climate and the species being grown.

Heating

Additional heating in a greenhouse can be provided by connection to the house heating; electric heaters; kerosene, solid fuel, oil or gas stoves. Most heaters can be controlled by a thermostat. An advantage of liquid petroleum gas and of kerosene heaters, is that they produce carbon dioxide and water vapor, which plants need in order to thrive. Solid fuel and coal gas heaters should have external flues, as they produce toxic fumes.

Cooling

Your greenhouse should have provision for cooling the interior, and short of leaving the door open, the simplest form of ventilation is a roof vent. These can be manually adjusted, but automatic vents are made, and they open at a pre-set temperature. A vent should be sited at the highest point of the structure to allow the hot air to escape, while cool air enters through a vent at a lower level; these lower vents should be manually operated. Ventilation can also be produced by exhaust fans, mounted high up on a vertical panel. If there is a prevailing wind, make sure that vents open on the downwind side.

Lighting

Light is essential in a greenhouse so that photosynthesis, the process by which plants convert light energy to chemical energy, to produce carbohydrates, can be carried out. A greenhouse should be positioned to obtain the maximum amount of daylight and the ideal site for a lean-to greenhouse is against a south facing wall (Northern Hemisphere). You may need to fit shades under the greenhouse roof, since plants can suffer if the sun's heat becomes too intense. Conversely, some plants may need encouragement, and will grow fast under artificial light, during winter months.

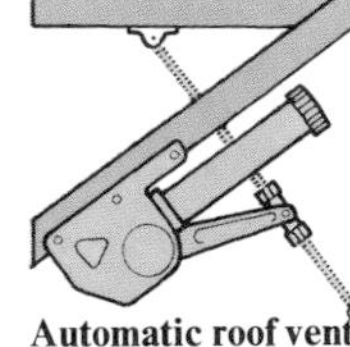

Automatic roof vent

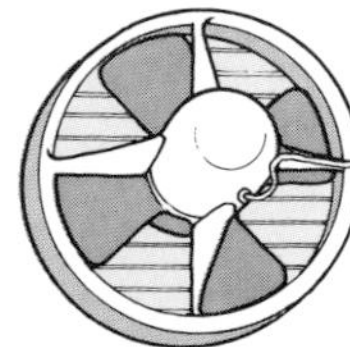

Exhaust fan

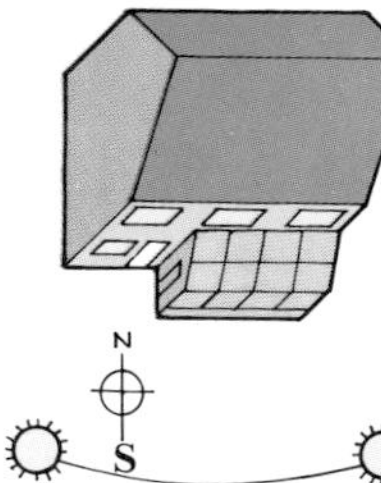

Path of winter sun

Positioning a greenhouse
Site your greenhouse on a south facing wall if possible. Try to avoid shadows cast by trees or adjacent buildings, bearing in mind that shadows are longer in winter.

Lean-to greenhouse
This is easier to build than other types, as it always has one rigid wall. However, a lean-to may block part of the light reaching any room beyond. Access from the house can be through an adjoining door. Such a structure can be connected to the house systems. It will benefit from heat loss from the house while helping to reduce it. Take care not to cause problems of damp when building on to the house.

Sun shades
These help to shut out sunlight when it becomes too strong. They operate by spring-loaded roller and track

Hanging baskets
Trailing plants can be displayed without taking up space on the staging

Exhaust fan
Although it consumes power, a fan is more effective than a roof vent

Automatic vent
This eliminates overheating by releasing hot air automatically

Shelves above staging
Provide space for small plants and make the most of available light

Wall-mounted cabinet
The safe place to lock away chemicals and fertilizers

Propagator
A miniature greenhouse, with its own heat and vent system

Vinyl plinth
A useful place to store bulky or heavy items

Slatted staging
A slatted bench mounted on brackets makes a large, aerated growing area

Shelf under staging
Seeds can germinate here before being moved into the light

Under bench storage
Suitable for large containers. Can also be lockable

Coved floor
This flooring is easy to clean, which is important if the greenhouse has direct access to main house

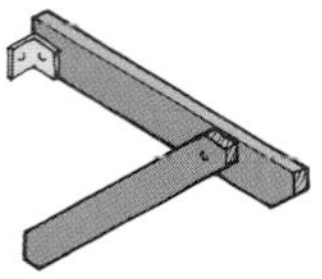

Staging

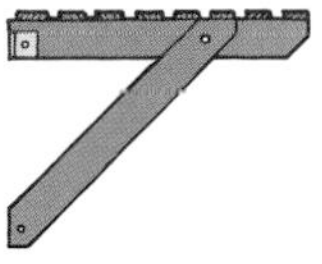

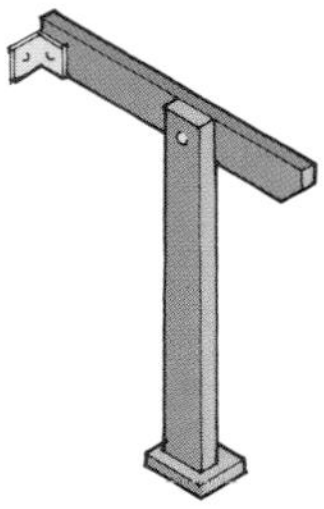

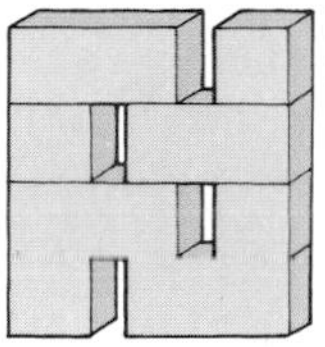

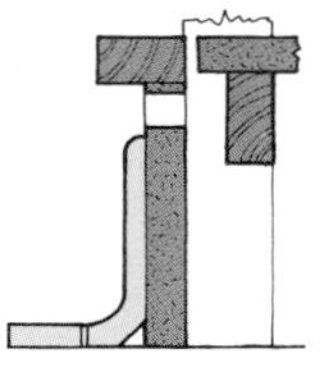

To provide your plants with plenty of light and circulating air they should be placed on slatted shelves, or staging. For wall-mounted staging – make brackets from 3 in. x 1 in. softwood. Cut top piece to required depth of staging, and make the diagonal piece the same length. Join together with a $2\frac{1}{2}$ in. carriage bolt and washer. Mark positions of brackets on the wall at 2 ft 6 in. centers, and fit the steel angle brackets with wall plugs, **1**. Cut ends of the diagonal as shown, and drill a clearance hole and counterbore for a $2\frac{1}{2}$ in. galvanized screw. Screw bracket in place at the top, and mark the position of the bottom hole so that top is horizontal. Drill, plug and screw in place. Where staging runs to a wall at one or both ends, screw a batten to the wall in place of a bracket. Where staging stops short the end brackets should have diagonal bracing. Mark the positions of the slats, **2**, leaving 1 in. gaps, on the two end brackets or battens, and one bracket in the middle. Mark positions of brackets on the battens, and pre-nail so that points just show. Nail battens in place using a heavy hammer pressed against underside of bracket when nailing. If the wall cannot bear the entire weight, substitute a vertical leg for the bracket diagonal, **3**.

You can make improvised staging that is easy to dismantle with 8 in. x 8 in. x 16 in. concrete blocks. Build a drywall leaving air gaps, **4**, and make the top with spacer battens, resting on top of the walls. Trestles are an alternative to block supports. Make legs from 2 in. x 2 in. sawn softwood; top rail from 3 in. x 1 in. and tie rails from 2 in. x 1 in.

Wall-mounted cabinet

Its high location makes the cabinet suitable for storing chemical weedkillers, fertilizers and other preparations needed in gardening. Ideally, the cabinet should have hinged, lockable doors and plastic trays on the shelves to catch leakage or accidental spillage from containers and bottles. Mount a fluorescent bulb under the front edge of the cabinet, and fix a baffle to shield your eyes from the direct light **5**. Alternatively, use lay-on doors that overhang the cabinet bottom.

Greenhouse bench

The bench shown is basically of the same construction as the one in the workshop (see p. 229). Drill 1 in. diameter ventilation holes in the plinth and in the uprights. Cover the junction between plinth and floor with vinyl floor covering or ceramic tiles **6**.

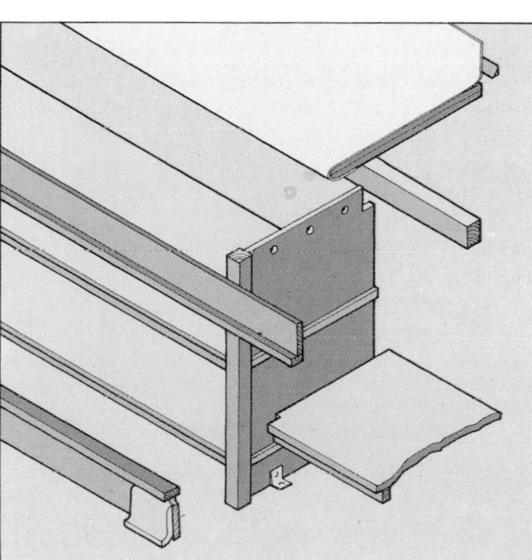

Modified worktop
Follow the instructions on p. 229 but in place of the hardboard facing round off the front edge and finish the surface with vinyl sheeting wrapped over the front edge and run up the wall at the back. Bond the vinyl in place with contact adhesive. Build a vinyl or tile covered plinth under the slatted staging to the same height and with similar coved junctions. This permits easier floor cleaning.

Utility Rooms

Clothes workshops

A combined sewing room and laundry is, in effect, a workshop, and will need as much careful planning as any other work area. Depending on the space available, you may have to plan separate areas for laundering clothes and for dressmaking, though ideally they should be combined in one workspace since both activities share certain pieces of equipment.

Laundry

A supply of hot and cold water is essential, and so the laundry room should be located as close as possible to other plumbed areas of the house. Basements which are situated below kitchens make suitable laundry rooms. Also, as the basement is usually large and open-plan, it is ideal for combining both sewing and laundering, as shown in the illustration. If space permits, store soiled laundry in this area in preference to a bathroom, and see the area is ventilated. Choose a washing machine with a large enough capacity to meet your family's needs and choose a dryer which is matched in capacity to the washing machine. This should be placed as near to the washer as possible. A useful addition is a sink to wash out stubborn stains, or for hand washing delicate garments.

Sewing area

You will need a large worktable for marking out and cutting patterns. A top of about 6 ft x 3 ft is ideal, and access from both sides is preferable. If space is limited, consider installing a folding or a trestle table which can be dismantled after use. Locate your sewing machine at right angles to the table so the weight of material is supported as you pass it through the machine. Your machine can be a permanent installation on the worktop if it has a dustproof cover. Alternatively, store it in a cabinet at the same level as the worktop; if in close proximity to the laundry, keep a bag of moisture-absorbing crystals in the cabinet to prevent rust attacking the machine. Store all sewing materials conveniently near to hand, and keep patterns and fabrics in drawers. There are a number of ironing boards designed to fold or stow away – choose a suitable type to install near your worktop, or employ a lightweight folding board which you can put in a tall closet or hang on the wall (see pp. 222-223).

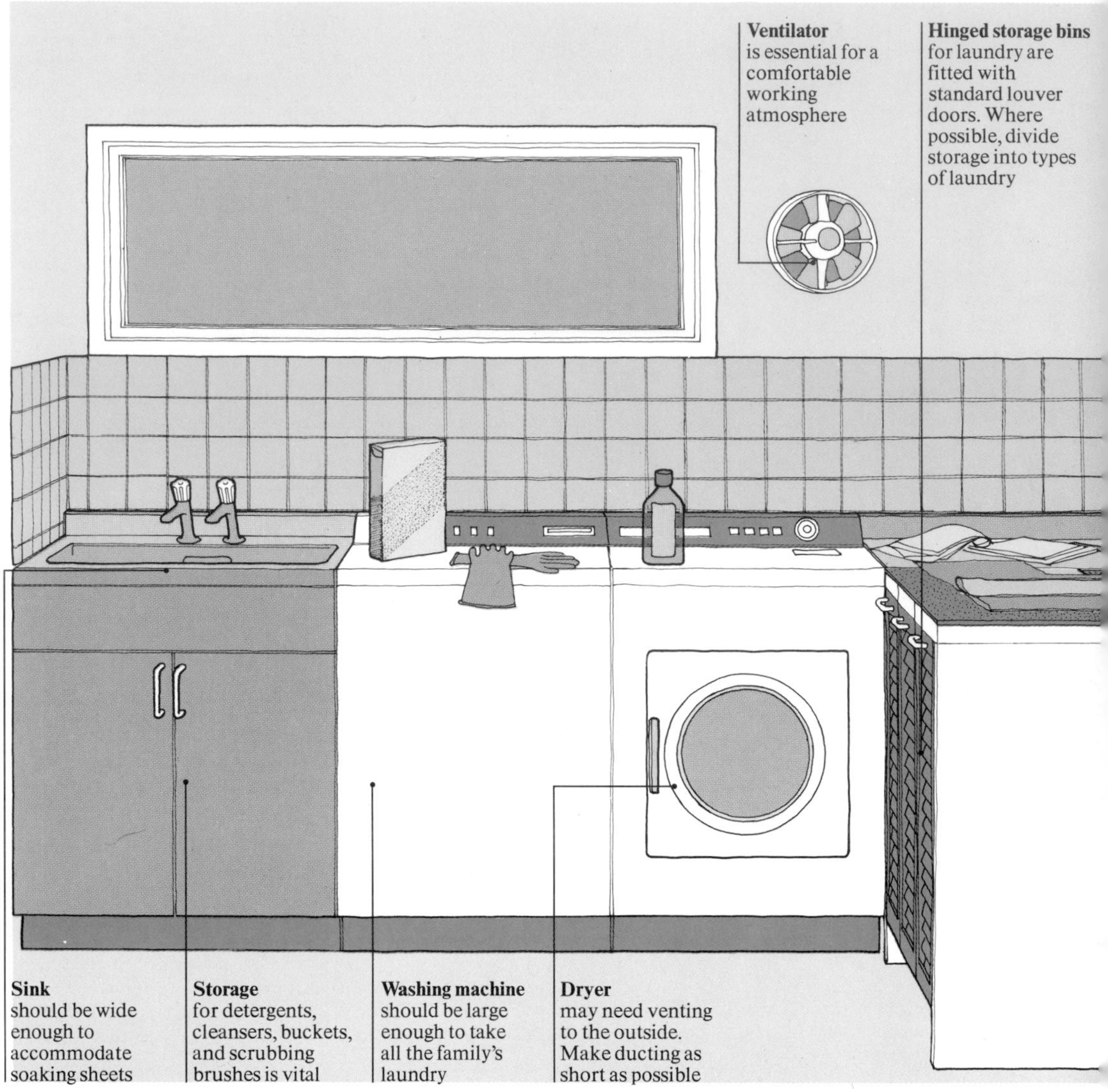

Ventilator is essential for a comfortable working atmosphere

Hinged storage bins for laundry are fitted with standard louver doors. Where possible, divide storage into types of laundry

Sink should be wide enough to accommodate soaking sheets

Storage for detergents, cleansers, buckets, and scrubbing brushes is vital

Washing machine should be large enough to take all the family's laundry

Dryer may need venting to the outside. Make ducting as short as possible

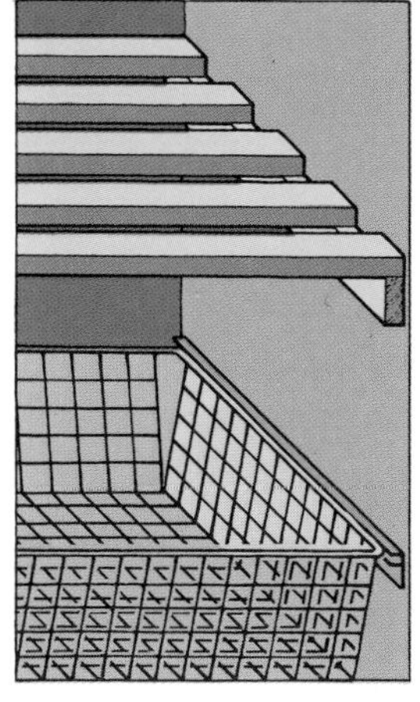

Linen cupboard
Store clean laundry in a heated, ventilated cupboard. Many homes incorporate the hot water tank in the cupboard as a heat source. You can fit a low level heater as an alternative. Have the shelves made of slatted wood, or use wire baskets, so that warm air can freely circulate.

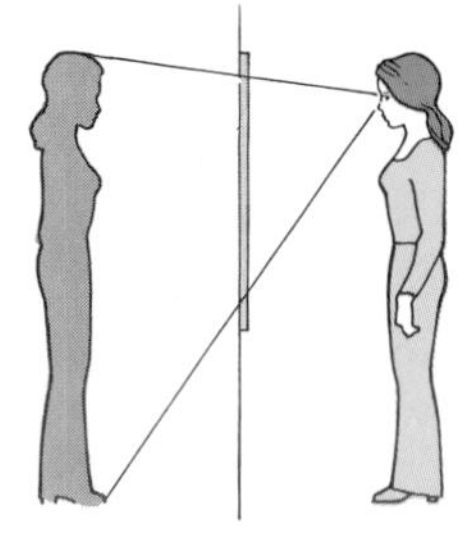

Full length mirror
A mirror is useful if you make your own clothes. It is unnecessary for it to run to the floor in order to see your whole figure, as this diagram proves.

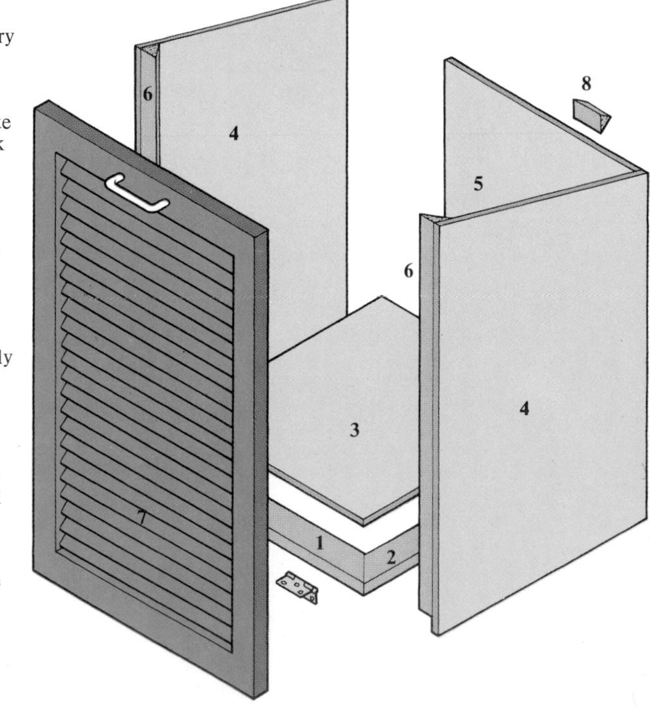

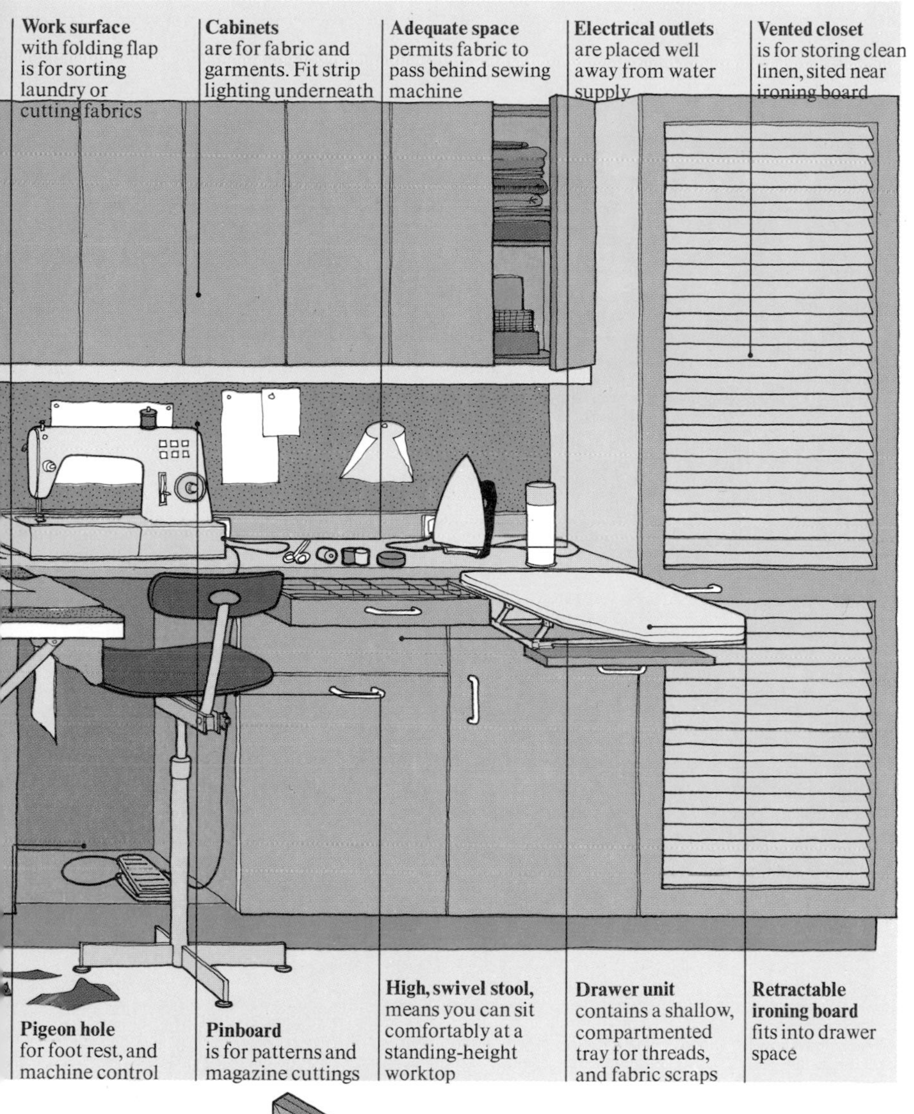

Hinged bin

Butt joint frame members **1** and *2* together. Nail and glue bottom **3** to frame. Cut angle on sides **4**, 4 in. lower at back end. Nail and glue back **5** to frame. Nail and glue sides to the frame and back with bottom edges flush. Plane top edge of back to match angle of sides. Glue triangular batten **6** flush with front edge of sides. Use C clamps to glue sides to front **7**, bottom frame should be $\frac{1}{2}$ in. up from bottom edge of front. Glue triangular block **8** in center of back. Attach "D" handle to front.

Base unit/cutting table

This base unit takes three hinged bins. Use lap joints to make top frame with members **1** and **2**, and to make bottom frame with members **3** and **4**. Center the bracket rails **5** at $10\frac{1}{2}$ in. from ends of top and bottom frames. Secure with dowel joints flush with back face of rails. Edge top of ends **6** with veneer. Screw top frame flush with top edge of ends, $1\frac{1}{4}$ in. from front edge. Use three $1\frac{3}{4}$ in. no. 8 c/s screws at each end. Screw bottom frame flush with bottom edge of ends, 3 in. from front edge, with same type screws. Nail and glue side battens **7** to ends, lining up with top and bottom frames. Nail and glue back **8** to frames. Nail and glue fixing battens **9** to inside of bottom frame. When the unit is in position, screw through battens into floor. Finish back **8** as required. Miter ends of worktop rails **10** and **11**, and nail and glue them to underside of worktops, **12**. Nail and glue fixing battens **13** to hinged flap to correspond with position of bracket rails **5**. Edge both worktops with plastic laminates. Use twelve $2\frac{1}{2}$ in. no. 8 c/s screws to fix worktop to base unit. Cover top surface of both worktops with $\frac{1}{4}$ in. thick cork tiles. Finish all surfaces with clear polyurethane. Screw hinged brackets in an open position to back of base unit into bracket rails. Position hinged flap on brackets, and screw in place with correct screws for bracket, 1 in. long. Screw butt hinge to bottom frame of hinged bins. Position bins in unit and screw hinges to base frame. Open bins and mark position of bolt on the front rail of base unit. Let bolt into the rail, and the strike plate into block **8**. A "spring bolt" will make the locking action automatic.

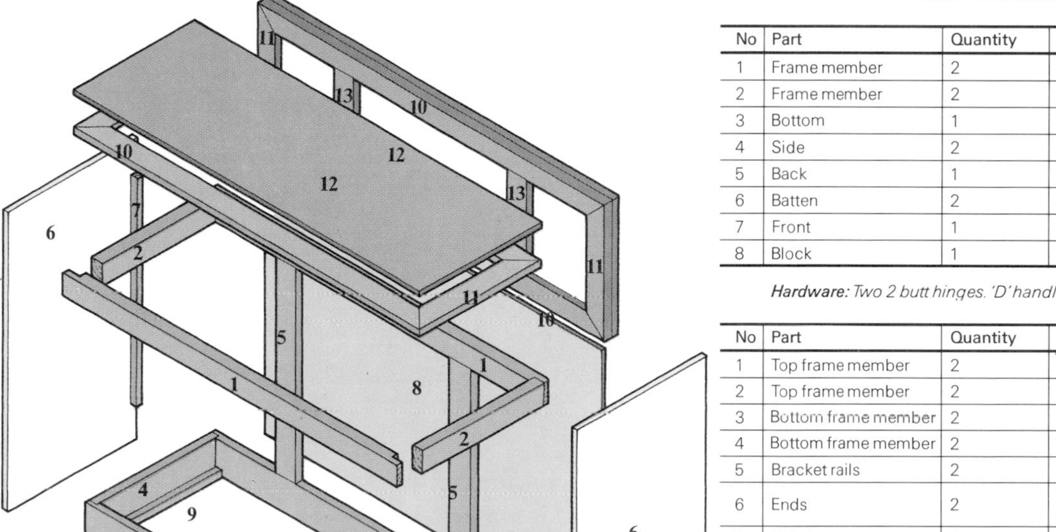

No	Part	Quantity	Length	Width	Th	Material
1	Frame member	2	14¼	2	1	Softwood
2	Frame member	2	15	2	1	Softwood
3	Bottom	1	15	14¼	¼	Plywood
4	Side	2	27	15⅜	⅜	Plywood
5	Back	1	23	15	⅜	Plywood
6	Batten	2	26	1	1	Triangular softwood
7	Front	1	30	15	1¼	Standard louvered door
8	Block	1	2	1½	1	Softwood

Hardware: Two 2 butt hinges. 'D' handle. ***NB*** *All dimensions are shown in inches.*

No	Part	Quantity	Length	Width	Th	Material
1	Top frame member	2	45¼	3	1½	Softwood
2	Top frame member	2	15⅝	3	1½	Softwood
3	Bottom frame member	2	45¼	5	1	Softwood
4	Bottom frame member	2	14⅛	5	1	Softwood
5	Bracket rails	2	27	3	1	Softwood
6	Ends	2	34¼	18	⅝	Plastic veneered particle board
7	Side battens	2	27	1	1	Softwood
8	Back	1	45¼	34¼	¼	Plywood
9	Fixing battens	2	13⅛	1	1	Softwood
10	Worktop rail	4	46½	3	1	Softwood
11	Worktop rail	4	18	3	1	Softwood
12	Worktop	2	46½	18	¾	Particle board
13	Fixing battens	2	13	3	1	Softwood

Hardware: Two 16 folding shelf brackets. 3 flushbolts. ***NB*** *All dimensions are shown in inches.*

Study

A working environment

Where you decide to do work at home will largely depend on the amount of time you spend on it. For occasional use, such as letter writing, you can make a small study in the leisure area, perhaps as part of a storage unit (see p. 217). If regular paperwork is involved, or if you run your business from your home, you will certainly need to set aside a room for this purpose and perhaps to install purpose-made units. Alternatively, you might consider building a study in a hallway, or on a landing, to employ unused space. The optimum height for a desk top is 2 ft 6 in. from the floor level, although a young person might find a lower height more comfortable. A typewriter should be supported at a level that allows your arms to be parallel to the floor when typing: the drawing on the right shows the typewriter on a peninsular work surface, positioned below the desk top. Insulate the room where possible, by lining the walls with cork tiles, or by erecting bookshelves – typewriters are fairly noisy, and should be further insulated by placing the machine on a rubber mat. Small items of stationery should be within easy reach: shallow trays or drawers are ideal for storing paper and envelopes, compartmented trays will hold paper clips, thumb tacks, spare ribbons, and so on. Aim for compactness so that you can reach for books and files without having to leave your chair.

Labeled file boxes
Clearly marked to show contents

Adjustable shelves
Keep reference books handy

Proper lighting
Correct siting avoids eyestrain (see p. 16)

Pinboard
Cork surface holds memos

Writing surface
is ideally 30 in. above floor level

Power outlet
should be installed near typewriter

Angled section
provides surface for additional reference material

Swivel chair
brings all work surfaces easily within reach

Peninsular worktop
Should be 2 in. lower than writing surface

Working space
Located either side of the typewriter for paper and notes

Mobile filing cabinet
Fits under the peninsular worktop

Constructing a work surface

The dimensions given here are only a guide, and may have to be altered to suit your personal needs. Make the typing unit **1** from $\frac{3}{4}$ in. particle board, 5 ft 3 in. long x 1 ft 6 in. wide. Thicken the edge with strips of $\frac{3}{4}$ in. x $1\frac{1}{2}$ in. particle board, glued all around the panel and mitered at the corners, **2**. To make the support panel **3**, edge lip a piece of particle board $\frac{3}{4}$ in. x 2 ft $1\frac{1}{4}$ in. x 1 ft 6 in. with plastic veneer or wood strip. Notch top corners to take edge battens of unit, and glue 2 in. x 1 in. softwood batten **4** flush with top edge. Glue panel to underside of top, after it has been covered. Glue 6 in. x 1 in. softwood rail **5** to underside of top and edge rail and join to support panel with two bolt and barrel nuts, or fit plastic insets in end of rail to take wood screws. Make a 2 in. x 2 in. softwood frame **6,** 5 ft long x 2 ft with an extension at the wall end to form the angled section of the top. Use rabbet and dado joints as shown. Cut a 2 in. x 2 in. softwood rail **7** to form the hypotenuse of the triangular section. This should be 1 ft 6 in. from the wall and front of work surface. Dado joint a crossrail **8**, centered 1 ft 6 in. from wall edge, to support butting edges of sections of worktop. Glue two pieces of $\frac{3}{4}$ in. particle board to form worktop **9**, flush with frame all around, and butting over the crossrail. Fill butt joint and all raw edges, take sharp corners off with sandpaper. Cover work surfaces with fabric-backed PVC. Glue fabric and wrap around edges, stapling underneath rails. Glue 2 in. x 2 in. wall battens **10** to underside of typing unit, and to the side of support rail. Screw both battens to wall. Lay working surface on typing unit, screwing through edge rails into wall.

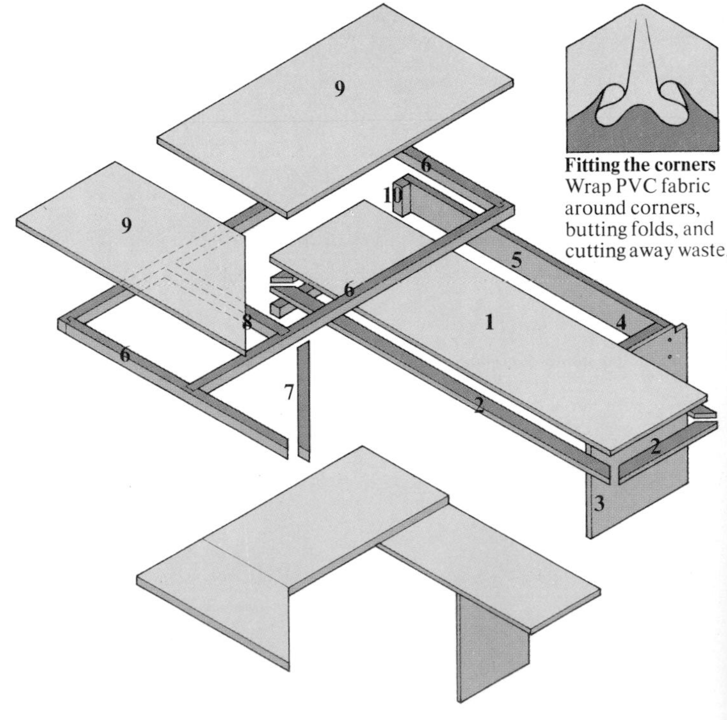

Fitting the corners
Wrap PVC fabric around corners, butting folds, and cutting away waste.

One Room Living

The Single Room

Comfort in a restricted space
A single room with a well-organized interior can provide most of the essential needs for a comfortable living area. If you plan it well, the limited space should not feel cramped, and it will have the advantage of being economical to maintain. Efficiency within a small area allows the occupant to concentrate on other activities. Such a room can offer inexpensive living for a student, privacy in a family home for an au pair, or a room for an elderly parent who may need constant attention yet who requires a degree of independence. Regardless of the age group, the activities will be broadly similar: sleeping, relaxing, storing, working and eating. These activities are unlikely to be limited to one person and there should be scope to entertain one or more people and space in which to move about comfortably.

Planning
Determine what you require from a single, living space: does a work area have priority over the kitchen area? Aim to make the space feel as generous as possible; even if the room itself is large, badly planned layouts can quickly make a room feel cramped. The overall size of the room may determine whether areas are open plan, linked with partitions, or separated by screens from floor to ceiling. Unless more than one person is occupying the room, an open plan scheme is more likely to be the final choice, especially in a room of limited size. One useful suggestion is to keep the floor as clear as possible by installing wall-hung units. Mirrors can be strategically placed to reflect the line of the walls, floor and ceiling to create an illusion of spaciousness.

Dividing the space
An interior that reveals every aspect at once can be less attractive than one that conceals certain areas, but has a linked scheme. The link could be a room divider, a folding screen or perhaps a curtain, used to separate areas visually, dividing the kitchen from the seating area, for instance, or the dining from the sleeping area. A floor-to-ceiling screen may provide you with an inexpensive divider, but would diminish the visual space. Open storage arranged across the room, or a shoulder-height folding screen (see p. 240) will separate areas at low level, yet create spaciousness when

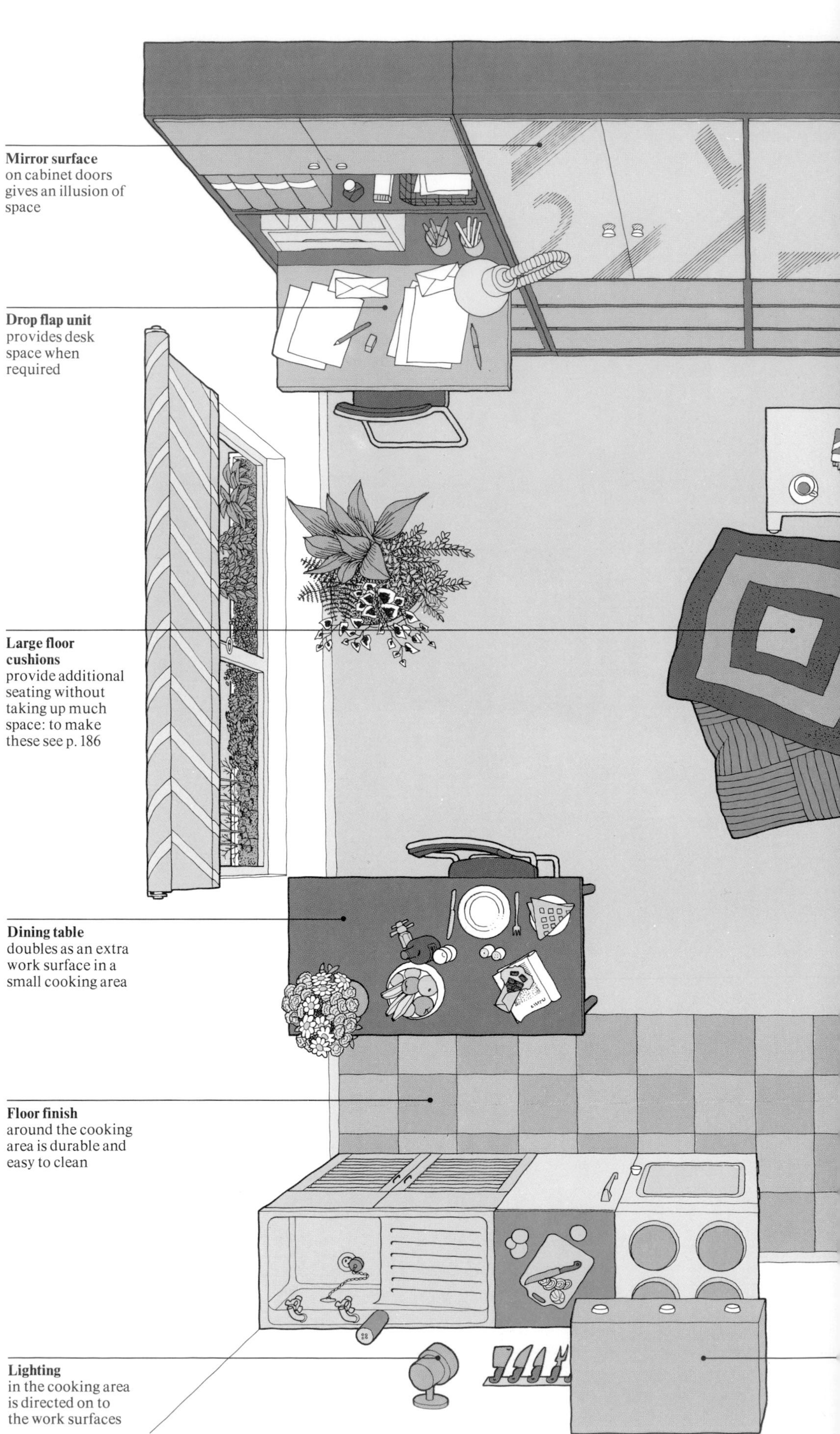

Unit
at head of bed provides shelving and storage space

Small tables
for informal meals or snacks are easily moved if fitted with casters

Bed with fitted drawers
provides integral storage space for bedcovers

Narrow clothes storage unit
stops drafts from door and is space-saving, as long as you have a pull-out hanging rail

Extractor hood
prevents cooking odors permeating living area

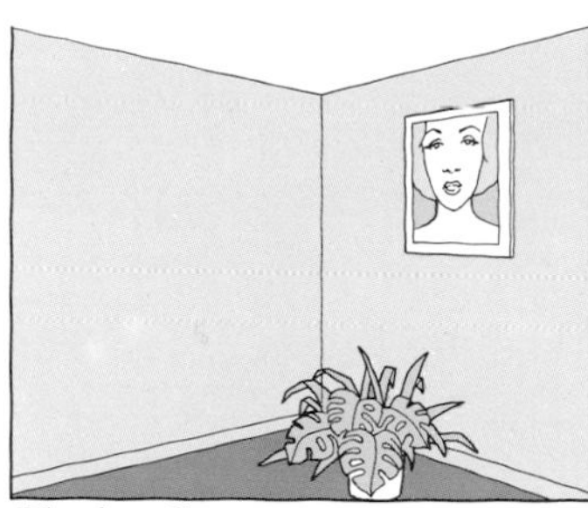

Blank wall areas
A framed picture or poster may seem the obvious solution. But there are other possibilities…

Reflecting space
A mirror creates an illusion of space if butted against reflected surface.

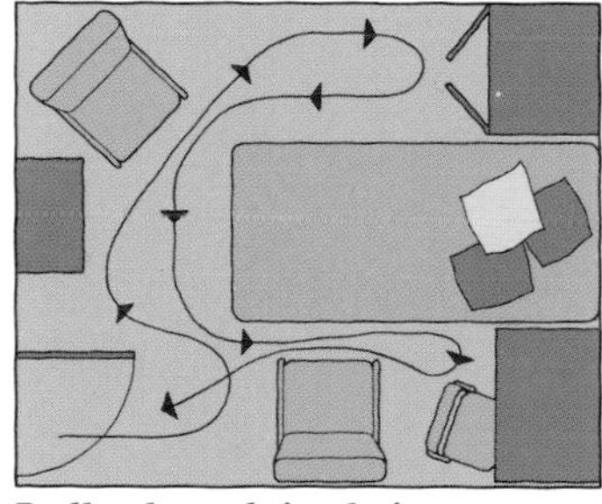

Badly-planned circulation
Narrow and complex passing areas can cause accidents, and are tiring.

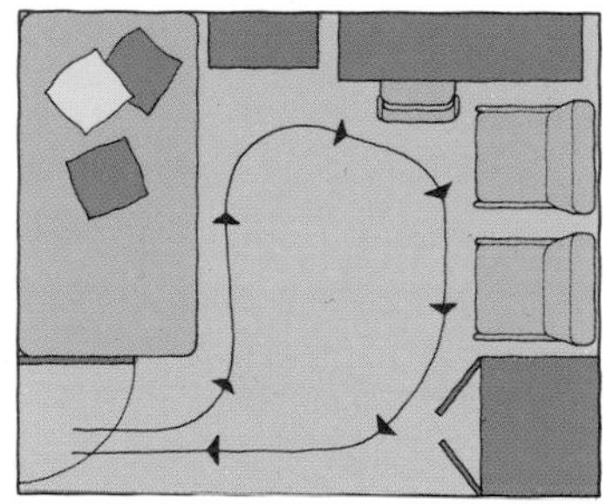

Well-planned areas
The same objects have been re-arranged to create better space and circulation.

Outdoor clothing storage
A ventilated closet with waterproof floor can be sited near the door.

you are standing up. Floor and wall finishes can also be used to create divided areas, by the simple application of color or texture or both. A kitchen area can be distinguished by a smooth, easy to clean floor finish and a wipe-down finish for the walls. The seating area might be carpeted and have floor cushions. Bear in mind, though, that you should limit the variations; space is created through unity rather than division by strong colors. Moreover, the areas may be seen all at one time, so the colors must harmonize (see pp. 24-25).

Furniture and appliances
Having planned the room's spatial appearance, you will need to consider those factors that determine where you put your furniture and appliances. The position of the doors and windows will affect where you place items; this is pretty basic, but there are other considerations that affect long-term planning: how well-equipped should your kitchen be, and how often will you entertain, and for how many people? Will you need a lavatory unit as well as a sink? Make a list of your needs, then draw a plan of the project and make paper cutouts of the furniture you aim to include, made to the same scale as the room. These can be moved around on the plan to determine the best space-saving arrangement (see pp. 12-13).

Combining your needs
Try and avoid basing your scheme on a current fashionable trend. You may not like it in six months' time, and it may not be the right solution for your particular room; there are probably only one or two fundamental arrangements that combine all your requirements as well as fitting the room. Where possible make the best use of a window in your arrangement, for it can greatly improve the feeling of space: it may even be the determining factor in your entire layout; the right decision at the start will avoid any unnecessary expense, particularly if you are including built-in units. As we have seen, the general, broader considerations are the first steps in successful planning. The more detailed considerations, such as where you hang your outdoor clothes, as shown on the left, or where to store items of food, will be dealt with on the following pages.

The Single Room

Practical planning
When you plan your living space, think about the normal activities likely to be carried out during the week. Position useful items to meet your daily requirements: a closet near the door, a stand to take an umbrella, a drop-leaf table that allows extra space and can be used as a work/dining table, a large wastepaper basket, and so on.

Cooking, washing and eating areas
The cooking area is best kept separate for practical reasons. It should include ample storage space. If possible it should be situated near the entrance way; groceries can be efficiently stored away, and the inevitable refuse from cooking can be easily removed without passing through the living area. The cooking area should be well-ventilated, although this depends on the position of the stove in relation to a window or outside wall.

Some form of personal washing facilities may be needed, perhaps in the form of a lavatory, or a shower if there is space. If the plumbing facilities are limited, it may be necessary to combine the lavatory basin with the kitchen sink: a plastic bowl in the sink is a good solution. Folding louvered doors are an attractive means of dividing the areas; they could be opened out to include the kitchen within the living space when you are entertaining friends. Unless the room is large enough to take a separate dining area, a folding or fixed counter dining table can be installed in the kitchen, with the benefit of being close to all the utensils. A low, occasional table is a useful addition to a living area, for general use and informal meals.

Seating area
If the cooking area is the "action" end of the room, the seating area should provide a comfortable, relaxed environment. This area could include low seating, a desk or hobby area, storage and perhaps the bed. This seating can, of course, take many forms depending on the amount of space: bean-bag chairs, big rectangular floor cushions filled with plastic or rubber foam, or a conventional upholstered sofa for relaxing in. Straight back dining or desk chairs are a less comfortable choice. Since you are likely to need more than one dining chair, it is sensible to have a couple of the folding type – director's chairs, for example. These can be stored away in a closet until needed.

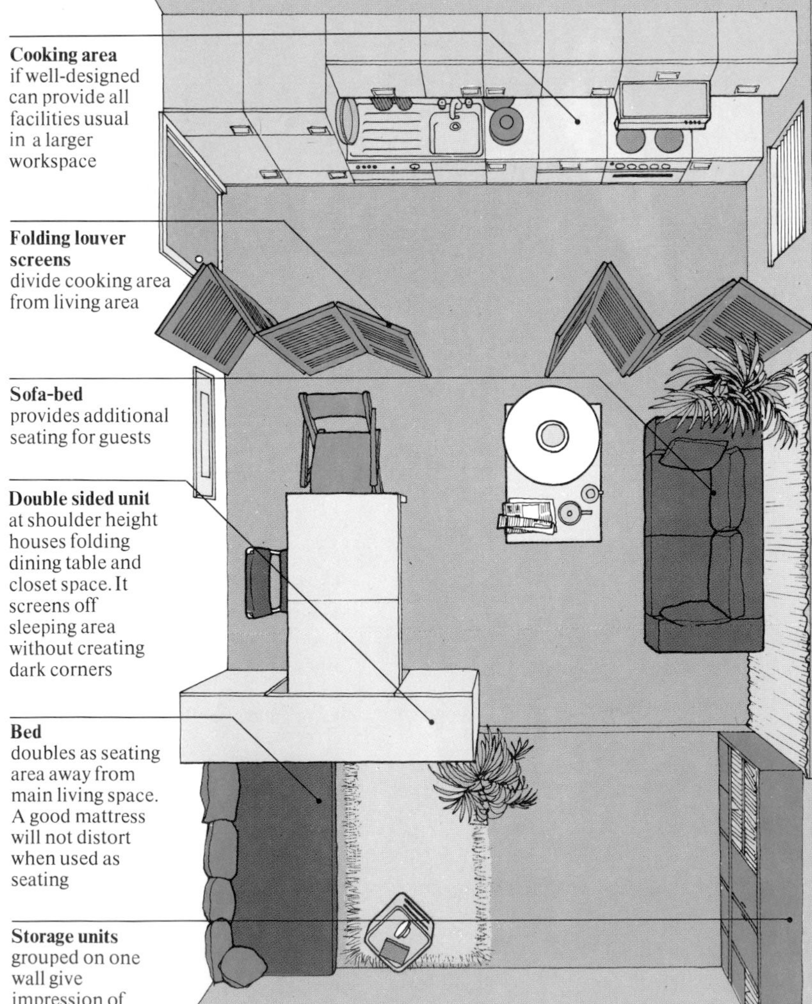

Swivel TV table
Designed for built-in furniture, this unit has a high load capacity and will turn 180°; the base simply screws into the furniture.

Shoulder height storage
This type of unit gives physical division of space without cutting it visually. It will store normal items but is also suitable for fold-away furniture, such as beds and tables.

Sleeping area

Unless you want the room to look like a bedroom with living space rather than a living room with sleeping space, avoid obvious bedroom features, such as soft, flouncy bedspreads, ornate headboards and dressing tables. Position the bed away from the window to avoid drafts. If the bed is situated in the seating area it can double up as a divan if pushed against the wall and covered with scatter pillows. This would provide adequate seating for occasional use only as a conventional bed does not have enough sitting support. A much better solution is to invest in a sofa-bed. For a young person or a couple on a limited budget a combined sleeping and seating arrangement could be constructed out of upholstered foam slabs used to cover part of the floor (see p. 240).

Bed covers should be stored away daily: a made-up bed spoils the illusion of a smart interior. Consider using a quilted coverlet, which will give you warmth and comfort, and is easy to store. Likewise there are a number of ingenious fittings for beds so that they can be folded away.

Storage area

However much storage you install, there never seems to be enough. Make an effort to limit your possessions to the essentials of everyday living. A unified storage system, whether built-in or free standing, will help you achieve a greater feeling of spaciousness, and is preferable to a variety of units randomly placed. The storage space should be provided with flexible interiors and include shelves, wire baskets or drawers and hanging rails for clothes. The doors can be solid to hide some items, and glassed-in to display others. Open shelving will add interest; mirror panels set in the back will create an image of space. There are, of course, many shelving systems available. A neat and effective way of closing them off, should you wish to do so, is by fitting shades to the top shelf, set slightly forward, to provide a simple screen. Additional storage space can be made by building a raised floor, with access to the space below through lift-off panels. If the room is high enough, you could have a builder construct a split-level floor. The upper deck may have restricted head room, but could be used very successfully as a sleeping area, giving you greater scope for one room living in the available space beneath.

1

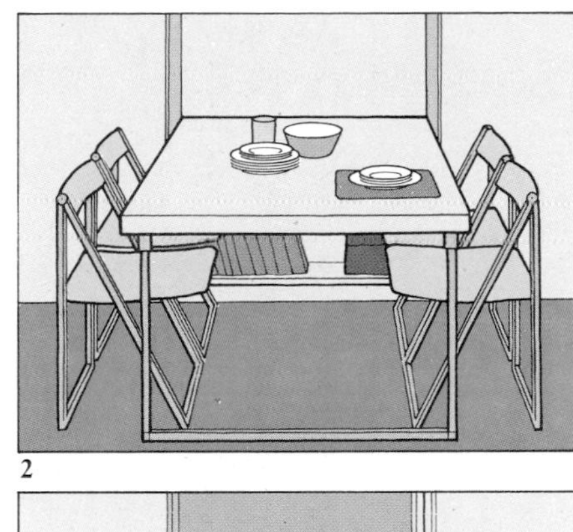

2

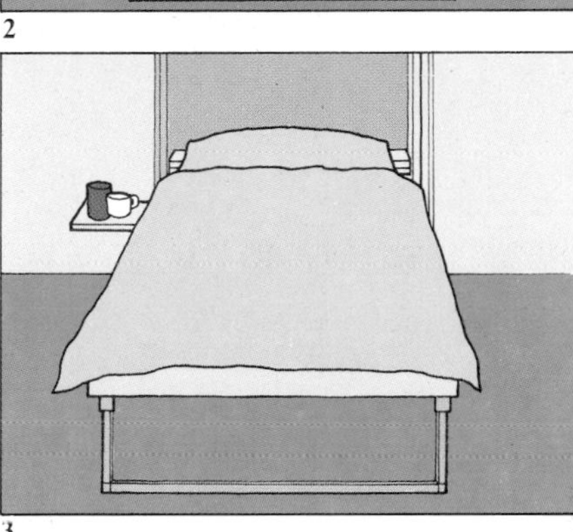

3

1 Pivot unit swings on its axis and is an integral part of the row of units. Unit combines a fold down bed and drop down table.

2 Table extends from unit and has supporting leg frame.

3 Drop down bed is behind swivel unit and folds away out of sight.

4

5

4 Open wall-mounted shelves make useful wall storage and worktop.

5 Roller shade fixed to upper shelf is used to screen off contents.

6

6 Raised floor allows plenty of room for storage beneath. Floor panels can be loose-laid for easy access. Battens screwed to the underside will locate them in the framework.

Single Room Furniture

Split level structures

The advantage of a heavy gauge steel structure, such as that shown on the right, is that you can build it yourself, and it requires no fixing to adjacent walls. There are several different systems but the type illustrated has cast collars with screw connectors, you merely plug in the tubes and tighten the screws with a small key. The structure is mounted on floor plates screwed to the floor. Alternative systems include slotted steel angle sections, bolted together with strengthening brackets. You can even make an efficient structure with large-bore steel plumbing, using the T joints and elbows with threaded fixings.

Slab floor cushions

To make the 30 in. square bordered cushions with 4 in. sides have 4 in. medium density foam slabs cut to 31 in. square. The lining and top cover, including borders, should measure 30 in. x 4 in. plus a $\frac{5}{8}$ in. hem all around, and the top and bottom panel 30 in. square plus a $\frac{5}{8}$ in. hem. Machine-stitch the covers, leaving one side seam open so you can turn the cover inside out and fit over the foam. Close the seam with slip-stitching after fitting. The addition of bands of nylon tape fastener, fitted around the edges of one face, will allow the cushion to be folded in two, as shown left, to be used as a back rest against the wall.

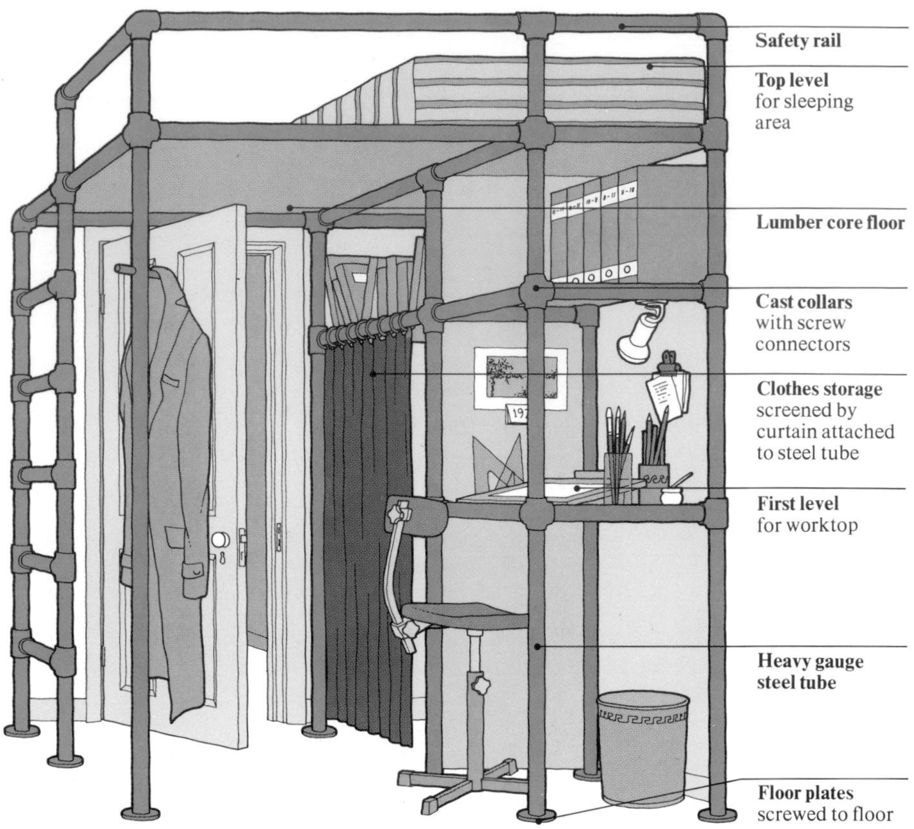

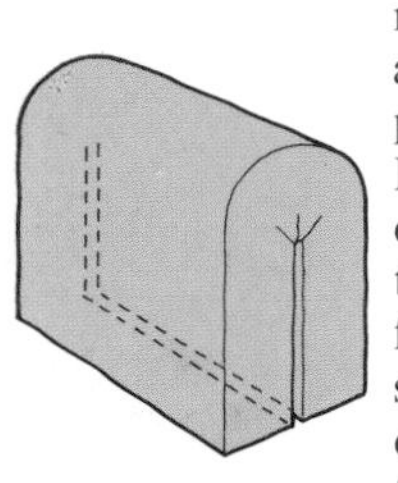

Folded slab cushion used as back rest

Folding screen

Cut panels as shown left from $\frac{1}{4}$ in. plywood as needed for the width of the screen. Round off the corners $\frac{3}{4}$ in. and smooth off the edges to match. Cut a pair of $\frac{1}{4}$ in. wide slots, $\frac{3}{4}$ in. apart, $\frac{3}{4}$ in. from the edges and 6 in. from each end: these are to take the straps. Paint panels. Make hinge straps from upholsterer's webbing or leather. Cut to length and mark sewing lines **A**. Fold ends over to form loops, align the marks and sew together, the ends folded back as in **B**. Fit the looped ends through the slots and fix with a length of $\frac{1}{4}$ in. dowel to make the hinge. Thread each pair in alternate directions, **C**. If the screen is not to be folded away, lightweight shelves can be added for display purposes. Make the shelves from $\frac{1}{4}$ in. plywood, cut into right angled triangles, with 12 in. sides forming the right angle. Fit two screw eyes in these sides, 2 in. from front and back corners. Cut small slots to take screw eye rings, at the required height in each screen panel. Lock in place by turning through 90°.

Screen panel

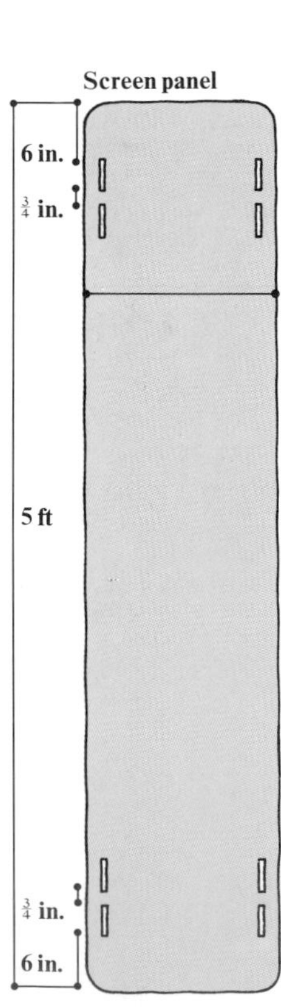

Split level structure

Safety rail
Top level for sleeping area
Lumber core floor
Cast collars with screw connectors
Clothes storage screened by curtain attached to steel tube
First level for worktop
Heavy gauge steel tube
Floor plates screwed to floor

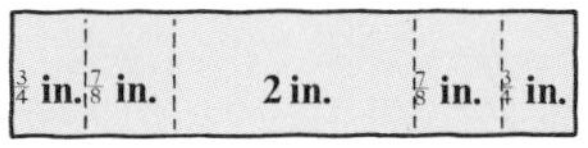

$\frac{3}{4}$ in. | $\frac{7}{8}$ in. | 2 in. | $\frac{7}{8}$ in. | $\frac{3}{4}$ in.

A

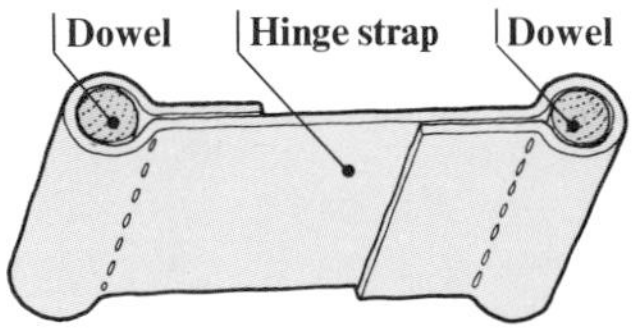

Dowel | Hinge strap | Dowel

Hinge detail

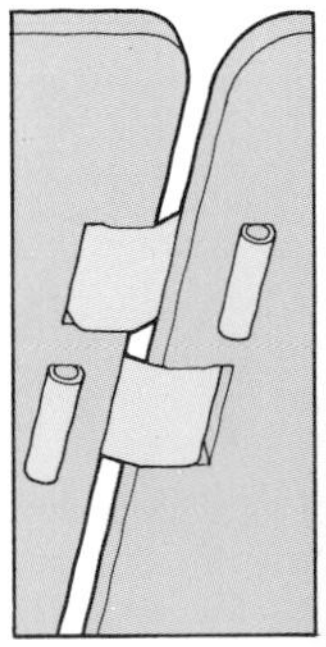

C Hinge fixing detail

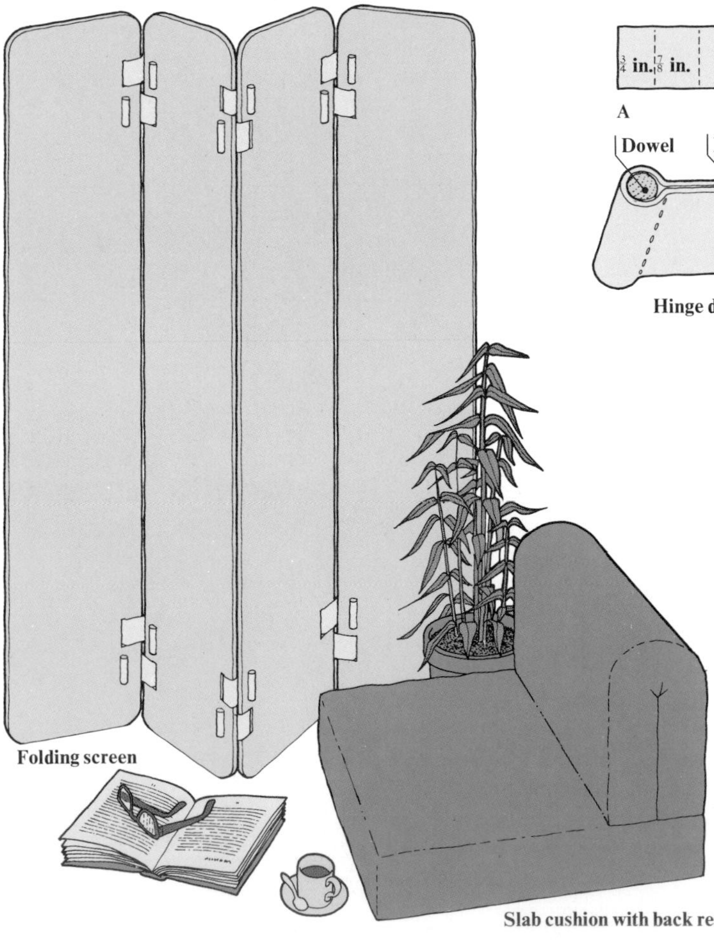

Folding screen

Slab cushion with back rest

Glossary & Index

Nails

Types and sizes

Nails are available in a wide range of types, sizes and finishes. The *common nail* has a heavy gauge and is used for rough framing work. The *box nail* is thinner, and is used for toenailing, framing and lighter work. The *casing nail* is of the same weight as the box nail, but has a conical head, which allows it to be driven below the surface with a nail set. These nails are used for the neat fixing of window and door casings, and for other finishing work. *Finishing nails* and *brads* are fine nails with small heads for fixing parquet flooring and light moldings to walls or furniture.

Nail sizes are expressed in units of length, represented by the letter "d" – the old abbreviation of the word "penny". The gauge of a nail increases with its length. The smallest size is 2d, and represents 1 in. The largest is 60d, or 6 in. in the common nail range (see chart). This system applies to common, box, casing and finishing nails. Brads and small box nails are sold by their actual length. Other special nails such as shingle nails are sold in one length only, or in different lengths but with the same gauge.

Nail finishes and uses

Nails are made from materials with different degrees of hardness and finish, so that each type is appropriate to a particular use: for strength, for protection against corrosion, or for gripping characteristics. The materials include iron, steel, copper, bronze, aluminum, stainless steel, and coatings such as zinc, cement or resin. In addition, special purpose nails have spiral threads or annular rings to increase their grip. In many examples the name of the nail describes the job for which it was designed: *drywall nails, shingle nails,* nails for *flooring, roofing* and *upholstering.* The *duplex nail* is one with a less obvious purpose. The duplex has two heads, the lower is used to clamp the work in the normal way, while the second head allows you to pull it out with a claw hammer; the nails are used for temporary fixtures. If you are not sure which nails to use, describe the job to your supplier. When buying nails it is better to overestimate the quantity, to avoid running short – the remainder can be kept for future use.

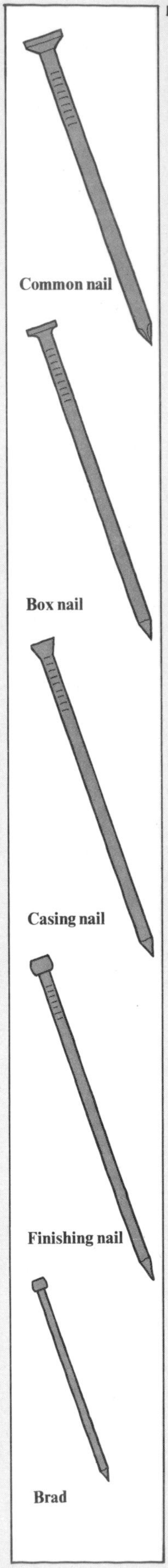

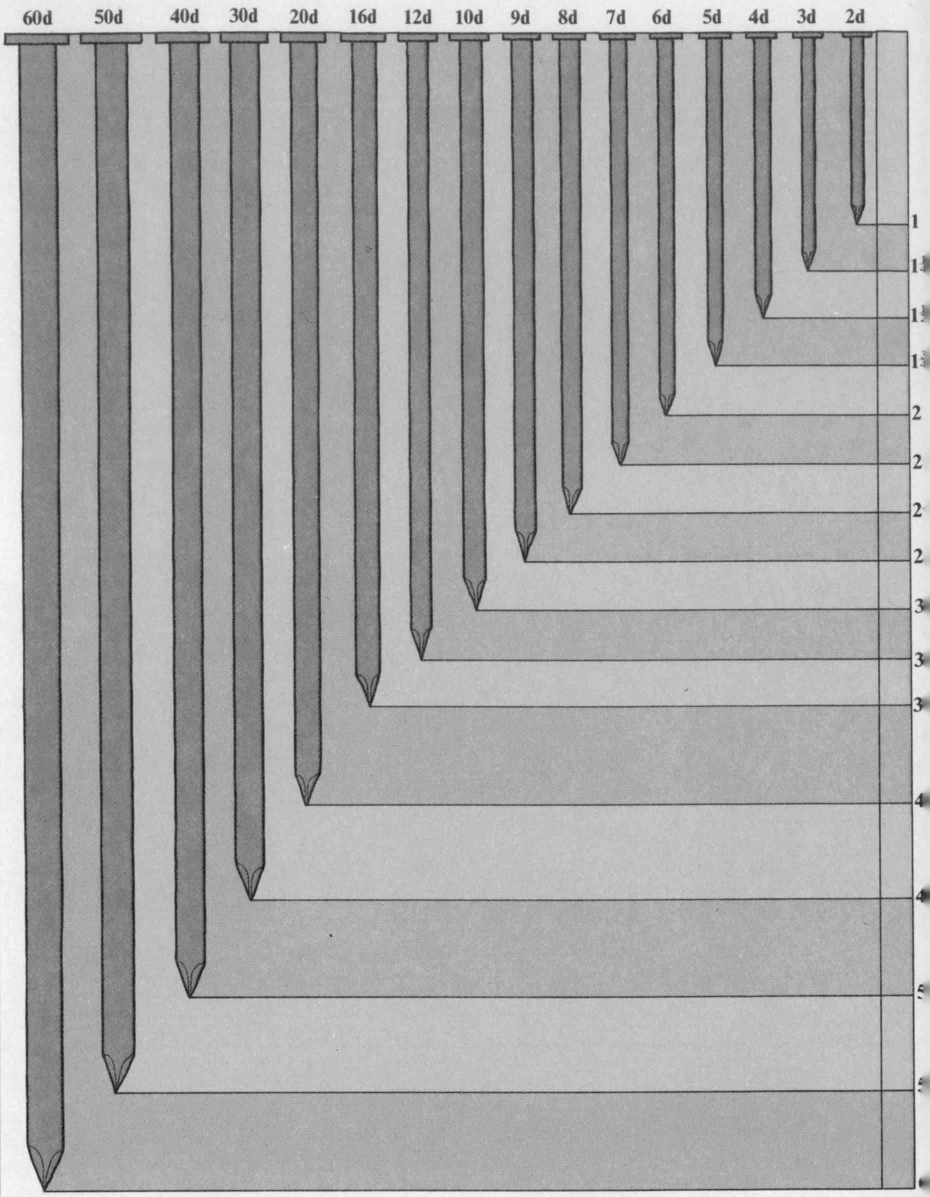

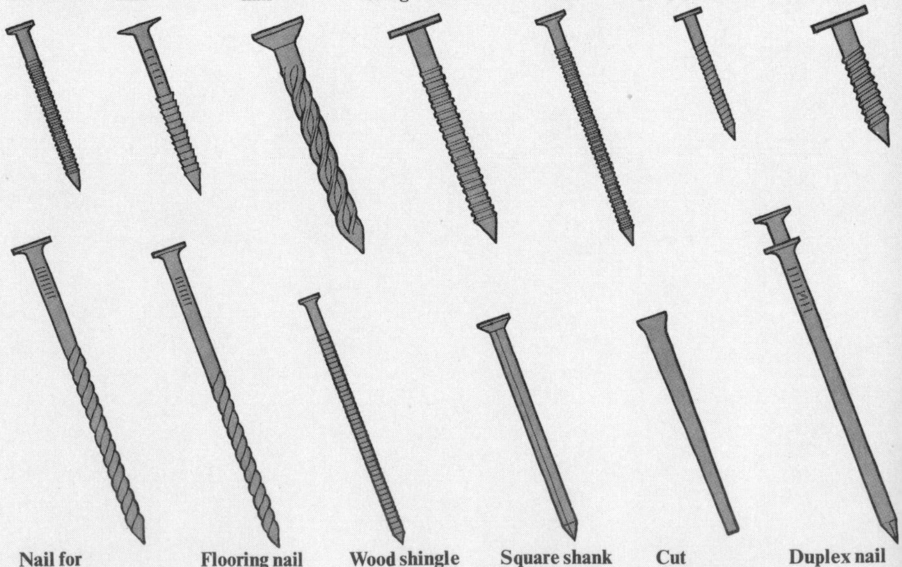

Lengths and gauges
Screw sizes are specified by the length and the gauge – the diameter of the shank (see chart). General purpose screws range from ¼ in. to 4 in., although specialist sizes may be smaller, and there are ones that go up to 6 in. Screws up to 1 in. increase by ⅛ in. increments; 1 in. to 3 in. by ¼ in. increments; 3 in. and longer by ½ in. increments. You select a screw for a particular job by its size, and this is largely determined by the material being fixed. With sheet material use a long, narrow screw for edge fixing, and short, wide screws for the face. For thick lumber use the size that will give the maximum gripping surface for its length. Always screw the thinner member to the thicker. When two equal thicknesses are being fixed together, use a screw length that falls just short of the combined thickness. For very thick wood sections, it is better to counterbore the head rather than use a very long screw; aim to have about two-thirds of the screw's length gripping into the lower member.

Head types
The length of a screw is measured from different points according to the head shape, which may be flat, round or oval.

Use flat head screws where the head must be flush or counterbored. The roundhead screw is used for assemblies that may be dismantled, or for fixing thin sheet material that cannot be countersunk. A flat washer is sometimes used with this type of screw. Oval head screws are a combination of the other two types, and are used for fine finished work, often in conjunction with screw washers, for increased gripping and a neater appearance. Screws are commonly made of steel, but brass screws are available, as are those with decorative or non-corrosive finishes, such as chrome and nickel-plate. Steel screws are the strongest, and should be employed when maximum grip is necessary, but they are liable to rust outdoors; a smear of grease will retard corrosion. As brass and plated screws are softer than steel ones, you should always drill pilot and shank holes to avoid straining them. If the wood is hard, drive a steel pilot screw of the same size to form the thread shape, then replace with the brass screw. Use them for decorative finishes.

Length	Shank numbers																	
¼ inch	0	1	2	3														
⅜ inch			2	3	4	5	6	7										
½ inch			2	3	4	5	6	7	8									
⅝ inch				3	4	5	6	7	8	9	10							
¾ inch					4	5	6	7	8	9	10	11						
⅞ inch							6	7	8	9	10	11	12					
1 inch							6	7	8	9	10	11	12	14				
1¼ inch								7	8	9	10	11	12	14	16			
1½ inch							6	7	8	9	10	11	12	14	16	18		
1¾ inch									8	9	10	11	12	14	16	18	20	
2 inch									8	9	10	11	12	14	16	18	20	
2¼ inch										9	10	11	12	14	16	18	20	
2½ inch													12	14	16	18	20	
2¾ inch														14	16	18	20	
3 inch															16	18	20	
3½ inch																18	20	24
4 inch																18	20	24
Twist bit sizes for round, flat and oval head screws in drilling shank and pilot holes																		
Shank hole Hard/softwood	1/16	5/64	3/32	7/64	1/8	1/8	5/32	5/32	3/16	3/16	7/32	7/32	1/4	1/4	9/32	5/16	11/32	3/8
Pilot hole Softwood	1/64	1/32	1/32	3/64	3/64	1/16	1/16	1/16	5/64	5/64	3/32	3/32	7/64	7/64	9/64	9/64	11/64	3/16
Pilot hole Hardwood	1/32	3/64	1/16	1/16	5/64	5/64	5/64	3/32	3/32	1/8	1/8	1/8	1/8	5/32	3/16	3/16	7/32	1/4

Choosing the right screw

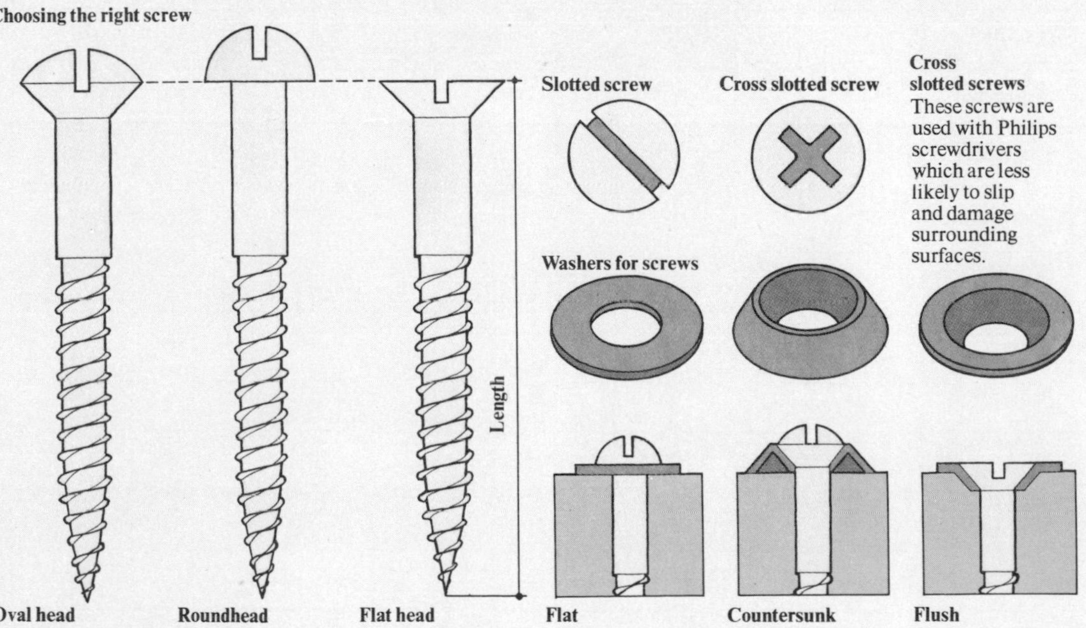

Adhesives

Types and applications
Adhesives are a versatile alternative to the more conventional fixing devices of screws and nails and they provide an invisible join. Most types of adhesive are made for a specific use, but some can be categorized as "general purpose" because they can be used to bond a wide variety of different materials. Epoxy and contact cements fall into this category, and may perform better than other special adhesives. The epoxies are particularly recommended for making strong joints, particularly over small areas, and with materials not easily cold-jointed, such as bonding metal to metal. Contact adhesives are best for hand-laying plastic laminates, the broad gluing area making an excellent bond. Contacts are not suitable for joining highly stressed joints such as those used in furniture making, because the glue line is rather thick and has a tendency to "creep" due to the rubbery nature of the adhesive. Obviously, a wood glue is a much better choice. There are a number of wood glues, each type having different properties. Some are ready-mixed, and dry by evaporation of the solvent which occurs when exposed to the air. Glues made in powder form contain a chemical hardener which is activated when mixed with water. Others have a separate hardener which is applied to one half of the joint, with an application of resin on the other. This has the advantage of preventing the setting taking place until the two halves are brought together, useful when working on a large item. There are waterproof glues for exterior work.

Gluing techniques
When you need to join two materials together with glue, there are certain points to follow if you want a good bond. Read the manufacturer's instructions carefully. The jointing parts should be clean, free from grease, and dry. Joints should be a good fit. In certain cases the materials should be roughened with abrasive paper. Apply enough glue to cover the surfaces, but not too generously as most will be squeezed out and wasted; too much glue will prevent a well-fitting mortise and tenon joint from closing. Wipe off excess glue from a joint before it sets. Some glues need clamping during the setting time. Where this is not practical, a technique known as "rub-jointing" can be used if the adhesive is the sticky type. The adhesive is applied to the part being jointed (usually a woodworking joint) and the two halves are rubbed together. Some of the adhesive is squeezed out, and the suction holds the joint until the glue sets. Adhesives work best when the gluing area is as large as possible. This is particularly important when making butt joints which rely entirely on the strength of the glue. If the glue is put on with a brush, remember to clean it afterwards, before the glue hardens. Most glues set at room temperature, but if conditions are cold, check that the glue is suitable. The following charts show types of adhesives available for most domestic jobs, and also their most important properties.

	Wood	Metal	Glass	Masonry	Ceramic	Plaster	Cork	Leather	Fabric	Carpet	Hardboard	Paper/ Cardboard	Acoustic Tiles	Rubber	Flexible Plastic	Rigid Plastic*	Stone
Wood	AB	CD	CD	CD	C	A					AC						CD
Metal	CD	CDG	DI	CD	CD	CD					C		C				CD
Glass	CD	DI	DGI	D	CDG	D								CI		CD	D
Masonry				D	D												D
Ceramic	F	AC	C	F	AC	F											F
Plaster	A	C	CD	C		A											
Cork	ACF	C		CF	C	ACF	C	C			ACF	AC	AC	C	C	C	CF
Leather	ACE	C	C	CG	CF	ACF		C	CF	CE	AC	AC			C	C	C
Fabric	ACE	C	C	ACE	C	AH	CE	CF	E	E	AEH	AEH	E	C	C	C	AC
Carpet	ACG	C	C	CE	CE	ACG	E	E	E	E	AC	ACE		C	C	C	CG
Hardboard	AC	C	CD	AC	CD	CG					ADC		C	C	C	C	AC
Paper/ Cardboard	ACH	CJ	CJ	ACH	ACJ	AH	AH	CE	CE		AEH	ACHJ		C	CJ	CJ	F
Acoustic Tiles	CF	CF		CF	CF	CF					CF		CF				F
Rubber	CF	CF	CF	CF	C	F	C			C	CF	C		C	C		CF
Flexible Plastic	CFG	CF	CF	CF	C	CF				C	CF	CF		C	GJ	CG	CF
Rigid Plastic*	CD	CD	CD	CD	CD	CD	C							C	C	CDG	CD
Stone		D	D	D	CD												D

Choosing the right adhesive
Use this cross-reference grid to help you find the adhesive needed to bond certain materials together. If you want to glue rubber to hardboard for example, the cross-reference gives you CF, Check the code below. This means that you can use either contact adhesive **C** or mastic **F**.

A. PVA
B. Synthetic resin
C. Contact
D. Epoxy
E. Latex
F. Mastic
G. Plastic
H. Glues and paste
I. Silicone sealant
J. Self adhesive tape.

**Acrylic, polystyrene, PVC; for best bond to itself use a brand name solvent adhesive specially designed for the plastic type.*

Code	Type	Uses	Description	Strength	Water resistance	Gap filling	Setting time (in hours)	Clamping	Cleaning agent	Brand name
A	PVA (Polyvinyl acetate)	Interior woodwork, general repairs for most materials.	White thick liquid available in flexible plastic bottles. Does not stain the work and dries clear. Non-toxic.	Very good	Poor	Fair	½ – 1	Yes	Water while liquid	Sears White Glue; Du Pont White Glue; Elmer's Glue-all.
B	Synthetic resin	Woodwork, interior or exterior. Furniture making. Boat building.	Resorcinol – syrup or powder with separate liquid hardener. Urea-formaldehyde – powder form contains hardener and mixed with water dries opaque cream color.	Excellent	Excellent Poor	Fair Very good	4 – 8	Yes	Warm water while liquid	Craftsman Plastic Resin; Sears Waterproof Resorcinol; Weldwood Plastic Resin.
C	Contact	Bonding sheet materials, laminate etc. General household repairs for most materials.	Rubber based adhesive. Applied to both parts, bonds on contact with firm pressure. Dries clear or yellow colored. Not suitable for stressed joints. Highly inflammable vapor.	Very good	Good	Poor	¼	No	Special solvent. Acetone	Sears Miracle Pliobond; Devco Rubber; Duro.
D	Epoxy	Tough general purpose adhesive for most materials. Will withstand boiling water.	Resin and hardener supplied in separate tubes for mixing in equal parts. Costly so use is limited to small jobs where strength is required. Made in fast and slow setting types. Dries clear.	Excellent	Excellent	Very good	¼ – 12	Yes	Methylated spirit while liquid	Elmer's Epoxy; Devcon Clear Epoxy; Epoxy 1177.
E	Latex	Bonds fabrics, cardboard, carpets and fibrous materials. Can be washed in hot water.	Natural rubber adhesive usually white, creamy consistency. Available in tubes or jars. Can be applied with a brush. Dries clear for a flexible joint.	Good	Good	Poor	¼ – 1	No	Lighter fluid	Sears Stitchless Mender; Devcon Patch; Franklin Carpet Adhesive.
F	Mastic	Flooring, tiling, paneling adhesives for fixing to concrete, lining boards etc.	Available in two basic types, rubber resin and synthetic latex. The former is solvent based, the latter water based. Some brands are applied to one surface, others to both. Application can be with notched spreader or caulking gun.	Good	Good	Good	Various	No	Petroleum solvent	Franklin Construction Adhesive; Ruscoe Pan-L-Bond.
G	Plastic	Model making. Repair work for ornaments made of glass, china, wood, plastics.	Usually a clear liquid supplied in tubes. Dries quickly and is transparent when set. Is moisture resistant and reasonably heat proof.	Good	Good	Poor	¼	Yes	Acetone	Scotch Super-Strength Adhesive; Duco Cement; Wilhold China & Glass Cement.
H	Glues & pastes	Wallpapering, collage. Repairing paper.	Made from various base materials including rubber, animal glues, flour pastes, vegetable derivatives. Available in powder or liquid form.	Good	Poor	Poor	½	No	Water	Le Page's Paper Cement; Carters Liquid Paste; Carters Rubber Cement.
I	Silicone sealant	Forms seals between sink or tub and walls. Bonds glass to glass for aquaria.	Thick creamy consistency, can be clear, white or pastel colored. Available in tubes. Does not change color when set.	Fair	Very good	Excellent	1 – 4	No	Solvent while liquid	Dow Silicone Adhesive; Sears Silicone Sealant; General Electric Silicone Seal.
J	Self adhesive tape	For quick fixing of paper and cardboard to a variety of materials.	Supplied on rolls in various widths. Can be clear tape or opaque colors. Made single or double sided.	Good	Poor	–	Instant	No	Lighter fluid	3 M's Tape.

Simple Geometry

Marking shapes and angles
A brief knowledge of simple plan-drawing geometry can be useful when measuring and marking up work. In addition to the marking instruments – 90° try square; combination square; adjustable level; measuring tape – a basic set of drawing instruments will help you to calculate bevels, shapes, and their sizes for any job. The instruments are: drawing board; T square; triangle with 45°, 90°, 45° angles and another having angles of 30°, 60°, 90°; protractor; and finally, a pair of compasses. Shapes can be drawn directly on to the material to be cut, or first worked out on paper or cardboard to make a template which is then drawn around. The template method can be a little less accurate. Which method is best depends on the material being marked, its size and its situation. The template method is more convenient when you need to mark out a number of repeat shapes.

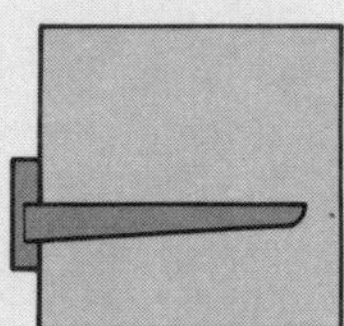

T square
Use in combination with the drawing board. Hold stock of square firmly against the side edge of board. Slide up and down to mark parallel horizontal lines.

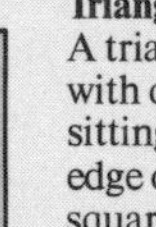

1

Triangle
A triangle is used with one side sitting on the top edge of the T square blade, to establish a line at a known angle to the base line, **1**.
You can mark angles in parallel by sliding the triangle along the T square. The T square can be tilted to draw any off-set angles, **2**.

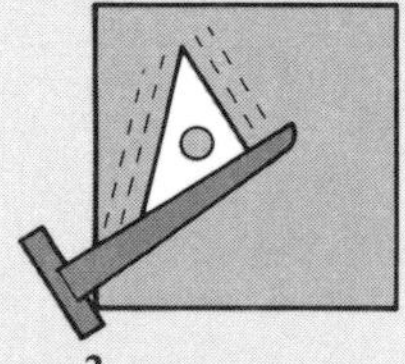

2

Protractor
A protractor is a 180° calibrated scale divided into 1° increments for marking angles. The center point of the base is set on a known point of a line, and the required angle ticked off around its outer edge. The center mark and tick are joined up with the aid of a straight edge. A protractor can also be used to check an angle already marked.

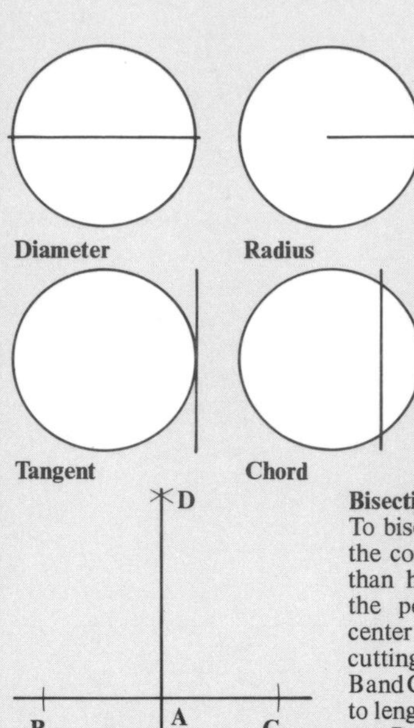

Simple geometry
There may be occasions when calibrated instruments cannot be used accurately. In such cases you can apply simple geometric techniques with the aid of compasses. Instructions which show you how to make various forms follow.

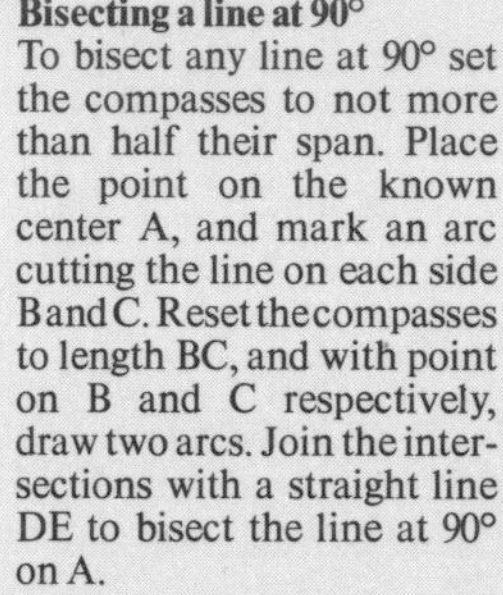

Bisecting a line at 90°
To bisect any line at 90° set the compasses to not more than half their span. Place the point on the known center A, and mark an arc cutting the line on each side B and C. Reset the compasses to length BC, and with point on B and C respectively, draw two arcs. Join the intersections with a straight line DE to bisect the line at 90° on A.

Bisecting any angle
To bisect any angle, set the compasses to a convenient radius and place the point at A. Mark off an arc BC. Place the point of the compasses on B and C and strike two arcs to meet at D. A line AD bisects the angle. A 90° right angle can be bisected in this way to give a 45° angle.

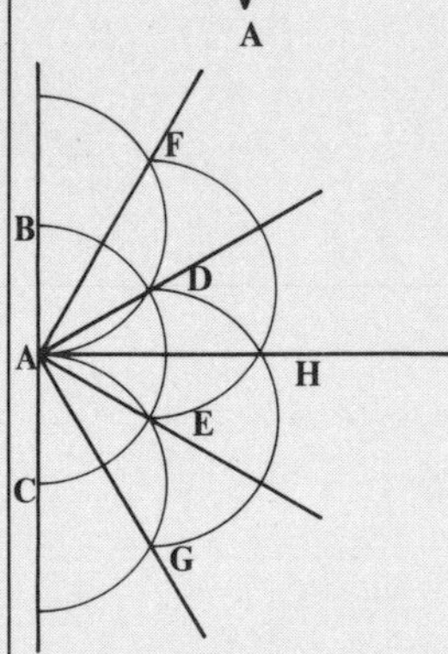

Dividing 180° into 30° angles
Set the compasses to a convenient radius and draw an arc centered on point A, to cut the base line at B and C. With the same radius strike an arc from points B and C. Strike two further arcs where the lines bisect at D and E. Draw straight lines between D, E, F, G, H and A.

Finding the center of a circle
Draw any line AB across the circle. Bisect this line as previously shown with the line CD. Now bisect line CD between the points D and E to give center of circle F.

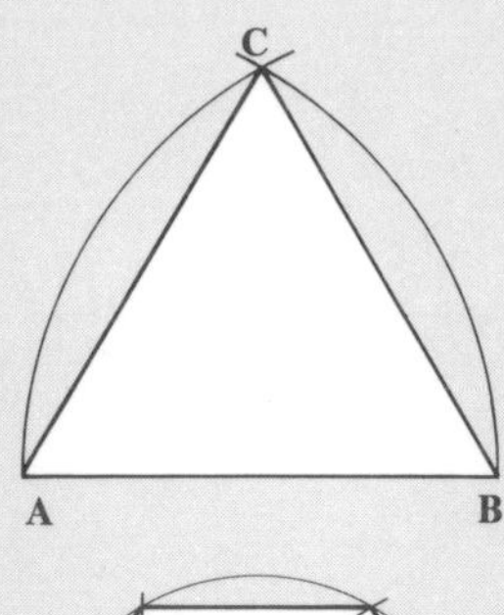

Drawing geometric shapes
Equilateral triangle
To draw an equal sided triangle with a side of known length AB, set a pair of compasses to this length. Strike arcs from points A and B. Join the intersection C with A and B.

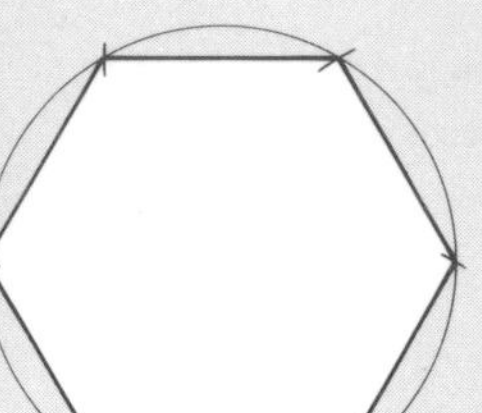

Hexagon
Draw a circle with a radius equal to the length of the hexagon side. With the compasses at this setting, strike off points around the circumference, centering the point on each intersection. It should divide exactly into six. Join up the intersections.

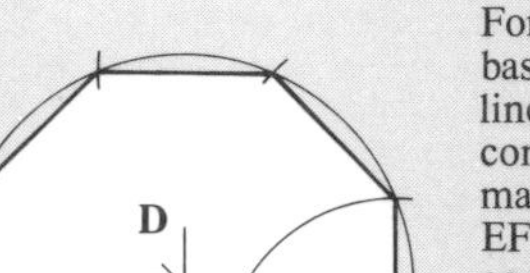

Octagon
For an octagon, draw a known base line AB. Bisect AB with line CD. Set a pair of compasses to half AB and mark an arc at E. Draw a line EF from E through B. Set the compasses to length AB and strike an arc from center B to cut line at G. Set the compasses on G and scribe a second arc to cut the first at HI. Draw a line through HI to give center of octagon at J. Draw a circle with radius AJ. Set the compasses to length AB and mark off remainder of sides on circle.

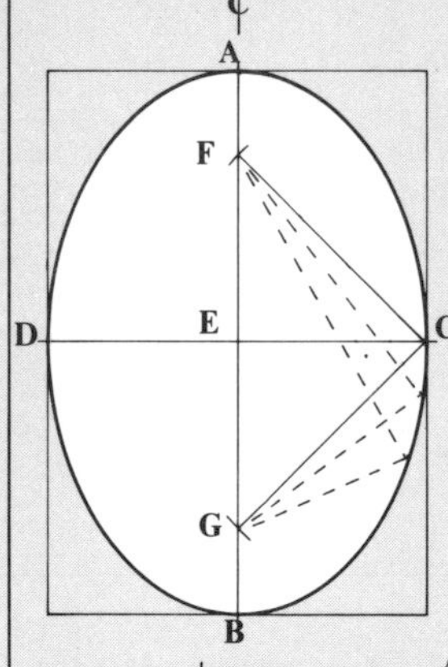

Ellipse
To draw an ellipse in a known rectangle, first bisect the rectangle with lines AB, CD. Set a pair of compasses to length AE, which is half of AB. With point on C, strike an arc at F and G. Drive fine nails on centers CFG to form pegs, and tie a taut loop of string around them. Pull out the nail at C, and using a pencil in its place, scribe the ellipse, keeping the line taut.

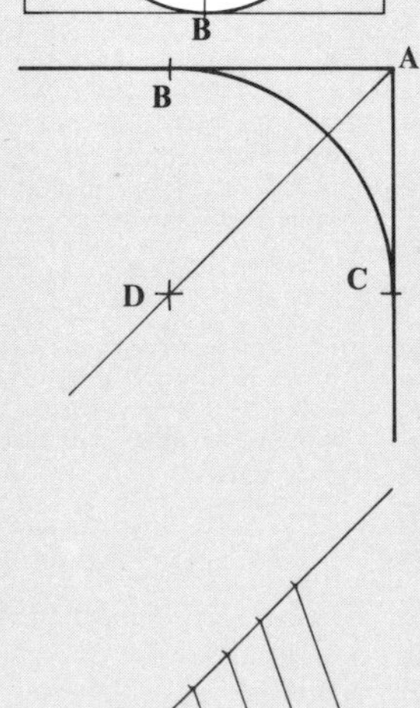

Marking a given radius on a right angle corner
To mark this radius, set the compass point on A and scribe an arc at B and C. With compasses on B and C, bisect angle at D. Set the compass on D and draw corner radius. This method marks a radius on a corner of any other angle. The center of the circle will always fall on the bisecting line AD.

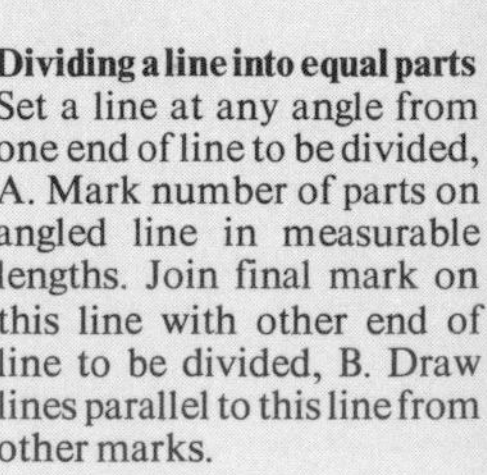

Dividing a line into equal parts
Set a line at any angle from one end of line to be divided, A. Mark number of parts on angled line in measurable lengths. Join final mark on this line with other end of line to be divided, B. Draw lines parallel to this line from other marks.

Calculating sizes

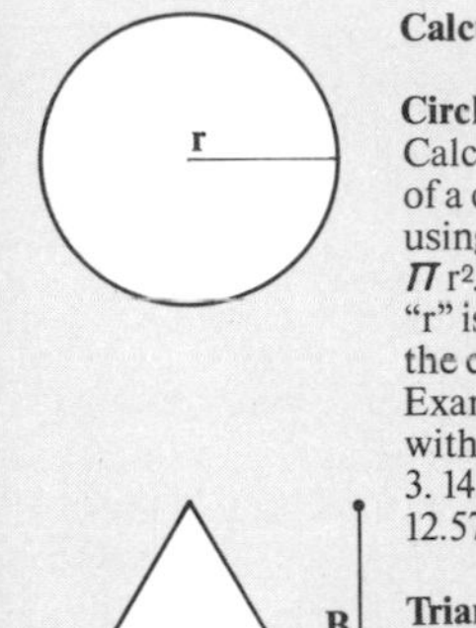

Circle
Calculate the area of a circle by using formula πr^2. $\pi = 3.14$, "r" is the radius of the circle. Example: a circle with 2 in. radius: 3.14×2^2in. = 12.57 sq. in.

Triangle
Calculate the area of a triangle with formula $\frac{A \times B}{2}$

Example:
$\frac{2.5 \text{ in} \times 3.5 \text{ in}}{2}$ = 4.375 sq. in.

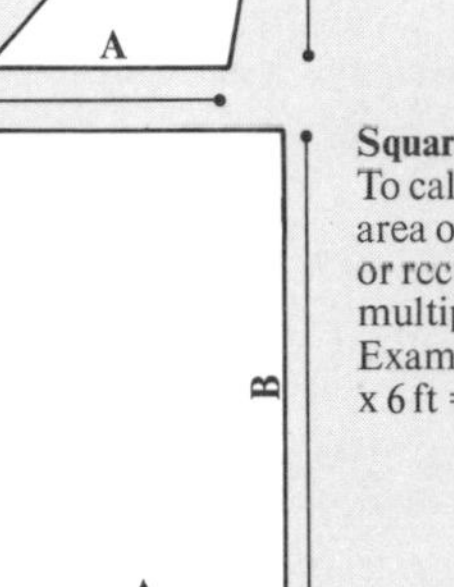

Square/rectangle
To calculate the area of a square or rectangle, multiply A x B. Example: 4.5 ft x 6 ft = 27 sq. ft.

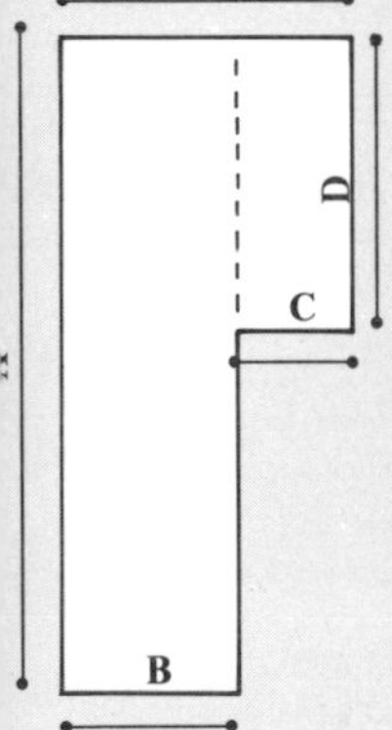

L-shaped room
You can calculate the area of an L-shaped room by dividing the shape into separate rectangles. Calculate the area of each and add the results together. Example:
Rectangle AB= 10 ft x 4 ft=40 sq. ft.
Rectangle CD= 3 ft x 4 ft= 12 sq. ft.
Total: 52 sq. ft.
If room has projections calculate its area and subtract from total.

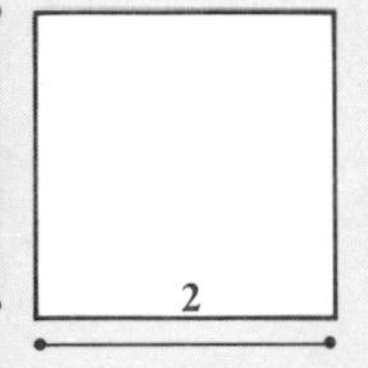

Perimeter
The perimeter of any straight sided figure is the sum of the length of the sides. Example: perimeter of square, left, is 8 (2+2+2+2).

Circumference
To calculate the circumference use the formula πD. π =3.14, D is the diameter of the circle. Example: a circle with an 8 in. diameter: 3.14x8 in. = 25.13 in.

Tile Chart

Area coverage

The chart gives the quantity of tiles of a particular size needed to cover a given area. To use the chart, work out the area to be covered. Check this figure in the left-hand column, look across the top line for the tile size you wish to use; the quantity of tiles you will need is shown where the two columns meet. For example: a wall measuring 10 ft x 8 ft = 80 sq. ft. To cover this wall with 4¼ in. x 4¼ in. tiles you will need 640 tiles. If the area falls between two of the figures in the chart, take the lower figure and note the quantity of tiles. Then check the balance which will fall between 1 and 4. Add this quantity to the lower figure to get the total needed. For example, for a wall measuring 64 sq. ft the nearest low figure in column 1 is 60. If you are using 4 in. x 4 in. tiles you will need 540. You are left with 4 sq. ft which gives you 36 tiles. The total needed for 64 sq. ft is therefore 540 plus 36= 576 tiles. For areas larger than those shown in column 1, divide the figure into units and add the totals. Where doors or windows occur, calculate their area and deduct from the total wall measurement.

Calculating for border tiles

It is rare that an estimated number of tiles will exactly fit an area without your having to use part tiles on borders and edges. To give a border of cut tiles of not less than half width, an allowance should be made for additional tiles to be cut to fit. An example is where you may have a rectangular area, with one long side and the other short. Look down the first column of the *Allowance Chart* for each measurement. Check against the tile size and then add the totals to find the extra tiles needed. Where fractions are shown for the larger tiles, unless part tiles are available you will have to buy the next whole number.

Tile Chart

Area in sq. ft	Sizes of tiles in inches						
	4 x 4	4¼ x 4¼	6 x 6	9 x 9	12 x 12	12 x 24	24 x 24
1	9	8	4	2	1	½	¼
2	18	16	8	4	2	1	½
3	27	24	12	6	3	1½	¾
4	36	32	16	8	4	2	1
5	45	40	20	9	5	2½	1¼
10	90	80	40	18	10	5	2½
15	135	120	60	27	15	7½	3¾
20	180	160	80	36	20	10	5
25	225	200	100	45	25	12½	6¼
30	270	240	120	54	30	15	7½
35	315	280	140	63	35	17½	8¾
40	360	320	160	72	40	20	10
45	405	360	180	81	45	22½	11¼
50	450	400	200	90	50	25	12½
55	495	440	220	99	55	27½	13¾
60	540	480	240	108	60	30	15
65	585	520	260	117	65	32½	16¼
70	630	560	280	126	70	35	17½
75	675	600	300	135	75	37½	18¾
80	720	640	320	144	80	40	20
85	765	680	340	153	85	42½	21¼
90	810	720	360	162	90	45	22½
95	855	760	380	171	95	47½	23¾
100	900	800	400	180	100	50	25

Allowance Chart

Length in feet	Width of tile in inches						
	4	4¼	6	9	12	(12 x 24)	24
1	3	3	2	2	1	See below	½
2	6	6	4	3	2		1
3	9	9	6	4	3		1½
4	12	12	8	6	4		2
5	15	15	10	7	5		2½
10	30	29	20	14	10		5
15	45	43	30	20	15		7½
20	60	57	40	27	20		10

N.B. In the case of 12 in. x 24 in. tiles refer to the appropriate columns depending on which way they are laid.

Glossary of Terms

A

Abrasive A rough-surfaced material used for grinding and polishing.
Aggregate Sand, rock and gravel-like materials used with cement to make concrete.
Air brick A perforated brick placed in a wall which provides ventilation by allowing air to pass through.
Air dried lumber Lumber that has been stacked and allowed to dry naturally.
Air pocket Empty space in a concrete wall caused by improper pouring.
Alloy A mixture of two or more metals.
Anchor bolt Bolt used to secure wood or steel to concrete.
Angle iron A reinforcement or support in the shape of an "L."
Anhydrous Moisture-free.
Aniline dyes Synthetically produced colors made from coal tar substances.
Antique To finish furniture so that it appears to be old and worn.
Aperture A wall opening for doors or windows.
Arch brick A wedge shaped brick used in constructing arches and curved masonry work.
Architrave Wooden door or window casing.
Asbestos Threadlike fibers of calcium and magnesium silicate used in fireproofing.
Asphalt A mineral material used widely for waterproofing on roofs, walls and floors.
Astragal A small beaded interior molding which acts as a stop for one of a pair of swinging doors.
Auger bit A spiral-shaped tool for boring holes in wood.
Awl A sharp-pointed tool for marking holes and scribing.

B

Backband A decorative molding applied to the outer edge of an interior window or door casing.
Backfill Earth which is replaced after excavating.
Backing Rubble used behind a finished masonry facing.
Backing bricks Cheaper bricks used behind the face ones.
Backsaw A fine-toothed saw with a stiff metal back used for accurate cutting.
Ballast Coarse gravel of sand, grit and stones.
Baluster A rail support in the shape of a small column.
Bar clamp A screw clamp used in woodworking with an adjustable stop mounted on a bar.
Baseboard A board placed around a room between the wall and the floor.
Batten A narrow strip of softwood lumber.
Batter board A temporary framework used in new foundations for locating corners.
Bay window A window or group of windows of several shapes supported by a foundation outside the main wall of a building.
Beading A narrow molding.
Beam A traversely-supporting structural member.
Beam ceiling A decorative ceiling with exposed beams which can be solid or imitation.
Bearing partition A partition which supports a vertical load.
Bearing wall A wall which supports a vertical load.
Bedding Mortar or putty used as a filling to ensure a firm bearing.
Bed joint A horizontal joint upon which bricks are placed.
Bed molding A molding used to cover an angle joint between two surfaces.
Bell and spigot joint The joint between the straight end of the spigot and the bell of the next pipe.
Bench hook A device to hold work in place on a bench which is used while sawing.
Benzene A powerful solvent.
Bevel The angle cut on the edge of a board or door, other than a right angle.
Biscuit tile A tile that is unglazed.
Blind nailing Nailing so that the heads are undiscernible on the work's surface.
Blind stop Rectangular molding used in window frame construction.
Blistering The formation of bubbles on painted or varnished surfaces.
Blower coil That part of an air conditioner which brings in warm air and disperses it as cool air.
Blowtorch A portable torch fired by gasoline.
Bond A strong and decorative mass formed by a regular arrangement of stones and bricks.
Bonding The joining of two surfaces or the agent which brings it about.
Bore A pipe's, cylinder's or hole's internal diameter.
Brace An inclined piece of lumber used to strengthen a building's framework.
Bracket A projecting support for a shelf or a strengthening device.
Brad A small thin nail with a deep head.
Brick veneer A decorative exterior wall finish of one brick's depth against a wood frame.
Bridging Pairs of diagonal braces fitted between floor joists which distribute the floor load.
BTU British Thermal Unit – a measurement used in air conditioning. 1 BTU=778.6 ft lbs.
Buffing compound A wax bonded soft abrasive in stick form.
Burr Some roughness or a small projection left on metal after cutting.
Bushing A device which protects insulated wires from abrasion by being packed tight against a conduit's end.
Butt To join two items together end-to-end without overlap.
Butt joint The junction at which the ends of two pieces of lumber meet.
BX cable Common term for flexible armored cable used in electric wiring.

C

Caliber The bore measurement or internal diameter.
Cantilevered Any rigid structure such as a beam or roof which extends beyond its vertical support.
Cant strip A triangular piece of wood placed under roof shingles or siding to ensure a slanting shape and to keep the roofing from cracking.
Cap A finished cement top of a chimney or wall; a fitting to close the end of a threaded pipe.
Cape chisel A narrow-bladed cold chisel for masonry work.
Capstan A wheel or other drum-shaped device to drive a belt.
Carpet strip A molding located beneath the baseboard to cover the gap between carpet and baseboard.
Casing The finished trim boards or molding around doors and windows, either inside or outside.
Caul A woodworking tool used to shape veneer to a curved surface.
Caulking compound A mastic material which is used to seal and waterproof the joints around windows and doors.
Chalk line A string coated with colored chalk which is used to make a straight line on a flat surface. If it is snapped after being fastened taut between two points it will produce an accurate measuring line on the surface.
Chamfer To remove the sharp edge of a board by planing it to a 45° angle.
Checking Cracks in the surface of wooden or painted surfaces.
Checkrails Beveled meeting rails of a double-hung window which are made thicker than the window to fill the gap between the top and bottom sash.
Chimney breast The projecting part of a wall above a fireplace.
Chuck A device which is attached to the head stock spindle of a rotating machine to hold work: adjustable jaws for holding drill bits in power or hand drills.
Circuit breaker A protective relay device which opens a circuit in case of an overload.
Clapboards Exterior house covering of wood siding.
Closure Part of a brick used to close the end of a course in a brick wall.
Cold chisel A wedge-like chisel used for cutting metals and masonry.
Common boards Lumber which is 1 in. thick and up to 12 in. wide.
Conduit A pipe or tube, usually of metal, in which wire is installed.
Cope To cut the end of molding to the shape of an adjoining molding piece.
Corbel out Building out from the wall's face one or more courses of brick or stone to form a support for beams.
Cornice A decorative exterior trim of molding or boards placed at the junction of roof and wall.
Counterbore To drill a larger, second hole in the original hole's center to a specified depth.
Countersink To shape a drilled hole in wood or metal using a cone-shaped tool to provide a recess for a flathead screw or bolt.
Course A layer of brick or stone.
Cradling Lumber used to support lath and plaster in vaulted ceilings.
Crimp To turn or close down the edge of a piece of sheet metal.

D

Dado A rectangular groove cut in wood across the wood's grain.
Damp proofing Treating a masonry wall to prevent water seeping through.
Doorhead The upper, horizontal part of a door's frame.
Doorstop A molding nailed to the inside face of a door frame against which the door closes.
Dormer A window which projects out from a sloping roof.
Double bend An S-shaped pipe fitting.
Downspout A pipe, usually of metal, used to carry rainwater from the roof to the ground.
Dry rot The decay of lumber to a powdery state brought about by fungal attacks in damp conditions.
Dry wall Interior covering materials which do not need to be mixed with water before applying.
Dutch door A two-part door where both parts act independently of each other.

E

Eaves The lower part of the roof, or overhang, which projects over an exterior wall.
Efflorescence A whitish deposit of water soluble salts on the surface of masonry or plaster.
End grain The wood grain exposed by cutting across the grain.
Escutcheon A protective plate in which a keyhole is cut.

F

Face The front of a wall; to cover with a new surface.
Face nail A nail driven perpendicular to the finished face.
Fascia Flat board or facing used as a trim.
Ferrule For paint brushes – the metal part between bristles and handle; for screwdrivers – the metal part between handle and blade.
File card A file cleaning brush with short fine wires.
Fireclay A heat resistant cement used to bond firebrick.
Fittings All those parts used to join pipes together.
Flashing Sheet metal or other material used on the roof around chimneys and vents to prevent water from entering.
Flue Chimney passageway which allows smoke, gas or fumes to rise.
Flush Condition describing adjacent surfaces which are level and fit evenly.
Flux A preparation which removes oxides from metals and inhibits oxidation while soldering.
Footing The foundation or support at the base or bottom of a wall or column.
Form A mold used to shape poured concrete.
Framing The wooden structure of a building which includes interior and exterior walls, floors, roof and ceiling.
French door A door where several wooden panels are replaced by glass panes.
French window A casement window which extends to the floor and can be used as a door.
Furring Narrow wood strips fastened to studs or masonry walls to provide a nailing base for wall materials.
Fuse A safety device which breaks an electric circuit on overloading.

G

Gables The triangular portions of a building contained between the slopes of a double-sloped roof.
Galvanized iron Rust inhibitive zinc-coated iron.
Garnet paper A red-colored abrasive.
Girder A large solid or built-up wood or steel beam used to support a concentrated load.
Glazing The process of fitting glass into windows or doors; the glass panes in window frames.
Ground An electrical connection to earth by means of rods or plates.
Grounds Strips of wood placed within a wall to provide a surface for plaster or other finishing material.
Grout A thin mortar used in filling the joints and cavities of masonry work.
Gusset An angle bracket or brace of wood or metal used to strengthen a corner.
Gutter A wood or metal trough attached to a building's edge to collect and conduct water.

H

Hardboard Wooden board made of compressed fiber.
Hawk A small board held by a handle underneath and used to hold mortar or plaster.
Header Horizontal beam placed between two long ones and perpendicular to them; a lintel.
Hot wire A wire carrying a current usually black.

I

I beam An I-shaped steel beam.
Insulation Electrical – materials which are poor conductors of electricity and are used to cover wires; Thermal – materials used to reduce the rate of heat flow.

J

Jamb The top and two sides of a window or door frame.
Joint To fit materials together; the place at which parts are joined together; method of fastening wooden parts together.
Jointing The way in which exterior mortar joints between brick or stone are finished.
Joists Wood or metal beams used to support floors and ceilings horizontally.
Junction box A distribution box where connections for several wires are made.

K

Kapok A fiber filler for pillows and mattresses.
Knocked down Structural units complete in various parts but unassembled.

L

Lacquer A finishing material that dries as its thinner or solvent evaporates.
Lampholder A socket for an electric light bulb.
Lap joint A joint where two pieces of wood overlap forming a single surface on both faces.
Lath Thin strip of wood nailed to wall stud to support plaster.
Light A pane of glass or that space in a window frame into which glass fits.
Lintel A supporting horizontal structural member over a door or window.
Lock nut A nut which is designed to remain tight once fixed.
Lock washer A washer which prevents nuts from loosening under vibration.
Louver A ventilating window of inclined horizontal slats.
Lumber Timber cut or planed to size for use as studs, boards, etc.

M

Main The principal circuit which supplies all others.
Mantel The shelf over the fireplace in front of the chimney.
Masonry Stone, brick, block or tile laid in mortar or concrete.
Mastic A pasty material used as a protective coating or cement.
Matched boards Tongue and groove boards.
Mat finish A non-glossy, dull surface.
Meeting rail The horizontal wood or metal rail separating upper and lower window sashes.
Metal lath A base for plaster made of metal sheet.
Mildew Mold formed by exposure to moisture.
Millwork Manufactured woodwork such as moldings, door frames, etc.
Miter To cut wood such as moldings or trim at a 45° angle so that when joined it forms a right angle.
Molding Any piece of wood, relatively narrow in size, cut to a special shape to provide an ornamental surface.
Mortar Masonry bonding material consisting of sand and cement.
Mortise A rectangular recess cut in a piece of wood to receive a tenon, or tongue.
Mullion A slender vertical divider separating units of a window or screen.
Muntins Vertical or horizontal dividers between window panes.
Muriatic acid Hydrochloric acid in a dilute form often used to clean brick.

N

Nail set A punch tool used for setting nail heads below a wood surface.
Nibbler A scissors-like tool for cutting irregular pieces of sheet metal.
Nippers Pincher tools with sharp cutting jaws.
Nipples Short pieces of pipe threaded at both ends and used for plumbing connections.
Nosing The rounded and projecting top edge of a stair tread.

O

Out of plumb Not vertical.
Overload Exceed the working capacity of a circuit.

P

Packing Soft, rope-like material which is pushed into plumbing joints to seal them.
Panel box A switch or fuse box in which branch currents are distributed.
Papier mache An easy-to-shape material made of paper and paste.
Pargeting A thin coat of plaster on a stone or brick wall applied for decorative purposes.
Particle board A formed panel made of wooden materials bonded together.
Parting strip A narrow piece of wood used in the center channel of a double-hung window to separate the two sashes.
Partition Any space-dividing wall.
Party wall Any wall used jointly by separate parties.
Pier A masonry column, usually rectangular, used to support other structures.
Pilot hole A small guide hole.
Plaster A mixture of lime, cement, sand and water with a strengthening agent used to cover walls and ceilings.
Plate glass A high quality flat polished glass.
Plinth A rectangular panel, normally the base of a cabinet.
Plumb bob A pointed, cone-shaped weight which hangs on a plumb or line and is used to determine verticality.
Plywood Thin, wooden sheets of an odd number glued together and laminated.
Pointing The finishing or filling of mortared joints.
Polyethylene Clear or black plastic pliable sheeting used in waterproofing.
Potted circuit An insulated circuit protected against humidity and temperature.
Prefabricated units Those items manufactured or assembled at a plant which require minimal on-site assembly.
Primer The first surface coat applied before or while painting; the material used to do this.
Putty A dough-like cement mixture used to set glass in frames and to fill in holes and cracks.

Q

Quarter round A three-sided molding with a curved face whose two remaining sides form a right angle.

R

Rabbet A continuous rectangular groove cut along the edge of a board at a 90° angle.
Radiant heat Heat produced by forced hot water systems with floor, ceiling or wall pipes or electrically heated panels.
Rafter The roof joists which support the covering boards.
Reaming The opening, widening or smoothing out of holes.
Reinforced concrete Concrete to which metal bars, rods or mesh are added to improve strength.

Glossary of Terms

Relay A magnetic switch.
Rendering The first coat of plaster on a brick or stone wall.
Retaining wall A barrier wall which resists lateral pressure and prevents earth movements.
Return bed A U-shaped plumbing joint.
Ripping Sawing wood in the direction of the grain.
Riser A vertical water supply pipe between stories; the upright part of a step.
Rivet A headed metal tack for fastening materials together.
Rough-in To install drainage and supply pipes before walls are finished during building construction.
Round nose chisel A cold chisel with a curved cutting edge used for chipping in filleted corners.

S

Sash The framework in a window which surrounds the glass.
Satin finish A painted surface having a dull luster.
Sawhorse A four-legged trestle support.
Scarfing The joining of the ends of two pieces of lumber with sloping lap joints so they appear continuous.
Score To incise along a cutting line.
Scratch coat The primary plaster application which provides a bonding for further coats.
Screed A thin layer of floor leveling compound; small strip of wood used as a plastering guide.
Scriber A sharp pointed steel tool, similar to a pencil, used for marking metal or wooden surfaces.
Service panel A fuse or circuit breaker box from which the electric circuits for a house emanate.
Setscrew A screw used to prevent rotary motion between two parts.
Shakes Thick, handsplit shingles; natural faults in timber.
Sheath The exterior protective covering of a wire or cable.
Sheathing Boards or prefabricated panels nailed to studs or rafters to provide a base for siding or roofing materials.
Shielded cables Wires or cables covered by a braided wire mesh.
Shims Thin strips of wood, often wedge-shaped, used for leveling wood members.
Shingles Thin pieces of wooden building material, with one end thicker than the other, which are overlapped to cover roofs and walls.
Shiplap boards Lumber with rabbeted edges that is joined with half-lap joints.
Shooting board A device for holding a plane at the proper angle for making accurate angular cuts.
Shoring Lumber which is used as a temporary brace during repairs.
Siding The exterior wall finish of a building.
Sill The lowest member of a structure's frame which is usually horizontal and supports the uprights.
Sill cock An outside faucet.
Siphonage The flow of liquid created by suction as a result of below atmospheric pressure.
Size A gelatin-like filling and sealing material.
Skirting Small wooden boards placed around the bottom of a room; the baseboard.
Sleepers Horizontally-laid lumber supporting floor joists.
Slip stone A sharpening stone with rounded edge for irregularly shaped woodworking tools.
Soffit The underside of a building's structural member.
Soft solders Any low temperature solders.
Solder Alloy of tin and lead; to join the surfaces of metals together with fused solder.
Solvent That liquid which is capable of dissolving a certain material.
Spacers Small pieces of wood used to hold concrete forms or tiles apart at desired distances.
Spackling compound A plaster filler paste.
Splicing The connecting of two wires together.
Stiles Vertical parts of doors.
Straight edge A leveling and measuring board with a straight edge.
Stretchers Bricks or blocks placed lengthwise in a wall.
Strike plate A jamb-mounted plate which receives the latch or bolt of a lock.
Striking off The leveling off of concrete to the top of forms or its shaping to the desired contour usually by means of a board.
Strut A rafter-supporting brace.
Stucco An exterior wall surface of a plaster-type material.
Stud Slender lumber or metal vertical piece used as a supporting surface for walls and partitions.
Subfloor Rough boards or plywood placed on floor joists to which the final finishing material is applied.
Sweating The condensation of moisture on a surface.
Switch A directing or controlling device for the current flow in a circuit.

T

Tamping The positioning and agitating of freshly poured concrete in the form.
Tenon A tongue-like projection cut in a piece of wood to fit into a mortise.
Terminal A mechanical device at which electrical connections are made.
Terra cotta Baked clay of a high quality.
Terrazzo A ground and polished flooring material of colored stone or marble embedded in cement.
T fitting A T-shaped water pipe or drain used to form branch lines off the main.
Thermoplastics Materials which soften and remain pliable under heat.
Thermostats Automatic control devices which operate on changes in temperature.
Thinwall Tubing for electric wires or conduits.
Thixotropic paints Those thick paints which when shaken or disturbed become fluid before reverting back to a jelly state.
Three-way switches Two switches which control an electric device from different locations.
Tie rods Metal or wooden rods used to bind together hard-to-join materials; steel rods used to hold concrete forms together while filling.
Timber Raw wood or sawed lumber of a size greater than 5 inches in width and thickness.
Toenail To drive a nail in at an angle in the initial material in order to penetrate another surface.
Toe of weld Junction of weld face and the base metal.
Toggle bolt An expanding fastener used when fixing screws to a hollow wall.
Toggle switch A switch operated by a movable lever or rocker button.
Tongue The projecting part of a board which fits into a groove.
Transom The window above a door.
Trap That part of a drain pipe whose function is to hold water and thus form a seal preventing sewer gases from entering.
Traversing Crossing the grain of wood.
Tread The horizontal member of a step.
Trim Those moldings and boards which are used to finish door and window openings or which are placed around the room at floor or ceiling level.
Truss A beam and steel rod triangular structure which supports loads over a long span.
Turn To shape wood or metal on a lathe.

U

U bolt A shaped bolt threaded on both ends.
Undercoat The second of three paint applications or the first coat in repainting; primer coat.
Underwriters' Laboratories A device and materials testing institution which determines standards of construction and performance.
Union A plumbing slip nut device used to join two threaded pipes without the need for dismantling them when disconnecting.

V

Valve A regulating device to control the flow of air or liquid.
Vapor barrier That construction material which prevents moisture penetrating walls and floors.
Veneer Thin sliced wooden sheets used for decorative purposes.

W

Wainscot An interior wall surface usually 3-4 ft above the floor which contrasts with an upper wall surface.
Wallboard A manufactured wood covering in sheet form.
Wall ties Metal wires or strips used to bind masonry tiers in cavity wall construction or which bind brick veneer to a wood frame wall.
Wash coat A thin covering coat, usually of shellac.
Water main The main water supply pipe.
Water table Projecting board or molding placed around the outside walls to shed rain water.
Weathering The making, finishing or treating of a surface to make it appear subject to the effects of weather.
Weather strips Plastic, metal, rubber or fabric pieces used around doors or windows to prevent drafts.
Welding A method of fastening metals by applying heat until the pieces fuse.
Wet rot Wood decay resulting from moisture and poor ventilation.
Whet To sharpen on a fine oil stone.
White coat The final plaster coat.
White wash A wall finishing material of slaked lime and water.
Winders Those stairs used on curved portions.
Wing nut An easily-turnable nut having wing-like projections.
Wiped joint A plumbing connection joining two pipes made by wiping solder around the joint.
Wire glass Glass containing wire mesh which prevents fragments scattering or shattering.
Wrecking bar A long steel bar used to pry up floorboards with a flat chisel point on one end and a curved claw on the other.

Y

Y joint A Y-shaped fitting used for connecting two diverging branches to the principal drain.

Index

A

B

C

Index

D

E

F

G

H

I

J

K

L

M

N

O

P

Index

All figures in italic type refer to illustrations.

Acknowledgments

DECORATING AND DO-IT-YOURSELF was conceived, edited and designed by **DORLING KINDERSLEY LIMITED**

Authors and Chief Contributors:
Albert Jackson and **David Day**

Graphic Design and Art Direction:
Simon Jennings

Designers:
Stephen Bull and **Debbie MacKinnon**

Contributing Editor:
Adrian Bailey

Editor:
Amy Carroll

Assistant Editor:
Sybil del Strother

Picture Researcher:
Caroline Lucas

AUTHORS' ACKNOWLEDGMENTS

We would like to acknowledge with gratitude the special talents of Simon Jennings who has worked with us from the outset to design and art direct this book. We also extend our particular thanks to: Stephen Bull and Debbie MacKinnon for their care and attention over the graphic presentation; Adrian Bailey, Amy Carroll and Sybil del Strother for their hard work in writing, styling and editing the text; Caroline Lucas for researching the photographs; Robin Harris for his multiple talents; and our thanks, with love, to Jacqueline Day and Pauline Jackson who by their support and patience have contributed as much as anyone else.

Albert Jackson
David Day

Special Contributors:
Adam Hardy
Pierre Junod
Garry Porter
Tricia Wastvedt
Dennis Young

Project Prototype Makers:
Bill Brooker
Richard Cooksey
Jacqueline Day
John Perkins
David Price

DORLING KINDERSLEY ARE GRATEFUL FOR THE ASSISTANCE PROVIDED BY THE FOLLOWING MANUFACTURERS AND ORGANIZATIONS:

Aaronson Brothers
Adjustable Clamp Co.
Aladdin Industries Inc.
American Brick & Stone Co.
American Standard Inc.
American Vinyl Co.
Armstrong Cork Co.
Barnes & Co.
Black & Decker Mfg. Co.
A. B. Boyd Co.
British Vita Co.
Carrier Corp.
Crown Decorative Products
Culligan Inc.
Fedders Corp.
General Electric Co.
B. F. Goodrich Chemical Co.
Habitat Designs Ltd
Häfele America Co.
Honeywell
Hotpoint Division of General Electric Co.
Interlübke
Kirsch Co.
Masonite Corp.
Minnesota Mining & Mfg. Co.
Montgomery Ward & Co.
Olin Corp.
Portland Cement Assn.
Rawlplug Co. Inc., The
Roto-Rooter Corp.
Schlage Lock Co.
Sears, Roebuck & Co.
Stanley Power Tools Division
Stanley Tools Division
Thiokol Chemical Corp.
Uniroyal Inc.
US Plywood Corporation
Westinghouse Electrical Corp.
Weyerhauser Co.
Woodfit Ltd

ARTISTS:

Allard Design Group (Terry Allen, Lyn Brookes, Roger Courthold, Bob Stoneman) *Pages: 62-63, 66-67, 84-85, 96-97, 108-109, 110-111, 112-113, 114-115, 116-117, 118-119, 120-121, 122-123, 124-125, 126-127, 166-167, 209, 224, 242-243.*
Arthur Baker *Pages: 34-35, 38-39, 42-43, 58-59, 80, 86-87.*
Brian Craker *Pages: 70-71, 90-91, 94-95, 98-99, 100-101, 102-103, 104-105, 106-107, 134-135, 136-137, 152-153, 154-155, 218-219, 234.*
Shirley Curzon *Pages: 16, 38-39, 164-165, 198-199.*
Robin Harris *Pages: 50-51, 54-55, 76-77, 82-83, 88-89, 92-93, 128-129, 130-131, 132-133, 138-139, 140-141, 142-143, 198-199, 206-207, 222-223, 226-227, 228-229, 230-231, 232-233.*
Brian Lewis/Colin Rattray *Pages: 162-163.*
Richard Lewis *Pages: 20-21, 24-25, 28-29, 65, 144-145, 146-147, 148-149, 150-151, 156-157, 158-159, 160, 178-179.*
Coral Mula *Pages: 8-9.*
Les Smith *Pages: 206-207, 212-213, 236-237, 238-239, 240.*
Technical Graphics Ltd (Charles Harvey, Brian Sayers, Keith Smith, Geoff Wicker) *Pages: 168-169, 170-171, 172-173, 176, 182-183, 186-187, 190, 194-195, 196, 202-203, 210, 216-217, 246-247.*

SPECIAL PHOTOGRAPHY:

Graham Henderson *Pages: 167, 170-171, 174-175, 178, 180-181, 184, 188-189, 192-193, 196, 200-201, 204, 208, 212-213, 220-221, 226-227.*
Peter Higgins *Pages: 4-5, 17, 25, 28-29, 33, 81, 161, 197, 205, 225.*

PICTURE SOURCES

Title page: *Daily Telegraph/ Patrick Thurston.*
Pages 6-7: *1. Liz Whiting/Tim Street-Porter 2. Liz Whiting/Tim Street-Porter 3. Camera Press 4. Camera Press 5. "Living Places" © Quick Fox 6. Michael Boys/Susan Griggs Agency*
Pages 10-11 *1. Camera Press 2. Michael Boys/Susan Griggs Agency 3. Michael Boys/Susan Griggs Agency 4. Camera Press 5. Graham Henderson 6. Maison Marie Claire*
Pages 14-15 *1. Liz Whiting 2. Interlübke 3. Graham Henderson 4. Jessica Strang*
Pages 18-19 *1. The Picture Library, Bow Street Studio 2. Liz Whiting/Tim Street-Porter 3. Good Housekeeping 4. The Picture Library, Bow Street Studio 5. The Picture Library, Bow Street Studio 6. "Living Places" © Quick Fox*
Pages 22-23 *1. Interlübke 2. Camera Press 3. Liz Whiting/Tim Street-Porter 4. Good Housekeeping 5. Jessica Strang*
Pages 26-27: *1-4. Interlübke*
Pages 30-31 *1. "Living Places" © Quick Fox 2. Interlübke 3. "Living Places" © Quick Fox 4. Bill McLaughlin 5. "Living Places" © Quick Fox 6. Bill McLaughlin 7. Interlübke 8. Bill McLaughlin*

PICTURE SOURCES

Pages 36-37 *1. Interlübke 2. Arthur Sanderson 3. "Living Places" © Quick Fox 4. Miele Co. 5. Miele Co. 6. Michael Boys/Susan Griggs Agency*
Pages 40-41 *1. Liz Whiting/Michael Nicholson 2. "Living Places" © Quick Fox 3. Bill McLaughlin 4. Maison Marie Claire 5. Interlübke 6. Good Housekeeping 7. Jessica Strang 8. Interlübke*
Pages 44-45 *1. Jessica Strang 2. Liz Whiting/Graham Henderson 3. Liz Whiting/Tim Street-Porter 4. Graham Henderson 5. Graham Henderson 6. Heidede Carstensen*
Pages 48-49 *1. Camera Press 2. Camera Press 3. Interlübke 4. Pentagram Design 5. Jessica Strang 6. Jessica Strang 7. Interlübke 8. "Living Places" © Quick Fox 9. Maison Marie Claire*
Pages 52-53 *1. Bill McLaughlin 2. Bill McLaughlin 3. Bill McLaughlin 4. Interlübke 5. Jessica Strang 6. Jessica Strang*
Pages 56-57 *1. Liz Whiting 2. Interlübke 3. Interlübke 4. Camera Press 5. Bill McLaughlin 6. Bill McLaughlin*
Pages 60-61: *1. Interlübke 2. Interlübke 3. Graham Henderson 4. Miele Co. 5. "Living Places" © Quick Fox 6. Liz Whiting 7. Miele Co.*
Page 64 *Gilchrist Studios*
Pages 66-67 *1. Berger Paints 2. Liz Whiting/Lavinia 3. Liz Whiting/ Tim Street-Porter 4. Maison Marie Claire 5. "Living Places" © Quick Fox*
Pages 70-71 *1. Interlübke 2. Michael Boys/Susan Griggs Agency 3. Interlübke 4. Interlübke 5. Interlübke 6. Bill McLaughlin 7. Liz Whiting*
Pages 74-75 *1. "Living Places" © Quick Fox 2. "Living Places" © Quick Fox 3. Interlübke 4. Michael Boys/ Susan Griggs Agency 5. Jessica Strang 6. "Living Places" © Quick Fox*
Pages 78-79 *1. Liz Whiting/Graham Henderson 2. The Picture Library, Bow Street Studio 3. Interlübke 4. Bill McLaughlin 5. Liz Whiting/Jerry Tubby 6. Liz Whiting/Jerry Tubby 7. Liz Whiting/ Graham Henderson 8. Interlübke*
Page 163 *1. Liz Whiting/Jerry Tubby 2. Liz Whiting/Tim Street-Porter 3. Michael Boys/Susan Griggs Agency 4. Liz Whiting/Tim Street-Porter*
Page 185 *1. Bill McLaughlin 2. Liz Whiting 3. Liz Whiting/Tim Street-Porter 4. Liz Whiting*
Page 188 *1. Michael Boys 2. Michael 2. Michael Boys*
Pages 192-193 *1. Graham Henderson 2. Graham Henderson 3. Good Housekeeping (design: Cindi Mufson ASID) 4. Graham Henderson 5. Liz Whiting/Graham Henderson 6. Graham Henderson*
Page 238 *Interlübke*

TYPESETTING
Diagraphic Typesetters, London
TJB Photosetting, London